ACAPULCO ORANGE BLOSSOM,
THE JAMES BOND MARTINI, APPLE DAIQUIRI,
PRICKLY PEAR MARGARITA, CAFÉ AZTECA,
KILANEA LAVA FLOW,
TEQUILA COCKTAIL, SPICED ORANGE BLOSSOM,
DUBONNET MANHATTAN, RASPBERRIES ROMANOFF,
STOLI CHOCOLATE MINTINI . . .

You'll find recipes for these and thousands of other exotic and delicious-sounding concoctions in this comprehensive bartender's guide. You'll also find out how the Bloody Mary got its name, how much is in a "tot" of liquor, as well as the difference between a *Shooter* and a *Shrub*, or between a *Fizz* and a *Flip*, and the meaning of such mixologist's terms as *Smash*, *Puff*, or *Bang!* With this remarkable guide, you'll be talking and serving and mixing drinks like a pro!

NEW EDITION
THE NEW
AMERICAN

BARTENDER'S GUIDE

JOHN J. POISTER is President of General Strategics, Inc., a New York–based communications consulting company and its TV–motion picture subsidiary, Poister Productions. He is also Executive Editor of its International News Features Network division which creates editorial subjects on travel, food, wine and spirits, entertainment, and the arts for print and broadcast media. He has written five books on food and wine.

THE
NEW
AMERICAN

BARTENDER'S
GUIDE
Second Edition

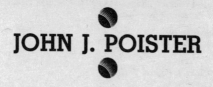

JOHN J. POISTER

A SIGNET BOOK

SIGNET
Published by New American Library, a division of
Penguin Putnam Inc., 375 Hudson Street,
New York, New York 10014, U.S.A.
Penguin Books Ltd, 27 Wrights Lane,
London W8 5TZ, England
Penguin Books Australia Ltd, Ringwood,
Victoria, Australia
Penguin Books Canada Ltd, 10 Alcorn Avenue,
Toronto, Ontario, Canada M4V 3B2
Penguin Books (N.Z.) Ltd, 182–190 Wairau Road,
Auckland 10, New Zealand

Penguin Books Ltd, Registered Offices:
Harmondsworth, Middlesex, England

First published by Signet, an imprint of New American Library,
a division of Penguin Putnam Inc.

First Printing, May 1989
First Printing, (Second edition) March 1999
10   9

FOR CAROL
With love and appreciation
for giving so much time and effort to this book.

PUBLISHER'S NOTE

Welcome to the world of the master mixologist, where one is offered a vast variety of recipes designed to please every taste. The reader is admonished to exercise moderation at all times, but especially when driving. If you are a host or proprietor, please consider arranging a safe alternative conveyance home for any guest who may have overindulged.

CONTENTS

Meaning of Symbols
Adjacent to Drink Names

☙ = CLASSIC

Classic or standard drink recipes
that have retained their popularity
over the years are designated by a ☙

N = NEW

New recipes that have been recently
introduced and which are not likely to be
found in older drink books are marked with an

○ = ORIGINAL

Original recipes or innovations
on standard recipes created by
the author are indicated by an

THE NEW MIXOLOGY

*"If good work came easy
everybody would be doin' it."*
—Louis Armstrong

The cocktail was born in the U.S. Precisely when and where remains a mystery, and while its roots run deep in the wine- and spirit-loving cultures of Europe, there is no doubt the cocktail is essentially an American phenomenon. It was a part of the adventurous frontier mentality that swept the country in the early nineteenth century. Because the cocktail was propelled by the Industrial Revolution from which great American fortunes were made, it is easy to understand why a slug of raw whiskey or a jolt of hell's fire rum that may have been acceptable during the post-Revolutionary War era wasn't the end-all for imbibers who could afford something better.

And better there was. Enterprising bartenders became famous for the signature drinks they created for their establishments, many of which have become classics. Thus, the foundations of what would become the New Mixology were laid. The legendary "Professor" Jerry Thomas invented the Martinez, which evolved into the dry Martini, and the Tom and Jerry, which still warms us on wintery nights. Tom Collins, who held forth at the Planter's Hotel in St. Louis, invented the famous tall cooler in 1858 that bears his name, as well as a popular version of the Planter's Punch which became the hostelry's signature libation. Johnnie Solon was much admired at New York's old Waldorf Bar for the special drinks he concocted for the "Waldorf Crowd"—J. Pierpont Morgan, John W. "Bet-a-Million" Gates, Richard Harding Davis, Colonel William F. "Buffalo Bill" Cody, Elbert H. Gary, and Mark Twain among them. For the hotel—the largest and most prestigious in New York City—he created the Bronx Cocktail, which became the Waldorf's famous signature drink.

The Edwardian period between the turn of the century and World War I was a period of great culinary progress. America's new, elegant hostelries and grand restaurants and bars equalled the best to be found anywhere in the world, with food and drink to match. American restaurateurs became accomplished at adapting French haute cuisine to their menus and British bartenders adopted many of our cocktails to their cocktail shakers and added some very good mixed drinks of their own. American rye and bourbon whiskeys found new markets and our infant California wine industry began showing great promise.

Then a terrible thing happened.

On January 16, 1920, America was plunged into the depths of Prohibition and those in the food, beverage, and hospitality industries predicted the end of the good life as they knew it. But it didn't happen. Instead of drying up the country, a whole generation of Americans learned about cocktails. The Roaring Twenties blasted off like a Stutz Bearcat. It was the era of the flapper, flaming youth, the raccoon coat, the speakeasy, bathtub gin, and something to carry it in—the hip flask.

Through the medium of the cocktail, the urge to seek new spirituous adventures spread across the Atlantic. Paris in the 1920s was filled with Americans as well as other expatriates. They gravitated to good saloons such as Harry's New York Bar and creative bartenders like Fernand Petiot, who is credited with inventing the Bloody Mary in 1924. Harry MacElhone, the proprietor, enjoyed inventing cocktails for the regulars. His most famous invention was the Sidecar, which later became the rage in America. He created Death in the Afternoon in honor of Ernest Hemingway's book of the same name. Hemingway would meet at Harry's with F. Scott Fitzgerald, George Gershwin, Gertrude Stein, and others who would indulge in genuine "American Hot Dogs" punctuated with Martinis. Hemingway, whose drinks were described as being "Napoleonic" in size and substance, preferred a large beer schooner brimming with cognac and champagne. He reportedly could drink quite a few of these without showing any ill effects.

Around the corner from Harry's and just a short walk to the Place Vendome was the most elegant watering place in Paris, the renowned Hotel Ritz. Hemingway and James Joyce delighted in the Ritz bars and the Ritz barmen Frank Meyer, Georges Sheuer, and Bertin, whom they considered master mixologists and good friends. One of Hemingway's favorites was Bertin's Ritz Special, and if he was feeling a little low, Georges would whip up a Ritz Special Pick-Me-Up (see Index). Over the years the Ritz remains unchanged; it is truly a palace devoted to fine food and memorable mixology.

London's Savoy Hotel has been a towering culinary success

since it opened in 1889. Auguste Escoffier was the first *chef des cuisines* and a genius in innovating and creating food dishes with surefire appetite appeal, especially for celebrity patrons including the likes of Nellie Melba and Luisa Tetrazzini, two great opera stars of the era. In such an exalted culinary climate the Savoy's beverage facilities were destined for greatness. The famed American Bar was opened in the late twenties under the direction of Harry Craddock, an American bartender who blended English finesse with American audacity in the cocktail shaker. One result of this approach was his famous invention, the White Lady (see Index). He could also make a formidable, crackling cold Martini back in the days when English barmen were stingy with ice cubes. Above all, Harry Craddock was a master mixologist and his legacy, *The Savoy Cocktail Book*, published in 1930, gives us a comprehensive peek of what Americans could expect when Prohibition was repealed (1933) and the Golden Age of Cocktails erupted free and unfettered. Repeal no doubt helped Franklin D. Roosevelt to easily win re-election as the American voters rallied to the battle cry, "He Brought Back Beer," and sang their post-Prohibition theme song, "Happy Days Are Here Again" with feeling.

Enter William Powell, who, as The Thin Man, popularized the classic stemmed Martini glass in his films—it was straight out of the trendsetting 1925 design show in Paris that introduced Art Deco to the world (*l'Exposition Internationale des Arts Decoratifs et Industriels Modernes*). That glass was to become the icon of the "Thirsty Thirties"—the beginning of the Golden Age of Cocktails—and sow the seeds of the New Mixology in America.

It's hard to imagine that in those early days during the Great Depression vodka was unknown in the United States and tequila's sunrise was far from dawning. American distillers were working hard to rebuild their whiskey-making capacity; English gin and Scottish Scotch were available again for legal import, but heavily taxed; cognac was considered a curiosity for the wealthy; and rum was looked down upon by the average consumer as something poor people drank with soda pop out of sheer desperation.

With the availability of quality gins, the first concoction to benefit was the Martini. It was now imbued with those wonderful, complex flavors which result from fine botanicals and expert blending. So, the redoubtable Martini went from equal parts of gin and vermouth to something in the neighborhood of a 20-to-1 ratio in the 1950s, and then eventually to straight gin on ice. It may have pleased its quaffer, but it could no longer be called a Martini or even a cocktail. Today a whole new generation of Martini drinkers, aided by professional bartenders who practice the disciplines of the New Mixology, are discovering the joys of beautifully balanced cocktails.

Rum that had been unfairly relegated to a "cheap-drink" status underwent a miraculous transformation in the late 1930s–early 1940s. Creative mixologists discovered rum—its many varieties, its wide range of flavors, and its mixability, especially with fruit juices. Pioneer entrepreneurs such as Don the Beachcomber (Don Beach) and Trader Vic (Victor Bergeron) built lavish, tropical theme restaurants offering a variety of exotic dishes combining Caribbean, Polynesian, and Chinese cuisines. For many patrons the drinks were the main event; they were studies in appetite appeal, which was unknown in the old speakeasies where patrons drank straight from a flask, glass jar, or coffee mug (in the event of a raid). Tropical fruit juices were expertly combined with several kinds of rums and liqueurs, various spices, and flavorings and presented in large, oversize cooler glasses; ceramic coconuts and pineapples; cups resembling voodoo masks; sea shells; tiki sculptures; and tumblers whittled out of real bamboo. These carefully constructed concoctions were often garnished with tropical garlands and orchids or other jungle flowers. The entire experience was made that much more effective when served against the background of subdued lights in a simulated native fishing village, accompanied by the night sounds of jungle birds and insects in the background.

The popularity of exotic rum drinks skyrocketed and many of these house specialties became famous signature drinks, like Trader Vic's Fog Cutter, Scorpion, and Shark's Tooth. Trader Vic lays claim to creating the Mai Tai, a classic rum drink if there ever was one. Not to be outdone, Don the Beachcomber created the Vicious Virgin, Never Say Die, Navy Grog, and the famous Zombie, which was cleverly promoted with the memorable admonition, "Only two drinks to a customer."

After the end of World War II, the pipelines began to fill up after a period of severe wartime shortages and the cocktail again underwent a revival. The success of rum creations stimulated a renewed interest in really stunning, showcase mixed drinks. It soon became apparent that not every bartender was equipped to create original, glamorous mixed drinks that not only looked good, but tasted as good as they looked. Hence the truism: all mixologists are bartenders, but not all bartenders are mixologists.

Cocktails took on a new life because there was a growing demand for classics as well as new inventions and most novice drinkers did not know one from another and didn't really care—they were enjoying exciting new experiences. Like the song says, "Everything Old Is New Again." All the old classics took on a new glitter and cocktail menus in the better bars were proud to feature the Pink Lady, Ramos Gin Fizz, Manhattan, Daiquiri, Singapore Sling, Sidecar, Jack Rose, Stinger, Bacardi, Old-Fashioned, Gimlet, Clover Club, Rob Roy, Phoebe Snow, Mimosa, Dubonnet Cocktail, Mint Julep, Whiskey Sour, Gin Rickey, Brandy Alexander, Sloe Gin Fizz, Champagne Cocktail, and Between the Sheets. Classics all, and deserving of the mixologist's magic touch. As for new inventions, the best was yet to come.

The year was 1946, a time of postwar shortages of just about anything to drink, unless it was milk or orange juice. A Los Angeles bar owner faced with the problem of getting potables for his customers thought that vodka might do in a pinch. Everyone who tried it in his bar said it was like drinking straight alcohol with no color, no smell, and no taste. Obviously, nobody was *that* thirsty. His mixologist's mind went to work. If, he reasoned, you have a distilled spirit with no flavor, you've got to provide it. He did. He mixed vodka with ginger beer and a little lime juice, served it with ice cubes in a copper mug, and named it the Moscow Mule (see Chapter 4). The rest is history.

The success of vodka is unmatched by any other distilled product. The fact that it had no discernible flavor of its own became a great marketing plus: Here was something that would *mix with anything*. The New Mixology was made for vodka. It would work in any mixed drink flavor combination, or it could be infused with flavor by the addition of fruit, herbs, or spices, as the Russians and the Poles have been doing for centuries.

By the late 1950s, vodka drinks were on everybody's top ten list. The Bloody Mary became an overnight bestseller. Vodka made great inroads into gin's traditional position as a summer cooler with tonic, and many Martini drinkers switched from gin to vodka. New vodka inventions proliferated with the White Russian, Kamikaze, Sea Breeze, Sex on the Beach, Bull Shot, Cape Codder, Fuzzy Navel, Harvey Wallbanger, Long Island Iced Tea, Screwdriver, and the Woo Woo becoming popular across the land.

The great lesson that we have learned from the successes in the spirit world is flavor is the thing we are chasing. During the Roaring Twenties many good-tasting drinks were invented, but for the average drinker, alcoholic potency or proof took precedence over taste because much that passed over the bars was of such poor quality.

Today, the New Mixology employs simple but effective methods to improve the results of drink-making, which you will find throughout this book. Remember, whether you are a professional or a home bartender, when creating drinks the goal is great flavor; and the axiom for mixologists may well be: Dream them up, mix them up, dress them up, set them up. If the flavor's there, watch them vanish. If it's missing, watch your guests vanish.

THE LANGUAGE OF MIXOLOGY

Just as there are many recipes for beef stew and it is called different names in different places, so too with beverage terminology. Names go in and out of style, and their meanings are changed by usage and the passage of time. The first name on our list is a good example. Originally an *apéritif* was a fortified, aromatized wine such as vermouth, which was and is popular throughout Europe as an appetizing beverage to be taken before a meal. Now it embraces a wide range of wines and spirits.

Apéritif. Originally a reference to an apéritif wine, fortified and aromatized by the addition of various herbs and spices, it was traditionally drunk before meals as a stimulant to the appetite. The term was also applied to various other wine concoctions of a proprietary nature such as Dubonnet, Byrrh, St. Raphael, and bitter-based liqueurs like Campari, Amer Picon, and even to bitters themselves such as Fernet Branca. Now the term encompasses pre-prandial spirits such as ouzo, Calisay, Pernod, Ricard, anesone; all kinds of cocktails; and even white table wine, which has become popular as a before-dinner drink in the U.S. Today, what constitutes an apéritif is of less importance than *when* it is imbibed. In other words, an apéritif is anything alcoholic taken prior to dining.

Bang! A term of our own invention used to identify double- or triple-flavor reinforced drinks such as Orange Bang! or Cherry Bang!—i.e., cherry juice, cherry liqueur, and cherry brandy.

Cobbler. A tall drink traditionally served in a highball or Collins glass filled with finely crushed ice and decorated with fresh fruit and mint sprigs. It may use any type of wine or spirit with or without a sweetener. The classic Cobbler from the gaslight era was made of sherry and pineapple syrup and various fresh fruit garnishes.

Chaser. A mixer that is tossed down the gullet after one has drunk a straight shot of whiskey or other spirit instead of being combined with a spirit in a glass. (See *Shooter.*) The Boilermaker originally was "a shot-and-a-beer," meaning a shot glass of whiskey followed by a beer chaser.

Cocktail. A combination of spirits (including wines) and flavorings, sweeteners, and garnishes of various kinds intended to be consumed before dining. Today the term "cocktail" is used interchangeably with apéritif. The usual cocktail recipe consists of a *base*, such as gin, whiskey, rum, brandy, vodka, or even a wine such as sherry, champagne, or in some cases a table wine; to which is added an *accent* spirit, e.g., triple sec, or a wine, e.g., Madeira; and often a *sweetener* (sugar syrup) or *flavoring* (orange juice) with or without garnishes (maraschino cherry). The *base*, *accent*, *sweetener* (if required), and *flavoring* is the basic formula for almost all cocktails. The exceptions are usually concoctions called cocktails that are no more like a cocktail than champagne is like a can of club soda.

Collins. Basically a sour in a tall glass with club soda or seltzer water. The famous Tom Collins made with gin has been extended to include everything from applejack (a Jack Collins) to Irish whiskey (Mike Collins). The John Collins is one you can win a bet on. If asked to describe it, many will say it is made with whiskey. Wrong! It is made with Hollands or jenever gin.

Cooler. There are many recipes for coolers, which all have these things in common: true coolers are made with ginger ale, club soda, or other types of carbonated beverage, and the rind of a lemon or orange, cut in a continuous spiral, with one end hooked over the rim of the glass. All coolers are served in tall glasses such as a Collins glass, which is sometimes called a cooler glass.

Crusta. A short drink of the sour type served in a glass that is completely lined with an orange or lemon peel cut in a continuous strip. Any spirit may be used as the base for this drink, but the Brandy Crusta was the prototype.

Cup. A punch-type drink that is made by the cup or glass instead of in a punch bowl.

Daisy. An oversize, sour-type drink sweetened with a fruit syrup such as raspberry and usually served in a large goblet with crushed ice and straws. (See *Fix.*)

Eggnog. A traditional Christmas holiday bowl containing a delectable combination of eggs, sugar, cream or milk, and brandy, rum, or bourbon served cold in individual cups in all its rich, creamy goodness. There are many old and famous recipes, including the Tom and Jerry, which is a hot Eggnog.

Fix. A sour-type drink similar to the Daisy and traditionally made with pineapple syrup and served with crushed ice in a large goblet with straws, if you wish.

Fizz. There are many fine old recipes for Fizzes, which are, as the name suggests, products of the old siphon bottle that "fizzed" the drink with a stream of bubbles as it was being made. The Gin Fizz is typical and similar to the Tom Collins. Other famous Fizzes such as the Ramos Gin Fizz, the Silver Fizz, and the Sloe Gin Fizz are not at all like a Tom Collins and are worth trying even without a siphon.

Flip. A creamy, cold drink made of eggs, sugar, and your favorite wine or spirit. The Brandy Flip and the Sherry Flip are perhaps best known. The Flip began in Colonial times as a hot drink made of spirits, beer, eggs, cream, and spices, mulled with a red-hot flip iron or flip dog that was plunged into the drink; hence the name, Flip.

Frappé. Anything served with finely crushed ice.

Grog. Originally a mixture of rum and water that was issued to sailors in the Royal Navy and later improved with the addition of lime juice and sugar. Now a Grog is any kind of drink, usually made with a rum base, fruit, and various sweeteners, and served either hot or cold in a large mug or glass. Reputedly named after Admiral Edward Vernon, who was called "Old Grog" because of the grogram cape he wore.

Highball. Any spirit served with ice and club soda in a medium to tall glass. Other carbonated beverages may be used, but if other ingredients are added, it is no longer a Highball.

Julep. A venerable drink made of Kentucky bourbon, sugar, mint leaves, and plenty of crushed ice. An American classic.

Lowball. A short drink consisting of spirits served with ice alone, or with water or soda in a short glass. Also called On-the-Rocks.

Mist. A glass packed with crushed ice to which spirits are added, usually straight.

Mulls. Wine or wine drinks that are heated and served as hot punches. Also called mulled wine from the time when drinks were heated with a red-hot poker, loggerhead, or flip iron.

Neat. A straight shot of any spirit taken in a single gulp without any accompaniment. Also called a Shooter.

Negus. A hot, sweet wine drink, with or without spices. Port or sherry is traditional. Named after Colonel Francis Negus, an eighteenth-century English luminary.

Nightcap. Any drink that is taken immediately before retiring. Milk punches, toddies, and short drinks such as liqueurs or fortified wines are favored.

On-the-Rocks. Any wine or spirit poured over ice cubes, usually in an Old Fashioned glass. Also called a *Lowball*.

Pick-Me-Up. Any concoction designed to allay the effects of overindulgence in alcoholic beverages.

Posset. An old English invention consisting of a mixture of hot wine, milk, and spices. Eggs were often used, with or without milk, and ale was sometimes used in combination with wine or used in place of it.

Puff. A combination of spirits and milk mixed in equal parts and topped with club soda. Usually served in an Old Fashioned glass.

Punch. A combination of spirits, wine, sweeteners, flavorings, fruit garnishes, and sometimes various carbonated beverages mixed in and served from a large bowl to a number of people. Individually made punches are called *Cups*.

Rickey. A drink made with gin or other spirit, lime juice, and club soda, usually served with ice in a small highball or Rickey glass, with or without sweetening. Named for Colonel Joe Rickey, an old-time Washington lobbyist.

Sangaree. A tall drink containing chilled spirits, wine, or beer, sometimes sweetened and given a good dusting with grated nutmeg. There are also recipes for hot Sangarees.

Shooter. A straight shot of whiskey or other kind of spirit taken neat. Also called a *Neat*.

Shrub. Spirits, fruit juices, and sugar, aged in a sealed container such as a cask or crock, then usually bottled.

Sling. A tall drink made with lemon juice, sugar, and spirits, usually served cold with club soda. The most famous Sling is the Singapore Gin Sling. There are also recipes for hot slings.

Smash. A short Julep made of spirits, sugar, and mint, usually served in an Old Fashioned glass.

Sour. A short drink made of lemon or lime juice, sugar, and spirits. The Whiskey Sour is the classic Sour, but it may be made with vodka, gin, rum, brandy, or various liqueurs, especially fruit-flavored cordials such as apricot, peach, etc.

Swizzle. Originally a tall rum cooler filled with cracked ice that was swizzled with a long twig or stirring rod or spoon rotated rapidly between the palms of the hands to produce frost on the glass. The Swizzle, a Caribbean invention, is made with any kind of spirit today and is traditionally served in a tall highball or Collins glass.

Syllabub. An old English recipe consisting of milk, cream, sugar, and spices, blended with sherry, port, or Madeira to produce a very sweet, creamy mixture that is often served in a sherbet glass as a dessert. In a more liquid form it may be drunk like a Posset. There are many variations of the Syllabub.

Toddy. Originally a hot drink made with spirits, sugar, spices such as cinnamon, cloves, etc., and a lemon peel mixed with hot water and served in a tall glass. Now a Toddy may be served cold with ice with any combination of spices and spirits.

Tot. A small amount of any beverage, a "short shot," "a wee dram," "a touch."

HOW TO TASTE A DRINK

Professional blenders depend to a great degree on their olfactory senses rather than their sense of taste. There are many reasons for this, but one important factor is that the sense of smell seems to hold up to extended sampling better than the sense of taste. The sense of smell, in fact, is essential to taste. Most people do not realize the significance of smell until they have severe nasal congestion and discover they have lost their sense of taste. Remembering flavors and aromas is another factor that is essential to tasting, since it is important to be able to recall specific sensory experiences when confronted with a similar scent or taste at another time and in another place. Since most people enjoy the taste of a beverage more than the aroma, the following checklist may be helpful for the nonprofessional in sampling and comparing spirits in their pristine state from the bottle, or in combination with other ingredients.

The author uses the following procedures in evaluating and ranking mixed-drink recipes as well as new distilled products. In the case of *unmixed* spirits, they are tested in sherry glasses, or *copitas*, which have been steam-cleaned without soap or detergents. Samples from freshly opened bottles are mixed with an equal portion of demineralized, distilled water at room temperature. No ice is used. Evaluations are made on color, aroma, flavor, body, aftertaste, and other perceptions relating to longevity of aroma, flavor intensity, smoothness or finish, and off-tastes suggesting chemical additives or woodiness from the barrel, sweetness, acidity, astringency, mustiness, corkiness, bitterness, or any other taste that is perceived as being unpleasant. Flavor accents, or "high notes," that give a beverage distinctively pleasant characteristics are noted in the most specific terms possible. For example, if a straight bourbon has overtones of spice, an effort should be made by the taster to define it. Is it similar to cinnamon, cloves, nutmeg, or is it herbal? If it is perceived as a nutty flavor (a popular descriptive term for certain brandies and fortified wines such as sherry and Madeira), what kind of a nutty flavor? Peanuts, hazelnuts, walnuts, and pecans are all nuts, but have very different flavors. A professional taster must fix a precise, definitive flavor or aromatic experience in his memory so that he can recall this sensory encounter at a future time when a similar (but not necessarily identical) situation arises. This ability to discriminate between subtleties of aroma and taste is one of the essential skills every professional taster or blender must have. Some say that it is a talent one is born with; others believe that much of this ability is acquired through experience.

The tasting/rating of mixed-drink concoctions is not nearly as demanding, and, for most, is more pleasant because the flavor differences are more obvious and require less concentration than that needed by a blender when comparing whiskey samples from different barrels of various ages from the same distillery. But whatever is being sampled, whether it be food or beverages, even the nonprofessional can learn to use his or her senses more effectively. The sense of smell is underused by most people. The proof of this can be demonstrated by asking a friend or associate to sample something to eat or drink. Most people immediately take a taste instead of first giving it a good sniffing. If you want to develop your sense of smell, start sniffing things like a dog. This is a good way to broaden your olfactory horizons and, along the way, you are certain to come across new sensory experiences that may surprise you.

Mixed drinks can be rated on these important factors:

1. Appearance   Appetite appeal is the main thing.

2. Aroma   Try to describe it to someone else.

3. Flavor   Describe first and subsequent impressions.

4. Refreshment Factor	Does it refresh? Is it zesty and satisfying? Does it perk you up?
5. Aftertaste	Does it leave a different taste in your mouth? Is it pleasant or out of keeping with the flavor experience?
6. Longevity Factor	Does it taste as good after a few more sips? After many sips?

When you try a new drink anywhere, even in an elegant restaurant, don't hesitate to take the time to evaluate it to your satisfaction:

Look at it. Does it look appealing, appetizing, tasty? Does it look refreshing? Does the color make you want to taste it?

Smell it. Really use your nose, not once but several times with a rest in between. Is your nose telling you about the ingredients that are in the drink? Is your nose filled with a heady, pleasant bouquet or just an odor that is flat and uninteresting?

Taste it. Take a small sip. Roll it around your mouth. Concentrate on your initial reaction. Now swallow it and remember the sensation. Take another sip and concentrate on the different taste experiences from different parts of your mouth. Try it again and suck in a little air with the liquid. Does it taste different the second and third time? How? In what way? Is it flavorful? In what way? Is it generally pleasant and satisfying? Is the residual aftertaste good? Does it leave you with a pleasant memory, a good impression? After you have had a whole drink, do you want another? Not right away? Maybe someday? Maybe never?

The same procedures are used in the tasting of wines with certain differences having to do with nomenclature and a profusion of descriptive terms that confuse even some professional vintners.

The key here is concentration. Many people never really know how to taste because from childhood they learn to eat without thinking, seldom use their noses in the eating process, become addicted to certain kinds of food and beverages (e.g., snack foods, ice cream, candy, cheeseburgers, and soft drinks) and are not motivated to try new gustatory experiences. The oft repeated phrase, "I *know* what I like," typifies an attitude that effectively blocks the objective investigation of new flavor experiences. For this reason, travel is a means of broadening one's culinary horizons. When in a foreign land we are often reluctantly forced to try new kinds of things to eat and drink, and frequently with rewarding results. The rapid growth of the popularity of table wines in America was a direct result of increasing travel abroad by Americans, both in the military and civilian life.

HOW TO MAKE A GOOD DRINK EVERY TIME

WHEN AND HOW TO POUR, STIR, SHAKE, AND WHIRL

Mastering the techniques of mixology is important to the amateur bartender as well as the professional, for in food and beverage preparation whether in the home or a five-star restaurant, *presentation* is a vital factor in the proper enjoyment of food and drink. Imagine dining in a fine restaurant and being subjected to an embarrassing display of ineptitude by a clumsy captain who in attempting to bone a beautifully prepared Dover sole turns it into a mangled mound of mush. Who could possibly relax at a bar littered with used cocktail napkins, puddles of melted ice, drippings from sloppily poured drinks, and unemptied ashtrays. This says something about the man or woman behind the bar. It says the person in charge doesn't give a damn, and the drinks that are dispensed will undoubtedly reflect this attitude.

Pouring properly requires practice. The experienced pro turns a jigger into a highball glass, pitcher, or shaker with a quick, smooth turn of the wrist that allows no spillage on the bar. The seasoned wine waiter, or sommelier, pours wine at the table with nary a drop to spot the fresh, white linen tablecloth, rotating the bottle ever so slightly each time to avoid drips and filling champagne glasses in stages so the foam never overflows on the table.

Then, of course, there are those who simply do not know how to serve properly. When a young, inexperienced bus boy in a restaurant splatters you with water drops while filling glasses at your table, it is annoying but forgivable. Not so with a professional bartender who is unable to pour a drink into your glass without spilling a portion of it on the bar, or who fills the glass so full that you inevitably dribble some of your cocktail on your clothes. There is also a new breed of bartender: always in a hurry. You order a Martini and he quickly fills a glass to the brim with cracked ice or mini-ice cubes (which pack together so tightly there is very little room for anything else), throws in a dash of vermouth, and then fills it to the rim with gin. No time to stir, or even to ask if you wanted the lemon twist he added gratuitously instead of the olive you prefer. Before you have a chance to ask for your olive, he's off to another part of the bar to hurriedly make another unmixed drink for another potentially dissatisfied customer. Contrast this performance with that of a famous Chicago bar where the barmen take pride in the fact that their Martinis are stirred at least a hundred times before they are served. Perhaps Martinis need not be stirred this much, but drinks do not mix themselves, and at least the customer gets the feeling that someone cares enough to take the time to do what is necessary, in his opinion, to produce an exemplary drink. After all, they say, every really good bartender has to be a little "stir crazy."

Drink recipes requiring the least amount of blending are stirred. Martinis and Manhattans are good examples of simple recipes that are stirred, not shaken. James Bond enjoys his Martinis shaken, not stirred, and there is nothing really wrong about this, since the aeration from the shaking, no doubt, improves the taste of the drink. Why not shake everything, if this is true? The reason is purely cosmetic. Mixing by electric blender or shaker using clear ingredients such as gin and vermouth results in a cloudy drink due to the dispersion of fine air bubbles. Even though the drink eventually clears up, it just isn't as attractive to many people as a sparkling, crystal-clear Martini shimmering in a cocktail glass. On the other hand, a drink recipe containing fruit juices is seldom as good-tasting when stirred as when well shaken or whipped in a blender.

The cocktail shaker was invented long ago for hard-to-mix drinks. This includes fruit-based drinks, recipes using dairy products such as cream and milk, and ingredients that must be mixed thoroughly, such as an egg or a thick sweetener like coconut syrup or honey. Old-time master bartenders like the legendary Harry Craddock of London's Savoy Hotel took great pride in their skill with the shaker, and some stoutly maintain that many drinks are better made by shaker than by blender. Craddock was fond of helping young bartenders with good advice: "Shake the shaker as hard as you can," he was quoted as saying. "Don't just rock it, you're trying to wake it up, not send it to sleep!"

However affectionately a bartender regards his shaker, there can be no doubt that the electric blender does a superb job in mixing certain exotic, so-called Polynesian drinks that call for a number of different ingredients. Moreover, the blender makes frappéed or "frozen" drinks such as the Margarita in much less time than a hand shaker. A strong case also can be made for the flavor enhancement of the blender through the process of aeration. Take a simple test: Open a carton container of orange juice and pour half into a cocktail shaker and half into an electric blender. Shake and mix the orange juice, with a little cracked ice if you wish, for exactly one minute and pour into glasses. Let your taste be the judge. From that day forward, let your motto be:

If the flavor has abated,
It snaps back when aerated.

Much good bartending is simply common sense and attention to detail. Many hallmarks of a good bar operation are just matters of good manners and good judgment. For example, serving a drink in a chilled glass, especially in warm weather, is far more appealing than in a glass that will warm the drink quickly. After all, stemmed glasses were invented so that one could hold a glass of chilled wine or an ice-cold cocktail without having it warmed by the heat of your hand.

When making any kind of mixed drink, do not ruin it by allowing it to drown as a result of too much ice meltage. Use plenty of ice—for most drinks, the more, the better—but mix them briskly and quickly and serve them *immediately*. By the same token, the recipient is well advised to drink his libation while it is crackling cold.

Common courtesy dictates that when a customer or guest drinks his drink and is ready for another, that a fresh start be made. Begin with a *new glass*, properly chilled, and it will look good and taste even better. Nothing is drearier than to refill a used glass. It is something that most of the better commercial bars would never do, but unfortunately, many home bartenders will commit this breach of good bar etiquette during the rush of the party.

MEASURES AND MEASURING

Cheat me on the price,
but don't cheat me on the goods.
   —Old New York garment-
   district saying

Everyone is entitled to fair measure. In the marketplace it is important because one buys—and sells—according to measures of various kinds. In the home, fair measure has nothing to do with getting value received for your money, but it has everything to do with making or getting a good drink.

Some bartenders, both professional and amateur, do not believe that accurate measuring of drinks is important. There are also good cooks who don't feel that measuring is important. Their argument seems convincing: "You've eaten my food and enjoyed it. Isn't that proof that measuring isn't really necessary?" The problem with the "pinch of this and a dab of that" school of cooking—and with the bartender who pours everything from shoulder height and never uses a measuring cup—is that they not only have difficulty in precisely duplicating their results, but, of much greater consequence, in producing accurate recipes that others can use with any degree of confidence. Many of us have had the experience of trying to get Grandmother's cake recipe without success until someone took the time to stand beside Grandmother, taking notes, checking and measuring every ingredient, and carefully describing the methods used from the flour sifting right through to the final icing and decoration. Even great chefs work from recipes in planning and preparing menus, and, of paramount importance, the others who work in the kitchen must know precisely how to prepare certain dishes. Drink recipes are without question much simpler than food recipes, but the difference between a good drink and a poor one is usually not the ingredients or the recipe, but the person behind the bar, wielding bottle, jigger, shaker, and spoon.

Experienced professional bartenders use the jigger-and-a-splash, the timed speed-pourer, or the "finger method" with a highball glass or mixing glass. But, remember, they have a lot of experience, and it is relegated to probably a dozen drinks that are ordered most of the time by most of the patrons—not counting *unmixed*, mixed drinks such as scotch and soda, Canadian on-the-rocks, bourbon and water, glass of white wine, etc. Many good bars make it a policy to pour generous drinks, especially for the regular customers. The jigger-and-a-splash usually ends up being a two-ounce drink. At the other end of the spectrum, the gyp-bar dispensing by the very same method delivers a wee bit more than an ounce. Then, there is the great middle ground—the big hotels and restaurants as well as bars that do a big business—where strict portion control dictates a measured drink. The ounce-and-a-half jigger is considered standard. The finger method is all right for home use but it is not accurate. Place two fingers around the bottom of the glass and fill the glass to the top of the uppermost finger. Now change glasses. A small glass gives you less and a fat glass gives you more. Slim fingers give you less and plump fingers give you more. That's not portion control. The speed-pourer timed by the bartender's count (usually a four-count) is fast and accurate in practiced hands, but is not recommended for home use because the amateur mixer does not have the volume to require either the speed-pourer or that particular mixing method. The home bartender is better off with a standard, double-ended metal jigger, as is the professional bartender who is using an unfamiliar recipe or a recipe calling for a number of ingredients and fractional measurements.

The mixologist is called upon to use other measures in addition to the jigger, especially when concocting a quantity of party-drink makings in advance or in the making of punches and other beverages for a multitude. This chart shows the relationship between various measures.

MIXOLOGIST'S MEASUREMENT CROSS-CHECK CHART

	Dashes	Barspoons	Teaspoons	Tablespoons	Ounces	Ponies	Milliliters	Jiggers	Wineglasses	Cups
Dash	1	⅓	⅙	1/18	1/36	1/36	0.81	1/54	1/144	1/288
Barspoon	3	1	½	⅙	1/12	1/12	2.43	1/18	1/48	1/144
Teaspoon	6	2	1	⅓	⅙	⅙	4.91	⅑	1/24	1/48
Tablespoon	18	6	3	1	½	½	14.75	⅓	⅛	1/16
Ounce	36	12	6	2	1	1	29.5	⅔	¼	⅛
Pony	36	12	6	2	1	1	29.5	⅔	¼	⅛
Milliliter	0.81	⅓	⅕	1/15	1/29	1/29	1	1/44	1/118	1/236
Jigger	54	18	9	3	1½	1½	44.25	1	⅜	⅕
Wine Glass	144	48	24	8	4	4	118	2⅔	1	½
Cup	288	96	48	16	8	8	236	5⅓	2	1

This chart is designed to be read across or vertically. The horizontal reading is for the equivalency of various measures. For example, by reading across you can find the equivalent of an ounce or a teaspoon. Reading down will tell you how many ounces are in a wineglass, etc. The relationship of common measures to one another underscores the importance of accurate measuring to produce predictable results.

MEASUREMENT RELATIONSHIPS—U.S. UNITS

These are useful measurements from a cup to a hogshead in case you are planning a lavish party.

1 cup = ½ pint = 8 fluid ounces = 2 gills
2 cups = 1 pint = 16 fluid ounces = 4 gills
4 cups = 2 pints = 1 quart = ¼ gallon
8 cups = 4 pints = 2 quarts = ½ gallon
16 cups = 8 pints = 4 quarts = 1 gallon
31½ gallons = 1 barrel
2 barrels = 1 hogshead

NEW METRIC SYSTEM MEASURES
FOR DISTILLED SPIRITS

Old Bottle Size	U.S. Measure	New Metric Measure	U.S. Measure	Servings (1½ oz.) Per Bottle
Miniature	1.6 oz.	50 ml.	1.7 oz.	1
Half pint	8 oz.	200 ml.	6.8 oz.	4½
Pint	16 oz.	500 ml.	16.9 oz.	11¼
Fifth	25.6 oz.	750 ml.	25.4 oz.	17
Quart	32 oz.	Liter	33.8 oz.	22
Half gallon	64 oz.	1.76 l.	59.2 oz.	39½

WINE BOTTLE MEASURES

Name	Metric Measure	U.S. Measure	Servings (4¼ oz.) Per Bottle
Split	187 ml.	6.3 oz.	1½
Tenth	375 ml.	12.7 oz.	3
Fifth	750 ml.	25.4 oz.	6
Quart	Liter—1000 ml.	33.8 oz.	8
Magnum	1.5 l.	50.7 oz.	12
Double Magnum	3 l.	101.4 oz.	24

Note: Serving sizes may be adjusted for large groups, but six servings per 750-ml. bottle of still wine is considered standard. In some cases, more servings are indicated for sparkling wines because it was in vogue at one time to serve champagne in a shallow saucer with a capacity of four ounces. But times change and the larger tulip glass, which is considered proper for sparkling wines, holds between six and eight ounces, so the six-per-bottle rule still holds. As has been pointed out in the section on gyp-bars and dull drinks, serving a skimpy drink is a false economy. Take the magnum and instead of a 4¼ ounce serving, you economize with a 3½ ounce serving. You will get two more glasses from the bottle, and your guests may wonder if you could afford to give a party. Or, if patrons are buying wine by the glass in a restaurant, the fact that they are getting a small serving will *not* go unnoticed. It's a fact: People would rather pay more for a substantial drink than to be served a miserly drink at any price.

MEASURES FOR FOOD ITEMS
FREQUENTLY USED IN DRINK PREPARATION

(The following measures are approximate.)

1 cup of *heavy cream*, when whipped, yields 2 cups.

A *pinch* of ground pepper or other powdered ingredient is that which can be held between the thumb and forefinger.

A *splash* is an imprecise measure left to the discretion of the cook or mixologist. It is more than a dash and generally conceded to be less than ½ ounce.

Depending on size, 4 to 6 *whole eggs* yield 1 cup; 8 to 11 *egg whites* yield 1 cup; and 12 to 14 *egg yolks* yield 1 cup.

1 *medium lemon* yields 3 tablespoons of juice.

1 *medium lemon* yields 1 tablespoon of grated rind.

1 *medium orange* yields ⅓ cup of juice.

1 *medium orange* yields 2 tablespoons of grated rind.

1 pound *granulated sugar* yields 2½ cups.

1 pound unsifted *confectioner's sugar* yields 4½ cups.

1 pound *brown sugar* yields 2½ cups.

GLASSWARE

Why is it that a drink always seems to taste better when served in a beautiful glass?

The answer, as every astute bartender, perceptive hostess, and experienced restaurateur knows, is presentation. As every caring chef knows, if something looks good, it will probably taste better. At the bar it is not only lovely crystal that counts, but the presentation of a drink, in the right kind of glass, clean, chilled, and properly garnished. In England, whiskey is often served in a stemmed glass similar to a wine goblet. Many Americans find it is an appealing way to serve a highball. The drink seems to have more importance than when served in a tumbler or ordinary highball glass. It also stays cold longer when held in the hand by the stem.

There are reasons why many drinks are served in special glasses. They usually look better, are made to hold just the right amount of liquid, and often stay cold longer. A Whiskey Sour will probably taste just as good in an Old Fashioned glass as it does in a Whiskey Sour glass, but somehow it wouldn't seem the same to a Whiskey Sour devotee. What about an Old Fashioned in a Whiskey Sour glass? Not likely. The heavy bottom of the Old Fashioned glass serves a purpose. A strong glass is needed to withstand the force that bartenders exert muddling sugar and bitters as well as fruit, which is the traditional method of preparing this drink.

Also, as every professional blender and wine connoisseur knows, certain glasses are designed to present maximum aroma from the glass to the taster. The brandy snifter is perhaps the best known among traditional glasses that enhance the bouquet of spirits. By the same token the large, globular burgundy wine glass is perfectly suited to the business of allowing a fine wine "room to breathe" and give off its rich, complex bouquet. Many experts are of the opinion that the Spanish copa or copita, the classic sherry wine glass that one finds everywhere in Spain, is the best glass ever made for "nosing," or scrutinizing the olfactory properties of a wine or spirit. For this reason you will find that master blenders in whiskey distilleries invariably are surrounded by an array of copas at the blending table.

Glasses that are not designed to potentiate the aroma of their contents still fulfill a special function. A tall Collins glass is made for coolers. Long drinks with ice cubes are not to be bolted down, but savored leisurely on a hot summer evening. Here, the cooling effect and refreshment is the thing, while aroma is a minor consideration. Other glasses like the stately Hurricane or chimney glass and the graceful, willowy stemmed liqueur glass are designed to glorify the drink that is being served. Such appetite-appealing presentation is an important part of going out for cocktails and dinner—and of the mystique or atmosphere that characterizes many outstanding restaurants. In fact, proper presentation is so important that some hotels and grand luxe restaurants have their own custom-designed glassware. Some shapes and designs have become popular enough to be adopted for general usage. The Delmonico glass, also known as the Whiskey Sour glass (or a version thereof) is named after a famous restaurant that flourished in New York at the turn of the century. The very tall Collins glass was devised and popularized by Don the Beachcomber for the Zombie and other tall specialty drinks, just as the original Tom Collins glass is an elongation of the traditional highball glass, which wasn't thought to be glamorous enough for a new generation of specialty, exotic drink creations.

There is nothing more complimentary to a finely made mixed drink or a rare wine than to have it presented to your guest in a lustrous, full-lead, cut crystal glass fashioned by Baccarat, Waterford, Orrefors, or Steuben. The feel, glint, clarity, and design of the crystal all combine to make the cocktail hour or dinner an important occasion. Unfortunately, expensive cut crystal is just not practical for even a five-star hotel or restaurant because of the amount of breakage in any commercial food service operation. However, there are sturdy, attractive makes of good-quality glassware that are suitable for bar and restaurant use. Of equal importance is having a variety of sizes and styles so that wine and mixed drinks may be properly and professionally dispensed. The principal kinds of glasses are:

Shot glass. The original bar measure seen littering saloon bars in a hundred Western movies. Designed to hold one drink ranging from a fraction of an ounce to two ounces or more. Some cleverly designed shot glasses appear to be enormous, but hold less than an ounce.

Pony glass. A stemmed glass holding one to two ounces for liqueurs and brandies.

Cocktail glass. A stemmed glass ranging in size from three to six ounces and with variously shaped bowls.

Highball glass. The familiar, straight-sided glass that usually has a capacity of eight to ten ounces. The present trend is to serve highballs in larger glasses.

Collins or chimney glass. An elongation of the highball glass that holds from ten to fourteen ounces.

Tall Collins or chimney glass. With a capacity of as much as sixteen ounces, this glass is usually used for exotic specialty drinks such as the Zombie or Singapore Sling.

Old Fashioned glass. Sometimes call a "rocks" glass because it is just the right size for a cocktail on-the-rocks or a whiskey and a splash of soda or water. Holds from eight to ten ounces.

Double Old Fashioned glass. With its fourteen- to sixteen-ounce capacity, this glass is becoming increasingly popular for all types of drinks.

Whiskey Sour glass. Sometimes called a Delmonico glass, this is the traditional glass for all kinds of sours. Holds from five to six ounces.

All-purpose balloon glass. Originally designed for wine drinking, this big—ten- to fourteen-ounce—glass is being used to serve everything from whiskey to beer and many kinds of cocktails and coolers. May be used when a large wine goblet is specified.

Sherry glasses. The American flared sherry glass holding about three ounces may be used for cordials and liqueurs, but the Spanish *copita*, the traditional flower-shaped sherry glass, is being used more frequently because it enables the drinker to enjoy the full aroma of whatever is in the glass. Capacity is slightly less than four ounces.

Brandy snifter. The classic blown-glass globular shape is designed to funnel all of the bouquet of a fine cognac, armagnac, or Spanish brandy to the brandy connoisseur's educated nose. It comes in many sizes ranging from four ounces to twenty-four ounces, and if you look diligently, you'll even come across some forty-eight-ounce snifters.

Champagne glasses. The champagne saucer, a stemmed glass, has been in use in the U.S. for a long time. It is relatively flat and shallow, disperses the bubbles in the wine rather quickly, and is also subject to spills at a crowded reception or party. It holds from four to six ounces (the larger size sometimes has a hollow stem), but can carry as little as two-and-a-half ounces in glasses used at glitzy tourist bars. The hollow stem is attractive but difficult to clean, so it isn't in general use except in private bars. The tulip glass, with a capacity of from six to nine ounces or more, is artfully designed to conserve the natural carbonation of champagne. It has been popular in Europe for many years and is coming into more common use in this country as *the* correct glass for sparkling wines.

Wineglasses. Wine may be drunk and enjoyed from almost any size or shape of glass. Red-wine glasses are usually much larger than white-wine glasses so that the bouquet of a full-bodied, robust Burgundy can be enjoyed to the fullest. White wines, with a few exceptions, are not strong on aroma or bouquet, thus the smaller glass, which is easier to chill, and since its contents are consumed more quickly, the wine stays properly cool. In recent years the "all-purpose" wineglass has been promoted aggressively. It is a good compromise for most people who are not in the habit of serving two or three table wines in the appropriate glass during dinner. Red wine fanciers lean toward a large glass with a capacity of sixteen ounces or more, but for many red wine lovers, the ten- to fourteen- ounce all-purpose glass will do nicely.

Beer glasses. Steins and schooners holding as much as a liter of suds were once looked upon as a mark of depravity by non-beer drinkers. But with a strong resurgence of draft beer underway, pint mugs and other large glasses are back in style again. It's the perfect way to drink fresh, foamy beer from the tap. For bottled-beer drinkers, the classic Pilsener glass, footed and shaped like an elongated V, is preferred. Pilsener glasses usually hold ten or twelve ounces of beer.

Specialty glasses. There are many special-purpose glasses that were designed or adapted for a new drink creation. The Irish coffee cup is an adaptation of the hot drink mug used for hot buttered rum and other winter warmers. There are flip glasses, fizz glasses, parfait glasses, water goblets, rickey glasses, compotes, ten-pin glasses, pousse-café glasses, lamp chimney glasses, Hurricane fourteen-ounce grog glasses, Savall glasses (half Hurricane size), Poco Grande ("Big Mouth"), Zombie glasses, slim cooler glasses holding fourteen-ounces to sixteen ounces, and punch cups. It is doubtful that even the largest bar will have all of these containers, but they all have their place in enhancing one's enjoyment of a favorite wine, beer, or mixed drink.

When shopping for glasses, bear in mind that the trend over the years has been to serve drinks in larger glasses. It not only looks better, but for the home bartender it *is* better since large glasses can accommodate many different types of drinks such as a Highball and a tall cooler and one needs less different shapes and sizes. It is interesting to look at old Art Deco cocktail glasses from the 1920s. Many of them held only about three ounces compared with today's four-to-six-ounce glasses. The same is true of wine glasses. Generally among wine lovers who have learned the importance of being able to savor the fragrance of the wine, the attitude seems to be: the bigger, the better.

TOOLS OF THE TRADE

Good tools are essential to good results, so it is important to obtain good basic equipment for the bar before stocking up on the many different kinds of gadgets and novelties that are available in every department store, housewares store, and gift shop.

Basics

Professional bartender's shaker set. Consisting of a sixteen-ounce mixing glass and metal top, this is a must. Get a fancy cocktail shaker if you like, but for the money the shaker set can't be beat.

Double-ended jigger. The standard metal jigger measures one-and-a-half fluid ounces in the large end and one fluid ounce in the small end. Check capacity with a chemist's graduate or have it checked by your pharmacist as home mixing cups are not precise enough.

Strainers. They come in all sizes and shapes. Get the regular professional bar strainer that fits the mixing glass in your shaker set.

Electric blenders. These high-speed mixers are essential for making many of today's popular mixed drinks. A good blender with a strong motor and variable speeds aerates most drinks in a way that no amount of shaking can accomplish. Some models have blades strong enough to frappé ice cubes (an ordinary blender needs ice cubes that are already cracked).

Corkscrews. Cork extractors come in many styles, but the secret to getting one that can really pull corks is to look for a *coil* and not a screw. The conventional screw-type cork-puller is not wide enough to get a good grip on a bad cork. The coil-type (it looks like a metal worm) does a better job because it is distributed through the cork in a wider area. There are four devices that are better than the old-fashioned corkscrew with a wooden handle, which requires the bottle opener to place the bottle between his legs and pull carefully in order to extract the cork without spilling the wine all over the floor. The **sommelier's corkscrew** (usually a coil) looks like a Swiss Army knife and holds a corkscrew, bottle opener, and a small knife for removing sealing materials from around the cork. It is small, portable, and does the job. The **gourmet** or **wing-type corkscrew** has two arms that rise when it is inserted into the cork. Press down on the arms or wings and the cork comes out. It is reliable in the hands of the inexperienced. The **double-action corkscrew** is ingenious in that once the screw is in the cork, the crossbar that doubles as a handle locks so that you continue turning and the cork is gradually extracted. The pulling—like the wing-type cork—is done by the device and not the bottle opener. Another excellent cork puller is the **Twistup** or cork-fork, which does not employ a screw or coil, but instead two prongs or tines attached to a sturdy handle that are inserted down into the neck of the bottle on each side of the cork. A gentle rocking motion will loosen the cork so that it may easily be extracted. Works well on spongy or crumbling corks that are too soft for a screw-type cork extractor.

Mixing spoons or barspoons. A long-handled spoon is indispensable for stirring mixed drinks, especially in a tall glass. The ten-inch stainless spoon is popular, but some prefer a twelve- or fourteen-inch length.

Measuring spoons. Buy the common kitchen-variety set of four nesting spoons. They are a necessity.

Ice bucket and ice tongs. Keeping a supply of ice by the bar for home entertaining eliminates the need to run back and forth to the refrigerator to get cubes. Ice tongs are a genteel way of serving ice in a drink, and sanitary too. Professional bartenders use an ice scoop, or *should*, since handling ice cubes and handling money is not a desirable combination.

Cutting board and knife. This is basic equipment for any bar and useful for all kinds of drink preparations. Buy a heavy, laminated board no more than eight inches in diameter, for easy storage.

Pitchers. Indispensable for home entertaining, pitchers are necessary for serving water and fruit juices and making stirred drinks such as the Martini and the Manhattan. Highballs for guests made with water from a pitcher rather than from the tap says something about the host.

Juice squeezers. Hand-held and electric juice squeezers are an important bar item. The new generation of compact electric juice squeezers is a real boon to drink-making.

Muddler. A good muddler is made of an extremely hard wood such as lignum vitae. It is used to crush condiments and muddle sugar, fruit, and mint for Juleps, Smashes, and Old Fashioneds.

Can and bottle openers. These housekeeping items seem unimportant until they are needed. Keep a sturdy bottle opener, a piercing can opener for soda, and an anchor opener for jars in the bar and another set in the kitchen. A snubber for stubborn jar lids and a conventional, key-operated can opener should be available if needed.

Optional Equipment

Electric ice crushers. These labor-saving devices are worth the price if you are going to make drinks like Mint Juleps or frappéed coolers for many guests because crushing ice by hand is tedious and a blender should not be used for extensive ice-crushing.

Wine cork retrievers. These gadgets are the only sure way to salvage corks that have been accidentally pushed down into the bottle. One simple, inexpensive French extractor consists of a wooden handle attached to three long wire rods with little prongs, turned inward, at the end. When the rods are thrust into the bottle they open and surround the cork. When the rods are pulled up, they close tightly around the cork, which is then pulled out.

Stirrers, coasters, and cocktail napkins. These basic hostess items are called for when guests come over for cocktails and add a nice touch. Coasters fulfill a valuable function in keeping rings from wet glasses from marring your furniture.

Champagne buckets and wine coolers. These are more than elegant accoutrements for entertaining; they fulfill an important function, since sparkling wines and still white wines lose their chill quickly in a warm dining room unless kept in a bucket or cooler. There are iceless wine chillers on the market and inexpensive wine coolers of conventional design using ice. The classic silver champagne bucket with handles, which looks much like a Grecian urn, is a compliment to anyone's dinner table. There are also sleek modern buckets with stands, which save table space.

Electric juice extractor. This valuable piece of equipment is not to be confused with the electric juicer for oranges, lemons, and limes. It is designed to extract liquid from fruits and vegetables (even nuts) that one normally could not squeeze using home kitchen equipment. Excellent for providing juices for unusual mixed drinks and a wide range of nonalcoholic mixed drinks.

Tap-Icer. Here is a wonderful little invention consisting of a convex steel weight attached to a nine-inch, flexible plastic handle. With a little wrist action it's a snap to crack ice cubes when making individual drinks. The springiness of the handle is the secret, and it has saved many a sore hand.

Gadgets, novelties, and heavy-duty equipment. All of these inventions and refinements have their place. Some are amusing, such as the vermouth atomizer for making Martinis, silver swizzle sticks for hurrying the bubbles out of your champagne and CO_2, corkscrews that push wine corks out of bottles by injecting gas into the bottle. The elegant brass decanting cradles for decanting old vintage wines, giant cork pullers that can disgorge a wine cork with one pull of the handle, temperature- and humidity-controlled wine vaults for the home holding several hundred bottles, and nitrogen-gas wine-preservation units represent the state of the art for serious wine connoisseurs. And for the mixologist, home bars are being custombuilt with such conveniences as dual sinks with running water, miniature refrigerators, and special racks to store glasses out of the way yet instantly accessible. The proliferation of ingenious gadgetry, the adaptation of professional heavy-duty equipment to home use, and the increasing popularity of electrically operated labor-saving devices reflect the broadening interest in the world of wines and spirits on the part of people everywhere.

THE SECRET OF EVERY WELL-MADE MIXED DRINK (AND THE MOST OFTEN IGNORED)

Ice. Ice that is pure, fresh, and really ice-cold is the least expensive, yet one of the most important, ingredients in any mixed beverage—and it is the most frequently overlooked even by experienced bartenders. After all, ice is ice. Right?

Wrong. It is true that all ice is frozen water, but there are other important factors to consider even with respect to the temperature of the ice being used.

The first consideration is generosity. Some bartenders, mistakenly believing they are doing a great service for their employers, make stingy drinks. But even a parsimonious barkeep can be lavish with ice. Every drink benefits from generous amounts of ice *properly used*. This does not mean lots of ice to make the weak, watery, pusillanimous cocktails that one is subjected to at gyp-bars and some big commercial hotel and restaurant beverage operations where everything is done by the numbers—to the customer's sorrow. A professional mixologist knows the importance of using ice in generous quantities to chill beverages thoroughly and quickly, while avoiding excessive ice meltage and drink dilution, which is a better way to lose customers than serving a cockroach in a cocktail. Patrons recognize that a bug can find its way into a glass, but a watery drink results from ineptness or the work of a niggardly bartender trying to save a few pennies.

The next factor is quality. All ice is not the same. Ice cubes made from tap water may impart an off taste to drinks due to chlorination and other chemical treatments to safeguard the municipal water supply. Ice stored in the proximity of other refrigerated or frozen food can quickly absorb odors that will definitely affect the quality of mixed drinks. Ice should be made from water that does not have a high mineral content and is not chemically treated—not an easy task for many city dwellers. The answer, of course, is a good grade of bottled water, preferably spring water rather than water that is simply filtered. Drinks made with ice that is pure and unadulterated really sparkle in both taste and appearance. And be sure to store "clean ice" in a freezer compartment that is not used to store other aromatic or strongly flavored foods.

Next to ice-cold drinks come ice-cold glasses and various ingredients for drink mixing. Glasses should always be chilled, especially in warm weather. As one savant said regarding drink temperatures, "A lukewarm drink makes a lukewarm guest." The methods of chilling glasses and ingredients are fairly obvious; it is simply a matter of taking the time to make this extra step a part of your drink-mixing routine.

Big bars and restaurants have cold cases under the bar where glasses, wines, fermented beverages, soft drinks, and fruit juices as well as other ingredients can be stored. This is the most convenient arrangement. Other methods involve plunging glasses upside down into a mound of crushed ice in the proximity of the bar, or filling glasses with cracked ice on the bar as the drink is being made. Punch makings should always be chilled in advance, since warm fruit juices and spirits poured into a punch bowl will melt the ice cake much too rapidly. There is nothing more insipid than a warm punch on a hot summer day. Other popular drinks that are served frequently such as Daiquiris, Martinis, Collinses, and Gimlets may be made with spirits from the freezer, where they are kept at 0°F. There is practically no ice meltage when these supercold rums, gins, and vodkas are used—which is not to everyone's taste. A little ice meltage may be good in that the libations are not quite so strong and the cocktail hour is prolonged for a civilized period of time. But the aficionado who savors the ultra-dry Martini finds zero-degree gin and vodka to his or her liking, all of which brings us to the question: How cold should cold be with respect to drink-making?

Ice cubes in a big commercial bar are usually brought in from an ice maker (not situated in the bar) in a large container, and poured into an ice compartment in the bar's well, where they remain until the supply is exhausted or melts away. This ice is not the same as that the home drink mixer uses when he reaches into his freezer for ice cubes from the ice tray. His ice cubes are usually large and quite cold. The commercial bar's ice cubes are almost always half-cubes or small discs that have been sitting in the well at room temperature. The cooling capacity of these different types of ice cubes and the meltage factor is far apart. For this reason the professional bartender needs to use a maximum amount of ice in his shaker and to make the drink with dispatch, whereas the home bartender (working under more leisurely conditions) needs to extend the mixing time so his drinks will not be too strong.

All ice is not equal. It is not alike in appearance, taste, or cooling ability, and the mixologist must take this into consideration, especially when making refreshments for the multitude. The home bartender is admonished to lay in a large supply of ice when entertaining. A safe rule is to arrange to buy commercially made ice. How much should you order? About twice as much as you think you will need. And if you are giving a lawn party or a barbecue in the backyard in mid-August, better make that three times as much.

A WORD ABOUT MIXERS

Besides ice, mixers—carbonated beverages such as club soda, ginger ale, lemon-lime, tonic, cola, and various fruit flavors—are the cheapest ingredients you will use to make an alcoholic mixed drink. When entertaining, buy top-quality mixers because they play an important part in the results you achieve when making highballs, Collinses, coolers, and other party drinks such as a punch. Even when capped with a good sealer or securely fastened by their own screw crown, mixers that have been opened lose their zip after a day or so. Don't use them for guests. Use freshly opened bottles that are well chilled in advance. As we all have experienced, opening a warm bottle of soda on a hot day showers the bartender and others nearby, but the worst thing is that a lot of the fizz that should be in the drink is on the floor.

GYP-BARS AND DULL DRINKS

He was so busy learning the tricks of the trade, he never learned the trade.

—Anonymous

Sooner or later every person who drinks will get caught in a gyp-bar. Contrary to popular belief, gyp-bars are found in some of the best places, not just in sleazy singles-bar mob scenes, tourist-trap nightclubs, and skid-row gin mills. In fact, the gyp-bar is more likely to be the product of greed than poverty, vice, or social degradation. And the root of this evil is often not the bartender, but a stingy restaurant owner, an ambitious, big-hotel beverage manager who wants to look good at the cash register, or a crooked tavern owner who is chiseling and skimming everything in sight to make a few extra bucks. And, yes, sometimes a misguided barkeep may be trying to ingratiate himself with the boss by cutting corners on his customers.

Whatever the reasons, it is the consumer who pays the price. Not only is he defrauded by paying more than he should for what he receives, but he must suffer through weak, watery, poorly made drinks, and in some cases, cheap, substandard liquor. The most common sign of a gyp-bar is a lousy drink. It could be a mistake, but usually it's someone behind the bar hoarding nickels and dimes at your expense. Considering the tremendous profitability of selling liquor by the drink: The difference between a good scotch and soda (usually standardized at a 1½-ounce serving, but frequently closer to 2 ounces in top drinking establishments) and a skimpy 1-ounce drink amounts to only pennies. A 750-ml. bottle of spirits will yield about 17 1½-ounce drinks or about 25 1-ounce drinks. If a bottle of ordinary bar vodka costs $6.00 (remember, he is *not* paying retail prices), 17 1½-ounce drinks will cost him $0.35 a drink, and 25 1-ounce drinks will cost him $0.24 a drink—a difference of $0.11 per drink. But those pennies mount up, you say. They do indeed, but considering the long-term negative effect of customer reaction to poorly made drinks, the proprietor might be far better off if he poured a good drink and charged accordingly. Unfortunately, this logic is lost on the professional chiseler. He will invariably charge the higher price and dispense the smaller drink.

Here are a few of the ways the gyp-bar operates to bilk its clientele:

Dice-ice. Many hotels and restaurants use ice cubes that are smaller than those you make at home in your refrigerator because they chill fast and are easier to handle. But the gyp-bar uses a tiny ice cube known as dice-ice since they are about the same size as dice or sugar cubes. Their function is to pack a highball or Old Fashioned glass so full there is very little space left for your drink. At a recent visit to a big airport terminal bar, we were served whiskey on-the-rocks in a small glass filled with dice-ice. When the contents were poured into another glass there was barely an ounce of liquid, including ice meltage. When this was called to the attention of one of the busy bartenders, he said offhandedly, "That's the regular drink. If you have a complaint, see the boss."

The cheap-shot. The standard glass measure, or shot glass, as it is often called, holds from one and a half to two ounces. Then there is the trick shot glass beloved by the gyp-bar. It is a masterpiece of illusion and surely must have been invented by a magician. It is a shot glass with a heavy bottom and actually appears to be larger than a standard shot glass. It has a white fill-line running around its circumference about a quarter of an inch from the rim. When the bartender serves you a highball, he usually fills it above the fill line so you feel you are receiving not only full measure but a little extra dividend as well. Some dividend! If you examine this cheap-shot glass from the top, you will see that it is conical in shape—wide at the top and ending up as a small point at the bottom of the glass. If you fill this glass to the top and pour the liquid into a standard measuring glass, you find you have been served the total of one ounce of liquid. The amount of liquid you get if your drink is poured to the fill-line is a generous five-eighths of an ounce, yet from the drinker's perspective it appears to be a big belt.

The frigger-jigger. The standard double-ended, or hourglass, jigger, usually made of metal—stainless steel, chrome-plated steel, or silver—has a capacity of one-and-a-half ounces at the large end and one ounce in the small end. From time to time you may come across some old-fashioned jiggers that are one-ounce/one-half-ounce combinations, but these are not in general use at most commercial bars. There are many different ways of measuring in the business of drink-making, but the one-and-a-half-ounce serving is now pretty much the rule—except at the gyp-bar. There are many ways of cheating on the portion served, and gyp-bars know them all. One method, unlike the "gyp-flip" and the "pygmy-pourer," takes no skill at all and involves the use of the frigger-jigger, sometimes just called the frigger. It looks like the standard double-ended jigger, but it has a false bottom so that the large end delivers only one ounce and the small end, one-half ounce. The frigger is so skillfully made that the only way to tell the frigger from the standard jigger is to actually measure the contents. However, since most bar patrons do not reach behind the bar to check the house measuring cup, only one's sense of taste can tell them that they are only receiving one ounce of spirits instead of one and a half ounces.

The gyp-flip. More sophisticated cheaters do not need phony jiggers or dice-ice, they can swindle you right before your very eyes by employing the technique known as the gyp-flip. You have, no doubt, often seen busy bartenders pour from the bottle into a jigger, quickly flip it into a glass, and then follow up with a quick pour directly into the glass. In an honest bar you are getting an ounce and a half *plus* by this method. In the dishonest bar you are getting less than the standard measure, since the bartender only fills the jigger a little more than half full on the first pour and just a tiny amount directly from the bottle. You are convinced you are getting a standard drink and a dividend. Actually, the gyp-flip only delivers a scanty one ounce and a wee bit more—quite a difference from the two-ounce drink you thought you were getting.

The pygmy-pourer. Most big bars today have their bottles equipped with "speed-pourers," actually corks that fit into the bottle with a curved metal spout that enables the bartender to quickly, and without spillage, pour from the bottle. Experienced bartenders can time the pouring with extreme accuracy so that exactly the right amount of liquid is delivered to shaker, blender, or glass. The "four count," with bottle inverted, will yield exactly one and a half ounces. With practice, the mixologist learns to count to four at exactly the right speed and pour the correct amount. It is all so simple. How can a gyp-bar find a way around this dispensing technique when the bartender, standing only a few feet away, is pouring drinks in plain view of everyone? Gypsters can always find a gimmick to give them an edge, so the pygmy-pourer was born. The pygmy-pourer looks exactly like the regular speed-pourer, except upon close inspection you will find that the opening at the top of the spout is the same length as the standard pourer, but only half the width. When the pygmy is poured to the count of four, it delivers half the amount delivered by the regular pourer. When viewed from the side, the stream from the pygmy-pourer looks the same as that dispensed by the speed-pourer; only your taste buds can tell you that you've received, and will pay for, a pygmy-sized drink.

The service-bar shuffle. Experienced drinkers imbibe at the bar. They know that the drinks are generally better when made out in the open and you can tell the bartender exactly how you want your drink prepared. Also, there is the incentive of the gratuity, the reward for good drinks and good service. Experienced drinkers also know that drinks made at the service-bar are usually less than generous and many times poorly made. Why? For very sound reasons. In a big bar or restaurant, where many people are served at tables in the dining room or cocktail lounge, the service-bar is often out of sight back in the kitchen area. You won't find the best bartenders stuck back in the service-bar, usually only the juniors, the apprentices. These mixers work alone, their only contacts are the cocktail servers, and if they pour light drinks and run a sloppy bar, no one will know or care unless the boss happens by. A service-bar in a gyp-joint is a license to steal, and nearly everyone at some time has been the victim of the service-bar shuffle. The signs of the gyp service-bar are well known: dice-ice, the "sly-ball," the "floater," cheap, off-brand liquor, "no-show" drinks, and dull, insipid cocktails.

(For the uninitiated, the slyball is an undersized highball glass with a capacity of six ounces instead of the standard eight to twelve ounces. The reason for this disparity is disarmingly simple: A weak, one-ounce measure would be unacceptable in a twelve-ounce highball glass unless it was packed with dice-ice, which would be a bit conspicuous. So the slyball is used in which the small measure of spirits is tolerable, at least to the unsophisticated drinker.)

If the service-bar is part of a gyp-bar operation, there may be a "midnight bottler" at work, so named since he plys his nefarious trade after the bar is closed. His job is to fill premium "call-brand" bottles (prestigious, well-known brand names that are advertised and promoted) with off-brand spirits such as a cheap, bulk scotch that is shipped in tanks to the U.S. to be rectified and bottled locally. So you order Chivas Regal, and the bottle may have been refilled in the dead of night with Loch Nowhere or Old MacSwigger. One evening an out-of-town friend hosted us for cocktails at a big, bustling hotel bar. He ordered his favorite drink, an Old Forester Old Fashioned. He got Old Overshoe. It was ghastly. He sent it back and got another drink with an Old Forester taste and aroma that didn't last beyond the second sip—a floater, an old routine in the repertoire of the service-bar shuffle. Our curiosity aroused, we returned the following evening, and our friend again ordered his favorite drink with the same disappointing results. Before he sent it back, we placed a small glass button in the Old Fashioned to see if the service bartender would mend his mischievous ways and send us the real premium bourbon that had been ordered instead of a spurious imitation. The "new" drink was back in a trice. My friend sniffed it and sampled it. Again it had a first blush of the real thing that did not last through the second tasting. Another floater? Sure enough, when we held up the glass to the light, our little button was resting on the bottom. Same old glass. Same old hooch. The same old service-bar shuffle. My friend might have received better treatment if he had been sitting at the bar, but if the bottles had been doctored by a midnight bottler, who knows?

There is no defense against the gyp-bar except to question anything that doesn't look, smell, or taste good to you. Speak up! If a drink is poorly made, warm, or watery, send it back. If a drink tastes weak, send it back. If you're paying for a premium gin in your Martini, make sure you get it and not Tinker Bell or some other off-brand. If you want a call-brand vodka in your Bloody Mary, you should get it, not Ivan the Terrible or some other obscure name. Some bars don't use any vodka in their Bloody Marys, as some investigative reporters learned when researching a story for a New York magazine. They discovered no-show Bloody Marys in one of the city's more elegant watering places through the simple expedient of taking samples of the drinks that were served at the bar and having them analyzed by a chemist. When confronted by the evidence, the owner, who charges top prices for his restaurant's drinks, said it was all a mistake, an oversight, and that it would never happen again. It *did* happen again. Some weeks later other samples were analyzed in a chemical laboratory, and again, nary a drop of alcohol could be found.

The only way gyp-bars and dull drinks can be eliminated is through vigilance on the part of consumers; perceptiveness (know what you're paying for); and a determined effort by everyone who patronizes a bar or restaurant to, as one old Scot put it, "get the worth of your money."

Awareness of what constitutes a good drink is a first step, whether one is drinking in a public place or in the privacy of one's home.

A COLLECTION OF FINE FLAVORINGS AND EXOTIC SWEETENERS

When drinks need sweetening, we immediately think of white sugar—granulated, superfine, or powdered (confectioners')—or brown varieties or sugar syrup—sometimes referred to in bartender's guides as simple syrup or, in very old drink recipe books, as gomme syrup. Since sugar crystals do not readily dissolve in alcohol, sugar syrup, which is easily made (mix 1 cup of water with 3 cups of sugar and boil for 5 minutes, bottle, and refrigerate), is essential for well-made mixed drinks with a minimum of shaking or blending.

Other commonly used sweeteners include honey, maple syrup, and fruit syrups such as grenadine. All have advantages and disadvantages. Honey is fine for flavor, but difficult to mix in a cold drink unless diluted with warm water in advance. Maple syrup is excellent, but has a very strong flavor, which limits its use as a drink sweetener. Grenadine is better for coloring than sweetening unless it is made from pomegranate juice in a high proportion to the syrup it is mixed with. Cheap grenadines are simply sugar syrups artificially colored and flavored, with a sickish-sweet, cloying taste that is all too evident if used in large amounts in a mixed-drink recipe.

Here are some sweeteners of various kinds that you may want to experiment with. Many are outstanding and contribute to the making of flavorful drinks:

Sirop de citron. A favorite with French cooks and bartenders. Its mild, lemony zestiness makes this acceptable in those recipes in which sweetened fresh lemon juice would be too acidic.

Almond syrup. This is a versatile sweetener for all kinds of tropical-style drinks. Also known as **orgeat syrup** or **sirop d'amandes,** this delightful flavoring may be used in recipes calling for almond extract.

Black currant syrup. Once unknown in bars in the U.S., **sirop de cassis** and its slightly alcoholic cousin, **crème de cassis,** is used in Kir and other vinous and spiritous mixed drinks.

Coffee syrup. This sweetener is used mainly in hot and cold drinks as a flavoring and sweetening agent. It may be used in any recipe in which a coffee flavor is desired.

Fruit syrups. Cherry, raspberry, strawberry, blueberry, gooseberry, and mulberry syrups are used for cooking and may be used in flavoring punches, coolers, and other exotic drinks. To prepare, filter fruit juice through cheesecloth and mix *thoroughly* with sugar (approximately 1 cup sugar to 2 cups juice, depending upon the sweetness of the fruit) and bring to a boil in a saucepan, filter again, and bottle. Most fruit syrups are also commercially available. All fruit syrups should be refrigerated after opening. The addition of vodka or grain neutral spirits (100 proof) will act as a preservative. One ounce of spirits to 10 ounces of syrup should suffice.

Falernum. This spicy, limey, somewhat fruity sweetener with overtones of ginger and almonds originated on the island of Barbados in the West Indies. It was originally concocted, no doubt, for rum drinks, and remains a superb flavoring for drinks made of various fruit juices and rum, gin, or vodka.

Orange syrup. This old-time flavoring dates from pre-refrigeration days when fresh oranges were not always available. It has been supplanted by the real thing, fresh or frozen, and orange liqueurs such as curaçao and triple sec, which are frequently used in mixed-drink recipes as sweeteners. It is still available commercially, although not always easy to find.

Red currant syrup. Along with its sister fruit syrup, cassis, *sirop de groseilles* is widely used in France as a flavoring in the kitchen. It also has many uses as a sweetener for beverages.

Coconut syrup. Coconut flavor has become increasingly popular in the U.S. in both food and beverage applications. Coconut syrup has many uses in the making of coolers, punches, and exotic, tropical-style drinks.

Artificial sweeteners. A teaspoon of cane sugar contains about 18 calories. Considering the high caloric content of most fruit-based mixed drinks, the use of synthetic sweeteners, unless one's carbohydrate intake is severely restricted, seems hardly worth the effort; but then, you shouldn't be drinking those sweet concoctions to begin with.

Molasses. Molasses is the product of cane juice reduced by boiling. Unsulfured molasses is considered the most desirable for ordinary kitchen uses. It has a role in the sweetening and flavoring of beverages because it is not as sweet as sugar and imparts a distinctive flavor to foods and mixed drinks. Blackstrap molasses is a product of the third boiling (the first boiling of cane juice is the best) and is as unpalatable and harsh as its name. Sorghum, the juice of sorgo, a cereal grass, is a thinner, slightly sour version of molasses and is used as a molasses substitute. Golden syrup is a processed residual molasses with a light, very agreeable flavor that makes it quite usable in a variety of food and drink recipes. Although treacle is synonymous for molasses in Great Britain, it is usually a mixture of molasses and corn syrup in the U.S. It is not considered a satisfactory substitute for molasses in most food recipes.

Corn syrup. This versatile sweetener has about half the sweetening power of cane sugar, but possesses excellent cooking and food-processing qualities. It is not commonly used in the making of mixed drinks, but has the advantage of smoothing out other ingredients in a mixture and has a more subtle sweetening effect than sugar. It is available in light and dark versions.

Jams, jellies, and preserves. While it might seem improbable that grape jelly, strawberry jam, or pineapple preserves would ever be used in the making of mixed drinks, these popular staples provide a vast, readily available, inexpensive source of delicious and flavorful sweeteners for punches, cocktails, and party drinks. Of course, jams, jellies, and preserves have been around forever—so long, in fact, that their rich source of flavor has lain untapped by America's mixologists. The electric blender has opened up all kinds of new possibilities, and now, once impossible tasks, such as making frappés quickly to order, are easily accomplished. So too are mixed drinks calling for a dab of orange marmalade, a spoonful of Damson plum preserves, or a dollop of black raspberry jelly.

In the creation of new mixed drinks, both alcoholic and non-alcoholic, the imaginative use of new kinds of flavorful sweeteners opens up new vistas for the innovative bartender.

A BATTERY OF BITTERS

Bitters live up to their name. They are aromatic mixtures of a variety of botanicals, such as seeds, roots, leaves, fruits, bark, and stems of various flora in an alcoholic base. Once prized for their medicinal qualities, bitters generally are used today as flavor catalysts and enhancers in the preparation of food recipes and a great variety of mixed drinks. Most are proprietary formulas made from closely guarded recipes. A few of these bitter concoctions have become famous as apéritifs rather than miniscule ingredients in mixed drinks to provide a flavor accent. Campari and Amer Picon are well-known examples. Other types of bitters are not intended for beverage use and should not be used for this purpose.

Master bartenders in the nineteenth century prided themselves on the imaginative and skillful use of various bitters to make a mixed drink more flavorful, unique, and perhaps even memorable enough to bring favored customers back for more. Legend has it that the first cocktail was made by a New Orleans apothecary, Antoine Peychaud, who mixed his family's secret bitters formula with brandy and regularly dispensed this mixture at his store located at 437 Royal Street.

Today the mixologist has a battery of bitters available to add subtle nuances of flavor to drinks of all kinds. Some of the famous old names, such as Boker's and Abbott's, as well as a fine imported orange bitters, may not be easy to find, but are surely worth the effort, since they have a valuable place in the world of creative drink-making.

Abbott's Bitters. This is a popular general-purpose preparation for food and beverage recipes made by the C.W. Abbott Co. of Baltimore, Maryland.

Amer Picon. A bitter formulation of cinchona bark, oranges, and gentian, which has become popular as an apéritif taken neat or mixed with vermouth, a dash of grenadine, or a soft drink. Made in France by Picon & Co. at Levallois Perret.

Angostura Aromatic Bitters. Introduced in 1824 from a recipe developed by a surgeon, Dr. Johann Gottlieb Benjamin Siegert, who served in the Prussian army under Marshal Blücher at the battle of Waterloo, Angostura bitters have become indispensable, in the opinion of many, for the making of a proper Pink Gin, Old Fashioned, or Manhattan cocktail. The name comes from the town of Angostura (Ciudad Bolivar), Venezuela, and not angostura bark, which is not used in its manufacture.

Boker's Bitters. This is a famous old name in aromatic bitters. Although it is not in wide distribution, correspondents report that they come across a bottle occasionally and eagerly snap it up.

Boonekamp Bitters. A Dutch product dating back to 1743, this bitters has a largely European following.

Calisay. This is a popular Catalonian specialty made in Barcelona from cinchona and other ingredients. It is more commonly served as an apéritif and as a *digestif* than used as an ingredient in mixed drinks, although it is called for in recipes that appear in old bar books.

Campari. This bitter apéritif with its distinctive brilliant red color and pungent quinine flavor has seemingly become the national drink of Italy. It is frequently drunk with soda or tonic water and is an essential ingredient for several cocktails such as the Negroni and the Americano.

China-Martini. This is another popular Italian bitter liqueur made by Martini and Rossi, and characterized by a quinine flavor and a syrupy consistency. It is not used generally as a cocktail ingredient, but is served rather as an apéritif and an after-dinner drink.

Fernet Branca. Originally compounded for use as a stomachic, Fernet Branca is popular with some drinkers as a hangover remedy. It is a complex, assertive combination of a variety of ingredients including cinchona bark, gentian, rhubarb, calamus, angelica, myrrh, chamomile, and peppermint. It is used as an apéritif to stimulate flagging appetites and as an ingredient in mixed drinks requiring a strong, bitter additive.

Jaegermeister. This complex, aromatic concoction containing some 56 herbs, roots, and fruits has been popular in Germany since its introduction in 1878. It may be used as a cocktail bitters, but is traditionally consumed as an apéritif or an after-dinner drink.

Orange Bitters. Specified in many mixed-drink recipes, orange bitters was very popular during the heyday of the cocktail in the World War I era and the Roaring Twenties that followed. The best orange bitters reputedly come from England, where famous old names such as Field, Son & Co. and Holloway's orange bitters were considered first-quality products.

Peychaud's Bitters. Purportedly derived from an ancient and closely guarded family recipe that Antoine Amedée Peychaud, a young French Creole, brought to New Orleans around the latter part of the eighteenth century. Peychaud, an apothecary, made his bitters famous in Louisiana by dispensing it from his pharmacy mixed with French brandy. It was later sold commercially by the L.E. Jung & Wulff Co. of New Orleans and became a staple for many mixed drinks because of its pungent bitter anise flavor. It is essential for making the Sazerac, a classic New Orleans libation.

Stonsdorfer. This is a German proprietary bitters popular as a *digestif*.

Underberg. Well known in Germany, where it is made, Underberg is reputed to work wonders in ameliorating hangovers and calming the morning-after "clangs."

Unicum. Here is a fine old name in bitters, made since 1840 by the venerable Viennese firm of Zwack, originally from Hungary and renowned for their outstanding clear fruit brandies.

Peach Bitters. Popular when Granddad rode home from his favorite saloon in a hansom cab, peach bitters, like many another ingredient that has gone out of style in the making of mixed drinks, will no doubt be rediscovered some day and become all the rage. In the meantime, you may have difficulty in finding a bottle of these bitters at your neighborhood store.

WHAT'S IN A NAME?

Bright with names that men remember,
Loud with names that men forget.
                                    —Swinburne

Many drink names are, sad to say, frivolous, overly cute, and inconsequential. Some are precious and contrived either to attract attention, arouse curiosity, or to appear trendy. Worst of all, many drinks that are basically similar except for minor differences have been given different names. You will find some in this book. It is not because of sloppy research or inattention to detail, but because in different parts of the world these concoctions are known by a particular name just as a strip sirloin steak is called a "strip steak" or a "shell steak" or a "New York cut," all names for the same thing in different parts of the country. Or the use of the term "rye" in the Northeast when it is not really rye whiskey that is being ordered, but blended whiskey. But if you order rye in Maryland or some parts of Delaware and Pennsylvania, you will get rye—straight rye whiskey.

Although most mixer's manuals are silent on the origin or significance of drink names, there are nevertheless, for the historically inclined, many meaningful names that were given to specific recipes in honor of a person, place, or event. You will find many drinks named after restaurants, bars, hotels, clubs, and resorts. Some of these names live on as the only vestiges of their birthplaces, which long ago succumbed to economic misfortune, natural calamities, or the juggernaut of urban renewal. Many drinks were named in honor of a distinguished or steady customer or a novel, stageplay, musical comedy, or a motion picture; some forgotten, but many well remembered. Stars of opera, ballet, stage, and screen have often been recipients of this special kind of liquid tribute. The list also includes kings and queens, presidents, political candidates who didn't make it; wars, battles, and peace treaties; athletic victories, civic events, and all manner of anniversaries in recognition of everything from the invention of the electric light to the one hundredth birthday of the Statue of Liberty.

Place names have always been popular, and in perusing this book you will find many, including a number of Indian names as well as drinks that have been named after cities and towns. There is scarcely a major city in the world that has not been lionized by its own specially created drink. And then, of course, there are many drink mixtures that have been named after family, friends, and business associates. If you feel like naming a cocktail after someone, invent a drink or take one you like and customize it to your own tastes. Who knows, you may like it so much, you'll do as so many others have done: Name it for yourself.

GIN: THE JOYS
OF JUNIPER

Get me out of this wet coat
and into a dry martini.
　　　　　　　—Robert Benchley

A well-made gin is a work of art. It is a product of the blender's talent and skill. Juniper, and the many botanicals (extracts from roots, leaves, bark seeds, etc., of plants) of which gin is composed, make up its essential quality and character. It is unaged and, except for dilution with water, is bottled just as it comes from the still. The first distillation results in a grain neutral spirit. After dilution with distilled water the neutral spirit is distilled once more in a gin still with all of the flavoring agents either mixed into the spirits or placed in racks and percolated by the spirit vapors during the redistillation process. Some American gins are compounded, which simply means that spirits are mixed with the essential oils of various botanicals without redistillation. Sometimes botanicals are added to the grain mash before it has been distilled the first time, and the entire process is carried out in a single distilling cycle. Every distiller has slightly different methods of achieving their desired result. The important thing to remember is that gin is a flavored spirit. Without flavorings it would not be gin. It would be vodka.

Every gin distiller has a treasured, secret recipe that is usually known to but a few and guarded like the crown jewels. What does gin contain? A broad spectrum of botanicals chosen from around the world for their particular flavor and aromatic qualities. Here is a typical sampling of ingredients with the omission of a secret ingredient or two: juniper berries (a primary ingredient), coriander seeds, angelica root, orris (iris) root, licorice, lemon peel, orange peel, almonds, cassia bark, cardamom seeds, anise, caraway seeds, fennel, cinnamon bark, bergamot, and cocoa.

As with so many spirituous inventions, gin began life as a

possible therapeutic specific for certain tropical diseases that sailors on Dutch East India Company ships were bringing back to the Netherlands in the seventeenth century. In the year 1650 Franciscus de la Boe, also known as Dr. Sylvius, a professor of medicine at the University of Leiden, was diligently searching for ways to cope with these exotic maladies from faraway places. It is recorded that he was unsuccessful in his research, but he did discover something else that had demonstrable medicinal qualities when taken in moderation: a spirituous infusion of juniper berries. Juniper had been used by physicians to help reduce fever with some success. Although this juniper infusion did not cure tropical afflictions, it had other benefits as a sedative; a mild diuretic; and a vasodilator that can be beneficial for many types of cardiac conditions; as well as a stimulant to the appetite and a tonic for the elderly.

Dr. Sylvius called his discovery "aqua vitae," which gives some hint as to the high esteem he held for his invention. His countrymen called it *jenever*, the Dutch name for juniper. The French named it *genièvre*, which, so the story goes, the English interpreted as having something to do with Geneva (which they later contracted to gin). Jenever (genièvre or genever) pertains to juniper the fruit, not Geneva the city. Jenever was also called Schiedam gin or Hollands gin, referring to the city and country of origin. Whatever the etymology, one thing seems to be well documented: English soldiers fighting in the Netherlands in the late seventeenth century tried the spirit, and liked its pungent, assertive flavor and piquant aroma. Because of its restorative powers, they christened it "Dutch courage," and took ample supplies of jenever back to England in the same manner that the armies of Henry II in 1170 brought whisky home from their forays in Ireland. In both instances it was much appreciated by the populace, since the English have never been diffident in matters of libationary pursuits.

In the later part of the seventeenth century, distilleries began to proliferate in England and the Netherlands, but the flavor characteristics of the spirits produced became quite different. In the Netherlands the center of the distilling industry was in Schiedam near the great port of Rotterdam, a strategic location (the grain poured in from as far away as Russia, and the spirits poured out). The popularity of jenever was accelerated by the war in progress with the French because imports of French brandy were shut off. The Dutch, who were great lovers of brandy, turned to jenever, and the distilleries of Schiedam covered the city with a pall of black smoke so dense it became known as the Black City, or Black Nazareth.

About the same time in England (1690) the Parliament under William of Orange passed "An Act for the Encouraging of the

Distillation of Brandy and Spirits from Corn." This not only was a great boon to British distillers, but the increased use of corn instead of barley malt made a difference in the flavor of English gin, which became more pronounced with the passing of time. English gin tended to be lighter in body and taste and eventually became famous as London dry gin with a characteristic crisp, clean juniper flavor. Jenever, on the other hand, retained its original full-bodied quality with a definite malty aroma and taste that reflects a high proportion of barley malt that is used in the mash.

Today, jenever is widely consumed in the Netherlands and is not used for cocktails because of its pronounced flavor, but rather drunk like Scandinavian *snaps*, or aquavit, neat or with quantities of wonderful Dutch beer. Jenever is aged, unlike London dry gin, and there is an old (*oude*) and a young (*jonge*) type of jenever, the latter being the most popular in the Netherlands, due, no doubt, to the fact that it is lighter and has less of a malt flavor than the old type.

London dry gin is made in the United States, and some of the American formulas have gained popularity on their own merits. The term "dry" has become outmoded, since almost all gin is dry today. An exception is Old Tom gin, which can be best described as a sweetened gin. It has become a rare commodity because the trend of popular tastes, as gauged by the relentless pursuit of the driest possible gin for the driest possible Martini, may be approaching absolute alcohol with barely a wisp of flavor. All of which means that Old Tom has become old hat. But don't count it out. Old things have a way of being recycled in the most improbable ways and at the most unexpected times.

Another distinguished gin is called Plymouth, not a brand but a type of English gin that is strongly flavored and quite aromatic. Tradition has it that the Royal Navy used Plymouth gin and Angostura bitters to concoct the first Pink Gin, a stomachic and a tonic that was used to guard against the ravages of loathsome and insidious tropical diseases. It didn't work any better than gin and quinine water for preventing malaria in India, Burma, and Malaysia for Her Majesty's forces during the days of the British Raj.

Aside from its apparent lack of efficacy in combating tropical diseases, gin is quite remarkable as a beverage. It is, aside from vodka, the most mixable of all those spirits having distinct flavors of their own, and for this reason mixed-drink recipes using gin as a base occupy large portions of every mixer's manual and bartender's guide.

ABBEY No. 1

1½ oz. gin
¾ oz. Lillet blanc
¾ oz. orange juice
Maraschino cherry or orange
    peel

Mix all ingredients, except cherry, with cracked ice and strain into a chilled cocktail glass. Garnish with cherry or orange peel.

ACACIA

2 oz. gin
½ oz. Benedictine
Dash kirsch
½ oz. lemon juice

Mix with cracked ice in a shaker or blender and strain into a chilled cocktail glass.

ADMIRAL BENBOW

2 oz. gin
1 oz. dry vermouth
½ oz. lime juice
Maraschino cherry

Pour all ingredients, except maraschino cherry, into a mixing glass with several ice cubes. Stir well and strain into a chilled Old Fashioned glass.

ADMIRAL COCKTAIL

2 oz. gin
¾ oz. lime juice
½ oz. Cherry Heering or
    Cherry Marnier

Mix with cracked ice in a shaker or blender and strain into a chilled cocktail glass.

ADMIRALTY COCKTAIL

1 oz. gin
½ oz. dry vermouth
½ oz. apricot brandy
1 tsp. lemon juice

Mix all ingredients with cracked ice in a shaker or blender. Pour into a chilled Old Fashioned glass.

ALASKA

1½ oz. gin
¾ oz. yellow Chartreuse
Several dashes orange
    bitters

Mix all ingredients with cracked ice in a shaker or blender. Strain into a chilled cocktail glass.

ALBEMARLE FIZZ

1½ oz. gin
½ oz. lemon juice
1 tsp. raspberry syrup
Several dashes framboise or
    raspberry schnapps
Club soda

Mix all ingredients with cracked ice in a shaker or blender and pour into a chilled highball glass. Add ice cubes if necessary and fill with club soda.

ALEXANDER'S BROTHER

1 oz. gin
1 oz. crème de cacao
1 oz. heavy cream

Mix all ingredients with cracked ice in a shaker or blender and strain into a chilled cocktail glass.

ALEXANDER'S SISTER

1½ oz. gin
½ oz. white or green crème
    de menthe
¾ oz. heavy cream

Mix all ingredients with cracked ice in a shaker or blender and strain into a chilled cocktail glass.

ALFREDO

1½ oz. gin
1½ oz. Campari
Orange peel

Mix all ingredients, except orange peel, with cracked ice in a shaker or blender. Pour into a chilled Old Fashioned glass. Twist orange peel over drink and drop in.

 ALMOND COCKTAIL

2 oz. gin
1 oz. dry vermouth
6 slivered almonds
Peach kernel, crushed
½ tsp. sugar syrup
1 tsp. kirsch
½ oz. peach brandy

Warm gin. Add almonds, peach kernel, and sugar syrup. Chill and pour mixture into a chilled Old Fashioned glass along with several ice cubes. Add remaining ingredients and stir.

BARTENDER'S SECRET NO. 1—Soda Gun

Beware the "soda gun" and how you use it. This invention is popular in big, busy bars, enabling bartenders (and others at the service end of the bar) to fill glasses with carbonated mixers at a machine-gun pace. The device consists of a battery of buttons and a pouring spout attached to a long hose that leads to storage tanks under the bar. At the press of a button the soda gun—also known as the "arm" or the "snake"—will dispense cola, lemon-lime soda, ginger ale, club soda, or water. It's a handy, time-saving gadget, good for busy bartenders, not so good for unbusy customers. Some people complain that frequently the carbonation is not what it should be, meaning that their drinks are flat, not bubbly. The more serious problem is the mixing of flavors from the small amount of residue left from the last filling. Super-premium spirits selling at super-premium prices deserve the best mixer money can buy, which explains why top bars use bottled mixers.

AMAGANSETT

1½ oz. gin
½ oz. dry vermouth
½ oz. Pernod
1 tsp. white crème de menthe

Mix all ingredients with cracked ice in a shaker or blender and strain into a chilled cocktail glass.

AMER PICON COOLER

1 oz. gin
1½ oz. Amer Picon
½ oz. Cherry Heering
1 tsp. sugar syrup or to taste
1 tsp. lemon juice
Club soda

Mix all ingredients, except club soda, with cracked ice in a shaker or blender and pour into a chilled highball glass. Fill with club soda.

ANITA'S SATISFACTION

1½ oz. dry gin
Several dashes grenadine
Several dashes Angostura bitters
Several dashes orange bitters

Mix all ingredients with cracked ice in a shaker or blender and strain into a chilled cocktail glass.

ANTIBES

1½ oz. dry gin
½ oz. Benedictine
2 oz. grapefruit juice
Orange slice

Mix all ingredients, except orange slice, with cracked ice in a shaker or blender and pour into a chilled Old Fashioned glass. Garnish with orange slice.

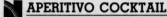 APERITIVO COCKTAIL

1½ oz. dry gin
1 oz. Sambuca Romana
   liqueur
Several dashes orange
   bitters

Blend all ingredients in a mixing glass with plenty of cracked ice and strain into a chilled cocktail glass.

APPIAN WAY

1½ oz. gin
½ oz. Strega
½ oz. amaretto
Orange slice

Mix all ingredients, except orange slice, with cracked ice in a shaker or blender and strain into a chilled cocktail glass. Decorate with orange slice.

ARUBA

1½ oz. gin
½ oz. curaçao
1 oz. lemon juice
1 egg white (for two drinks)
1 tsp. orgeat or Falernum
   syrup

Mix all ingredients with cracked ice in a shaker or blender and strain into a chilled cocktail glass.

ASCOT

1 oz. gin
½ oz. dry vermouth
½ oz. sweet vermouth
1 tsp. anisette
Generous dash Angostura
   bitters
Lemon peel

Mix all ingredients, except lemon peel, with cracked ice in a shaker or blender and strain into a chilled cocktail glass. Twist lemon peel over drink and drop into glass.

AVIATION

1½ oz. gin
½ oz. lemon juice
½ tsp. maraschino liqueur
½ tsp. apricot brandy

Mix all ingredients with cracked ice in a shaker or blender and strain into a chilled cocktail glass.

BACK BAY BALM

1½ oz. gin
3 oz. cranberry juice
½ oz. lemon juice
Several dashes orange
   bitters
Club soda

Pour all ingredients, except club soda, into a chilled highball glass with several ice cubes and stir gently. Fill with club soda.

BALI HAI

1 oz. gin
1 oz. light rum
1 oz. okolehao
1 oz. lemon juice
3 oz. lime juice
1 tsp. orgeat or sugar syrup
   to taste
Brut champagne

Mix all ingredients, except champagne, with cracked ice in a shaker or blender. Pour into a chilled Collins glass and fill with cold champagne.

BARBARY COAST

¾ oz. gin
¾ oz. light rum
¾ oz. scotch
¾ oz. white crème de cacao
¾ oz. cream

Mix all ingredients with cracked ice in a shaker or blender and pour into a chilled Old Fashioned glass.

BARNEGAT BAY COOLER

2 oz. gin
3 oz. pineapple juice
½ oz. lime juice
1 tsp. maraschino liqueur
Club soda or lemon-lime
   soda or ginger ale

Mix all ingredients with cracked ice in a shaker or blender. Pour into a chilled double Old Fashioned glass.

BARNUM

1½ oz. gin
½ oz. apricot brandy
Several dashes Angostura
  bitters
Several dashes lemon juice

Mix all ingredients with cracked ice in a shaker or blender and strain into a chilled cocktail glass.

BAYARD FIZZ

2 oz. gin
½ oz. maraschino liqueur
1 oz. lemon juice
1 tsp. raspberry syrup
Club soda
2 raspberries

Mix all ingredients, except club soda and raspberries, with cracked ice in a shaker or blender and strain into chilled highball glass. Fill with club soda, stir gently, and garnish with raspberries.

BEAULIEU BUCK

2 oz. gin
½ oz. Cointreau
Several dashes dry vermouth
Ginger ale
Lime wedge

Mix all ingredients, except ginger ale and lime wedge, with cracked ice in a shaker or blender and pour into a chilled highball glass. Fill with ginger ale and squeeze lime over drink and drop into glass.

BEEKMAN PLACE COOLER

1½ oz. gin
1 oz. sloe gin
3 oz. grapefruit juice
½ oz. sugar syrup
Club soda

Mix all ingredients, except soda, with cracked ice in a shaker or blender and pour into a chilled Collins glass. Fill with cold club soda and stir gently.

BEE'S KNEES

1½ oz. gin
1 tsp. honey
Several dashes lemon juice
  or to taste

Mix all ingredients with cracked ice in a shaker or blender. Strain into a chilled cocktail glass.

BELGRAVIA

1 oz. gin
½ oz. Dubonnet blanc
1 tsp. maraschino liqueur
3 oz. champagne or dry
    sparkling wine
Orange peel

Mix all ingredients, except wine and orange peel, in a mixing glass with ice and strain into a chilled wine goblet. Fill with champagne. Twist orange peel over drink and drop into glass.

BERLINER

1½ oz. gin
½ oz. kümmel
½ oz. dry vermouth
½ oz. lemon juice

Mix all ingredients with cracked ice in a shaker or blender and strain into a chilled cocktail glass.

BERMUDA COCKTAIL

1½ oz. dry gin
1 oz. apricot brandy
½ oz. lime juice
1 tsp. Falernum or sugar
    syrup
Dash grenadine
Orange peel
½ tsp. curaçao

Mix all ingredients, except orange peel and curaçao, with cracked ice in a shaker or blender and pour into a chilled Old Fashioned glass. Twist orange peel over drink and drop into glass and top with curaçao.

BERMUDA HIGHBALL

1 oz. gin
1 oz. brandy
1 oz. dry vermouth
Club soda or ginger ale

Pour all ingredients, except club soda, into a chilled highball glass with several ice cubes. Fill with club soda or ginger ale.

BETWEEN THE SHEETS No. 2

1 oz. gin
1 oz. brandy
1 oz. Cointreau

Mix all ingredients with cracked ice in a shaker or blender and strain into a chilled cocktail glass.

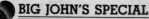 **BIG JOHN'S SPECIAL**

3 oz. grapefruit juice
1½ oz. gin
1 oz. vodka
1 oz. orange juice
Several dashes orange
    flower water
4 maraschino cherries
Several dashes maraschino
    cherry juice
Wedge preserved cocktail
    orange

Mix all ingredients with crushed ice in a blender or shaker until frappéed. Serve in double Old Fashioned glass.

BISCAYNE

1 oz. gin
½ oz. light rum
½ oz. Forbidden Fruit
½ oz. lime juice
Lime slice

Mix all ingredients, except lime slice, with cracked ice in a shaker or blender and strain into a chilled cocktail glass. Garnish with lime slice.

BISCAYNE BREAKFAST JOY

2 oz. gin
½ oz. frozen grapefruit
    concentrate
1 oz. frozen orange juice
    concentrate
1 tsp. orgeat syrup
Several dashes grenadine
Several dashes kirsch

Mix all ingredients with cracked ice in a shaker or blender. Pour into a chilled Old Fashioned glass.

BISHOP'S COCKTAIL

2 oz. gin
2 oz. ginger wine

Mix all ingredients with cracked ice in a shaker or blender and strain into a chilled cocktail glass.

BITER

1½ oz. gin
¾ oz. green Chartreuse
¾ oz. lemon juice
Dash Pernod

Mix with cracked ice in a shaker or blender and strain into a chilled cocktail glass.

BLOODHOUND

1½ oz. gin
½ oz. sweet vermouth
½ oz. dry vermouth
1 tsp. strawberry liqueur
Several whole strawberries

Mix all ingredients with cracked ice in a blender and pour into a chilled cocktail glass.

BLOOMSBURY BLAST

1½ oz. gin
1½ oz. medium sherry
½ tsp. sweet vermouth
½ tsp. dry vermouth
¼ oz. curaçao
¼ oz. cherry brandy
¼ oz. crème de cacao
1 oz. lemon or lime juice

Mix all ingredients with plenty of cracked ice in a shaker or blender and pour into a large, chilled wine goblet.

BODEGA BOLT

1 oz. gin
1 oz. fino or amontillado
   sherry
Club soda
Lime peel

Pour gin and sherry into chilled highball glass with several ice cubes and fill with club soda. Stir gently and twist lime peel over drink and drop into glass.

BONNIE PRINCE

1½ oz. gin
½ oz. Lillet blanc
¼ oz. Drambuie
Orange peel

Mix all ingredients, except orange peel, with cracked ice in a shaker or blender and strain into a chilled cocktail glass. Twist orange peel over drink and drop into glass.

BORDEAUX COCKTAIL

1 oz. gin
¾ oz. Cordial Médoc
½ oz. dry vermouth
½ oz. lemon juice

Mix all ingredients with cracked ice in a shaker or blender and strain into a chilled cocktail glass.

BOOMERANG No. 2

1½ oz. gin
¾ oz. dry vermouth
Several dashes Angostura bitters
Several dashes maraschino liqueur
Lemon peel

Mix all ingredients, except lemon peel, with cracked ice in a shaker or blender and strain into a chilled cocktail glass. Twist lemon peel over drink and drop into glass.

BOTANY BAY

2 oz. gin
4 oz. orange juice
4 oz. grapefruit juice
1 oz. boysenberry syrup

Mix with cracked ice in a shaker or blender and pour into a chilled double Old Fashioned glass.

BRAVE COW

1½ oz. gin
1½ oz. Kahlua
Lemon peel

Pour gin and coffee liqueur into a chilled Old Fashioned glass with several ice cubes. Twist lemon peel over drink and drop into glass and stir.

BRISTOL COCKTAIL

1½ oz. gin
½ oz. ruby port
Several dashes Pernod

Mix all ingredients with cracked ice in a shaker or blender and pour into a chilled cocktail glass.

BRITTANY

1½ oz. gin
½ oz. Amer Picon
½ oz. orange juice
½ oz. lemon juice
1 tsp. sugar syrup
Orange peel

Mix all ingredients, except orange peel, with cracked ice in a shaker or blender and strain into a chilled cocktail glass. Twist orange peel over drink and drop into glass.

BRITTANY FIZZ

1 oz. gin
1 oz. brandy
1 oz. dry vermouth
Club soda
Lemon peel

Mix all ingredients, except club soda and lemon peel, with cracked ice in a shaker or blender and pour into a chilled highball glass. Fill with club soda and twist lemon peel over drink and drop into glass.

BROKEN SPUR

1 oz. gin
1½ oz. white port
1 oz. sweet vermouth
1 tsp. anisette
1 egg yolk

Mix all ingredients with cracked ice in a shaker or blender. Pour into a chilled Old Fashioned glass.

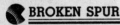 BRONX COCKTAIL, The Original

1½ oz. gin
½ oz. orange juice
Dash dry vermouth
Dash sweet vermouth

Mix all ingredients with cracked ice in a shaker and strain into a chilled cocktail glass.

Johnnie Solon, a famous bartender at the old **Waldorf-Astoria Hotel in New York,** is credited with inventing this drink.

BRONX COCKTAIL

1½ oz. gin
½ oz. dry vermouth
½ oz. sweet vermouth
1 oz. orange juice

Mix all ingredients with cracked ice in a shaker or blender and strain into chilled cocktail glass.

For a dry Bronx cocktail, omit sweet vermouth.

BRONX GOLDEN

1½ oz. gin
½ oz. dry vermouth
½ oz. sweet vermouth
1 oz. orange juice
1 egg yolk

Mix all ingredients with cracked ice in a shaker or blender and strain into a chilled cocktail glass.

BRONX SILVER

1½ oz. gin
½ oz. dry vermouth
½ oz. sweet vermouth
1 oz. orange juice
1 egg white

Mix all ingredients with cracked ice in a shaker or blender and strain into a chilled cocktail glass.

BRYN MAWR COCKTAIL

1½ oz. gin
½ oz. apricot liqueur
½ oz. lime juice
1 tsp. grenadine

Mix all ingredients with cracked ice in a shaker or blender and pour into a chilled cocktail glass.

THE BULLDOG CAFE

½ oz. gin
½ oz. rye
½ oz. sweet vermouth
½ oz. brandy
Several dashes triple sec or
  orange bitters

Mix all ingredients with cracked ice in a shaker or blender and strain into a chilled glass.

B.V.D.

¾ oz. gin
¾ oz. light rum
¾ oz. dry vermouth

Mix all ingredients with cracked ice in a shaker or blender and strain into a chilled cocktail glass.

CABARET No. 1

1½ oz. gin
1½ oz. Dubonnet rouge
Several dashes Angostura
  bitters
Several dashes Pernod
Maraschino cherry

Mix all ingredients, except maraschino cherry, with cracked ice in a shaker or blender and strain into a chilled cocktail glass. Garnish with cherry.

CABARET No. 2

1½ oz. gin
½ oz. dry vermouth
½ oz. Benedictine
Several dashes Angostura
   bitters
Maraschino cherry

Stir all ingredients, except cherry, in a mixing glass with cracked ice and strain into a chilled cocktail glass. Garnish with cherry.

CAFÉ DE PARIS

2 oz. gin
½ oz. heavy cream
1 tsp. Pernod
1 egg white (for two drinks)

Mix all ingredients with cracked ice in a shaker or blender and strain into a chilled cocktail glass.

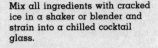

CAGNES-SUR-MER

1½ oz. gin
½ oz. Forbidden Fruit
½ oz. curaçao
2 oz. orange juice
½ tsp. lemon juice
Several dashes orange
   bitters
Club soda
Orange slice

Mix all ingredients, except club soda and orange slice, with cracked ice in a shaker or blender and pour into chilled Collins glass. Fill with club soda and garnish with orange slice.

CANNES CHAMPAGNE CUP

1 oz. gin
Several dashes Angostura
   bitters
Several dashes prunelle or
   framboise
Several dashes crème de
   cassis
Orange peel

Pour gin, bitters, prunelle, and cassis into a chilled highball glass with several ice cubes. Fill with champagne. Stir gently and twist orange peel over drink and drop into glass.

CARMEN CAVALLERO

1 oz. gin
¾ oz. dry vermouth
¾ oz. dry sherry
Dash curaçao

Pour all ingredients into a mixing glass with several ice cubes. Stir and strain into a chilled cocktail glass.

CHANTICLEER

2 oz. gin
1 oz. lemon juice
½ oz. raspberry syrup or to taste
1 egg white (for two drinks)

Mix all ingredients with cracked ice in a shaker or blender and pour into a chilled Old Fashioned glass.

CHATHAM

1½ oz. gin
½ oz. ginger-flavored brandy
½ oz. lemon juice
1 tsp. sugar syrup
Small section of preserved ginger

Mix all ingredients, except ginger, with cracked ice in a shaker or blender and strain into a chilled cocktail glass. Garnish with ginger.

CHERRY BANG!

1½ oz. gin
½ oz. Cherry Marnier
¼ oz. maraschino liqueur
½ oz. lemon juice
Several dashes kirsch
Maraschino cherry

Mix all ingredients, except kirsch and cherry, with cracked ice in a shaker or blender and strain into chilled cocktail glass. Garnish with cherry and top with kirsch.

CHERRY COBBLER

1½ oz. gin
½ oz. Cherry Heering
½ oz. crème de cassis
½ oz. lemon juice
½ oz. sugar syrup
Lemon slice
Maraschino cherry

Mix all ingredients, except lemon slice and cherry, with cracked ice in a shaker or blender and pour into chilled Old Fashioned glass. Garnish with lemon slice and maraschino cherry.

CHOCOLATE SOLDIER

1½ oz. gin
1 oz. Dubonnet rouge
½ oz. lime juice

Mix all ingredients with cracked ice in a shaker or blender and pour into a chilled Old Fashioned glass.

CLARIDGE COCKTAIL

1½ oz. gin
1 oz. dry vermouth
½ oz. apricot brandy
½ oz. triple sec

Mix all ingredients with cracked ice in a shaker or blender and strain into a chilled cocktail glass.

CLOISTER

1½ oz. gin
½ oz. yellow Chartreuse
½ oz. grapefruit juice
1 tsp. lemon juice
1 tsp. sugar syrup or to taste

Mix all ingredients with cracked ice in a shaker or blender and strain into a chilled cocktail glass.

 CLOVER CLUB

1½ oz. gin
1 oz. lime juice
½ oz. grenadine
1 egg white (for two drinks)

Mix all ingredients with cracked ice in a shaker or blender and strain into a chilled cocktail glass.

COCO CHANEL

1 oz. gin
1 oz. Kahlua or Tia Maria
1 oz. heavy cream

Mix all ingredients with cracked ice in a shaker or blender and strain into a chilled cocktail glass.

COCONUT GIN

1½ oz. gin
¼ oz. cream of coconut
¾ oz. lemon juice
¼ oz. maraschino cherry juice or 1 tsp. maraschino cherry liqueur

Mix all ingredients with cracked ice in a shaker or blender and strain into a chilled cocktail glass.

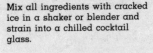 COLONY CLUB

1½ oz. gin
1 tsp. anisette
Several dashes orange bitters

Mix all ingredients with cracked ice in a shaker or blender and strain into a chilled cocktail glass.

CONNECTICUT BULLFROG

2 oz. gin
½ oz. light or gold rum
½ oz. lemon juice
½ oz. maple syrup or to taste

Mix all ingredients with cracked ice in a shaker or blender and strain into a chilled cocktail glass.

COPENHAGEN DREAM

1½ oz. gin
½ oz. aquavit
½ oz. lemon juice
1 tsp. sugar syrup or to taste
1 tsp. heavy cream
1 egg white (for two drinks)

Mix all ingredients with cracked ice in a shaker or blender and pour into a chilled Old Fashioned glass.

CORDIAL MÉDOC SOUR

1½ oz. gin
¾ oz. Cordial Médoc
½ oz. lemon juice
Orange slice

Mix all ingredients, except orange slice, with cracked ice in a shaker or blender and strain into a chilled Whiskey Sour glass. Garnish with orange slice.

 ## CORNELL COCKTAIL

2 oz. gin
½ oz. maraschino liqueur or
  to taste
1 egg white (for two drinks)

Mix with cracked ice in a shaker or blender and strain into a chilled cocktail glass.

CORONADO

1½ oz. gin
½ oz. curaçao
2 oz. pineapple juice
Several dashes kirsch
Maraschino cherry

Mix all ingredients, except maraschino cherry, with cracked ice in a shaker or blender and pour into a chilled Old Fashioned glass. Garnish with cherry.

COSTA DEL SOL

1½ oz. gin
1 oz. apricot brandy
1 oz. Cointreau or curaçao

Mix all ingredients with cracked ice in a shaker or blender and pour into a chilled Old Fashioned glass.

CRIMSON

2 oz. gin
½ oz. lemon juice
1 tsp. grenadine
1 oz. port

Mix all ingredients, except port, with cracked ice in a shaker or blender. Pour into a chilled highball glass and top with port float.

CRISTIFORO COLUMBO

1½ oz. gin
½ oz. Campari
4 oz. orange juice
Dash grenadine
Club soda
Dash curaçao

Mix all ingredients, except club soda and curaçao, with cracked ice in a shaker or blender and pour into a chilled highball glass. Fill with club soda and top with dash of curaçao.

DAMN THE WEATHER

1 oz. gin
½ oz. sweet vermouth
1 oz. orange juice
1 tsp. curaçao

Mix all ingredients with cracked ice in a shaker or blender and pour into a chilled Old Fashioned glass.

DANISH GIN FIZZ

1½ oz. gin
¾ oz. Cherry Heering
¼ oz. kirsch
½ oz. lime juice
½ oz. sugar syrup
Club soda
Lime slice

Mix all ingredients, except club soda and lime slice, with cracked ice in a shaker or blender and strain into a chilled Collins glass. Fill with club soda and garnish with lime slice.

DARB

1 oz. gin
1 oz. dry vermouth
1 oz. apricot brandy
½ oz. lemon juice
1 tsp. sugar syrup or to taste

Mix all ingredients with cracked ice in a shaker or blender and strain into a chilled cocktail glass.

DARBY

1½ oz. gin
½ oz. lime juice
½ oz. grapefruit juice
1 tsp. sugar syrup

Mix all ingredients with cracked ice in a shaker or blender and strain into a chilled cocktail glass.

DEMPSEY

1 oz. gin
1 oz. applejack or calvados
1 tsp. sugar syrup or to taste
2 dashes Pernod
2 dashes grenadine

Mix all ingredients with cracked ice in a shaker or blender and pour into a chilled Old Fashioned glass.

DERBY No. 1

1½ oz. gin
Several dashes peach bitters
Mint sprigs

Mix all ingredients, except mint sprigs, with cracked ice in a shaker or blender. Pour into a chilled Old Fashioned glass and garnish with mint sprigs.

● DEVIL'S SMILE

1 oz. gin
1 oz. brandy
1 oz. triple sec
1 oz. lemon juice
Dash amaretto

Mix all ingredients with cracked ice in a shaker or blender and strain into a chilled cocktail glass.

◥ DIAMOND HEAD

1½ oz. gin
½ oz. curaçao
2 oz. pineapple juice
1 tsp. sweet vermouth

Mix all ingredients with cracked ice in a shaker or blender. Strain into chilled cocktail glass.

DIXIE

1 oz. gin
½ oz. Pernod
½ oz. dry vermouth
1–2 oz. orange juice
Several dashes grenadine

Mix all ingredients with cracked ice in a shaker or blender and strain into a chilled Old Fashioned glass.

DIXIE DELIGHT

1 oz. gin
1 oz. Southern Comfort
1 oz. dry vermouth
½ tsp. sugar syrup
Several dashes Pernod

Mix all ingredients with cracked ice in a shaker or blender and strain into a chilled cocktail glass.

DOCTOR'S ORDERS

1 oz. gin
1 oz. cognac
1 oz. Forbidden Fruit
Several dashes lemon juice

Mix all ingredients with cracked ice in a shaker or blender. Strain into a chilled champagne saucer glass.

DOCTOR YES

1½ oz. gin
½ oz. crème de cacao
½ oz. amaretto

Mix all ingredients with cracked ice in a shaker or blender and strain into a chilled cocktail glass.

DOUGLAS FAIRBANKS

2 oz. gin
¾ oz. apricot brandy
1 oz. lemon juice
1 tsp. sugar syrup or to taste
1 egg white (for two drinks)

Mix with cracked ice in a shaker or blender and strain into a chilled cocktail glass.

DRAKE GIN SOUR

2 oz. gin
1 tsp. lemon juice
1 tsp. orgeat syrup or sugar syrup
1 egg white (for two drinks)

Mix all ingredients with cracked ice in a shaker or blender and strain into a chilled Whiskey Sour glass.

Created for the **Drake Hotel, Chicago.**

⚫ DUBONNET COCKTAIL

1½ oz. gin
1½ oz. Dubonnet rouge
Lemon peel

Mix all ingredients, except lemon peel, with cracked ice in a shaker or blender and pour into a chilled Old Fashioned glass. Twist lemon peel over drink and drop into glass.

DUNDEE

1 oz. gin
¾ oz. scotch
½ oz. Drambuie
½ oz. lemon juice
Lemon peel

Mix all ingredients, except lemon peel, with cracked ice in a shaker or blender and pour into a chilled Old Fashioned glass. Twist lemon peel over drink and drop into glass.

DUQUESNE CLUB

1½ oz. gin
½ oz. amaretto
½ oz. lime juice
Dash grenadine

Mix all ingredients with cracked ice in a shaker or blender and strain into a chilled cocktail glass.

ELK

1 oz. gin
1 oz. prunelle
Several dashes dry vermouth

Mix all ingredients with cracked ice in a shaker or blender and pour into a chilled Old Fashioned glass.

FERNET BRANCA COCKTAIL

2 oz. gin
½ oz. Fernet Branca
½ oz. sweet vermouth

Mix all ingredients with cracked ice in a shaker or blender and strain into a chilled cocktail glass.

FILBY

2 oz. gin
¾ oz. amaretto
½ oz. dry vermouth
½ oz. Campari
Orange peel

Stir all ingredients, except orange peel, with cracked ice in a mixing glass and pour into a chilled cocktail glass. Garnish with orange peel.

FINE AND DANDY

1½ oz. gin
¾ oz. triple sec
¾ oz. lemon juice
Dash Angostura or orange
    bitters

Mix all ingredients with cracked
ice in a shaker or blender and
strain into a chilled cocktail
glass.

FOGHORN

2 oz. gin
Ginger beer
Lemon slice

Pour gin into a chilled highball
glass with several ice cubes. Fill
with ginger beer and garnish
with lemon slice.

FRANKENJACK COCKTAIL

1 oz. gin
½ oz. dry vermouth
½ oz. apricot brandy
½ oz. Cointreau
Maraschino cherry

Mix all ingredients, except maraschino cherry, with cracked ice
in a shaker or blender and pour
into a chilled Old Fashioned
glass. Decorate with cherry.

FROTH BLOWER COCKTAIL

2 oz. gin
1 tsp. grenadine
1 egg white (for two drinks)

Mix all ingredients with cracked
ice in a shaker or blender and
pour into a chilled Old Fashioned glass.

GALE FORCE

1½ oz. gin
¾ oz. gold rum
3 oz. orange juice
½ oz. lemon juice
Several dashes of 151-proof
    Demerara rum or Jamaica
    rum

Mix all ingredients with cracked
ice in a shaker or blender and
pour into a chilled Old Fashioned glass.

 **THE GATE OF HORN**

2 oz. gin
½ oz. curaçao
2 oz. orange juice
1 oz. grapefruit juice
Dash orgeat syrup or to taste
Several dashes orange
    flower water

Mix with cracked ice in a shaker
or blender and pour into a
chilled wine goblet.

 **GEISHA CUP**

1½ oz. gin
1 oz. apricot brandy
2 oz. orange juice
2 oz. grapefruit juice
Maraschino cherry

Mix all ingredients, except maraschino cherry, with cracked ice
in a shaker or blender and serve
in a chilled Collins glass. Garnish with cherry.

GENOA

¾ oz. gin
¾ oz. grappa
½ oz. Sambuca Romana
½ oz. dry vermouth
Green olive

Mix all ingredients, except green
olive, with cracked ice in a
shaker or blender and strain into
a chilled cocktail glass. Garnish
with olive.

GEORGE V COCKTAIL

1½ oz. gin
1 oz. Lillet blanc
1 tsp. Cointreau
Several dashes orange
    bitters

Mix all ingredients with cracked
ice in a shaker or blender and
strain into a chilled cocktail
glass.

 THE GILDED ORANGE No. 1

2 oz. gin
½ oz. dark Jamaica rum
2 oz. orange juice
1 oz. orgeat syrup or to taste
Several dashes orange
    bitters
Dash lemon juice
Orange peel

Mix all ingredients, except orange peel, with cracked ice in a
shaker or blender and pour into
a chilled Old Fashioned glass.
Twist orange peel over drink
and drop into glass.

GILROY

1 oz. gin
1 oz. cherry brandy
½ oz. dry vermouth
½ oz. lemon juice
Several dashes orange
   bitters

Mix all ingredients with cracked
ice in a shaker or blender and
pour into a chilled Old Fashioned glass.

 ## GIMLET No. 1

2 oz. gin
¼ oz. Rose's lime juice
Lime slice

Mix all ingredients with cracked
ice in a shaker or blender and
pour into a chilled Old Fashioned glass. Garnish with lime
slice.

GIMLET No. 2

2 oz. gin
½ oz. fresh lime juice
Lime peel

Mix all ingredients, except lime
peel, vigorously with cracked ice
in a mixing glass and pour into
a chilled Old Fashioned glass.
Twist lime peel over drink and
drop into glass.

 ## GIN AND BITTERS Pink Gin

2–3 oz. gin
½ tsp. Angostura bitters

Mix gin and bitters in a glass
with ice cubes until chilled.
Strain into a chilled Old Fashioned glass without ice, since
this drink is traditionally served
neat.

GIN & GINGER

1½ oz. gin
Ginger ale
Lemon peel

Pour gin into chilled highball
glass with several ice cubes.
Twist lemon peel over drink and
drop in. Fill with ginger ale. Stir
gently.

 GIN AND TONIC

2 oz. gin
Tonic water
Lime wedge

Pour gin into chilled Collins glass with several ice cubes. Fill with tonic water and squeeze lime wedge over drink and drop into glass.

GIN BOLOGNESE

1 oz. gin
½ oz. Fernet Branca
½ oz. orange bitters
Lemon peel

Mix all ingredients, except lemon peel, with cracked ice in a shaker or blender. Strain into a chilled cocktail glass. Twist lemon peel over drink and drop into glass.

GIN CASSIS

1½ oz. gin
½ oz. lemon juice
½ oz. crème de cassis

Mix all ingredients with cracked ice in a shaker or blender and pour into a chilled Old Fashioned glass.

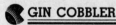 GIN COBBLER

2 oz. gin
1 tsp. sugar syrup or orgeat
    syrup
Club soda
Orange slice

Mix gin and syrup with cracked ice in a double Old Fashioned glass and fill with cold club soda. Stir gently and garnish with orange slice.

GIN DAISY

2–3 oz. gin
1 oz. lemon juice
¼ oz. raspberry syrup or
    grenadine
½ tsp. sugar syrup or to taste
Club soda
Orange slice or mint sprigs

Mix all ingredients, except club soda and orange slice, with cracked ice in a shaker or blender and pour into a chilled highball glass. Fill with cold club soda and garnish with orange slice.

GIN FIZZ

2–3 oz. gin
½ oz. sugar syrup
Juice of ½ lemon
Juice of ½ lime
Club soda
Maraschino cherry

Mix all ingredients, except
cherry and club soda, in a
shaker or blender and pour into
a chilled highball glass and fill
with cold club soda. Garnish
with cherry.

 ## GINGERINE

2 oz. gin
4 oz. tangerine juice
4 oz. grapefruit juice
Dash sugar syrup or to taste
Dash grenadine or raspberry
   syrup

Mix with cracked ice in a shaker
or blender and pour into a
chilled double Old Fashioned
glass.

 ## THE GIN-GER MAN

2 oz. gin
4 oz. orange-grapefruit juice
2 oz. cranberry juice
1 tablespoon ginger
   marmalade
Orange slice

Mix all ingredients, except orange slice, with cracked ice in a
shaker or blender and pour into
a chilled double Old Fashioned
glass. Garnish with orange slice.

 ## GIN-GER MAN No. 2

2 oz. gin
4 oz. orange juice
2 oz. grapefruit juice
½ oz. orgeat syrup or to taste
1 tablespoon ginger
   marmalade

Mix with cracked ice in a shaker
or blender and pour into a
chilled Collins glass.

 ## GIN MILK PUNCH

1½ oz. gin
5 oz. milk
1 tsp. sugar syrup
Pinch of ground nutmeg

Mix all ingredients, except nutmeg, with cracked ice in a
shaker or blender and pour into
a chilled highball glass. Sprinkle
with ground nutmeg.

GIN RAY

2 oz. gin
1 oz. light rum
3 oz. orange juice
1 oz. lemon juice
1 tsp. orgeat syrup or sugar
   syrup
Several dashes maraschino
   liqueur

Mix all ingredients with cracked ice in a shaker or blender and pour into a chilled double Old Fashioned glass.

 GIN RICKEY

1½ oz. gin
Club soda
Juice of ½ lime

Pour gin into a chilled highball glass with several ice cubes. Fill with club soda, add lime juice, and stir gently.

GIN SIDECAR

1½ oz. gin
¾ oz. triple sec
1 oz. lemon juice

Mix all ingredients with cracked ice in a shaker or blender and pour into a chilled Old Fashioned glass.

GIN SLING

2–3 oz. gin
1 oz. lemon juice
½ oz. orgeat or sugar syrup
   or to taste
Club soda or water

Mix gin, lemon juice, and syrup with cracked ice in a double Old Fashioned glass and fill with cold club soda or water. Stir well.

GIN SMASH No. 1

6 mint leaves
1½ oz. gin
½ oz. peppermint schnapps
½ oz. lemon juice
½ oz. sugar syrup
Lemon slice
Mint sprig

Muddle mint leaves, gin, schnapps, lemon, and sugar syrup in a double Old Fashioned glass with a little water. Add cracked ice, stir well, and garnish with lemon slice and mint sprig.

GIN SMASH No. 2

Mint leaves
2 oz. gin
½ oz. curaçao
½ oz. lime juice
Dash orange bitters
Lemon slice
Several mint sprigs
Club soda

Muddle mint leaves, gin, curaçao, lime juice, and orange bitters in a chilled Old Fashioned
glass until well mixed. Add
crushed ice and garnish with
lemon slice and mint sprigs. Add
a splash of club soda and stir
well.

GIN SOUR

2–3 oz. gin
1 oz. lemon juice
1 tsp. sugar syrup or to taste
Orange slice
Maraschino cherry

Mix all ingredients, except orange slice and maraschino
cherry, with cracked ice in a
shaker or blender and strain into
a chilled Whiskey Sour glass.
Decorate with fruit.

GOLDEN FIZZ

2–3 oz. gin
1 oz. lemon or lime juice
1 tsp. sugar syrup or to taste
1 egg yolk
Club soda
Lemon or lime slice

Mix all ingredients, except fruit
slice, with cracked ice in a
shaker or blender and pour into
a chilled Collins glass. Fill with
cold club soda, stir gently, and
garnish with fruit slice.

GOLDEN DAWN

2 oz. gin
¾ oz. apricot liqueur
2 oz. orange juice
Juice of ½ lime
Dash grenadine or raspberry
   syrup

Mix with cracked ice in a shaker
or blender and strain into a
chilled cocktail glass.

GOODBYE DOLLY

1½ oz. gin.
½ oz. maraschino liqueur
1 tsp. grenadine
1 egg white (for two drinks)
1 tsp. Parfait Amour or
   anisette

Mix all ingredients but the last with cracked ice in a shaker or blender. Strain into a chilled cocktail glass. Add a float of Parfait Amour or anisette.

 GRADEAL SPECIAL

1½ oz. gin
¾ oz. light rum
¾ oz. apricot brandy or
   apricot liqueur
1 tsp. sugar syrup

Mix with cracked ice in a shaker or blender and strain into a chilled cocktail glass.

If apricot liqueur is used, omit sugar syrup.

GRAND MOMENT

1½ oz. gin
¾ oz. Grand Marnier
½ oz. lime juice
1 egg white (for two drinks)

Mix all ingredients with cracked ice in a shaker or blender. Pour into a chilled brandy snifter.

GRAND PASSION

2 oz. gin
1 oz. La Grande Passion
Several dashes Angostura
   bitters

Mix all ingredients with cracked ice in a shaker or blender and pour into a chilled cocktail glass.

GRAND ROYAL FIZZ

2 oz London dry gin
Juice of ½ lemon
Several dashes maraschino
   liqueur
1 tsp. confectioner's sugar or
   to taste
1 tbsp. heavy cream
Club soda

Mix all ingredients, except club soda, with cracked ice in a shaker or blender and serve in a chilled highball glass. Top with club soda and stir gently.

GRANVILLE

1½ oz. gin
¼ oz. Grand Marnier
¼ oz. calvados
¼ oz. lemon juice

Mix all ingredients with cracked ice in a shaker or blender and strain into a chilled cocktail glass.

GRAPEFRUIT COCKTAIL

1½ oz. gin
1 oz. grapefruit juice
1 tsp. maraschino liqueur
Maraschino cherry

Mix all ingredients, except maraschino cherry, with cracked ice in a shaker or blender and strain into a chilled cocktail glass. Garnish with cherry.

GRAPE VINE

1½ oz. gin
2 oz. grape juice
1 oz. lemon juice
½ oz. sugar syrup
Dash grenadine

Pour all ingredients into a chilled Old Fashioned glass with several ice cubes and stir well.

BARTENDER'S SECRET NO. 2—Crystal Check

Clean, sparkling glassware adds to the appeal of any drink. But don't rely on either home or institutional dishwashers to give you spotless glasses every time. As every bartender knows, water spots (not dirt) are the problem, and, occasionally, grease smears from lipstick. Always check glasses that come from the dishwasher against the light to see if the detergent is doing its job. If glasses are hand-washed, use two towels: one for drying and one for polishing. Change towels frequently. From a hygienic standpoint, air-drying after washing is best. If washing glasses in a home dishwasher, do not remove glasses after the final rinse cycle. Give them time to dry in the heat before removing.

GREAT DANE

1 oz. gin
½ oz. dry vermouth
½ oz. Cherry Heering
1 tsp. kirsch
Lemon peel

Mix all ingredients, except lemon peel, with cracked ice in a shaker or blender and strain into a chilled cocktail glass. Twist lemon peel over drink and drop into glass.

GREAT SECRET

1½ oz. gin
¾ oz. *Lillet blanc*
*Several dashes Angostura
    bitters*
Orange peel

Mix all ingredients, except orange peel, with cracked ice in a shaker or blender and strain into a chilled cocktail glass. Twist orange peel over drink and drop into glass.

GREENBRIER COLLINS

2 oz. gin
½ oz. *lemon juice*
1 tsp. *white crème de
    menthe*
1 tsp. *sugar syrup*
Club soda
Mint sprigs

Mix all ingredients, except club soda and mint leaves, with cracked ice in a shaker or blender and pour into a chilled Collins glass. Fill with cold club soda, stir gently, and garnish with mint sprigs.

Created for **The Greenbrier, White Sulphur Springs, West Virginia.**

GREEN DRAGON

1½ oz. gin
1 oz. *green crème de menthe*
½ oz. *kümmel*
½ oz. *lemon juice*
*Several dashes peach or
    orange bitters*

Mix all ingredients with cracked ice in a shaker or blender and strain into a chilled cocktail glass.

GREEN LAGOON

1 oz. gin
1 oz. *green crème de menthe*
2–3 oz. *pineapple juice*

Mix all ingredients with cracked ice in a shaker or blender and strain into a chilled cocktail glass.

GUARDS COCKTAIL

1½ oz. gin
½ oz. *sweet vermouth*
½ oz. *curaçao*

Pour all ingredients into a chilled Old Fashioned glass with several ice cubes and stir until well mixed.

HABIT ROUGE

1½ oz. gin
1½ oz. grapefruit juice
1½ oz. cranberry juice
1 tsp. maple syrup or honey

Mix all ingredients with cracked ice in a shaker or blender and pour into a chilled wine goblet or cocktail glass.

HARLEM COCKTAIL

1½ oz. gin
1 oz. pineapple juice
1 tsp. maraschino liqueur
1 tbsp. diced canned
pineapple

Mix all ingredients in a blender with cracked ice and pour into a chilled Old Fashioned glass.

HASTY COCKTAIL

1½ oz. gin
½ oz. dry vermouth
½ tsp. grenadine
Several dashes Pernod

Mix all ingredients with cracked ice in a shaker or blender and strain into a chilled cocktail glass.

HAWAIIAN

1½ oz. gin
1 oz. pineapple juice
1 egg white (for two drinks)
Several dashes orange
bitters

Mix all ingredients with cracked ice in a shaker or blender and strain into a chilled cocktail glass.

HAWAIIAN COOLER

1½ oz. gin
4 oz. pineapple juice
½ oz. orgeat syrup
Club soda
Maraschino cherry

Mix all ingredients, except club soda and cherry, with cracked ice in a shaker or blender and pour into a double Old Fashioned glass. Fill with cold club soda and stir gently. Garnish with a cherry.

HAWAIIAN ORANGE BLOSSOM

1½ oz. gin
1 oz. curaçao
2 oz. orange juice
1 oz. pineapple juice

Mix all ingredients with cracked ice in a shaker or blender and strain into a chilled Whiskey Sour glass.

● HOFFMAN DOLAN FIZZ

1½ oz. gin
¾ oz. apricot brandy
1 tsp. anisette or Pernod
1 tsp. lemon juice
Club soda
Lemon peel
½ apricot

Mix all ingredients, except club soda, lemon peel, and apricot, with cracked ice in a shaker or blender and pour into a chilled Collins glass. Fill with club soda, twist lemon peel over drink and drop in glass. Garnish with apricot.

THE HOMESTEAD SPECIAL

1½ oz. gin
½ oz. blackberry liqueur
½ oz. lime juice

Mix all ingredients with cracked ice in a shaker or blender and strain into a chilled cocktail glass.

Created for **The Homestead, Hot Springs, Virginia.**

HYANNIS HIATUS

1½ oz. gin
Cranberry juice
Orange slice

Pour gin into chilled double Old Fashioned glass with several ice cubes. Fill with cranberry juice and garnish with orange slice.

◤ ISTRIAN SMILING

1½ oz. gin
1 oz. crème de cassis
1 tsp. Mandarine Napoleon
Tonic water

Stir gin, cassis, and Mandarine liqueur with ice in a mixing glass and pour into a tall highball glass. Add ice cubes and fill with cold tonic water.

JAMAICA GLOW

1½ oz. gin
½ oz. dry red wine
¼ oz. dark Jamaica rum
½ oz. orange juice
Lime slice

Mix all ingredients, except lime slice, with cracked ice in a shaker or blender and strain into a chilled cocktail glass. Decorate with lime slice.

 THE JAY BIRD

2 oz. gin
1 oz. sloe gin
2 oz. pineapple juice
Dash orgeat syrup
Pineapple stick

Mix all ingredients, except pineapple, with cracked ice in a shaker or blender and serve in a chilled Collins glass. Garnish with pineapple stick.

JEWEL

1 oz. gin
1 oz. sweet vermouth
1 oz. green Chartreuse
Several dashes orange
  bitters
Lemon peel

Mix all ingredients, except lemon peel, with cracked ice in a shaker or blender and strain into a chilled Old Fashioned glass. Twist lemon peel over drink and drop into glass.

JOAN COLEMAN'S COCKTAIL

1½ oz. gin
½ oz. maraschino liqueur
1 egg white (for two drinks)
Dash orange flower water

Mix all ingredients with cracked ice in a shaker or blender and strain into a chilled cocktail glass.

JOCKEY CLUB

2 oz. gin
½ tsp. crème de noyaux
½ tsp. lemon juice
Several dashes Angostura
  bitters
Several dashes orange
  bitters

Mix all ingredients with cracked ice in a shaker or blender and strain into a chilled Old Fashioned glass.

JOHN'S IDEA

1½ oz. Seagram's Extra Dry
   Gin
¾ cup orange juice
1–2 tsp. Piña Colada mix or
   to taste

Mix all ingredients with cracked
ice in a shaker or blender and
strain into a chilled Collins
glass.

Created for the Seagrams Distillers Co. by the author

JOULOUVILLE

1 oz. gin
½ oz. apple brandy
½ oz. sweet vermouth
½ oz. lemon juice
Several dashes grenadine

Mix all ingredients with cracked
ice in a shaker or blender and
strain into a chilled cocktail
glass.

JUDGE, JR.

1 oz. gin
1 oz. light rum
½ oz. lemon juice
1 tsp. grenadine

Mix all ingredients with cracked
ice in a shaker or blender and
strain into a chilled cocktail
glass.

JUAN-LES-PINS COCKTAIL

1 oz. gin
¾ oz. Dubonnet blanc
½ oz. apricot brandy
Dash lemon juice
Maraschino cherry

Mix all ingredients, except maraschino cherry, with cracked ice
in a shaker or blender and
strain into chilled cocktail glass.
Garnish with cherry.

JUPITER COCKTAIL

1½ oz. gin
¾ oz. French vermouth
1 tsp. Parfait Amour or
   crème de violette
1 tsp. orange juice

Mix all ingredients with cracked
ice in a shaker or blender and
strain into a chilled cocktail
glass.

As with any gin-vermouth combination, feel free to change the
proportions to suit individual
tastes.

KCB

1½ oz. gin
¼ oz. kirsch
Several dashes apricot
   brandy
Several dashes lemon juice
Lemon peel

Mix all ingredients, except
lemon peel, with cracked ice in
a shaker or blender and strain
into a chilled cocktail glass.
Twist lemon peel over drink and
drop into glass.

KENSINGTON CHEER

1½ oz. gin
3 oz. green ginger wine
2 oz. orange juice
Club soda
Slice of candied ginger

Mix all ingredients, except club
soda and ginger, with cracked
ice in a shaker or blender and
pour into a chilled highball
glass. Fill with club soda, stir
gently, and garnish with candied
ginger.

KEY CLUB COCKTAIL

1½ oz. gin
½ oz. dark Jamaica rum
½ oz. Falernum
½ oz. lime juice
Pineapple stick

Mix all ingredients, except pineapple stick, with cracked ice in a
shaker or blender and strain into
a chilled cocktail glass. Decorate
with pineapple.

KNOCKOUT

1 oz. gin
1 oz. dry vermouth
1 oz. Pernod
Dash lemon juice
Maraschino cherry

Mix all ingredients, except maraschino cherry, with cracked ice
in a shaker or blender and
strain into a chilled cocktail
glass. Decorate with cherry.

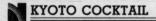 KYOTO COCKTAIL

1½ oz. gin
½ oz. dry vermouth
½ oz. melon liqueur
Dash lemon juice

Mix all ingredients with cracked
ice in a shaker or blender and
strain into a chilled cocktail
glass.

LA CÔTE BASQUE COCKTAIL

1½ oz. gin
½ oz. Forbidden Fruit
½ oz. triple sec
Several dashes orange
  bitters

Mix all ingredients with cracked ice in a shaker or blender and strain into chilled cocktail glass.

LADBROKE ROAD COCKTAIL

1½ oz. gin
1 oz. strawberry liqueur
½ oz. lemon juice
Dash triple sec
Club soda
Lemon peel
1 whole strawberry

Mix all ingredients, except club soda, lemon peel, and strawberry, with cracked ice in a shaker or blender and strain into a chilled Collins glass. Fill with club soda and twist lemon peel over drink and drop in. Garnish with strawberry.

LADYFINGER

1 oz. gin
½ oz. Cherry Heering or
  Cherry Marnier
½ oz. kirsch

Mix all ingredients with cracked ice in a shaker or blender and pour into a chilled Old Fashioned glass.

LEAP FROG

1½ oz. gin
½ oz. lemon juice
Ginger ale

Mix gin and lemon juice with cracked ice in a tall highball or Collins glass and fill with cold ginger ale.

LE COQ D'OR

1 oz. gin
½ oz. dry vermouth
½ oz. triple sec
½ oz. apricot brandy
Maraschino cherry

Mix all ingredients, except maraschino cherry, with cracked ice in a shaker or blender and pour into a chilled Old Fashioned glass. Decorate with cherry.

LE TOUQUET COCKTAIL

1½ oz. gin
½ oz. calvados
½ oz. light rum
¼ oz. Grand Marnier
Club soda
Orange peel

Mix all ingredients, except club soda and orange peel, with cracked ice in a shaker or blender and pour into a chilled highball glass. Fill with club soda and twist orange peel over drink and drop into glass.

LILLET NOYAUX

½ oz. gin
1½ oz. Lillet blanc
1 tsp. crème de noyaux
Orange peel

Mix all ingredients, except orange peel, with cracked ice in a shaker or blender and strain into a chilled cocktail glass. Twist orange peel over drink and drop into glass.

LILLIAN LANGELL

2 oz. gin
Several dashes crème yvette
Several dashes orange
  flower water
1 egg white (for two drinks)

Mix all ingredients with cracked ice in a shaker or blender and strain into a chilled cocktail glass.

LITTLE DEVIL

1 oz. gin
1 oz. gold rum
½ oz. triple sec
½ oz. lemon juice

Mix all ingredients with cracked ice and strain into a chilled cocktail glass.

LONDON COCKTAIL No. 1

1½ oz. gin
¾ oz. triple sec
½ oz. lemon juice

Mix all ingredients with cracked ice in a shaker or blender and pour into a chilled cocktail glass.

LONDON COCKTAIL No. 2

1½ oz. gin
Several dashes maraschino
  liqueur
Several dashes orange
  bitters
Several dashes sugar syrup
  or to taste

Mix all ingredients with cracked
ice in a shaker or blender and
strain into a chilled cocktail
glass.

LONDON FRENCH "75"

1½ oz. gin
Juice of ½ lemon
1 tsp. sugar syrup
Brut champagne

Mix gin, lemon juice, and sugar
syrup with cracked ice in a
shaker or blender and pour into
a chilled Collins glass. Add ice
cubes and fill with cold
champagne.

LONE TREE

¾ oz. gin
¾ oz. dry vermouth
¾ oz. sweet vermouth
Several dashes orange
  bitters
Olive

Mix all ingredients, except olive,
with cracked ice in a shaker or
blender and strain into a chilled
cocktail glass. Garnish with
olive.

LORELEI

1½ oz. gin
½ oz. green crème de
  menthe
¼ oz. kümmel
¼ oz. lemon juice

Mix all ingredients with cracked
ice in a shaker or blender and
strain into a chilled cocktail
glass.

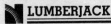 LUMBERJACK

1 oz. gin
½ oz. applejack
½ oz. Southern Comfort
½ oz. maple syrup

Mix all ingredients with cracked
ice in a shaker or blender and
strain into a chilled cocktail
glass.

MAIDEN'S BLUSH No. 1

1½ oz. gin
1 tsp. curaçao
½ tsp. lemon juice
½ tsp. grenadine

Mix all ingredients with cracked ice in a shaker or blender and strain into a chilled Whiskey Sour glass.

MAIDEN'S BLUSH No. 2

2½ oz. gin
¾ oz. Pernod
½ tsp. grenadine

Mix all ingredients with cracked ice in a shaker or blender and strain into a chilled cocktail glass.

MAIDEN'S PRAYER No. 1

1½ oz. gin
¾ oz. Cointreau
¼ oz. orange juice
¼ oz. lemon juice

Mix all ingredients with cracked ice in a shaker or blender and strain into a chilled cocktail glass.

MAIDEN'S PRAYER No. 2

1½ oz. gin
½ oz. Lillet blanc
¼ oz. lemon juice
¼ oz. orange juice

Mix all ingredients with cracked ice in a shaker or blender. Strain into a chilled cocktail glass.

Some recipes specify ¼ oz. calvados and ¼ oz. apricot brandy in place of lemon and orange juices.

MAINBRACE No. 1

1½ oz. gin
¾ oz. triple sec or curaçao
1 oz. grape juice

Mix all ingredients with cracked ice in a shaker or blender and strain into a cocktail glass.

MAINBRACE No. 2

1 oz. gin
1 oz. curaçao
1 oz. grapefruit juice

Mix all ingredients with cracked ice in a shaker or blender. Strain into a chilled cocktail glass.

MANDARINE FIZZ

1 oz. gin
1 oz. *Mandarine Napoleon*
2 oz. orange or tangerine
   juice
½ oz. sugar syrup
Club soda
Tangerine wedge

Mix all ingredients, except club soda and tangerine wedge, with cracked ice in a shaker or blender and strain into a chilled highball glass. Fill with club soda and garnish with tangerine wedge.

MARIEMONT SPECIAL

1 oz. gin
1 oz. dry vermouth
1 oz. orange juice
1 tsp. grenadine
Dash triple sec

Mix all ingredients with cracked ice in a shaker or blender and pour into a chilled Old Fashioned glass.

MARMALADE COCKTAIL

2 oz. gin
1 oz. lemon juice
1 tbsp. orange marmalade

Mix all ingredients with cracked ice in a blender and pour into a chilled cocktail glass.

MATINEE

1½ oz. gin
½ oz. sambuca
½ oz. lime juice
1 tsp. heavy cream
1 egg white (for two drinks)
Pinch of ground nutmeg or
   cinnamon

Mix all ingredients, except spice, with cracked ice in a shaker or blender and strain into a chilled cocktail glass. Sprinkle with ground nutmeg or cinnamon.

MARTINI Basic recipe. See page 110 for Martini Variations.

2 oz. gin
½ tsp. dry vermouth or to
   taste
Olive or lemon *twist*

Stir gin and vermouth in a mixing glass with plenty of ice and strain into a chilled cocktail glass. Garnish with olive or lemon twist.

MAYFAIR

1½ oz. gin
½ oz. apricot-flavored brandy
3 oz. orange juice
Dash grenadine

Mix all ingredients with cracked ice in a shaker or blender and strain into a chilled cocktail glass.

MELON COCKTAIL No. 1

1½ oz. gin
½ oz. maraschino liqueur
½ oz. lemon juice
Maraschino cherry

Mix all ingredients, except cherry, with cracked ice in a shaker or blender and strain into a chilled cocktail glass.

MELON COCKTAIL No. 2

1½ oz. gin
¾ oz. melon liqueur
½ oz. triple sec
½ oz. lemon juice

Mix all ingredients with cracked ice in a shaker or blender and strain into a chilled cocktail glass.

MERRY WIDOW

1 oz. gin
1 oz. dry vermouth
Several dashes Pernod
Several dashes Benedictine
Several dashes Peychaud's
    bitters or Angostura bitters
Lemon peel

Mix all ingredients, except lemon peel, with cracked ice in a shaker or blender and strain into a chilled cocktail glass. Twist lemon peel over drink and drop into glass.

BARTENDER'S SECRET NO. 3—Martini Fixings

The conventional Martini employs traditional garnishes: the lemon peel and the green olive. The Gibson, an extra-dry Martini using tiny bottled pearl onions, was, when it became popular, considered to be a rather daring innovation. Nowadays, Martini makers and drinkers are experimenting with a wide range of garnishes with rewarding results. Here are some variations that are used individually, not in combination: chili pepper; lime or orange twist; dill-pickle slice; capers; anchovies; avocado slice; artichoke heart; radish slice; water-chestnut sliver; pickled green bean; button mushrooms marinated in vermouth; baby eggplants steeped in white wine vinegar; olives stuffed with anchovies or onion or almonds; olives marinated in port, sherry, or Madeira; and even garlic slices or sliver of Bermuda onion. There is no end to creative garnishes. The classic Martini seems to be strong enough to stand up to anything in the way of additives. As every bartender knows, there is no accounting for individual taste.

◥ MICHEL'S PASSION

2 oz. gin
1 oz. dry vermouth
1 oz. *La Grande Passion*
Orange peel

Mix all ingredients, except orange peel, with cracked ice in a shaker or blender and strain into a chilled cocktail glass. Twist orange peel over drink and drop into glass.

MILLION DOLLAR COCKTAIL

1½ oz. gin
¾ oz. sweet vermouth
½ oz. pineapple juice
1 tsp. grenadine
1 egg white (for two drinks)

Mix all ingredients with cracked ice in a shaker or blender and strain into a chilled cocktail glass.

MILLIONAIRE COCKTAIL No. 1

1½ oz. gin
¾ oz. Pernod
1 egg white (for two drinks)
Dash anisette

Mix all ingredients with cracked ice in a shaker or blender and pour into a chilled cocktail glass.

MISSISSIPPI MULE

1½ oz. gin
¼ oz. crème de cassis
¼ oz. lemon juice

Mix all ingredients with cracked ice in a shaker or blender and pour into a chilled Old Fashioned glass.

MOLDAU

1½ oz. gin
½ oz. plum brandy
½ oz. orange juice
½ oz. lemon juice
Brandied cherry

Mix all ingredients, except brandied cherry, with cracked ice in a shaker or blender and pour into a chilled cocktail glass. Garnish with cherry.

MOLL COCKTAIL

1 oz. gin
1 oz. sloe gin
1 oz. dry vermouth
Dash orange bitters

Mix with cracked ice in a shaker or blender and strain into a chilled cocktail glass.

MONKEY GLAND

1½ oz. gin
¾ oz. orange juice
Several dashes Benedictine
Several dashes grenadine

Mix all ingredients with cracked ice in a shaker or blender and strain into a chilled cocktail glass.

MONTREAL COCKTAIL

1 oz. gin
1 oz. Cherry Marnier
1 oz. orange juice
1 oz. lime juice
½ oz. sugar syrup or to taste

Mix all ingredients with cracked ice in a shaker or blender and strain into a chilled cocktail glass.

MOONSHOT

1½ oz. gin
3 oz. clam juice
Dash red pepper sauce

Combine all ingredients in a mixing glass with several ice cubes. Strain into a chilled Whiskey Sour glass.

MORNING JOY

1 oz. gin
1 oz. crème de banane
2 oz. orange juice

Mix all ingredients with cracked ice in a shaker or blender and strain into a chilled Whiskey Sour glass.

 MORNING KISS

¾ oz. gin
¾ oz. apricot brandy
1 oz. orange juice
Brut champagne

Mix all ingredients, except champagne, with cracked ice in a shaker or blender and strain into a large, chilled wine goblet. Fill with cold champagne and stir gently.

MORNING SUN

2 oz. gin
2 oz. grapefruit juice
2 oz. orange juice
½ tsp. maraschino cherry juice
Dash Angostura bitters
Maraschino cherry

Mix all ingredients, except maraschino cherry, with cracked ice in a blender. Pour into a chilled double Old Fashioned glass and garnish with maraschino cherry.

MOULIN BLEU

1½ oz. gin
1½ oz. Pernod
Orange slice

Pour all ingredients into a chilled Old Fashioned glass with several ice cubes and stir and garnish with orange.

MULE'S HIND LEG

¾ oz. gin
¾ oz. apple brandy
¾ oz. Benedictine
¾ oz. apricot brandy
¾ oz. maple syrup or to taste

Mix all ingredients with cracked ice in a shaker or blender and pour into a chilled cocktail glass.

This is the original recipe. Modern versions sometimes utilize more gin and apple brandy in proportion to other ingredients.

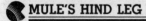 NEGRONI

2 oz. gin
½ oz. sweet vermouth
¾ oz. Campari
Orange peel

Blend all ingredients, except orange peel, with cracked ice in a mixing glass and strain into a chilled cocktail glass. Twist orange peel over drink and drop into glass.

NEW ORLEANS GIN FIZZ

3 oz gin
1 oz. cream or half-and-half
Juice of ½ lemon
1 egg white (for two drinks)
Dash vanilla extract
Dash orange flower water
1 oz. simple syrup or to taste
Club soda

Mix all ingredients, except club soda, with cracked ice in a shaker or blender and pour into a large chilled highball glass; top with club soda and stir gently.

When this classic drink was invented in the ninteenth century, soda was dispensed from a syphon bottle. As was the custom, a squirt from the syphon was used to give a drink a little fizz, hence the name.

NEWPORT COOLER

1½ oz. gin
½ oz. brandy
½ oz. peach liqueur
Several dashes lime juice
Ginger ale or lemon-lime
  soda

Mix all ingredients, except soda, in a chilled Collins glass with ice cubes. Fill with ginger ale or lemon-lime soda.

NIGHT TRAIN

2 oz. gin
1 oz. Cointreau
½ oz. lemon juice
Dash kirsch

Mix all ingredients with cracked ice in a shaker or blender and strain into a chilled cocktail glass.

THE NOON BALLOON

2 oz. gin
3 oz. orange juice
1 oz. grapefruit juice
1 oz. cranberry juice
½ oz. Falernum or sugar
  syrup to taste
Maraschino cherry

Mix all ingredients, except cherry, with cracked ice in a shaker or blender and serve in a chilled double Old Fashioned glass.

NORMANDY COCKTAIL No. 2

1½ oz. gin
¾ oz. calvados or applejack
½ oz. apricot brandy
Several dashes lemon juice

Mix all ingredients with cracked ice in a shaker or blender and pour into a chilled cocktail glass.

NORMANDY NIP

1½ oz. gin
¾ oz. calvados
½ oz. lemon juice
½ oz. sugar syrup

Mix all ingredients with cracked ice in a shaker or blender and strain into a chilled cocktail glass.

NYACK COCKTAIL

1 oz. gin
¾ oz. cherry brandy
½ oz. dry vermouth

Mix all ingredients with cracked ice in a shaker or blender and strain into a chilled cocktail glass.

OPERA

1½ oz. gin
¾ oz. Dubonnet rouge
½ oz. maraschino liqueur
Orange peel

Mix all ingredients, except orange peel, with cracked ice in a shaker or blender and strain into a chilled cocktail glass. Twist orange peel over drink and drop into glass.

ORANGE BANG! No. 2

1½ oz. gin
1 oz. orange juice
½ oz. triple sec or curaçao
Several dashes orange bitters
1 large orange wedge

Mix gin, orange juice, triple sec, and orange bitters with cracked ice in a shaker or blender and strain into a chilled cocktail glass. Garnish with orange wedge.

ORANGE BLOSSOM

1½ oz. gin
1 oz. orange juice
Orange slice

Mix all ingredients, except orange slice, with cracked ice in a shaker or blender. Strain into a chilled cocktail glass. Decorate with orange slice.

● ORGEAT COCKTAIL

2 oz. gin
1 oz. lemon juice
¾ oz. orgeat syrup or to taste
1 egg white (for two drinks)

Mix with cracked ice in a shaker or blender and strain into a chilled cocktail glass.

OUR HOME

1 oz. gin
1 oz. peach brandy
½ oz. dry vermouth
Dash lemon juice
1 egg white (for two drinks)

Mix all ingredients with cracked ice in a shaker or blender and strain into a chilled cocktail glass.

PALL MALL

1 oz. gin
1 oz. sweet vermouth
1 oz. dry vermouth
1 tsp. white crème de menthe
Several dashes orange bitters

Pour all ingredients into a mixing glass with several ice cubes and strain into a chilled cocktail glass.

THE PANDA

1 oz. gin
1 oz. calvados or applejack
1 oz. slivovitz
1 oz. orange juice
Dash sugar syrup or to taste

Mix with cracked ice in a shaker or blender and strain into a chilled cocktail glass.

PARISIAN

1 oz. gin
1 oz. dry vermouth
1 oz. crème de cassis

Pour all ingredients into a mixing glass with several ice cubes. Stir and strain into a chilled cocktail glass.

PARK AVENUE COCKTAIL

1½ oz. gin
½ oz. cherry brandy
½ oz. lime juice
¼ oz. maraschino liqueur

Mix all ingredients with cracked ice in a shaker or blender and strain into a chilled cocktail glass.

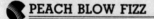 PASSION CUP No. 1

2 oz. gin
2 oz. orange juice
1 oz. passion fruit juice
1 oz. Piña Colada mix or
   equal parts of pineapple
   juice and coconut milk
Maraschino cherry

Mix all ingredients, except cherry, with cracked ice in a shaker or blender and pour into a chilled wine goblet. Garnish with maraschino cherry.

PEACH BLOW FIZZ

2–3 oz. gin
1 oz. lemon juice
1 oz. heavy cream
1 tsp. sugar syrup or to taste
4 mashed strawberries
Club soda

Mix all ingredients, except club soda, with cracked ice in a shaker or blender and pour into a chilled highball glass. Fill with club soda and stir gently.

BARTENDER'S SECRET NO. 4—Cocktail Scents

Many mixed drinks are enhanced by garnishes such as lemon, lime, and orange peel as well as olives, cherries, and onions. Many bartenders will twist a lemon peel (to release the essential oils) and rub it around the rim of a cocktail glass when making a Martini, for example. The lemony aroma and taste enhance the drink. Why not try it with lime, orange, and even an olive or maraschino cherry? The suggestion of flavor on the rim of the glass gives a hint of the enjoyment of a well-made cocktail that awaits the drinker.

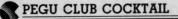 **PEGU CLUB COCKTAIL**

1½ oz. gin
¾ oz. orange curaçao
1 tsp. lime juice
Dash Angostura bitters
Dash orange bitters

Mix all ingredients with cracked ice in a shaker or blender and strain into a chilled cocktail glass.

PENDENNIS CLUB COCKTAIL

1½ oz. gin
¾ oz. apricot brandy
½ oz. lime juice
1 tsp. sugar syrup
Several dashes Peychaud's
  bitters

Mix all ingredients with cracked ice in a shaker or blender and strain into a chilled cocktail glass.

PIMLICO COOLER

1½ oz. gin
3 oz. orange juice
Ginger ale

Pour gin and orange juice into a chilled highball glass with ice cubes and fill with cold ginger ale. Stir gently.

PINEAPPLE MINT COOLER

2 oz. gin
½ oz. peppermint schnapps
1 oz. lemon juice
3 oz. pineapple juice
½ oz. sugar syrup
Club soda
Pineapple stick
Green cherry (optional)

Mix all ingredients, except club soda, pineapple stick, and green cherry, with cracked ice in a shaker or blender and pour into a chilled highball glass. Fill with club soda and garnish with fruit.

 PINK GIN

2–3 oz. gin
Angostura bitters to taste

Mix gin and bitters with plenty of ice in a mixing glass and strain into a chilled cocktail or Old Fashioned glass.

PINK LADY

1½ oz. gin
1½ oz. applejack or calvados
1 oz. lemon juice
1 tsp. sugar syrup or to taste
1 tsp. grenadine
1 egg white (for two drinks)

Mix all ingredients with cracked ice in a shaker or blender and strain into a chilled cocktail glass.

PINK PANTHER No. 2

1½ oz. gin
¾ oz. dry vermouth
½ oz. crème de cassis
1 oz. orange juice
1 egg white (for two drinks)

Mix all ingredients with cracked ice in a shaker or blender and strain into a chilled cocktail glass.

PINK ROSE

1½ oz. gin
1 tsp. lemon juice
1 tsp. heavy cream
1 egg white
Several dashes grenadine

Mix all ingredients with cracked ice in a shaker or blender and strain into a chilled cocktail glass.

 **POLISH SIDECAR**

1 oz. gin
¾ oz. blackberry liqueur or blackberry brandy
¾ oz. lemon juice
4 fresh blackberries (optional)

Mix all ingredients, except fresh blackberries, with cracked ice in a shaker or blender and pour into a chilled glass. Garnish with blackberries.

If blackberry brandy is used, it may be necessary to sweeten drink with sugar syrup.

PRÉ CATELAN COCKTAIL

1½ oz. gin
1 oz. Parfait Amour
Several dashes lemon juice

Mix all ingredients with cracked ice in a shaker or blender and strain into a chilled cocktail glass.

 **PRINCETON**

1½ oz. gin
¾ oz. port
Several dashes orange
    bitters
Lemon peel

Mix all ingredients, except
lemon peel, with cracked ice in
a shaker or blender and strain
into a chilled cocktail glass.
Twist lemon peel over drink and
drop into drink.

PRUNELLE ALEXANDER

1½ oz. gin
1 oz. prunelle
1 oz. heavy cream
Pinch ground cinnamon

Mix all ingredients, except cinnamon, with cracked ice in a
shaker or blender and strain into
a chilled cocktail glass. Sprinkle
with cinnamon.

 **PUERTO BANUS COCKTAIL**

1½ oz. gin
1 oz. Cherry Marnier
1 tsp. fino sherry or dry
    vermouth

Mix all ingredients with cracked
ice in a shaker or blender and
strain into a chilled cocktail
glass.

PUNT E MES NEGRONI

½ oz. gin or vodka
½ oz. Punt e Mes
½ oz. sweet vermouth
Orange peel

Mix all ingredients, except orange peel, with cracked ice in a
shaker or blender and strain into
a chilled cocktail glass. Twist orange peel over drink and drop
into glass.

PUNXATAWNY PHIL

1 oz. gin
1 oz. light rum
1 tsp. lemon juice
Dash grenadine
Ginger ale

Mix all ingredients, except ginger ale, with cracked ice in a
shaker or blender. Pour into a
chilled highball glass and fill
with cold ginger ale.

RADNOR COCKTAIL

1 oz. gin
1 oz. apricot brandy
1 tsp. lemon juice
½ tsp. sugar syrup
½ tsp. grenadine

Mix all ingredients with cracked ice in a shaker or blender. Strain into a chilled cocktail glass.

 RAMOS GIN FIZZ

2 oz. gin
½ oz. lime juice
½ oz. lemon juice
1 tsp. sugar syrup
1 tsp. heavy cream
Several dashes orange
  flower water
1 egg white (for two drinks)
Club soda

Mix all ingredients, except club soda, with cracked ice in a shaker or blender and pour into a tall Collins glass. Fill with cold club soda and stir gently.

RED CLOUD

1½ oz. gin
¾ oz. apricot liqueur
½ oz. lemon juice
1 tsp. grenadine
Dash Angostura bitters

Mix all ingredients with cracked ice in a shaker or blender and strain into a chilled cocktail glass.

RED LIGHT No. 1

1 oz. gin
2 oz. sloe gin
1 oz. lemon juice
Maraschino cherry

Mix all ingredients, except cherry, with cracked ice in a shaker or blender and strain into a chilled cocktail glass. Garnish with cherry.

 THE RED LION COCKTAIL

1 oz. gin
1 oz. Grand Marnier
½ oz. orange juice
½ oz. lemon juice

Mix all ingredients with cracked ice in a shaker or blender and strain into a chilled cocktail glass.

RENDEZVOUS

1½ oz. gin
½ oz. kirsch
½ oz. Campari or to taste
Lemon peel

Mix all ingredients, except
lemon peel, with cracked ice in
a shaker and strain
into a chilled cocktail glass.
Twist lemon peel over drink and
drop into glass.

ROADTOWN RAMMER

1½ oz. gin
½ oz. curaçao
½ oz. dry vermouth
½ oz. pineapple juice

Mix all ingredients with cracked
ice in a shaker or blender and
strain into a chilled cocktail
glass.

ROCKY GREEN DRAGON

1 oz. gin
¾ oz. green Chartreuse
½ oz. cognac

Mix all ingredients with cracked
ice in a shaker or blender and
pour into a chilled cocktail
glass.

ROMAN COOLER

1½ oz. gin
¾ oz. Punt e Mes
½ oz. lemon juice
½ oz. sugar syrup
Dash sweet vermouth
Club soda
Orange peel

Mix all ingredients, except club
soda and orange peel, with
cracked ice in a shaker or
blender and pour into a chilled
highball glass. Fill with club
soda, stir, and twist orange peel
over drink and drop into glass.

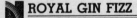 ROYAL GIN FIZZ

1½ oz. gin
½ oz. Grand Marnier
1 oz. lemon juice
½ oz. sugar syrup
1 egg
Club soda
Maraschino cherry

Mix all ingredients, except soda
and cherry, with cracked ice in a
shaker or blender and pour into
a chilled Collins glass. Fill with
cold club soda and garnish with
a cherry.

ROYAL ORANGE BLOSSOM

1½ oz. gin
¾ oz. Grand Marnier
3 oz. orange juice
1 tsp. orgeat syrup or honey

Mix all ingredients with cracked ice in a shaker or blender and strain into a chilled cocktail glass.

RUSSIAN COCKTAIL No. 2

1 oz. gin
1 oz. vodka
½ oz. white crème de cacao
½ oz. crème de noyaux

Mix all ingredients with cracked ice in a shaker or blender and pour into a chilled cocktail glass.

SAN REMO COCKTAIL

2 oz. gin
½ oz. dry vermouth
1 oz. Strega

Mix all ingredients with cracked ice in a shaker or blender and strain into a chilled cocktail glass.

● SECRET FLOWER

2 oz. gin
2 oz. orange juice
2 oz. grapefruit juice
½ tsp. maraschino liqueur or to taste
¼ tsp. orange flower water

Mix with cracked ice in a shaker or blender and strain into a chilled wine goblet. Float a drop or two of orange flower water on top of drink.

SELF-STARTER

1 oz. gin
½ oz. Lillet blanc
1 tsp. apricot brandy
Several dashes Pernod

Mix all ingredients with cracked ice in a shaker or blender and strain into a chilled cocktail glass.

● SEVILLE

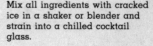

1½ oz. gin
½ oz. fino sherry
½ oz. orange juice
½ oz. lemon juice
½ oz. sugar syrup or to taste

Mix all ingredients with cracked ice in a shaker or blender and pour into a chilled Old Fashioned glass.

SHEAPARD'S SUFFERING BASTARD

Angostura bitters
1½ oz. gin
1½ oz. brandy
1 tsp. Rose's lime juice
Ginger beer
Mint sprig
Cucumber slice
Orange or lemon slice

Swirl bitters around a chilled 14-oz. double Old Fashioned glass so it is thoroughly coated and discard excess bitters. Add several ice cubes to glass along with gin, brandy, and lime juice, mix well, and fill glass with cold ginger beer. Stir gently and garnish with mint, cucumber, and orange or lemon slice.

SILVER BULLET

2 oz. gin
1 oz. kümmel
1 oz. lemon juice

Mix all ingredients with cracked ice in a shaker or blender. Strain into a chilled cocktail glass.

SILVER STALLION

2 oz. gin
1 oz. lemon juice
1 oz. lime juice
1 scoop vanilla ice cream
Club soda

Mix all ingredients except club soda with cracked ice in a shaker or blender and pour into a chilled double Old Fashioned glass. Fill with club soda and stir gently.

Shake or blend only for a few seconds until smooth.

 **SINGAPORE SLING**

2 oz. gin
1 oz. cherry brandy or
    Cherry Heering
Juice of ½ lemon
Dash Benedictine
Club soda
Lemon slice
Mint sprig (optional)

Mix gin, brandy, lemon juice, and Benedictine with a splash of soda or water in a shaker with cracked ice and strain into a 12-oz. Collins glass that has been well chilled. Add ice cubes, fill with cold club soda, stir gently, and garnish with lemon slice and mint sprig.

If you use a red, fruity cherry brandy or a cherry liqueur, then no additional sweetening is required. If you use a kirsch, you may want to add some sugar syrup.

 SLOE BOAT TO CHINA

2 oz. gin
1 oz. sloe gin
4 oz. orange juice
4 oz. grapefruit juice

Mix with cracked ice in a shaker or blender and serve in a double Old Fashioned glass. Add additional ice if needed.

SNOWBALL

1 oz. gin
¼ oz. white crème de menthe
¼ oz. anisette or Pernod
¼ oz. crème de violette
¼ oz. heavy cream

Mix all ingredients with cracked ice in a shaker or blender and strain into a chilled champagne saucer glass.

 THE SPICED ORANGE BLOSSOM

2 oz. gin (or vodka)
4 oz. orange juice (suggest freshly squeezed)
Dash maraschino cherry juice
Dash Angostura bitters
2 maraschino cherries
Pinch of cinnamon

Mix all ingredients with cracked ice in a blender and pour into a chilled double Old Fashioned glass.

STAR DAISY

1 oz. gin
1 oz. apple brandy
1 oz. lemon juice
1 tsp. sugar syrup
¼ tsp. curaçao

Mix all ingredients with cracked ice in a shaker or blender and strain into a chilled wine goblet.

◣ STEAMBOAT GIN

1½ oz. gin
¾ oz. Southern Comfort
½ oz. grapefruit juice
½ oz. lemon juice

Mix all ingredients with cracked ice in a shaker or blender and strain into a chilled cocktail glass.

BARTENDER'S SECRET NO. 6—Flavor Mist

A legendary Martini maker in a bar on Chicago's Michigan Avenue famous for its generous, well-made Martinis delights in using an atomizer connected to a vermouth bottle to make very, very, very dry Martinis for the regulars. It not only works efficiently, but Martini devotees are tantalized by the aroma of vermouth from the clouds of mist that are generated as each Martini is made at the bar. The atomizer may also be used effectively to "top" certain cocktails with aromatic spirits such as Pernod, crème de menthe, kirsch, Cointreau, and even Angostura bitters. Apparently spraying certain highly scented liqueurs and brandies into the atmosphere increases the intensity of the aroma. It is also quite economical, for a little squirt of crème de violette or Drambuie seems to go a long way.

STRAWBERRY BLOW FIZZ

1½ oz. gin
½ oz. strawberry liqueur or strawberry schnapps
1 oz. cream
½ oz. lemon juice
¼ cup frozen strawberries, thawed (including syrup)
1 tsp. Falernum or sugar syrup
Club soda

Mix all ingredients, except club soda, with cracked ice in a shaker or blender, and pour into a chilled Old Fashioned glass. Add more ice, if you wish, and fill with club soda.

STREGA SOUR

1½ oz. gin
½ oz. *Strega*
½ oz. lemon juice
Lemon slice

Mix all ingredients, except lemon slice, with cracked ice in a shaker or blender and strain into a chilled cocktail glass. Garnish with lemon slice.

SUTTON HOUSE SPECIAL

1½ oz. gin
½ oz. *peppermint schnapps*
½ oz. sugar syrup
½ oz. lemon juice
6 mint leaves

Mix all ingredients, except mint leaves, with cracked ice in a shaker or blender. Pour into a chilled double Old Fashioned glass and bruise mint leaves with a bar spoon and add additional cracked ice. Stir vigorously.

TANGIER

1 oz. gin
1 oz. *triple sec*
1 oz. *Mandarine Napoleon*
Orange peel

Mix all ingredients, except orange peel, with cracked ice in a shaker or blender and strain into a chilled cocktail glass. Garnish with orange peel.

TANGO

1½ oz. gin
¼ oz. sweet vermouth
¼ oz. dry vermouth
1 oz. orange juice
Several dashes curaçao or
   triple sec

Mix all ingredients with cracked ice in a shaker or blender and pour into a chilled Old Fashioned glass.

THE TANQUERAY EMERALD No. 1

1½ oz. *Tanqueray* gin
¾ oz. green Chartreuse
¾ oz. lime juice
1 egg white *(for two drinks)*
Minted green cherry
   (optional)

Mix all ingredients, except green cherry, with cracked ice in a shaker or blender and strain into a chilled cocktail glass.

Created for Tanqueray by the author.

THE TANQUERAY EMERALD No. 2

1½ oz. Tanqueray gin
½ oz. Rose's lime juice
Dash blue curaçao
Lime slice

Mix all ingredients, except lime slice, in a shaker or blender and strain into a chilled cocktail glass.

Created for Tanqueray by the author.

 THE TANQUERAY EMERALD No. 3

1½ oz. Tanqueray gin
½ oz. green crème de menthe
1 oz. cream or half-and-half

Mix all ingredients with cracked ice in a shaker or blender and strain into a chilled cocktail glass.

Created for Tanqueray by the author.

TOM COLLINS

2–3 oz. gin
1½ oz. lemon juice
½ oz. sugar syrup or to taste
Club soda
Maraschino cherry

Mix all ingredients, except soda and cherry, in a tall Collins glass with ice, fill with club soda, and garnish with cherry.

 TRAVELER'S JOY

1 oz. gin
1 oz. cherry liqueur
1 oz. lemon juice

Mix with cracked ice in a shaker or blender and strain into a chilled cocktail glass.

TROPICAL COCKTAIL

2 oz. gin
1 oz. frozen pineapple juice concentrate
1 oz. guava nectar
½ oz. La Grande Passion
Orange peel

Mix all ingredients, except orange peel, with cracked ice in a shaker or blender and pour into a chilled Old Fashioned glass. Twist orange peel over drink and drop into glass.

TUTTI-FRUTTI

3 oz. gin
1 oz. maraschino liqueur
1 oz. amaretto
2 oz. diced apples
2 oz. diced pears
2 oz. diced peaches

Mix all ingredients with cracked ice in a blender until smooth. Pour into a chilled highball glass.

ULANDA

1½ oz. gin
¾ oz. Cointreau
Several dashes Pernod

Mix all ingredients with cracked ice in a shaker or blender and pour into a chilled cocktail glass.

UNION LEAGUE CLUB

1½ oz. gin
1 oz. ruby port
Several dashes orange
    bitters
Orange peel

Mix all ingredients, except orange peel, with cracked ice in a shaker or blender and pour into a chilled cocktail glass. Garnish with orange peel.

VALENCIA COCKTAIL No. 2

1½ oz. gin
1 oz. dry sherry
Lemon peel

Pour gin and sherry into a mixing glass with several ice cubes. Stir well and strain into a chilled cocktail glass. Twist lemon peel over drink and drop into glass.

VELVET KISS

1 oz. gin
½ oz. crème de banane
½ oz. pineapple juice
1 oz. heavy cream
Dash grenadine

Mix all ingredients with cracked ice in a shaker or blender and strain into a chilled cocktail glass.

VERA'S THEME

2 oz. gin
Several dashes crème yvette
1 egg white (for two drinks)

Mix all ingredients with cracked ice in a shaker or blender and pour into a chilled Old Fashioned glass.

VERMONT VIGOR

1½ oz. gin
1 oz. lemon juice
½ oz. maple syrup or to taste

Mix all ingredients with cracked ice in a shaker or blender and pour into a chilled Old Fashioned glass.

VERNE'S LAWYER

1½ oz. gin
½ oz. apple brandy or calvados
¼ oz. lime juice
Several dashes grenadine

Mix all ingredients with cracked ice in a shaker or blender. Pour into a chilled cocktail glass.

VERONA COCKTAIL

1 oz. gin
½ oz. sweet vermouth
1 oz. amaretto
Dash or two of lemon juice
Orange slice

Mix all ingredients, except orange slice, with cracked ice in a shaker or blender and pour into a chilled Old Fashioned glass. Garnish with orange slice.

VIVIAN'S JURY

1½ oz. gin
½ oz. dry vermouth
½ oz. blue curaçao
Several dashes Pernod

Mix all ingredients with cracked ice in a shaker or blender. Strain into a chilled cocktail glass.

WARDAY'S COCKTAIL

1 oz. gin
1 oz. sweet vermouth
1 oz. calvados or applejack
1 tsp. yellow Chartreuse

Mix all ingredients with cracked ice in a shaker or blender and strain into a chilled cocktail glass.

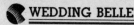# WEDDING BELLE

1 oz. gin
1 oz. Dubonnet rouge
½ oz. cherry brandy
1 oz. orange juice

Mix all ingredients with cracked ice in a shaker or blender and pour into a chilled cocktail glass.

WENDY FOULD

¾ oz. gin
¾ oz. Cointreau
¾ oz. apricot brandy
Orange slice

Mix all ingredients, except orange slice, with cracked ice in a shaker or blender and strain into chilled cocktail glass. Garnish with orange slice.

WHITE BABY No. 2

1 oz. gin
1 oz. Cointreau or triple sec
1 oz. heavy cream

Mix all ingredients with cracked ice in a shaker or blender and strain into a chilled cocktail glass.

# WHITE CARGO No. 1

2½ oz. gin
½ oz. maraschino liqueur
Dash dry white wine
1 scoop vanilla ice cream

Mix in a blender until smooth, adding a little extra white wine if necessary. Serve in a chilled wine goblet.

WHITE CARGO No. 2

2 oz. gin
Several dashes cream sherry
¼ cup vanilla ice cream
Maraschino cherry

Mix all ingredients, except maraschino cherry, for a few seconds in a blender until smooth. Pour into chilled parfait or sherbet glass and garnish with cherry.

WHITE LILY

1 oz. gin
1 oz. Cointreau
1 oz. light rum
Dash of Pernod

Mix all ingredients with cracked ice in a blender or shaker and strain into a chilled cocktail glass.

WHITE ROSE

1½ oz. gin
¾ oz. maraschino liqueur
2 oz. orange juice
½ oz. lime juice
1 tsp. sugar syrup
1 egg white (for two drinks)

Mix all ingredients with cracked ice in a shaker or blender and strain into a chilled cocktail glass.

WHITEOUT

1½ oz. gin
1 oz. white crème de cacao
1 oz. heavy cream

Mix all ingredients with cracked ice in a shaker or blender and strain into a chilled cocktail glass.

XANTHIA

1 oz. gin
1 oz. cherry brandy
1 oz. yellow Chartreuse

Mix all ingredients with cracked ice in a shaker or blender and pour into a chilled cocktail glass.

Martini Variations

The Martini in all of its many versions, proportions, and formulations is unquestionably the emperor of cocktails. A gin Martini is the classic cocktail, and although the vodka-based Martini (see page 157) has become enormously popular, purists still consider the gin Martini the only real version of this redoubtable—and controversial—drink.

An apocryphal story illustrates the strong and divergent opinions that surround the ceremonial protocol involved in concocting a proper Martini. It seems a U.S. Air Force pilot was in the habit of carrying a small bottle of gin and vermouth, a jar of olives, a mixing spoon, and large metal cup in his survival kit. Upon seeing the kit for the first time, his copilot said, "How on earth will those Martini makings ever help you if you're lost in the jungle?" The pilot replied, "If I'm lost out in the middle of nowhere, all I have to do is start making a Martini and sure enough, somebody will appear out of the bushes and say, 'That's no way to make a Martini!' "

Every Martini drinker has a special preference for the kind of gin and vermouth that is used, the garnish that is added, and even the number of ice cubes that are put into the mixing glass. As to mixing techniques, some say it should be stirred briefly so as "not to bruise the gin." A head bartender at a distinguished Chicago club famous for their great Martinis insists that Martinis must be stirred "at least a hundred times." Some devotees, including James Bond, prefer their Martinis "shaken, not stirred." Shaking aerates the mixture, so perhaps the flavor is improved slightly, but most people do not find the cloudy drink that results very appealing. There are even strong feelings about whether everything, including all the ingredients, should be chilled in advance. Some keep their gin stored in the freezing compartment of their refrigerator. Others stoutly maintain that the resulting drink is too strong because there is insufficient ice meltage. And when it comes to meltage, almost everyone agrees that a watery Martini is *totally unacceptable*.

A stormy debate can be generated instantly if one broaches the subject of proportions of gin vis-à-vis vermouth. Bernard DeVoto wrote a classic essay in *Harper's* magazine way back in 1949 in which he set forth an iron-bound principle which stated that the ideal ratio was precisely 3.7 parts of gin to one part of vermouth. Times have changed, and although DeVoto's formula makes a very pleasant drink, it would never suit those Martini lovers, who, like Winston Churchill, maintained that the world's finest Martini involved nothing more than glancing at the vermouth bottle (unopened) while pouring gin into the mixing glass.

Aside from serious experimentation with regard to the right ratio between gin and vermouth, there is considerable division of opinion as to additives. Purists are convinced that even a drop of lemon essence squeezed from a lemon peel is a violation of the integrity of this hallowed potation. The more audacious mixologist will use accents such as a minim (a minim is approximately one to two drops and is precisely 0.061610 milliliter) or two of scotch, Pernod, curaçao, various bitters, crème de menthe, or whatever seems to add zest to the palate of the brash, restless, or jaded drinker. Obviously, if a dry cocktail sherry or a white wine vinegar in place of vermouth makes an exemplary cocktail in the opinion of the imbiber, then who can say that these things are adulterants rather than flavor enhancers?

Much is made of the dryness quotient of Martinis. Once a 12-to-1 Martini was considered potent, then came the 20-to-1 version. Of course we all know where this kind of one-upmanship leads: to straight gin chilled with ice. This is what some bars, including New York's famed "21" Club, serve when a valued customer asks for a *very* dry Martini. As one of their bartenders put it, "It is the only way you can convince some people that you have made the driest Martini possible in accordance with their request." Straight gin on the rocks is not a Martini or even a cocktail. It is a straight shot, a shooter, a rammer, a belt, or whatever you wish to call it, but not a mixed drink by any standard.

The cocktail that is believed to be the progenitor of the Martini is the Martinez, invented in the middle of the nineteenth century in San Francisco by a legendary bartender of the day, Jerry Thomas. The original recipe was 4-to-1—not four parts gin to one of vermouth, but the other way around, including a dash of bitters and two dashes of maraschino liqueur. In the Roaring Twenties a proper Martini was made with a large proportion of vermouth by today's tastes. Now, after hearing tales of the thousand-to-one Martini, it seems that a new generation of drinkers have discovered the Martini and are drinking them very much the way Bernard DeVoto did in the late forties.

The Martini controversy is bound to continue and will never be resolved, but there are a few basics that almost everyone seems to subscribe to: Use the best ingredients, gin, vermouth, olives, etc., or at least what you consider to be the best. Use plenty of ice and make your drink with dispatch so it is crisp and crackling cold, and serve immediately in a chilled glass. By the same token, Martinis should be consumed while bright and fresh. They do not improve if left to warm to room temperature or to dilute if served on the rocks. As to additives or garnishes, this is purely a matter of personal taste. No matter what seems trendy or in, a good rule to follow is, if you don't like your Martini a certain way, don't drink it that way. This elegant concoction is meant to be enjoyed, to each his or her own. After all, that's why it was invented in the first place.

The following recipes are for various Martinis and the many Martini variations that have proliferated through the years.

ALLIES

1 oz. gin
1 oz. dry vermouth
Several dashes kümmel

Mix all ingredients with cracked ice in a shaker or blender. Pour into a chilled Old Fashioned glass.

ATTA BOY

2 oz. gin
1 oz. dry vermouth
½ tsp. grenadine
Lemon peel

Mix all ingredients, except
lemon peel, with cracked ice in
a shaker or blender and strain
into a chilled cocktail glass.
Twist lemon peel over drink and
drop into drink.

 ## BALMORAL MARTINI

2 oz. Bombay Gin
Several dashes dry
  vermouth, or to taste
Several dashes of Scotch
  whisky
Lemon twist

Stir gin and vermouth with ice
in a pitcher and strain into a
chilled cocktail glass. Float
Scotch whisky on top of drink
and garnish with lemon twist.

Created by the author for Carillon Importers, Ltd.

BLUE SAPPHIRE MARTINI

2 oz. Bombay Sapphire Gin
Several dashes dry
  vermouth, or to taste
¼ oz. blue curaçao
Orange peel cut into a long,
  thin swirl

Stir all ingredients, except orange peel, with ice in a pitcher
and strain into a chilled cocktail
glass. Garnish with orange peel.

Created by the author for Carillon Importers, Ltd.

DUTCH MARTINI

2 oz. Dutch jenever gin
½ tsp. dry vermouth
Lemon peel

Pour gin and dry vermouth into
mixing glass with plenty of ice
cubes. Stir briskly and strain
into a chilled cocktail glass.
Twist lemon peel over drink and
drop into glass.

FINO MARTINI

2 oz. gin
¼ oz. fino sherry
Lemon twist or olive

Pour gin and fino sherry into mixing glass with several ice cubes.
Stir well and strain into a
chilled cocktail glass. Twist
lemon peel over drink and drop
into glass or garnish with olive.

GIBSON

2½ oz. gin
Several dashes dry vermouth
Cocktail onions

Pour gin and dry vermouth into mixing glass with ice cubes. Stir briskly and strain into a chilled cocktail glass. Garnish with cocktail onions.

GIN AND IT

1 oz. gin
1 oz. sweet vermouth

Combine in a chilled cocktail glass without ice.

This is the original recipe. It may also be made with dry vermouth. Modern tastes opt for more gin, less vermouth, and ice.

GOLF MARTINI

1½ oz. gin
1 tsp. dry vermouth or to taste
Several dashes Angostura bitters
Green olive

Pour gin, dry vermouth, and Angostura bitters in mixing glass and stir vigorously with ice cubes for one minute. Strain into a chilled cocktail glass and garnish with an olive.

GREENLEE'S MARTINI

1 Cornichon gherkin with juice
2 oz. Bombay Sapphire Gin

Pour a little juice from a jar of Cornichon gherkins into a chilled Martini glass and swirl around so that the inside of glass is covered. Slice a Cornichon lengthwise except for a section at the top. Squeeze the uncut section between thumb and forefinger so that the slices spread apart like a fan, and place in the bottom of the glass. Pour gin into a mixing glass with ice and add ¼ tsp. of the Cornichon juice. Stir briskly and strain into Martini glass.

This house special was named for R. Scott Greenlee, executive chef of **The Pollard, Red Lodge, Montana.**

HAWAIIAN MARTINI

1½ oz. gin
½ tsp. dry vermouth
½ tsp. sweet vermouth
½ tsp. pineapple juice

Mix all ingredients with cracked ice in a shaker or blender and strain into a chilled cocktail glass.

HOFFMAN HOUSE

1½ oz. gin
½ oz. dry vermouth
Dash orange bitters
Olive

Stir gin, vermouth, and bitters with ice and strain into a chilled cocktail glass. Garnish with olive.

IMPERIAL

1½ oz. gin
1½ oz. dry vermouth
Several dashes maraschino liqueur
Several dashes Angostura bitters
Olive

Mix all ingredients, except green olive, with cracked ice in a shaker or blender and strain into a chilled cocktail glass. Garnish with olive.

JAMES BOND'S MARTINI

3 oz. Tanqueray Gin
1 oz. Stolichnaya Vodka
½ oz. blonde Lillet vermouth
Large slice of lemon zest

Add all ingredients, except lemon zest, to a shaker three-quarters full of cracked ice and shake rapidly for two minutes. Strain immediately into a chilled Martini glass and garnish with lemon zest (the colored outside part of the peel) that has been carefully sliced into a graceful spiral. This cocktail should be consumed with dispatch while crackling cold, before temperature and evaporation interfere with its enjoyment.

MADAME DU BARRY'S MARTINI

2 oz. gin or vodka
¼ oz. curaçao
¼ oz. lemon juice
1 tsp. maraschino liqueur
1 egg white (for two drinks)
Cherry
Orange slice

Mix all ingredients, except orange slice, with cracked ice in a shaker or blender and strain into a chilled cocktail glass. Garnish with orange slice.

Created by the author for Beverage Media, Ltd.

 ## MARINER'S MARTINI

2–3 oz. gin
White wine vinegar with anchovies
Lemon twist or olive

In a mixing glass add plenty of ice, gin, and several drops of white wine vinegar in which fillets of anchovies have been steeped. Stir briskly and strain into a chilled brandy snifter. Add one or two anchovies and twist lemon peel over drink and drop into glass, or garnish with olive.

To prepare anchovies and vinegar, open a 2 oz. can of anchovies and drain on paper towels to remove *all* oil and steep in white vinegar for several days in refrigerator. When vinegar has a slight anchovy flavor, it is ready to use.

THE MARTINEZ Forerunner of the Martini

Dash of bitters
2 dashes maraschino liqueur
1 pony Old Tom gin
1 wine glass vermouth
¼ slice lemon

Mix all ingredients, except lemon, in a shaker with cracked ice and strain into a chilled cocktail glass.

Original recipe advised adding two dashes of "gum (sugar) syrup, if the guest prefers it very sweet."

MARTINI MELONZONA A LA MEDICI

2–3 oz. gin
White wine vinegar (in
    which baby eggplant
    have been steeped)
Lemon twist

Drain a jar of preserved baby eggplant and replace liquid with white wine vinegar; let steep in the refrigerator for several days. Pour gin into a mixing glass with ice cubes and add a few drops of vinegar from jar. Stir briskly and strain into a chilled brandy snifter. Garnish with one or two baby eggplant that have been drained on paper towels and decorate with lemon twist.

MARTINI MIGNON

2 oz. Bombay Sapphire Gin
¼ blonde Lillet vermouth
Orange slice (preferably
    steeped in Grand Marnier
    for a few hours)

Stir gin and vermouth with ice in a pitcher and strain into a chilled cocktail glass. Garnish with orange slice.

Created by the author for **Carillon Importers, Ltd.**

MARTINI ROMANA

1½ oz. gin
½ tsp. dry vermouth
Several dashes Campari

Pour all ingredients into a mixing glass with plenty of ice and stir briskly. Strain into a chilled cocktail glass.

MÉDOC MARTINI

2 oz. gin
½ tsp. dry vermouth
½ oz. Cordial Médoc

Mix all ingredients with cracked ice in a mixing glass and strain into a chilled cocktail glass.

NEWBURY

1½ oz. gin
1½ oz. sweet vermouth
Several dashes curaçao
Lemon peel
Orange peel

Mix all ingredients, except fruit peels, with cracked ice in a shaker or blender and strain into a chilled cocktail glass. Twist lemon and orange peels over drink and drop into glass.

PAISLEY MARTINI

2 oz. gin
½ tsp. dry vermouth
½ tsp. scotch

Mix all ingredients with plenty of cracked ice in a shaker or blender and strain into a chilled cocktail glass.

PALM ISLAND MARTINI

1½ oz. gin
½ oz. dry vermouth
¼ oz. white crème de cacao

Mix all ingredients with cracked ice in a shaker or blender and pour into a chilled Old Fashioned glass.

Vermouth and crème de cacao should be adjusted to individual tastes.

PEGGY COCKTAIL

1½ oz. gin
½ oz. vermouth
Generous dash Dubonnet
Generous dash Pernod

Stir all ingredients with ice in a mixing glass and strain into a chilled cocktail glass.

PERFECT MARTINI

1½ oz. gin
½ tsp. dry vermouth
½ tsp. sweet vermouth
Green olive

Mix all ingredients, except green olive, with cracked ice in a mixing glass and strain into a chilled cocktail glass. Garnish with olive.

RACQUET CLUB

1½ oz. gin
½ oz. dry vermouth
Dash orange bitters

Stir all ingredients with ice in a mixing glass and strain into a chilled cocktail glass.

 ROLLS-ROYCE No. 1

1½ oz. gin
½ oz. dry vermouth
½ oz. sweet vermouth
Several dashes Benedictine

Stir all ingredients in a mixing glass with ice and strain into a chilled cocktail glass.

SAKETINI

2 oz. gin
¼ oz. sake
Green olive or lemon twist

Mix all ingredients, except olive or lemon twist, with cracked ice in a shaker or blender and strain into a chilled cocktail glass. Garnish with olive or lemon twist.

SICILIAN MARTINI

1½ oz. gin
¼ oz. dry vermouth
½ oz. dry Marsala
Lemon peel

Pour gin, dry vermouth, and dry Marsala into mixing glass with ice cubes. Stir briskly and strain into a chilled cocktail glass. Twist lemon peel over drink and drop into glass.

 SWEET MARTINI

2 oz. gin
½ oz. sweet vermouth
Dash orange bitters
Orange peel

Pour gin, vermouth, and bitters into a mixing glass with ice cubes. Mix well and strain into a chilled cocktail glass. Twist orange peel over drink and drop into glass.

THIRD DEGREE

1½ oz. gin
½ oz. dry vermouth
½ tsp. Pernod

Stir all ingredients with ice in a mixing glass and strain into a chilled cocktail glass.

WEMBLEY No. 1

1½ oz. gin
½ oz. vermouth
¼ oz. calvados or applejack

Stir all ingredients with ice in a mixing glass and strain into a chilled cocktail glass.

YALE COCKTAIL

1½ oz. gin
½ oz. dry vermouth
Several dashes orange bitters
Several dashes maraschino liqueur

Stir in a mixing glass with cracked ice and strain into a chilled cocktail glass.

VODKA: THE GREAT WHITE SPIRIT

> Drinking is the joy of the Rus!
> —Grand Prince Vladimir,
>   First Czar of all
>   the Russias

Vodka, now the largest-selling category of spirits in the United States, is a highly refined liquor that, after processing, has no discernible taste, color, or odor. Unlike whiskey, vodka is distilled at a high proof (190 proof or about 95% pure alcohol) and thus is free of congeners, esters, botanicals, and those elements that give other kinds of spirits their distinctive flavor, aroma, and color. Contrary to popular belief, vodka is rarely made from potatoes today. Most of the better imported vodkas— and all vodkas distilled in the U.S.—are made from grain.

America's love affair with vodka began late in life—in 1946, to be exact, a period of severe war-caused shortages that had stripped liquor dealers' shelves of nearly all the old favorite brands. In those days vodka was known only vaguely as a beverage that people drink in Chekhov plays, Tolstoy novels, and in films about dashing cossacks and the brothers Karamazov roistering to strains of gypsy violins amid shouts of "Nazdorovye."

In their frantic search for something resembling potable spirits, it seems that some enterprising hedonists stumbled upon bottles of Smirnoff vodka, an obscure product that had been distilled in this country since the mid-1930s. The discovery was, as its ultimate impact upon the populace indicates, a noteworthy event, the magnitude of which was unsuspected at the time. The Smirnoff label, emblazoned with czarist crowns and royal regalia, represented not only a fine-quality distilled beverage, but, of even greater significance, had the unique characteristics of being tasteless, colorless, and odorless. As the Smirnoff folks were wont to say in their advertising, "It leaves you breathless"—a selling proposition of some consequence to a generation of Americans spending millions of dollars annually on mouthwash, chewing gum, and assorted breath purifiers.

The turning point came in the late 1940s when Smirnoff used an alien mule to propel its product to new popularity throughout the land. The Moscow Mule, in case you don't remember, was a refreshing combination of Smirnoff vodka, half a lime, and ginger beer served in a copper mug. It still is regarded in the spirits industry as one of the greatest promotions of its kind, and if you come across any of the old copper mugs inscribed with the picture of a mule, snap them up, since they are collector's items.

In the years that followed, many other distinguished brands have emerged; some like Smirnoff with authentic Russian antecedents and others Russian only in name, as well as a host of imports such as Stolichnaya (Russia), Wyborowa (Poland), Absolut (Sweden), Finlandia (Finland), and vodkas from such improbable places as Turkey, Israel, England, Ireland, and China.

In the United States, vodka by law is defined as "neutral spirits so distilled, or so treated after distillation with charcoal or other materials, as to be without distinctive character, aroma, taste, or color." The only differences among the various brands are the types of grain used, the distillation methods, the filtration techniques, and the water used to control the alcoholic strength. These strictures do not necessarily apply to vodkas made in foreign countries. A case in point is Stolichnaya, a vodka distilled in Russia. If you sip a little Stolichnaya on the rocks, you will detect a subtle flavor, a quite distinctive nuance for which some people with highly educated palates are willing to pay a premium price.

The Russians have contributed importantly to the art of distilling vodka. The techniques of filtering vodka through charcoal, which gives the finished product its "clean" taste, was discovered in 1810 by a Russian pharmaceutical chemist, Andrey Albanov. This process is used by nearly all distillers today.

The improvement in the smoothness, quality, and taste resulting from Albanov's charcoal filtration techniques brought vodka to new heights of popularity in Russia. At one point it is estimated that there were more than four thousand vodka brands being sold in the country. It has traditionally been tossed off neat with zakuski or appetizers such as smoked salmon, sturgeon, and eel, and, of course, freshly salted caviar, herring, smoked tongue, and exotic comestibles such as fish pie made from the head and cheeks of large sturgeon. It is reported that the Russian nobility, apparently in an attempt to emulate the lavish culinary bacchanalia of ancient Rome, enjoyed such delicacies as pate of songbirds and jellied wild boar's head, while downing large amounts of vodka before, during, and after the various courses. This practice, although somewhat attenuated, persists today in Russia and especially the Scandinavian countries, where the Swedish *smörgåsbord* and the Danish *kolde bord* are enjoyed to the accompaniment of cold akvavit and beer.

The practice of flavoring vodka is an ancient one, dating to the earliest mentions of vodka in Poland during the reign of Boleslaus I (992–1025), and in Russia, where twelfth-century records make numerous allusions to *zhiznennia voda* (water of life). Flavoring of vodka with various fruits and herbs is said to have originated with housewives who did not enjoy the raw taste of the early, crude distillates. Besides vodkas that are flavored by the distiller, even today the stuffing of citrus fruit peel, anise, basil, or black currants into a bottle of vodka to produce subtleties of flavor through the venerable process of infusion is common practice in Russian households.

As to the often raised question as to who was the first to invent vodka, the Russians or the Poles, historical writings provide clues, but no definitive answers. The Poles had their Boleslaus I, who made vodka drinking a royal custom during the tenth century. The Russians are quick to point out that also in the tenth century, Grand Prince Vladimir, the first Czar of a completely unified Russia, is supposed to have exclaimed upon being told that the use of vodka was contrary to the religious law of his Moslem subjects, "But drinking is the joy of the Rus!"

In spite of vodka's strong Russian image, the Poles, quietly but with firm conviction, claim to be the true originators of vodka. In addition to massive historical documentation that indicates that vodka was in common use in Poland in the fourteenth century, they point out that vodka (or *wodka* as it is spelled in Polish) is a diminutive term for water, springing originally from the Latin *aqua vitae* or "water of life." The Poles also contend that when their country was partitioned in 1795 (between Austria, Prussia, and Russia), Russia annexed the major part of their vodka distilling industry. In spite of this, they say, even today more Polish vodka is exported to Russia than to any other country.

The most telling argument of all, perhaps, is Wodka Wyborowa, a superb product made by Agros, a Polish state-operated trade organization. Like Stolichnaya, it is a clean-tasting vodka with an ephemeral bouquet and a subtle flavor. If your taste buds are alert, you might detect a whisper of rye or some fleeting mineral taste from the type of water used. In any event, Wodka Wyborowa is an experience worth repeating.

The popularity of vodka spread from Russia and Poland throughout northern Europe, where its restorative properties in helping combat the ravages of long, freezing winter nights were especially appreciated. The Scandinavians flavored their vodkas with caraway, dill, and other herbs and spices—and called the end result *akvavit* (or *aquavit* from *aqua vitae*). Elsewhere in this chapter we shall explore some of the delightful ways of using this bracing spirit.

For many years in Sweden, an unflavored akvavit called *renat brännvinn* has been popular. As the consumption of vodka increased in America, the Scandinavians began to export their high-quality neutral spirits with considerable success. Finlandia, noted for its striking ice-sculptured packaging, has built up a loyal following in this country. *Renat brännvinn* was introduced to the U.S. market as Absolut Vodka in a starkly modern bottle that immediately attracted the attention of quality-import vodka enthusiasts. Its bright, clean, zesty qualities combined with aggressive marketing has made it the top-selling imported vodka in the country.

The best way to sample vodka is to take it neat, as old-world vodka drinkers do, in one gulp, or to pour an ounce over ice, savor the bouquet, if any, swirl a few drops around the mouth, and swallow. Some purists are adamant that you should not swallow any spirit you are taste-testing—but if you don't, you will never be able to really judge the aftertaste. More important is the water your ice is made from, since this can affect the taste. This detail is often overlooked not only by tasters, but wary tourists who eschew the tap water in a foreign country, and then proceed to guzzle drinks cooled with ice made from tap water.

The great white spirit is an international affair that will titillate your taste buds, and at times puzzle your palate, but you should always find it refreshing and satisfying, as the "water of life" was meant to be.

Vodka's universal and growing popularity has produced important sub-classifications within the category, some of which have reached the level of cult subjects. The Bloody Mary and the Vodka Martini in all of their many forms and variations are good examples. Flavored vodkas and the practice of flavoring them in the home are also subjects worthy of special attention.

Following the main body of vodka drink recipes in this chapter are special sections on the Bloody Mary, page 160; Vodka Martini, page 169; flavored vodka (including do-it-yourself recipes and distilled specialties such as aquavit), page 174; and a collection of light, low-alcoholic concoctions called "Splash Drinks" for those who desire to drink moderately, page 182.

ALEXANDER NEVSKY COCKTAIL

1 oz. vodka
1 oz. apricot liqueur
½ oz. lemon juice
4 oz. orange juice
Orange slice

Mix all ingredients, except orange slice, in a shaker or blender with cracked ice and pour into a chilled wine goblet. Garnish with orange slice.

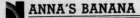 ANNA'S BANANA

1½ oz. vodka
1 oz. lime juice
½ small ripe banana, peeled and sliced
1 tsp. orgeat syrup or honey
Lime slice

Mix all ingredients, except lime slice, with cracked ice in a blender until smooth. Strain into a chilled wine glass and garnish with lime slice.

BANANA BALM

1½ oz. vodka
½ oz. banana liqueur
1 tsp. lime juice
Club soda
Mint sprigs

Mix vodka and banana liqueur with cracked ice in a shaker or blender. Pour into a chilled highball glass. Fill with club soda. Stir gently. Garnish with mint sprigs.

BEAU RIVAGE

1½ oz. vodka
1 tsp. sugar syrup
1 tsp. Pernod
1 cucumber slice (lengthwise)

Mix all ingredients, except cucumber, with cracked ice in a shaker or blender and pour into an Old Fashioned glass. Decorate with cucumber slice.

BARTENDER'S SECRET NO. 7—Beer Care

Don't overchill beer. It makes the beer look cloudy, suppresses the head, and interferes with the flavor. The 45 degree (F) range is just about right, give or take a few degrees. Ale and stout are best when served around 55 degrees because of their more complex flavors. Bottled beer should be stored in a cool place and away from sunlight. If a bottle or can of beer has no fizz when poured into a glass, discard it. It may be spoiled. And never wash beer mugs or glasses in soap and water. It destroys the head. Instead, wash in a solution of salt or soda and air dry.

BEER BUSTER

2 oz. 100-proof vodka, ice cold
Several dashes Tabasco sauce
Beer or ale, ice cold

Pour all ingredients into chilled beer mug and stir gently.

BELLINSKY

3 oz. pureed peach
1 tsp. maraschino liqueur or to taste
1 oz. Stolichnaya Peach Vodka
Brut champagne

Be sure to use a fresh peach when making this drink recipe. Puree ripe peach by forcing it through a sieve and spoon into a large, chilled wine goblet and sweeten to taste with maraschino liqueur. Add vodka and fill with cold champagne.

Created by the author for Carillon Importers, Ltd.

BELMONT STAKES

1½ oz. vodka
½ oz. gold rum
½ oz. strawberry liqueur
½ oz. lime juice
½ tsp. grenadine
Orange slice

Mix all ingredients, except orange slice, with cracked ice in a shaker or blender. Strain into a chilled cocktail glass. Garnish with orange slice.

BLACKHAWK

1½ oz. vodka
½ oz. blackberry brandy
½ oz. lime juice
Lime slice

Mix all ingredients, except lime slice, with cracked ice in a shaker or blender. Strain into a chilled cocktail glass and garnish with lime slice.

 BLACK RUSSIAN

1½ oz. vodka
¾ oz. Kahlua

Mix both ingredients with cracked ice in a shaker or blender. Pour into a chilled Old Fashioned glass.

To make a Black Magic, add several dashes lemon juice.

BARTENDER'S SECRET NO. 8—Invisible Pepper

When making Bloody Marys or other drinks requiring pepper, perceptive bartenders, mindful that a pinch of black pepper on the surface of a drink is about as appetizing as a used cigar, follow the custom of French chefs, who for many years have used ground *white* pepper in cream soups, salad dressings, and light sauces. It is not only invisible to the casual observer, but blends better than ground black pepper. The flavoring imparted is about the same.

 BLOODY MARY This is the basic recipe. See page 160 for Bloody Mary variations.

2 oz. vodka
4–6 oz. tomato juice
1 tsp. lemon juice
¼ tsp. Worcestershire sauce
Several dashes Tabasco
  sauce
Pinch white pepper
Several pinches celery salt
  or to taste
½ tsp. chopped dill (fresh or
  dried)

Mix all ingredients well with cracked ice and serve in a chilled Collins glass with additional ice cubes if needed.

BLUE LAGOON

1½ oz. vodka
½ oz. blue curaçao
1½ oz. pineapple juice
Several dashes green
  Chartreuse
Pineapple slice

Mix all ingredients, except pineapple slice, with cracked ice in a shaker or blender. Strain into a chilled cocktail glass. Decorate with pineapple slice.

BLUE LOU

2 oz. vodka
1 oz. blue curaçao
Several dashes kirsch

Mix all ingredients with cracked ice in a shaker or blender. Strain into a chilled cocktail glass.

BLUE SHARK

1 oz. vodka
1 oz. tequila
Several dashes blue curaçao

Mix all ingredients with cracked ice in a blender or shaker and pour into a chilled Old Fashioned glass.

BORODINO

1 oz. vodka
1 oz. gin
1 oz. triple sec

Mix all ingredients with cracked ice in a shaker or blender. Strain into a chilled cocktail glass.

 THE BOTTOM LINE

1½ oz. vodka
½ oz. Rose's lime juice
Tonic water
Lime slice

Mix vodka and lime juice with ice cubes in a highball glass and fill with tonic. Garnish with lime slice.

BOYAR

2 oz. vodka
½ oz. dry vermouth
¼ oz. kümmel

Mix all ingredients with cracked ice in a shaker or blender and strain into a chilled cocktail glass.

 BRIDGETOWN GIMLET

2½ oz. vodka
½ oz. Rose's lime juice
½ oz. fresh lime juice
½ oz. Falernum or to taste

Mix all ingredients with cracked ice in a shaker or blender and pour into an Old Fashioned glass.

BULLFROG

1½ oz. vodka
4 oz. limeade
1 tsp. triple sec
Lime slices

Mix all ingredients, except lime slices, with cracked ice in a shaker or blender and pour into a chilled double Old Fashioned glass. Garnish with lime slices.

BULL ROAR

2 oz. vodka
4 oz. beef bouillon, beef
    consommé, or beef broth
½ oz. lemon juice
½ tsp. Bovril beef extract
Dash Tabasco sauce
Dash A-1 sauce
Dash Worcestershire sauce
Pinch freshly ground white
    pepper

Mix all ingredients with cracked ice in a mixing glass and pour into a chilled Old Fashioned glass.

BULL SHOT

1½–2 oz. vodka
4 oz. beef consommé or beef
    bouillion
1 tsp. lemon juice
Several dashes
    Worcestershire sauce
Several dashes Tabasco
    sauce (optional)
½ tsp. horseradish (optional)
Pinch celery salt or celery
    seed (optional)

Mix all ingredients with ice cubes in a chilled double Old Fashioned glass.

BUTTER CREAM

1 oz. vodka
1½ oz. butterscotch schnapps
3 oz. Irish cream

Mix all ingredients with ice in a chilled double Old Fashioned glass.

THE CAMP FIRE CLUB COOLER

4 oz. vodka
2 oz. Piña Colada mix
4 oz. grapefruit juice
4 oz. orange juice

Mix all ingredients with cracked ice in shaker or blender and pour into chilled Collins glasses. Makes 2 drinks.

Created for the Camp Fire Club of America, Chappaqua, New York.

 **CAPE CODDER**

1½ oz. vodka
Dash lime juice
4 oz. cranberry juice
1 tsp. sugar syrup or to taste

Mix all ingredients with cracked ice in a shaker or blender and strain into a chilled double Old Fashioned glass.

 **CAROL'S DELIGHT**

1½ oz. vodka
4 oz. orange juice
½ oz. cherry-flavored brandy
1 tsp. Falernum or to taste

Mix all ingredients with cracked ice in a shaker or blender and serve in a chilled double Old Fashioned glass.

CAYMAN CUP

1½ oz. vodka
½ oz. triple sec
2 oz. mango nectar
2 oz. orange juice
½ oz. lemon juice
Mango or peach slices

Mix all ingredients, except mango slices, with cracked ice in a shaker or blender. Pour into a chilled Collins glass. Decorate with fruit slices.

CHERRY ORCHARD

1½ oz. vodka
1 oz. kirsch
1 oz. cherry liqueur
Dash lemon juice

Mix all ingredients with cracked ice in a shaker or blender and pour into a chilled cocktail glass.

CHERRY RUM FIX

1 tsp. confectioner's sugar
Water
1 oz. vodka
1 oz. light rum
½ oz. Cherry Heering or
    Cherry Marnier
½ oz. lemon juice
Brandied cherry
Lemon slice

Muddle sugar and water in a chilled double Old Fashioned glass until sugar is dissolved and add all other ingredients, except cherry and lemon slice. Mix well with ice cubes or cracked ice and garnish with cherry and lemon slice.

CHIQUITA

1½ oz. vodka
½ oz. banana liqueur
¼ cup bananas, sliced
½ oz. lime juice
1 tsp. orgeat syrup or sugar
   syrup

Mix all ingredients with cracked ice in a shaker until smooth. Pour into chilled deep-saucer champagne glass.

CIRCASSIAN CREAM

1 oz. vodka
½ oz. sweet vermouth
1 oz. heavy cream
½ oz. curaçao
½ oz. white crème de cacao

Mix all ingredients with cracked ice in a shaker or blender. Pour into a chilled Old Fashioned glass.

 COFFEE COOLER

1½ oz. vodka
1 oz. Kahlua
1 oz. heavy cream
4 oz. iced coffee
1 scoop coffee ice cream

Mix all ingredients, except ice cream, with cracked ice in a shaker or blender. Pour into a chilled double Old Fashioned glass and top with coffee ice cream.

COLD COFFEE CHANTILLY

1 oz. vodka
1 oz. coffee schnapps
3 oz. heavy cream
½ oz. triple sec

Mix all ingredients with cracked ice in a shaker or blender and pour into a chilled wine glass or brandy snifter.

COPACABANA BANANA

1 oz. vodka
1 oz. gold rum
1 oz. lime juice
1 tsp. orgeat syrup
½ banana, peeled and sliced
1 tsp. banana liqueur

Mix all ingredients, except banana liqueur, with cracked ice in a blender and pour into a chilled wine goblet and top with banana liqueur.

 CORAL REEF

1½ oz. vodka
2 oz. *Malibu* or *CocoRibe*
6 fresh strawberries or tbsp.
　strawberry preserves

Mix all ingredients with cracked ice in a blender and pour into a chilled wine goblet.

CORTINA COCKTAIL

1½ oz. vodka
1½ oz. white port
1 tsp. *Campari*
Dash grenadine

Stir all ingredients in a mixing glass with ice and pour into a chilled cocktail glass.

 CORTINA CUP

1 oz. vodka
½ oz. white crème de cacao
½ oz. sambuca
½ oz. heavy cream

Mix all ingredients with cracked ice in a blender until smooth. Strain into chilled cocktail glass.

COSMOPOLITAN

1½ oz. vodka
1 oz. *Cointreau*
1 oz. cranberry juice
½ oz. lime juice
Orange peel

Mix all ingredients, except orange peel, with cracked ice in shaker or blender and strain into a chilled cocktail glass. Garnish with orange peel.

COSSACK CHARGE

1½ oz. vodka
½ oz. cognac
½ oz. cherry brandy

Mix all ingredients with cracked ice in a shaker or blender and pour into a chilled cocktail glass.

COSSACK COFFEE GROG

1½ oz. vodka
1 oz. *Kahlua, Tia Maria,* or
　crème de cacao
½ cup black coffee, chilled
¼ tsp. vanilla extract
¼ tsp. ground cinnamon
1 scoop chocolate ice cream

Mix all ingredients with a small amount of crushed ice in a blender and serve in a chilled double Old Fashioned glass.

THE COUNTESS COCKTAIL

1 oz. vodka
1 oz. Cherry Heering
½ oz. triple sec
1½ oz. orange juice
1½ oz. grapefruit juice

Mix all ingredients with cracked ice in a shaker or blender and pour into a chilled Old Fashioned glass.

COUNT OF PARIS

1 oz. vodka
1 oz. cognac
½ oz. anisette
½ oz. triple sec

Mix all ingredients with cracked ice in a shaker or blender. Strain into a chilled cocktail glass.

 COUNT STROGANOFF

1½ oz. vodka
¾ oz. white crème de cacao
½ oz. lemon juice

Mix all ingredients with cracked ice in a shaker or blender. Strain into a chilled cocktail glass.

COW-COW COOLER

1½ oz. vodka
¾ oz. root beer schnapps
Root beer
Large scoop vanilla ice cream

Combine vodka and root beer schnapps in a chilled Collins glass with ice cubes and fill with cold root beer. Drop in ice cream scoop.

CRIMEA COOLER

1½ oz. vodka
3 oz. grapefruit juice
½ oz. crème de cassis
Ginger ale
Mint sprig (optional)
Orange slice

Mix vodka, grapefruit juice, and cassis with cracked ice in a shaker or blender and pour into a chilled Collins glass. Fill with cold ginger ale and garnish with mint sprig and orange slice.

CZARINA

1 oz. Stolichnaya Raspberry
  Vodka
1 oz. Bailey's Irish Cream
1 oz. half-and-half or light
  cream
1 tsp. maraschino liqueur

Mix all ingredients, except maraschino, with cracked ice in a
shaker or blender and serve in a
chilled stemmed glass. Top with
maraschino liqueur.

Created by the author for Carillon Importers, Ltd.

 **THE DRAKE COOLER**

1½ oz. vodka
1 oz. sloe gin
4 oz. pineapple juice
4 oz. grapefruit juice
Dash Falernum or simple
  syrup to taste

Mix all ingredients with cracked
ice in a shaker or blender and
pour into a tall chilled Collins
glass.

Created for Drake University,
Des Moines, Iowa.

DUBROVNIK

1½ oz. vodka
¾ oz. slivovitz
½ oz. lemon juice
½ tsp. sugar syrup

Mix all ingredients with cracked
ice in a shaker or blender and
pour into a chilled cocktail
glass.

 **DUBONNET FIZZ No. 1**

1 oz. vodka
3 oz. Dubonnet rouge
Club soda
Lemon peel

Mix vodka and Dubonnet with
several ice cubes in a highball
glass and fill with club soda.
Twist lemon peel over drink and
drop in.

EGGHEAD

1½ oz. vodka
4 oz. orange juice
1 egg

Mix all ingredients with cracked
ice in a blender until smooth
and pour into a chilled Old Fashioned glass.

FLORIDA JOY

1½ oz. Absolut Citron Vodka
4 oz. grapefruit juice
½ oz. triple sec
Lemon slice

Mix all ingredients, except lemon slice, with cracked ice in a shaker or blender and pour into a chilled highball glass. Garnish with lemon slice.

Created by the author for Absolut Vodka.

FLYING GRASSHOPPER

1½ oz. vodka
½ oz. green crème de
    menthe
½ oz. white crème de
    menthe

Mix all ingredients with cracked ice in a shaker or blender and pour into a chilled Old Fashioned glass.

THE FRACTURED FRIAR

1½ oz. vodka
¾ oz. Frangelico

Add ice cubes to a chilled Old Fashioned glass, pour in vodka and Frangelico, and stir well.

Conceived by Florence Eichin.

 ## FUZZY NAVEL No. 2

1 oz. vodka
½ oz. peach schnapps
6 oz. orange juice
Orange slice

Mix all ingredients, except orange slice, with cracked ice in a shaker or blender and pour into a chilled Collins glass.

GAZPACHO MACHO

1½ oz. vodka or tequila
2 oz. gazpacho soup
2 oz. beef bouillon
½ oz. lemon juice
Dash Tabasco sauce
Dash Worcestershire sauce
Pinch freshly ground white
    pepper
Pinch celery salt
1 tsp. dry sherry

Mix all ingredients, except sherry, with cracked ice in a mixing glass and pour into a chilled Old Fashioned glass. Float sherry on top.

GENOA

1½ oz. vodka
2 oz. orange juice
¾ oz. Campari

Mix all ingredients with cracked ice in a blender or shaker and pour into a chilled Old Fashioned glass.

◣ GEORGIA PEACH

1½ oz. vodka
¾ oz. peach-flavored brandy
1 tsp. peach preserves
1 tsp. lemon juice
1 slice canned or fresh peach, peeled and chopped

Mix all ingredients with cracked ice in a blender until smooth and pour into a chilled double Old Fashioned glass.

GINGERSNAP

3 oz. vodka
1 oz. Stone's ginger wine
Club soda

Combine vodka and ginger wine with several ice cubes in a double Old Fashioned glass. Fill with soda and stir gently.

◣ GINZA MARY

1½ oz. vodka
1½ oz. V-8 or tomato juice cocktail
1½ oz. sake
½ oz. lemon juice
Several dashes Tabasco sauce
Dash soy sauce or to taste
Pinch freshly ground white pepper

Mix all ingredients with cracked ice in a mixing glass and pour into a chilled Old Fashioned glass.

THE GODMOTHER

1½ oz. vodka
¾ oz. Amaretto di Saronno

Mix with ice cubes in a chilled Old Fashioned glass.

GOLDEN FROG

½ oz. vodka
½ oz. Galliano
½ oz. Strega
½ oz. lemon juice

Mix all ingredients with cracked ice in a blender until smooth. Pour into a chilled cocktail glass.

GREEN DRAGON

2 oz. Stolichnaya vodka
1 oz. green Chartreuse

Mix with cracked ice in a shaker or blender and strain into a chilled cocktail glass.

GREEN ISLAND

1½ oz. vodka
3 oz. pineapple juice
Juice of 1 lime
½ tsp. sugar syrup
½ oz. green crème de menthe
Pineapple spear

Mix all ingredients, except crème de menthe and pineapple spear, with cracked ice in a shaker or blender and pour into a chilled Hurricane glass. Top with float of green crème de menthe and garnish with pineapple spear.

GYPSY

2 oz. vodka
½ oz. Benedictine
1 tsp. lemon juice
1 tsp. orange juice
Orange slice

Mix all ingredients, except orange slice, with cracked ice in a shaker or blender and strain into a chilled cocktail glass. Garnish with orange slice.

GYPSY SPELL

1½ oz. vodka
½ oz. Benedictine
½ oz. brandy
Several dashes curaçao

Mix all ingredients with cracked ice in a shaker or blender and strain into a chilled cocktail glass.

 HANLEY SPECIAL

2 oz. vodka
1 oz. gin
⅔ cup tangerine juice
Falernum to taste (sugar syrup may also be used)

Mix with cracked ice in a shaker or blender and pour into a chilled double Old Fashioned glass.

 HARVEY WALLBANGER

1½ oz. vodka
4 oz. orange juice
½ oz. Galliano

Pour vodka and orange juice into a chilled Collins glass with several ice cubes and stir well. Top with Galliano float.

 HAVERFORD HOOKER

4 oz. vodka or gin
1 oz. orgeat syrup or to taste
½ pint vanilla ice cream
Club soda
Mint sprigs (Optional)

Mix all ingredients, except soda and mint, with cracked ice in a shaker or blender and pour into a chilled double Old Fashioned glass. If mixture is too thick, add a little soda and stir gently. Garnish with mint sprigs.

Created for the Haverford School, Haverford, Pennsylvania.

THE ICE PICK

1½ oz. vodka
Iced tea
Lemon wedge

Fill a highball or Collins glass with several ice cubes and vodka and fill with iced tea. Squeeze lemon over drink and drop into glass.

 INEZ COCKTAIL

1 oz. vodka
1 oz. brandy
1 oz. cream sherry
2 oz. dry red wine
½ oz. Swedish Punsch
2 oz. orange juice
Dash sugar syrup or to taste

Mix all ingredients with cracked ice in a shaker or blender and pour into chilled cocktail glasses. Makes 2 drinks.

JAEGERMEISTER

1½ oz. vodka
½ oz. kümmel
½ oz. lime juice
Lime peel

Mix all ingredients, except lime peel, with cracked ice in a shaker or blender. Strain into a chilled cocktail glass. Twist lime peel over drink and drop in.

 **JUNGLE JIM**

1 oz. vodka
1 oz. crème de banane
1 oz. milk

Mix with cracked ice in a shaker or blender and pour into a chilled Old Fashioned glass.

KEMPINSKY FIZZ

1½ oz. vodka
½ oz. crème de cassis
1 tsp. lemon juice
Ginger ale, bitter lemon
  soda, or club soda

Pour all ingredients, except soda, into chilled highball glass with ice. Fill with soda and stir gently.

KIEV CUP

1½ oz. 100-proof vodka
½ oz. Cherry Heering
½ oz. lime juice
Dash cherry brandy

Mix all ingredients, except brandy, with cracked ice in a shaker or blender and strain into a chilled cocktail glass. Top with cherry brandy.

 KIEV SUNDAE

1 oz. Stolichnaya Cinnamon
  Vodka
¾ oz. white crème de cacao
¾ oz. Bailey's Irish Cream
1 large scoop vanilla ice
  cream
1 tsp. Stolichnaya Raspberry
  Vodka
Whipped cream (optional)

Mix all ingredients, except Raspberry Vodka and whipped cream, with cracked ice in a blender for about ten seconds until texture is thick and smooth. Do not over-mix. Pour into a large, chilled wine goblet and float Raspberry Vodka on top. Add a dollop of whipped cream, if you wish, and serve with a teaspoon.

Created by the author for Carillon Importers, Ltd.

KRETCHMA

1 oz. vodka
1 oz. crème de cacao
½ oz. lemon juice
½ tsp. grenadine

Mix all ingredients with cracked ice in a shaker or blender. Strain into a chilled cocktail glass.

KURANT CASSIS

1½ oz. Absolut Kurant Vodka
½ oz. crème de cassis
4 oz. grapefruit juice

Mix all ingredients with cracked ice in a shaker or blender and pour into a chilled double Old Fashioned glass.

Created by the author for Absolut Vodka.

KURANT IMPERIAL KIR

1 oz. Absolut Kurant Vodka
1 oz. crème de cassis
Brut champagne or white wine

Mix vodka and cassis with several ice cubes in a chilled wine goblet. Remove ice cubes and fill with cold champagne or white wine.

Created by the author for Absolut Vodka.

KURANT JUICE BREAK

1½ oz. Absolut Kurant Vodka
2 oz. orange juice
2 oz. pineapple juice
½ oz. Grand Marnier
Orange slice
Maraschino cherry

Mix all ingredients, except orange slice and cherry, with cracked ice in a shaker or blender and pour into a chilled cooler glass. Garnish with orange slice and cherry.

Created by the author for Absolut Vodka.

KURANT SUNRISE

2 oz. Absolut Kurant Vodka
3 oz. orange juice
2 oz. cranberry juice
½ oz. sloe gin
Orange slice

Mix all ingredients, except orange slice, with cracked ice in a shaker or blender and pour into a chilled Collins glass. Garnish with orange slice.

Created by the author for Absolut Vodka.

KURANT TOREADOR

1½ oz. Absolut Kurant Vodka
4 oz. grapefruit juice
½ oz. oloroso sherry

Mix all ingredients with cracked ice in a shaker or blender and pour into a chilled Old Fashioned glass.

Created by the author for Absolut Vodka.

LE DOYEN

1 oz. vodka
1 oz. crème de banane
1 oz. cream

Mix all ingredients with cracked ice in a shaker or blender. Strain into a chilled cocktail glass.

LIEUTENANT KIJE COCKTAIL

1 oz. vodka
1 oz. apricot liqueur
1 oz. orange juice

Mix all ingredients with cracked ice in a shaker or blender and strain into a chilled cocktail glass.

 LIEUTENANT KIJE'S KOLADA

1½ oz. Stolichnaya
   Strawberry Vodka
½ oz. light rum
½ small ripe banana
¼ cup fresh strawberries
3 oz. pineapple juice
1 oz. coconut cream or to
   taste
Pineapple stick or slice

Mix all ingredients, except pineapple stick, with cracked ice in a blender until texture is smooth and creamy. Pour into a chilled Hurricane glass and garnish with pineapple stick or slice.

Created by the author for Carillon Importers, Ltd.

MADAME DE MONTESPAN

1 oz. vodka
½ oz. white crème de cacao
½ oz. curaçao
1 oz. heavy cream

Mix all ingredients with cracked ice in a shaker or blender. Pour into a chilled cocktail glass.

MOSCOW MILK TODDY

1½ oz. vodka
½ oz. grenadine
4 oz. milk
Powdered cinnamon

Mix all ingredients, except cinnamon, with cracked ice in a shaker or blender and pour into a chilled Old Fashioned glass. Top with powdered cinnamon.

MOSCOW MULE

2–3 oz. vodka
1 tsp. lime juice
Ginger beer
Lime slice or wedge

Pour vodka and lime juice in a chilled coffee mug or a highball glass with several ice cubes. Stir and fill with ginger beer. Garnish with lime.

This is the original Moscow Mule from the **Cock n' Bull Restaurant, Los Angeles.**

MOTHER'S WHISTLER

1½ oz. vodka
4 oz. pineapple juice
½ oz. orgeat syrup
Dash kirsch
Pineapple stick

Mix all ingredients, except pineapple stick, with cracked ice in a shaker or blender and pour into a chilled Old Fashioned glass. Decorate with pineapple.

MOSCVATINI

1½ oz. Stolichnaya vodka
1 oz. kümmel
Black olive

Mix with cracked ice in a mixing glass and strain into a chilled cocktail glass. Garnish with black olive.

NEVSKY PROSPECT

1½ oz. vodka
½ oz. light rum
½ oz. curaçao
¼ oz. lime juice
1 tsp. sugar syrup or to taste

Mix all ingredients with cracked ice in a shaker or blender, and strain into a chilled cocktail glass.

NINOTCHKA'S NIGHT CAP

1 oz. vodka
½ oz. gold rum
½ oz. coffee liqueur
4 oz. milk

Mix all ingredients with ice in a chilled Old Fashioned glass.

OMSK PEACH

1½ oz. vodka
½ oz. peach brandy
½ oz. orgeat syrup or to taste
1 tsp. lemon juice
1 ripe peach peeled and
  diced or canned peach,
  diced

Mix all ingredients with cracked ice in a blender until smooth and serve in a chilled wine goblet.

ORANGE BANG! No. 1

2 oz. vodka
4 oz. fresh orange juice
½ oz. curaçao
½ cup orange sections, fresh
  or canned

Mix all ingredients with cracked ice in a shaker or blender and pour into a chilled double Old Fashioned glass.

ORANGE DELIGHT

1 oz. vodka
1 oz. curaçao
½ oz. lime juice
½ oz. lemon juice
4 oz. orange juice
Orange slice

Mix all ingredients, except orange slice, with cracked ice in a shaker or blender. Pour into a chilled double Old Fashioned glass. Garnish with orange slice.

PASSION CUP No. 2

1 oz. vodka
1 oz. Jamaica rum
½ oz. La Grande Passion
½ oz. lemon juice
Lemon peel

Mix all ingredients, except lemon peel, with cracked ice in a shaker or blender. Pour into a chilled Old Fashioned glass. Twist lemon peel over drink and drop in.

PAVLOVA COCKTAIL

1½ oz. vodka
¾ oz. light rum
½ oz. strawberry liqueur
1 fresh strawberry (optional)

Mix all ingredients, except strawberry, with cracked ice in a shaker or blender and strain into a chilled cocktail glass. Garnish with strawberry.

PAVLOVA PEACH

1½ oz. Stolichnaya Peach
   Vodka
2 oz. cranberry juice
2 oz. orange juice
Peach slice

Mix all ingredients with cracked
ice in a blender or shaker and
serve in a chilled double Old
Fashioned glass with several ice
cubes. Garnish with peach
slice.

Created by the author for Carillon Importers, Ltd.

 ## PEACH BUCK

1½ oz. vodka
½ oz. peach brandy
½ oz. lemon juice
Ginger ale
Peach slice

Mix all ingredients, except ginger ale and peach slice, with
cracked ice in a shaker or
blender and pour into chilled
highball glass. Fill with ginger
ale and garnish with peach
slice.

PEACH TREE STREET

1½ oz. vodka
¾ oz. peach schnapps
3 oz. cranberry juice
3 oz. orange juice
Peach slice

Mix all ingredients, except
peach slice, with cracked ice in
a shaker or blender and pour
into a chilled wine goblet. Garnish with peach slice.

PETER'S CHEER

1 oz. vodka
1 oz. Cherry Heering
½ oz. dry vermouth
2 oz. orange juice

Mix all ingredients with cracked
ice in a shaker or blender. Strain
into a chilled cocktail glass.

PETROGRAD PUNCH

1½ oz. vodka
3 oz. grapefruit juice
2 oz. Concord grape wine

Mix vodka and grapefruit juice
with cracked ice in a shaker or
blender and pour into a chilled
wine goblet. Top with wine float.

PETROUCHKA

1 oz. vodka
½ oz. light rum
½ oz. strawberry liqueur
1 tsp. lime juice
Dash grenadine
Brut champagne
1 fresh strawberry

Mix vodka, rum, strawberry liqueur, lime juice, and grenadine with cracked ice in a shaker or blender and pour into a large, chilled wine goblet. Fill with cold champagne and garnish with strawberry.

PILE DRIVER

2 oz. vodka
3 oz. prune juice
½ tsp. lemon juice

Stir well with ice in a double Old Fashioned glass.

PINE VALLEY No. 2

1½ oz. vodka
½ oz. peppermint schnapps
Limeade or lemon-lime soda
Lime slice

Pour vodka and schnapps into a chilled Collins glass with ice cubes. Add limeade or soda and stir gently. Garnish with lime slice.

PINK PEARL

2½ oz. vodka
4 oz. grapefruit juice
1 oz. maraschino cherry juice
1½ oz. Rose's lime juice
Maraschino cherry

Mix all ingredients, except cherry, with cracked ice in a shaker or blender. Strain into a chilled double Old Fashioned glass. Garnish with maraschino cherry.

THE PINK PUSSYCAT

2 oz. vodka
4 oz. orange juice
2 oz. cranberry juice
¼ oz. maple syrup or to taste

Mix all ingredients with cracked ice in a shaker or blender and pour into a chilled double Old Fashioned glass.

BARTENDER'S SECRET NO. 9—Iced Spirits

To freeze a bottle of vodka or akvavit in a block of ice is not only a very fashionable way to serve these spirits crackling cold in pony glasses, to be quaffed neat with caviar or whatever else is being offered as an hors d'oeuvre, but it is a practical way of ensuring your spirits will be properly iced. One method is to cut the top off a half-gallon milk carton and fill with water and place a bottle of spirits in the center of the carton, place in freezing compartment standing vertically and fill with additional water until the carton is filled to the rim. After ice is frozen solid, remove carton and save for use in replacing ice meltage when the cake of ice is served at room temperature. Bottle may be stored in the carton in the freezer and additional water added for refreezing ice block as needed.

PLUM BOB

2 oz. vodka or gin
Juice of 2 ripe red plums
2 tbsp. plum jelly
Juice of ½ lemon
Sugar syrup to taste
Lemon-lime soda

Mix all ingredients, except lemon-lime soda, with cracked ice in a shaker or blender and pour into a chilled double Old Fashioned glass. Fill with soda and stir gently.

POLYNESIAN PEPPER POT

1½ oz. vodka
¾ oz. gold rum
4 oz. pineapple juice
½ oz. orgeat syrup or sugar syrup
½ tsp. lemon juice
1 tbsp. cream
Several dashes Tabasco sauce
¼ tsp. cayenne pepper
Curry powder

Mix all ingredients, except curry powder, with cracked ice in a shaker or blender. Pour into a chilled double Old Fashioned glass and sprinkle with curry powder.

This was intended to be a hot, spicy drink. Seasonings should be adjusted to personal tastes.

PRINCE IGOR COCKTAIL

1½ oz. vodka
¾ oz. Grand Marnier
4 oz. orange juice
1 tsp. grenadine

Mix all ingredients, except grenadine, with cracked ice in a shaker or blender. Pour into a chilled double Old Fashioned glass and top with grenadine.

◗ PRINCE IGOR'S NIGHTCAP

1 oz. Stolichnaya Coffee
  Vodka
1 oz. Bombay Sapphire Gin
1 oz. light cream
Grated cinnamon

Mix all ingredients with cracked ice in a shaker or blender and serve in a chilled stemmed glass. Sprinkle with grated cinnamon.

Created by the author for Carillon Importers, Ltd.

◗ PRINCESS ALEXANDRA

1½ oz. Stolichnaya Vanilla
  Vodka
1 oz. white crème de cacao
1 oz. cream or half-and-half
Pinch grated nutmeg

Mix all ingredients, except nutmeg, in a shaker or blender with cracked ice and strain into a chilled cocktail glass. Sprinkle with nutmeg.

Created by the author for Carillon Importers, Ltd.

PROVINCETOWN PLAYHOUSE

1 oz. vodka
1 oz. gold rum
3 oz. cranberry juice
½ oz. sugar syrup or to taste
Dash lime juice

Mix all ingredients in a chilled Old Fashioned glass with several ice cubes.

PRUSSIAN SALUTE

1½ oz. vodka
½ oz. blackberry brandy
½ oz. slivovitz
½ oz. triple sec

Mix all ingredients with cracked ice in a shaker or blender. Strain into a chilled cocktail glass.

PUERTO PLATA

1½ oz. vodka
½ oz. banana liqueur
2 oz. pineapple juice
½ oz. orgeat syrup
1 tsp. lemon juice

Mix all ingredients with cracked ice in a shaker or blender. Strain into a chilled Old Fashioned glass.

PURPLE PASSION

1½ oz. vodka
2–3 oz. grape juice
Ginger ale or club soda

Mix vodka and grape juice with ice cubes in a Collins glass and fill with ginger ale or soda. Stir gently.

PUSHKIN'S MILK SHAKE

1 oz. Stolichnaya Coffee
    Vodka
½ oz. Stolichnaya Orange
    Vodka
1 cup cold milk or half-and-
    half
Two generous tbsps.
    powdered cocoa, or to
    taste
Whipped cream
Grated nutmeg

Mix coffee and orange vodkas, cocoa, and milk in a shaker or blender and pour into a chilled stemmed glass. Top with whipped ceam and sprinkle with nutmeg.

Created by the author for Carillon Importers, Ltd.

PUSHKIN'S PUNCH

1 oz. vodka
1 oz. Grand Marnier
Dash lime juice
Dash orange bitters
Champagne or dry sparkling
    wine

Mix all ingredients, except wine, with cracked ice in a blender or shaker. Strain into a large chilled wine goblet and fill with chilled champagne. Stir gently.

QUAKER CITY COOLER

1 oz. vodka
3 oz. chablis
½ oz. sugar syrup
½ oz. lemon juice
Several dashes vanilla
    extract
1 tsp. grenadine

Mix all ingredients, except grenadine, in a shaker or blender with cracked ice and pour into a chilled wine goblet. Top with grenadine.

RACING DRIVER

2 oz. vodka
1 oz. sloe gin
3 tbsp. frozen orange juice
    concentrate
3 maraschino cherries
Dash kirsch

In blender with cracked ice combine vodka, sloe gin, orange juice, and cherries. Add ice, continuing to blend until mixture is very thick and smooth. Pour into sherbet glasses and top with kirsch. Serves two.

 RAINY SUNDAY

2 oz. vodka
2 oz. gin
3 oz. orange juice
3 oz. grapefruit juice
Generous tbsp. orange
    sections
Generous tbsp. grapefruit
    sections
Dash simple syrup or to taste
Several dashes orange
    flower water

Mix all ingredients with plenty of cracked ice in a shaker or blender and pour into double Old Fashioned glasses. Makes 2 drinks.

 RASPBERRIES ROMANOFF

1 oz. Stolichnaya Raspberry
    Vodka
½ oz. triple sec or curaçao
Several fresh raspberries
    (optional)
Brut champagne
Several dashes of
    kirschwasser

Add chilled vodka, triple sec or curaçao, and fresh raspberries to a large, chilled stemmed glass, and fill with cold champagne. Sprinkle a few drops of kirschwasser on top.

Created by the author for Carillon Importers, Ltd.

RASPUTIN'S REVENGE

1½ oz. 100-proof vodka
1 oz. cognac
1 oz. Grand Marnier
1 oz. lime juice
Several dashes orange
    bitters or Angostura bitters
Orange slice

Mix all ingredients, except orange slice, with cracked ice in a shaker or blender and strain into a cocktail glass or a Whiskey Sour glass and garnish with orange slice.

THE RED BIRD

2 oz. vodka
1 oz. sloe gin
3 oz. cranberry juice
3 oz. orange juice

Mix all ingredients with cracked ice in a shaker or blender and pour into a chilled double Old Fashioned glass.

RED LIGHT No. 2

1½ oz. vodka
1 oz. cranberry liqueur
Dash lime juice

Pour all ingredients into a chilled cocktail glass with several ice cubes. Stir gently.

THE ROMANOFF APPLE

1½ oz. vodka
¼ oz. calvados or applejack
½ oz. lime juice
1 tsp. sugar syrup
¼ cup chopped apples, cored and pared

Mix all ingredients with cracked ice in blender until smooth and pour into a chilled champagne saucer.

ROSE COLLINS

3 oz. vodka
1½ oz. sloe gin
2 packages of dry Tom Collins mix or 2 oz. lemon or lime concentrate
1 egg white

Mix all ingredients with plenty of cracked ice in a blender and pour into chilled double Old Fashioned glasses. Makes 2 drinks.

RUSSIAN BEAR

1 oz. vodka
1 oz. dark crème de cacao
1 oz. heavy cream

Mix all ingredients with cracked ice in a shaker or blender and strain into a chilled cocktail glass.

RUSSIAN COCKTAIL

1 oz. vodka
1 oz. gin
1 oz. white crème de cacao

Mix all ingredients with cracked ice in a shaker or blender and strain into a chilled cocktail glass.

 **RUSSIAN COFFEE**

½ oz. vodka
1½ oz. coffee liqueur
1 oz. heavy cream

Mix all ingredients with cracked ice in a blender and pour into a chilled brandy snifter.

RUSSIAN PORT

1 oz. vodka
1 oz. white port wine
Dash Angostura bitters

Mix all ingredients in a mixing glass with cracked ice and strain into a chilled cocktail glass.

RUSSIAN ROB ROY

1½ oz. vodka
½ oz. dry vermouth
½ oz. scotch
Lemon twist

Stir all ingredients, except lemon twist, in a mixing glass and pour into a chilled cocktail glass. Garnish with lemon twist.

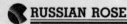 **RUSSIAN ROSE**

2 oz. vodka
½ oz. grenadine
Dash orange bitters

Mix all ingredients with cracked ice in a mixing glass and strain into a chilled cocktail glass.

RUSSIAN WOLFHOUND

Pinch salt
1½ oz. vodka
2 oz. bitter lemon soda
2 oz. grapefruit juice

Moisten rim of a chilled wine goblet with several dashes bitter lemon soda, and roll rim in salt. Pour vodka, grapefruit juice and remaining bitter lemon soda into glass with several ice cubes. Stir gently.

SALTY DOG

Pinch salt
Pinch granulated sugar
Lime wedge
2 oz. vodka
Grapefruit juice

Mix salt and sugar and spread out on a sheet of aluminum foil or wax paper. Wipe the rim of an Old Fashioned glass with lime wedge and roll glass in salt-sugar mixture until rim is evenly coated. Fill chilled glass with several ice cubes, vodka, and grapefruit juice and stir.

◤ SAMOVAR SLING

2 oz. vodka
½ oz. Benedictine
½ oz. cherry brandy
½ oz. lemon juice
Several dashes Angostura
    bitters
Several dashes orange
    bitters
Club soda

Mix all ingredients, except club
soda, with cracked ice in a
shaker or blender. Pour into a
chilled Collins glass, fill with
cold club soda, and stir gently.

◤ SCREWDRIVER

1½ oz. vodka
4 oz. orange juice
Orange slice

Pour vodka and orange juice into
a chilled double Old Fashioned
glass with several ice cubes. Stir
and decorate with orange slice.

SEA BREEZE No. 1

2 oz. vodka
3 oz. grapefruit juice
3 oz. cranberry juice

Mix all ingredients with cracked
ice in a shaker or blender and
pour into a chilled highball
glass.

SEA BREEZE No. 2

1½ oz. vodka
4 oz. grapefruit juice
1 oz. cranberry liqueur
Orange slice

Mix all ingredients, except orange slice, with cracked ice and
pour into a chilled highball
glass. Garnish with orange slice.

◤ SEA GARDEN COCKTAIL

2 oz. vodka
2 oz. tomato juice
2 oz. V-8 juice
2 oz. clam juice
½ tsp. lemon juice
½ tsp. finely chopped dill
2–3 dashes Worcestershire
    sauce
2–3 dashes Tabasco sauce

Mix all ingredients with cracked
ice in a shaker or blender and
pour into a chilled Collins glass.

SERGE'S SUNSHINE

1½ oz. vodka
4 oz. grapefruit juice
½ oz. triple sec

Mix all ingredients with cracked ice in a shaker or blender and pour into a highball glass.

 ## SEWICKLEY HUNT STIRRUP CUP

1½ oz. vodka
½ oz. sloe gin
4 oz. orange-grapefruit juice

Mix with cracked ice in a blender or shaker and pour into a silver stirrup cup or a double Old Fashioned glass.

SEX ON THE BEACH

1 oz. vodka
1 oz. peach schnapps
3 oz. cranberry juice
3 oz. orange or pineapple juice

Add several ice cubes to a highball glass, pour in all ingredients, and stir briskly.

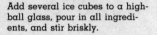 ## SHOSTAKOVICH SHAKE

2 oz. Stolichnaya Coffee Vodka
½ oz. Stolichnaya Vanilla Vodka
½ oz. Agavero Liqueur or simple syrup to taste
5 oz. whole milk
1 tsp. Stolichnaya Cinnamon Vodka

Mix all ingredients, except Cinnamon Vodka, with ¼ cup cracked ice in a shaker or blender and strain into a large chilled wine goblet. Float Cinnamon Vodka on top. Adjust ingredients to taste.

Created by the author for Carillon Importers, Ltd.

SIBERIAN SUNSET

2 oz. vodka
1 oz. raspberry or cherry or strawberry liqueur
½ oz. lime juice

Mix all ingredients with cracked ice in a shaker or blender and strain into a chilled cocktail glass.

SILENT GEORGE

1½ oz. vodka
½ oz. peppermint schnapps
4 oz. pineapple juice
Fresh pineapple slice

Mix all ingredients, except pine-apple slice, with cracked ice in a shaker or blender and pour into a double Old Fashioned glass. Garnish with pineapple.

 ## SLOW COMFORTABLE SCREW

1 oz. vodka
¾ oz. Southern Comfort
¾ oz. sloe gin
Fresh orange juice

Add several ice cubes to a chilled highball glass and pour in vodka, Southern Comfort, and sloe gin. Stir well and fill with orange juice.

SOVIET COCKTAIL

1½ oz. vodka
½ oz. dry vermouth
½ oz. amontillado sherry
Lemon peel

Mix all ingredients, except lemon peel, with cracked ice in a shaker or blender and strain into a chilled cocktail glass. Twist lemon peel over drink and drop into glass.

 ## ST. PETERSBURG

2 oz. vodka
¼ tsp. orange bitters
1 orange wedge

Pour vodka and bitters into mix-ing glass with several ice cubes. Stir until very cold and pour into a chilled Old Fashioned glass. Score peel of orange wedge with tines of fork and drop into drink.

THE STEVERINO

1 oz. vodka
2 oz. dry red wine
1 oz. pineapple juice
Several dashes triple sec

Mix all ingredients with cracked ice in a shaker or blender and strain into a chilled wine glass.

Created for Steve Allen, com-poser, writer, and motion picture and TV star.

STOLI FREEZE

1 oz. Stolichnaya vodka
Several grindings of black or
    white pepper

Place bottle of vodka in freezer
for several hours (or store there
permanently) and chill a small
pony or sherry glass. Fill chilled
glass with ice cold vodka and
grind pepper on top.

STRAW HAT

1 oz. vodka
2 oz. Malibu or CocoRibe
¼ cup fresh strawberries
Several whole strawberries

Mix all ingredients, except for
strawberries to be used for garnish, with cracked ice in a
shaker or blender until smooth
and pour into a chilled wine goblet and garnish with
strawberries.

STROGANOFF SLING

1½ oz. Stolichnaya
    Raspberry Vodka
½ oz. Bombay Gin
½ oz. maraschino liqueur
1 oz. lemon juice
1 tsp. superfine sugar or to
    taste
Club soda
Maraschino cherry
Orange slice

Mix all ingredients, except club
soda, maraschino cherry, and orange slice, in a tall, chilled
cooler glass. Add several ice
cubes and fill with cold club
soda. Stir gently and garnish
with cherry and orange slice.

Created by the author for Carillon Importers, Ltd.

 SUPER LEMON COOLER

1½ oz. Absolut Citron Vodka
3 oz. tonic water
3 oz. bitter lemon soda
Lemon slice

Mix vodka, tonic, and bitter
lemon with ice cubes in a
chilled Collins glass. Garnish
with lemon slice.

Created by the author for Absolut Vodka.

SURFER'S COLA

1½ oz. vodka
½ oz. cola schnapps
Canada Dry Half-and-Half
Lemon slice

Combine vodka and cola
schnapps in a Collins glass with
ice cubes. Fill with Half-and-Half
and garnish with lemon slice.

SURREY RUFF

1½ oz. vodka
3 oz. tonic water
3 oz. bitter lemon soda
Lemon or lime wedge

Mix all ingredients, except lemon or lime wedge, in a chilled Collins glass with cracked ice and squeeze lemon or lime over drink and drop wedge into glass.

 **TAMARA LVOVA**

1 oz. Stolichnaya Strawberry
   Vodka
1 oz. Rhum Barbancourt
1 oz. crème de cacao
Scoop vanilla ice cream
Whipped cream
1 large strawberry

Mix all ingredients, except whipped cream and strawberry, in a blender for about 10 seconds until creamy. Do not overmix. Serve in a chilled stemmed glass, top with whipped cream, and garnish with strawberry.

Created by the author for Carillon Importers, Ltd.

 TEANECK COOLER

1½ oz. Absolut Citron Vodka
3 oz. grape juice
Ginger ale
Lemon slice

Mix vodka and grape juice with ice cubes in a chilled Collins glass and fill with cold ginger ale. Garnish with lemon slice.

Created by the author for Absolut Vodka.

TIMOCHENKO'S TOT

2 oz. vodka
½ oz. gin or light rum
½ oz. amaretto
4 oz. orange juice or equal
   parts orange and
   grapefruit juice

Mix all ingredients with cracked ice in a shaker or blender and pour into a chilled wine goblet.

TO RUSSIA WITH LOVE

1½ oz. Stolichnaya Vanilla
   Vodka
½ oz. maraschino liqueur
½ oz. coconut rum
1 oz. cream or half-and-half
1 egg white (for two drinks)
Maraschino cherry

Mix all ingredients, except cherry, with cracked ice in a shaker or blender and strain into a chilled cocktail glass. Garnish with cherry.

Created by the author for Carillon Importers, Ltd.

TORTOLA GOLD

1 oz. vodka
1 oz. gold rum
½ oz. La Grande Passion
2 oz. pineapple juice
½ oz. lemon juice
Mint sprigs

Mix all ingredients, except mint sprigs, with cracked ice in a blender until smooth. Strain into a chilled Collins glass. Garnish with mint sprigs.

 ## TROIKA TAMER

1 oz. Stolichnaya Peach
   Vodka
1 oz. Amaretto di Saronno
½ oz. sloe gin
½ oz. lemon juice

Mix all ingredients with cracked ice in a shaker or blender and serve in a chilled cocktail glass or an Old Fashioned glass with ice cubes.

Created by the author for Carillon Importers, Ltd.

VANYA'S STRAWBERRY FIZZ

1½ oz. Stolichnaya
   Strawberry Vodka
1 oz. cranberry juice
6 large strawberries
Lemon-lime soda
1 large strawberry

Mix all ingredients, except soda and one large strawberry for garnish, in a shaker or blender with cracked ice. When mixture is smooth, pour into a chilled Collins glass and fill with cold lemon-lime soda. Add ice cubes, if necessary, and garnish with large strawberry.

Created by the author for Carillon Importers, Ltd.

VODKA COOLER

1½ oz. vodka
½ oz. sweet vermouth
½ oz. lemon juice
½ oz. sugar syrup
Club soda

Mix all ingredients, except club soda, with cracked ice in a shaker or blender. Pour into a chilled Collins glass and fill with club soda.

 ## VODKA GIMLET No. 1

2 oz. vodka
½ oz. Rose's lime juice

Combine all ingredients in a mixing glass with several ice cubes, stir, and strain into a chilled cocktail glass.

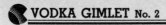 **VODKA GIMLET** No. 2

1½ oz. vodka
1 oz. fresh lime juice
½ oz. sugar syrup

Mix all ingredients with cracked ice in a shaker or blender and strain into a chilled Old Fashioned glass.

 **VODKA GRAND MARNIER**

1½ oz. vodka
½ oz. Grand Marnier
½ oz. lime juice
Orange slice

Mix all ingredients, except orange slice, with cracked ice in a shaker or blender and pour into a chilled cocktail glass. Garnish with orange slice.

 **VODKA GRASSHOPPER**

½ oz. vodka
¾ oz. green crème de menthe
¾ oz. white crème de cacao

Mix all ingredients with cracked ice in a shaker or blender and strain into a chilled cocktail glass.

VODKA MARTINI

Basic recipe. See page 169 for Vodka Martini variations.

2–3 oz. vodka
Dash dry vermouth or to taste
Lemon peel or olive

Combine vodka and vermouth in a mixing glass with a generous amount of ice cubes. Stir quickly but thoroughly and strain into a chilled cocktail glass. Garnish with lemon peel or olive.

The secret of a good Vodka Martini is thorough mixing with a great deal of ice in a matter of seconds to minimize ice meltage. Vermouth proportions are critical since this provides the flavor of the drink. It must be adjusted for individual tastes.

 **VODKA SOUR**

1½–2 oz. vodka
¾ oz. lemon juice
1 tsp. sugar syrup
Lemon slice
Maraschino cherry

Mix all ingredients, except lemon slice and maraschino cherry, with cracked ice in a shaker or blender. Strain into a chilled Whiskey Sour glass and garnish with lemon slice and cherry.

◗ VODKA STINGER

1½ oz. vodka
1 oz. white crème de menthe

Mix vodka and crème de menthe with cracked ice in a mixing glass and strain into a chilled cocktail glass.

VOLGA BOATMAN

1½ oz. vodka
1 oz. cherry-flavored brandy
1 oz. orange juice
Maraschino cherry

Mix all ingredients, except maraschino cherry, with cracked ice in a shaker or blender and strain into a chilled cocktail glass. Garnish with cherry.

◗ THE VULGAR BOATMAN

1½ oz. vodka
¾ oz. cherry liqueur
¼ oz. dry vermouth
½ oz. lemon juice
¼ tsp. kirsch
Dash orange bitters

Mix all ingredients with cracked ice in a shaker or blender and strain into a chilled cocktail glass.

◖ WAIKIKI COMBER

1½ oz. vodka
6 oz. guava juice
½ oz. fresh lime juice
½ oz. black raspberry
  liqueur

Mix all ingredients, except raspberry liqueur, with cracked ice in a shaker or blender and pour into a chilled Collins glass. Over the back of a spoon, pour in raspberry liqueur.

WARSAW

1½ oz. vodka
½ oz. blackberry liqueur
½ oz. dry vermouth
1 tsp. lemon juice
Lemon peel

Mix all ingredients, except lemon peel, with cracked ice in a shaker or blender and strain into chilled cocktail glass. Twist lemon peel over drink and drop into glass.

WHITE CARNATION

1½ oz. vodka
1½ oz. lemon juice
1 oz. pineapple juice
Club soda

Mix all ingredients, except for club soda, in a shaker or blender and pour into a Collins glass. Fill with club soda and stir gently.

WHITE RUSSIAN

1½ oz. vodka
1 oz. white crème de cacao
¾ oz. heavy cream

Mix all ingredients with cracked ice in a shaker or blender and strain into a chilled cocktail glass.

WHITE WITCH

1 oz. vodka
1 oz. white crème de cacao
½ cup vanilla ice cream

Mix all ingredients in a blender at low speed for 10 seconds. Spoon into a chilled sherbet glass or wine goblet.

WOO WOO

1½ oz. vodka
1 oz. peach schnapps
4 oz. cranberry juice

Put several ice cubes in a high-ball glass, add ingredients, and stir briskly.

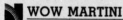

WOW MARTINI

3 oz. Belvedere Vodka
¼ oz. Blandy's 5-year-old
   Sercial Madeira
Lemon peel

Pour all ingredients, except lemon peel, into an ice-filled mixing glass and stir at least 50 times with a bar spoon. Strain into a well-chilled Martini glass and garnish with lemon peel.

Created by Andrea Immer, Beverage Director, Windows of the World, New York.

YORSH

1½ oz. vodka
12 oz. mug of beer

You may quaff the vodka neat and follow it with a mug of beer, or you may pour the vodka into the beer and drink them together.

Bloody Mary Lore
and Variations

If the Moscow Mule helped make vodka famous in America, then the Bloody Mary surely helped make it profitable. In a very short time, perhaps ten years, vodka came from out of nowhere and was propelled to the heights, becoming the best-selling spirit in the land. And the Bloody Mary, far and away the most popular vodka drink in America, has won its place in the pantheon of classic mixed drinks alongside the Martini, Daiquiri, Manhattan, and that other redoubtable vodka creation, the Screwdriver.

What is the origin of this famous drink? There are many fanciful stories regarding the birth of the Bloody Mary and some misconceptions about the drink itself. This much we do know: The Bloody Mary was (a) invented a long time ago; (b) originally was a simple concoction made up of nothing more than vodka and tomato juice with perhaps a pinch of salt and pepper, and, just maybe, a dash of lemon juice; (c) was formulated as a cocktail, not a tall drink; and (d) that it originated not in America—where many good things happen—but in France, where many good things also happen.

Harry's New York Bar in Paris is generally credited as being the birthplace of the Bloody Mary. Located at 5 Rue Daunou between the Rue de la Paix and the Avenue de l'Opera, not far from another world-famous bar, the Ritz, Harry's was a font of new drink creations and lays claim to such classics as the Sidecar. In the early 1920s Harry's Bar was a gathering place for American expatriates living in Paris, such as Ernest Hemingway and F. Scott Fitzgerald. Legend has it that George Gershwin plinked out themes for "An American in Paris" on the downstairs piano while Gertrude Stein scribbled poetic fragments on the dining room's tablecloths. Among the regulars were the Dolly Sisters and the Prince of Wales, who would stop by now and again for a nightcap.

Perhaps the glamorous and gifted clientele that frequented Harry's inspired the staff to be creative and innovative. One who rose to the challenge was Fernand Petiot, a bartender born in America of French parents. One day in 1924 he concocted the first Bloody Mary. The authentic, original recipe for this drink, according to Andy MacElhone, son of Harry MacElhone (the Harry of Harry's New York Bar) is as follows:

"In a cocktail shaker, place plenty of ice,
a pinch of salt, some black pepper,
two ounces of vodka, and some tomato juice.
All of these should be well shaken and
poured into a tumbler."

"This caught the fancy of the morning trade," Mr. MacElhone
said in a 1977 interview. "Although some of the clients insisted
that it should be more spiced up, whereupon Pete added red
pepper, lemon juice, and Worcestershire sauce, and four or
five drops of Tabasco to his recipe."

Other accounts insist that the original recipe was simply
vodka and tomato juice mixed with ice. Then came the salt,
pepper, and lemon juice. Worcestershire sauce came even
later, and Tabasco entered the picture long after that, although
the McIlhenny Company, makers of Tabasco sauce, insists it
was used early on and that a proper Bloody Mary cannot be
made without it.

As the popularity of the Bloody Mary grew, so did specula-
tion as to the origin and significance of such a vivid, unappe-
tizing name. Here are some of the theories that have been
proposed:

The Bloody Mary was a house specialty of the Bucket of
Blood Club in Chicago, a long-vanished hangout for news-
papermen in the 1920s, where the membership met regularly
for the purpose of drinking themselves under the table.

Bloody Mary was coined by a bartender at Harry's New York
Bar whose girlfriend, Mary, was always late for dates and to
whom he referred in a fit of pique as "that bloody Mary!"

Bloody Mary was a legendary character in the South Seas
who became famous as a result of the musical South Pacific,
based upon James Michener's Tales of the South Pacific.

Bloody Mary alluded to a Scottish queen known for her
vengeful ways, which earned her the name Bloody Mary. The
name was supposedly coined by Harry MacElhone, one of the
owners of Harry's Bar and a Scot.

Joseph Scaialom, a legendary barman from Cairo's Sheap-
ard's Hotel and later maître d' at the Four Seasons and Windows on the World in New York, claims that the real Bloody
Mary was invented in Manhattan at Vladimir's Bar long before
Petiot's concoction. He maintains the name Vladimir was cor-
rupted to Bloody Meyer, which later became Bloody Mary.

Take your choice. The Scottish connection makes more sense
to me than the other explanations. In any event, I believe most
people would rather drink a Bloody Mary than speculate as to
the origin of the name, the inventor, or the original formula.

As with every significant innovation, a host of challengers crawl out from behind the back of the bar to vie for a place of honor as the originator. One thing we do know with some certainty is that Fernand Petiot returned to his native land in 1934 and brought his invention with him, and in his capacity as a bartender at New York's distinguished St. Regis Hotel introduced the Bloody Mary to a thirsty and appreciative generation of Americans.

A thorough perusal of the St. Regis Hotel bar, kitchen, and banquet department files, through the courtesy of Mr. August Ceradini, general manager of this venerable U.S. birthplace of the Bloody Mary, failed to reveal any startlingly new information on the subject, nor did that legendary paper napkin with the original recipe written on it in pencil by the inventor come to light. But Petiot's St. Regis version of the Bloody Mary—then called the "Red Snapper" for reasons of propriety (the hotel did not feel the name "Bloody Mary" was proper for a genteel clientele)—is a matter of record.

RED SNAPPER

1½ oz. vodka
2 oz. tomato juice
1 dash lemon juice
2 dashes salt
2 dashes black pepper
2 dashes cayenne pepper
3 dashes Worcestershire
  sauce

Add the salt, pepper, Worcestershire sauce, and lemon juice to a shaker glass. Then add ice, vodka, and tomato juice. Shake, pour into a highball glass, garnish, and serve.

There have been changes over the years, some good, some not so good. The most radical, in the opinion of purists, is the switch from a short drink, a cocktail, to a tall drink on-the-rocks. They also decry the substitution of lime juice for lemon juice. When drinks become classics, the ingredient variations, mixing techniques, and opinions proliferate like mushrooms after a summer shower. Craig Claiborne, the food editor of *The New York Times*, for one, has definite ideas as to what constitutes "the best Bloody Mary in town." He stoutly maintains that the best Bloody Marys are made by "our favorite barman, Jimmy Fox, who presides over the Blue Bar in the Algonquin Hotel on the edge of New York's theater district." And here is Jimmy's recipe:

ALGONQUIN BLOODY MARY

1½ oz. vodka
4 oz. tomato juice
Salt and freshly ground
 black pepper to taste
Juice of half a lime
1 tsp. Worcestershire sauce
4–6 dashes Tabasco sauce
1 lime wedge

Ideally, a Bloody Mary should be shaken, using a bartender's standard glass and metal cocktail shaker set. Add the vodka, tomato juice, and so on to the metal container. Fill the glass container with ice, the smaller the cubes the better. Invert the glass into the metal container and shake quickly nine times. If the drink is shaken excessively, the tomato juice may separate. Immediately strain the Bloody Mary into a glass and serve with a lime wedge dropped in. Yield: one cocktail.

As the Bloody Mary's popularity soared, it was only natural that many variations would appear, using a variety of spirits and seasonings. People may be intrigued momentarily by the prospect of trying a Bloody Mary made with tequila, aquavit, or even rum and whiskey, but they quickly return to vodka because it is a perfect foil for tomato juice and other seasonings that are used. But when it comes to spices, sauces, and other flavoring agents, everyone, it seems, has a favorite additive. Some like to use V-8 juice in place of tomato juice, or a more or less equal mixture of beef consommé or bouillon or straight beef consommé and no tomato juice. Clam juice added to tomato juice in a ratio of one part clam juice to two parts tomato juice appeals to the seafood set, and health buffs have been known to lace their Bloody Marys with sauerkraut juice.

In the realm of condiments, there are many options to be explored. Celery salt imparts a crisp accent flavor to a Bloody Mary, although some prefer celery seed instead so as not to add to the saltiness imparted by the Worcestershire sauce. And speaking of sauces, try A-1 in place of, or in addition to, Worcestershire sauce in your next Bloody Mary. It adds quite a different flavor tone and makes a zesty, spicy drink. Herbs have been used with great success. Try some chopped fresh dill in your next Bloody Mary, or you may prefer oregano or tarragon or sweet basil. Onion lovers enjoy chopped chives or scallions in their drink, and some even have used a few drops of garlic from a garlic press. Tex-Mex food fans have used chopped jalapeño peppers with some success, but it results in a libation that is just too hot for most palates. A nominal amount of fresh horseradish is a much vaunted "secret ingredient" used by some bartenders, and it does add extra zip to a Bloody Mary. Flavoring variations are limited only by your own imagination. Texans toss in hot barbecue sauce, San Franciscans are said to savor a good dollop of soy sauce, Spanish go for anchovy paste, and Bostonians delight in crushed capers.

There are many Bloody Mary variations, ranging from the Virgin Mary (also called the Contrary Mary because of the absence of alcohol) to the O Sole Maria, made with Galliano or grappa. Others with humorous as well as flavorful qualities are: the Shamrock Mary (Irish whiskey), Sake Mary (sake), Bonnie Mary (scotch), Bloody Maria (also called Tequila Maria and Mexicali Mary), Danish Mary (akvavit), Red Marija (slivovitz), Bloody Bull (equal parts beef consommé and tomato juice), Hot Beefy Mary (beef bouillon), Nautical Mary (clam juice and tomato juice), and La Bonne Maria (cognac). There are undoubtedly others and perhaps a few that haven't even been thought of yet.

BLOODHOUND

1½ oz. vodka
½ oz. dry sherry
4 oz. tomato juice
Dash lemon juice
Pinch salt
Pinch white pepper
Lime slice

Mix all ingredients, except lime slice, in a Collins glass with ice and garnish with lime slice.

BLOODY BLOSSOM

1½ oz. vodka
3 oz. orange juice
3 oz. tomato juice
Mint sprig (optional)

Mix vodka and juices in a shaker or blender with cracked ice and pour into a Collins glass. Garnish with mint.

BLOODY BREW

1½ oz. vodka
3 oz. beer
4 oz. tomato juice
Pinch salt
Dill pickle spear

Mix all ingredients, except pickle spear, gently in a highball or Collins glass with ice. Garnish with pickle.

Proportions of beer to tomato juice should be adjusted to individual tastes. Condiments may be added as in a basic Bloody Mary.

BLOODY BULL

2 oz. vodka
3 oz. V-8
3 oz. beef bouillon, beef
    broth, or beef consommé
½ oz. lemon juice
Dash Tabasco sauce
Dash Worcestershire sauce
Pinch freshly ground white
    pepper

Mix all ingredients with cracked ice in mixing glass and pour into a chilled Old Fashioned glass.

BLOODY MARIE

1½–2 oz. vodka
4 oz. tomato juice
¼ oz. lemon juice
½ tsp. Pernod
Several dashes
    Worcestershire sauce
Several dashes Tabasco
    sauce
Salt to taste
Freshly ground white pepper
    to taste

Mix all ingredients, except salt and pepper, with cracked ice in a mixing glass and strain into a chilled double Old Fashioned glass.

BOMBAY MARY

1½ oz. vodka
4 oz. tomato juice
½ tsp. curry powder or to
    taste
Pinch ground coriander
Pinch celery seed or celery
    salt
Dash soy sauce or to taste
Dash Worcestershire sauce
Dash Tabasco sauce
Dash lemon juice

Mix all ingredients with cracked ice in a 14-oz. double Old Fashioned glass.

Seasonings should be adjusted for individual tastes.

BORSCHT BELT

2 oz. vodka
4 oz. beet borscht
Several dashes Worcestershire
   sauce or to taste
Several dashes lime juice
Several dashes Tabasco
   sauce
Sour cream or yogurt

Mix all ingredients, except sour cream or yogurt, in a Collins glass or a double Old Fashioned glass with cracked ice. Top with a dollop of sour cream or yogurt.

BROODY MALY

2 oz. vodka
4 oz. tomato juice
½ oz. lemon juice
Pinch white pepper
Pinch celery salt
1 egg white (for two drinks)
Several dashes oyster sauce
Several fresh celery tops or
   leaves (optional)

Mix all ingredients with cracked ice in a blender until smooth and pour into a chilled highball glass.

CLAM DIGGER

2 oz. vodka
4 oz. V-8
2 oz. clam juice
2 tsp. lemon juice
Several dashes Tabasco sauce
Dash Worcestershire sauce
Pinch freshly ground white
   pepper

Mix all ingredients with cracked ice in a mixing glass and pour into a chilled highball glass.

CLAM UP

2 oz. vodka
2 oz. clam juice
3 oz. tomato juice
Several dashes lemon juice
Several dashes
   Worcestershire sauce
Several dashes Tabasco sauce
Pinch white pepper
Pinch chopped dill

Mix all ingredients with cracked ice in a shaker or blender. Pour into a chilled highball glass.

◤ COCK 'N' BULL SHOT

1½ oz. vodka
2 oz. chicken consommé
2 oz. beef bouillon, beef
    consommé, or beef broth
½ oz. lemon juice
Dash Tabasco sauce
Dash Worcestershire sauce
Pinch freshly ground white
    pepper
Pinch celery salt

Mix all ingredients with cracked ice in a mixing glass and pour into a chilled Old Fashioned glass.

THE HAPPY MARY

2 oz. vodka
4–6 oz. V-8 juice
1 tsp. lime juice
Several dashes Tabasco
    sauce
Several dashes
    Worcestershire sauce
Generous pinch white
    pepper
Generous pinch celery salt
Generous pinch oregano or
    dill or tarragon

Mix all ingredients with cracked ice in a mixing glass and pour into a double Old Fashioned glass.

◤ MEL TORMÉ'S BLOODY MARY

1½ oz. vodka
4 oz. tomato juice
4 slices cucumber, peeled
4–6 slices of celery
1 slice Bermuda onion, diced
Pinch white pepper
Dash Tabasco sauce
Dash Worcestershire sauce
Celery stalk

Mix all ingredients, except celery stalk, with cracked ice in a blender and pour into a chilled highball glass. Garnish with celery stalk. Add additional tomato juice, if necessary.

THE RED LION INN BLOODY MARY

1 oz. vodka
¾ cup tomato juice
2 dashes lemon juice
4 dashes Worcestershire
    sauce
2 to 3 drops Tabasco sauce
2 dashes each salt and
    pepper
¼ tsp. horseradish sauce
Celery stalk
Lime wedge

Combine vodka, lemon juice, and seasonings in a Hurricane glass. Add cracked ice and stir well. Garnish with stalk of celery and wedge of lime.

A house specialty of **The Red Lion Inn, Stockbridge, Massachusetts.**

SMOKY MARY

1½ oz. vodka
4 oz. Tomato juice
½ oz. lemon juice
½ oz. barbecue sauce
Dash Tabasco
Dash Worcestershire sauce
Lemon slice

Mix all ingredients with cracked ice in a double Old Fashioned glass. Garnish with lemon slice.

◣ SUN-DRIED TOMATO BLOODY MARY

1½ oz. Absolut Vodka infused
    with sun-dried tomatoes
    (see below)
3 oz. tomato juice
3 oz. V-8 juice
Pinch celery salt
Pinch black pepper
Dash Tabasco sauce
Dash horseradish
Dash lemon juice

Put all ingredients into a large, chilled highball glass, add ice and mix well. To infuse vodka used in this drink, pour 4 oz. of vodka into a glass container with a tight-fitting top. Add four sun-dried tomatoes, cover, and let stand for at least two days. When ready to use, strain and discard tomatoes. If you age this infusion longer, after a week replace old tomatoes with fresh ones.

This house specialty is a signature drink of **The Hilton at Short Hills, New Jersey.**

SWEDISH CLAM DIGGER

2 oz. aquavit
6-oz. can Clamato
Dash Worcestershire sauce
Dash lemon juice
Dash Tabasco sauce
Several pinches of chopped
   dill

Mix all ingredients, except dill, in a large Collins glass or a double Old Fashioned glass with cracked ice and sprinkle with chopped dill.

VELVET MARY

1½ oz. vodka
4 oz. tomato juice
½ oz. lemon juice
½–1 tbsp. grated horseradish
1 egg white (for two drinks)
Several dashes
   Worcestershire sauce
Several dashes Tabasco
   sauce

Mix all ingredients with cracked ice in a shaker or blender. Pour into a chilled Collins glass.

Vodka: Martini Variations

The Vodka Martini is rapidly overtaking its sibling, the Gin Martini, which for many years occupied the number-one position as America's favorite mixed drink. Times change, and the growth of vodka, which can only be described as meteoric, reflects the tastes of the nation. The Vodka Martini has a clean, uncomplicated flavor and the perception of lightness and dryness that makes it a winner.

There are many ways to make a Vodka Martini, ranging from a goodly portion of vermouth to just a whisper or none at all. And there are a variety of garnishes that provide zest and variety. At the moment, the Cajun Martini (made with either gin or vodka) is the rage, and every bar that features them has its own special recipe.

No matter how you like your Martinis, there is one rule that should always be followed—and is, invariably, by master bartenders. Use plenty of ice, and mix the drink thoroughly and quickly so there is a minimum amount of ice meltage, but a great deal of chill. The glasses, as we remind you in every recipe in this book, must be *crackling cold*. The Martini should be consumed with dispatch while it is still crisply cold.

ABSOLUT KURANT MARTINI No. 2

2 oz. *Absolut Kurant Vodka*
¼ oz. *dry sherry*
Black olive or Greek olive

Stir vodka and sherry in pitcher with ice cubes and strain into a chilled stemmed glass. Garnish with black or Greek olive.

Created by the author for Absolut Vodka.

THE ALEXANDER NEVSKY MARTINI

2 oz. *Stolichnaya Raspberry Vodka*
1 oz. *Bombay Sapphire Gin*
4 *fresh raspberries*
Framboise or kirschwasser (optional)

Blend vodka and gin with a generous quantity of ice in a mixing glass and strain into a chilled Martini glass with fresh raspberries. Sprinkle a few drops of framboise or kirschwasser over the top the the the drink.

Created by the author for Carillon Importers, Ltd.

ALMOND JOY MARTINI

2 oz. *Absolut Vodka*
Several dashes crème de noyaux or almond extract or amaretto
3–4 *toasted almonds*

Stir vodka and crème de noyaux with ice in a pitcher and strain into a chilled cocktail glass. Garnish with toasted almonds.

Created by the author for Absolut Vodka.

CAJUN KING MARTINI

1½ oz. *Absolut Pepper Vodka*
½ oz. *Absolut Citron Vodka*
Dash dry vermouth or to taste
Pickled jalapeño pepper
Lemon peel

Mix pepper and citron vodkas and vermouth with ice in a small pitcher or mixing glass and strain into a chilled cocktail glass. Add jalapeño pepper; twist lemon peel over drink and drop into glass.

Created by the author for Absolut Vodka.

CAJUN MARTINI No. 1

1½–2 oz. vodka
Dash dry vermouth or to
taste
Large jalapeño pepper

Mix vodka and vermouth with
plenty of ice, rapidly and briskly,
and strain into a chilled cocktail
glass. Garnish with pepper.

CAJUN MARTINI No. 2

1½–3 oz. vodka
Dash dry vermouth
1 thin slice garlic
Several slices of pickled
jalapeño pepper
Several pickled cocktail
onions, blotted to remove
vinegar taste

An hour or so before you mix
Martinis, let vodka steep with
garlic, pepper, and onions in a
sealed container in the refrigerator or freezer. Mix in a mixing
glass with plenty of ice and
strain into a chilled cocktail
glass. Garnish with a pepper
slice or onions.

CHAMBORTINI

1½ oz. Stolichnaya Orange
Vodka
½ oz. Chambord
Maraschino cherry

Combine vodka and Chambord
in a shaker with ice. Shake well
and strain into a chilled Martini
glass. Garnish with cherry.

This is a house specialty of
Fechin Inn, Taos, New Mexico.

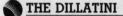 THE CHRIS PAVONE MARTINI

2 oz. Stolichnaya Orange
Vodka
¼ oz. Cointreau or triple sec
Several dashes Angostura
Bitters
Orange or lemon peel

Mix all ingredients, except orange or lemon peel, with plenty
of ice in a mixing glass, stir
briskly, and strain into a chilled
Martini glass. Garnish with orange or lemon peel.

● THE DILLATINI

1½–2½ oz. vodka
Dash of dry vermouth or to
taste
Kosher dill pickle stick

Mix vodka and vermouth in a
mixing glass with plenty of ice
and strain into a chilled cocktail
glass. Garnish with dill pickle.

HEAVENLY MARTINI

2 oz. *Bombay Gin or Absolut Vodka*
½ oz. *Grand Marnier*
½ oz. *maraschino liqueur, or to taste*
1 egg white (for two drinks)
Maraschino cherry

Mix all ingredients, except cherry, with ice in a blender and pour into a chilled wine glass. Garnish with cherry. Adjust maraschino liqueur for desired sweetness.

Created by the author for Carillon Importers, Ltd.

 ## ITALIAN MARTINI

2 oz. *Absolut Vodka*
Dash sweet vermouth, or to taste
Dash Campari, or to taste
Orange peel

Stir all ingredients with ice in a pitcher and strain into a chilled cocktail glass. Garnish with orange peel.

Created by the author for Absolut Vodka.

MIKHAIL'S MARTINI

2 oz. *Stolichnaya Coffee Vodka*
¼ oz. *Stolichnaya Vanilla Vodka*
Several coffee beans

Stir coffee and vanilla vodkas with a generous amount of ice in a pitcher. Strain into a chilled Martini glass and add coffee beans.

Created by the author for Carillon Importers, Ltd.

 ## MUSCOVY MARTINI

1 oz. *Stolichnaya Cinnamon Vodka*
1 oz. *Stolichnaya Orange Vodka*
½ oz. *triple sec*
½ oz. *orange juice*
Pinch powdered cinnamon
Orange peel

Stir all ingredients, except powdered cinnamon, with ice cubes in a mixing glass and strain into a chilled Martini glass. Twist orange peel over drink and drop into glass. Sprinkle a little powdered cinnamon over drink.

Created by the author for Carillon Importers, Ltd.

OCHI CHERNYA

2 oz. vodka
¼ oz. dry vermouth
¼ oz. sweet vermouth
1 large black olive

Mix rapidly with plenty of ice in a mixing glass and strain into a chilled cocktail glass. Garnish with a black olive.

From the Russian Tea Room, New York.

THE ROLATINI

2 oz. vodka
Dash dry vermouth
1 Rolaids tablet

Mix vodka and vermouth in a mixing glass with plenty of ice and strain into a chilled cocktail glass. Garnish with a Rolaids tablet instead of an olive or lemon peel.

For harried advertising people. The Rolaids tablet will perhaps soften the impact of the dry Martini after a full day with a difficult client.

SPANISH VODKA MARTINI

2½ oz. vodka
½ oz. dry sherry
Lemon peel

Mix vodka and sherry with cracked ice in a mixing glass and strain into a chilled cocktail glass. Twist lemon peel over drink and drop into glass.

STOLI CHOCOLATE MINTINI

1½ oz. Stolichnaya Chocolate Vodka
1 oz. white crème de menthe
1 oz. cream
1 mint sprig

Mix all ingredients, except mint sprig, with cracked ice in a shaker or blender and strain into a chilled Martini glass. Garnish with mint sprig.

Created by the author for Carillon Importers, Ltd.

VODKA GIBSON

2–3 oz. vodka
½–1 tsp. dry vermouth or to
   taste
Pearl onions, pickled

Mix vodka and vermouth in a
mixing glass with plenty of ice,
very rapidly so as to limit ice
meltage and strain into a chilled
cocktail glass. Garnish with several pickled pearl onions after
blotting them on paper towels to
prevent residual vinegar flavor
from affecting the drink.

Flavored Vodkas

Distilled spirits take on the flavor and character of the mash
used in the distilling process. In the case of spirits made at
very high proof from low flavor-intensive grains such as corn,
wheat, rice, or barley—and spirits that have been processed
into grain neutral spirits—flavors must be added to the spirits
by rectifying (redistilling), infusion, maceration, or percolation.

The addition of such things as pepper, buffalo grass, or orange peel to vodka is flavoring by means of infusion or maceration, a common practice in eastern European households,
dating from the fifteenth century and probably much earlier.
London dry gin and akvavit are, in a real sense, flavored "vodkas." Gin is made by distilling a fermented grain mash, which
yields alcohol as high as 190 proof. At this point it is, practically speaking, a "vodka." It is then reduced in proof by the
addition of distilled water and redistilled with assorted botanicals that provide the flavor and aroma. It is reduced in proof
and bottled immediately. There is no aging. Akvavit is made
in the same way. This process of flavoring could be done by
infusion (similar to making a cup of tea), except for the fact
that distillation yields an end product with more intense flavor
and aroma than is possible by infusion.

A wide variety of liqueurs and cordials through the years
have been made by the infusion method, and, in fact, all homemade liqueurs are traditionally produced in this manner since
stills are either impractical or illegal for home use. Since the
base, except when brandy is used, is grain neutral spirits, the
end product is in reality a flavored vodka. In Sweden, little
flavoring kits are sold so that unflavored vodka (renat brän-
vinn) may be flavored at home. These flavors approximate
popular liqueur flavors as well as herbs, fruits, and spices.
These are reminiscent of the gin-making kits that were sold

in drugstores during Prohibition to make what became known as "bathtub gin."

From the earliest times there was a need to flavor these spirits not because they were bland, but rather because they were harsh and raw and laced with noxious impurities. The custom parallels that of the ancient Greeks and Romans, who doused their wine with all manner of herbs, fruits, flower blossoms, and other botanicals to preserve the vintage and make the wine palatable.

The Russians and the Poles have a long tradition of flavoring vodkas. Some of the more popular, traditional homemade vodka flavors are: *pertsovka* (vodka infused with black-and-white peppercorns, reputedly a great favorite with Peter the Great); *zubrovka* (vodka flavored with buffalo grass); *starka* (vodka aged in old wine casks for as much as ten years and steeped in apple and pear leaves); *okhotnitchya* (known as "hunter's vodka" and flavored with herbs and berries); *chesnochnaya* (an infusion of pepper, garlic, and dill); and *limonovka* (lemon- or orange-flavored vodka). For special occasions, a "jubilee vodka," *yubileyneya osobaya*, laced with brandy and honey, was much in vogue.

The neutral state of vodka cries out for experimentation. The imaginative cook and the innovative mixologist will delight, as in times past, in trying new flavorings. Here are some that have been used in the past; it is quite obvious when scanning this list, only the bounds of individual tastes limit the inventive pursuit of new flavor experiences.

Fruits of all kinds have been used with success, including cherries and cherry pits, tangerines, lemons, oranges, grapefruit, cranberries, raspberries, black currants, blueberries, apricots and apricot pits, apples, plums, peaches, and pineapple. Coffee beans, tea, fennel, vanilla beans, saffron, coriander, absinthe (or absinthe substitutes), almonds, cumin, mint, bitter orange, hazelnuts, red peppers, anise, violets, caraway, cardamom, cocoa, lingonberries, cedar, dill, juniper, cornflowers, sage, cinnamon, and rose petals compose a partial listing of ingredients that have been utilized as flavoring agents. Actually, anything that is not toxic may be steeped in vodka and the essential flavor extracted by the time-honored infusion process.

Some flavored vodkas are now bottled by distillers, such as Stolichnaya Pertsovka and Absolut Peppar, and are readily available in the U.S. If the present trend continues, it is likely other flavors will be introduced into the market. Meanwhile, there is nothing to prevent you from trying out some of your favorite flavors on your own. Here are some tips on vodka flavoring:

Select a good-grade vodka that will make it all worthwhile.

Use the original bottle for flavoring or, if you decide to use a decanter or other container, make sure it is clean and odor-free. If using fruits and herbs, buy them fresh rather than using canned fruit or dried herbs. If using spices, pass over any old caraway seeds or cinnamon sticks and buy them fresh. The flavor difference is worth it. Seal container tightly after adding ingredients and steep for twenty-four to forty-eight hours, turning the bottle several times daily. Do not leave strong-flavored ingredients to steep too long because the flavor can become harsh. Garlic, lemon peel, anise, cumin, coriander, and peppers can become overpowering if infused for extended periods. After vodka has been infused, store in the refrigerator or freezer. Small amounts of flavoring substances may be left in the bottle for decoration, such as a sprig of dill or mint or a thin spiral of orange peel.

Here are some representative recipes:

ANISE VODKA

1 liter vodka
1 tbsp. anise seeds or to taste
Sprig of fresh tarragon or fennel (optional)

Put anise seeds into vodka and steep for 24 hours, turning bottle from time to time to circulate anise. Check flavor, strain vodka into a new container, decorate with a sprig of tarragon or fennel, and store in refrigerator or freezer.

APRICOT VODKA

1 liter vodka
1 dozen dried apricots, diced
6 apricot kernels (optional)

Put diced apricot into vodka and infuse for 24 hours, turning bottle from time to time to circulate apricots. Apricot kernels may be used for a more intense, bitter flavor. Check flavor and strain into a new container. Store in refrigerator or freezer.

BASIL VODKA

1 liter vodka
1 dozen fresh basil leaves

Wash leaves and put into bottle for about 24 hours at room temperature. Turn bottle several times to circulate leaves. Check for flavor. Remove vodka from leaves and store in refrigerator or freezer. A sprig of basil may be added for decorative purposes.

CUCUMBER VODKA

1 liter vodka
1 medium cucumber

Scrub cucumber and peel. Cut into thin, lengthwise strips and put into vodka. Steep at room temperature for 48 hours, turning bottle occasionally to circulate cucumber. Check flavor and steep for a longer period if stronger flavor is desired. Strain into new container and store in refrigerator or freezer.

GARLIC AND DILL VODKA

1 liter vodka
1 or 2 garlic cloves
Several sprigs of fresh dill
Half dozen peppercorns
  (optional)

Bruise garlic to release flavor and put into vodka with dill sprigs and a few peppercorns, if you wish. Steep for about 24 hours at room temperature, turning the bottle every so often to circulate ingredients. Check flavor and strain into a new bottle. Store in refrigerator or freezer. A sprig of dill may be kept in the bottle for decorative purposes.

GINGER VODKA

1 liter vodka
Fresh ginger root

Peel a section of ginger root long enough so that a dozen slices ⅛-inch thick can be cut. Quarter slices and put into bottle and steep for about 48 hours at room temperature, turning bottle occasionally to circulate ginger. Check flavor and steep longer for more intensive flavor. Strain into a new container and store in freezer.

LEMON-PEPPER VODKA

1 liter vodka
4 dozen black-and-white
  peppercorns, mixed
Peel of 1 lemon

Put peppercorns into vodka and peel lemon so that only the yellow, outer peel (zest) is used and put into bottle. Steep for 24 to 48 hours, turning bottle occasionally. Check flavor and strain into a new container. Store in refrigerator or freezer.

RASPBERRY VODKA

1 liter vodka
2 cups sugar
1 lb. fresh red raspberries
Large container with tightly
    fitting lid

Add vodka, sugar, and raspberries to large container, cover, and store in a cool, dark place. Every week open container and stir well. After about two months, strain liquid through a fine sieve into a bottle and store in refrigerator or freezer.

This is a traditional and widely used method of flavoring vodka, and works well with any fresh fruit.

The following five original recipes were developed especially for Absolut Peppar Vodka by the author.

 CLAM SHOT

1½ oz. Absolut Peppar Vodka
3 oz. fresh or bottled clam
    juice
Several dashes
    Worcestershire sauce
Dash lemon juice
Dash Tabasco sauce
½ tsp. horseradish

Mix all ingredients with cracked ice in a double Old Fashioned glass.

Created by the author for Absolut Vodka.

CREOLE MARTINI

1½–2 oz. Absolut Peppar
    Vodka
Dash dry vermouth or to
    taste
Large pepperoncini (pickled
    medium-hot pepper)

Rapidly mix vodka and vermouth with plenty of ice in a mixing glass and strain into a chilled cocktail glass and garnish with pepperoncini (which may be eaten as drink is consumed).

Created by the author for Absolut Vodka.

NAUTICAL MARY

1½ oz. Absolut Peppar Vodka
3 oz. tomato juice or V-8
    juice
3 oz. clam juice
½ tsp. horseradish
Several dashes
    Worcestershire sauce
Several dashes Tabasco
    sauce
½ tsp. lemon juice or to taste
Several pinches of chopped
    dill

Mix all ingredients with cracked
ice in a mixing glass and pour
into a double Old Fashioned
glass.

Created by the author for Absolut Vodka.

 PEPPER BULL

1½ oz. Absolut Peppar Vodka
5 oz. beef consommé
Generous dashes
    Worcestershire sauce
1 tsp. lemon juice
Pinch of celery salt or celery
    seed (optional)

Mix all ingredients with ice in a
double Old Fashioned glass.

Created by the author for Absolut Vodka.

SURF AND TURF

1½–2 oz. Absolut Peppar
    Vodka
3 oz. beef consommé
3 oz. clam juice
½ tsp. lemon juice
Several dashes Tabasco
    sauce
Several dashes
    Worcestershire sauce

Mix all ingredients with ice in a
14-oz. double Old Fashioned
glass.

Proportions of clam juice to consommé may be adjusted. Some
prefer 2 parts consommé to 1
part clam juice.

Created by the author for Absolut Vodka.

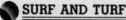

Akvavit

Aquavit or Akvavit (depending on whether you are drinking
it in Denmark, Sweden, or Norway) is, with respect to social
custom, tradition, and culinary habit, what vodka is to Russia,
cognac is to France, scotch is to Great Britain, tequila is to

Mexico, and ouzo is to Greece, to use just a few rather obvious analogies. Actually, aquavit occupies a special place in the Scandinavian dining protocol since it is consumed *with* food, and not drunk as a cocktail or an apéritif. In the U.S. there is no spirit that is comparable, since generally we consume only wine or beer with food.

As a matter of historical record, the first license to sell aquavit in Sweden was granted in 1498, just six years after the discovery of America. The practice of flavoring aquavit with herbs has gone on for generations, dating back to the days when every housewife had a small herb garden for growing various botanicals that were used in cooking and for medicinal purposes. Sweden produces many excellent aquavits, the best known of which is Absolut. O.P. Anderson is another popular brand, and it is deliciously flavored with a combination of anise, caraway, and fennel. Herrgard's Aquavit is flavored with caraway and whisky and aged in old cherry casks, which gives it a very smooth, intriguing taste. Skåne (pronounced "skona") is a mild aquavit produced in southern Sweden and is a big seller in Scandinavia. Linie Aquavit is made in Oslo, Norway, and the label usually carries the name of the ship on which it was stored during its aging, the theory being that spirits aged this way benefited greatly from the rocking of the ship on the high seas. Probably the best-known aquavit in America is the Danish Akvavit, produced in the city of Aalborg, which is an excellent product with a clean, crisp, refreshing caraway flavor.

The custom in Scandinavian countries is to drink *snaps*, or aquavit, crackling cold in little pony glasses accompanied by glasses of cool beer. The aquavit is quaffed in one gulp, with or without a beer chaser, to lusty shouts of *skål!* And all the while, you are enjoying a vast array of delicacies from the smorgasbord table, which in Denmark is called the *kolde bord*, as aquavit and beer are traditionally taken together with food at the table.

As good as aquavit is neat, it also provides an unusual flavor dimension to a number of mixed drinks. Here are some selected, original recipes that were developed for the U.S. importers of Aalborg Akvavit by the author.

AALBORG SOUR

2 oz. *Aalborg Akvavit*
Juice of ½ lemon
1 tsp. sugar syrup or *to taste*

Mix all ingredients with cracked ice in a shaker or blender and strain into a chilled cocktail glass.

AKVATINI

2-3 oz. Aalborg Akvavit
Dash dry vermouth or to
taste
Anchovy olive or lemon
twist

Mix akvavit and vermouth with
plenty of ice in a mixing glass
and strain into a chilled cocktail
glass. Garnish with an anchovy
olive or secure a rolled anchovy
and a green olive together with
a toothpick or drop in lemon
twist.

 ## COPENHAGEN COCKTAIL

1 oz. Aalborg Akvavit
1 oz. gin
Dash dry vermouth or to
taste
Large stuffed olive

Stir all ingredients, except olive,
in a mixing glass with ice and
strain into a chilled cocktail
glass. Garnish with olive.

 ## DANISH BORSCHT

1-2 oz. Aalborg Akvavit
4 oz. cold beet borscht
Dash Tabasco sauce
Dash lemon juice
Yogurt or sour cream

Mix all ingredients, except yogurt or sour cream, in a shaker
or blender and pour into a double Old Fashioned glass. Top
with a generous dollop of yogurt
or sour cream.

 ## THE DANISH BULL

2 oz. Aalborg Akvavit
4 oz. beef consommé or beef
bouillon
1 tsp. lemon juice
½ tsp. Worcestershire sauce
or to taste
Several pinches celery salt
or celery seed.

Mix all ingredients with cracked
ice in a double Old Fashioned
glass.

 ## MIDNIGHT SUN

1½ oz. Aalborg Akvavit
1 oz. grapefruit juice
½ oz. lemon juice
1 tsp. sugar syrup or to taste
Dash grenadine
Orange slice

Mix all ingredients, except orange slice, with cracked ice in a
shaker or a blender and pour
into a chilled cocktail glass. Garnish with orange slice.

THE ÖRESUND

2 oz. Aalborg Akvavit
2 oz. V-8 juice
2 oz. tomato juice
2 oz. clam juice
½ tsp. lemon juice
½ tsp. Worcestershire sauce
Pinch finely chopped dill
Pinch finely chopped parsley
Sprig of fresh dill

Mix all ingredients, except dill sprig, with cracked ice in a shaker or a blender and pour into a large Collins glass. Decorate with dill sprig.

TIVOLI COCKTAIL

1½ oz. Aalborg Akvavit
¼ oz. kirsch
1 oz. lime juice
1 tsp. sugar syrup or to taste
1 oz. cream

Mix all ingredients with cracked ice in a shaker or a blender and strain into a chilled wine goblet.

The Light Drink Concept—
A "Splash" of Spirits

The powerhouse potations of the Roaring Twenties were in vogue because the quality of bootleg spirits in this country was atrocious, so, as a consequence, men and women of the Jazz Age drank for effect rather than flavor. Partly in an attempt to mask the taste of crudely made gin and whiskey, some truly abominable concoctions were foisted upon unsophisticated, gullible drinkers. Some of these mixtures survive today, as do some of the old bar guides where they may still be found, but drinking habits and tastes have changed. Now it is no longer fashionable to swig brutally strong mixtures nor is it considered smart to drink to excess. Drinking in moderation is now very much the order of the day, not only for reasons of health and fitness, but perhaps more important: the realization that people must drink responsibly. And there is a growing grassroots opinion that maintains that if driving an automobile is required, people should not drink at all—meaning not even a sip of anything alcoholic.

Moderation is a growing trend, and somewhere between the never-never land of the jumbo 20-to-1 Martini on the one hand and the club soda on the rocks with a wedge of lime on the other is a middle ground of moderate drink recipes that are imaginative and satisfying and that fulfill the primary objective of the cocktail hour: to induce fleet conversation, to give a lift to the spirit without obliterating the evening that follows, to quicken the appetite, and to provide a happy opportunity to enjoy friends, relax, and banish the cares of the day. Recognizing the need for a new generation of truly moderate mixed drinks, we were asked by Heublein, Inc., to develop some appetizing concoctions using the "splash" concept involving a very modest amount of spirits. In the case of the 27 recipes that follow in this section, the amount of vodka specified is only a half ounce instead of the traditional one-and-one-half ounces. This concept and the recipes that resulted became known as the "Smirnoff Splash." The recipes are simple, easy to make, and, according to consumer-tasting panels, flavorful and satisfying. No, these drinks are not drunk-proof any more than beer and wine or anything alcoholic is. If you drink too much alcohol in any form, you will become intoxicated. But if you are in the habit of taking two cocktails before dinner, try one of these Smirnoff Splash drinks. If you stick to two, you'll automatically be taking in less alcohol and calories than if you imbibed standard mixed drinks.

The following recipes were created especially for Heublein, Inc., and Smirnoff Vodka by the author.

 BEACHCOMBER

3 oz. dry red wine 3 oz. cranberry juice Splash of vodka (½ oz.) Lemon twist	Stir with ice and serve in a chilled highball glass with ice. Add lemon.

BEAULIEU

4 oz. champagne 2 oz. orange juice 2 oz. grapefruit juice Splash of vodka (½ oz.) Dash grenadine	Mix all ingredients, except champagne, in a blender with ice and pour into a chilled Collins glass. Add champagne and stir gently.

CADIZ

3 oz. Harvey's Bristol Cream Splash of vodka (½ oz.) 2–3 dashes Angostura bitters	Stir all ingredients with ice in a chilled Old Fashioned glass.

 COBLENZ COOLER

3 oz. *Rhine wine*
Splash of vodka (½ oz.)
Club soda
Orange slice

Serve chilled wine in a chilled highball glass with ice. Add vodka and fill with soda. Garnish with orange slice.

COLOMBE d'OR

4 oz. *champagne*
2 dashes orange curaçao
Splash of vodka (½ oz.)
Dash Angostura bitters

Gently stir chilled ingredients, which have been stored in refrigerator for a day, and serve in a chilled stemmed glass.

GAMIN

3 oz. *white wine*
Splash of vodka (½ oz.)
Dash or two of cherry brandy
Club soda

Stir all spirits in a chilled Collins glass with ice. Fill with soda.

 GILDED LILY

3 oz. *Lillet blanc*
Splash of vodka (½ oz.)
Orange slice

Stir with ice, strain, and pour into a chilled stemmed glass. Add orange slice.

 GOLDEN ROOSTER

1 oz. *dry vermouth*
1 oz. *medium sherry*
Splash of vodka (½ oz.)
Lemon twist

Stir with ice, strain, and pour into a chilled stemmed glass. Add lemon twist.

HARVEY'S CIDER

4 oz. *apple cider*
Splash of vodka (½ oz.)
2–3 dashes Harvey's Bristol Cream

Stir with ice and serve in a chilled stemmed glass.

KIRNOFF FIZZ

4 oz. champagne
½ oz. crème de cassis
Splash of vodka (½ oz.)

Chill ingredients in refrigerator
and stir gently in a chilled
stemmed glass.

 ## LÀ CAMELIA

3 oz. dry white wine
Splash of vodka (½ oz.)
2 dashes apricot brandy

Stir all ingredients with ice in a
mixing glass, strain and serve in
a chilled stemmed glass.

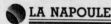 ## LA NAPOULE

3½ oz. dry white wine
Splash of vodka (½ oz.)
½ oz. crème de cassis

Chill ingredients in refrigerator
and stir in a chilled stemmed
glass.

 ## LE CHEVAL BLANC

3 oz. chablis
Splash of vodka (½ oz.)
2–3 dashes maraschino
  liqueur

Stir all ingredients with ice.
Strain and serve in a chilled
stemmed glass.

 ## LEFT BANK

3 oz. St. Raphael
Splash of vodka (½ oz.)
Dash triple sec
Lime
Club soda

Stir spirits with ice in a chilled
10-oz. Collins glass. Add ice,
dash of lime, and fill with club
soda.

 ## MERRY DU BARRY

3 oz. rosé wine
Splash of vodka (½ oz.)
1 tsp. crème de cassis

Stir all ingredients with ice in a
chilled goblet.

PAPARAZZI No. 1

2 oz. Campari
Splash of vodka (½ oz.)
Quinine water
Lime

Stir Campari and vodka with ice and pour into a chilled Collins glass. Fill with quinine water and add a squeeze of lime.

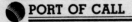 PORT OF CALL

3 oz. tawny port
Splash of vodka (½ oz.)
Dash orange curaçao

Stir port and vodka with ice, add orange curaçao, and serve in a chilled stemmed glass.

QUAI d'ORSAY

2 oz. Byrrh
2 oz. dry vermouth
Splash of vodka (½ oz.)
Orange slice

Stir spirits with ice in a chilled stemmed glass. Garnish with orange slice.

 REGATTA

4 oz. champagne
Splash of vodka (½ oz.)
1–2 dashes mirabelle or pear
    brandy

Chill ingredients in refrigerator and stir gently in a chilled stemmed glass.

RIGHT BANK

3 oz. dry vermouth
Splash of vodka (½ oz.)
Club soda
Orange slice

Stir spirits in a chilled Collins glass. Add ice and club soda.

 RIVIERA TONIC

3 oz. soave
3 oz. quinine water
Splash of vodka (½ oz.)
Orange slice

Chill ingredients in refrigerator and add to a chilled Collins glass. Add ice and stir. Garnish with orange slice.

ROSTANG

3 oz. dry red wine
Splash of vodka (½ oz.)
2 dashes orange curaçao

Stir all ingredients with ice in a chilled stemmed glass.

 RUE ROYALE

4 oz. champagne
Splash of vodka (½ oz.)
Dash of framboise or kirsch

Chill ingredients in refrigerator, serve in a chilled stemmed glass and stir gently.

 SMIRNOFF MIMOSA

3 oz. champagne
3 oz. orange juice
Splash of vodka (½ oz.)

Chill ingredients in refrigerator, serve in a chilled stemmed glass and stir gently.

 TOVARICH

1 oz. sweet vermouth
1 oz. Campari
Splash of vodka (½ oz.)
Club soda
Orange peel

Stir spirits well in a chilled high-ball glass with ice. Fill with soda. Add orange peel.

 **TROIKA**

1 oz. sloe gin
Splash of vodka (½ oz.)
4 oz. orange juice

Mix all ingredients with cracked ice in a blender and serve in a large chilled goblet.

TROIS MARCHES

3 oz. Dubonnet rouge
Splash of vodka (½ oz.)
2–3 dashes orange curaçao
Club soda
Orange slice

Stir spirits with ice in a chilled Collins glass. Fill with soda; add orange slice.

RUM: A TASTE OF THE TROPICS

> Boy, bring a bowl of china here
> Fill it with water cool and clear;
> Decanter with Jamaica ripe,
> A spoon of silver, clean and bright,
> Sugar twice fin'd in pieces cut,
> Knife, sieve and glass in order out,
> Bring forth the fragrant fruit, and then
> We're happy till the clock strikes ten.
> —Benjamin Franklin
> *Poor Richard's Almanac*

One of the great pleasures of traveling in the Caribbean is the opportunity to become intimately acquainted with a wide variety of different rums found throughout the islands. No other spirit category offers rum's infinite variety of flavor and taste experiences. The availability of an array of fresh, exotic tropical fruits and spices helps explain why rum drinks made in the U.S. with less than fresh tropical fruits "don't taste the same." It is the rums themselves, however, that really make the difference. Almost every island of consequence makes its own rum, only a few of which are exported to foreign shores.

Exploring different rum types is an exciting and challenging culinary adventure. One may begin with something as basic as a Martini, which can be made dusty dry with the light white rums of Puerto Rico; or try a sturdy, flavorful Rum Sour made with the gold rums of Barbados and the Dominican Republic. A festive punch has seldom been put to lips that could not be improved by the addition of the rich, dark, full-bodied rums of Jamaica or Demerara. Tall, frosty coolers develop tantalizing overtones with the addition of a Haitian rum while the dry, pungent rums of the French West Indies bring elegant accents to even mundane cocktails; when sipped from a snifter like fine cognac, a Martinique rum reportedly made Ernest Hemingway exclaim that it was "the perfect antidote for a rainy day."

Rums appear even in unlikely places (countries not thought of as rum-producing areas) such as Colombia, which produces the mellow, amber Ron Medellin, distilled in the city of the same name. And neighboring Venezuela makes an outstanding gold rum, Cacique Ron Anejo, which, like Ron Medellin, occasionally appears on dealers' shelves in the U.S. Nearby Trinidad is a treasure trove of excellent but little known rums such as Old Oak, Ferdi's 10-Years-Old, and Siegert's Bouquet rum. Those powerhouse, spicy, dark, pungent rums from the Demerara River area of Guyana, which run as high as 151-proof, were no doubt the self-same spirits described by a Colonial writer as being "strong enough to make a rabbit bite a bulldog." These rums are produced by two respected firms: Hudson's Bay and Lemon Hart & Sons.

The rums of Barbados have happily been discovered by American rum drinkers. Although Mount Gay is the best known in the U.S., there are other excellent brands with the typical smoothness, flavor, and finesse of Bajan gold rums such as Cockspur, Cockade, and Alleyne Arthur's. Other jewels of the islands worthy of special mention are Bermudez rum, a velvety smooth product made in the Dominican Republic; Rhum Barbancourt, a classic rum of exceptional quality made in Haiti; the wonderful, pungent Rhums of Martinique such as Rhum La Mauny, Rhum Clément, Rhum Saint-James, and Rhum Negrita; robust British Navy Pusser's Rum from the British Virgin Islands (used as the Royal Navy's rum ration for nearly 300 years) and, of course, the great company of aromatic, full-bodied rums from Jamaica carrying such famous names as Myers's, Appleton, and Captain Morgan.

Credit for the bourgeoning popularity of rums of all kinds in the U.S. must go to the highly respected firm of Bacardi & Company, Ltd., which began corporate life in the year 1862 in Santiago de Cuba. The first plant consisted of a shed housing an ancient, cast-iron pot still, a few fermenting tanks, and some aging barrels. The tin-roofed shed also housed a colony of fruit bats; hence, the bat trademark that appears on every bottle of Bacardi rum. From these meager beginnings Bacardi has grown into the producer of the world's largest-selling brand of spirits, with distribution in 175 different countries. The firm's dedication to quality has been the driving force behind the success of this famous brand.

Rum is the product of sugarcane. Unlike spirits made from grain, such as whiskey, the juice from the cane can be fermented directly into alcohol instead of having to be converted first from starch to sugar. After the juice is pressed from the sugarcane, it is boiled, reduced, and clarified. The heavy sugar syrup that results is processed into sugar and molasses. To start the fermentation process, a little molasses is removed from the batch, diluted, and taken to the laboratory, where a tiny portion of yeast is added. The yeast is a vital part of the entire process. Every rum distiller has its own special strain of yeast, which is a closely guarded trade secret. In the case of Bacardi, their yeast strain was developed more than a century ago.

After the yeast has grown sufficiently—a week or ten days—this fermentation culture is added to molasses in the fermenting tanks. The fermentation process usually takes about seventy-two hours. Then the fermented batch is distilled in continuous-column stills more than four stories high. These modern stills differ from the old-fashioned pot still in that live steam is used to draw off the distillate at very high proofs, which eliminates certain impurities that can produce harshness in the end product. The process is continuous, whereas in the pot still, spirits can only be made in batches. After distillation is completed, the rums are aged in barrels (American white oak is preferred) until they have matured. At the proper time the blender proceeds to "marry" rums of various ages and from different batches until the precise blend is achieved with the proper color, bouquet, flavor, smoothness, and balance.

Rum and rum drinks are very much a part of the American heritage. By the end of the seventeenth century rum was the most quaffed spirit in the American colonies. And by all accounts, the Colonials were a hard-drinking lot, and, considering some of the concoctions that were in vogue, "hard" is used advisedly. Some of the popular libations of the day were Kill-Divil, Stonewall and Bogus, Coo-Woo, Whistle-Belly Vengeance, and Rattle-Skull. The latter consisted of a large peg of rum mixed with brandy, wine, and porter (a dark, full-bodied malt brew similar to stout), and seasoned with lime peel and nutmeg.

The Flip also was all the rage with our founding fathers and no doubt gave them both sustenance and comfort during the trying times of the American Revolution. It is the only mixed drink recipe that has survived to the present, and with the omission of one ingredient, the Flip is made today with the same basic recipe that was used over two hundred years ago.

Flips were made as both hot and cold drinks, but the hot version was extremely popular, as were all mulled potations during those days without central heating. The hot Flip was made by mixing rum and beer with beaten eggs, cream, and spices, then mulled with a red-hot poker known as a "flip-iron," "flip-dog," or "loggerhead." During heated discussions over hot drinks, so the story goes, loggerheads sometimes were used to drive home a point. This is believed to be the origin of the phrase "being at loggerheads."

During the eighteenth century the Caribbean was known as the Spanish Main, an appellation that was not recognized by the British navy, American privateers, or the motley assortment of pirates, freebooters, and rogues who sailed the high seas. One thing all could agree to, however, was that Grog was the most popular drink to be had, whether in port or at sea. This forerunner of the highball was simply rum mixed with water. The Grog was standard issue to sailors in the Royal Navy and is named for Admiral Edward Vernon, who was nicknamed "Old Grog" for his habit of wearing a grogram cape and for cutting the rum ration with generous amounts of water to prevent drunkenness aboard ship.

Legend has it that Henry Morgan, the notorious British buccaneer, improved the grog ration by adding lime juice to prevent scurvy among his crew. If he added a little sugar, he might well have been remembered and revered as the inventor of the Daiquiri (which came later and originated in, and was named for, a small village of the same name not far from the original Bacardi distillery in Cuba).

For those who would like to expand their spiritous horizons, a Caribbean Rum Baedeker has been provided for the adventurous who would consider a trip to exciting and exotic places, and the opportunity to experience new and different rum drinks a smashing way to have a holiday.

A Caribbean Rum Baedeker

Country	Indigenous Rum Brands
Antigua	Cavalier Antigua Rum
Barbados	Alleyne Arthur's Special Old Barbados Rum
	Cockade Fine Rum
	Cockspur 5 Star
	Gosling's Choicest Barbados Rum
	Lamb's Navy Rum (rums from Barbados, Guayana, Jamaica, and Trinidad blended and bottled in London)
	Lightbourn's Selected Barbados Rum
	Old Brigand Rum (Alleyne Arthur)
	Malibu
	Mount Gay "Eclipse" Rum
	Mount Gay Sugar Cane Brandy (ten years old)

Country	Indigenous Rum Brands
Bermuda	Gosling's Black Seal
Brazil	Janeiro Cachaca Toucana Cachaca
Cuba	Casa Merino 1889 Havana Club Ron Matusalem (*Note:* Santiago de Cuba was the site of the original Bacardi distillery.)
Colombia	Ron Viejo de Caldas Ron Medellin Tres Esquinas
Costa Rica	Ron Viejo Especial
Dominican Republic	Barceló Ron Bermudez Brugal Macorix Siboney
Ecuador	Ron San Miguel
Guatemala	Ron Botran Ron Zacapa
Guyana	Lemon Hart & Sons Finest Demerara Rum Hudson's Bay Demerara Rum (Both of these rums are bottled in the U.K.)
Haiti	Rhum Barbancourt Barbancourt Rhum Liqueurs
Jamaica	Appleton C.J. Wray Coruba Daniel Finzi Fine Old Rum Gilbey's Governor General Jamaica Rum Hudson's Bay Jamaica Rum (bottled in the U.K.) Kelly's Jamaica Rum Captain Morgan Myers's Rum Rumona Jamaica Rum Liqueur Skol Wray & Nephew

Country	Indigenous Rum Brands
French West Indies	Rhum Saint-James
	Rhum Clément
	Liqueur Créole Clément
	Rhum Bally
	Rhum La Mauny
	Rhum Martinique
	Rhum Negrita
	(bottled in Bordeux)
Nicaragua	Ron Flor de Cana
Panama	Abuelo
	Carta Vieja
	Cortez
	Admiral Nelson
Puerto Rico	Bacardi
	Calypso
	Captain Morgan
	Ron Carioca
	Ron Castillo
	Boca Chica
	Don Q
	Grenado
	Ron Llave
	Myers's Rum
	Ron Merito
	Palo Viejo
	Ronrico
	Ron del Barrilito
	Ron Matusalem
	Trigo
St. Lucia	Jos. Jn. Baptiste Crystal
	Clear White Rum
St. Vincent	Sunset St. Vincent Rum
Virgin Islands (British)	Aristocrat
	British Navy Pusser's Rum
	Caribaya
	Carnival
	Carta Vieja

Country	Indigenous Rum Brands
Virgin Islands (U.S.)	Cruzan Rum
	Gold Award
	Laird's Five O'Clock
	McCormick
	Old St. Croix
	Poland Spring
	Pott Rum
	Redrum
	Ron Chico
	Ron Popular
Trinidad	Fernandes "Vat 19"
	Ferdi's 10-Year-Old
	Old Oak Rum
	Siegert's Bouquet Rum
Venezuela	Cacique Ron Añejo
	Ocumare Amazonas
	Pampero

Note: This partial listing of Caribbean rums does not include private label brands.

ACAPULCO

1½ oz. light rum
½ oz. triple sec
½ oz. lime juice
1 tsp. sugar syrup or to taste
1 egg white (for two drinks)
Mint leaves, slightly torn

Mix all ingredients, except mint leaves, with cracked ice in a shaker or blender, strain into a chilled cocktail glass, and garnish with mint.

● ADMIRAL NELSON

1 oz. light rum
1 oz. gin
1 tsp. triple sec
½ oz. lime juice
Orange slice

Mix all ingredients, except orange slice, with cracked ice in a shaker or blender and pour into a chilled Old Fashioned glass. Garnish with orange slice.

ADMIRAL VERNON

1½ oz. light rum
½ oz. Grand Marnier
½ oz. lime juice
1 tsp. orgeat syrup

Mix all ingredients with cracked ice in a shaker or blender and strain into a chilled cocktail glass.

 ADOLPH'S ALM

1½ oz. light rum
½ oz. amaretto
½ oz. lime juice
1 tsp. maraschino liqueur or sugar syrup
Dash orange bitters

Mix all ingredients with cracked ice in a shaker or blender and strain into a chilled cocktail glass.

AMERICAN FLYER

1½ oz. light rum
¼ oz. lime juice
½ tsp. sugar syrup or to taste
Champagne or sparkling wine

Mix all ingredients, except champagne, with cracked ice in a shaker or blender and strain into a chilled wine goblet. Fill with chilled champagne.

ANDALUSIA

¾ oz. light rum
¾ oz. brandy
¾ oz. dry sherry
Several dashes Angostura bitters

Combine all ingredients in a mixing glass with several ice cubes, stir well, and strain into a chilled cocktail glass.

ANKLE BREAKER

1½ oz. 151-proof Demerara rum
1 oz. cherry brandy
1 oz. lemon or lime juice
1 tsp. sugar syrup or to taste

Mix all ingredients with cracked ice in a shaker or blender and pour into a chilled Old Fashioned glass.

APPLE DAIQUIRI

1½ oz. light Puerto Rican
    rum
½ oz. calvados or applejack
½ oz. lemon juice
1 tsp. sugar syrup or to taste
Dash apple juice
Apple wedge

Mix all ingredients, except apple wedge, in a shaker or blender with cracked ice and strain into a chilled cocktail glass. Garnish with apple wedge.

APPLE PIE

1½ oz. light rum
¾ oz. sweet vermouth
½ oz. calvados
1 tsp. lemon juice
Dash grenadine
Dash apricot brandy

Mix all ingredients with cracked ice in a shaker or blender and strain into a chilled cocktail glass.

APRICOT LADY

1½ oz. light rum
1 oz. apricot-flavored brandy
    or apricot liqueur
½ oz. curaçao
½ oz. lime juice
1 egg white (for two drinks)
Orange slice

Mix all ingredients, except orange slice, with cracked ice in a shaker or blender at low speed for fifteen seconds, pour into a chilled Old Fashioned glass, and garnish with fruit slice.

APRICOT PIE

1½ oz. light Puerto Rican
    rum
½ oz. sweet vermouth
1 oz. apricot brandy
1 tsp. lemon juice
Dash grenadine

Mix all ingredients with cracked ice in a shaker or blender and pour into a chilled cocktail glass.

ARAWAK PUNCH

1½ oz. gold Jamaica rum
½ oz. passion fruit juice or
    pineapple juice
½ oz. lime juice
1 tsp. orgeat syrup

Mix all ingredients with cracked ice in a shaker or blender, and pour into a chilled Old Fashioned glass.

AZTECA Aztec Cocktail

1½ oz. light rum or tequila
1 oz. Kahlua
1 oz. crème de cacao
Dash curaçao

Mix all ingredients with cracked ice in a shaker or blender and strain into a chilled cocktail glass.

BACARDI

1½ oz. light or gold Bacardi rum
½ oz. lime juice
½ tsp. grenadine

Mix all ingredients with cracked ice in a shaker or blender and pour into a chilled cocktail glass.

BACARDI SPECIAL

1½ oz. light Bacardi rum
¾ oz. gin
1 oz. lime juice
1 tsp. grenadine

Mix with cracked ice in a shaker or blender and strain into a chilled cocktail glass.

BAHIA DE BOQUERON

1½ oz. light Puerto Rican rum
½ oz. triple sec
1 oz. orange juice
½ oz. lime juice
Lemon-lime soda
Lemon and lime slices

Mix all ingredients, except soda and lemon and lime slices, with cracked ice in a shaker or blender and pour into a chilled Collins glass. Fill with soda, stir gently, and garnish with lemon and lime slices.

BANANA DAIQUIRI

1½ oz. light rum
½ oz. lime juice
1 tsp. sugar syrup or crème de banane
⅓ ripe banana, sliced

Mix all ingredients with cracked ice in a blender until smooth and pour into a chilled cocktail glass.

BANANA RUM

½ oz. white rum
½ oz. banana liqueur
½ oz. orange juice

Mix all ingredients with cracked ice in a shaker or blender, and strain into a chilled cocktail glass.

BANYAN COCKTAIL

1½ oz. gold rum
¾ oz. apricot brandy
½ oz. lime juice
½ oz. orgeat syrup or sugar
   syrup to taste
Dash grenadine

Mix with cracked ice in a shaker or blender and strain into a chilled cocktail glass.

BARBADOS PLANTER'S PUNCH

3 oz. Barbados gold rum
Juice of 1 lime
1 tsp. sugar syrup or to taste
Dash Angostura bitters
Water or club soda
Ripe banana slice
Orange slices
Maraschino cherry
Pinch ground nutmeg

Mix all ingredients except banana, orange slices, cherry, and nutmeg, with cracked ice in a shaker or blender and pour into a large, chilled Collins glass. Garnish with banana, orange slices, and maraschino cherry. Sprinkle ground nutmeg on top.

BARRANQUILLA BUCK

1½ oz. light Colombian rum
   (Medellin or Tres
   Esquinas)
½ oz. Falernum
1 oz. lemon juice
Club soda
Orange slice

Mix all ingredients, except club soda and orange slice, with cracked ice in a shaker or blender and pour into a chilled Old Fashioned glass. Fill with club soda and garnish with orange slice.

BATIDA DE PIÑA

2–3 oz. light rum
⅔ cup crushed pineapple
1 tsp. sugar syrup
Mint sprig (optional)

Mix all ingredients, except mint sprig, with cracked ice in a blender until smooth, and pour into a chilled double Old Fashioned glass. Garnish with mint sprig.

BEACHCOMBER

1½ oz. light rum
½ oz. Cointreau
½ oz. lime juice
Several dashes maraschino
   liqueur

Mix all ingredients with cracked
ice in a shaker or blender and
strain into a chilled cocktail
glass.

BEACHCOMBER'S GOLD

1½ oz. light rum
½ oz. dry vermouth
½ oz. sweet vermouth

Combine all ingredients with
several ice cubes in a mixing
glass, stir well, and strain into a
chilled cocktail glass.

 BEEKMAN PLACE COFFEE

1 cup hot black coffee
2 cinnamon sticks
1 oz. Tia Maria
1½ oz. dark Jamaica rum
Dash amaretto
1 scoop chocolate ice cream
Whipped cream
Pinch ground nutmeg

Prepare coffee and let steep with
cinnamon sticks until it is cool.
Chill in refrigerator (remove cinnamon sticks) along with other
ingredients. Chill blender bowl.
Add chilled coffee, Tia Maria,
rum, and amaretto to blender
and mix well. Add scoop of ice
cream and blend for no more
than 3 seconds. Pour into a
chilled highball glass, top with a
generous helping of whipped
cream, and sprinkle with
nutmeg.

BEE'S KISS No. 1

1½ oz. light Puerto Rican
   rum
1 tsp. honey
1 tsp. heavy cream

Mix all ingredients with cracked
ice in a shaker or blender and
strain into a chilled cocktail
glass.

BEE'S KNEES No. 2

1½ oz. gold rum
½ oz. orange juice
½ oz. lime juice
1 tsp. sugar syrup or to taste
Several dashes curaçao
Orange peel

Mix all ingredients, except orange peel, with cracked ice in a
shaker or blender and strain into
a chilled cocktail glass. Twist orange peel over drink and drop
into glass.

BETWEEN THE SHEETS

¾ oz. light rum
¾ oz. brandy
¾ oz. Cointreau
½ oz. lemon juice

Mix all ingredients with cracked ice in a shaker or blender and strain into a chilled cocktail glass.

⬤ BITCH'S ITCH

2 oz. 86-proof Demerara rum
½ oz. white crème de cacao
½ oz. triple sec
1 oz. lime juice
½ oz. Falernum or sugar
  syrup to taste
1 tsp. 151-proof Demerara
  rum
Pinch ground cinnamon
Pinch ground nutmeg

Mix all ingredients, except 151-proof rum, cinnamon, and nutmeg, with cracked ice in a shaker or blender and pour into a large Collins glass. Top with a float of 151-proof rum and sprinkle with cinnamon and nutmeg.

⬤ BLACK STRIPE No. 2 Cold

2 oz. dark Jamaica rum
½ oz. golden molasses
½ oz. lemon juice

Mix with cracked ice in a blender and pour into a chilled cocktail glass.

BLACK WITCH

1½ oz. gold rum
½ oz. pineapple juice
1 tsp. dark Jamaica rum
1 tsp. apricot brandy

Mix all ingredients with cracked ice in a shaker or blender and strain into a chilled cocktail glass.

BLUE MOUNTAIN

1½ oz. Jamaica rum
¾ oz. vodka
¾ oz. Tia Maria
2 oz. orange juice

Mix all ingredients with cracked ice in a shaker or blender. Pour into a chilled Old Fashioned glass.

BLUE MOUNTAIN COOLER

2 oz. light rum
½ oz. triple sec or curaçao
½ oz. lemon juice
1 tsp. blueberry syrup
Club soda
Fresh blueberries (optional)
Lemon slice

Mix all ingredients, except club soda, blueberries, and lemon slice, with cracked ice in a shaker or blender and pour into a chilled Collins glass. Fill with club soda and garnish with a few blueberries and lemon slice.

BOCA CHICA COFFEE

2 oz. dark or gold Jamaica rum
1 scoop vanilla or mocha ice cream
Cold black coffee

Mix rum and ice cream in a chilled highball or double Old Fashioned glass until smooth but not too melted. Fill with cold black coffee and stir once or twice only.

BOLERO

1½ oz. light rum
¾ oz. apple brandy or applejack
Several dashes sweet vermouth
Lemon peel

Mix all ingredients, except lemon peel, with ice in a mixing glass, stir briskly, and strain into a chilled cocktail glass. Twist lemon peel over drink and drop into glass.

 BONAIRE BOOTY

½ oz. gold rum
½ oz. amaretto
1 oz. chocolate almond liqueur
1 oz. cream

Mix with cracked ice in a blender and pour into a chilled cocktail glass.

BONGO COLA

1½ oz. gold Barbados, Haitian, and Jamaica rum
1 oz. Tia Maria
2 oz. pineapple juice
Dash kirsch
Dash lemon juice
Cola
Maraschino cherry

Mix rum, Tia Maria, pineapple juice, kirsch, and lemon juice with cracked ice in a shaker or blender and pour into a tall, chilled Collins glass. Add several ice cubes, fill with cold cola, stir gently, and garnish with a cherry.

BON TON COCKTAIL

1 oz. gold Barbados rum
1 oz. Southern Comfort
½ oz. Grand Marnier
½ tsp. lemon juice
Several dashes orange
  bitters

Mix all ingredients with cracked ice in a shaker or blender and strain into a chilled cocktail glass.

BURMA BRIDGE BUSTER

1 oz. light rum
½ oz. brandy
¼ oz. Cherry Heering
½ oz. lemon juice
1 tsp. sugar syrup or to taste

Mix all ingredients with cracked ice in a shaker or blender and pour into a chilled cocktail glass.

Created for the 490th Bombardment Squadron of the 10th and 14th Air Forces.

BUSHRANGER

1 oz. light rum
1 oz. Dubonnet rouge
Several dashes Angostura
  bitters
Lemon peel

Mix all ingredients, except lemon peel, with cracked ice in a shaker or blender and strain into a chilled cocktail glass. Twist lemon peel over drink and drop in.

CALICO JACK

1 oz. dark Jamaica rum
1 oz. rye or bourbon
½ oz. lemon juice
½ oz. sugar syrup or to taste

Mix all ingredients with cracked ice in a shaker or blender and strain into a chilled cocktail glass.

CALYPSO COCKTAIL

1½ oz. gold Trinidad rum
1 oz. pineapple juice
½ oz. lemon juice
1 tsp. Falernum or sugar
  syrup to taste
Dash Angostura bitters
Pinch grated nutmeg

Mix all ingredients except nutmeg with cracked ice in a shaker or blender and strain into a chilled cocktail glass. Sprinkle with nutmeg.

CANEEL BAY CREAM

1½ oz. *light rum*
½ oz. *white crème de cacao*
½ oz. *coffee liqueur*
1 oz. *light cream*

Mix all ingredients with cracked ice in a shaker or blender and strain into a chilled cocktail glass.

CANNES-CANNES

1½ oz. *light rum*
1½ oz. *gin*
½ oz. *Cointreau*
3 oz. *grapefruit juice*
Orange slice

Mix all ingredients, except orange slice, with cracked ice in a shaker or blender, pour into a chilled Old Fashioned glass, and garnish with orange slice.

 CANTALOUPE CUP

1½ oz. *light Puerto Rican rum*
⅓ cup *ripe cantaloupe, diced*
½ oz. *lime juice*
½ oz. *orange juice*
½ tsp. *sugar syrup or to taste*
Cantaloupe slice, cut long and slim

Mix all ingredients, except cantaloupe slice, with cracked ice in a blender until smooth and pour into a chilled Old Fashioned glass. Garnish with cantaloupe slice.

CARDINAL COCKTAIL No. 1

2 oz. *light rum*
½ oz. *amaretto or crème de noyaux*
½ oz. *triple sec*
1 oz. *lime juice*
½ tsp. *grenadine*
Lime slice

Mix all ingredients, except lime slice, with cracked ice in a shaker or blender and pour into a chilled Old Fashioned glass. Garnish with lime slice.

CASA BLANCA

2 oz. *gold Jamaica rum*
¼ tsp. *curaçao*
¼ tsp. *maraschino liqueur*
1 tsp. *lime juice*
Dash Angostura bitters

Mix all ingredients with cracked ice in a shaker or blender and strain into a chilled cocktail glass.

CAT CAY COCKTAIL

1½ oz. Haitian rum or
   Martinique rum
½ oz. Grand Marnier
½ oz. lime juice
Lemon peel

Mix all ingredients, except
lemon peel, with cracked ice in
a shaker or blender. Strain into
a chilled cocktail glass, twist
lemon peel over drink, and drop
into glass.

CHALULA CREAM

1½ oz. gold Jamaica rum
½ oz. maraschino liqueur
½ oz. lime juice
1 tsp. heavy cream
1 egg white (for two drinks)

Mix all ingredients with cracked
ice in a shaker or blender and
strain into a chilled cocktail
glass.

CHAPULTEPEC

1 oz. light rum
¾ oz. brandy
¼ oz. sweet vermouth
¼ oz. tequila
1 tsp. sugar syrup or to taste

Mix all ingredients with plenty
of cracked ice in a shaker or
blender and pour into a chilled
Whiskey Sour glass.

CHARLES DARDEN

½ oz. dark rum
1½ oz. apricot liqueur
2 oz. orange juice
½ oz. lemon juice
Dash grenadine
Champagne
Orange slice

Mix all ingredients, except orange slice and champagne, with
crushed ice in a blender. Pour
the mixture into a chilled wine
goblet and top with champagne.
Decorate with orange slice.

A house specialty created by
Eric Gaultier, chief bartender,
Hotel Gaunahani, Saint-Barthél-
emy, French West Indies.

CHARLOTTE AMALIE CELEBRATION CUP

1½ oz. light Virgin Islands
   rum
1 oz. Cherry Heering
1 oz. lemon juice
1 tsp. sugar syrup or to taste
2 oz. lemon-lime soda
Lemon slice

Mix all ingredients, except soda
and lemon slice, with cracked
ice in a shaker or blender and
pour into a chilled double Old
Fashioned glass. Fill with cold
lemon-lime soda and garnish
with lemon slice.

 **CHEERY COKE**

2 oz. *Jamaica rum*
Several dashes cherry
    brandy or cherry cordial
Cola
Lemon peel

Combine rum, brandy, and a little cola in a chilled double Old Fashioned glass and stir well. Fill with cold cola and stir gently. Twist lemon peel over drink and drop into glass.

CHERRY DAIQUIRI

1½ oz. *light rum*
½ oz. *Cherry Heering*
½ oz. *lime juice*
Several dashes *kirsch*
Lime peel

Mix all ingredients, except lime peel, with cracked ice in a shaker or blender and strain into a chilled cocktail glass. Twist lime peel over drink and drop into glass.

CHICAGO FIZZ

1 oz. *gold rum*
1 oz. *port*
½ oz. *lemon juice*
1 tsp. *sugar syrup or to taste*
1 egg white (for two drinks)
Club soda

Mix all ingredients, except club soda, with cracked ice in a shaker or blender. Strain into a chilled Collins glass and fill with cold club soda.

CHICKASAW COCKTAIL

1 oz. *gold rum*
1 oz. *Southern Comfort*
½ oz. *curaçao*
1 tsp. *lemon juice*
Several dashes orange
    bitters

Mix all ingredients with cracked ice in a shaker or blender and strain into a chilled cocktail glass.

CHI-CHI

2 oz. *light rum*
5 oz. *pineapple juice*
½ oz. *blackberry brandy*

Mix rum and pineapple juice with cracked ice in a shaker or blender and pour into a chilled highball glass. Top off with blackberry brandy.

2 oz. gold Barbados rum
1 tsp. curaçao
½ oz. passion fruit juice
Several dashes grenadine
Several dashes Angostura
   bitters

Mix all ingredients with cracked ice in a shaker or blender and strain into a chilled cocktail glass.

 ## COCONUT BANG! No. 1

1 oz. light rum
1 oz. coconut rum
½ oz. coconut juice
½ oz. coconut cream
   (canned)
1 oz. orange juice
2 oz. fresh coconut, cut in
   small pieces
½ oz. lemon juice

Drain the water or juice from a coconut by puncturing the "eyes" at one end and drain into a tumbler. There should be sufficient liquid in the average coconut to make 3 or 4 drinks. Crack coconut with a hammer and remove meat by using a table knife. Coconut meat may be frozen for future use. Mix all ingredients in a blender with cracked ice until smooth and pour into a chilled Hurricane or chimney glass.

Many coconut recipes call for using the coconut shell as a drinking glass. This looks great in photos taken in exotic tropical settings, but almost never works well due to the fact that the coconut was never designed to be used as a drinking vessel. Use a big glass. It eliminates a lot of spilled drinks.

 ## COCONUT BANG! No. 2

1½ oz. coconut rum
2 oz. pineapple juice
1 oz. lime juice
½ oz. coconut syrup
1 tsp. CocoRibe or Malibu
Fresh coconut, grated

Mix all ingredients, except grated coconut, with cracked ice in a shaker or blender. Pour into a chilled double Old Fashioned glass and sprinkle with grated coconut.

COLUMBIA

1½ oz. light rum
½ oz. raspberry syrup or
    raspberry or cherry
    liqueur
½ oz. lemon juice
1 tsp. kirschwasser

Mix all ingredients with cracked ice in a shaker or blender and strain into a chilled cocktail glass.

CONTINENTAL

1½ oz. light rum
½ oz. green crème de
    menthe
½ oz. lime juice
1 tsp. sugar syrup or to taste

Mix all ingredients with cracked ice in a shaker or blender and strain into a chilled cocktail glass.

CORKSCREW

1½ oz. light rum
½ oz. dry vermouth
½ oz. peach liqueur
Lime slice

Mix all ingredients, except lime slice, with cracked ice in a shaker or blender, strain into a chilled cocktail glass, and garnish with lime slice.

CORONADO GOLD

1½ oz. gold rum
1 oz. brandy
½ oz. lemon juice
½ oz. sugar syrup or to taste
1 egg yolk

Mix all ingredients with cracked ice in a blender and pour into a chilled Whiskey Sour glass.

COZUMEL COFFEE COCKTAIL

1 oz. Barbados or Mexican
    gold rum
1 oz. coffee liqueur
1 oz. triple sec

Mix all ingredients with cracked ice in a shaker or blender and strain into a chilled cocktail glass.

BARTENDER'S SECRET NO. 10—Creative Containers

Exotic rum drinks deserve exotic presentation in some novel or unusual glass. So reasoned Trader Vic when he was introducing his elegant liquid inventions in an atmosphere of a romantic, tropical island hideaway. No container, if attractive, was too bizarre for his Polynesian potations. Trader Vic used flower vases, pottery bowls, ceramic mugs shaped like skulls, and even ceramic pineapples and coconuts. China rum kegs and footed tiki bowls (decorated with South Seas religious figures) were used for communal drinks. All kinds of glassware were utilized to make drinks look appealing, important, and romantic. A big beer schooner or a king-size brandy snifter properly garnished with fruits and flowers has a certain allure that one does not feel when the same drink is served in a highball glass. It is not usually necessary to shop around for rare and unusual glassware to achieve an exotic effect when serving party drinks to your guests. Instead of serving a Rum Collins in a Collins glass, try using a tall pilsener beer glass (if it has a small stem, so much the better) or a big wine goblet. Those oversize brandy snifters that are used only occasionally will give an aura of importance to any tall drink. Footed iced-tea glasses, parfait, and sherbet glasses, even tall water goblets, can add just the right touch to cocktails and coolers. Search the back of the cupboard. Those heavy coffee mugs you thought you'd never use again might be just the thing for your next party.

CREOLE CUP

1½ oz. light rum
Beef bouillon or consommé
1 tsp. lemon juice
Several dashes Tabasco
  sauce
Several dashes
  Worcestershire sauce
Pinch celery salt
Pinch white pepper

Put several ice cubes into a chilled double Old Fashioned glass. Add rum, bouillon, lemon juice, and seasonings and stir well.

CUBA LIBRE

2 oz. light, gold, or dark rum
Cola, ice cold
Wedge of lemon or lime

Half fill a chilled highball or Collins glass with ice cubes, add rum, and fill with cold cola. Stir gently and squeeze lemon or lime wedge over drink and drop into glass.

CUBANO ESPECIAL

1½ oz. light Cuban or Puerto
    Rican rum
½ oz. curaçao
½ oz. lime juice
½ oz. pineapple juice
Pineapple slice

Mix all ingredients, except pineapple slice, with cracked ice in a shaker or blender, pour into a chilled cocktail glass, and garnish with pineapple slice.

CULROSS

1 oz. gold rum
½ oz. Lillet blanc
½ oz. apricot brandy
½ oz. lemon juice

Mix all ingredients with cracked ice in a shaker or blender and pour into a chilled cocktail glass.

CURAÇAO COOLER

1 oz. dark Jamaica rum
1 oz. curaçao
1 oz. lime juice
Club soda
Orange slice

Mix all ingredients, except club soda and orange slice, with cracked ice in a shaker or blender. Pour into a chilled highball glass, fill with cold club soda, and garnish with orange slice.

DAIQUIRI

2 oz. light rum
Juice of ½ lime
½ tsp. sugar syrup or to taste

Mix all ingredients with cracked ice in a shaker or blender and strain into a chilled cocktail glass.

DAIQUIRI DARK

2 oz. *Jamaica rum*
½ oz. *lime juice*
1 tsp. *Falernum or sugar
    syrup to taste*

Mix all ingredients with cracked
ice in a shaker or blender and
strain into a chilled cocktail
glass.

DEMERARA DROP-SHOT

2 oz. *90-proof Demerara rum*
½ oz. *coconut cream*
½ oz. *lemon juice*

Mix all ingredients with cracked
ice in a blender and pour into a
chilled Old Fashioned glass.

DERBY SPECIAL

1½ oz. *light rum*
½ oz. *Cointreau*
1 oz. *orange juice*
½ oz. *lime juice*

Mix all ingredients with cracked
ice in a blender and pour into a
chilled cocktail glass.

DEVIL'S TAIL

1½ oz. *gold rum*
½ oz. *vodka*
½ oz. *apricot liqueur*
½ oz. *lime juice*
½ tsp. *grenadine*
Lime peel

Mix all ingredients, except lime
peel, with cracked ice in a
blender and pour into a chilled
cocktail glass. Twist lime peel
over drink and drop into glass.

 DOCTOR FUNK

½ *lime*
½ *lemon juice*
1 tsp. *sugar syrup*
Dash grenadine
2–3 oz. *dark Jamaica,
    Haitian, or Martinique
    rum*
Club soda
½ tsp. *Pernod or Herbsaint*

Fill a mixing glass with ice
cubes and squeeze lime into
glass (reserve shell). Add all
other ingredients, except soda
and Pernod, and stir briskly.
Strain into a chilled, tall Collins
glass, add additional ice cubes,
fill with cold club soda, and top
off with Pernod and lime shell.

DOUBLOON

1 oz. Jamaica rum
1 oz. light rum
1 oz. 151-proof rum
1 oz. grapefruit juice
1 oz. orange juice
Several dashes orange
  curaçao
Several dashes Pernod
Orange slice
Maraschino cherry

Mix all ingredients, except orange slice and maraschino cherry, with cracked ice in a shaker or blender. Pour into a chilled double Old Fashioned glass and garnish with fruit.

THE DRINKING MAN'S FRUIT CUP

2 oz. gold Barbados rum
1 oz. dark Jamaica rum
1 oz. cranberry juice
1 oz. orange juice
1 heaping tbsp. orange and
  grapefruit sections
Lemon-lime soda

Mix all ingredients, except soda, with cracked ice in a blender and pour into a chilled Collins glass. Fill with cold lemon-lime soda and stir gently.

DRY HOLE

1 oz. light rum
½ oz. apricot brandy
½ oz. Cointreau
½ oz. lemon juice
Club soda

Mix all ingredients, except club soda, with cracked ice in a shaker or blender, pour into a chilled highball glass, and fill with cold club soda.

This is a specialty drink of **The Petroleum Club of Houston.**

EL SALVADOR

1½ oz. light rum
¾ oz. Frangelico
½ oz. lime juice
1 tsp. grenadine

Mix all ingredients with cracked ice in a shaker or blender and strain into a chilled cocktail glass.

⬤ AN ENHANCED PLANTER'S PUNCH

2½ oz. dark Jamaica rum
1 oz. curaçao
2 oz. orange juice
1 oz. pineapple juice
1 oz. lime or lemon juice
Falernum, orgeat, or sugar
    syrup to taste
Dash grenadine
Club soda
Pineapple slice
Orange slice
Maraschino cherry

Mix all ingredients, except soda, pineapple and orange slices, and cherry, with cracked ice in a shaker or blender and pour into a large, chilled Collins glass. Fill with cold club soda and stir gently. Garnish with pineapple and orange slices and cherry.

EYE OPENER No. 1

1½ oz. light rum
1 tsp. triple sec
1 tsp. white crème de cacao
1 tsp. sugar syrup
½ tsp. Pernod
1 egg yolk

Mix all ingredients with cracked ice in a shaker or blender and strain into a chilled cocktail glass.

EYE OPENER No. 2

2 oz. dark Jamaica rum
2 oz. Barbados rum
½ oz. curaçao
2 oz. orange juice
1 oz. grapefruit juice
1 oz. sweetened lemon juice
    or liquid Whiskey Sour
    mix

Mix all ingredients with cracked ice in a shaker or blender and pour into a chilled double Old Fashioned glass.

FER DE LANCE

2 oz. Jamaica rum
1 oz. lime juice
1 oz. orange juice
½ oz. sugar syrup
1 tsp. 151-proof Demerara
    rum

Mix all ingredients, except Demerara rum, with cracked ice in a shaker or blender and pour into a chilled cocktail glass. Float Demerara rum on top.

FERN GULLY

1 oz. dark Jamaica rum
1 oz. light rum
½ oz. coconut cream
1 oz. orange juice
½ oz. lime juice
½ oz. amaretto or crème de
   noyaux

Mix all ingredients with cracked ice in a shaker or blender and serve in a chilled cocktail glass or wine goblet.

52ND STREET

1½ oz. dark Jamaica rum
1 oz. lemon juice
½ oz. cognac
½ oz. Cointreau
1 tsp. grenadine

Mix with plenty of ice in a blender until frappéed and serve in a chilled champagne glass.

FIG LEAF

1 oz. light rum
1 oz. sweet vermouth
½ oz. lime juice
Several dashes Angostura
   bitters
Lemon peel

Mix all ingredients, except lemon peel, with cracked ice in a shaker or blender and strain into a chilled cocktail glass. Twist lemon peel over drink and drop into glass.

FIJI FIZZ

1½ oz. dark Jamaica rum
½ oz. bourbon
1 tsp. Cherry Marnier
Several dashes orange
   bitters
4 oz. cola
Lime peel

Mix all ingredients, except cola and lime peel, with cracked ice in a shaker or blender, pour into a chilled Collins glass, fill with cold cola, and garnish with lime peel.

FORT DE FRANCE

1½ oz. gold rum
½ oz. brandy
½ oz. pineapple juice
1 oz. lime juice
1 tsp. Cointreau
Lime slice

Mix all ingredients, except lime slice, with cracked ice in a shaker or blender and pour into a chilled Collins glass. Garnish with lime slice.

 FROGDON

1 oz. gold rum
½ oz. dark Jamaica rum
½ oz. cranberry liqueur
1 oz. lime juice
½ oz. sugar syrup or to taste
1 egg white (for two drinks)

Mix all ingredients with cracked ice in a shaker or blender and pour into a chilled Old Fashioned glass.

FROZEN DAIQUIRI

2 oz. light rum
½ oz. lime juice
1 tsp. sugar

Mix all ingredients with plenty of crushed ice in a blender at low speed for a few seconds until snowy and pour into a chilled deep-saucer champagne glass.

FROZEN GUAVA DAIQUIRI

1½ oz. light rum
1 oz. guava nectar
½ oz. lime juice
1 tsp. crème de banane (optional)

Mix all ingredients with plenty of crushed ice in a blender for a few seconds until snowy and pour into a chilled deep-saucer champagne glass.

FROZEN PASSION

1½ oz. light Puerto Rican rum
½ oz. La Grande Passion
½ oz. lime juice
½ oz. orange juice
1 tsp. lemon juice

Mix all ingredients with plenty of crushed ice in a blender for a few seconds until snowy and pour into a chilled deep-saucer champagne glass.

FROZEN PEACH DAIQUIRI

1½ oz. light Puerto Rican rum
½ oz. lime juice
1 heaping tbsp. fresh, canned, or frozen peaches, diced
½ oz. syrup from canned or frozen peaches or sugar syrup

Mix all ingredients with plenty of crushed ice in a blender for a few seconds until snowy and pour into a chilled deep-saucer champagne glass.

FROZEN PINEAPPLE DAIQUIRI

1½ oz. light Puerto Rican
  rum
½ oz. lime juice
½ tsp. pineapple syrup or
  crème de banane
2 oz. canned pineapple,
  finely chopped

Mix all ingredients with plenty
of crushed ice in a blender for a
few seconds until snowy and
pour into a chilled deep-saucer
champagne glass.

FT. LAUDERDALE

1½ oz. gold rum
½ oz. sweet vermouth
½ oz. orange juice
½ oz. lime juice
Preserved cocktail orange
  section

Mix all ingredients, except orange section, with cracked ice in
a shaker or blender and pour
into a chilled Whiskey Sour
glass. Garnish with orange
section.

GEORGIA RUM COOLER

2–3 oz. light rum
½ oz. lemon juice
1 tsp. Falernum
Dash grenadine
1 tsp. salted peanuts
Club soda
Pinch of ground cinnamon

Mix all ingredients, except club
soda and cinnamon, with
cracked ice in a blender at high
speed for 30 seconds, pour into a
chilled Collins glass, and fill
with cold club soda. Stir gently
and sprinkle with ground
cinnamon.

GOLDEN GATE

1 oz. light rum
½ oz. gin
½ oz. white crème de cacao
1 oz. lemon juice
1 tsp. 151-proof Demerara
  rum
1 tsp. Falernum or orgeat
  syrup to taste
Orange slice

Mix all ingredients, except orange slice, with cracked ice in a
shaker or blender, pour into a
chilled Old Fashioned glass, and
garnish with orange slice.

GRAND OCCASION COCKTAIL

1½ oz. light rum
½ oz. Grand Marnier
½ oz. white crème de cacao
½ oz. lemon juice

Mix with cracked ice and pour into a chilled cocktail glass.

GUANABANA

1½ oz. light rum
1 oz. guanabana (soursop) nectar
1 tsp. lime juice

Mix all ingredients with cracked ice in a shaker or blender and strain into a chilled cocktail glass.

GUANABARA GUAVA

2 oz. gold rum
½ oz. maraschino liqueur
1½ oz. guava nectar
Juice of ½ lemon
½ oz. pineapple juice
1 tsp. coconut syrup or to taste
Lemon-lime soda
Lemon slice

Mix all ingredients, except soda and lemon slice, with cracked ice in a shaker or blender, pour into a chilled Collins glass, and top with cold club soda. Stir gently and garnish with lemon slice.

HAPPY APPLE

1½ oz. gold Barbados rum
3 oz. sweet apple cider
½ oz. lemon juice
Lime peel

Mix all ingredients, except lime peel, with cracked ice in a shaker or blender and pour into a chilled Old Fashioned glass. Twist lime peel over drink and drop into glass.

HAMMERHEAD

1 oz. gold rum
1 oz. amaretto
1 oz. curaçao
Dash Southern Comfort

Mix all ingredients with cracked ice in a shaker or blender and strain into a chilled cocktail glass.

HAMMERTOE

1½ oz. light rum
½ oz. curaçao
½ oz. lime juice
1 tsp. amaretto

Mix all ingredients with cracked ice in a shaker or blender and pour into a chilled Old Fashioned glass.

HAVANA BANANA FIZZ

1½ oz. light rum
2 oz. pineapple juice
1 oz. lime juice
⅓ ripe banana, sliced
Several dashes Peychaud's bitters
Bitter lemon soda

Mix all ingredients, except soda, with cracked ice in a blender until smooth. Pour into a chilled highball glass and fill with cold bitter lemon soda.

HAVANA BANDANA

2 oz. light Cuban or Puerto Rican rum
½ oz. lime juice
1 very ripe banana, sliced
Dash banana liqueur

Mix all ingredients, except banana liqueur, with cracked ice in a blender until smooth and pour into a chilled double Old Fashioned glass. Float dash of banana liqueur on top.

HAVANA CLUB

1½ oz. light rum
½ oz. dry vermouth

Mix all ingredients with cracked ice in a shaker or blender and strain into a chilled cocktail glass.

HONEY BEE

2 oz. light Puerto Rican rum
½ oz. honey
½ oz. lemon juice

Mix all ingredients with cracked ice in a shaker or blender and strain into a chilled cocktail glass.

HOP TOAD

1 oz. light rum
1 oz. apricot brandy
1 oz. lime juice

Mix all ingredients with cracked ice in a shaker or blender and strain into a chilled cocktail glass.

HURRICANE

1 oz. light rum
1 oz. gold rum
½ oz. passion fruit syrup
½ oz. lime juice

Mix all ingredients with cracked ice in a shaker or blender and strain into a chilled cocktail glass.

IBO LELE

2 oz. gold Haitian or
   Barbados rum
½ oz. 151-proof Demerara
   rum
½ oz. orgeat syrup or to taste
1 tsp. cream
1 egg (for two drinks)
Pinch of ground nutmeg

Mix all ingredients, except nutmeg, with cracked ice in a shaker or blender and strain into a chilled wine glass. Sprinkle with ground nutmeg.

INDEPENDENCE SWIZZLE

2 oz. Trinidad rum (Ferdi's,
   Old Oak, or Siegert's)
Juice of ½ lime
1 tsp. honey or to taste
Several dashes Angostura
   bitters
Lime slice

Mix all ingredients, except lime slice, with crushed ice in a tall, chilled Collins glass with a swizzle stick. Sometimes it is better to dissolve honey with a little water before trying to mix it in a cold drink. Garnish with lime slice.

A swizzle stick may be made from a small twig with many little branches or you may substitute a long spoon.

IPSWICH SWITCHELL

2 oz. light rum
1 oz. cranberry juice
1 tsp. sugar syrup or to taste
Dash lime juice

Mix all ingredients with cracked ice in a shaker or blender and strain into a chilled double Old Fashioned glass filled with crushed ice.

ISLAND ICED TEA

1 oz. light rum
½ oz. dark Jamaica rum
1 cup iced tea, cold
1 tsp. Falernum or sugar
  syrup to taste
Dash lemon juice
Dash 151-proof Demerara
  rum
Lemon slice
Mint sprig (optional)

Mix light rum, Jamaica rum, tea, syrup, and lemon juice in a tall, chilled highball or Collins glass, add ice, and top with 151-proof rum. Garnish with lemon slice and mint sprig.

BARTENDER'S SECRET NO. 11—Exotic Fruits

Time was that tropical fruits in most of the U.S. were limited to oranges, lemons, grapefruits, limes, bananas, pineapples, and coconuts (the latter, not really a fruit but a seed, is included here because it is a popular mixed-drink ingredient). Thanks to jet transportation, increased demand for exotic tropical fruits, and important technological improvements in food processing, new kinds of tropical fruits are becoming available. Sweet, syrupy papaya, mango, and guava nectars are being replaced with appetizing juice drinks that are a boon to the professional bartender and the home drink maker. These are now becoming available in supermarkets. Rare tropical fruits like the soursop, sweetsop, custard apple, mammee apple, akee, and Malay apple will no doubt find their way to grocery-store shelves. It wasn't long ago that the kiwi, passion fruit, and the papaya were just curiosities. When more exotic fruits become readily available, mixologists will have a field day and the rum drinker will be the beneficiary.

ISLAND SCHOONER FLOAT

1 oz. Bacardi Premium Black
  Rum
4 oz. chilled cola
2 scoops vanilla ice cream
Maraschino cherry

In a chilled fountain glass combine rum, cola, and ice cream with an iced-tea spoon. Do not overmix. Garnish with a cherry. Serve with an iced-tea spoon.

Created by the author for Bacardi Imports, Inc., Miami.

ISLAND SUNRISE

2 oz. Bacardi Premium Black
  Rum
6 oz. orange juice
1½ oz. heavy cream
2 tbsp. superfine sugar or to
  taste
Orange slice

Mix all ingredients, except orange slice, with cracked ice in a shaker or blender and strain into a chilled wine goblet. Garnish with orange slice.

Created by the author for Bacardi Imports, Inc., Miami.

ISLE OF THE BLESSED COCONUT

1½ oz. light rum
½ oz. lime juice
½ oz. lemon juice
½ oz. orange juice
1 tsp. cream of coconut
1 tsp. orgeat syrup or to taste

Mix all ingredients with cracked ice in a blender until smooth and pour into a chilled deep-saucer champagne glass.

ISLE OF PINES

1½ oz. light Puerto Rican rum
½ oz. lime juice
1 tsp. peppermint schnapps
6 mint leaves

Mix all ingredients with plenty of crushed ice in a blender for a few seconds until snowy and pour into a chilled cocktail glass. Serve with a straw.

JADE

1½ oz. gold Barbados rum
½ tsp. green crème de menthe
½ oz. lime juice
½ tsp. curaçao
1 tsp. sugar syrup or to taste
Lime slice

Mix all ingredients, except lime slice, with cracked ice in a shaker or blender, strain into a chilled cocktail glass, and garnish with lime slice.

JAMAICA EGG CREAM

1½ oz. dark Jamaica rum
1 oz. gin
1 oz. light cream
1 tsp. lemon juice
1 tsp. sugar syrup or to taste
Club soda

Mix all ingredients, except club soda, with cracked ice in a shaker or blender, pour into a chilled highball glass, and fill with cold club soda.

Inspired by the New York City Egg Cream drink, which contains no egg or cream.

JAMAICA MULE

1½ oz. light Jamaica rum
½ oz. dark Jamaica rum
½ oz. 151-proof rum
½ oz. Falernum or sugar
  syrup
½ oz. lime juice
Ginger beer
Pineapple stick
1 section preserved ginger
  (optional)

Mix all ingredients, except ginger beer, pineapple, and ginger, with cracked ice in a shaker or blender and pour into a chilled Collins glass. Fill with cold ginger beer and stir gently. Garnish with pineapple stick and ginger.

JAMAICA PEACH

1½ oz. dark Jamaica rum
1½ oz. peach brandy
2 oz. orange juice
2 oz. pineapple juice
1 oz. grapefruit juice
1 oz. guava juice
Several dashes Falernum
Pineapple stick
Orange slice

Mix all ingredients, except pineapple stick and orange slice, in a shaker or blender with cracked ice and pour into a chilled double Old Fashioned glass. Garnish with pineapple stick and orange slice.

JAMAICA STONE FENCE

2 oz. dark Jamaica rum
6 oz. apple cider, chilled
Cinnamon stick
Pinch grated nutmeg

Stir rum and cider with ice in a mixing glass and pour into a double Old Fashioned glass. Garnish with cinnamon and nutmeg.

JAMBO JACK

2 oz. dark Jamaica rum
½ oz. curaçao
½ oz. apricot brandy
1 oz. lime juice
½ oz. orgeat syrup or
  Falernum
Pineapple stick

Mix all ingredients, except pineapple stick, with cracked ice in a shaker or blender and pour into chilled highball glass. Garnish with pineapple stick.

JAVIER SAAVEDRA

1 oz. dark Jamaica rum
1 oz. white tequila
2 oz. pineapple juice
1 oz. grapefruit juice
Orange slice

Mix all ingredients, except orange slice, with cracked ice in a shaker or blender, strain into a chilled cocktail glass, and garnish with orange slice.

JOLLY ROGER

1 oz. light rum
1 oz. Drambuie
½ oz. lime juice
Several dashes scotch
Club soda

Mix all ingredients, except club soda, with cracked ice in a shaker or blender. Pour into a chilled highball glass and fill with club soda.

J.P.'S PUNCH

1½ oz. light Puerto Rican
   rum
1 oz. dark Jamaica rum
2 oz. orange juice
1 oz. pineapple juice
½ oz. lime juice
½ sliced ripe banana
Maraschino cherry

Mix all ingredients, except cherry, with cracked ice in a shaker or blender and serve in a double Old Fashioned glass. Garnish with a cherry.

JU-JU

1 oz. Haitian or Martinique
   rum
1 oz. Southern Comfort
1 oz. orange juice
½ oz. lime juice
1 tsp. Falernum or orgeat
   syrup
½ ripe banana, sliced

Mix with cracked ice in a blender until smooth and pour into a chilled Collins glass.

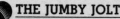 **THE JUMBY JOLT**

½ oz. gold Jamaica rum
½ oz. gin
½ oz. scotch
½ oz. lime juice
1 tsp. sweet vermouth
1 tsp. cherry brandy
Maraschino cherry

Mix all ingredients, except maraschino cherry, with cracked ice in a shaker or blender and pour into a chilled Collins glass. Garnish with cherry.

KAMEHAMEHA RUM PUNCH

1 oz. light rum
1 oz. blackberry brandy
2 oz. pineapple juice
½ oz. lemon juice
½ oz. sugar syrup or to taste
1 tsp. dark Jamaica rum
Pineapple stick

Mix all ingredients, except Jamaica rum and pineapple stick, with cracked ice in a shaker or blender. Pour into chilled highball glass, top with float of Jamaica rum, and garnish with pineapple stick.

BARTENDER'S SECRET NO. 12—Coconut Control

Fresh ripe coconuts are troublesome to prepare, but worth it in terms of flavor dividends for both food and drink preparation. When buying a coconut, select one that is heavy in the hand and full of liquid which can be plainly heard when coconut is shaken. First puncture the "eyes" at one end of the shell with an ice pick and drain out liquid and save. It may be frozen or kept in the refrigerator for a day or two. If you wish to use the shell as a container, saw it in half and remove coconut meat by inserting a long, thin, flexible kitchen knife in between shell and meat and pry out. Remove brown skin with a vegetable parer and shred with a grater or chop in a blender by adding just a few pieces at a time. Some cooks find it easier to open the shell and extract the meat by baking the whole coconut in an oven for about 15 minutes at 325°; the shell is then easily cracked open. If you wish to make coconut milk, chop meat in blender with about ¼ cup of water for a small coconut. Use milk in place of water for coconut cream. Add the liquid you drained from the coconut for more intense flavor. Strain mixture and use for drink-making. If more liquid is needed, return coconut meat to blender and repeat the process.

KE-KALI-NEI-AU

1½ oz. light rum
½ oz. kirsch
1½ oz. passion fruit juice
1 oz. lemon juice
½ oz. orgeat or sugar syrup
   to taste
1 oz. dark Jamaica rum
1 coconut shell, halved
Red hibiscus and assorted
   tropical fruits (optional)

Mix all ingredients, except Jamaica rum, coconut, hibiscus, and assorted fruits, with cracked ice in a shaker or blender. Pour into coconut shell, top with float of Jamaica rum, and garnish with red hibiscus and assorted fruits. Serve with straws.

To prepare coconut, puncture "eyes" and drain out water.* Saw coconut in half and place open end up in a cup, small dish, or ashtray so that it will not fall over when filled with liquid. If coconuts are not available, use any large decorative glass.

*Save water for punches and other tropical rum drinks.

KEMPI COLADA

1½ oz. Myers's dark rum
½ oz. cream of coconut
1½ oz. light cream or half-
   and-half
4 oz. apple juice
½ apple (Granny Smith)
¼ oz. powdered cinnamon
Apple slice (for garnish)
Cherry

Mix all ingredients, except apple slice and cherry, with cracked ice in a shaker or blender and pour into a chilled Hurricane glass. Garnish with apple slice and cherry.

This drink is a house specialty of the **Kempinski Hotel Gravenbruch, Frankfurt, Germany.**

KENT CORNERS COMFORT

1½ oz. dark Jamaica rum
½ oz. lime juice
1 tsp. maple syrup
Lime slice

Mix all ingredients, except lime slice, with cracked ice in a shaker or blender, pour into a chilled Old Fashioned glass, and garnish with lime slice.

KILAUEA KUP

1½ oz. gold rum
½ oz. crème de banane
4 oz. pineapple juice
1 oz. Rose's lime juice
1 tsp. coconut rum
Orange slice
Maraschino cherry

Mix all ingredients, except coconut rum, orange slice, and maraschino cherry, with cracked ice in a shaker or blender and pour into a chilled Collins glass. Top with coconut rum and garnish with fruit.

KILL DIVIL

2 oz. light or gold rum
1 oz. brandy
½ oz. honey or to taste
Several pinches of freshly grated ginger

Stir all ingredients with a little water until honey is dissolved, add cracked ice, and stir again until cold. Pour into a chilled Old Fashioned glass and add additional ice if necessary.

KINGSTON No. 1

1½ oz. dark Jamaica rum
¾ oz. kümmel
¾ oz. orange juice
Dash Pimiento Dram

Mix with cracked ice in a shaker or blender and strain into a chilled cocktail glass.

KINGSTON No. 2

1½ oz. dark Jamaica rum
¾ oz. gin
Juice of ½ lime
1 tsp. grenadine or to taste

Mix with cracked ice in a shaker or blender and strain into a chilled cocktail glass.

KINGSTON COCKTAIL

1½ oz. dark Jamaica rum
1 oz. Tia Maria
1 tsp. lime juice

Mix all ingredients with cracked ice in a shaker or blender and strain into a chilled cocktail glass.

KINGSTON COFFEE GROG

1½ oz. gold Jamaica rum
1½ oz. Tia Maria
½ tsp. powdered instant coffee
½ tsp. sugar syrup or to taste

Mix all ingredients in a mixing glass with ice until coffee powder is dissolved and strain into a chilled Delmonico glass.

KOKO HEAD

2 oz. light rum
½ oz. triple sec
½ oz. pineapple liqueur or apricot liqueur
1 oz. lime juice
Lime slice

Mix all ingredients, except lime slice, with cracked ice in a shaker or blender, pour into a chilled Old Fashioned glass, and garnish with lime slice.

KUAI KUP

3 oz. light rum
4 oz. pineapple juice
2 oz. orange juice
½ oz. passion fruit juice
Pineapple slice

Mix all ingredients, except pineapple slice, with cracked ice in a shaker or blender and pour into a chilled double Old Fashioned glass. Garnish with pineapple slice.

 LALLAH ROOKH

1½ oz. light rum
¾ oz. cognac
½ oz. crème de vanille or vanilla extract
1 tsp. sugar syrup or to taste
1 generous tbsp. whipped cream

Mix all ingredients, except whipped cream, with cracked ice in a shaker or blender and serve in a chilled wine goblet and top with whipped cream.

LEMON RUM ICE

2 oz. *light rum*
4 oz. *lemon ice, sorbet, or sherbet*

Chill blender bowl, rum and lemon ice in freezer before making this drink. Spoon out a generous ½ cup of lemon ice and add to blender bowl with chilled rum. Turn blender on for 3 seconds. Spoon mixture into a chilled wine goblet. Serve with spoon and straw.

The secret to this drink is to mix quickly so ice does not get mushy. Thus everything must be well chilled in advance.

LIMBO COCKTAIL

2 oz. *light rum*
½ oz. *crème de banane*
1 oz. *orange juice*

Mix all ingredients with cracked ice in a shaker or blender and strain into a chilled cocktail glass.

 LITTLE DIX MIX

1½ oz. *dark Jamaica rum*
½ oz. *crème de banane*
½ oz. *lime juice*
1 tsp. *curaçao*

Mix all ingredients with cracked ice in a shaker or blender and pour into a chilled Old Fashioned glass.

Created for **Little Dix Bay in the British Virgin Islands.**

LOCO COCO

1½ oz. *light rum*
½ oz. *crème de cacao*
1 oz. *cream of coconut*
1 oz. *lemon juice*
1 tsp. *coconut rum*
Club soda
Lemon slice
Maraschino cherry

Mix all ingredients, except club soda, lemon slice, and cherry, with cracked ice in a shaker or blender and pour into a chilled Collins glass. Fill with cold club soda, stir gently, and garnish with fruit.

 **LOMA LOMA LULLABY**

1½ oz. light rum
1 oz. passion fruit syrup or
    La Grande Passion
1 oz. lime juice
1 egg white (for two drinks)
1 tsp. 151-proof Demerara rum

Mix all ingredients, except Demerara rum, with cracked ice in a blender and pour into a chilled Whiskey Sour glass. Top with Demerara rum.

LONDON DOCK COOLER

1½ oz. Jamaica or gold rum
3 oz. claret
½ oz. kirsch
½ oz. Falernum or to taste
Orange peel

Mix all ingredients, except orange peel, into a chilled highball glass with several ice cubes and stir well. Twist orange peel over drink and then drop into glass.

BARTENDER'S SECRET NO. 13—Spill Aids

Spills happen under the best of circumstances. Fast action can often prevent permanent damage to a dress or suit. Red wine stains are particularly stubborn. The affected area should be bathed with club soda or cold water immediately, followed by liquid detergent or mild bar soap (Ivory), which is rubbed into stain. The same treatment should be used on coffee stains. Club soda is a handy, inexpensive grease-cutter that some bartenders use to clean wood and stainless-steel surfaces as well as spots from their customers' jackets and ties.

LOUISIANA PLANTER'S PUNCH

1½ oz. gold rum
¾ oz. bourbon
¾ oz. cognac
½ oz. sugar syrup or orgeat
    syrup
1 oz. lemon juice
Several dashes Peychaud's
    bitters
Several dashes Herbsaint or
    Pernod
Lemon slice
Orange slice
Club soda (optional)

Mix all ingredients, except lemon and orange slices and club soda, with cracked ice in a shaker or blender and pour into a chilled highball glass. Garnish with fruit slices. Fill with cold soda if you wish.

MAGENS BAY

1½ oz. light rum
½ oz. apricot brandy
1 oz. orange juice
1 oz. lime juice
½ oz. sugar syrup or to taste
Orange slice
Maraschino cherry

Mix all ingredients, except orange slice and maraschino cherry, with cracked ice in a shaker or blender and strain into a chilled cocktail glass. Garnish with orange slice and maraschino cherry.

MAHUKONA

1½ oz. light rum
½ oz. triple sec
½ oz. lemon juice
Several dashes rock-candy
    syrup or orgeat syrup
Several dashes Angostura
    bitters
Pineapple slice
Mint sprigs (optional)

Mix all ingredients, except pineapple slice and mint sprigs, with cracked ice in a shaker or blender. Pour into a chilled Collins glass and garnish with pineapple slice and mint.

 MAI KAI NO

1 oz. light rum
1 oz. dark Jamaica rum
½ oz. 151-proof Demerara
    rum
1 oz. lime juice
½ oz. orgeat syrup
½ oz. passion fruit juice or
    La Grande Passion
Club soda
Pineapple or orange slice
Mint sprig (optional)

Mix all ingredients, except fruit slice and mint, with cracked ice in a shaker or blender and pour into a tall, chilled Collins glass. Fill with club soda and garnish with fruit slice and mint sprig.

MAI TAI

1 oz. Jamaica rum
1 oz. Martinique rum
½ oz. curaçao
Juice of 1 lime
¼ oz. rock-candy syrup
¼ oz. orgeat syrup
Lime peel
Mint sprig
Pineapple stick

Mix all ingredients, except lime peel, mint, and pineapple, with cracked ice in a shaker or blender and pour into a chilled double Old Fashioned glass. Garnish with lime peel, mint sprig, and pineapple stick.

This is Trader Vic's original recipe.

MALLARD'S REEF

1½ oz. gold Jamaica rum
½ oz. Galliano
2 oz. orange juice
Dash grenadine
Orange slice
Maraschino cherry

Mix all ingredients, except orange slice and cherry, with cracked ice in a shaker or blender and serve in a chilled wine goblet. Garnish with orange slice and cherry.

 MAMBO PUNCH

2 oz. Haitian rum
½ oz. curaçao
2 oz. orange juice
1 oz. pineapple juice
¾ oz. lime juice
½ oz. tamarind syrup,
   Falernum, or sugar syrup,
   or to taste
½ ripe banana, sliced

Mix all ingredients with cracked ice in a blender and pour into a chilled double Old Fashioned glass.

MANDINGO GRINGO

1½ oz. Jamaica dark rum
½ oz. crème de banane
2 oz. pineapple juice
1 oz. orange juice
½ oz. lime juice

Mix all ingredients with cracked ice in a blender at low speed for 15 seconds and pour into a chilled Old Fashioned glass.

MANGO DAIQUIRI

2 oz. light rum
1 oz. curaçao
2 oz. mango juice or nectar
½ oz. lime juice
½ oz. sugar syrup or to taste

Mix with plenty of cracked ice in a blender until frappéed and pour into a chilled wine glass. Serve with straws.

MARACAS BEACH BOLT

2 oz. 151-proof Demerara rum
½ oz. curaçao or triple sec
1 oz. lime juice
Mint leaves (optional)

Mix all ingredients, except mint leaves, with cracked ice in a shaker or blender. Pour into a chilled Old Fashioned glass and garnish with mint.

MARTINIQUE COOLER

1½ oz. rum
½ oz. Mandarine Napoleon
1 oz. lime juice
½ oz. orgeat or sugar syrup to taste
Lime slice

Mix all ingredients, except lime slice, with cracked ice in a blender, pour into a chilled highball glass, and garnish with lime slice.

MARY PICKFORD

1½ oz. light Martinique rum
¼ oz. maraschino liqueur
¼ oz. grenadine
1½ oz. pineapple juice

Mix all ingredients with cracked ice in a shaker or blender and pour into a chilled cocktail glass.

 MAUNA LANI FIZZ

2 oz. gold rum
½ oz. 151-proof rum
3 oz. pineapple, finely chopped
½ oz. lemon juice
½ oz. pineapple juice
½ oz. orgeat syrup or sugar syrup to taste
1 egg white (for two drinks)
Club soda
Lime slice

Mix all ingredients, except club soda and lime slice, with cracked ice in a blender until smooth and pour into a chilled highball glass. Fill with club soda and garnish with lime slice.

MARIE GALANTE

1 oz. light rum
½ oz. triple sec
1 oz. grapefruit juice
½ oz. La Grande Passion

Mix all ingredients with cracked ice in a shaker or blender and strain into a chilled cocktail glass.

 MAYAGUEZ WATERMELON COOLER

2 oz. light Puerto Rican rum
1 oz. melon liqueur
½ oz. lime juice
½ oz. sugar syrup or to taste
1 cup watermelon, seeded and diced
Lime slice

Mix all ingredients, except lime slice, with cracked ice in a blender at low speed for 15 seconds and pour into a chilled double Old Fashioned glass. Garnish with lime slice.

MERENGUE COFFEE

1 oz. light rum
1 tsp. Kahlua
1 tsp. crème de cacao
Scoop coffee ice cream
5 oz. cold black coffee

Mix all ingredients in blender until smooth and pour into a large, chilled coffee mug. Do not overmix.

MESA VERDE

1½ oz. light rum
½ oz. lemon juice
4 oz. pineapple juice
1 tsp. green crème de menthe

Mix all ingredients, except crème de menthe, with cracked ice in a shaker or blender, pour into a chilled highball glass, and top with crème de menthe.

MEXICANO

2 oz. light rum
½ oz. kümmel
1 oz. orange juice
Several dashes Angostura bitters

Mix all ingredients with cracked ice in a shaker or blender and pour into a chilled cocktail glass.

MIKE DEVCICH'S BAHAMA MAMA

1 oz. light rum
1 oz. coconut rum
2 oz. orange juice
2 oz. pineapple juice
½ oz. grapefruit juice
Dash grenadine

Mix with cracked ice in a shaker or blender and strain into a chilled double Old Fashioned glass.

 ## MINT CONDITION

1½ oz. light rum
½ oz. peppermint schnapps
1 oz. guava, mango, or
    papaya juice (nectar)
Several dashes grenadine

Mix all ingredients, except grenadine, with cracked ice in a shaker or blender. Pour into a chilled Delmonico glass and float grenadine on top.

 ## MIXED BLESSING

1½ oz. Puerto Rican rum
½ oz. 151-proof Demerara
    rum
2 tbsp. crushed pineapple
4 oz. pineapple juice
½ oz. Falernum or to taste
Several dashes lime juice

Mix all ingredients with cracked ice in a blender until smooth and pour into a chilled double Old Fashioned glass.

MOBAY COCKTAIL

1½ oz. dark Jamaica rum
½ oz. Dubonnet rouge
Several dashes Grand
    Marnier
Lemon peel

Mix all ingredients, except lemon peel, with cracked ice in a shaker or blender, and strain into a chilled cocktail glass. Twist lemon peel over drink and drop in.

MOJITO

½ lime
1 tsp. sugar
Several mint sprigs
2 oz. light rum
Club soda (optional)

Squeeze lime juice into a chilled double Old Fashioned glass, add sugar and mint, and muddle until sugar is dissolved. Fill glass with crushed ice and pour in rum. Swizzle until glass frosts, adding additional crushed ice and rum as needed. Garnish with mint sprig and serve with straws. You may top off drink with cold club soda if you wish, or some prefer a dash of dark Jamaica rum.

MOLOKINI FIZGIG

1 oz. light rum
½ oz. amaretto
½ oz. white crème de cacao
1 oz. pineapple juice
1 oz. orange
2 oz. cream or half-and-half
1 whole egg (for two drinks)
Pineapple stick

Mix all ingredients with cracked ice in a blender and serve in a large chilled balloon glass. Decorate with a long pineapple stick.

MORNE FORTUNE

1½ oz. light rum
½ oz. brandy
2 oz. orange juice
½ oz. lemon juice
1 tsp. orgeat syrup
Dash orange flower water or orange bitters

Mix all ingredients, except orange flower water, with cracked ice in a shaker or blender, strain into a chilled cocktail glass, and top with orange flower water or bitters.

MORNING DIP

1½ oz. gold Puerto Rican rum
1 tsp. maraschino liqueur
1 oz. orange juice
1 tsp. Falernum or sugar syrup to taste

Mix with cracked ice in a shaker or blender and strain into a chilled cocktail glass.

MORNING JOY

1½ oz. gold rum
Grapefruit juice
1 tsp. sloe gin

Pour rum into chilled highball glass with several ice cubes, fill with grapefruit juice, and stir well. Top with sloe gin.

THE MORRO CASTLE COOLER El Castillo Morro Frio

1 oz. light Puerto Rican rum
¾ oz. triple sec
3 oz. orange juice
3 oz. Brut champagne

Mix all ingredients, except champagne, with cracked ice in a shaker or blender and pour into a chilled Collins glass. Add cold champagne and stir gently.

Created by the author for Rums of Puerto Rico, New York.

MYRTLE BANK PUNCH

1½ oz. 151-proof Demerara rum
Juice of ½ lime
1 tsp. grenadine
1 tsp. sugar syrup or to taste
½ oz. maraschino liqueur

Mix all ingredients, except maraschino liqueur, with cracked ice in a shaker or blender and pour into a chilled highball glass. Top off with a maraschino float.

NANCY FRIEDMAN'S BLUE MEANIE

3 oz. light Bermudez rum
1 oz. Parfait Amour
1 oz. lemon juice
Dash triple sec
Maraschino cherry

Mix all ingredients, except triple sec and cherry, with cracked ice in a shaker or blender and serve in a chilled cocktail glass. Garnish with cherry and top off with a dash of triple sec.

NAVY GROG

1 oz. light or gold Puerto Rican rum
1 oz. dark Jamaica rum
1 oz. 86-proof Demerara rum
½ oz. orange juice
½ oz. guava juice
½ oz. lime juice
½ oz. pineapple juice
½ oz. orgeat syrup or to taste
Lime slice
Mint sprig (optional)

Mix all ingredients, except lime slice and mint sprig, with cracked ice in a shaker or blender and pour into a chilled double Old Fashioned glass. Garnish with lime slice and mint sprig.

NEW ORLEANS BUCK

1½ oz. light Haitian rum
1 oz. orange juice
½ oz. lime juice
Several dashes Peychaud's
   bitters (optional)
Ginger ale
Lime slice

Mix all ingredients, except ginger ale and lime slice, with cracked ice in a shaker or blender, pour into a chilled Collins glass, and fill with cold ginger ale. Garnish with lime slice.

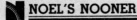 NOEL'S NOONER

1 oz. dark Jamaica rum
1 oz. gin
1 oz. dry red wine
1 oz. orange juice
Lime slice

Mix all ingredients, except lime slice, with cracked ice in a shaker or blender, pour into a chilled Old Fashioned glass, and garnish with lime slice.

OCHO RIOS

1½ oz. dark Jamaica rum
1 oz. guava nectar
½ oz. heavy cream
½ oz. lime juice
1 tsp. Falernum or sugar
   syrup to taste

Mix all ingredients with cracked ice in a blender and pour into a chilled cocktail glass.

ORCABESSA FIZZ

1 oz. Jamaica rum
1 oz. coconut rum or coconut
   liqueur
2 oz. pineapple juice
½ oz. lime juice
Club soda
Pineapple slice

Mix all ingredients, except club soda and pineapple slice, with cracked ice in a shaker or blender. Pour into a chilled highball glass, fill with cold club soda, and garnish with pineapple slice.

OUTRIGGER No. 1

1½ oz. gold rum
¾ oz. Benedictine
½ oz. lime or lemon juice
½ tsp. sugar or to taste

Mix all ingredients with cracked ice in a shaker or blender and strain into a chilled cocktail glass.

Created by the author for Benedictine Whitbread Enterprises, Inc.

OUTRIGGER No. 2

1 oz. gold rum
1 oz. brandy
1 oz. triple sec
½ oz. lime juice

Mix all ingredients with cracked ice in a shaker or blender and strain into a chilled cocktail glass.

PAGO PAGO

2 oz. gold Barbados rum
½ tsp. white crème de cacao
½ tsp. green Chartreuse
½ oz. pineapple juice
½ oz. lime juice

Mix all ingredients with cracked ice in a shaker or blender and pour into a chilled Old Fashioned glass.

PALM BAY SPECIAL

1½ oz. light rum
½ oz. lemon juice
1 tsp. honey or to taste
Champagne
Pineapple slice

Mix all ingredients, except pineapple slice and champagne, in a shaker or blender. Strain into chilled goblet and fill with cold champagne. Garnish with pineapple slice.

PALM ISLAND

1½ oz. gold rum
1½ oz. Grand Marnier

Pour rum and Grand Marnier into a chilled Old Fashioned glass with several ice cubes and stir well.

PANCHO VILLA No. 2

1 oz. light rum
1 oz. gin
1 oz. apricot liqueur or
apricot brandy
1 tsp. cherry brandy
1 tsp. pineapple juice

Mix all ingredients with cracked ice in a shaker or blender and strain into a chilled cocktail glass.

PARISIAN BLONDE

1 oz. dark Jamaica rum
1 oz. triple sec
1 oz. heavy cream

Mix with cracked ice in a shaker
or blender and strain into a
chilled cocktail glass.

A PASSIONATE DAIQUIRI

1½ oz. light rum
½ oz. lime juice
½ oz. sugar syrup or to taste
½ oz. passion fruit juice

Mix all ingredients with cracked
ice in a shaker or blender and
strain into a chilled cocktail
glass.

PEACH DAIQUIRI

2 oz. light rum
½ oz. lime juice
1 tsp. sugar syrup or to taste
½ ripe peach, fresh, canned,
   or frozen, diced

Mix all ingredients with cracked
ice in a blender until smooth
and pour into a chilled wine
glass.

PEARL DIVER

1 oz. Malibu
¾ oz. Midori
3 oz. pineapple juice
1 oz. sweet-and-sour mix
Cherry
Pineapple slice

Mix all ingredients, except
cherry and pineapple, with
plenty of ice in a blender for 15
seconds until mushy. Pour into a
large red-wine glass and garnish with a cherry and a pineapple slice.

This is a special signature drink
of the **Turnberry Isle Resort &
Club, Aventura, Florida.**

PELICAN BAY

1 oz. gold Puerto Rican rum
¾ oz. crème de banane
¼ oz. Pernod

Mix all ingredients with cracked
ice in a shaker or blender and
strain into a chilled cocktail
glass.

▨ PENSACOLA

1½ oz. light Barbados rum
½ oz. guava nectar
½ oz. orange juice
½ oz. lemon juice
1 tsp. La Grande Passion
  (optional)

Mix all ingredients with cracked
ice in a blender until smooth
and pour into a chilled deep-
saucer champagne glass.

▨ PENSACOLA COLA

1½ oz. gold rum
½ oz. Cherry Marnier
Cola
Lemon peel

Mix rum, Cherry Marnier, and
cold cola in a tall, chilled Collins glass with ice cubes. Stir
gently and twist lemon peel over
drink and drop into glass.

▨ PEPPER TREE PUNCH

2 oz. light Jamaica rum
1 oz. dark Jamaica rum
1 oz. lime juice
1 tsp. sugar syrup or orgeat
  syrup
Several dashes Angostura
  bitters
Pinch of ground cinnamon
Pinch of cayenne pepper

Mix all ingredients in blender
with cracked ice and serve in
chilled double Old Fashioned
glass.

PILOT BOAT

1½ oz. dark Jamaica rum
1 oz. crème de banane
2 oz. lemon or lime juice

Mix all ingredients with cracked
ice and strain into a chilled cocktail glass.

▨ PIÑA COLADA

2 oz. gold rum
2 oz. cream of coconut
4 oz. pineapple juice
Pineapple stick
Maraschino cherry

Mix all ingredients, except pineapple stick and maraschino
cherry, with cracked ice in a
shaker or blender and pour into
a chilled Collins glass. Garnish
with fruit.

PINEAPPLE BANG!

2 oz. *light Hawaiian rum*
1 oz. *crème d'anana or*
    pineapple schnapps
½ oz. *lime juice*
½ cup *pineapple sherbet*
1 heaping tbsp. *diced fresh*
    or canned pineapple
Pineapple stick

Mix all ingredients, except pineapple stick, with cracked ice in a blender until smooth and pour into a chilled chimney glass or a double Old Fashioned glass. Garnish with pineapple stick.

 **PINEAPPLE BLUSH**

2 oz. *light rum*
½ oz. *crème de noyaux*
3 oz. *crushed pineapple*
Maraschino cherry

Mix all ingredients, except cherry, with plenty of cracked ice in a blender until frappéed and pour into a chilled double Old Fashioned glass. Garnish with cherry.

PINEAPPLE DAIQUIRI

2 oz. *light rum*
½ oz. *Cointreau*
3 oz. *pineapple juice*
¼ oz. *lime juice*

Mix all ingredients with plenty of cracked ice in a blender until frappéed and pour into a chilled wine glass.

PINK MERMAID

1½ oz. *light rum*
½ oz. *lime juice*
1 tsp. *heavy cream*
1 tsp. *grenadine*
1 egg white *(for two drinks)*

Mix with cracked ice in a shaker or blender and strain into a chilled cocktail glass.

PINK RUM AND TONIC

2 oz. *light rum*
½ oz. *lime juice*
1 tsp. *grenadine*
Tonic water
Lime slice

Mix all ingredients, except tonic water and lime slice, with cracked ice in a shaker or blender and pour into a chilled Collins glass. Fill with cold tonic water and garnish with lime slice.

PINK VERANDA

1 oz. gold Puerto Rican rum
½ oz. dark Jamaica rum
1½ oz. cranberry juice
½ oz. lime juice
1 tsp. sugar
1 egg white (for two drinks)

Mix all ingredients with cracked ice in a shaker or blender and pour into a chilled Old Fashioned glass.

PINO FRIO

1½ oz. light rum
2 oz. pineapple juice
½ oz. lemon juice
2 pineapple slices, cubed
Dash Falernum
Mint sprigs (optional)

Mix all ingredients, except mint sprigs, with cracked ice in a blender at high speed for a few seconds, pour into a chilled Collins glass, and garnish with mint sprigs.

PIRATE'S JULEP

6 mint leaves
1 tsp. orgeat syrup or sugar syrup
Several dashes Peychaud's bitters or Pernod
2–3 oz. gold Jamaica rum
1 tsp. Mandarine Napoleon or curaçao
Mint sprig
Powdered sugar

Muddle mint leaves in a chilled double Old Fashioned glass with syrup. Add bitters and fill glass with crushed ice and pour in rum. Swizzle until glass frosts, adding more ice if necessary. Top with liqueur and garnish with a mint sprig dusted with powdered sugar.

PISCADERA BAY

1½ oz. Jamaica rum
½ oz. curaçao
½ oz. Falernum or sugar syrup
½ oz. lime juice
1 tsp. cherry brandy
Dash Angostura bitters
Maraschino cherry
Orange slice

Mix all ingredients, except maraschino cherry and orange slice, with cracked ice in a shaker or blender. Pour into a chilled double Old Fashioned glass and garnish with fruit.

PLANTER'S PUNCH The Original

1½–2 oz. Myers's dark rum
3 oz. orange juice
Juice of ½ lemon or lime
1 tsp. superfine sugar
Dash grenadine
Orange slice
Maraschino cherry

Mix all ingredients, except orange slice and cherry, with cracked ice in a shaker or blender and pour into a tall, chilled Collins glass. Garnish with orange slice and cherry.

The Myers's Rum people lay claim to the origination and popularization of the Planter's Punch, and this is the original recipe that appears on the back label of Myers's Rum.

PLANTER'S PUNCH No. 2

2 oz. Puerto Rican rum
1 oz. dark Jamaica rum
½ oz. sugar syrup or
   Falernum to taste
1 oz. lime juice
Several dashes Angostura
   bitters
Club soda
Orange slice
Lemon slice

Mix all ingredients, except club soda, orange, and lemon slices, with cracked ice in a shaker or blender. Pour into a chilled Collins glass, fill with cold club soda, and garnish with orange and lime slices.

PLANTATION PUNCH

1½ oz. dark Jamaica rum
¾ oz. Southern Comfort
1 tsp. brown sugar or to taste
1 oz. lemon juice
Club soda
Orange slice
Lemon slice
1 tsp. port

Mix all ingredients, except soda, fruit slices, and port, with cracked ice in a shaker or blender and pour into a tall Collins glass. Fill with cold club soda, garnish with fruit, and top with port.

PLAYBOY COOLER

1½ oz. gold rum
1½ oz. Kahlua
3 oz. pineapple juice
½ oz. lemon juice or lime juice
Cola
Maraschino cherry

Mix all ingredients, except cola and maraschino cherry, with cracked ice in a shaker or blender and pour into chilled highball glass. Fill with cola and garnish with cherry.

POISTERIZER

2½ oz. Barbados rum
1 oz. orange juice
1 oz. pineapple juice
1 oz. coconut cream
Lemon-lime soda
½ oz. 151-proof Demerara rum

Mix all ingredients, except soda and Demerara rum, with ice in a shaker or blender and pour into a tall, chilled Collins glass. Fill with lemon-lime soda and top with Demerara rum.

POKER COCKTAIL

1½ oz. light rum
¾ oz. sweet vermouth
Orange peel

Mix rum and vermouth with cracked ice in a shaker or blender and strain into a chilled cocktail glass. Twist orange peel over drink and drop into glass.

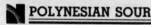 **POLYNESIAN SOUR**

1½ oz. light rum
½ oz. La Grande Passion
1 oz. orange juice
½ oz. lemon juice
1 oz. pineapple juice
½ tsp. rock-candy syrup or
    sugar syrup or to taste
Pineapple slice

Mix all ingredients, except pineapple, with cracked ice in a shaker or blender, strain into a chilled Whiskey Sour glass, and garnish with pineapple slice.

POMME DE ANTILLAIS Antilles Apple

1½ oz. gold Martinique rum
½ oz. calvados
½ oz. sweet vermouth
Lemon peel

Mix all ingredients, except lemon peel, with cracked ice in a shaker or blender and pour into a chilled cocktail glass. Twist lemon peel over drink and drop into glass.

 **POOLABANGA SLING**

1½ oz. gold rum
2 oz. orange juice
½ oz. lime juice
½ oz. Falernum
1 tsp. cherry brandy
Club soda
Mint sprigs (optional)

Mix all ingredients, except mint, with cracked ice in a shaker or blender and pour into a chilled highball glass and fill with cold club soda. Garnish with mint.

Created for **Poolabanga Island,** a tropical jewel.

PORT ANTONIO

1 oz. gold rum
½ oz. dark Jamaica rum
½ oz. Tia Maria
½ oz. lime juice
1 tsp. Falernum
Lime slice

Mix all ingredients, except lime slice, with cracked ice in a shaker or blender, pour into a chilled Old Fashioned glass, and garnish with lime slice.

POTTED PARROT

1½ oz. gold rum
½ oz. orange curaçao
3 oz. orange juice
1 oz. lemon juice
1 tsp. orgeat syrup
1 tsp. rock-candy syrup
Mint sprigs (optional)
1 tsp. 151-proof Demerara
  rum

Mix all ingredients, except mint sprigs and 151-proof rum, with cracked ice in a shaker or blender, strain into a chilled double Old Fashioned glass, and garnish with mint. Float Demerara rum on top.

PRESIDENTE COCKTAIL No. 1

1½ oz. light rum
½ oz. dry vermouth
½ oz. curaçao
Dash grenadine
Lemon peel

Mix all ingredients, except lemon peel, with cracked ice in a shaker or blender and pour into a chilled cocktail glass. Twist peel over drink and drop into glass.

PRESIDENTE COCKTAIL No. 2

1½ oz. light rum
1 oz. orange juice
Several dashes grenadine

Mix all ingredients with cracked ice in a shaker or blender and pour into a chilled cocktail glass.

 PUNTA DEL ESTE

1½ oz. light rum
½ oz. white crème de cacao
½ oz. light coconut rum
  (CocoRibe or Malibu)
2 oz. pineapple juice
1 oz. cranberry juice
1 oz. cream

Mix all ingredients with cracked ice in a blender and pour into a chilled Collins glass. Add additional ice if needed.

PUSHKIN'S PUNCH

2 oz. dark Jamaica rum
1 oz. triple sec
Juice of 1 lemon
Juice of 1 lime
2 oz. orange juice
Orgeat syrup to taste
Dash Angostura bitters

Mix with cracked ice in a shaker or blender and serve in a tall, chilled Collins glass.

PUSSER'S PAIN KILLER

4 oz. British Navy Pusser's Rum
4 oz. pineapple juice
1 oz. orange juice
1 oz. coconut cream or syrup
Orange slice

Mix all ingredients, except orange slice, with cracked ice in a shaker or blender and pour into a chilled Collins glass. Garnish with Union Jack flag.

QUARTER DECK

1½ oz. dark Jamaica rum
¾ oz. cream sherry
1 tsp. lime juice

Mix all ingredients with cracked ice in a shaker or blender and strain into a chilled cocktail glass.

RAMPART STREET PARADE

1 oz. light rum
¾ oz. crème de banane
½ oz. Southern Comfort
1 oz. lime juice

Mix all ingredients with cracked ice in a shaker or blender and strain into a chilled cocktail glass.

RANGIRORA MADNESS

2 oz. dark Jamaica rum
2 oz. pineapple juice
2 oz. orange juice
Bitter lemon soda
1 tsp. 151-proof Demerara rum
Maraschino cherry
Pineapple slice

Mix all ingredients, except lemon soda, 151-proof rum, pineapple, and maraschino cherry, with cracked ice in a shaker or blender and pour into a large, chilled highball glass. Fill with bitter lemon soda, top with float of 151-proof rum, and garnish with pineapple and cherry.

This incurable tropical malady can be alleviated only by large amounts of Demerara rum.

ROADTOWN SPECIAL

2 oz. *light Virgin Islands rum*
½ *lime*
Ginger beer

Pour rum into a chilled highball glass with several ice cubes. Squeeze lime over drink and drop into glass. Fill with cold ginger beer and stir gently.

ROSE HALL

1 oz. *dark Jamaica rum*
½ oz. *crème de banane*
1 oz. *orange juice*
1 tsp. *lime juice*
Lime slice

Mix all ingredients, except lime slice, with cracked ice in a shaker or blender, pour into a chilled cocktail glass, and garnish with lime slice.

RUM AND BITTER LEMON

1½ oz. *light, gold, or dark rum*
Bitter lemon soda
Lemon slice

Pour rum and bitter lemon soda into a chilled highball glass with several ice cubes and stir gently. Garnish with lemon slice.

RUM BEGUINE

1½ oz. *Martinique rum or Haitian rum*
2 oz. *sauterne, chilled*
2 oz. *pineapple juice*
1 oz. *lemon juice*
½ oz. *sugar syrup or Falernum to taste*
Several dashes *Peychaud's bitters or Angostura bitters*
Pineapple slice

Mix all ingredients, except pineapple slice, with cracked ice in a shaker or blender and pour into a chilled Collins glass. Garnish with pineapple.

RUM BLOODY MARY

1½ oz. light Puerto Rican
   rum
4 oz. tomato juice
½ oz. lime juice or lemon
   juice
Several dashes
   Worcestershire sauce
Several dashes Tabasco
   sauce
Pinch of freshly ground
   pepper
Pinch of celery salt

Stir all ingredients well with
cracked ice in a mixing glass
and pour into a chilled highball
glass.

RUM BUCK

1½ oz. light rum
½ oz. lime juice
Ginger ale, chilled
Lime slice
Toasted almonds, grated
   (optional)

Mix rum and lime juice with
cracked ice in a shaker, pour
into a chilled Collins glass, and
fill with cold ginger ale. Stir
gently and garnish with lime
slice and sprinkle top with
grated almonds.

RUM COLLINS

2 oz. light or gold rum
1 tsp. sugar syrup
½ lime
Club soda

Combine rum and sugar syrup
in chilled Collins glass and stir.
Squeeze in juice of lime, drop in
peel, fill with club soda, add several ice cubes, and stir gently.

RUM DUBONNET

1 oz. light rum
1 oz. Dubonnet rouge
1 tsp. lime juice
Lime peel

Mix all ingredients, except lime
peel, with cracked ice in a
shaker or blender and strain into
a chilled cocktail glass. Twist
lime peel over drink and drop
into glass.

RUM OLD FASHIONED

1 tsp. sugar syrup
Splash water
Several dashes Angostura
    bitters
2-3 oz. gold Barbados,
    Haitian, or Martinique
    rum, or gold or dark
    Jamaica rum
Lemon peel
Orange peel

Stir syrup and water in a chilled Old Fashioned glass, add bitters and rum. Mix well and add ice. Garnish with lemon and orange peel. Add additional water if you wish.

RUM MARTINI

2 oz. light Puerto Rican rum
Dash dry vermouth or to
    taste
Olive stuffed with almond or
    lemon peel

Combine rum and dry vermouth in mixing glass with several ice cubes, stir well, and strain into a chilled cocktail glass. Garnish with stuffed olive or twist lemon peel over drink and drop into glass.

RUM ROYALE

1½ oz. Bacardi Premium
    Black Rum
1½ oz. cold black coffee
½ cup vanilla ice cream
Cinnamon stick
Pinch ground cinnamon

Mix rum, coffee, and ice cream in a chilled wine goblet until slightly slushy. Garnish with cinnamon stick and sprinkle with ground cinnamon.

Created by the author for Bacardi Imports, Inc., Miami.

RUM ROSE

1 oz. dark Jamaica rum
1 oz. light Jamaica rum
1 oz. Rhum Negrita
2 oz. orange juice
Falernum or simple syrup to
    taste
Dash grenadine
Lemon-lime soda

Mix all ingredients, except soda, with cracked ice in a shaker or blender and pour into a chilled double Old Fashioned glass. Fill with lemon-lime soda and stir gently.

 **RUM RUNNER**

1½ oz. gold rum
½ oz. blackberry-flavored
   brandy
½ oz. crème de banane
4 oz. orange juice
Dash Falernum or grenadine

Mix all ingredients with cracked
ice in a shaker or blender and
serve in a chilled Squall glass
or a wine goblet.

RUM SCREWDRIVER

2 oz. light Puerto Rican rum
4–6 oz. orange juice
Orange slice

Mix rum and orange juice in a
blender with cracked ice and
pour into a chilled Collins glass.
Garnish with orange slice.

RUM AND SHERRY

1½ oz. light rum
¾ oz. amontillado sherry
Maraschino cherry

Combine rum and sherry in a
mixing glass with several ice
cubes and stir well. Strain into a
chilled cocktail glass and garnish with maraschino cherry.

 RUM SOUR

2 oz. light or dark rum
Juice of ½ lime
1 tsp. sugar syrup or to taste
1 tsp. orange juice (optional)
Orange slice
Maraschino cherry

Mix all ingredients, except orange slice and cherry, with
cracked ice in a shaker or
blender and strain into a chilled
Whiskey Sour glass. Garnish
with orange slice and cherry.

 RUMBO

2 oz. gold Haitian or
   Barbados rum
1 oz. dark Jamaica rum
2 oz. orange juice
2 oz. guava juice
Dash lime juice

Mix with cracked ice in a shaker
or blender and pour into a
chilled double Old Fashioned
glass.

SAN JUAN No. 1

1½ oz. light rum
¾ oz. brandy
1 tsp. grenadine
½ oz. lime juice

Mix all ingredients with cracked ice in a shaker or blender and strain into a chilled cocktail glass.

SAN JUAN No. 2

1½ oz. light or gold Puerto
    Rican rum
1 oz. grapefruit juice
1 oz. lime juice
½ oz. cream of coconut or to
    taste
1 tsp. 151-proof Demerara
    rum

Mix all ingredients, except 151-proof rum, with cracked ice in a blender until smooth. Pour into a chilled wine goblet and top with a float of 151-proof rum.

● SAN JUAN SUNDOWNER

1½ oz. Bacardi Premium
    Black Rum
2 oz. orange juice
2 oz. pineapple juice
Bitter lemon or lemon-lime
    soda
Orange slice

Mix rum, orange juice, and pineapple juice with cracked ice in a shaker or blender and pour into a tall, chilled Collins glass. Add several ice cubes and fill with bitter lemon soda. Stir gently and garnish with orange slice.

Created by the author for Bacardi Imports, Inc., Miami.

BARTENDER'S SECRET NO. 14—Flavor Catalysts

The flavor enhancement of rum-based fruit drinks, as well as those made with other spirits such as gin and vodka, can be effectively accomplished by the use of fruit-flavored liqueurs. Triple sec, curaçao, peach liqueur, maraschino, apricot liqueur, crème de noyaux, anisette, sloe gin, crème de menthe, crème de cacao, kümmel, amaretto, and crème de cassis are all well-known and readily available. In addition to these generic flavors, there are many distinguished proprietary liqueurs, which when used with good judgment contribute new and unusual flavor dimensions to various mixed drinks.

Here are some especially good flavor catalysts: Benedictine, Chartreuse (green for intense flavor, yellow for fragrance), Grand

Marnier, Cherry Heering, Cointreau, Galliano, Kahlua, Tia Maria, Drambuie, Frangelico, Chambord, and Irish Mist. There are many others, of course. Accomplished mixologists use these complex and comparatively expensive formulations as elegant sweeteners (most liqueurs have a high sugar level), as aromatic floats on top of drinks, as a foil or flavor accent to balance or modify another dominant taste, or to create a more interesting flavor in a conventional, "cliché" drink recipe.

The new, flavor-intensive schnapps products such as peach, pear, apple, and other fruit, spice, candy, and soft drink flavors are excellent for giving old drink recipes a new zest.

SANTA MARTA SLING

2 oz. *light Colombian or Puerto Rican rum*
½ oz. *lime juice*
1 tsp. *coconut syrup*
Club soda
1 tsp. *amaretto*

Mix all ingredients, except club soda and amaretto, with cracked ice in a shaker or blender and pour into a chilled Old Fashioned glass. Fill with club soda, stir gently, and top with amaretto float.

SAVANE

1½ oz. *light rum*
½ oz. *banana liqueur*
1 oz. *lemon juice*
1 tsp. *Falernum*

Mix all ingredients with cracked ice in a shaker or blender and strain into a chilled cocktail glass.

SEA HAWK

1 oz. *dark Jamaica rum*
½ oz. *Barbados rum*
½ oz. *Bermuda Gold liqueur*
Dash Cointreau
Dash grenadine
Juice of 1 lime
Juice of ½ orange

Mix with cracked ice in a shaker or blender and strain into a silver mug filled with shaved ice.

Originated by Bru Mysak of New York's "21" Club.

SEPTEMBER MORN

2–3 oz. *light rum*
½ oz. *lime juice*
1 tsp. *grenadine*
1 *egg white*

Mix all ingredients with cracked ice in a shaker or blender and strain into a chilled cocktail glass.

SEVILLA No. 1

1 oz. dark Jamaica rum
1 oz. sweet vermouth
Orange peel

Mix rum and vermouth with cracked ice in a shaker or blender and strain into a chilled cocktail glass. Twist orange peel over drink and drop into glass.

SEVILLA No. 2

1½ oz. light rum
1½ oz. port
1 egg
½ tsp. sugar syrup or to taste
Freshly grated nutmeg

Mix rum, port, egg, and sugar syrup with cracked ice in a blender and pour into a chilled cocktail glass. Sprinkle with grated nutmeg.

SCORPION

2 oz. light Puerto Rican rum
1 oz. brandy
2 oz. orange juice
1½ oz. lemon juice
½ oz. orgeat syrup
Gardenia

Mix all ingredients, except flower, with shaved ice in a blender and pour into a chilled wine goblet. Garnish with a gardenia.

This is an original Trader Vic's recipe.

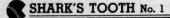 SHARK'S TOOTH No. 1

1 oz. 151-proof Puerto Rican rum
Juice of ½ lime (save shell)
½ oz. lemon juice
Dash grenadine
Dash rock-candy syrup
Club soda

Mix all ingredients, except club soda, in a shaker or blender with ice and pour into a large pilsener glass. Fill with cold club soda and add lime shell for garnish. Stir gently.

This is an original Trader Vic's recipe.

SHARK'S TOOTH No. 2

1 oz. dark Jamaica rum
1 oz. Haitian, Martinique, or Barbados gold rum
¼ oz. sloe gin
1 oz. lemon juice
Several dashes passion fruit syrup or nectar
Club soda

Mix all ingredients, except club soda, with cracked ice in a shaker or blender and pour into a chilled double Old Fashioned glass. Fill glass with cold club soda and stir gently.

SHANGHAI

1½ oz. dark Jamaica rum
½ oz. anisette
1 oz. lemon juice
Several dashes grenadine

Mix all ingredients with cracked ice in a shaker or blender and pour into a chilled cocktail glass.

SHANGO

2 oz. Haitian rum
1 tsp. 151-proof Demerara rum
2 oz. pineapple juice
½ oz. lemon juice
½ oz. Falernum or sugar syrup
Bitter lemon soda
Lemon slice

Mix all ingredients, except soda and lemon slice, with cracked ice in a shaker or blender and pour into a chilled Collins glass. Fill with bitter lemon soda, stir gently, and garnish with fruit slice.

BARTENDER'S SECRET NO. 15—Tropical Toppings

Toppings for exotic, tall coolers and party drinks have been the hallmarks of this kind of refreshment since the practice was begun by establishments such as Trader Vic's and Don the Beachcomber when they wanted to popularize their so-called Polynesian-type rum drinks in the 1930s. The fact that nobody in Polynesia had ever seen one of these elegant, show-case libations is unimportant. The ingredients (fruits, spices, and flavorings from faraway places combined with rare rums), the toppings (aromatic liqueurs), and the decorations (hibiscus, orchids, and gardenias) proclaimed to adoring patrons: "This is what is drunk in a tropical paradise." Toppings will add luster and enjoyment to almost any drink, tropical or not. Sometimes a dash, splash, or a teaspoon of spirits such as brandy or a high-proof rum is used as a float on top of a drink, but more often the choice is a liqueur.

SKULL CRACKER

4 oz. light rum
1 oz. white crème de cacao
1 oz. pineapple juice
1 oz. lemon juice
Lime slice

Mix with cracked ice in a shaker or blender and serve in a chilled wine goblet. Makes a pirate-sized portion for one, or it may be shared with a piratess.

SLEDGEHAMMER

¾ oz. gold rum
¾ oz. brandy
¾ oz. calvados or applejack
Dash Pernod

Mix all ingredients with cracked ice in a shaker or blender and strain into a chilled cocktail glass.

SLOPPY JOE'S No. 1

1 oz. light rum
1 oz. dry vermouth
½ tsp. triple sec
½ tsp. grenadine
Juice of 1 lime

Mix with cracked ice in a shaker or blender and strain into a chilled cocktail glass.

SPEIGHTSTOWN SWIZZLE

1½ oz. Barbados rum
1 oz. calvados or applejack
1 tsp. lime juice
1 tsp. orgeat syrup or
   Falernum
Several dashes Angostura
   bitters

Mix all ingredients with cracked ice in a shaker or blender and pour into a chilled Old Fashioned glass.

● SPICE ISLAND

2 oz. gold rum
½ oz. CocoRibe
½ oz. Captain Morgan
   Spiced Rum
3 oz. orange juice
2 oz. red grape juice
2 oz. cranberry juice

Mix with cracked ice in a shaker or blender and pour into a chilled 16-oz. Zombie glass.

STRAWBERRY COLADA

2–3 oz. gold Puerto Rican or
   Virgin Islands rum
4 oz. Piña Colada mix
1 oz. fresh or frozen
   strawberries
1 tsp. strawberry schnapps or
   liqueur

Mix all ingredients, except strawberry schnapps and whole strawberry, with cracked ice in a blender until smooth, pour into a chilled Pilsener glass, and top with strawberry schnapps or liqueur and a whole strawberry.

STRAWBERRY DAIQUIRI

1½ oz. light rum
½ oz. lime juice
1 tsp. sugar syrup or to taste
6 large fresh or frozen
  strawberries

Mix with cracked ice in a
blender until smooth and pour
into a chilled cocktail glass.

ST. VINCENT SURPRISE

1½ oz. gold rum
½ oz. triple sec
1 tsp. Pernod
1 oz. lime juice
½ ripe banana, sliced

Mix all ingredients with cracked
ice in a blender and pour into a
chilled wine goblet.

 SUFFERIN' SWEDE

2½ oz. Haitian or Barbados
  gold rum
1 heaping tbsp. lingonberries
4 oz. orange juice
2 oz. grapefruit juice
½ oz. Falernum or to taste

Mix with cracked ice in a
blender until lingonberries are
well whipped into other ingredients. Pour into a chilled double
Old Fashioned glass. Add more
ice if necessary.

SUGAR MILL TOT

1½ oz. gold rum
Juice of 1 lime
Light molasses to taste

Mix all ingredients with cracked
ice in a shaker or blender and
serve in an Old Fashioned glass.

SUNDOWNER No. 2

2 oz. light rum
½ oz. lime juice
Tonic water
Dash triple sec
Dash grenadine

Mix all ingredients, except tonic
water, with cracked ice in a
shaker or blender and pour into
a chilled highball glass. Fill
with cold tonic water and stir
gently.

SURINAM SUNDOWNER

1½ oz. 86-proof Demerara
   rum or dark Jamaica rum
½ oz. sweet vermouth
½ oz. gin
Several dashes Angostura
   bitters

Combine all ingredients in a
mixing glass with several ice
cubes, stir well, and strain into a
chilled cocktail glass.

 SUTTON PLACE SLING

2 oz. dark Jamaica rum
2 oz. orange juice
Several dashes Angostura
   bitters
Several dashes lime juice
Several dashes maraschino
   cherry juice
Bitter lemon soda
1 tsp. 151-proof rum

Mix all ingredients, except
lemon soda and 151-proof rum,
with cracked ice in a shaker or
blender and pour into a chilled
Collins glass. Fill with bitter
lemon soda, stir gently, and top
with float of 151-proof rum.

SWEET N' SILKY

1 oz. light rum
1 oz. triple sec
1 oz. heavy cream

Mix all ingredients with cracked
ice in a shaker or blender and
strain into a chilled cocktail
glass.

TAHITI CLUB

2 oz. light or gold rum
½ oz. pineapple juice
½ oz. lime juice
½ oz. lemon juice
½ tsp. maraschino liqueur
Orange slice

Mix all ingredients, except orange slice, with cracked ice in a
shaker or blender and pour into
a chilled Old Fashioned glass.
Garnish with orange slice.

⬤ TE HONGI

3 oz. Jamaica, Barbados, or
   Haitian gold rum
3 oz. orange juice
3 oz. pineapple juice
2 oz. apricot nectar
1 oz. lemon juice
Falernum or simple syrup to
   taste
Dash grenadine
Ginger ale
Orange slice
Maraschino cherry

Mix all ingredients, except ginger ale, orange slice, and maraschino cherry, with cracked ice in a shaker or blender and pour into a 16-oz. Hurricane or chimney glass. Add more ice if necessary and fill with cold ginger ale. Stir and garnish with orange and cherry.

⬤ TIGER'S MILK No. 1

1½ oz. Bacardi Anejo Gold
   Rum
1½ oz. cognac
4–6 oz. half-and-half
Sugar syrup to taste
Grated nutmeg or cinnamon

Mix all ingredients, except ground spice, with cracked ice in a shaker or blender and pour into a chilled wine goblet. Dust with grated nutmeg or cinnamon.

TOBAGO CAYS

1½ oz. gold rum
½ oz. lime juice
½ oz. sugar syrup
½ tsp. maraschino liqueur
½ tsp. Pernod

Mix all ingredients, except Pernod, with cracked ice in a blender until smooth. Pour into a chilled wine goblet and top with Pernod.

⬤ TOM TOM A Real Head Pounder

1 oz. Haitian rum
1 oz. coconut rum
1 oz. brandy
½ oz. La Grande Passion
1 oz. lemon juice
1 oz. pineapple juice
1 oz. orange juice
Orange slice
Mint sprig

Mix all ingredients, except mint sprig and orange slice, with cracked ice in a blender and strain into a chilled Hurricane glass. Garnish with mint sprig and orange slice.

TORRIDO

2 oz. Haitian or Martinique
   rum
½ tsp. Benedictine
½ oz. lime juice
1 tsp. grenadine
Dash Pernod

Mix all ingredients, except Pernod, with cracked ice in a shaker or blender and pour into a chilled cocktail glass. Top with Pernod float.

TORRIDORA COCKTAIL

1½ oz. light rum
½ oz. Tia Maria
¼ oz. heavy cream
1 tsp. 151-proof Demerara
   rum

Mix all ingredients, except 151-proof rum, with cracked ice in a shaker or blender and strain into a chilled cocktail glass. Top with float of 151-proof rum.

TORTOLA MILK PUNCH

2–3 oz. British Navy Pusser's
   Rum
1 tsp. coconut cream or
   orgeat syrup or Falernum
   to taste
6 oz. milk
Pinch powdered cinnamon
Pinch powdered nutmeg

Mix rum, sweetener, and milk with cracked ice in a blender or shaker and pour into a chilled Collins glass. Sprinkle with spices.

TRADE WINDS

2 oz. gold Barbados rum
½ oz. slivovitz
½ oz. lime juice
½ oz. Falernum or orgeat
   syrup

Mix with plenty of cracked ice and frappé in a blender. Serve in a chilled cocktail glass.

TROPICAL BIRD

1 oz. gold rum
½ oz. dark Jamaica rum
½ oz. dry vermouth
½ oz. lemon juice
1 tsp. raspberry syrup
Lemon peel

Mix all ingredients, except lemon peel, with cracked ice in a shaker or blender and strain into a chilled cocktail glass. Twist lemon peel over drink and drop into glass.

TWELVE GAUGE GROG

1½ oz. dark Jamaica rum
¾ oz. 151-proof Demerara rum
2 oz. orange juice
1 oz. lemon juice
1 tsp. sugar syrup or to taste
Several dashes Angostura bitters
Grapefruit soda
Orange slice
Maraschino cherry

Mix all ingredients, except grapefruit soda, orange slice, and maraschino cherry, with cracked ice in a shaker or blender and pour into a tall, chilled Collins glass. Fill with cold grapefruit soda, stir gently, and garnish with fruit.

 **UNDERTOW**

1 oz. gold Jamaica rum
1 oz. gin
½ oz. crème de noyaux
1 oz. lime juice
1 tsp. guava syrup or passion fruit syrup
Lime peel

Mix all ingredients, except lime peel, with cracked ice in a blender and pour into a chilled double Old Fashioned glass. Garnish with lime peel.

VERACRUZ COCKTAIL

1½ oz. gold Mexican rum
½ oz. dry vermouth
2 oz. lime juice
1 oz. sugar syrup or to taste
1 oz. pineapple juice

Mix all ingredients with cracked ice in a shaker or blender and pour into a chilled Old Fashioned glass.

VICTORIA PARADE

1½ oz. gold Jamaica rum
1 oz. Southern Comfort
4 oz. iced tea
½ oz. lemon juice
1 tsp. orgeat or sugar syrup
Club soda

Combine all ingredients, except club soda, with several ice cubes in a chilled Collins glass, stir well, and top off with a splash of cold club soda.

VILLA HERMOSA

1½ oz. dark Jamaica rum
½ oz. Kahlua
1 oz. heavy cream

Mix all ingredients with cracked ice in a shaker or blender and strain into a chilled cocktail glass.

VIÑA DEL MAR COOLER

1½ oz. light rum
¼ oz. kirsch
4 oz. orange juice
Ginger ale, chilled
Lime peel

Mix all ingredients, except ginger ale and lime peel, with cracked ice in a shaker or blender, pour into a chilled Old Fashioned glass, and fill with ginger ale. Twist lime peel over drink and drop into glass.

WAIKOLOA FIZZ

1½ oz. Barbados rum
½ oz. Jamaica rum
3 oz. pineapple juice
½ oz. passion fruit juice
1 tsp. coconut syrup
Lemon-lime soda
Lime slice

Mix all ingredients, except lemon-lime soda and lime slice, with cracked ice in shaker or blender and pour into a chilled Collins glass. Fill with lemon-lime soda, stir gently, and garnish with lime slice.

WHITE LION

1½ oz. dark Jamaica rum
1 oz. lemon juice
½ oz. Falernum or orgeat syrup or to taste
Several dashes raspberry syrup
Several dashes Angostura bitters

Mix all ingredients with cracked ice in a shaker or blender and pour into a chilled cocktail glass.

WHITE PIGEON

1½ oz. light rum
¾ oz. anisette

Mix all ingredients with cracked ice in a shaker or blender and pour into a chilled cocktail glass.

WHITE WITCH

1 oz. light Jamaica rum
½ oz. white crème de cacao
½ oz. Cointreau
½ lime
Club soda
Mint sprigs coated with
    powdered sugar

Mix all ingredients, except lime, club soda, and mint sprigs, with cracked ice in a shaker or blender and pour into a chilled Collins glass. Squeeze in lime juice, fill with cold club soda, and stir gently. Garnish with sugar-dusted mint sprigs.

This is an original Trader Vic's recipe.

WINDWARD PASSAGE

1½ oz. light rum
3 oz. pineapple juice
1 tsp. crème de cassis
1 tsp. kirsch

Mix all ingredients with cracked ice in a shaker or blender and strain into a chilled cocktail glass.

XANGO

1½ oz. light rum
½ oz. Cointreau
1 oz. grapefruit juice
Lemon peel

Mix all ingredients, except lemon peel, with cracked ice in a shaker or blender and strain into a chilled cocktail glass. Twist lemon peel over drink and drop into glass.

XYZ COCKTAIL

2 oz. dark Jamaica rum
1 oz. Cointreau
1 oz. lemon juice

Mix all ingredients with cracked ice in a shaker or blender and pour into a chilled cocktail glass.

YAKA-HULA-HICKY-DULA

1½ oz. dark rum
1½ oz. dry vermouth
1½ oz. pineapple juice

Mix all ingredients with cracked ice in a shaker or blender and strain into a chilled cocktail glass.

 ZAMBOANGA

1½ oz. gold Philippines rum
   (Tanduay)
½ oz. sweet vermouth
½ oz. triple sec
1 oz. lime juice
1 tsp. maple syrup or light
   molasses to taste

Mix all ingredients with cracked ice in a blender until smooth and pour into a chilled wine goblet.

THE ZOMBIE

2 oz. light Puerto Rican rum
1 oz. dark Jamaica rum
½ oz. 151-proof Demerara
   rum
1 oz. curaçao
1 tsp. Pernod or Herbsaint
1 oz. lemon juice
1 oz. orange juice
1 oz. pineapple juice
½ oz. papaya or guava juice
   (optional)
¼ oz. grenadine
½ oz. orgeat syrup or sugar
   syrup to taste
Mint sprig (optional)
Pineapple stick

Mix all ingredients, except mint and pineapple stick, with cracked ice in a blender and pour into a tall, chilled Collins glass. Garnish with mint sprig and pineapple stick.

This is a re-creation of the original Zombie recipe by Don the Beachcomber.

BRANDY: THE REGAL SPIRIT

> Claret is the liquor for boys;
> port for men; but he who aspires
> to be a hero must drink brandy.
> —Dr. Samuel Johnson

Brandy, the most universal, venerable, and perhaps the most readily available of all spirits in the world, was, according to some historians, probably the first product resulting from the invention of the still. It has not been called *eau-de-vie*—the water of life—frivolously. In Europe during the Middle Ages, pure water was unknown in the cities and waterborne diseases were rampant, a condition that prevailed through the nineteenth century and wreaks havoc in parts of Europe even today. This explains why frail Tiny Tim, along with many of his peers, swigged down a pint of ale with his breakfast. It explains the popularity of tea and coffee, not to mention wine, and spirits made from wine, fruits, and grains.

In medieval times eau-de-vie of various kinds were endowed with great medicinal properties. In 1250 Arnaud de Villeneuve wrote of the almost magical properties of spirits to alleviate sickness and prolong life. And the spirit at hand came from the Charentes region, which borders the Atlantic midway between the Pyrenees and Brittany, the capital of which is Cognac. The very name summons forth images of oaken casks, cob-webbed bottles, and crystal brandy snifters yielding the incomparable bouquet of a fifty-year-old cognac being sipped and savored by candlelight at the end of a memorable evening of haute cuisine.

Cognac, the royal family of the brandy world, is made by a distinguished group of distillers located in the strictly delimited Cognac region. The area has been subdivided, by French government decree, into seven parts: *Grande Champagne, Petite Champagne, Borderies, Fin Bois, Bons Bois, Bois*

Ordinaires, and *Bois Communs*. The two Champagne districts are considered the premier producing sections by many connoisseurs, but the entire area regularly makes an exemplary brandy by any standard. The "Champagne" designation has no connection with the bubbly wine made far to the north, but refers to a geologic division of the area which separates the Champagne districts from the Bois subdivisions.

Cognac is distilled in large alembics that resemble the distilling apparatus used by the alchemists of the Middle Ages. The distilling process, which is carried out in two stages, is a delicate procedure requiring constant attention. After distillation the cognac is put into oak casks made of wood from the forests of Limousin or Tronçais and ages for as long as sixty or seventy years. This is considered maximum, since cognac aged too long loses much of its character. During the aging period, which is carried out above ground in *chais*, or storehouses, a great deal of the brandy is lost by evaporation through the porous oak. This is a necessary part of the maturation process. It is called, philosophically perhaps, *la part des anges*—the angel's share. After blending, the cognac is bottled and, unlike wine, the aging stops. Thus, a bottle of cognac aged for ten years and bottled in 1890 is still only a ten-year-old brandy.

There is much confusion in the minds of many cognac lovers about the meaning of all the stars and letters that have traditionally adorned cognac labels. In recent years terms have been regulated by the French government if the designation refers to age, i.e., V.O., "Very Old," which signifies that it is not *very* old, but at least four-and-a-half years old, and V.S.O.P., "Very Superior Old Pale," another popular designation, signifies that the brandy has been aged as long as ten years. Every distiller has premium cognacs with appellations such as "Napoleon," "Extra," etc., which can be quite old, but certainly not aged in oak since the Battle of Waterloo. Apart from minimum age requirements by law, the actual age is left to the integrity and honesty of the individual cognac producer.

Some of the leading cognac brands are Curvoisier, Hennessy, Martell, and Remy Martin. Many lesser-known brands are also outstanding, including names such as Hine, Camus, Otard, Monnet, Bisquit-Dubouche, Delamain, and L. de Salignac.

Armagnac is France's other great brandy. It is distilled in the Armagnac region of southwestern France in Gascony, home of d'Artagnan, who was immortalized by Alexander Dumas in *The Three Musketeers*. Armagnac is made like cognac in great pot stills, aged in oak, and carefully blended to achieve its distinctive flavor, which has been described as earthy, full-bodied, and nutty, with floral overtones of violets and a hint of fruit such as plums, prunes, peaches, or grapes. Each armagnac lover finds a distinguishing flavor, scent, or aftertaste that is described subjectively. Some important brands include Cles de Ducs, De Montal, Lapostolle, Larressingle, Loubere, Sempe, Caussade, and Montesquiou.

Normandy in northwestern France produces many good things to eat and drink, such as Camembert cheese and calvados apple brandy, which has become famous for its crisp, clean, apple flavor. It is similar to American applejack, but with more finesse—the result of aging as long as ten to fifteen years. Calvados may be enjoyed before, after, and even during meals. The custom of drinking a tot of calvados as a *digestif* in the middle of a meal is known as "Trou Normand." It is supposed to enhance one's appetite for the courses to come and many people maintain that it performs this task admirably. The best calvados comes from a small section of Normandy designated by the French government as *Pays d'Auge* and is so stated on the label, i.e., *Calvados du Pays d'Auge*. This certifies that this calvados was made in pot stills (as opposed to continuous stills) and is double-distilled in the same way cognac is produced. Outstanding brands of calvados are available in the U.S. such as Bizouard, Boulard, Busnel, Cardinal, Herout Fils, Normandie, and Rollon. But if you want to experience calvados at its best try twenty-year-old Boulard X.O.

French distillers also make a wide range of fruit brandies. These are clear eau-de-vie called *alcools blanc*. Pear brandy made from the Williams or Bartlett pear is particularly well-known and frequently is bottled with a whole pear inside. Framboise from raspberries, fraise from strawberries, mirabelle from plums, and kirsch from cherries are all popular. These and other fruit brandies also are made by distillers in Switzerland, Germany, Hungary, Croatia, and the United States. A brandy distilled from grape pomace (skins and pulp remaining after the juice or wine has been removed from the grape press or fermenting vat) is popular in Burgundy. It is called *marc*, and like *grappa*, the Italian pomace brandy, when unaged can be quite strong and assertive, although these pomace brandies, including those made by California distillers, have their devotees.

California brandies are on the rise and at this writing account for three out of every four bottles of brandy sold in the U.S. Most of the brandy produced is made from a large proportion of Thompson Seedless and Flame Tokay grapes and a sprinkling of other grape varieties using continuous stills. By law California brandy must be aged for two years in oak barrels, but it is usually held longer, which makes for a smoother product. The end result is a brandy that is light, clean, and fruity with a definite grape flavor that may vary from slightly dry to sweet. In addition to traditional, post-prandial brandy-snifter sipping, California brandies also lend themselves to the making of mixed drinks, which has, no doubt, been an important factor in their increasing popularity. Good representative brands include Christian Brothers, Cresta Blanca, Petri, Italian Swiss Colony, Lejon, Coronet VSQ, E & J Brandy, A.R. Morrow, Aristocrat, Paul Masson Conti Royal, Royal Host, as well as many winery labels such as Korbel, Almaden, and Beaulieu, who market brandies under their respective names.

Having spent much time in Spain, I have developed a taste for Spanish brandies shipped from Jerez de la Frontera in the "Sherry Triangle" of southern Spain by Pedro Domecq, Duff Gordan, Sandeman, and others among the great sherry producers. Most Spanish brandies are not made from sherry wines, as many suppose, but from wines that are produced in La Mancha, an area south of Madrid made famous as the home base of Don Quixote. Spanish brandies have a distinctive character that carries overtones of sherry, perhaps from aging in casks that were used for sherry wine. The flavor and bouquet are pronounced, sometimes pungent, with a slightly sweet aftertaste and a nutty quality. Some of the most distinguished Spanish brandies are Carlos I and Fundador made by Pedro Domecq; Capa Negra from Sandeman; and Cardinal Mendoza produced by Sanchez Romate.

Many countries produce excellent brandies with unique qualities that are not found anywhere else. Metaxa from Greece (almost a liqueur due to the addition of sugar); Asbach-Uralt from Germany; and Pisco brandy from Peru (produced in Ica, an oasis in the coastal desert, a four-hour drive along the sea south of Lima, where logically nothing should grow) are prime examples of good spirits made in countries not generally thought of as brandy producers. Other examples are Mexico, the source of the popular Presidente brandy and South Africa, which produces K.W.V. brandy in the beautiful wine-growing area near Cape Town.

Brandy has an historic and universal appeal. Its restorative qualities are well-known, and its function as a digestive at the end of a meal is appreciated by gourmet and gourmand alike. And the mixability and versatility of brandy in various cocktails and other libations will, it is hoped, be amply demonstrated in the recipes that follow.

A.J.

1½ oz. calvados or applejack
1½ oz. grapefruit juice
Several dashes grenadine

Mix all ingredients with cracked ice in a shaker or blender and pour into a chilled cocktail glass.

ADRIENNE'S DREAM

2 oz. brandy
½ oz. peppermint schnapps
½ oz. white crème de cacao
½ oz. lemon juice
½ tsp. sugar syrup or to taste
Club soda
Mint sprig

Mix all ingredients, except soda and mint, with cracked ice in a shaker or blender and pour into a chilled Collins glass. Fill with cold club soda and garnish with mint sprig.

ALABAMA

1 oz. brandy
1 oz. curaçao
½ oz. lime juice
½ tsp. sugar syrup or to taste
Orange peel

Mix all ingredients, except orange peel, with cracked ice in a shaker or blender and strain into a chilled cocktail glass. Twist orange peel over drink and drop into glass.

 ALABAMA SLAMMA

1 oz. cognac
½ oz. blackberry brandy
1 oz. coffee brandy
½ oz. dry vermouth
½ oz. amaretto
1 oz. lemon juice

Mix all ingredients with cracked ice in a shaker or blender and pour into a chilled brandy snifter.

ALABAMMY BOUND

1 oz. brandy
1 oz. Southern Comfort
1 oz. lemon juice
½ tsp. sugar syrup or to taste
Mint sprig

Mix all ingredients, except mint sprig, with cracked ice in a shaker or blender, strain into a chilled cocktail glass, and garnish with mint.

ALEXANDER'S SISTER

1½ oz. brandy
1 oz. white crème de menthe
1 oz. heavy cream

Mix all ingredients with cracked ice in a shaker or blender and pour into a chilled cocktail glass.

This cocktail may also be made with gin in place of brandy.

ALHAMBRA

1½ oz. brandy
½ oz. fino sherry
½ oz. Drambuie
Orange slice
Lemon peel

Mix all ingredients, except orange slice and lemon peel, with cracked ice in a shaker or blender and pour into a chilled Old Fashioned glass. Garnish with orange slice, then twist lemon peel over drink, and drop into glass.

AMBASSADOR WEST

1½ oz. brandy
1 oz. gin
1 tsp. dry vermouth
Green olive

Combine brandy, gin, and dry vermouth in a mixing glass with several ice cubes, stir well, and strain into a chilled cocktail glass. Twist lemon peel over drink and drop in, or garnish with cocktail olive.

AMBROSIA FOR TWO

3 oz. brandy
3 oz. apple brandy
Several dashes raspberry
    syrup or raspberry liqueur
Champagne

Mix all ingredients, except champagne, with cracked ice in a shaker or blender and pour equally into two chilled wine glasses. Fill each glass with cold champagne.

◤ AMBULANCE CHASER

2 oz. cognac
¼ oz. port
1 egg yolk
Several dashes
    Worcestershire sauce
Several grindings white
    pepper

Mix with cracked ice in a blender and pour into a chilled cocktail glass.

AMERICAN ROSE

1½ oz. brandy
1 tsp. grenadine
½ fresh peach, peeled and
  mashed
Several dashes Pernod
Champagne

Mix all ingredients, except champagne, with cracked ice in a shaker or blender and pour into a chilled wine goblet. Fill with champagne and stir gently.

APPLE BANG!

2 oz. calvados or applejack
3 oz. apple cider
Several dashes lemon juice
1 egg white (for two drinks)
Club soda (optional)
1 tsp. apple schnapps

Mix all ingredients, except soda and apple schnapps, with cracked ice in a shaker or blender and pour into a chilled, large wine goblet. Fill with cold club soda and add additional ice if needed. Top with apple schnapps.

APPLE BLOSSOM No. 1

1½ oz. brandy
1 oz. apple juice
1 tsp. lemon juice
Lemon slice

Mix all ingredients, except lemon slice, with cracked ice in a shaker or blender, strain into a chilled cocktail glass, and garnish with lemon slice.

APPLE BLOSSOM No. 2

1½ oz. applejack
1 oz. apple juice
½ oz. lemon juice
1 tsp. maple syrup
Lemon slice

Mix all ingredients, except lemon slice, with cracked ice in a blender at low speed for 15 seconds, pour into a chilled deep-saucer champagne glass, and garnish with lemon slice.

 APPLE BLOW FIZZ

2-3 oz. applejack or calvados
¼ tsp. lemon juice
1 tsp. sugar syrup or to taste
1 egg white (for two drinks)
Club soda

Mix all ingredients, except soda, with cracked ice in a shaker or blender and pour into a chilled highball glass. Add ice cubes if necessary and fill with cold club soda. Stir gently.

APPLE BRANDY COCKTAIL

2 oz. applejack or calvados
½ tsp. lemon juice
½ tsp. grenadine

Mix all ingredients with cracked ice in a shaker or blender and strain into a chilled cocktail glass.

APPLE BRANDY FRAPPÉ

1½ oz. applejack or calvados
½ oz. lime juice
1 tsp. sugar syrup or to taste
1 egg white (for two drinks)

Mix with plenty of cracked ice in a blender for a few seconds until slushy and pour into a chilled wine glass.

APPLE BRANDY COOLER

2 oz. brandy
1 oz. light rum
4 oz. apple juice
½ oz. lime juice
 tsp. Falernum or sugar
  syrup to taste
1 tsp. dark Jamaica rum
Lime slice

Mix all ingredients, except dark rum and lime slice, with cracked ice in a shaker or blender and pour into a chilled Collins glass. Top with float of dark rum and garnish with lime slice.

◤ APPLE BUCK

1½ oz. applejack
½ oz. lemon juice
1 tsp. ginger-flavored brandy
Ginger ale
Preserved ginger

Mix all ingredients, except ginger ale and preserved ginger, with cracked ice in a shaker or blender and pour into a chilled highball glass. Fill with cold ginger ale, stir gently, and garnish with ginger.

APPLE BYRRH

1½ oz. calvados
½ oz. dry vermouth
½ oz. Byrrh
½ tsp. lemon juice
Lemon peel

Mix all ingredients, except lemon peel, with cracked ice in a shaker or blender and pour into a chilled Old Fashioned glass. Twist lemon peel over drink and drop into glass.

APPLE CART

1 oz. applejack
¾ oz. Cointreau or curaçao
½ oz. lemon juice

Mix all ingredients with cracked ice in a shaker or blender and strain into a chilled cocktail glass.

APPLE DUBONNET

1½ oz. calvados or applejack
1½ oz. Dubonnet rouge
Lemon slice

Mix all ingredients, except lemon slice, with cracked ice in a shaker or blender, pour into a chilled Old Fashioned glass, and garnish with lemon slice.

APPLE FIZZ

2 oz. apple brandy
4 oz. apple juice
Dash lime juice
Club soda
Lime slice

Combine all ingredients, except lime slice, in a chilled Collins glass with several ice cubes, stir gently, and garnish with lime slice.

APPLE GINGER SANGAREE

1½ oz. apple brandy
¾ oz. green-ginger wine
1 tsp. sugar syrup
Ground nutmeg

Mix all ingredients, except nutmeg, with cracked ice in a shaker or blender, pour into a chilled goblet, and sprinkle with nutmeg.

APPLE KNOCKER

3 oz. apple brandy
½ oz. sweet vermouth
4 oz. orange juice
½ oz. sugar syrup or to taste
1 tsp. lemon juice

Mix all ingredients with cracked ice in a shaker or blender and pour into a chilled Collins glass. Add additional ice if necessary.

APPLE RUM-DUM

1 oz. applejack
1 oz. light rum
½ oz. lime juice
½ oz. orgeat syrup or sugar
  syrup to taste
Club soda
Orange peel
Lemon peel

Mix all ingredients, except soda, orange and lemon peels, with cracked ice in a shaker or blender and pour into a chilled Collins glass. Add additional ice and fill with cold club soda. Twist orange and lemon peels over drink and drop into glass.

APPLE SIDECAR

1½ oz. apple brandy
½ oz. triple sec
½ oz. lime juice

Mix all ingredients with cracked ice in a shaker or blender and pour into a chilled cocktail glass.

APPLE SWIZZLE

1½ oz. applejack
1 oz. light rum
½ oz. lime juice
1 tsp. sugar syrup or to taste
Dash Angostura bitters

Mix with cracked ice in a shaker or blender and pour into a chilled Old Fashioned glass. Add more ice if necessary.

APPLEJACK COLLINS

2 oz. applejack
1 oz. lemon juice
1 tsp. sugar syrup
Several dashes orange
  bitters
Club soda, chilled
Lemon slice

Mix all ingredients, except club soda and lemon slice, with cracked ice in a shaker or blender and pour into a chilled Collins glass. Fill with club soda, stir gently, and garnish with lemon slice.

APPLEJACK DAISY

1½ oz. applejack
½ oz. lime juice
1 tsp. raspberry syrup
Club soda, chilled
1 tsp. ginger brandy
Lime slice

Mix all ingredients, except club soda, ginger brandy, and lime slice, with cracked ice in a shaker or blender and pour into a chilled highball glass. Fill with club soda, stir gently, and top with float of ginger brandy. Garnish with lime slice.

APPLEJACK MANHATTAN

1¾ oz. applejack
¾ oz. sweet vermouth
Dash orange bitters
Maraschino cherry

Combine all ingredients, except maraschino cherry, in a mixing glass with several ice cubes, stir well, and strain into a chilled cocktail glass. Garnish with cherry.

APPLEJACK SOUR

2 oz. applejack
1 oz. lemon juice
1 tsp. sugar syrup or to taste

Mix all ingredients with cracked ice in a shaker or blender and strain into a chilled cocktail glass.

APOLLO COOLER

1½ oz. Metaxa
½ oz. lemon juice
Ginger ale
Lemon slice
1 tsp. ouzo

Mix brandy and lemon juice with cracked ice in a shaker or blender and pour into a chilled highball glass. Fill with ginger ale, stir gently, and garnish with lemon slice. Top with ouzo.

APRICOT BRANDY FIZZ

2 oz. apricot-flavored brandy
Several dashes grenadine
Orange slice
Lemon peel
Club soda

Pour brandy and grenadine into a chilled Old Fashioned glass with several ice cubes, add lemon peel and orange slice, fill with cold club soda, and stir gently.

APRICOT BRANDY SOUR

2 oz. apricot brandy
1 oz. lemon juice
1 tsp. sugar syrup or to taste
Lemon slice

Mix all ingredients, except lemon slice, with cracked ice in a shaker or blender and strain into a chilled cocktail glass. Garnish with lemon slice.

APRICOT PIE

1 oz. apricot brandy
1 oz. light rum
½ oz. sweet vermouth
1 tsp. lemon juice
Several dashes grenadine
Orange peel

Mix all ingredients, except orange peel, with cracked ice in a shaker or blender and pour into a chilled Old Fashioned glass. Twist orange peel over drink and drop into glass.

APRICOT LADY

1 oz. apricot brandy
1½ oz. light rum
½ oz. lime juice
1 tsp. curaçao
1 egg white (for two drinks)
Orange slice

Mix all ingredients, except orange slice, with cracked ice in a shaker or blender, pour into a chilled cocktail glass, and garnish with orange slice.

APRICOT No. 1

2 oz. apricot brandy
1 oz. orange juice
1 oz. lemon juice
Several dashes gin

Mix all ingredients with cracked ice in a shaker or blender and pour into a chilled cocktail glass.

APRICOT No. 2

1½ oz. apricot brandy
½ oz. gin
1 oz. orange juice
½ oz. lemon or lime juice
1 tsp. orgeat syrup

Mix with cracked ice in a shaker or blender and strain into a chilled cocktail glass.

 ## B&B

1 oz. cognac
1 oz. Benedictine

Pour into a brandy snifter and swirl until well blended.

B&B COLLINS

2 oz. cognac
½ oz. lemon juice
1 tsp. sugar syrup or to taste
Club soda
½ oz. Benedictine
Lemon slice

Mix all ingredients, except club soda, Benedictine, and lemon slice, with cracked ice in a shaker or blender and pour into a chilled Collins glass. Fill with club soda, stir gently, and top with float of Benedictine. Garnish with lemon slice.

BALTIMORE BRACER

1 oz. brandy
1 oz. anisette
1 egg white (for two drinks)

Mix all ingredients with cracked ice in a shaker or blender and pour into a chilled cocktail glass.

BART FARRELL'S FIZZ

1 oz. brandy
1 oz. pineapple juice
½ oz. lemon juice
Several dashes maraschino liqueur
Club soda
Dash Angostura or orange bitters

Mix all ingredients, except club soda and bitters, with cracked ice in a shaker or blender and pour into a chilled highball glass. Fill with club soda, top with bitters, and stir gently.

BARTON SPECIAL

1½ oz. calvados
¾ oz. gin
¾ oz. scotch
Lemon peel

Mix all ingredients, except lemon peel, with cracked ice in a shaker or blender and pour into a chilled Old Fashioned glass. Twist lemon peel over drink and drop into glass.

BATEAUX MOUCHE

1½ oz. cognac
½ oz. Dubonnet blanc
½ oz. lemon juice
1 tsp. sugar syrup
½ oz. curaçao

Mix all ingredients, except curaçao, with cracked ice in a shaker or blender and strain into a chilled cocktail glass. Top with curaçao float.

BASIN STREET BALM

1 oz. brandy
½ oz. peach brandy
½ oz. lemon juice
1 tsp. peach schnapps or
    kirsch
Orange slice

Mix all ingredients, except orange slice, with cracked ice in a shaker or blender and strain into a chilled cocktail glass. Garnish with orange slice.

BBC

2 oz. blackberry-flavored
    brandy
Cola
Lemon slice

Pour brandy into a chilled Collins glass with ice cubes and fill with cold cola. Garnish with lemon slice.

 BEACH STREET COOLER

1½ oz. brandy
½ oz. curaçao
½ oz. lemon juice
Cola

Mix brandy, curaçao, and lemon juice with cracked ice in a shaker or blender and pour into a chilled Collins glass. Fill with cold cola. Stir gently.

BELMONT PARK

1 oz. apple brandy
1 oz. apricot brandy
½ oz. gin
½ oz. orange juice
Several dashes grenadine

Mix all ingredients, except grenadine, with cracked ice in a shaker or blender and pour into a chilled cocktail glass. Top with grenadine float.

BESS-ARLENE

1½ oz. brandy
½ oz. curaçao
Club soda
Dash Pernod

Pour brandy and curaçao over ice in a chilled Collins glass and fill with cold club soda. Add a dash of Pernod and stir gently.

 BETSY ROSS

1½ oz. brandy
1½ oz. port
1 egg yolk
1 tsp. sugar syrup or to taste
Several dashes curaçao
Several dashes Angostura
    bitters
Ground nutmeg (optional)

Mix all ingredients, except nutmeg, with cracked ice in a shaker or blender and strain into a chilled cocktail glass. Sprinkle with ground nutmeg, if you wish.

BETWEEN THE SHEETS

1½ oz. cognac
1 oz. light rum
¾ oz. curaçao or triple sec
½ oz. lemon juice

Mix with cracked ice in a shaker or blender and strain into a chilled cocktail glass.

BEVERLY HILLS COOLER

1 oz. brandy
½ oz. Benedictine
3–4 oz. orange juice
Champagne
Gardenia or orchid (optional)

Mix brandy, Benedictine, and orange juice with cracked ice in a shaker or blender and strain into a chilled brandy snifter or Squall glass. Fill with cold champagne and garnish with a gardenia or orchid (or flower of your choice).

BIG APPLE

2 oz. applejack
½ oz. amaretto
3 oz. apple juice
1 tbsp. applesauce
Ground cinnamon

Mix all ingredients, except cinnamon, with cracked ice in a blender until smooth. Serve in a chilled parfait glass and sprinkle with cinnamon.

BLACKJACK

1 oz. blackberry brandy
1 oz. brandy
1 oz. heavy cream

Mix all ingredients with cracked ice in a shaker or blender and pour into a chilled cocktail glass.

BOMBAY

1 oz. brandy
1 oz. dry vermouth
½ oz. sweet vermouth
½ tsp. curaçao
Dash of Pernod
Orange slice

Mix all ingredients, except orange slice, with cracked ice in a shaker or blender, pour into a chilled Old Fashioned glass, and garnish with orange slice.

BOOSTER

2 oz. brandy
1 oz. curaçao
1 egg white (for two drinks)
Pinch of ground nutmeg

Mix all ingredients, except ground nutmeg, with cracked ice in a shaker or blender and pour into a chilled cocktail glass. Sprinkle with nutmeg.

 **BOSOM CARESSER No. 1**

1½ oz. brandy
½ oz. triple sec or curaçao
1 egg yolk
1 tsp. grenadine

Mix all ingredients with cracked ice in a shaker or blender and strain into a chilled cocktail glass.

BOSOM CARESSER No. 2

1 oz. brandy
1 oz. Madeira
½ oz. triple sec

Stir all ingredients with ice in a mixing glass and strain into a chilled cocktail glass.

BOSTON BLACKIE

2 oz. blackberry-flavored brandy
Bitter lemon soda
Lime wedge

Add brandy to a chilled Collins glass with ice cubes and fill with cold bitter lemon soda. Stir gently and garnish with lime wedge.

BRANDANA FRAPPÉ

1½ oz. applejack or calvados
½ oz. crème de banane
½ oz. lime juice
Orange slice

Mix applejack, banana liqueur, and lime juice with plenty of cracked ice in a blender for a few seconds until slushy and pour into a chilled wine glass. Garnish with orange slice.

BRANDANA COOLER

1½ oz. brandy
¾ oz. crème de banane
½ oz. lemon juice
Club soda, chilled
Lemon wedge
Banana slice

Mix all ingredients, except club soda, lemon and banana slices, with cracked ice in a shaker or blender and pour into a chilled Collins glass. Fill with club soda, stir gently, and garnish with lemon wedge and banana slice.

BRANDIED APRICOT

1½ oz. brandy
½ oz. apricot brandy
½ oz. lemon juice
Canned or dried apricot

Mix all ingredients, except apricot, with cracked ice in a shaker or blender and strain into a chilled cocktail glass. Garnish with an apricot.

BRANDY ALEXANDER

1½ oz. brandy
1 oz. crème de cacao
1 oz. heavy cream

Mix all ingredients with cracked ice in a shaker or blender and strain into a chilled cocktail glass.

BRANDY BUCK

1½ oz. brandy
¼ oz. white crème de menthe
½ oz. lemon juice
Ginger ale, chilled
Several seedless grapes

Mix all ingredients, except ginger ale and grapes, with cracked ice in a shaker or blender and pour into a chilled highball glass. Fill with club soda, stir gently, and garnish with seedless grapes.

BRANDY CASSIS

1½ oz. brandy
¼ oz. crème de cassis or to taste
½ oz. lemon juice
Lemon peel

Mix all ingredients, except lemon peel, with cracked ice in a shaker or blender and strain into a chilled cocktail glass. Twist lemon peel over drink and drop into glass.

BRANDY CHAMPERELLE

½ oz. curaçao
½ oz. yellow Chartreuse
½ oz. anisette
½ oz. cognac

Prechill all ingredients, and, in the order listed, carefully pour each into a chilled sherry glass using the bowl of a barspoon so that each floats on the one beneath it.

BRANDY COBBLER

2–3 oz. brandy
1 tsp. curaçao or maraschino or peach liqueur
1 tsp. pineapple syrup or sugar syrup to taste
Orange slice
Maraschino cherry

Fill a chilled glass goblet about three-quarters full of cracked ice and add brandy, liqueur, and syrup. Stir briskly with bar spoon until glass begins to frost. Garnish with orange slice and cherry.

BRANDY CRUSTA

Spiral peel of a medium orange or large lemon
Lemon slice
Superfine sugar
2–3 oz. brandy
½ oz. lemon juice
½ oz. maraschino liqueur
Several dashes Angostura bitters
Maraschino cherry

Cut a thin, even spiral from an orange or lemon after cutting off the ends of the fruit. Rub the rim of a chilled wine goblet with lemon slice and roll rim in superfine sugar until well coated. Mix brandy, lemon juice, maraschino liqueur and bitters with cracked ice in a shaker or blender and pour into goblet that has been lined with orange or lemon spiral. Garnish with maraschino cherry.

BRANDY DAISY

2–3 oz. brandy
Juice of ½ lemon
½ oz. raspberry syrup or grenadine
1 tsp. sugar syrup
Club soda
Peach slice or orange slice
Pineapple stick
Maraschino cherry
Dash Pernod or maraschino liqueur (optional)

Mix brandy, lemon juice, raspberry, and sugar syrup with cracked ice in a shaker or blender and pour into a chilled wine goblet and add additional cracked ice. Stir briskly until goblet is frosted. Fill with cold club soda and garnish with fruits. A dash of Pernod is sometimes used to top off drink.

BRANDY EGGNOG

2–3 oz. brandy
½ oz. sugar syrup or to taste
1 cup milk
1 egg
Freshly ground nutmeg

Mix all ingredients, except nutmeg, with cracked ice in a shaker or blender and strain into a chilled highball glass. Sprinkle with nutmeg.

BRANDY FIX

2–3 oz. brandy
1 tsp. sugar syrup
1 tsp. water
Juice of ½ lemon

Add all ingredients to a chilled double Old Fashioned glass and fill with cracked ice. Stir until glass frosts. Serve with a straw, if you wish.

 BRANDY FIZZ

2–3 oz. brandy
1½ oz. lemon juice or half lime and lemon juice
½ oz. sugar syrup or to taste
Club soda

Mix all ingredients, except soda, with cracked ice in a shaker or blender and pour into a chilled highball glass. Add additional ice cubes if necessary and fill with cold club soda.

BRANDY FLIP

2 oz. brandy
1 egg
1 tsp. sugar syrup or to taste
½ oz. cream (optional)
Ground nutmeg

Mix all ingredients, except nutmeg, with cracked ice in a blender and pour into a chilled wine glass. Sprinkle with nutmeg.

BRANDY GUMP

2–3 oz. brandy
½ oz. lemon juice
½ tsp. grenadine

Mix all ingredients with cracked ice in a shaker or blender and strain into a chilled cocktail glass.

BRANDY JULEP

6 mint leaves
1 tsp. sugar syrup or honey
Brandy
Mint sprig
Powdered sugar

Place mint leaves in a chilled double Old Fashioned glass and add syrup or honey and a little cold water. Muddle leaves until bruised and fill glass with shaved or finely crushed ice. Fill with brandy and churn with a barspoon until glass frosts. Add more ice and brandy and churn until well frosted. Garnish with mint sprig and dust it with powdered sugar.

BRANDY MANHATTAN

2 oz. brandy
½ oz. sweet or dry vermouth
Dash Angostura bitters
Maraschino cherry

Combine brandy, sweet vermouth, and Angostura bitters in a mixing glass with several ice cubes, stir well, and strain into a chilled cocktail glass. Garnish with maraschino cherry.

BRANDY MELBA

1½ oz. brandy
½ oz. peach schnapps
¼ oz. raspberry liqueur
½ oz. lemon juice
Several dashes orange
  bitters
Peach slice

Mix all ingredients, except peach slice, with cracked ice in a shaker or blender, strain into a chilled cocktail glass, and garnish with peach slice.

BRANDY MILK PUNCH

2 oz. brandy
8 oz. milk
1 tsp. sugar syrup
Pinch of ground nutmeg

Mix all ingredients, except ground nutmeg, with cracked ice in a shaker or blender, pour into a chilled double Old Fashioned glass, and sprinkle with nutmeg.

BRANDY OLD FASHIONED

1 sugar cube
Several dashes Angostura
   bitters
3 oz. brandy
Lemon peel

Place sugar cube in a chilled
Old Fashioned glass and sprinkle with bitters and a dash of
cold water. Muddle sugar cube
until dissolved. Add ice cubes
and brandy. Twist lemon peel
over drink and drop into glass.

 ## BRANDY SANGAREE

½ tsp. superfine sugar
Dash water
2–3 oz. brandy
Ground nutmeg

Dissolve sugar with a little
water in a chilled double Old
Fashioned glass, add ice cubes
and brandy. Stir well and sprinkle with ground nutmeg.

 ## BRANDY SCAFFA No. 1

½ oz. raspberry syrup
½ oz. maraschino liqueur
½ oz. green Chartreuse
½ oz. cognac

In a sherry or parfait glass carefully pour in the ingredients, in
the exact order listed, using the
round bottom of a spoon so they
remain separated. This traditional recipe is similar to a
pousse-café and a champerelle,
using various ingredients poured
in layers and never mixed, except by the drinker.

 ## BRANDY SCAFFA No. 2

1½ oz. cognac
1½ oz. maraschino liqueur
Dash Angostura bitters

Mix all ingredients with ice
cubes in a chilled double Old
Fashioned glass.

BRANDY SOUR

2 oz. brandy
1 oz. lemon juice
½ oz. orange juice (optional)
1 tsp. sugar syrup or to taste
Maraschino cherry

Mix all ingredients, except
cherry, with cracked ice in a
shaker or blender, strain into a
chilled Whiskey Sour glass, and
garnish with cherry.

◣ BRONX CHEER

2 oz. apricot brandy
6 oz. raspberry soda
Orange peel

Mix brandy and soda with ice cubes in a chilled Collins glass. Twist orange peel over drink and drop into glass.

BULL'S MILK

2 oz. brandy
½ oz. dark Jamaica rum
6 oz. milk
1 tsp. sugar syrup or to taste
Pinch cinnamon or nutmeg

Mix all ingredients, except spice, with cracked ice in a shaker or blender and pour into a chilled highball glass. Sprinkle with spice.

◣ CALIFORNIA COLA

1½ oz. brandy
½ oz. triple sec
Cola
Lemon slice

Pour brandy and triple sec over ice in a chilled Collins glass and fill with cold cola. Garnish with lemon slice.

◣ CALIFORNIA DREAMING

2 oz. apricot brandy
4 oz. orange soda
1 scoop orange sherbet

Mix with cracked ice in a blender for a few seconds until smooth. Serve in a parfait glass.

CANDY COCKTAIL

1 oz. brandy
1 oz. Galliano
Dash maraschino liqueur
2 scoops orange sherbet
Chocolate chips

Mix all ingredients, except chocolate chips, with cracked ice in a blender until smooth and pour into a chilled wine goblet. Sprinkle chocolate chips on top.

CAPTAIN KIDD

1½ oz. brandy
1 oz. dark Jamaica rum
1 oz. crème de cacao
Orange slice
Maraschino cherry
Pineapple stick

Mix all ingredients, except orange slice, maraschino cherry, and pineapple stick, with cracked ice in a shaker or blender and pour into a chilled Delmonico glass. Garnish with fruit.

CARROL

1½ oz. brandy
¾ oz. sweet vermouth
Maraschino cherry

Mix all ingredients, except maraschino cherry, with cracked ice in a shaker or blender, pour into a chilled cocktail glass, and garnish with cherry.

CHAMPAGNE COOLER

1 oz. brandy
1 oz. Cointreau
Champagne
Mint sprigs

Pour brandy and Cointreau into a chilled Squall glass or wine goblet, fill with champagne, and stir gently. Garnish with mint sprigs.

CHAMPAGNE DREAM

Dash Pernod
½ oz. cognac
½ oz. curaçao
Dash maple syrup
Brut champagne

Rinse a large, chilled champagne tulip glass with Pernod. In a mixing glass add several ice cubes, cognac, curaçao, and maple syrup and strain into champagne tulip. Fill with cold champagne and stir gently.

CHAMPS ELYSEES

1½ oz. cognac
½ oz. yellow Chartreuse
½ oz. lemon juice
1 tsp. sugar syrup or to taste
Dash Angostura bitters

Mix all ingredients with cracked ice in a shaker or blender and pour into a chilled cocktail glass.

 CHERRY BERRY

1½ oz. blackberry-flavored
    brandy
½ oz. cherry brandy
6 oz. black-cherry soda
Maraschino cherry

Pour brandies into a tall, chilled Collins glass with ice cubes and fill with cold black-cherry soda. Stir gently. Garnish with cherry.

CHERRY BLOSSOM

1½ oz. brandy
¾ oz. cherry brandy or
   cherry liqueur
½ oz. curaçao
½ oz. lemon juice
¼ oz. grenadine
1 tsp. sugar syrup or to taste

Mix all ingredients with cracked ice in a shaker or blender and strain into a chilled cocktail glass.

CHERRY HILL

1 oz. brandy
1 oz. cherry brandy
½ oz. dry vermouth
Orange peel

Mix all ingredients, except orange peel, with cracked ice in a shaker or blender and pour into a chilled cocktail glass. Twist orange peel over drink and drop into glass.

CHICAGO

Lemon wedge
Superfine sugar
1½ oz. brandy
Dash curaçao
Dash Angostura bitters
Champagne

Moisten the rim of a chilled wine goblet with lemon wedge and roll rim in sugar until evenly coated. Mix brandy, curaçao, and bitters with cracked ice in a mixing glass and strain into goblet. Fill with cold champagne.

CLASSIC

Lemon wedge
Superfine sugar
1½ oz. brandy
½ oz. curaçao
½ oz. maraschino liqueur
½ oz. lemon juice
Lemon peel

Moisten rim of a chilled cocktail glass with a lemon wedge and dip rim in superfine sugar until evenly coated. Mix brandy, curaçao, maraschino liqueur, and lemon juice with cracked ice in a shaker or blender and strain into cocktail glass. Twist lemon peel over drink and drop into glass.

CNOSSUS COOLER

1½ oz. Metaxa
Several dashes Angostura
 bitters
5 oz. pineapple juice
Maraschino cherry
Orange slice

Mix brandy and bitters in a chilled highball glass with several ice cubes and stir. Add pineapple juice and garnish with cherry and orange slice.

 COCOA MOCHA

2 oz. coffee-flavored brandy
Chocolate soda
Cinnamon stick

Pour brandy over ice in a double Old Fashioned glass and fill with cold chocolate soda. Garnish with cinnamon stick.

COFFEE COCKTAIL No. 1

1 oz. brandy
1 oz. Cointreau
1 oz. cold black coffee

Shake with cracked ice and pour into a chilled parfait glass.

COFFEE COCKTAIL No. 2

1½ oz. brandy
¾ oz. port
Several dashes curaçao
Several dashes sugar syrup
 or to taste
1 egg yolk
Ground nutmeg

Mix all ingredients, except nutmeg, with cracked ice in a blender and strain into a chilled cocktail glass. Sprinkle with nutmeg.

 COFFEE FIZZ

2 oz. coffee-flavored brandy
2 oz. milk or half-and-half
1 egg (optional)
Cream soda
Pinch ground cinnamon

Mix brandy, milk, and egg with cracked ice in a blender and pour into a chilled Collins glass. Fill with cream soda, add additional ice, if necessary, and sprinkle with cinnamon.

COFFEE FLIP

1 oz. cognac
½ oz. port
4 oz. coffee
½ tsp. sugar syrup
1 egg
Pinch of ground nutmeg

Mix all ingredients, except ground nutmeg, with cracked ice in a shaker or blender, pour into a chilled Squall glass or wine goblet. Add additional ice, if necessary. Sprinkle with nutmeg.

 COLD DECK

1½ oz. brandy
¾ oz. sweet vermouth
¾ oz. peppermint schnapps
　or white crème de menthe

Mix all ingredients with cracked ice in a shaker or blender and strain into a chilled cocktail glass.

For a Dry Cold Deck, substitute a dry vermouth in place of sweet vermouth.

CORPSE REVIVER

1½ oz. applejack
¾ oz. brandy
½ oz. sweet vermouth

Mix with cracked ice in a shaker or blender and strain into a chilled cocktail glass.

DANISH KISS

1½ oz. applejack
1 oz. Cherry Heering
1 oz. cream

Mix with cracked ice in a shaker or blender and strain into a chilled cocktail glass.

DEAUVILLE

1 oz. brandy
¾ oz. apple brandy
½ oz. triple sec or Cointreau
½ oz. lemon juice

Mix all ingredients with cracked ice in a shaker or blender and strain into a chilled cocktail glass.

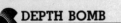 DEPTH BOMB

1¼ oz. apple brandy
1¼ oz. brandy
Several dashes lemon juice
Several dashes grenadine

Mix all ingredients with cracked ice in a shaker or blender and pour into a chilled cocktail glass.

DONNA'S DELIGHT

1½ oz. brandy
1 oz. apricot brandy
½ oz. amaretto

Mix with plenty of cracked ice in a blender for a few seconds and pour into a chilled cocktail glass.

DOROTHY JOHNSON'S JOY

1 oz. brandy
1 oz. port
½ cup vanilla ice cream

Mix all ingredients in a blender for a few seconds until smooth and pour into a chilled parfait glass.

DOUBLE BRANDY FLIP

1 oz. brandy
1 oz. apricot brandy
½ oz. sugar syrup
1 egg
Ground nutmeg

Mix all ingredients, except ground nutmeg, with cracked ice in a shaker or blender, strain into a chilled cocktail glass, and sprinkle with nutmeg.

 EAST INDIA

1½ oz. brandy
½ oz. curaçao
½ oz. pineapple juice
Dash Angostura bitters

Mix with cracked ice in a shaker or blender and strain into a chilled cocktail glass.

EAU-DE-V.I.P.

1½ oz. brandy
½ oz. apricot brandy
½ oz. triple sec
½ oz. lemon juice
½ tsp. sugar or to taste
Dash maraschino liqueur
Lemon slice

Mix all ingredients, except lemon slice, with cracked ice in a shaker or blender and pour into a chilled balloon glass. Garnish with lemon slice.

ELYSEE PALACE

1 oz. cognac
½ oz. raspberry liqueur
Brut champagne
½ tsp. framboise

Stir cognac and raspberry liqueur with several ice cubes in a mixing glass until well chilled. Pour into a chilled tulip glass, fill with cold champagne, and top with a framboise float.

ESCOFFIER COCKTAIL

1½ oz. calvados
¾ oz. Cointreau
¾ oz. Dubonnet rouge
Dash Angostura bitters
Maraschino cherry

Blend calvados, Cointreau, Dubonnet, and bitters with cracked ice in a mixing glass. Stir briskly and strain into a chilled cocktail glass. Garnish with maraschino cherry.

FANTASIO

1 oz. brandy
¾ oz. dry vermouth
1 tsp. white crème de cacao
1 tsp. maraschino liqueur

Mix all ingredients with cracked ice in a shaker or blender and pour into a chilled cocktail glass.

FJORD

1 oz. brandy
½ oz. aquavit
1 oz. orange juice
½ oz. lime juice
1 tsp. grenadine

Mix all ingredients with cracked ice in a shaker or blender and strain into a chilled cocktail glass.

FLAG

1½ oz. apricot brandy
Several dashes curaçao
1 tsp. crème yvette
1 oz. dry red wine

Mix apricot brandy and curaçao with cracked ice in a shaker or blender. Pour crème yvette into a chilled Old Fashioned glass, then carefully strain brandy and curaçao mixture over a barspoon so that the mixture floats on top of the crème yvette. Top with red wine float.

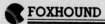 **FOXHOUND**

1½ oz. brandy
½ oz. cranberry juice
1 tsp. kümmel
1 tsp. lemon juice
Lemon slice

Mix all ingredients, except lemon slice, with cracked ice in a shaker or blender, pour into a chilled Old Fashioned glass, and garnish with lemon slice.

FRENCH CONNECTION

1½ oz. cognac
¾ oz. Amaretto di Saronno

Mix with ice cubes in a chilled Old Fashioned glass.

 FROUPE

1½ oz. brandy
1½ oz. sweet vermouth
1 tsp. Benedictine

Blend all ingredients in a mixing glass with several ice cubes, stir well, and strain into a chilled cocktail glass.

 **FRUIT PASSION**

1½ oz. brandy
½ oz. triple sec
½ oz. cherry liqueur
½ oz. lemon juice
Dash raspberry syrup or
    grenadine

Mix with cracked ice in a shaker or blender and strain into a chilled cocktail glass.

FUZZY BROTHER

1½ oz. brandy
½ oz. peach schnapps
4 oz. orange juice

Mix with cracked ice in a shaker or blender and serve in a chilled double Old Fashioned glass. Add additional ice, if necessary.

 GAZETTE

1½ oz. brandy
1 oz. sweet vermouth
1 tsp. lemon juice
1 tsp. sugar syrup

Mix all ingredients with cracked ice in a shaker or blender and pour into a chilled cocktail glass.

GEORGIA PEACH FIZZ

1½ oz. brandy
½ oz. peach brandy
½ oz. lemon juice
1 tsp. crème de banane
1 tsp. sugar syrup
Club soda
Fresh or brandied peach
  slice

Mix all ingredients, except club soda and peach slice, with cracked ice in a shaker or blender and pour into a chilled Collins glass. Fill with club soda, stir gently, and garnish with peach slice.

GINGER JONES

1½ oz. brandy
½ oz. ginger brandy
1 oz. orange juice
½ oz. lime juice
½ oz. sugar syrup or to taste
Preserved ginger

Mix all ingredients, except preserved ginger, with cracked ice in a shaker or blender and pour into a chilled Old Fashioned glass. Garnish with ginger.

GOLDEN CHAIN

1 oz. cognac
1 oz. Galliano
½ oz. lime juice
Dash yellow Chartreuse
Lime slice

Mix all ingredients, except lime slice, with cracked ice in a shaker or blender and strain into a chilled cocktail glass. Garnish with lime slice.

GOLDEN SLIPPER

1 oz. apricot brandy
1 oz. yellow Chartreuse
1 egg yolk

Mix all ingredients with cracked ice in a shaker or blender and pour into a chilled cocktail glass.

GOLF EL PARAISO

¾ oz. apple brandy
¾ oz. light rum
½ oz. orange juice
½ oz. lemon juice
¼ oz. grenadine
Orange slice

Mix all ingredients, except orange slice, with cracked ice in a shaker or blender and pour into a chilled Old Fashioned glass. Garnish with orange slice.

GOLFE JAUN

1½ oz. brandy
½ oz. maraschino liqueur
1 oz. pineapple juice
½ oz. lemon juice
½ tsp. kirsch

Mix all ingredients, except kirsch, with cracked ice in a shaker or blender and strain into a chilled cocktail glass. Top with a kirsch float.

THE GOOD DOCTOR

2 oz. coffee-flavored brandy
2 oz. half-and-half or cream
Dr Pepper or black raspberry
  soda
Pinch powdered cinnamon

Mix brandy and half-and-half with cracked ice in a shaker or blender and pour into a chilled highball glass. Fill with cold Dr Pepper and additional ice, if necessary. Sprinkle with cinnamon.

GOODNIGHT SWEETHEART COCKTAIL

1 oz. cognac
1 oz. apricot brandy
1 oz. port
1 tsp. sugar syrup or to taste
1 egg yolk
Lemon peel
Pinch of ground cinnamon

Mix all ingredients, except lemon peel and ground cinnamon, with cracked ice in a shaker or blender and pour into a chilled wine goblet. Twist lemon peel over drink and drop into glass.

GRANADA

1 oz. brandy
1 oz. fino sherry
½ oz. curaçao
Tonic water
Orange slice

Mix all ingredients, except tonic water and orange slice, with cracked ice in a shaker or blender and pour into a chilled highball glass. Fill with cold tonic, stir gently, and garnish with orange slice.

GRAND APPLE

1 oz. calvados
½ oz. cognac
½ oz. Grand Marnier
Lemon peel
Orange peel

Pour calvados, cognac, and Grand Marnier in a mixing glass with several ice cubes, stir well, and pour into a chilled Old Fashioned glass. Twist lemon and orange peels over drink and drop into glass.

GRANT PARK

1½ oz. apricot-flavored
    brandy
2 oz. orange juice
1 oz. lemon juice
½ oz. orgeat syrup or to taste

Mix with cracked ice in a shaker
or blender and pour into a
chilled cocktail glass.

GRENADIER

1½ oz. brandy
¾ oz. ginger-flavored brandy
Freshly grated ginger
Dash sugar syrup or to taste

Mix with ice cubes in a pitcher
and strain into a chilled cocktail
glass.

HALF MOON STREET

2 oz. brandy
1 oz. pineapple juice
½ oz. lemon juice
½ oz. sugar syrup
Several dashes lime juice
Club soda
Several dashes 151-proof
    Demerara rum
Orange slice

Mix all ingredients, except club
soda, rum, and orange slice,
with cracked ice in a shaker or
blender and pour into a chilled
Collins glass. Add several ice
cubes, fill with soda and float of
rum. Garnish with orange slice.

HARVARD

1½ oz. brandy
½ oz. sweet vermouth
¼ oz. lemon juice
1 tsp. grenadine
Dash Angostura bitters

Mix all ingredients with cracked
ice in a shaker or blender and
strain into a chilled cocktail
glass.

HIGH APPLEBALL

2 oz. apple brandy
Ginger ale or club soda
Lemon peel

Pour apple brandy into a chilled
highball glass with several ice
cubes, fill with ginger ale, and
stir gently. Twist lemon peel
over drink and drop into glass.

HO-HO-KUS POCUS

1 oz. applejack
1 oz. brandy
Several dashes bourbon

Mix all ingredients with cracked ice in a shaker or blender and pour into a chilled cocktail glass.

HONEYMOON

1½ oz. apple brandy
¾ oz. Benedictine
1 oz. lemon juice
Several dashes curaçao

Mix all ingredients with cracked ice in a shaker or blender and pour into a chilled cocktail glass.

HOTEL DU CAP

1 oz. applejack
½ oz. apricot brandy
¾ oz. lemon juice
1 tsp. grenadine
Dash orange bitters

Mix all ingredients with cracked ice in a shaker or blender and strain into a chilled cocktail glass.

ICHBIEN

2 oz. calvados
½ oz. curaçao
2 oz. milk or cream
1 egg yolk
Ground nutmeg

Mix all ingredients, except nutmeg, with cracked ice in a shaker or blender and strain into a chilled Delmonico glass. Sprinkle with nutmeg.

IMPERIAL HOUSE FRAPPÉ

1½ oz. port
¾ oz. brandy
1 egg yolk
Freshly grated nutmeg

Mix port, brandy, and egg yolk with plenty of cracked ice in a blender until slushy and pour into a chilled wine glass.

INCA PUNCH

1 oz. Pisco
½ oz. triple sec
1 oz. dry red wine
1½ oz. orange juice
1½ oz. pineapple juice
Mint sprig

Mix all ingredients, except mint sprig, with cracked ice in a shaker or blender and pour into a chilled Squall glass or wine goblet. Garnish with mint sprig.

JACK-IN-THE-BOX

1½ oz. applejack
1 oz. pineapple juice
1 oz. lemon juice
*Several dashes Angostura
bitters*

Mix all ingredients with cracked ice in a shaker or blender and pour into a chilled cocktail glass.

JACK RABBIT

1½ oz. applejack
½ oz. lemon juice
½ oz. orange juice
1 tsp. maple syrup or to taste

Mix all ingredients with cracked ice in a shaker or blender and strain into a chilled cocktail glass.

JACK ROSE

2 oz. applejack
½ oz. lime or lemon juice
1 tsp. grenadine

Mix all ingredients with cracked ice in a shaker or blender and strain into a chilled cocktail glass.

JANET HOWARD

2 oz. brandy
1¼ oz. orgeat syrup
*Several dashes Angostura
bitters*

Mix with cracked ice in a shaker or blender and strain into a chilled cocktail glass.

JAPANESE

2 oz. brandy
¼ oz. orgeat syrup
¼ oz. lime juice
Dash Angostura bitters
Lime peel

Mix all ingredients, except lime peel, with cracked ice in a shaker or blender and strain into a chilled cocktail glass. Twist lime peel over drink and drop into glass.

BARTENDER'S SECRET NO. 16—Fresh Ice

Fresh ice. No, it doesn't refer to freshening someone's glass with additional ice. It is an important consideration, especially for the home bartender. Ice that has been kept for a long time in a freezer not only will take on odors from meats, fish, and vegetables stored nearby but will become stale with the passage of time. You probably have experienced the flat, musty taste of water that has been stored for a long period of time in a sealed container or the unpleasant odor from an empty jar that has been closed and stored away in the back of a cupboard. Old ice can give an off-taste and odor to many mixed drinks, particularly those that require a generous amount of ice in their making. So, do as good hosts and experienced mixologists do: use fresh ice. It's the cheapest ingredient in any drink, so you might as well go first class.

JEAN LAFITE'S FRAPPÉ

1½ oz. brandy
1 oz. medium or dark Jamaica rum
½ oz. lemon or lime juice
1 tsp. orgeat syrup or Falernum
1 egg yolk

Mix with a generous amount of cracked ice in a blender for a few seconds until slushy and spoon into a chilled wine goblet.

JEAVONS HEAVEN

1 oz. cognac
1 oz. green Chartreuse

Mix with plenty of cracked ice in a blender for a few seconds and serve in a chilled cocktail glass.

JULY 4TH SALUTE

1 oz. cherry brandy
1 oz. white crème de cacao
1 oz. cream

Mix with cracked ice in a shaker or blender and strain into a chilled cocktail glass.

KAHLUA TOREADOR

2 oz. brandy
1 oz. Kahlua
1 egg white (for two drinks)

Mix all ingredients with cracked ice in a shaker or blender and pour into a chilled cocktail glass.

KATINKA'S PALINKA

2 oz. Zwack Barack Palinka
   apricot brandy
½ oz. lemon juice
1 tsp. sugar syrup or to taste
Club soda
Orange slice

Mix all ingredients, except club soda and orange slice, with cracked ice in a shaker or blender and pour into a chilled highball glass. Fill with club soda and garnish with orange slice.

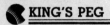 KING'S PEG

2–3 oz. cognac
Brut champagne

Pour cognac into a chilled wine goblet with several ice cubes and fill with cold champagne.

KISS THE BOYS GOODBYE

1 oz. brandy
1 oz. sloe gin
¼ oz. lemon juice
1 egg white (for two drinks)

Mix all ingredients with cracked ice in a shaker or blender and strain into a chilled cocktail glass.

KUHIO KOOLER

½ cup crushed pineapple
½ oz. sugar syrup or to taste
2 oz. brandy
Several dashes raspberry
   syrup
Club soda
Lemon peel
Pineapple stick

Combine crushed pineapple and sugar syrup in a mixing glass and muddle fruit. Add brandy, raspberry syrup, and several ice cubes and stir well. Pour into a chilled highball glass, fill with club soda, and stir gently. Twist lemon peel over drink and drop in. Garnish with pineapple stick.

LA GRANDE CASCADE

1 oz. brandy
½ oz. Parfait Amour
½ oz. lemon juice
½ oz. orange juice
Several dashes Cointreau

Mix all ingredients with cracked ice in a shaker or blender and pour into a chilled cocktail glass.

Created for the grand **Belle Epoque** restaurant in the Bois de Boulogne, **Paris.**

LA JOLLA

1½ oz. brandy
½ oz. crème de banane
¼ oz. lemon juice
1 tsp. orange juice

Mix all ingredients with cracked ice in a shaker or blender and strain into a chilled cocktail glass.

LAKE COMO

1½ oz. brandy
¾ oz. Tuaca
Lemon peel

Combine brandy and Tuaca liqueur in a mixing glass with several ice cubes, stir well, and pour into a chilled Old Fashioned glass. Twist lemon peel over drink and drop into glass.

LALLAH ROOKH COCKTAIL No. 2

1½ oz. cognac
½ oz. Jamaica rum
¼ oz. sugar syrup
¼ oz. vanilla extract
1 tsp. heavy cream

Mix all ingredients with cracked ice in a shaker or blender and pour into a chilled Old Fashioned glass.

LAYER CAKE

1 oz. crème de cacao
1 oz. brandy
1 oz. heavy cream
Halved maraschino cherry
    (optional)

Prechill all ingredients, including the Delmonico glass you will use to make this drink. Using a barspoon, carefully pour each liquid ingredient into the glass in layers in the order listed. Cut a cherry in half and carefully place the cut-end down on cream so it floats on top.

LE CAGNARD

2 oz. brandy
½ oz. Amer Picon
Lemon peel
Orange peel

Combine brandy and Amer Picon in a mixing glass with several ice cubes, stir well, and pour into a chilled Old Fashioned glass. Twist lemon and orange peels over drink and drop into glass.

LIBERTY

1½ oz. calvados
¾ oz. light rum
Several dashes sugar syrup
Maraschino cherry

Mix all ingredients, except maraschino cherry, with cracked ice in a shaker or blender, strain into a chilled cocktail glass, and garnish with cherry.

LIANO

1 oz. cognac
½ oz. Galliano
½ oz. Grand Marnier

Mix with cracked ice in a shaker or blender and strain into a chilled cocktail glass.

 ### LOUDSPEAKER

1 oz. brandy
1 oz. gin
¼ oz. Cointreau
½ oz. lemon juice

Mix with cracked ice and strain into a cocktail glass.

 ### MALIBU MOCHA

1½ oz. brandy
½ oz. crème de cacao
Cola
Maraschino cherry

Pour brandy and crème de cacao over ice in a chilled Collins glass and fill with cold cola. Garnish with cherry.

MARCONI WIRELESS

1½ oz. apple brandy
½ oz. sweet vermouth
Several dashes orange
  bitters

Mix all ingredients with cracked ice in a shaker or blender and pour into a chilled cocktail glass.

 ### MARGO MOORE

1½ oz. brandy
¾ oz. light rum
Several dashes curaçao
Bitter lemon soda

Pour brandy and rum over ice in a chilled Collins glass, add dashes of curaçao, and fill with cold bitter lemon soda. Stir gently.

MAYFAIR COCKTAIL

1 oz. cognac
1 oz. Dubonnet rouge
½ oz. lime juice
1 tsp. sugar syrup
Several dashes Angostura
    bitters
Orange peel

Mix all ingredients, except orange peel, with cracked ice in a shaker or blender and strain into a chilled cocktail glass. Twist orange peel over drink and drop into glass.

MÉDOC COCKTAIL

1½ oz. brandy
½ oz. Cordial Médoc
½ oz. lemon juice
Orange peel

Mix all ingredients, except orange peel, with cracked ice in a shaker or blender and strain into a chilled cocktail glass. Twist orange peel over drink and drop into glass.

MEMPHIS BELLE

1½ oz. brandy
¾ oz. Southern Comfort
½ oz. lemon juice
Several dashes orange
    bitters

Mix with cracked ice in a shaker or blender and strain into a chilled cocktail glass.

MERION'S CRICKET

2 oz. apricot brandy
½ oz. sloe gin
½ oz. lime juice

Mix all ingredients with cracked ice in a shaker or blender and pour into a chilled cocktail glass.

MERRY WIDOW No. 2

1½ oz. cherry brandy
1 oz. maraschino liqueur
Maraschino cherry

Mix all ingredients, except maraschino cherry, with cracked ice in a shaker or blender. Strain into a chilled cocktail glass and garnish with cherry.

METAXA ORANGE SOUR

1½ oz. Metaxa
¾ oz. Stolichnaya Orange
   Vodka
½ oz. lemon juice
½ oz. orange juice
1 tsp. sugar or to taste
Orange slice
Maraschino cherry

Mix all ingredients, except orange slice and cherry, with cracked ice in a shaker or blender and pour into a chilled Whiskey Sour glass. Adjust portions to suit your taste and garnish with orange slice and cherry.

Created by the author for Carillon Importers, Ltd.

MIKADO

1½ oz. brandy
Several dashes curaçao
Several dashes crème de
   noyaux
Several dashes orgeat syrup
Several dashes Angostura
   bitters

Mix all ingredients with cracked ice in a shaker or blender and pour into a chilled cocktail glass.

MONMOUTH PARK

1 oz. calvados
½ oz. white port
½ oz. apricot brandy
½ oz. lemon juice
Orange slice

Mix all ingredients, except orange slice, with cracked ice in a shaker or blender and strain into a chilled cocktail glass. Garnish with orange slice.

 ## THE MOOCH

2 oz. apricot brandy
6 oz. lemon-lime soda
Lemon twist

Mix brandy and soda with ice cubes in a chilled highball glass. Twist lemon peel over drink and drop into glass.

MOONRAKER

1½ applejack or calvados
¾ oz. light rum
½ oz. lime juice
½ oz. orgeat syrup or
   Falernum to taste
Apple slice

Mix all ingredients, except apple slice, with cracked ice in a shaker or blender and pour into a chilled Squall glass. Garnish with apple slice.

MONTPARNASSE

½ oz. cognac
1 tsp. kirsch
Dash orange bitters
1 tsp. orgeat syrup
Brut champagne
¼ cup lemon or orange ice

Mix cognac, kirsch, bitters, and syrup with cracked ice in a shaker or blender and strain into a chilled Squall or large tulip glass. Fill almost to the brim with cold champagne and top with lemon or orange ice float.

 MOON RIVER

1½ oz. brandy
½ oz. peppermint schnapps
Lemon-lime soda
Dash grenadine

Pour brandy and schnapps over ice in a chilled Collins glass, fill with cold soda, and stir gently. Top with a dash of grenadine.

MORNING

1 oz. brandy
1 oz. dry vermouth
Several dashes Pernod
Several dashes curaçao
Several dashes maraschino liqueur
Several dashes orange bitters
Maraschino cherry

Mix all ingredients, except maraschino cherry, with cracked ice in a shaker or blender, pour into a chilled Old Fashioned glass, and garnish with cherry.

MOTHER SHERMAN

1½ oz. apricot brandy
1 oz. orange juice
Several dashes orange bitters

Mix all ingredients with cracked ice in a shaker or blender and pour into a chilled cocktail glass.

MUSCATEL FLIP

2 oz. brandy
4 oz. muscatel wine
¼ oz. heavy cream
1 egg
1 tsp. sugar syrup or to taste
Ground nutmeg

Mix all ingredients, except nutmeg, with cracked ice in a blender until smooth. Serve in chilled parfait glass and sprinkle with nutmeg.

NEWTON'S GRAVITY APPLE

1½ oz. apple brandy
½ oz. curaçao or triple sec
Several dashes Angostura
  bitters

Mix all ingredients with cracked ice in a shaker or blender and strain into a chilled cocktail glass.

NINE-PICK

1 oz. brandy
1 oz. Pernod
1 oz. Cointreau
1 egg yolk

Mix all ingredients with cracked ice in a shaker or blender and pour into a chilled Delmonico glass.

NORMANDY COLLINS

2 oz. calvados
½ oz. lemon juice
1 tsp. sugar syrup
1 tsp. cream
1 egg white (for two drinks)
Club soda
Lime slice
Maraschino cherry

Mix all ingredients, except club soda, lime slice, and maraschino cherry, with cracked ice in a shaker or blender and pour into a chilled Collins glass. Fill with club soda, stir gently, and garnish with lime slice and cherry.

NORMANDY GOLD

1 oz. calvados
1 oz. gin
1 oz. apricot liqueur
1 oz. orange juice
Several dashes grenadine

Mix with cracked ice in a shaker or blender and strain into a chilled cocktail glass.

OAK ROOM SPECIAL

1 oz. cherry brandy
1 oz. brandy
1 oz. crème de cacao
1 egg white (for two drinks)

Mix all ingredients with cracked ice in a shaker or blender and strain into a chilled cocktail glass.

⬤ ODD McINTYRE

1 oz. brandy
1 oz. Cointreau or triple sec
1 oz. Lillet blanc
½ oz. lemon juice

Mix with cracked ice in a shaker or blender and strain into a chilled cocktail glass.

OLYMPIC

1 oz. brandy
1 oz. curaçao
1 oz. orange juice

Mix all ingredients with cracked ice in a shaker or blender and pour into a chilled cocktail glass.

OOM PAUL

1 oz. calvados or applejack
1 oz. Dubonnet rouge
Several dashes Angostura
   bitters

Mix all ingredients with cracked ice in a shaker or blender and pour into a chilled cocktail glass.

ORIENTA POINT

1 oz. brandy
1 oz. gin
Several dashes dry vermouth
Green olive

Mix all ingredients, except green olive, with cracked ice in a shaker or blender, strain into a chilled cocktail glass, and garnish with olive.

PANCHO VILLA No. 1

1 oz. brandy
1 oz. white or gold tequila
1 oz. light rum
1 tsp. cherry brandy or
   cherry liqueur
4 oz. pineapple juice

Mix all ingredients with cracked ice in a shaker or blender and pour into a chilled wine goblet.

PAVILION CAPRICE COOLER

½ oz. honey
4 oz. grapefruit juice,
   unsweetened
½ oz. lemon juice
1½ oz. peach brandy
1 egg white (for two drinks)

Blend honey, grapefruit juice, and lemon juice with a barspoon until honey is dissolved. Pour mixture into a blender with cracked ice and add brandy and egg white and blend until smooth. Serve in a chilled Squall glass or brandy snifter.

◤ PEACH FUZZ

1½ oz. peach brandy
½ oz. white crème de cacao
1 oz. heavy cream
1 tsp. apple schnapps

Mix all ingredients, except apple schnapps, with cracked ice in a shaker or blender and pour into a chilled cocktail glass. Top with a float of apple schnapps.

PEACHTREE SLING

1½ oz. brandy
¾ oz. peach brandy
½ oz. lemon juice
¼ oz. sugar syrup or to taste
Club soda
Brandied or fresh peach slice
1 tsp. peach liqueur

Mix all ingredients, except soda, peach slice, and peach liqueur, with cracked ice in a shaker or blender and pour into a chilled Collins glass. Fill with cold club soda and garnish with peach slice. Top off with peach liqueur float.

PEAR BRANDY FIZZ

1½ oz. pear brandy
1 tsp. lime juice
Club soda
Lemon peel
Pear strips (sliced
   lengthwise)

Pour brandy and lime juice in a chilled highball glass with several ice cubes, fill with club soda, and stir gently. Twist lemon peel over drink and drop into glass. Garnish with pear strips.

● PETER PIPER'S PINEAPPLE POP

1½ oz. apple brandy
½ oz. framboise
½ oz. pineapple juice
Lemon-lime soda
Pineapple stick

Mix all ingredients, except soda and pineapple stick, with cracked ice in a shaker or blender and pour into a chilled Collins glass. Fill with cold lemon-lime soda and garnish with pineapple stick.

PHILADELPHIA SCOTSMAN

1 oz. apple brandy
1 oz. port
1 oz. orange juice
Club soda

Mix all ingredients except club soda with cracked ice in a shaker or blender and pour into a chilled highball glass. Fill with club soda and stir gently.

 PHOEBE SNOW

1½ oz. cognac
1½ oz. Dubonnet rouge
Dash Pernod

Mix all ingredients with cracked ice in a shaker or blender and strain into a chilled cocktail glass.

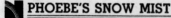 PHOEBE'S SNOW MIST

1 oz. cognac
1 oz. Dubonnet rouge
¼ oz. Pernod
1 egg white (for two drinks)
Lemon peel

Mix all ingredients, except lemon peel, with cracked ice in a shaker or blender and pour into a chilled Old Fashioned glass. Twist lemon peel over drink and drop into glass.

PINK WHISKERS

1 oz. apricot brandy
½ oz. dry vermouth
1 oz. orange juice
1 tsp. grenadine
Several dashes white crème de menthe
1 oz. port

Mix all ingredients, except port, with cracked ice in a shaker or blender and pour into a chilled cocktail glass. Top with a port float.

PISCO PUNCH

3 oz. Pisco
1 tsp. lime juice
1 tsp. pineapple juice
Several pineapple chunks

Mix all ingredients with plenty of cracked ice until smooth and pour into a chilled Squall glass or wine glass.

PISCO SOUR

2 oz. Pisco
½ oz. lemon juice
½ oz. sugar syrup
1 egg white (for two drinks)
Several dashes Angostura
    bitters

Mix all ingredients, except Angostura bitters, with cracked ice in a shaker or blender and strain into a chilled Whiskey Sour glass. Top with several dashes Angostura bitters.

PLACE VENDOME

1 oz. gin
1 oz. Cointreau
1 oz. apricot brandy

Mix with cracked ice in a shaker or blender and strain into a chilled cocktail glass.

POLONAISE

1½ oz. brandy
½ oz. blackberry brandy or
    blackberry liqueur
½ oz. dry sherry
Dash lemon juice

Mix all ingredients with cracked ice in a shaker or blender and pour into a chilled Old Fashioned glass.

POOP DECK

1 oz. blackberry brandy
½ oz. brandy
½ oz. port

Mix all ingredients with cracked ice in a shaker or blender and pour into a chilled cocktail glass.

PORT BEAM

1 oz. brandy
1 oz. ruby port
½ oz. lemon juice
¼ oz. maraschino liqueur
Orange slice

Mix all ingredients, except orange slice, with cracked ice in a shaker or blender, pour into a chilled cocktail glass, and garnish with orange slice.

PRAIRIE OYSTER

1 egg
1½ oz. brandy
Several dashes
  Worcestershire sauce
Dash cayenne powder
Dash Tabasco sauce
Dash celery salt

Separate egg and carefully place egg yolk, unbroken, in a Delmonico glass. Add all other ingredients and drink all together with egg yolk in a single swallow.

PRINCE ALBERT'S SALUTE

2 oz. cognac
2 oz. kümmel

Swirl cognac and kümmel in a brandy snifter until well blended. Add ice cubes, if you wish.

PRINCE OF WALES

1 oz. brandy
1 oz. Madeira
¼ oz. curaçao
Several dashes Angostura
  bitters
Champagne
Orange slice

Mix all ingredients, except champagne and orange slice, with cracked ice in a shaker or blender and pour into a chilled Squall glass or wine goblet. Fill with champagne, stir gently, and garnish with orange slice.

PRINCESS MARY'S PRIDE

1½ oz. calvados
¾ oz. Dubonnet rouge
½ oz. dry vermouth

Mix all ingredients with cracked ice in a shaker or blender and pour into a chilled cocktail glass.

QUAKER

1½ oz. brandy
1 oz. light rum
½ oz. lemon juice
½ oz. raspberry syrup
Lemon peel

Mix all ingredients, except lemon peel, with cracked ice in a shaker or blender and strain into a chilled cocktail glass. Twist lemon peel over drink and drop into glass.

RADNOR HUNT

1½ oz. mirabelle
1 oz. orange juice
½ oz. lemon juice
1 tsp. sugar syrup

Mix all ingredients with cracked ice in a shaker or blender and pour into a chilled stirrup cup or cocktail glass.

RAFFAELLO

½ oz. Pisco
½ oz. Galliano
½ oz. sweet vermouth
Dash Angostura bitters
Dash Grand Marnier

Mix with cracked ice in a shaker or blender and serve on the rocks in an Old Fashioned glass.

RASPBERRY RICKEY

1½ oz. framboise
½ oz. lime juice
1 tsp. sugar syrup or to taste
Club soda
6 fresh raspberries

Mix all ingredients, except raspberries and club soda, with cracked ice in a shaker or blender and strain into a chilled Squall or large tulip glass. Fill with cold club soda, add ice cubes if necessary, and garnish with raspberries.

RITTENHOUSE SQUARE

1½ oz. cognac
1 oz. curaçao
½ oz. anisette
Brandied cherry

Mix all ingredients, except brandied cherry, with cracked ice in a shaker or blender, strain into a chilled Old Fashioned glass, and garnish with cherry.

 ROYAL SMILE

2 oz. applejack
1 oz. gin
½ oz. lemon juice
1 tsp. grenadine

Mix with cracked ice in a shaker or blender and strain into a chilled cocktail glass.

RUSH STREET

1½ oz. brandy
½ Mandarine Napoleon
½ oz. lemon juice
Several dashes orgeat or
    sugar syrup

Mix with cracked ice in a shaker
or blender and strain into a
chilled cocktail glass.

SADDLE RIVER SECRET

2 oz. applejack
½ oz. triple sec
1 oz. apple juice
1 oz. cranberry juice
½ oz. lime or lemon juice
½ tsp. maple syrup or sugar
    syrup
Apple or lemon slice
½ tsp. 151-proof Demerara
    rum

Mix all ingredients, except fruit
slice and rum, with cracked ice
in a shaker or blender and pour
into chilled Squall glass or wine
goblet. Garnish with fruit slice
and top with rum float.

SARATOGA

2 oz. brandy
½ tsp. maraschino liqueur
1 oz. crushed pineapple or
    pineapple juice
Several dashes Angostura
    bitters

Mix all ingredients with cracked
ice in a blender and strain into
a chilled cocktail glass.

SAVOY HOTEL

1 oz. crème de cacao
1 oz. Benedictine
1 oz. cognac

Pour each ingredient carefully
into a chilled sherry glass using
the back of a barspoon so that
each ingredient floats upon the
one beneath it.

From **The Savoy, London.**

 SAVOY TANGO

1½ oz. apple brandy
1 oz. sloe gin

Combine all ingredients in a mixing glass with several ice cubes and stir well. Strain into a chilled cocktail glass.

From **The Savoy, London.**

SHARKY PUNCH

2 oz. calvados
½ oz. rye whiskey
1 tsp. sugar syrup
Club soda

Mix all ingredients, except club soda, with cracked ice in a shaker or blender and pour into a chilled Old Fashioned glass. Fill with cold club soda and stir gently.

SIDECAR

1½ oz. brandy
¾ oz. curaçao or triple sec
½ oz. lemon juice

Mix all ingredients with cracked ice in a shaker or blender and strain into a chilled cocktail glass.

From **Harry's New York Bar, Paris.**

SINK OR SWIM

1½ oz. brandy
½ oz. sweet vermouth
Several dashes Angostura bitters

Mix all ingredients with cracked ice in a shaker or blender and strain into a chilled cocktail glass.

SIR RIDGEWAY KNIGHT

1 oz. brandy
¾ oz. yellow Chartreuse
¾ oz. triple sec
Several dashes Angostura bitters

Mix with cracked ice in a shaker or blender and strain into a chilled cocktail glass.

SIR WALTER RALEIGH

1½ oz. brandy
¾ oz. light rum
1 tsp. curaçao
1 tsp. lime juice
1 tsp. grenadine

Mix all ingredients with cracked ice in a shaker or blender and pour into a chilled cocktail glass.

SLEDGE HAMMER

1 oz. brandy
1 oz. applejack
1 oz. dark Jamaica rum
Several dashes Pernod

Mix all ingredients with cracked ice in a shaker or blender and pour into a chilled cocktail glass.

SLEEPY HEAD

3 oz. brandy
Orange peel
4–5 mint leaves
Ginger ale

Pour brandy into a chilled high-ball glass with ice cubes. Twist orange peel over drink and drop into glass. Add mint leaves, which are slightly bruised, and fill with cold ginger ale. Stir gently.

SLIVOVITZ FIZZ

2 oz. slivovitz (plum brandy)
½ oz. lime juice
1 tsp. sugar syrup
Club soda
Plum slice

Mix brandy, lime juice, and sugar with cracked ice in a shaker or blender and pour into a chilled highball glass. Add more ice if necessary and fill with cold club soda. Garnish with plum slice.

SLOE BRANDY

2 oz. brandy
½ oz. sloe gin
1 tsp. lemon juice

Mix all ingredients with cracked ice in a shaker or blender and strain into a chilled cocktail glass.

SLOPPY JOE'S No. 2

1 oz. brandy
1 oz. port
1 oz. pineapple juice
½ tsp. triple sec
½ tsp. grenadine

Mix with cracked ice in a shaker or blender and strain into a chilled cocktail glass.

SOUTH PACIFIC

1½ oz. brandy
1 oz. gin or vodka
3 oz. grapefruit, pineapple, or orange juice
½ oz. lemon juice

Mix all ingredients with cracked ice in a shaker or blender and strain into a chilled Whiskey Sour glass.

SOUTHERN CROSS

1½ oz. brandy
½ oz. triple sec
Tonic water
Lime wedge

Pour brandy and triple sec over ice into a chilled Collins glass and fill with cold tonic water. Garnish with lime wedge.

SOUTH STREET SEAPORT

1 oz. brandy
1 oz. Madeira
¼ oz. dry vermouth
Lemon peel

Mix all ingredients, except lemon peel, with cracked ice in a shaker or blender and pour into a chilled Old Fashioned glass. Twist lemon peel over drink and drop into glass.

SPECIAL ROUGH

1½ oz. apple brandy
1½ oz. brandy
Several dashes Pernod

Mix all ingredients with cracked ice in a shaker or blender and pour into a chilled cocktail glass.

STINGER

1½ oz. brandy
1½ oz. white crème de menthe

Mix all ingredients with cracked ice in a shaker or blender and strain into a chilled cocktail glass.

STONE FENCE

2–3 oz. applejack
Several dashes Angostura
   bitters
Sweet apple cider

Pour applejack and bitters over ice cubes in a double Old Fashioned glass and fill with cold cider.

STRAWBERRY ROAN

2 oz. brandy
½ oz. lemon juice
½ oz. sugar syrup
1 tsp. strawberry liqueur

Mix all ingredients with cracked ice in a shaker or blender and strain into a chilled cocktail glass.

TANTALUS

1 oz. brandy
1 oz. lemon juice
1 oz. Forbidden Fruit

Mix all ingredients with cracked ice in a shaker or blender and pour into a chilled cocktail glass.

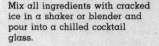 THE WHIP

1½ oz. brandy
¾ oz. sweet vermouth
¾ oz. dry vermouth
½ tsp. curaçao
Several dashes Pernod

Mix all ingredients with cracked ice in a shaker or blender and pour into a chilled cocktail glass.

333

1½ oz. calvados
1½ oz. Cointreau
1½ oz. grapefruit juice

Mix with cracked ice in a shaker or blender and strain into a chilled cocktail glass.

TORPEDO

1½ oz. calvados
¾ oz. brandy
Dash gin

Mix all ingredients with cracked ice in a shaker or blender and pour into a chilled cocktail glass.

TULIP

1 oz. apple brandy
¾ oz. apricot brandy
½ oz. sweet vermouth
½ oz. lemon juice

Mix all ingredients with cracked ice in a shaker or blender and pour into a chilled cocktail glass.

TUXEDO PARK

1½ oz. apple brandy
½ oz. white crème de menthe
Several dashes Pernod

Mix all ingredients with cracked ice in a shaker or blender and pour into a chilled brandy snifter.

VALENCIA

2 oz. apricot brandy
1 oz. orange juice
Several dashes orange bitters
Champagne (optional)

Mix all ingredients with cracked ice in a shaker or blender and pour into a chilled cocktail glass.

Some recipes call for chilled champagne, in which case use a large tulip glass or a wine goblet.

VANITY FAIR

1½ oz. applejack
½ oz. cherry brandy
½ oz. maraschino liqueur
1 tsp. amaretto or crème de noyaux

Mix all ingredients, except amaretto, with cracked ice in a shaker or blender and serve in a chilled cocktail glass. Top with a float of amaretto or crème de noyaux.

VIA VENETO

1½ oz. brandy
½ oz. sambuca
½ oz. lemon juice
1 tsp. sugar syrup
1 egg white (for two drinks)

Mix all ingredients with cracked ice in a shaker or blender and pour into a chilled Old Fashioned glass.

WASHINGTON

1½ oz. brandy
1 oz. dry vermouth
½ tsp. sugar syrup
Several dashes Angostura
  bitters

Mix all ingredients with cracked ice in a shaker or blender and strain into a chilled cocktail glass.

 WATERBURY

2 oz. cognac
½ oz. lemon juice
1 tsp. sugar syrup
1 egg white (for two drinks)
Several dashes grenadine

Mix all ingredients with cracked ice in a shaker or blender and pour into a chilled cocktail glass.

 WEEP NO MORE

1½ oz. cognac
1½ oz. Dubonnet rouge
1½ oz. lime juice
Dash maraschino liqueur

Mix all ingredients with cracked ice in a shaker or blender and strain into a chilled cocktail glass.

WHITEHALL CLUB

1 oz. brandy
½ oz. gin
½ oz. Grand Marnier
2 oz. orange juice
1 oz. lemon juice
½ oz. sugar syrup

Mix all ingredients with cracked ice in a shaker or blender and strain into a chilled parfait glass.

WHITE WAY

1 oz. cognac
1 oz. anisette
1 oz. Pernod

Combine all ingredients in a mixing glass with ice cubes and strain into a chilled cocktail glass.

WIDOW'S KISS

1 oz. applejack
½ oz. Benedictine
½ oz. yellow Chartreuse
Dash Angostura bitters
Fresh strawberry (optional)

Mix all ingredients, except strawberry, with cracked ice in a shaker or blender, strain into a chilled cocktail glass, and garnish with strawberry, if you wish.

WILLAWA

1½ oz. brandy
¾ oz. Galliano
¾ oz. cherry brandy
¾ oz. cream
Ground nutmeg

Mix all ingredients, except nutmeg, with cracked ice in a shaker or blender and strain into a chilled cocktail glass.

YELLOW PARROT

1 oz. brandy
1 oz. Pernod
1 oz. yellow Chartreuse

Mix all ingredients with cracked ice in a shaker or blender and pour into a chilled cocktail glass.

YOKOHAMA MAMA

1½ oz. brandy
½ oz. melon liqueur
Several dashes amaretto

Mix with cracked ice in a shaker or blender and strain into a chilled cocktail glass.

ZACK IS BACK WITH THE ZWACK

2 oz. Zwack's Barack Palinka apricot brandy
Dash dry vermouth or to taste
1–2 pepperoncini or other type of medium-hot pepper

Blend brandy and vermouth in a small pitcher or mixing glass with plenty of ice and stir briskly. Pour into a chilled cocktail glass and garnish with pepperoncini or medium-hot pepper.

BOURBON, BLENDS, AND CANADIAN WHISKY

> Did you ever hear of Captain Wattle?
> He was all for love
> and a little for the bottle.
> —Anonymous

Bourbon was not the first spirit distilled in the New World, but its widespread popularity has made it the most famous American whiskey. Over the years it has won recognition and respect as a true American "original" along with the turkey, baseball, hot dogs, apple pie, and, of course, corn, which made bourbon possible. During Colonial times, rum, distilled from molasses in New England, was the big drink, mainly because it was readily available and cheap. Brandy, port, and Madeira were popular with the affluent, but beyond the means of ordinary people, since they had to be imported from Europe at great cost.

Early in the eighteenth century Scotch, Irish, and Dutch settlers began making whiskey in various parts of Maryland, Virginia, and Pennsylvania, with the result that rye and barley became important cash crops. Farmers in outlying areas soon discovered that while a horse could carry only four bushels of grain to market, it could carry two kegs of whiskey—which represented two dozen bushels of grain after its conversion into spirits. Consequently, distilling became an important part of farming. In the early days of the republic it was estimated that there were over five thousand stills operating in western Pennsylvania alone.

This tremendous whiskey output presented a tempting tax source to Alexander Hamilton, the secretary of the treasury, who was hard-pressed to pay off the debts incurred by the government when financing the American Revolution. As a result, in 1791 an excise tax was placed on whiskey production. The distiller-farmers—an independent breed—didn't like it and ruffled the feathers of more than a few tax collectors (with a little tar thrown in for good measure). President George Washington responded by sending in the militia in 1794 to show the farmers that, then as now, Uncle Sam has the last word in tax matters. The government, as every American history student learns, quickly put down the Whiskey Rebellion. Nary a shot was fired, and the principle of the federal government's right to tax the products of American enterprise was firmly established.

To evade the long arm of the tax collector, many farmers pushed west into Native American territory, and it was in southern Indiana and over the Appalachians in the bluegrass country of Kentucky that they found a haven. More important was the wonderful water supply, essential to distilling good whiskey. This was provided by a unique geological phenomenon: a vast limestone mantel that runs underground through parts of Indiana and Kentucky. The water that passes through this limestone layer is naturally filtered, and is, as they say, "as sweet as a baby's kiss." Add to this an abundance of corn (it was more plentiful than rye), and all the elements for a truly fine native whiskey were in place.

Evan Williams of Louisville is generally credited as being the first distiller in Kentucky who plied his trade full-time, not just as a sideline. His whiskey, apparently, was not held in high esteem, however, for in 1783 he was reprimanded by the Louisville town council for bringing whiskey to an official meeting. And not only that, he received a further citation for the poor quality of the whiskey that he brought to the meeting!

Williams's whiskey probably was no worse than many. Distilling was not a precise art on the American frontier and was looked upon more as a means of preserving the harvest than a method of making a fine-flavored, aged, and mellow "sippin' whiskey." Much of the whiskey was produced haphazardly, and quality control was undreamed of in those early times. The beneficial effects of keeping spirits in wooden casks to age was well-known, but most producers were impatient to get their whiskey to market and so the "aging process" was determined by how long it took a pack horse to make the trip to town.

In the year 1789, or thereabouts, the Rev. Elijah Craig, a Baptist minister and sometime distiller, made an interesting discovery. He aged some corn whiskey in a charred oak barrel instead of the usual wooden container, which was uncharred. The resulting whiskey was not only smoother and mellower, but possessed a different flavor that was far superior to that made by traditional methods. It soon became apparent that a new name was needed for the new whiskey. The Reverend Craig lived in Georgetown, Kentucky, and since wines and spirits are frequently named for their places of origin, Georgetown was, no doubt, considered—and promptly discarded. The naming of a new product after a town named for an English monarch was not considered astute marketing, especially in those days. Why not name the new whiskey after the county in which Georgetown was located? A splendid idea. Besides, the county was named for another royal family—in France—who had aided the American cause during the Revolution. Thus, the new spirit became known far and wide as *bourbon*.

Although aging in charred oak was a boon to the finished product, other primitive methods for making distilled spirits remained, as illustrated by the manner in which alcoholic content was determined or "proved." Whiskey was mixed with gunpowder in equal proportions and ignited. If the mixture burned with a wavering yellow flame, it was too low in alcohol. If it burned rapidly with a bright blue flame, it was too strong. What was wanted was a blue flame that burned steadily, indicating to the still-man that the whiskey was about 50 percent alcohol. That is, 100 proof. This is the origin of the term "proof" used to this day to indicate alcoholic content.

Today bourbon is available in varying strengths as a straight whiskey ranging from 80 to 100 proof and slightly over; as a *blend* of straight whiskeys; as a sweet- or sour-mash bourbon; as a Kentucky or Tennessee bourbon; and as a regular or a bottled-in-bond whiskey. If all this seems somewhat confusing, here is a simplified explanation for the bourbon buyer:

Straight bourbon is the most common form in which this type of whiskey is marketed. There are also blended bourbons that, unlike straight bourbons, are whiskeys from various distilleries, made at different times. They are labeled "blended bourbon" as opposed to "straight bourbon," which must be made during the same distilling period and at the same distillery. In a blend, by law, the age given must be that of the youngest whiskey used.

Bourbon, in whatever form, must, according to federal law, be made of a grain formula containing at least 51 percent corn (other grains usually used are barley and rye) and aged in new charred oak barrels. Bourbon can be made anywhere in the U.S., but most of it, perhaps as much as 80 percent, comes from Kentucky. Tennessee whiskey, often called "Tennessee bourbon," is straight whiskey that may be made from a mash containing at least 51 percent corn or *any other grain*. It is filtered through charcoal to give it its characteristic flavor. Some Tennessee whiskeys have been promoted with a good deal of homespun kitsch, but the fact is, if it is a straight whiskey, it cannot legally contain any additives other than water. So except for the mash formula and the length of time it is aged in wood, Tennessee bourbon is like any other straight whiskey. Fine straight whiskeys are produced from other grains besides corn, rye being the classic example because it was one of the first whiskeys produced in the New World. Rye whiskey has a distinctive, full-bodied rye flavor and is not to be confused with ordinary blended whiskeys, which for many years in the Northeastern United States were called "ryes." True to their American Colonial roots, fine straight rye whiskeys are still produced in parts of Pennsylvania and Maryland.

There seems to be much confusion in many people's minds about the terms "sour mash" and "sweet mash," the former being heavily promoted to bourbon drinkers as part of the mystique of the master distiller who employs sour mash in some arcane way to make the "real thing." These terms refer to the yeasting process. They have nothing to do with a sweet or sour taste in the finished product. Sour mash is the preferred yeasting process for making bourbon. It means that a certain proportion of the mash used must contain stillage or spent liquids (sans alcohol) that remain from the previous distillation. This is mixed with fresh mash and fermented for the new batch. Sweet mash contains no stillage from the previous distillation. In other words, it is made from scratch, with nothing remaining from the old batch. It is doubtful that anyone but a professional spirits blender could tell whether a whiskey was made with sweet or sour mash.

Many people are under the impression that the term "bottled-in-bond" is a guarantee of quality. It is not. The Bottled-in-Bond Act passed by Congress in the 1890s allowed distillers to bottle certain distilled spirits without the necessity of paying the Internal Revenue excise taxes until the product was withdrawn from the warehouse to be sold. Certain conditions prevailed. Only straight whiskeys could qualify, meaning that they had to be distilled at one location, be 100 proof in strength, and be aged four years in wood. The whiskey was stored in a bonded warehouse under U.S. Treasury Department custody. There is no U.S. government certification, actual or implied, of the quality of the spirits held in bond. A poor whiskey placed in bond will undergo only a cosmetic transformation (on the label of the bottle), meaning it will change from a poor whiskey to a bonded poor whiskey.

If you count all the straight and blended bourbons on the market and add in all the private labels, it is estimated that there are about 500 brands available to the consumer. Reading whiskey labels doesn't give the buyer a clue as to what is inside the bottle except that it is whiskey. The best way to get to know bourbon is to indulge in a program of taste testing. A good way to begin is to mix a tot of whiskey with an equal amount of water (good spring water without a pronounced mineral taste) and sample it like the professional tasters do. When you find a bourbon that you like above all the rest, stick with it.

A Single Barrel, Small Batch Sampler

In the world of fine bourbons, the top of the line are whiskeys that are made in small batches under the expert eye of the distiller and those very special barrels that he selects to be bottled, undiluted, directly from the wood. Here is a blue ribbon selection. Each has its own unique qualitites, and for this reason we have made no effort to rank them. If you could sample them all, and pick one bourbon you like above all the rest, then that is the best choice for you. Individual tastes play an important role in the business of eating and drinking. In the final analysis, no one can tell you what you should like or dislike.

- **Baker's Kentucky Straight Bourbon,** Small Batch, 107 proof, seven years old.
- **Blanton's Single-Barrel Kentucky Straight Bourbon,** 93 proof.
- **Booker's Kentucky Straight Bourbon,** Small Batch, 126.1 proof, seven years, eight months old.
- **Hancock's Reserve Single-Barrel Kentucky Straight Bourbon,** 89 proof.
- **Jack Daniel's Single-Barrel Straight Tennessee Whiskey,** 94 proof.
- **Knob Creek Kentucky Straight Bourbon,** Small Batch, 100 proof, nine years old.
- **Maker's Mark Kentucky Straight Bourbon Limited Edition,** 101 proof.
- **Rock Hill Farms Single-Barrel Kentucky Straight Bourbon,** 100 proof.
- **Wild Turkey Kentucky Spirit Single-Barrel Kentucky Straight Bourbon,** 101 proof.

A Bourbon Classic

The most famous of the renowned classic bourbon drinks is unquestionably the Mint Julep. There are as many recipes as there are bartenders, and countless heated arguments have ensued over which recipe, hallowed by tradition and the benediction of time, will best convey—with authenticity, integrity, and professionalism—the blessings of flavor, bouquet, and well-being that are the hallmarks of a fine, aged bourbon.

Here is a recipe that was sent by an acquaintance who prides himself on the making of a good Mint Julep:

A REAL, HONEST-TO-GOD MINT JULEP

Practically everybody has heard of a Mint Julep, but few mixologists know how to concoct one properly. Mint Juleps originated in Williamsburg, Virginia, back in the seventeenth century, and the original Mint Julep has never been bettered. Here it is:

Break, and drop into a silver or pewter tankard with handle, fifteen or twenty (depending on size of leaves) fresh, I repeat, fresh mint leaves. Add a scant teaspoon of granulated sugar and two tablespoons of water. Then muddle the leaves until well crushed and sugar is dissolved. Fill tankard with finely crushed ice. Pour (don't measure) enough bourbon into tankard to come to about an inch below rim. After thoroughly stirring, add crushed ice to just below rim and float thereon a teaspoon of Barbados rum. Place three or four sprigs of mint into mixture, allowing mint to protrude several inches above rim. When imbibing, shove your nose into mint and sniff and quaff at the same time. Oh boy! My mouth is watering.

I've found that the ideal main ingredient in the julep is a 90 or 100 proof, sour-mash Kentucky bourbon. Ezra Brooks is just right, and I recommend it highly. Light Mount Gay rum makes an excellent float.

If you are expecting visitors, whip up enough juleps and place them in freezer for not more than a half hour before serving. Or, if you are expecting quite a few guests, I suggest that you prepare beforehand, a mash of muddled mint leaves, sugar, and water, always adhering strictly to the proportions in the recipe. Also, save time by readying sprigs of mint to stick their noses in. If you insist on starting with a frosted tankard, all right. Personally, I can never wait for a tankard to frost, and actually it doesn't enhance the taste of the nectar one whit.

I wish to God there'd been mint on Parris Island—and bourbon.

Sincerely,
Ben Finney

 **AMALFI COCKTAIL**

1½ oz. bourbon
1 oz. lemon juice
½ oz. Galliano
1 tsp. orgeat syrup
Club soda

Mix all ingredients, except club soda, in a shaker or blender with cracked ice. Pour into a chilled Collins glass. Fill with club soda.

ANCHORS AWEIGH

1 oz. bourbon
2 tsp. triple sec
2 tsp. peach brandy
2 tsp. maraschino liqueur
2 tbsp. heavy cream
Several drops of maraschino
  cherry juice

Mix all ingredients with cracked ice in a shaker or blender. Pour into a chilled Old Fashioned glass.

 **BANK HOLIDAY**

½ oz. bourbon
½ oz. Galliano
½ oz. crème de cacao
½ oz. brandy
1–2 oz. sweet cream

Mix all ingredients with cracked ice in a shaker or blender and strain into a chilled cocktail glass.

BEEF AND BOURBON

1½ oz. bourbon
4 oz. beef consommé or
  bouillon
Juice of ½ lemon
Several dashes
  Worcestershire sauce
Pinch celery seed or celery
  salt
Cucumber sticks (optional)

Stir all ingredients, except cucumber, with ice in a double Old Fashioned glass and garnish with cucumber sticks.

BISCAYNE MANHATTAN

1½ oz. bourbon
½ oz. sweet vermouth
2 oz. orange juice
Several dashes yellow
    Chartreuse
Orange slice

Mix all ingredients, except orange slice, with cracked ice in a shaker or blender, strain, and serve in a chilled cocktail glass. Garnish with orange slice.

BLIZZARD

3 oz. bourbon
1 oz. cranberry juice
1 tbsp. lemon juice
2 tbsp. sugar syrup

Mix all ingredients with plenty of cracked ice in a shaker or blender until drink is frosty. Serve in a chilled highball glass.

BLUE GRASS BLUES

1 oz. bourbon
1 oz. dry vermouth
Several dashes Angostura
    bitters
Several dashes of blue
    curaçao
Lemon peel

Mix all ingredients, except lemon peel, in a shaker or blender with cracked ice. Serve in a chilled Old Fashioned glass. Twist the lemon peel over the drink and drop in.

BLUE GRASS COCKTAIL

1½ oz. bourbon
1 oz. pineapple juice
1 oz. lemon juice
1 tsp. maraschino liqueur

Mix all ingredients with cracked ice in a shaker or blender. Strain into a chilled cocktail glass.

BOURBON A LA CRÈME

2 oz. bourbon
1 oz. dark crème de cacao
Several vanilla beans

Combine all ingredients in a shaker or blender with cracked ice and chill in the refrigerator for one hour. When ready, mix well and strain into a chilled cocktail glass.

BOURBON BRANCA

2 oz. bourbon
1 tsp. Fernet Branca
Lemon twist (optional)

Stir bourbon and Fernet Branca
with cracked ice in a chilled Old
Fashioned glass. If you wish,
add a twist of lemon.

BOURBON CARDINAL

2 oz. 100-proof bourbon
1 oz. grapefruit juice
1 oz. cranberry juice
½ oz. lemon juice
2 tsp. sugar or sugar syrup to
    taste
Generous dash maraschino
    cherry juice
2 maraschino cherries

Mix all ingredients with cracked
ice in blender and serve in a
chilled goblet.

BOURBON COBBLER

1½ oz. bourbon
1 oz. Southern Comfort
1 tsp. peach-flavored brandy
2 tsp. lemon juice
1 tsp. sugar syrup
Club soda
Peach slice

Mix all ingredients, except soda
and peach slice, with cracked
ice in a shaker or blender. Pour
into a chilled highball glass,
add ice cubes, fill with soda,
and decorate with peach slice.

BOURBON COLLINS No. 1

1½ oz. bourbon
½ oz. lime juice
1 tsp. sugar syrup or to taste
Club soda
Lime peel (optional)

Mix the bourbon and lime juice
with cracked ice in a shaker or
blender. Pour into a chilled 12-oz.
Collins glass and fill with club
soda. If you wish, twist the lime
peel and drop into the drink.

BOURBON COLLINS No. 2

2 oz. 100-proof bourbon
½ oz. lemon juice
1 tsp. sugar syrup or to taste
Several dashes of
    Peychaud's bitters
Club soda
Lemon slice (optional)

Mix all ingredients, except soda
and lemon slice, with cracked
ice in a shaker or blender. Pour
into a chilled highball glass and
fill with club soda. Decorate with
a lemon slice, if you wish.

BOURBON COOLER

3 oz. bourbon
½ oz. grenadine
1 tsp. sugar syrup or to taste
Several dashes peppermint
    schnapps
Several dashes orange
    bitters (optional)
Club soda
Pineapple stick
Orange slice
Maraschino cherry

Mix all ingredients, except soda, pineapple, orange slice, and cherry, in a blender or shaker with cracked ice. Pour into a chilled, tall Collins glass and fill with club soda. Garnish with fruit.

BOURBON CURE

2 oz. bourbon
1 oz. Dubonnet Blanc
1 tsp. Vieille Cure
Orange peel

Mix all ingredients, except the orange peel, with cracked ice in a shaker or blender. Pour into a chilled Old Fashioned glass. Twist the orange peel over the drink and drop in.

 BOURBON DAISY

1½ oz. bourbon
½ oz. lemon juice
1 tsp. grenadine
Club soda
1 tsp. Southern Comfort
Orange slice
Pineapple stick

Mix the bourbon, lemon juice, and grenadine with cracked ice in a shaker or blender. Pour into a chilled highball glass and fill with club soda. Float Southern Comfort on top. Garnish with an orange slice and pineapple stick.

BOURBON MILK PUNCH

1½ oz. bourbon
3 oz. milk or half-and-half
1 tsp. honey or sugar syrup
Dash vanilla extract
Nutmeg, grated

Mix all ingredients, except the nutmeg, in a shaker or blender with cracked ice. Pour into a chilled Old Fashioned glass. Sprinkle with nutmeg.

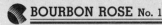 **BOURBON ROSE** No. 1

1½ oz. bourbon
1 oz. triple sec
4 oz. orange juice
Grenadine

Mix all ingredients, except grenadine, with cracked ice in a shaker or blender and pour into a chilled highball glass. Float some grenadine on top.

BOURBON ROSE No. 2

1½ oz. bourbon
½ oz. dry vermouth
½ oz. crème de cassis
¼ oz. lemon juice

Mix all ingredients with cracked ice in a shaker or blender. Serve in a chilled Old Fashioned glass.

BOURBON SATIN

1 oz. bourbon
1 oz. white crème de cacao
1 oz. heavy cream

Mix all ingredients with cracked ice in a shaker or blender. Strain into a chilled cocktail glass.

 **BOURBON SIDECAR**

1½ oz. bourbon
¾ oz. curaçao or triple sec
½ oz. lemon juice

Mix all ingredients with cracked ice in a shaker or blender and strain into a chilled cocktail glass.

BOURBON SLOE GIN FIZZ

1 tsp. sugar syrup or to taste
½ tsp. lemon juice
1½ oz. bourbon
¾ oz. sloe gin
Club soda
Lemon slice
Maraschino cherry

Pour syrup, lemon juice, bourbon, and sloe gin into a 14-oz. Collins glass, add a little cracked ice, and mix well. Add additional ice, fill with club soda, and garnish with lemon slice and cherry.

BOURBON SOUR

2 oz. bourbon
Juice of ½ lemon
½ tsp. sugar or sugar syrup
Orange slice

Mix all ingredients, except orange slice, in a shaker or blender with cracked ice. Strain into a chilled Whiskey Sour glass. Garnish with a slice of orange.

BRIGHTON PUNCH

1 oz. bourbon
1 oz. cognac
¾ oz. Benedictine
Juice of ½ lemon
Juice of ½ orange
1 tsp. sugar syrup or to taste
Club soda
Orange slice

Mix all ingredients, except soda and orange slice, with cracked ice in a shaker or blender and pour into a chilled highball or Collins glass. Fill with soda, stir gently, and garnish with orange slice.

CHAMPAGNE JULEP

Several sprigs of mint
1 tsp. sugar syrup
3 oz. bourbon
Brut champagne or dry
    sparkling wine.

Remove a half-dozen mint leaves from sprig and put them in a tall Collins glass with syrup and muddle. Fill glass two-thirds full with cracked ice, pour in bourbon, and stir briskly. Add additional ice if necessary and fill with ice-cold champagne or sparkling wine. Stir gently and garnish with a large mint sprig.

CHURCHILL DOWNS COOLER

1½ oz. bourbon
1 oz. crème de banane
½ oz. triple sec
3 oz. pineapple juice
½ oz. lemon juice
Club soda
Pineapple slice
Maraschino cherry

Mix all ingredients, except soda, pineapple slice, and cherry, with cracked ice in a shaker or blender and pour into a 14-oz. Collins glass and fill with soda. Garnish with pineapple slice and cherry.

COLONEL LEE'S COOLER

1 oz. bourbon
1 oz. brandy
2 tsp. triple sec
4 oz. ginger ale

Mix the bourbon, brandy, and triple sec with cracked ice in a chilled highball glass and gently stir. Fill with ginger ale.

COMMODORE COCKTAIL No. 2

1½ oz. bourbon
¾ oz. white crème de cacao
½ oz. lemon juice

Mix all ingredients with cracked ice in a shaker or blender and strain into a chilled cocktail glass.

COOL COLONEL

1½ oz. bourbon
1 oz. Southern Comfort
3 oz. strong tea, chilled
½ oz. lemon juice
1 tsp. sugar syrup or to taste
Club soda
Lemon peel

Mix all ingredients, except soda and lemon peel, in a shaker or blender with cracked ice. Pour into a chilled, tall Collins glass, fill with soda, and twist lemon peel over drink and drop into glass.

CRESCENT CITY SPECIAL

2 oz. bourbon
1 tsp. Herbsaint or Pernod
½ tsp. orgeat or sugar syrup
Several dashes Peychaud's bitters
Lemon twist

Stir all ingredients, except lemon twist, in a double Old Fashioned glass with ice, twist lemon peel over drink, and drop in glass.

DEER JUICE

1½ oz. bourbon
2 oz. sweet-and-sour mix
2 oz. orange juice
4 oz. 7-Up
Several dashes lemon juice
Dash grenadine

Mix bourbon, sweet-and-sour mix, and orange juice with cracked ice in a shaker or blender and pour into a large, chilled cooler glass with several ice cubes. Fill with cold 7-Up, stir gently, and top with a squeeze of lemon juice and a dash of grenadine.

This is a house specialty of **Loews Santa Monica Beach Hotel, Santa Monica, California.**

DERBY DAY SPECIAL

1 oz. bourbon
1 oz. heavy cream
1 oz. crème de banane
Dash Grand Marnier

Mix all ingredients with cracked ice in a shaker or blender. Serve in a chilled Old Fashioned glass.

 A DRY MAHONEY

6 parts bourbon (2½ oz.)
1 part dry vermouth (½ oz.)
Lemon peel

Stir all ingredients, except lemon peel, with ice and strain into a chilled cocktail glass. Twist lemon peel over drink and drop rind in glass. Serve with an ice cube or two on the side in a second glass.

This is a New York ad man's version of the classic dry Manhattan.

EASTERLY

1 oz. Pernod
1 oz. bourbon or gold rum
½ oz. amaretto
4 oz. pineapple juice

Mix all ingredients with cracked ice in a shaker or blender and serve in a chilled 12-oz. Collins glass.

FATHER'S MILK

1½-2 oz. bourbon
1 tsp. sugar syrup or to taste
1 cup milk
Nutmeg (optional)

Mix bourbon and syrup with milk in a tall highball glass with cracked ice and dust with grated nutmeg. For a frothy drink, mix in blender and pour into a highball glass.

FLINTLOCK

1½ oz. bourbon
½ oz. applejack
1 tsp. lemon juice
Several dashes grenadine
Several dashes peppermint
    schnapps

Mix all ingredients with cracked ice in a shaker or blender. Strain into a chilled cocktail glass.

FORESTER

1½ oz. bourbon
¾ oz. cherry liqueur
1 tsp. lemon juice
Maraschino cherry

Mix all ingredients, except cherry, with cracked ice in a shaker or blender. Pour into a chilled Old Fashioned glass. Garnish with cherry.

THE FONTAINEBLEU SIDECAR

2 oz. bourbon
1 oz. curaçao or Cointreau
Juice of ½ lemon
Grand Marnier float

Mix all ingredients, except Grand Marnier, with cracked ice in a shaker or blender and pour into a chilled wine goblet. Float a teaspoon or two of Grand Marnier on top.

FRENCH TWIST

1½ oz. bourbon
1½ oz. brandy
½ oz. Grand Marnier
1 tsp. lemon juice

Mix all ingredients with cracked ice in a shaker or blender. Strain into a chilled cocktail glass.

FROZEN MINT JULEP

2 oz. bourbon
1 oz. lemon juice
1 oz. sugar syrup
6 small mint leaves
Mint sprig

Muddle mint leaves with bourbon, lemon juice, and syrup in a bar glass. Put all ingredients, except mint sprig, in a blender with finely crushed ice and mix at high speed for no longer than 15 seconds or until ice becomes mushy. Serve in a chilled double Old Fashioned glass and garnish with a sprig of mint.

GINZA

2 oz. bourbon
1 oz. sake
1 tsp. sugar syrup or to taste
1 tsp. lemon juice
Orange slice

Mix all ingredients, except orange, with cracked ice in a shaker or blender. Pour into a chilled cocktail glass. Garnish with orange slice.

GOLDEN GLOW

1½ oz. bourbon
½ oz. Jamaica rum
2 oz. orange juice
1 tsp. lemon juice
Falernum or sugar syrup to
    taste
Dash grenadine

Mix all ingredients, except grenadine, with cracked ice in a shaker or blender, strain, and pour into a chilled cocktail glass. Top with a grenadine float.

GRENOBLE COCKTAIL

1½ oz. bourbon
½ oz. framboise
½ oz. triple sec
1 oz. orange juice
1 tsp. orgeat syrup

Mix all ingredients with cracked ice in a shaker or blender. Serve in a chilled cocktail glass.

 HAWAIIAN EYE

1½ oz. bourbon
½ oz. crème de banane
1 oz. Kahlua
3–4 oz. pineapple juice
1 oz. heavy cream
Dash Pernod (optional)
1 egg white
Pineapple slice
Cherry

Mix all ingredients, except pineapple slice and cherry, with cracked ice in a shaker or blender at high speed for 15 seconds. Pour into a chilled highball glass. Garnish with a pineapple slice and cherry.

HEARN'S COCKTAIL

¾ oz. bourbon or Irish
    whiskey
¾ oz. sweet vermouth
¾ oz. Pernod
Several dashes Angostura
    bitters

Mix all ingredients with cracked ice in a shaker or blender. Serve in a chilled Old Fashioned glass.

 ## HUNTRESS COCKTAIL

1 oz. bourbon
1 oz. cherry liqueur
1 oz. heavy cream
Dash triple sec

Mix all ingredients thoroughly in a shaker or blender with cracked ice. Strain and serve in a chilled cocktail glass.

ITALIAN STALLION

1½ oz. bourbon
½ oz. Campari
½ oz. sweet vermouth
Dash Angostura bitters
Lemon peel

Stir all ingredients, except lemon peel, with ice in a pitcher and strain into a chilled cocktail glass. Twist lemon peel over drink and drop into glass.

JAMAICA SHAKE

1½ oz. bourbon
1 oz. Jamaica dark rum
1 oz. heavy cream

Mix all ingredients with cracked ice in a shaker or blender. Strain into a chilled cocktail glass.

 ## KENTUCKY CHAMPAGNE COCKTAIL

1 oz. 100-proof bourbon
½ oz. peach liqueur
Several dashes bitters
Champagne
Peach slice

Mix the bourbon, peach schnapps, and bitters in a chilled wine goblet and stir with ice cubes. Fill with champagne. Garnish with peach slice.

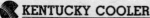 ## KENTUCKY COOLER

1½ oz. bourbon
¾ oz. brandy
1 oz. lemon juice
2 tsp. sugar syrup or to taste
Club soda
Barbados rum

Mix all ingredients, except soda and rum, in a shaker or blender with cracked ice. Pour into a chilled 14-oz. Collins glass, add ice, and fill with club soda. Add a float of rum.

KENTUCKY ORANGE BLOSSOM

1½ oz. bourbon
½ oz. triple sec
1 oz. orange juice
Lemon peel

Mix all ingredients, except lemon peel, with cracked ice in a shaker or blender. Pour into a chilled Old Fashioned glass. Twist the lemon peel over the drink and drop in.

KEY WEST COCKTAIL

1½ oz. bourbon
1 oz. orange juice
1 oz. pineapple juice
1 tsp. lemon juice
Several dashes Angostura
    bitters
Orgeat or sugar syrup to
    taste

Mix all ingredients with cracked ice in a shaker or blender. Pour into a chilled Old Fashioned glass.

 LITTLE COLONEL

2 oz. bourbon
1 oz. Southern Comfort
1 oz. lime juice

Mix all ingredients with cracked ice in a shaker or blender and strain into a chilled cocktail glass. If a sweeter drink is desired, add more Southern Comfort.

LOUISVILLE STINGER

1 oz. bourbon
1 oz. light rum
2 tsp. white crème de cacao
2 tsp. white crème de
    menthe

Mix all ingredients with cracked ice in a shaker or blender. Serve in a chilled cocktail glass.

MAN O' WAR

2 oz. bourbon
1 oz. orange curaçao
½ oz. sweet vermouth
Juice of ½ lime

Mix all ingredients with cracked ice in a shaker or blender. Pour into a chilled cocktail glass.

MANHATTAN, BOURBON

1½–2 oz. bourbon
½ oz. sweet vermouth
Dash bitters (optional)
Maraschino cherry

Pour the bourbon, vermouth, and bitters in a shaker along with ice cubes and stir. Strain into a chilled cocktail glass. Garnish with a maraschino cherry.

MILLIONAIRE COCKTAIL No. 2

1½ oz. bourbon
½ oz. Pernod
Several dashes curaçao
Several dashes grenadine
1 egg white (for two drinks)

Mix all ingredients with cracked ice and strain into a chilled cocktail glass.

 ## MINT CONDITION

¾ oz. bourbon
¾ oz. peppermint schnapps
¾ oz. vodka
½ oz. Kahlua

Mix all ingredients with cracked ice in a shaker or blender. Serve in a chilled Whiskey Sour glass.

MIRAMAR

2½ oz. bourbon
½ oz. Benedictine

Mix ingredients with cracked ice in a shaker or blender. Strain into a chilled cocktail glass.

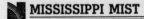 ## MISSISSIPPI MIST

1½ oz. bourbon
1½ oz. Southern Comfort

Pour bourbon and Southern Comfort into an Old Fashioned glass. Fill with crushed ice and gently stir.

NEVINS COCKTAIL

1½ oz. bourbon
½ oz. apricot liqueur
1 oz. grapefruit juice
1 tsp. lemon juice
Several dashes Angostura
  bitters

Mix all ingredients with cracked ice in a shaker or blender. Serve in an Old Fashioned glass.

NEW ORLEANS COCKTAIL

1½ oz. bourbon
½ oz. Pernod
Dash orange bitters
Several dashes Angostura
　bitters
Dash anisette
Sugar syrup to taste
Lemon peel

Mix all ingredients, except lemon peel, with cracked ice in a shaker or blender. Pour into a chilled Old Fashioned glass. Twist the lemon peel over drink and drop in.

 **OLD FASHIONED**

1½–2 oz. bourbon, blended
　whiskey, Canadian, or rye
Dash water
Dash sugar syrup or to taste
Dash or two Angostura
　bitters

Mix all ingredients in an Old Fashioned glass and add several ice cubes (no fruit).

PADDOCK SPECIAL

2 oz. bourbon
1 oz. green crème de menthe
Juice of ½ lime
1 tsp. sugar syrup or to taste
6 small mint leaves
Club soda
Mint sprig

Add bourbon, crème de menthe, lime juice, syrup, and mint leaves to a bar glass and muddle leaves well. Put into a blender with cracked ice and mix well. Pour into a chilled Collins glass and fill with soda. Garnish with mint sprig.

PADUCAH PALOOKAH

1½ oz. bourbon
½ oz. apricot-flavored brandy
Juice of ½ lime
1 tsp. sugar syrup or to taste
Dash grenadine
Lime slice
Maraschino cherry

Mix all ingredients, except lime slice and cherry, with cracked ice in a shaker or blender and strain into a chilled Old Fashioned glass. Garnish with lime slice and cherry.

PAPARAZZI No. 2

1½ oz. bourbon
½ oz. sweet vermouth
½ oz. Fernet Branca
Several dashes anesone
  liqueur or Pernod

Mix all ingredients with cracked ice in a shaker or blender. Strain into a chilled cocktail glass.

POLO DREAM

1½–2 oz. bourbon
1 oz. orange juice
¾ oz. orgeat syrup or to taste

Mix with cracked ice in a shaker or blender and strain into a chilled cocktail glass.

PORT LIGHT

2 oz. bourbon
½ oz. La Grande Passion or
  passion fruit juice
½ oz. honey
1 oz. lemon juice
1 egg white (for two drinks)
Mint sprigs (optional)

Mix all ingredients, except mint sprigs, with cracked ice in a shaker or blender and pour into a Collins glass. Garnish with mint.

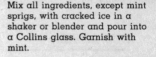 PRESBYTERIAN

2–3 oz. bourbon
Ginger ale
Club soda

Pour bourbon into a chilled highball glass, add ice cubes, and fill with equal parts of ginger ale and club soda.

PRIDE OF PADUCAH

2 oz. bourbon
1 oz. dark crème de cacao
1 oz. heavy cream
Several almonds, toasted
  and slivered

Mix all ingredients, except almonds, in a shaker or blender with cracked ice. Pour into a chilled Old Fashioned glass. Decorate with slivered almonds.

QUICK AND EASY MINT JULEP

Several mint sprigs
1 tsp. superfine sugar
1 tsp. water
3 oz. bourbon

Muddle mint sprigs in a double Old Fashioned glass with sugar and water until sugar is dissolved. Fill glass with finely crushed ice and add bourbon. Stir briskly with an iced-tea spoon. Garnish with a mint sprig.

RANGOON SWOON

1 oz. bourbon
1 oz. triple sec
1 oz. crème de banane
Juice of 1 lemon
3 oz. pineapple juice

Mix all ingredients with cracked ice in a shaker or blender and serve in a large, chilled glass.

This is a special house drink of the **Rangoon Racquet Club, Beverly Hills.**

RED ROVER

1½ oz. bourbon
½ oz. sloe gin
½ oz. lemon juice
1 tsp. sugar syrup
Lemon slice
Peach slice (optional)

Mix all ingredients, except lemon and peach slices, in a shaker or blender with cracked ice, strain and pour into a chilled cocktail glass. Garnish with the lemon slice and peach slice.

 ## RODEO DRIVE RAMMER

1½ oz. bourbon
½ oz. peach brandy
½ oz. curaçao
½ oz. Jamaica rum
3 oz. orange juice
1 tsp. orgeat syrup,
    Falernum, or sugar syrup
Club soda
Pineapple slice
Maraschino cherry

Mix all ingredients, except soda, pineapple, and cherry, with cracked ice in a shaker or blender and pour into a 14-oz. Collins glass. Fill with soda, stir gently, and garnish with pineapple and cherry.

ROUND HILL SPECIAL

1½ oz. bourbon
½ oz. Jamaica dark rum
2 tsp. orange juice
2 tsp. lemon juice
1 tsp. orgeat syrup

Mix all ingredients with cracked
ice in a shaker or blender. Strain
into a chilled cocktail glass.

ROYAL ROOST

¾ oz. bourbon or rye
¾ oz. Dubonnet rouge
Several dashes curaçao
Several dashes Pernod
Pineapple slice
Orange slice
Lemon peel
Generous dashes Peychaud's
    bitters (optional)

Mix all ingredients, except orange and pineapple slices,
lemon peel, and bitters, with
cracked ice in a mixing glass
and strain into a chilled Old
Fashioned glass with several ice
cubes. Garnish with fruit and top
with bitters.

ROYAL WHISKEY SOUR

2 oz. bourbon, rye, Canadian
    or blended whiskey
Juice of ½ lemon
1 tsp. sugar syrup or to taste
2 brandied maraschino
    cherries

Mix all ingredients with cracked
ice in a blender until cherries
are chopped fine and pour into a
Whiskey Sour glass.

S.S. MANHATTAN

1½ oz. bourbon
½ oz. Benedictine
2 oz. orange juice

Mix all ingredients with cracked
ice in a shaker or blender and
pour into a chilled cocktail
glass.

SARATOGA FIZZ

1½ oz. bourbon
1 tsp. lemon juice
1 tsp. lime juice
1 tsp. sugar syrup or to taste
1 egg white
Club soda
Maraschino cherry

Mix all ingredients, except club
soda and cherry, with cracked
ice in a shaker or blender. Pour
into a chilled highball glass and
fill with cold club soda. Garnish
with cherry.

SAVANNAH SATIN

1½ oz. Pernod
1 oz. gin, bourbon, or light rum
1 oz. light cream
1 egg white (for two drinks)
1 tsp. sugar or to taste

Mix all ingredients with cracked ice in a shaker or blender and serve in a chilled cocktail glass.

SEAGIRT COCKTAIL

1½ oz. bourbon
2 oz. grapefruit juice
1 oz. cranberry juice
½ tsp. orgeat syrup

Mix all ingredients with cracked ice in a shaker or blender. Strain into a chilled cocktail glass.

SHERRY TWIST No. 3

1½ oz. bourbon or blended whiskey
¾ oz. cocktail sherry
Lemon peel

Pour the bourbon or blended whiskey and sherry into a shaker with cracked ice and stir. Strain into a chilled cocktail glass. Twist the lemon peel over drink and drop in.

SMOOTH SAILING

2 oz. bourbon
2 oz. half-and-half or cream
Club soda

Mix bourbon and cream with cracked ice in a shaker or blender and strain into a chilled Old Fashioned glass. Fill with cold club soda and stir gently.

SOUTHERN GINGER

1½ oz. 100-proof bourbon
1 tsp. ginger-flavored brandy
1 tsp. lemon juice
Ginger ale
Lemon twist

Mix all ingredients, except ginger ale and lemon twist, with cracked ice in a shaker or blender and pour into a double Old Fashioned glass. Fill with ginger ale, twist lemon over drink, and drop peel into glass.

SOUTHSIDE

6 mint leaves
1 tsp. sugar syrup or to taste
Juice of ½ lemon
1½–2 oz. bourbon
Spring water

Muddle mint leaves in sugar and lemon juice, add bourbon, a little spring water, crushed ice, and muddle again. Garnish with additional mint leaves if you wish.

SPRING HOUSE SOUR

1½ oz. bourbon
½ oz. peppermint schnapps
1 tbsp. lemon juice
1 tsp. sugar syrup or to taste
Mint sprig (optional)
Maraschino cherry

Mix all ingredients, except mint and cherry, in a shaker or blender with cracked ice and pour into an Old Fashioned glass. Garnish with mint sprig and cherry.

 ## STINGER SOUR

1½ oz. bourbon
1 tbsp. lemon juice
Several dashes peppermint
   schnapps
Sugar syrup to taste

Mix all ingredients with cracked ice in a shaker or blender. Serve in a chilled cocktail glass.

SWEET AND SOUR BOURBON

1½ oz. bourbon
4 oz. orange juice
Pinch or two sugar
Pinch salt
Maraschino cherry

Mix all ingredients, except cherry, in a shaker or blender with cracked ice and pour into a Whiskey Sour glass. Garnish with cherry.

THREE-BASE HIT

1 oz. bourbon
1 oz. light rum
1 oz. brandy
2 tsp. lemon juice
Falernum or sugar syrup to
   taste

Mix all ingredients with cracked ice in a shaker or blender. Strain into a chilled cocktail glass.

TIVOLI COCKTAIL

1½ oz. bourbon
½ oz. sweet vermouth
½ oz. aquavit
Dash Campari

Mix all ingredients with cracked ice in a shaker or blender and strain into a chilled cocktail glass.

 TROLLEY COOLER

2 oz. bourbon
Pineapple juice
Cranberry juice

Pour the bourbon into a highball glass to which ice has been added. Fill the glass with equal parts of pineapple and cranberry juices and stir.

WALDORF COCKTAIL

1½ oz. bourbon
¾ oz. Pernod
½ oz. sweet vermouth
Dash Angostura bitters

Stir with ice and strain into a chilled cocktail glass.

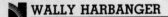 WALLY HARBANGER

1 oz. bourbon
½ oz. Galliano
1 oz. lemon juice
1 tsp. sugar syrup
Sprig of mint (optional)

Mix all ingredients, except mint sprig, with crushed ice in a shaker or blender. Serve in a chilled Old Fashioned glass. Decorate with a sprig of mint.

 WARD EIGHT

1½–2 oz. bourbon
1 oz. lemon juice
1 oz. orange juice
Sugar syrup to taste
Dash grenadine

Mix all ingredients with cracked ice in a shaker or blender and strain into a chilled cocktail glass.

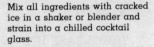 WHIRLAWAY

2 oz. bourbon
1 oz. curaçao
Several dashes Angostura bitters
Club soda

Mix all ingredients, except soda, in a blender or shaker with cracked ice. Pour into a chilled Old Fashioned glass and top with club soda.

1½ oz. 100-proof bourbon
½ oz. 86-proof Demerara rum
1 oz. lemon juice
1 oz. orange juice
1 oz. grapefruit juice
1 tbsp. sugar or sugar syrup
   to taste
Dash maraschino cherry
   juice

Mix all ingredients with cracked ice in a shaker or blender and pour into double Old Fashioned glass.

151-proof Demerara rum may be used for the hearty drinker.

WHISPER OF A KISS

1½ oz. bourbon
¾ oz. apricot liqueur
½ tsp. lemon juice
1 tsp. grenadine

Mix with cracked ice in a shaker or blender, strain, and serve in a chilled cocktail glass.

Blended Whiskey

Blended whiskey is a combination of various straight whiskeys, grain spirits, and, in some cases, light whiskeys. The whiskeys and spirits are carefully selected by the blender to produce a flavorful, well-balanced, smooth, and harmonious formula that can be precisely duplicated and quality-controlled over an extended period of time on a full production basis. The blend must contain at least 20 percent straight whiskeys while the remainder may be grain neutral spirits (spirits distilled out at 190 proof or more, which are later reduced in proof for blending purposes), or grain spirits (neutral spirits that are aged in wood to produce a certain amount of mellowing and delicate flavor overtones), or light whiskeys, or any combination thereof.

Much of the whiskey that is popular today is blended. This reflects a growing trend toward lighter food and beverages of all kinds. By the term "lighter," in the popular sense, we mean not only light-bodied but less filling. It is the general desire for a lack of heaviness that explains a gradual movement in the American brewing industry away from the traditional rich, hoppy, full-bodied European-style beers and ales and toward a pale, dry, light-bodied product with high carbonation and far less intensity of flavor.

Light whiskeys, themselves a relatively recent category in

distilled spirits in the U.S., are distilled at high proofs, over 160, and stored in seasoned, or used, charred oak containers. The resulting whiskey has much less flavor presence than a straight whiskey. It is valuable in making blended whiskey because it can be used to replace grain neutral spirits in the blend, thus giving more character to the finished product while still retaining a light body.

Watching a master blender at work is fascinating, and will give anyone a new appreciation of the complexities involved in developing a blended whiskey. He sits at a large, round, revolving table. Lining the edge of the table will be as many as sixty glasses. Sherry glasses are best for nosing spirits samples because their modified tulip shape concentrates the aroma. Each glass has an identification code inscribed on its foot. A watch crystal is placed on top of the glass to prevent evaporation. The blender, using nose and mouth and drawing upon a prodigious memory for all the nuances of taste and smell, proceeds to move from glass to glass, noting colors— ranging from clear through straw, fawn, sand, beige, tan, and amber to rich walnut, dark mahogany, and tobacco brown— sniffing, tasting, comparing, remembering other scents and flavors from other times. His concentration is broken only when he pauses to make notes. If he is creating a new blended whiskey, he and his assistants may check hundreds of samples from the spirits "library." The final selection for the blend, after testing many, many combinations, may comprise as many as 50 different distilled components.

The care that is taken in the blending laboratory to keep unwanted and extraneous elements from interfering with the blending process is vital, for the blender must keep his senses sharp and in tune. The glasses are all steam-cleaned to prevent a soap or detergent residue from building up. Each sample is reduced to exactly 40 proof (20 percent alcohol) by adding demineralized spring water to the whiskey. The serious whiskey drinker need not be this fastidious, but it should be noted that spring water used as a mixer (as well as to make ice cubes) will in many cases markedly improve the flavor of whiskey over a drink made with tap water. The problem of detergent residue in glasses is not relegated to the laboratory. It is evident at wine tastings, where large numbers of glasses are required, some of which have not been properly rinsed. It is also the bane of the beer drinker. Improperly washed glasses are a principle cause of beer prematurely losing its head.

Anyone can enhance his or her enjoyment of spirits by taking some cues from the professional blender. The nose is paramount in the tasting process. Some blenders say that they can tell more about a sample by smelling it than tasting it. So use your nose when trying a drink, even a mixed one. Give it a good sniff before you drink it and concentrate on the sensations and impressions your olfactory senses are sending you. Wine aficionados consider smelling essential to the appreciation of wine; so it is with whiskey. A carefully made whiskey deserves to be savored and enjoyed like a fine wine.

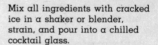 AUNT GRACE'S PACIFIER

2 oz. *blended whiskey*
1 oz. *raspberry syrup*
Club soda

Pour blended whiskey and raspberry syrup into a chilled Old Fashioned glass and stir well. Add several ice cubes and fill with club soda.

BANDANA

1½ oz. *blended whiskey*
¾ oz. *banana liqueur*
1 tsp. *lemon juice*
1 tsp. *orange juice*

Mix all ingredients with cracked ice in a shaker or blender. Strain into a chilled cocktail glass.

BARBIZON COCKTAIL

1½ oz. *blended whiskey*
½ oz. *Benedictine*
Several dashes Cointreau
Juice of ½ lime or ¼ lemon

Mix all ingredients with cracked ice in a shaker or blender. Strain into a chilled cocktail glass.

 BERRY PATCH

1½ oz. *blended whiskey*
1 oz. *blackberry brandy*
½ oz. *lemon juice*
½ oz. *grenadine*

Mix all ingredients with cracked ice in a shaker or blender, strain, and pour into a chilled cocktail glass.

BLACK HAWK

1 oz. *blended whiskey*
1 oz. *sloe gin*
½ oz. *lemon juice*
Maraschino cherry

Mix all ingredients, except cherry, with cracked ice in a shaker or blender. Strain into a chilled cocktail glass. Garnish with a maraschino cherry.

BLENDED COMFORT

2 oz. blended whiskey
1 oz. Southern Comfort
½ oz. dry vermouth
1 oz. orange juice
1 oz. lemon juice
¼ peach, skinned
Lemon slice
Orange slice

Mix all ingredients, except orange and lemon slices, with cracked ice in a shaker or blender. Pour into a chilled Collins glass. Garnish with a slice of orange and slice of lemon.

BLUE GRASS VELVET

1½ oz. blended whiskey
½ oz. Benedictine
2 tsp. lemon juice

Mix all ingredients with cracked ice in a shaker or blender. Strain into a chilled cocktail glass.

 BOILERMAKER

1½ oz. blended whiskey
12 oz. mug or Pilsener glass
   of beer

Drink the whiskey straight and immediately follow with a beer chaser. Some prefer to pour the whiskey into the beer and quaff them together.

BOSS TWEED SPECIAL

1 oz. blended whiskey
1 oz. light rum
1 oz. brandy
1 oz. lemon juice
1 tsp. sugar syrup or to taste
Several dashes Angostura
   bitters

Mix all ingredients with cracked ice in a shaker or blender and serve in a chilled Old Fashioned glass

BOSUN'S MATE

1 oz. blended whiskey
1 oz. ruby port
1 oz. Jamaica rum
Several dashes Angostura
   bitters

Mix all ingredients with cracked ice in a shaker or blender and strain into a chilled Old Fashioned glass.

BOTOFOGO COCKTAIL

1 oz. blended whiskey
1 oz. sweet vermouth
Several dashes Amer Picon

Mix all ingredients with cracked ice in a shaker or blender and strain into a chilled cocktail glass.

CABLEGRAM

2 oz. blended whiskey
1 tsp. sugar syrup
½ oz. lemon juice
Ginger ale

Mix all ingredients, except ginger ale, with cracked ice in a shaker or blender. Pour into a chilled highball glass and fill with ginger ale.

 CANDY PANTS

1½ oz. blended whiskey
½ oz. cherry-flavored brandy
1 tsp. lemon juice
Sugar syrup to taste
Dash grenadine

Mix all ingredients with cracked ice in a shaker or blender, strain, and serve in a chilled cocktail glass.

CHAPEL HILL

1½ oz. blended whiskey
½ oz. curaçao
½ oz. lemon juice
Orange slice

Mix all ingredients, except orange slice, with cracked ice in a shaker or blender. Pour into a chilled cocktail glass. Decorate with a slice of orange.

COFFEE EGGNOG

1½ oz. blended whiskey
1 oz. Kahlua
6 oz. milk
1 oz. heavy cream
1 tsp. sugar syrup
½ tsp. instant coffee
1 egg
Ground cinnamon

Mix all ingredients, except cinnamon, with cracked ice in a shaker or blender and strain into a chilled Collins glass. Sprinkle with ground cinnamon.

COMMODORE No. 1

1½ oz. blended whiskey
½ oz. strawberry liqueur
½ oz. lime juice
2 oz. orange juice
Dash orange bitters

Mix all ingredients with cracked ice in a shaker or blender. Strain into a chilled cocktail glass.

CONTINENTAL PERFECT

1 oz. blended whiskey
1 oz. dry vermouth
1 oz. sweet vermouth
Several dashes Angostura
    bitters
1 orange section

Mix all ingredients, except orange, with cracked ice in a shaker or blender. Pour into a chilled Old Fashioned glass. Garnish with orange section.

DANNY'S DOWNFALL

1 oz. blended whiskey
1 oz. gin
1 oz. sweet vermouth

Pour all ingredients into a mixing glass and stir with ice cubes. Strain into a chilled cocktail glass.

DELTA

1½ oz. blended whiskey
½ oz. Southern Comfort
½ oz. lime juice
½ tsp. sugar syrup
Orange slice
Fresh peach slice

Mix all ingredients, except orange and peach slices, with cracked ice in a shaker or blender. Pour into a chilled Old Fashioned glass. Garnish with orange and peach slices.

DERBY FIZZ

1½ oz. blended whiskey
1 tsp. curaçao
1 tsp. sugar syrup
1 tsp. lemon juice
1 egg
Club soda

Mix all ingredients, except club soda, with cracked ice in a shaker or blender. Strain into a chilled highball glass. Fill with club soda.

DERBY No. 2

1 oz. blended whiskey
½ oz. sweet vermouth
½ oz. white curaçao
½ oz. lime juice
Mint sprig (optional)

Mix all ingredients, except mint sprig, with cracked ice in a shaker or blender. Pour into a chilled Old Fashioned glass. Decorate with a mint sprig.

DE RIGUEUR

1½ oz. blended whiskey
½ oz. grapefruit juice
2 tsp. honey

Mix all ingredients with cracked ice in a shaker or blender. Strain into a chilled cocktail glass.

DINAH

1½ oz. blended whiskey
½ oz. lemon juice
1 tsp. honey or sugar syrup
½ tsp. peppermint schnapps
Mint sprig

Mix all ingredients, except schnapps and mint, with cracked ice in a shaker or blender and strain into a chilled cocktail glass. Garnish with a mint sprig and a float of peppermint schnapps.

BARTENDER'S SECRET NO. 17—Frosting Glasses

Frosting glasses, mugs, or tankards is as important to the proper presentation of special drinks such as the Mint Julep as a pastry chef's ingenious decorations on a layer cake or petit four. To make your drinks look appetizing and crackling cold be sure that the glass or mug is *completely dry* on the outside, since moisture retards frosting and if the glass is wet enough it won't frost at all. For best results, place dry glasses in freezer for an hour or so before using. Metal, such as copper, pewter, or silver frost best and look elegant. A note of caution: Do not hold mug with bare hand. It will melt frost. Use a glove or bar towel.

DIXIE DRAM

2 oz. blended whiskey
½ oz. white crème de
  menthe
¼ oz. lemon juice
½ tsp. sugar syrup
Several dashes curaçao

Mix all ingredients with cracked ice in a shaker or blender. Pour into a chilled Old Fashioned glass.

DORADO

1½ oz. blended whiskey
6 oz. orange juice
1 tsp. liquid Piña Colada
  mix
Several dashes grenadine
Pineapple stick
Maraschino cherry

Mix all ingredients, except fruit, with cracked ice in a shaker or blender and pour into a 10- or 12-oz. Collins glass. Garnish with fruit.

EDEN ROC FIZZ

1½ oz. blended whiskey
1 egg white (for two drinks)
½ oz. lemon juice
1 tsp. sugar syrup
1 tsp. Pernod
Club soda

Mix all ingredients, except club soda, with cracked ice in a shaker or blender. Pour into a chilled highball glass and fill with club soda.

FLAVIO'S SPECIAL

1½ oz. blended whiskey
½ oz. sweet vermouth
½ oz. Grand Marnier
Dash orange bitters

Pour all ingredients into a mixing glass with several ice cubes and gently stir. Strain into a chilled cocktail glass.

FRISCO SOUR

1½ oz. blended whiskey
¾ oz. Benedictine
1 tsp. lemon juice
1 tsp. lime juice
Dash grenadine (optional)
Orange slice

Mix all ingredients, except orange slice, in a shaker or blender, with cracked ice and strain into a Whiskey Sour glass. Garnish with orange slice.

GINGER JOLT

1½ oz. blended whiskey
¾ oz. ginger-flavored wine
Slice ginger root
Club soda

Pour whiskey and wine into a highball glass with ice cubes. Smash ginger root with a hammer, mallet, or the side of a meat cleaver and drop into drink. Fill with club soda.

GINGER SNAP

1 oz. blended whiskey
1 oz. ginger-flavored brandy
6 oz. cola
Several dashes lemon juice

Stir all ingredients with ice in a 10-oz. Collins glass.

GLOOM LIFTER

1½ oz. blended whiskey
¾ oz. brandy
½ oz. raspberry liqueur
1 tsp. sugar syrup or to taste
1 tsp. lemon juice
1 egg white (for two drinks)

Mix all ingredients with cracked ice in a shaker or blender. Pour into a chilled Old Fashioned glass.

GRAPEFRUIT COOLER

2 oz. blended whiskey
4 oz. grapefruit juice
½ oz. red currant syrup
¼ oz. lemon juice
½ orange slice
½ lemon slice

Mix all ingredients, except orange and lemon slices, with cracked ice in a shaker or blender. Pour into a chilled Collins glass with several ice cubes. Garnish with fruit slices.

 ## GUIDO'S SPECIAL

1½ oz. blended whiskey
¾ oz. dry vermouth
1 oz. pineapple juice
Club soda
Dash sambuca

Mix all ingredients, except club soda and sambuca, with cracked ice in a shaker or blender. Pour into a chilled Collins glass with additional cracked ice. Fill with club soda and float sambuca on top.

HAWAII SEVEN-O

1½ oz. blended whiskey
½ oz. amaretto
6 oz. orange juice
1 heaping tsp. Piña Colada
  mix

Mix all ingredients with cracked ice in a shaker or blender and serve in a 10-oz. Collins glass. Use more Piña Colada mix if a sweeter drink is desired.

 ## HENRY MORGAN'S GROG

1½ oz. blended whiskey
1 oz. Pernod
½ oz. Jamaica dark rum
1 oz. heavy cream
Ground nutmeg

Mix all ingredients, except nutmeg, with cracked ice in a shaker or blender. Pour into a chilled Old Fashioned glass. Sprinkle with ground nutmeg.

 ## HORSE'S NECK

1 lemon
2–3 oz. blended whiskey
Ginger ale

Peel the lemon in one continuous strip and place in a chilled Collins glass. Pour in whiskey and ice cubes and squeeze a few drops of lemon juice into glass. Fill with ginger ale and stir gently.

 ## INDIAN RIVER COCKTAIL No. 1

1½ oz. blended whiskey
¼ oz. raspberry liqueur
¼ oz. sweet vermouth
½ oz. grapefruit juice

Mix all ingredients with cracked ice in a shaker or blender. Pour into a chilled Old Fashioned glass.

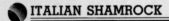 ## ITALIAN SHAMROCK

1½ oz. blended whiskey
½ oz. peppermint schnapps
½ oz. amaretto
1½ oz. milk

Mix all ingredients with cracked ice in a shaker or blender, strain, and pour into a chilled cocktail glass.

JAPANESE FIZZ

2 oz. blended whiskey
¾ oz. port
½ oz. lemon juice
1 tsp. sugar syrup
Club soda
Orange peel
Pineapple stick

Mix all ingredients, except club soda, orange, and pineapple, with cracked ice in a shaker or blender. Pour into a chilled highball glass and fill with club soda. Twist orange peel over drink and drop in. Garnish with a pineapple stick.

JUNIOR LEAGUE

1½ oz. blended whiskey
1 oz. anisette
Maraschino cherry

Mix all ingredients, except cherry, with cracked ice in a shaker or blender. Strain into a chilled cocktail glass. Garnish with a maraschino cherry.

KEY BISCAYNE

1½ oz. blended whiskey
½ oz. curaçao
½ oz. sweet vermouth
Juice of ½ lime
Mint sprig (optional)

Mix all ingredients, except mint sprig, with cracked ice in a shaker or blender. Strain into a chilled cocktail glass. Garnish with a sprig of mint.

 ## KONA COOLER

1½ oz. blended whiskey
¾ oz. white crème de cacao
6 oz. pineapple juice
Pineapple slice
Maraschino cherry

Mix all ingredients, except fruit, with cracked ice in a shaker or blender and serve in a 10-oz. Collins glass. Garnish with fruit.

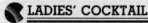 ## LADIES' COCKTAIL

1½ oz. blended whiskey
1 tsp. anisette
Several dashes Pernod
Several dashes Angostura
   bitters
Pineapple stick

Mix all ingredients, except pineapple stick, with cracked ice in a shaker or blender and strain into a chilled Old Fashioned glass. Garnish with a pineapple stick.

LAWHILL COCKTAIL

1½ oz. blended whiskey
½ oz. dry vermouth
¼ tsp. Pernod
¼ tsp. maraschino liqueur
½ oz. orange juice
Dash Angostura bitters

Mix all ingredients with cracked ice in a shaker or blender. Strain into a chilled cocktail glass.

 ## LORD RODNEY

1½ oz. blended whiskey
¾ oz. Jamaica rum
1 tsp. coconut syrup
Dash of white crème de cacao

Mix all ingredients with cracked ice in a shaker or blender. Strain into a chilled cocktail glass.

 ## LOS ANGELES COCKTAIL

4 oz. blended whiskey
1 oz. lemon juice
2 oz. sugar syrup or to taste
Several dashes sweet vermouth
1 egg

Mix all ingredients with cracked ice in a shaker or blender and pour into chilled Old Fashioned glasses. Serves two.

 ## MADEIRA COCKTAIL

1½ oz. blended whiskey
1½ oz. Malmsey Madeira
1 tsp. grenadine
Dash lemon juice
Orange slice

Mix all ingredients, except orange, with cracked ice in a shaker or blender. Pour into a chilled Old Fashioned glass. Decorate with orange slice.

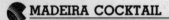 ## MANHATTAN, The Original

1½–2 oz. blended whiskey
¼–½ oz. sweet vermouth
Dash Angostura bitters
Maraschino cherry (optional)

Mix all ingredients with plenty of ice in a mixing glass or pitcher and strain into a chilled cocktail glass.

Amount of vermouth should be adjusted to individual taste.

See page 368 for Manhattan variations.

BARTENDER'S SECRET NO. 18—Tap Water

The simplest mixer in the world—water—can make or break a drink. Heavily treated or chlorinated tap water will flatten the flavor of premium whiskey faster than you can say, "I'll have another." If you compare your favorite scotch or bourbon with tap water and a good spring water, your taste buds will quickly show you the difference. Ice cubes made with spring water are also a flavor saver, and they'll look crystal clear in your glass.

MANHASSET

1½ oz. blended whiskey
¼ oz. dry vermouth
¼ oz. sweet vermouth
½ oz. lemon juice
Lemon peel

Mix all ingredients with cracked ice in a shaker or blender. Strain into a chilled cocktail glass. Twist lemon peel over drink and drop in.

MAY COCKTAIL

1½ oz. blended whiskey
¼ oz. kirschwasser
¼ oz. strawberry liqueur
May wine, chilled
Lemon slice

Mix all ingredients, except wine and lemon slice, with cracked ice in a shaker or blender. Pour into a chilled Old Fashioned glass. Fill with May wine and stir. Decorate with a slice of lemon.

MARTHA WASHINGTON

1½ oz. blended whiskey
¾ oz. cherry liqueur
1 tsp. lemon juice
Several dashes grenadine
    (optional)
Maraschino cherry

Mix all ingredients, except cherry, with cracked ice in a shaker or blender, strain, and serve in a chilled cocktail glass. Garnish with cherry.

NEW ORLEANS OLD FASHIONED

½ tsp. sugar syrup
*Several dashes Angostura
  bitters*
2 tsp. water or club soda
1½–2 oz. blended whiskey
*Several dashes Peychaud's
  bitters*
Lemon peel

Combine sugar, bitters, and water or club soda in a mixing glass and stir until sugar dissolves. Add the blended whiskey along with several ice cubes, thoroughly stir, and top with Peychaud's bitters. Twist lemon peel over drink and drop in.

NEW WORLD

1½ oz. blended whiskey
½ oz. lime juice
1 tsp. grenadine
Lime peel

Mix all ingredients, except lime peel, with cracked ice in a shaker or blender. Strain into a chilled cocktail glass and twist lime peel over drink and drop in.

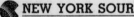 NEW YORKER

1½ oz. blended whiskey
½ oz. lime juice
1 tsp. sugar syrup or to taste
Dash grenadine
Lemon peel
Orange peel

Mix all ingredients, except lemon and orange peels, with cracked ice in a shaker or blender. Strain into a chilled cocktail glass and twist lemon peel and orange peel over drink and drop in.

NEW YORK SOUR

2 oz. blended whiskey
½ oz. lemon juice
1 tsp. sugar syrup or to taste
½ oz. dry red wine
½ slice of lemon

Mix blended whiskey, lemon juice, and sugar with cracked ice in a shaker or blender. Pour into a chilled Whiskey Sour glass and top with dry red wine and stir. Decorate with a slice of lemon.

NORMANDY JACK

1½ oz. blended whiskey
¾ oz. applejack or calvados
½ oz. lemon juice
1 tsp. sugar syrup or to taste

Mix all ingredients with cracked ice in a shaker or blender. Strain into a chilled cocktail glass.

OH, HENRY!

1½ oz. blended whiskey
¼ oz. Benedictine
3 oz. ginger ale
Lemon wedge

Stir all ingredients, except lemon wedge, in a chilled Old Fashioned glass with ice. Garnish with lemon wedge.

OLD ORCHARD SOUR

2 oz. blended whiskey
½ oz. lemon juice
½ oz. lime juice
1 tsp. sugar syrup or to taste
1 tsp. strawberry cordial
Club soda

Mix all ingredients, except club soda, with cracked ice in a shaker or blender. Pour into a chilled Collins glass. Fill with club soda.

ORLY BIRD

1½ oz. blended whiskey
1 tbsp. sweet vermouth
Several dashes Pernod
Several dashes cherry
    brandy

Mix all ingredients with cracked ice in a shaker or blender. Strain into a chilled cocktail glass.

● PAINTED PONY

1 oz. blended whiskey
1 oz. Grand Marnier
¾ oz. orange juice
¾ oz. lemon juice
1 tsp. grenadine

Mix all ingredients with cracked ice in a shaker or blender, strain, and serve in a chilled cocktail glass.

PARK LANE

1½ oz. blended whiskey
½ oz. sloe gin
1 tsp. lemon juice
½ tsp. sugar syrup or to taste

Mix all ingredients with cracked ice in a shaker or blender. Strain into a chilled cocktail glass.

PEACH TREE STREET

1½ oz. blended whiskey
1 oz. Southern Comfort
Several dashes orange
    bitters
Maraschino cherry

Mix all ingredients, except
cherry, with cracked ice in a
shaker or blender. Strain into a
chilled cocktail glass. Decorate
with a maraschino cherry.

PERE BISE

1½ oz. blended whiskey
½ oz. Cherry Marnier
¼ oz. lemon juice
1 egg white (for two drinks)
Dash Pernod

Mix all ingredients with cracked
ice in a shaker or blender. Pour
into a chilled Whiskey Sour
glass.

PINK ALMOND

1 oz. blended whiskey
½ oz. crème de noyaux
½ oz. orgeat syrup or
    amaretto
½ oz. kirsch
½ oz. lemon juice
Lemon slice

Mix all ingredients, except
lemon slice, with cracked ice in
a shaker or blender. Pour into a
chilled Whiskey Sour glass. Decorate with lemon slice.

POIRE WILLIAM'S FIZZ

1½ oz. blended whiskey
2–3 oz. grapefruit juice
½ oz. pear brandy
Club soda

Pour all ingredients, except club
soda, in a chilled highball glass
with ice cubes. Fill with club
soda and stir gently.

 PREAKNESS

2 oz. blended whiskey
¼ oz. sweet vermouth
¼ oz. Benedictine
Dash Angostura bitters

Pour all ingredients into a mixing glass with several ice cubes,
gently stir, and strain into a
chilled cocktail glass.

▨ PRINCE VALIANT

1½ oz. blended whiskey
1 tsp. white crème de
   menthe or peppermint
   schnapps
Dash orange bitters

Pour all ingredients into an Old Fashioned glass and stir with ice.

 RATTLESNAKE

1½ oz. blended whiskey
1 tsp. lemon juice
1 tsp. sugar syrup
1 egg white (for two drinks)
Several dashes Pernod

Mix all ingredients with cracked ice in a shaker or blender. Pour into a chilled Old Fashioned glass.

RED ROOSTER

1 oz. blended whiskey
3 oz. St. Raphael, Byrrh, or
   Dubonnet rouge
Several dashes lemon juice
Lemon or orange twist

Stir all ingredients, except fruit peel, in a double Old Fashioned glass with ice. Twist peel over drink and drop in glass.

▨ RED VELVET SWING

1½ oz. blended whiskey
½ oz. sloe gin
1 tsp. lemon juice
2 tsp. confectioner's sugar or
   to taste

Mix all ingredients with cracked ice in a shaker or blender, strain, and serve in a chilled cocktail glass.

ROSE HALL NIGHTCAP

1 oz. blended whiskey
1 oz. Pernod
1 oz. heavy cream
1 tsp. dark crème de cacao

Mix all ingredients, except crème de cacao, with cracked ice in a shaker or blender. Pour into a chilled Old Fashioned glass. Add a float of dark crème de cacao.

RUE DE RIVOLI

1 oz. blended whiskey
1 oz. dry vermouth
1 oz. Dubonnet rouge
1 oz. orange juice
½ orange slice

Combine all ingredients in a mixing glass with several ice cubes and stir thoroughly. Pour into a chilled Old Fashioned glass.

ST. CLOUD COCKTAIL

1 oz. blended whiskey
1 oz. Pernod
1 oz. cream
Ground nutmeg

Mix all ingredients, except nutmeg, with cracked ice in a shaker or blender. Pour into a chilled cocktail glass. Sprinkle with ground nutmeg.

BARTENDER'S SECRET NO. 19—Glass Care

Before putting a load of dirty glasses in the dishwasher, check for lipstick on the rims. A little pre-wash spray helps get rid of these stains, which a home dishwasher cannot always remove completely. Fine crystal should be hand-washed, never put into a dishwasher. If washing in hard water, a half ounce of vinegar added to your sink makes your glasses bright and shiny. Dishes and glasses washed by hand should be placed in a rack and allowed to air dry. If your fine lead crystal becomes dusty as a result of infrequent use, never polish with a cloth; it will scratch the glass. They must be washed by hand and air dried.

ST. LOUIS COCKTAIL

1½ oz. blended whiskey
½ oz. Southern Comfort
1 tsp. orgeat syrup or
    amaretto
2 tsp. lime juice
Lime slice

Mix all ingredients, except lime slice, with cracked ice in a shaker or blender. Strain into a chilled cocktail glass. Decorate with lime slice.

7 & 7

1½ oz. Seagram's 7-Crown
   blended whiskey
4 oz. 7-Up soda

Pour blended whiskey into a
chilled highball glass with several ice cubes. Add 7-Up and stir
gently.

The following eight recipes were created by the author for the
Seagram Distillers Company.

 7 OF CLUBS

1½ oz. Seagram's 7-Crown
   blended whiskey
¾ oz. peppermint schnapps
6 oz. Coca-Cola

Stir with ice in a 10-oz. Collins
glass.

 7 OF DIAMONDS

1½ oz. Seagram's 7-Crown
   blended whiskey
1 oz. crème de cassis
Dash lemon juice

Mix all ingredients with cracked
ice in a shaker or blender,
strain, and pour into a chilled
cocktail glass.

7 OF HEARTS

1½ oz. Seagram's 7-Crown
   blended whiskey
½ oz. amaretto
6 oz. orange juice
1 tsp. grenadine

Stir with cracked ice in a 10- or
12-oz. Collins glass or mix with
ice in a shaker or blender.

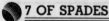 **7 OF SPADES**

1½ oz. Seagram's 7-Crown
   blended whiskey
¾ oz. amaretto
6 oz. cola
Dash lemon juice (optional)

Stir all ingredients with cracked
ice in a 10-oz. Collins glass.

7 STINGER

1 oz. Seagram's 7-Crown
   blended whiskey
1 oz. peppermint schnapps

Mix with cracked ice in a shaker
or blender, strain, and serve in a
chilled cocktail glass.

7 VEILS

1½ oz. Seagram's 7-Crown
   blended whiskey
1 oz. pineapple juice
1 oz. lemon juice
¾ oz. white crème de cacao
1 tsp. grenadine

Mix all ingredients with cracked
ice in a shaker or blender,
strain, and serve in a chilled
cocktail glass.

SHAMROCK-7

1 oz. Seagram's 7-Crown
   blended whiskey
½ oz. white crème de cacao
½ oz. peppermint schnapps
1 oz. milk

Mix all ingredients with cracked
ice in a shaker or blender,
strain, and pour into a chilled
cocktail glass.

SHERRY & 7

1½ oz. Seagram's 7-Crown
   blended whiskey
¾ oz. cocktail sherry
Maraschino cherry

Mix sherry and whiskey with
cracked ice in a pitcher, strain,
and serve in a chilled cocktail
glass. Garnish with cherry.

 SKY CLUB SPECIAL

1½ oz. blended whiskey
½ oz. gold rum
3 oz. orange juice

Pour all ingredients into a mixing glass with several ice cubes
and gently stir. Strain into a
chilled cocktail glass.

 ## SOUTHERN FIZZ

1½ oz. blended whiskey or
  bourbon
½ oz. Southern Comfort
½ oz. lemon juice
2 oz. orange juice
1 tsp. orgeat syrup
Club soda

Mix all ingredients, except club
soda, in a shaker or blender
with cracked ice and pour into a
14-oz. Collins glass. Fill up with
club soda and stir gently.

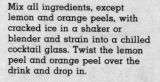 ## STONYBROOK

1½ oz. blended whiskey
½ oz. triple sec
½ oz. crème de noyaux
1 egg white (for two drinks)
Lemon peel
Orange peel

Mix all ingredients, except
lemon and orange peels, with
cracked ice in a shaker or
blender and strain into a chilled
cocktail glass. Twist the lemon
peel and orange peel over the
drink and drop in.

 ## SUMMER FIZZ

1½ oz. blended whiskey
3 oz. grapefruit juice
1 tsp. strawberry liqueur
Club soda

Pour all ingredients, except club
soda, into a chilled highball
glass with ice cubes. Fill with
the club soda and stir gently.

 ## THE SUNSET GUN

4 oz. blended whiskey, rye,
  or bourbon
6 cloves
1 oz. curaçao
Several dashes orange
  bitters

Pour whiskey into a glass, add
cloves, cover, and let steep for
about an hour. Remove cloves,
pour whiskey into a shaker or
blender with cracked ice, add curaçao, and mix well. Strain into
chilled cocktail glasses and top
with orange bitters. Return
cloves to glasses or put in some
new ones.

This drink is for two, to be
mixed immediately following retreat, when the sunset gun is
fired and the flag lowered.

TEMPTATION COCKTAIL

1½ oz. blended whiskey
½ oz. Dubonnet rouge
Several dashes curaçao
Several dashes Pernod
Orange peel
Lemon peel

Mix all ingredients, except fruit peels, with cracked ice in a shaker or blender, strain into a chilled cocktail glass, and twist peels over drink and drop into glass.

TOMMY LATTA

1½ oz. blended whiskey
½ tsp. dry vermouth
½ tsp. sweet vermouth
Several dashes lemon juice
Dash sugar syrup or to taste

Mix all ingredients with cracked ice in a shaker or blender and strain into a chilled cocktail glass.

 TOM NEUBERGER'S TODDY

1 tsp. honey
2 oz. water
2 oz. blended whiskey
Dash maraschino liqueur
Lemon peel and cinnamon
   stick

Combine honey and water in a chilled Old Fashioned glass and stir until sugar dissolves. Add the blended whiskey and maraschino along with several ice cubes. Stir well. Twist lemon peel over the drink, drop in, and garnish with cinnamon stick.

VINCENNES

1½ oz. blended whiskey
1 oz. Dubonnet rouge
½ oz. triple sec
Dash Pernod
Lime peel

Combine all ingredients, except lime peel, in a mixing glass with several ice cubes and stir thoroughly. Strain into a chilled cocktail glass. Twist lime peel over the drink and drop in.

 **WATERLOO**

1½ oz. blended whiskey
¾ oz. Mandarine Napoleon
1 tsp. lemon juice
1 tsp. sugar syrup or to taste
Club soda
Orange slice

Mix all ingredients, except club soda and orange slice, with cracked ice in a shaker or blender. Strain into a chilled Old Fashioned glass. Top with club soda. Decorate with orange slice.

WHIPPET

1½ oz. blended whiskey
½ oz. peppermint schnapps
½ oz. white crème de cacao

Mix all ingredients with cracked ice in a shaker or blender. Strain into a chilled cocktail glass.

 **WHISKEY COBBLER**

1 tsp. sugar syrup
1 tsp. orgeat syrup or
   amaretto
2 oz. blended whiskey
Dash curaçao
Mint sprig (optional)

Fill a large wine goblet with finely crushed ice, pour in sugar syrup, orgeat or amaretto, and churn with a barspoon until well mixed. Add more ice if necessary and pour in whiskey. Continue churning until frost begins to form on the outside of goblet. Throw in a dash of curaçao and garnish with a mint sprig.

WHISKEY CURAÇAO FIZZ

2 oz. blended whiskey
½ oz. curaçao
1 oz. lemon juice
1 tsp. sugar
Club soda
Orange slice

Mix all ingredients, except club soda and orange slice, with cracked ice in a shaker or blender. Pour into a chilled Collins glass with several ice cubes and fill with club soda. Garnish with orange slice.

 **WHISKEY DAISY**

2 oz. blended whiskey or
   bourbon
1 tsp. red currant syrup,
   raspberry syrup, or
   grenadine
½ oz. lemon juice
Club soda (optional)
1 tsp. yellow Chartreuse
Slice of lemon

Mix all ingredients, except club soda, Chartreuse, and lemon slice, with cracked ice in a shaker or blender. Pour into a chilled highball glass. Fill with club soda, if you wish. Add a float of yellow Chartreuse and decorate with a lemon slice.

Other floats are used with the daisy such as curaçao, maraschino liqueur, Grand Marnier, green Chartreuse, Benedictine, and Galliano, to name a few.

WHISKEY FIZZ

1½ oz. blended whiskey
Several dashes Angostura
   bitters
½ tsp. sugar syrup or to taste
Club soda

Mix whiskey, bitters, and sugar
in a chilled highball glass with
ice and fill with club soda.

 ## WHISKEY RICKEY

1½ oz. blended whiskey
Juice of ½ lime
1 tsp. sugar syrup
Club soda
Lime peel

Mix whiskey, lime juice, and
sugar in a Collins glass with
cracked ice, fill with club soda,
and twist lime peel over drink
and drop into glass.

ZAGREB COCKTAIL

2 oz. blended whiskey
½ oz. slivovitz
1 tsp. lemon juice
1 tsp. sugar syrup
Club soda
Pineapple stick

Mix all ingredients, except club
soda and pineapple stick, with
cracked ice in a shaker or
blender. Strain into a chilled
wine glass. Fill with club soda.
Decorate with pineapple.

MANHATTAN VARIATIONS

CARACAS MANHATTAN

1½ oz. blended whiskey
¾ oz. sweet vermouth
1 tsp. Benedictine
Several dashes Amer Picon
1 egg white (for two drinks)
Maraschino cherry

Mix all ingredients, except maraschino cherry, with cracked ice
in a shaker or blender. Pour into
a chilled Old Fashioned glass.
Garnish with a maraschino
cherry.

DANISH MANHATTAN

1½ oz. blended whiskey
¼ oz. kirschwasser
¼ oz. Cherry Heering

Mix all ingredients with cracked
ice in a shaker or blender. Strain
into a chilled cocktail glass.

MANHATTAN, DRY

1½–2 oz. blended whiskey
¼–½ oz. dry vermouth
Dash Angostura bitters
 (optional)
Lemon peel

Mix all ingredients with plenty of ice in a mixing glass or a pitcher and strain into a chilled cocktail glass. Twist lemon peel over drink and drop into glass.

 **DUBONNET MANHATTAN**

1½ oz. blended whiskey
1 oz. Dubonnet rouge
Maraschino cherry

Mix all ingredients, except cherry, with cracked ice in a shaker or blender. Pour into a chilled Old Fashioned glass. Garnish with maraschino cherry.

◥ **MANHATTAN COOLER**

1½ oz. blended whiskey
½ oz. dry vermouth
½ oz. amaretto
2 oz. orange juice
1 oz. lemon juice
Club soda

Mix all ingredients, except club soda, with cracked ice in shaker or blender. Pour into a chilled Collins glass. Fill with club soda.

MARIA'S MANHATTAN

1½ oz. blended whiskey
½ oz. dry vermouth
½ oz. strawberry liqueur

Pour all ingredients in a mixing glass with several ice cubes and stir well. Strain into a chilled cocktail glass.

◣ **OLD-FASHIONED MANHATTAN**

1½ oz. blended whiskey
1½ oz. sweet vermouth
Maraschino cherry

Mix all ingredients with cracked ice in a shaker or blender. Pour into a chilled cocktail glass. Garnish with a maraschino cherry.

PARISIAN MANHATTAN

1½ oz. blended whiskey
½ oz. sweet vermouth
Several dashes Amer Picon
Maraschino cherry

Mix all ingredients with cracked ice in a shaker or blender. Strain into a chilled cocktail glass. Garnish with a cherry.

MANHATTAN, PERFECT

1½–2 oz. blended whiskey
½ oz. sweet vermouth
¼ oz. dry vermouth
Dash Angostura bitters
  (optional)
Lemon peel or maraschino
  cherry

Mix all ingredients with cracked ice in a mixing glass or pitcher and strain into a chilled cocktail glass. Garnish with lemon peel or maraschino cherry.

ROSEY MANHATTAN

1½ oz. blended whiskey
½ oz. dry vermouth
½ oz. raspberry liqueur

Mix all ingredients with cracked ice in a shaker or blender. Strain into a chilled cocktail glass.

SWISS MANHATTAN

1½ oz. blended whiskey
½ oz. dry vermouth
½ oz. kirsch
Several dashes Angostura
  bitters (optional)

Mix all ingredients with cracked ice in a shaker or blender. Serve in a chilled Old Fashioned glass.

Canadian Whisky

Canadian whiskies are all blends of spirits made from cereal grains such as wheat, rye, corn, and barley. By law, they must be at least three years old, though in practice, most Canadians are six years old or more. They are characterized by a delicate flavor, a very light body, and a smoothness that is brought about by aging in wood. Like American blended whiskeys, Canadians have a high level of mixability because the flavors are not strong or trenchant. Like other blended whiskeys, Canadian whiskies are referred to as "rye" in certain parts of the U.S. This is incorrect, since these blends may contain some rye, but probably not more so than that which is found in American blends. Canadian whisky, while similar to other blends, has unique qualities of its own and a pleasant, unobtrusive character that makes it particularly appealing to those who do not enjoy what they perceive to be a strong whisky taste. As a base for mixed drinks, Canadian whisky is outstanding.

ALASKAN CRUISE

1½ oz. Canadian whisky
¾ oz. crème de banane
2 oz. lime juice
3 oz. orange juice
½ tsp. sugar or to taste

Mix all ingredients with cracked ice in a shaker or blender and pour into a tall, chilled cooler glass with ice.

A house specialty of the **Pan Pacific Vancouver Hotel, Canada.**

ASPEN CRUD

3 large scoops vanilla ice cream
5 oz. milk
4 oz. Maker's Mark Bourbon
Whipped cream

Blend all ingredients, except whipped cream, until thick and creamy (consistency of a thick milk shake). Serve in a chilled Hurricane glass. Top with whipped cream.

This is a house specialty of **Hotel Jerome and The J-Bar, Aspen, Colorado.**

BONAVENTURE COCKTAIL

1½ oz. Canadian whisky
½ oz. Cherry Marnier
½ oz. lemon juice
½ oz. orange juice

Mix all ingredients with cracked ice in a shaker or blender. Pour into a chilled Old Fashioned glass.

CANADIAN AND CAMPARI

1 oz. Canadian whisky
½ oz. Campari
1 oz. dry vermouth
Lemon peel

Mix all ingredients, except lemon peel, with cracked ice in a shaker or blender. Strain into a chilled cocktail glass. Twist lemon peel over drink and drop in.

CANADIAN APPLE

1½ oz. Canadian whisky
½ oz. calvados
1½ tsp. sugar syrup
1 tsp. lemon juice
Several pinches powdered cinnamon
Lemon slice

Mix all ingredients, except lemon slice, with cracked ice in a shaker or blender. Pour into a chilled Old Fashioned glass. Garnish with a slice of lemon.

CANADIAN BLACKBERRY COCKTAIL

1½ oz. Canadian whisky
½ oz. blackberry brandy or
  blackberry liqueur
½ oz. orange juice
1 tsp. lemon juice
1 tsp. sugar syrup

Mix all ingredients with cracked ice in a shaker or blender. Serve in a chilled Old Fashioned glass. If blackberry liqueur is used in place of blackberry brandy, you may want to omit sugar syrup.

CANADIAN COCKTAIL

1½ oz. Canadian whisky
½ oz. curaçao
½ oz. lemon juice
1 tsp. sugar syrup (optional)
Dash Angostura bitters

Mix all ingredients with cracked ice in a shaker or blender. Pour into a chilled Old Fashioned glass.

CANADIAN DAISY

1½ oz. Canadian whisky
½ oz. lemon juice
1 tsp. raspberry syrup
Club soda
1 tsp. brandy
Whole raspberries (optional)

Mix the Canadian whisky, lemon juice, and raspberry syrup with cracked ice in a shaker or blender. Pour into a chilled highball glass and fill with club soda. Add a float of brandy. Garnish with whole raspberries.

CANADIAN DOG'S NOSE

2 oz. Canadian whisky
4 oz. tomato juice, chilled
1 tsp. Worcestershire sauce
½ tsp. Tabasco sauce
6 oz. cold beer
Freshly ground black pepper
Salt

Pour the Canadian whisky, tomato juice, Worcestershire sauce, and Tabasco sauce into a shaker with ice cubes and stir well. Pour into a chilled Collins glass. Add beer while slowly stirring. Sprinkle with salt and ground black pepper.

CANADIAN HURRICANE

1½ oz. Canadian whisky
½ oz. white crème de
  menthe
½ oz. dry gin
Juice of ½ lemon

Mix all ingredients with cracked ice in a shaker or blender. Strain into a cocktail glass.

CANADIAN LUMBERJILL

1½ oz. Canadian whisky
6 oz. orange juice
½ oz. Piña Colada mix, or to taste
½ oz. amaretto liqueur
Orange wheel

Mix all ingredients, except orange wheel, with cracked ice in a shaker or blender and serve in a chilled highball glass with several ice cubes. Garnish with orange wheel.

CANADIAN MANHATTAN

1½–2 oz. Canadian whisky
½ oz. sweet vermouth
Dash Angostura bitters (optional)
Maraschino cherry

Pour whisky, vermouth, and bitters into a shaker with ice cubes. Stir gently and strain into a chilled cocktail glass. Garnish with a maraschino cherry.

CANADIAN MOUNTY

1½ oz. Canadian whisky
1 oz. cranberry liqueur
1 oz. orange juice
1 tsp. lemon juice

Mix all ingredients with cracked ice in a shaker or blender. Pour into a chilled Old Fashioned glass.

CANADIAN OLD FASHIONED

1½ oz. Canadian whisky
½ tsp. curaçao
Dash lemon juice
Dash Angostura bitters
Lemon peel
Orange peel

Mix all ingredients, except lemon and orange peels, with cracked ice in a shaker or blender. Pour into a chilled Old Fashioned glass. Twist lemon and orange peel over drink and drop in.

CANADIAN PINEAPPLE FIX

1½ oz. Canadian whisky
½ oz. maraschino liqueur
½ oz. pineapple juice
½ oz. lemon juice
Pineapple stick

Mix all ingredients, except pineapple stick, with cracked ice in a shaker or blender. Pour into a chilled Old Fashioned glass. Decorate with a pineapple stick.

CANADIAN STONE FENCE

1½ oz. Canadian whisky
½ oz. triple sec
2 oz. apple cider
1 tsp. sugar syrup

Mix all ingredients with cracked ice in a shaker or blender. Strain into a chilled cocktail glass.

 CANADIAN SUNRISE

4 oz. fresh orange juice
2 oz. cranberry juice
½ oz. lemon juice
1½ oz. Canadian Club
½ oz. maple syrup or to taste
Orange wheel

Mix all ingredients, except orange wheel, with cracked ice in a shaker or blender and pour into a chilled double Old Fashioned glass. Garnish with orange wheel.

Created by the author for Hiram Walker & Sons, Inc.

 COMMONWEALTH COCKTAIL

1¾ oz. Canadian whisky
½ oz. Van der Hum
1 tsp. lemon juice
Orange peel

Mix all ingredients, except orange peel, with cracked ice in a shaker or blender. Pour into a chilled cocktail glass. Twist orange peel over drink and drop in.

CORDIAL CANADIAN

1 oz. Canadian whisky
1 oz. dry vermouth
1 oz. Cordial Médoc
Maraschino cherry

Pour ingredients into a shaker without ice and stir thoroughly. Pour into a chilled Old Fashioned glass with ice and garnish with cherry.

 **DOG SLED**

2 oz. Canadian whisky
2 oz. orange juice
1 tbsp. lemon juice
1 tsp. grenadine

Mix all ingredients with cracked ice in a shaker or blender. Pour into a chilled Old Fashioned glass.

BARTENDER'S SECRET NO. 20—Simple Sweetener

Since sugar and alcohol do not readily mix, busy professional bartenders use superfine sugar or, better yet, simple sugar syrup to speed up the mixing process. A good working formula is two cups sugar to one cup water. Mix sugar with cold water in a saucepan and boil for five minutes or until all sugar is dissolved and the syrup is clear. Cool and bottle. It will last a considerable period of time and save considerable time in drink-making, especially for a large number of guests.

8ᵉ ARRONDISSEMENT Canadian Ward Eight

2 oz. Canadian whisky
½ oz. lemon juice
½ tsp. grenadine
1 tsp. maple syrup or sugar
    syrup
Slice of lemon

Mix all ingredients, except lemon slice, with cracked ice in a shaker or blender. Pour into a chilled cocktail glass. Garnish with a slice of lemon.

ESQUIMAUX CREME

1½ oz. Canadian whisky
1 oz. Grand Marnier
1 oz. heavy cream
1 tsp. lemon juice
1 egg
Nutmeg, grated
Cinnamon, powdered

Mix all ingredients, except nutmeg and cinnamon, with cracked ice in a shaker or blender. Pour into a chilled wine goblet and sprinkle with nutmeg and cinnamon.

FROBISHER FIZZ

1½ oz. Canadian whisky
1 oz. peppermint schnapps
¼ oz. white crème de cacao
1 egg white (for two drinks)
Club soda

Mix all ingredients, except club soda, with cracked ice in a shaker or blender. Pour into a chilled double Old Fashioned glass and fill with club soda.

FRONTENAC COCKTAIL

1½ oz. Canadian whisky
½ oz. Grand Marnier
Several dashes kirschwasser
Dash orange bitters

Mix all ingredients with cracked ice in a shaker or blender. Pour into a chilled cocktail glass.

 ## HABITANT COCKTAIL

1½ oz. Canadian whisky
1 oz. lemon juice
1 tsp. maple syrup
Orange slice
Cherry

Mix all ingredients, except orange slice and cherry, with cracked ice in a shaker or blender. Strain into a chilled cocktail glass. Decorate with a slice of orange and cherry.

 ## IRISH CANADIAN SANGAREE

1 oz. Canadian whisky
½ oz. Irish Mist
½ oz. orange juice
½ oz. lemon juice
Nutmeg, grated

Pour whisky, Irish Mist, orange and lemon juices into a chilled Old Fashioned glass and stir with ice. Dust with nutmeg.

 ## IRISH MOUNTY

1½ oz. Canadian whisky
1 oz. Irish Mist
½ oz. heavy cream
Nutmeg, grated

Mix all ingredients, except nutmeg, with cracked ice in a shaker or blender. Strain into a chilled cocktail glass and sprinkle with nutmeg.

LAKE LOUISE COCKTAIL

1½ oz. Canadian whisky
½ oz. amaretto
½ oz. heavy cream

Mix all ingredients with cracked ice in a shaker or blender. Strain into a chilled cocktail glass.

LA RESERVE COCKTAIL

1½ oz. Canadian whisky
½ oz. yellow Chartreuse
2 oz. orange juice

Mix all ingredients with cracked ice in a shaker or blender. Strain into a chilled cocktail glass.

 **MAMMAMATTAWA**

1½ oz. Canadian whisky
½ oz. Drambuie
¼ oz. cherry brandy

Mix all ingredients with cracked ice in a shaker or blender. Serve in a chilled cocktail glass.

MOOSE JAW

1½ oz. Canadian whisky
1 oz. apple brandy
1 tsp. grenadine or sugar
    syrup
1 tsp. lemon juice
Several dashes peppermint
    schnapps

Mix all ingredients in a shaker or blender with cracked ice. Pour into a chilled Old Fashioned glass.

 **MT. TREMBLANT**

1 oz. Canadian whisky
½ oz. dry vermouth
½ oz. Grand Marnier
½ oz. cranberry liqueur

Mix all ingredients with cracked ice in a shaker or blender. Strain into a chilled cocktail glass.

THE MUSKOKA COCKTAIL

1½ oz. Canadian whisky
½ oz. scotch
1 oz. orange juice
½ oz. lemon juice
1 tsp. maple syrup or sugar
    syrup
Dash grenadine

Mix all ingredients with cracked ice in a shaker or blender. Strain into a chilled Whiskey Sour glass.

 **OPENING** No. 1

1½ oz. Canadian whisky
1 tsp. sweet vermouth
1 tsp. grenadine

Stir with ice in a pitcher or mixing glass and strain into a chilled cocktail glass.

QUEBEC COCKTAIL

1½ oz. Canadian whisky
½ oz. Amer Picon
½ oz. maraschino liqueur
½ oz. dry vermouth

Mix all ingredients with cracked ice in a shaker or blender. Strain into a chilled cocktail glass.

 STE. AGATHE COCKTAIL

1½ oz. Canadian whisky
¾ oz. Cointreau
1 tsp. grenadine
½ oz. lemon juice
Lemon peel

Mix all ingredients, except lemon peel, with cracked ice in a shaker or blender. Strain into a chilled cocktail glass. Twist lemon peel over drink and drop in.

SASKATOON STINGER

2 oz. Canadian whisky
1 oz. peppermint schnapps or
    white crème de menthe
Lemon peel

Pour whisky and peppermint schnapps into a chilled Old Fashioned glass with ice cubes and stir gently. Twist lemon peel over drink and drop in.

SINGAPORE COCKTAIL

1½ oz. Canadian whisky
¾ oz. sloe gin
¼ oz. Rose's lime juice
½ oz. lemon juice
Cucumber peel

Mix all ingredients, except cucumber peel, with cracked ice in a shaker or blender. Pour into a chilled Old Fashioned glass. Garnish with a cucumber peel.

 TROIS RIVIERES

1½ oz. Canadian whisky
¾ oz. Dubonnet rouge
½ oz. triple sec
Orange peel

Mix all ingredients, except orange peel, with cracked ice in a shaker or blender. Strain into a chilled cocktail glass. Twist orange peel over drink and drop in.

VANCOUVER COCKTAIL

2 oz. Canadian whisky
1 oz. Dubonnet rouge
½ oz. lemon juice
1 egg white (for two drinks)
½ tsp. maple syrup or sugar
   syrup
Several dashes orange
   bitters (optional)

Mix all ingredients with cracked ice in a shaker or blender. Pour into a chilled cocktail glass.

Rye

 BAL HARBOUR COCKTAIL

1½ oz. rye
½ oz. dry vermouth
1 oz. grapefruit juice
Maraschino cherry

Mix all ingredients, except cherry, with cracked ice in a shaker or blender. Strain into a with maraschino cherry.

BLINKER

1½ oz. rye
2 oz. grapefruit juice
1 tsp. grenadine

Mix all ingredients with cracked ice in a shaker or blender. Pour into a chilled cocktail glass.

ELK'S OWN

1½ oz. rye
¾ oz. port
Juice of ½ lemon
1 egg white
1 tsp. powdered sugar
Pineapple stick

Mix all ingredients, except pineapple, with cracked ice in a shaker or blender. Pour into a chilled Old Fashioned glass. Garnish with pineapple stick.

 **FRISCO COCKTAIL**

1½ oz. rye
1½ oz. Benedictine
½ oz. lemon juice
Orange peel

Mix all ingredients, except orange peel, in a shaker or blender with cracked ice and strain into a chilled cocktail glass. Garnish with orange peel.

FOX RIVER

1½ oz. rye
½ oz. dark crème de cacao
Several dashes orange
   bitters or peach bitters
Lemon peel

Mix all ingredients, except
lemon peel, with cracked ice in
a shaker or blender. Pour into a
chilled cocktail glass. Twist
lemon peel over drink and drop
in.

FRUITY OLD FASHIONED

1½ oz. rye
1 oz. sugar syrup
1 tsp. cherry juice
Several dashes Angostura or
   orange bitters
Peach slice or pineapple
   slice
Orange slice
Maraschino cherry
Lemon peel
Whole strawberry (optional)

Mix all ingredients, except fruit
and lemon peel, with cracked ice
in a chilled Old Fashioned
glass. Garnish with strawberry,
orange slice, and maraschino
cherry. Twist lemon peel over
drink and drop in along with
strawberry.

HESITATION

1½ oz. rye
1½ oz. Swedish Punsch
Several dashes lemon juice

Mix all ingredients with cracked
ice in a shaker or blender. Pour
into a chilled cocktail glass.

HUNTER'S COCKTAIL

1½ oz. rye
½ oz. cherry brandy
Maraschino cherry

Pour rye and cherry brandy into
an Old Fashioned glass with ice.
Stir well. Garnish with maraschino cherry.

INDIAN RIVER COCKTAIL No. 2

1 oz. rye
1 oz. dry vermouth
2 oz. orange juice
Several dashes raspberry
   syrup

Mix all ingredients with cracked
ice in a shaker or blender. Pour
into a chilled Old Fashioned
glass.

KUNGSHOLM COCKTAIL

1 oz. rye
1 oz. Swedish Punsch
2 oz. orange juice
½ oz. raspberry syrup
Several dashes Pernod

Mix all ingredients with cracked ice in a shaker or blender. Pour into a chilled double Old Fashioned glass.

LAFAYETTE

1½ oz. rye
¼ oz. dry vermouth
¼ oz. Dubonnet rouge
Several dashes Angostura
   bitters

Mix all ingredients with cracked ice in a shaker or blender. Pour into a chilled Old Fashioned glass.

LISBON COCKTAIL

1½ oz. rye
2 oz. port
½ oz. lemon juice
1 tsp. sugar syrup or to taste
1 egg white (for two drinks)

Mix all ingredients with cracked ice in a shaker or blender. Pour into a chilled Old Fashioned glass.

 LORD BALTIMORE'S CUP

½ tsp. sugar syrup or to taste
Several dashes Angostura
   bitters
1 oz. rye
Champagne
Several dashes Pernod

Combine sugar and Angostura bitters in chilled wine goblet. Add rye and several ice cubes. Fill with champagne and add a float of Pernod.

MONTE CARLO

1½ oz. rye
½ oz. Benedictine
Several dashes Angostura
   bitters

Mix all ingredients with cracked ice in a shaker or blender. Pour into a chilled cocktail glass.

NEW YORK

1½ oz. rye
½ oz. lime juice
1 tsp. sugar syrup
Several dashes grenadine
Orange peel

Mix all ingredients, except orange peel, with cracked ice in a shaker or blender. Pour into a chilled Old Fashioned glass. Twist orange peel over drink and drop in.

 NORMANDY COOLER

1 oz. rye
1 oz. calvados
1 tsp. sugar syrup
Club soda
Lemon slice

Mix all ingredients, except club soda, with cracked ice in a shaker or blender. Pour into a chilled highball glass and fill with club soda. Garnish with lemon slice.

 OPENING No. 2

1½ oz. rye
¼ oz. sweet vermouth
Dash grenadine
Dash maraschino liqueur

Mix all ingredients with cracked ice in a shaker or blender. Pour into a chilled cocktail glass.

PERFECT RYE MANHATTAN

2 oz. rye
½ tsp. sweet vermouth
½ tsp. dry vermouth
Several dashes Angostura
   bitters
Maraschino cherry

Mix all ingredients, except cherry, with cracked ice in a shaker or blender. Strain into a chilled cocktail glass. Garnish with maraschino cherry.

PINK RYE

1½ oz. rye
Several dashes Angostura
   bitters

Fill an Old Fashioned glass with crushed ice, pour in rye, add bitters and stir well.

RED TOP

1½ oz. rye
½ oz. lemon or lime juice
1 tsp. sugar syrup
1 egg white (for two drinks)
½ oz. claret

Mix all ingredients, except claret, with cracked ice in a shaker or blender. Strain into a chilled Whiskey Sour glass. Top with claret.

● ROARING TWENTIES MANHATTAN

1 oz. rye
2 oz. dry or sweet vermouth
Several dashes orange
    bitters

Mix all ingredients with cracked ice in a mixing glass. Serve in a chilled cocktail glass.

ROCK AND RYE COOLER

1 oz. rock and rye
1 oz. vodka
1 tsp. lime juice
Lemon-lime soda
Lime slice

Mix all ingredients, except soda and lime slice, with cracked ice in a shaker or blender. Pour into a chilled highball glass. Fill with lemon-lime soda. Garnish with lime slice.

ROCKY RIVER COCKTAIL

1 oz. rye
1 oz. apricot brandy
1 tsp. lemon juice
Sugar syrup to taste
Maraschino cherry

Mix all ingredients, except cherry, with cracked ice in a shaker or blender. Strain into a chilled cocktail glass. Decorate with maraschino cherry.

ROSE HALL RYE TODDY

1 oz. rye
1 oz. Jamaica rum
Juice of ½ lime
1 oz. sugar syrup or
    Falernum to taste

Mix all ingredients with cracked ice in a shaker or blender. Pour into a chilled Old Fashioned glass.

RYE FIZZ

1½ oz. rye
Dash Angostura bitters
Dash sugar syrup
Club soda

Combine rye, bitters, and syrup in a mixing glass. Stir well. Pour into a chilled highball glass along with several ice cubes. Fill with club soda.

 RYE FLIP

1½ oz. rye
1 egg
1 tsp. sugar syrup
Ground nutmeg

Mix all ingredients, except nutmeg, with cracked ice in a shaker or blender. Strain into a chilled brandy glass. Sprinkle with ground nutmeg.

 **RYE MANHATTAN**

1½ oz. rye
¼ oz. sweet vermouth
Maraschino cherry

Mix rye and vermouth in a mixing glass with cracked ice and strain into a chilled cocktail glass. Garnish with cherry. For a drier drink, substitute dry vermouth in place of sweet and use lemon twist in place of cherry.

SHAKER HEIGHTS

½ oz. rye
½ oz. gin
½ oz. sweet vermouth
½ oz. brandy
Several dashes orange
  bitters

Mix all ingredients with cracked ice in a shaker or blender. Strain into a chilled cocktail glass.

STRØGET COCKTAIL

2 oz. rye
1 oz. Cherry Heering
½ oz. lemon juice

Mix all ingredients with cracked ice in a shaker or blender and strain into a chilled cocktail glass.

TENNESSEE

2 oz. rye
1 oz. maraschino liqueur
½ oz. lemon juice

Mix all ingredients with cracked ice in a shaker or blender. Serve in a chilled cocktail glass.

 T.N.T. COCKTAIL No. 1

1½ oz. rye
1½ oz. Pernod

Mix both ingredients with cracked ice in a shaker or blender. Serve in a chilled cocktail glass.

WHITEHALL COCKTAIL

1½ oz. rye
½ oz. lime juice
½ oz. Benedictine
Several dashes Angostura
  bitters

Mix all ingredients with cracked ice in a shaker or blender. Serve in a chilled cocktail glass.

YASHMAK

1½ oz. rye
¾ oz. dry vermouth
½ oz. Pernod
Several dashes Angostura
  bitters
Sugar syrup to taste

Mix all ingredients with cracked ice in a shaker or blender. Pour into a chilled highball glass.

IN SEARCH OF IRISH SPIRITS AND THE SCOTCH MYSTIQUE

> I've taken more good from alcohol
> than alcohol has taken from me.
> —Winston Churchill

No one knows precisely when the Irish invented whiskey, but invent it they did, and, as many an Irishman truly believes, in terms of civilized blessings this event ranks in stature with the discovery of fire and the invention of the wheel.

The art of distillation had been around for several thousand years, for Aristotle wrote of it three centuries before the birth of Christ. It was known in ancient Egypt and Mesopotamia as well as China and some other parts of the Far East, but the Saracens are generally credited with introducing distilling to the modern era. The use of the alembic (an Arabic word), which is very similar in appearance and function to the old-fashioned copper-pot still, to manufacture potable spirits eluded man until the sixth century. This is about the time when the Celts came upon their momentous discovery. The English, never ones to be shy about raising a goblet at the drop of a cork, gave the name "whiskey" to the Gaelic *uisce beatha* (meaning "water of life") after the army of Henry II returned to England in 1170 from a foray to the Emerald Isle. The expedition was undistinguished except for a protracted and enthusiastic sampling of the native distilled beverages.

Word of this golden elixir spread throughout the realm, and it ultimately became a favorite potation in royal circles. Queen Elizabeth I was known to take a tot or two, possibly through the good offices of her friend and confidant, Sir Walter Raleigh, who was presented with a puncheon of homemade whiskey by the Earl of Cork when he was en route to the New World. Even the czar of all the Russias, Peter the Great, preferred Irish whiskey over vodka and said so in no uncertain terms. "Of all the wines," he proclaimed, "the Irish is the best." By the end of the eighteenth century Ireland was awash with whiskey stills—more than two thousand according to the tax collectors, who, then as now, were not welcome in the glens and hollows of the back country.

Having invented whiskey, it follows as surely as night shall follow the day that one must have a place to drink it. The parlor wouldn't do in olden days, for that was a family room. It must be a public place and accessible to all. Enter the public house, i.e., the pub.

If the Irish didn't invent the pub, they surely turned it into a most lasting national institution. Today, throughout the length of the republic, from Malin Head in the north to Mizen Head in the south, there are reportedly some ten thousand pubs. They are very much an integral part of the cultural life and the social fabric of the land. An Irish pub, whether a bright and brassy emporium in Dublin, or a humble wayside bar at a village crossroad in Donegal or Kerry, must be experienced to be appreciated. The Irish pub is at once a haven, forum, recreation center, retreat, snack bar, and saloon, but—first and foremost—a drinking establishment. It is here you will find arrayed along the back bar, behind great ebony tap handles bearing the names Guinness Stout, Smithwick's ale, and Harp beer, the distinguished company of Irish whiskeys: Dunphy's, John Jameson, Old Bushmill's, Murphy's, Paddy, Power's, and Tullamore Dew, to name the most popular brands. Currently, Bushmill's and Jameson are available in the U.S.

You also will find something else in every Irish pub: the opportunity to do exactly what you want to do. You can drink quietly, enjoy a light meal of "pub grub," read your newspaper, have a go at the dart board, or socialize. The latter, for most, is a great attraction. It is said that an Irishman won't walk across the street for a free drink, but will travel a mile or two for some good conversation. True or not, you'll find plenty of good conversation in Irish pubs without any question, for the Irish are a gregarious lot—friendly, outgoing, articulate, and loquacious, all of which is aided by a few drams of good Irish whiskey or a pint or two of Guinness.

Having frequented more than a few pubs on several visits to Ireland, I have often marveled at feeling so fit the morning after a night out in a pub. Aside from the natural stimulation of pleasant surroundings and friendly encounters, I have concluded that the care and aging that go into the making of Irish whiskey has a salutary effect (in moderate quantities, of course) on the human organism.

Irish whiskey, like scotch, is made from barley and water,

but unlike scotch, the malted and unmalted barley used to make Irish whiskey is dried in smokeless kilns, whereas the Scots dry their barley over peat fires, thus accounting for the smoky flavor of scotch. During the great potato famines of the early nineteenth century it was feared there would be a world shortage of Irish spirits by some who believed that Irish whiskey is the product of potatoes. This bit of misinformation came about, no doubt, from the fact that illicit whiskey is known in Ireland as "poteen," a name derived from the pot stills that are an essential part of the bootlegger's paraphernalia.

The basic process of making whiskey is quite simple on paper, but in practice requires considerable skill and experience. The barley, malted and unmalted (malting is achieved by allowing barley to sprout and stopping the growing process at just the right time by kiln drying), is ground along with other cereal grains such as rye, wheat, and corn, mixed with water, and cooked in huge tuns, or tanks. Then yeast is added, and the mixture is allowed to ferment for several days. The first of three distillations takes place in large pot stills after which the whiskey—raw, powerful, and crystal clear—is placed in oak casks and allowed to age from four to fifteen years. After sampling and testing when the maturation process has been completed, the whiskey is reduced in alcoholic strength by the addition of distilled water until it reaches 80 proof and allowed to "rest" for a time before being bottled. The result is a whiskey that is full-bodied, smooth, mellow, and possessed of a distinctive barley malt flavor. Irish whiskey is highly regarded by those who know and respect fine whiskey. It deserves more exposure than simply as a basic ingredient for Irish Coffee, as delectable as that worthy libation may be, for it is excellent on-the-rocks with a little water, club soda, or other mixers, and in a wide range of mixed drinks.

In and around the softly rolling, verdant counties of southern Ireland (palm trees grow in Kerry), 'tis said that soil in Tipperary and Waterford is so rich that a toothpick stuck in the sod will sprout in a fortnight. Here nature's bounty seems endless, and dairy products from Cork are legend. It was the richness of Ireland's cream that softened and smoothed out the resulting flavor of coffee, and Irish whiskey in Irish Coffee. What if, someone may have surmised, we leave out the coffee and just combine a little whiskey and cream? They did and it was delicious and a whole new liquor category began to take shape. R.& A. Bailey Co., Ltd., of Dublin found a way to homogenize spirits and cream so that after bottling it would have a reasonable shelf life without refrigeration under most climatic conditions. In the brief time since its birth in 1979, Bailey's Original Irish Cream Liqueur has rocketed to a sales level of one million cases per year, making it, according to industry sources, the number-one selling liqueur in the world. This success story has encouraged a host of similar proprietary liqueurs made with Irish whiskey and various flavorings blended with fresh cream. All are quality products and include such brands as Carolans, the number-two Irish cream liqueur; Waterford, made by Irish Distillers International, who own and control all of the major whiskey production in Ireland; O'Darby's; and Emmett's, and, no doubt, others which have not yet crossed my lips. One thing is certain, all of the cream liqueurs seem to have an irresistible appetite appeal for many, many people, even those who are not disposed to be whiskey drinkers. Perhaps therein lies the secret of its success: It tastes more like an adult milk shake than an alcoholic beverage. And apparently that's a taste that a lot of people like.

In Tullamore, very near to the geographical center of Ireland, another remarkable spiritous product is made by the Irish Mist Liqueur Company, Ltd., which in a relatively brief period of time has achieved recognition as one of the world's great proprietary liqueurs. Irish Mist is exciting to the palate and to the imagination, for it is believed by members of the Williams family, who created the liqueur from an old formula, that Irish Mist may be a re-creation of the lost heather wine of Ireland.

Now, if you don't know about heather wine you haven't been reading any Irish folklore lately. According to legend, heather wine was made from a closely guarded recipe by "the little people," or fairies. It also was said to be the favorite tonic of the Tuatha de Danann, an ancient Irish race endowed with magical powers since driven underground by the Celts, where, some say, they flourish to this day. Nevertheless, there are enough historical references, folklore notwithstanding, to convince many scholars that heather wine did indeed exist. Heather wine is alluded to in Irish song and story and records dating back to the pagan era of Irish history. And then it was gone.

The date of that disappearance is 1691, a year of great rebellion, when the "Wild Geese," the Irish nobility, fled Ireland. It is said that they took the secret of heather wine with them. Nobody really knows the whereabouts of the ancient formula. It remains a mystery. As the story goes, some of the Irish exiles later joined the army of Maria Theresa, the empress of Austria, where they served with distinction. So one fine day when the Williams family received a visitor from Austria bearing an ancient recipe purported to be the lost secret of heather wine, the pieces seemed to fit together. More important than the credibility of the visitor was the formula itself. It stood up to close scrutiny and tested out beyond all expectations. So when you quaff some Irish Mist, "the legendary liqueur," you just might be sampling Ireland's lost heather wine. In any event, the experience is a pleasant one.

Whether the real secret of heather wine has been recovered or not, I do not know, but it surely fires the imagination with another kind of spirit—the spirit of Ireland's glorious past. You sense it when you stand on the brow of the Hill of Tailte watching the sun set across the Blackwater River that runs through the gently rolling Meath countryside. Here was held the ancient festival of Aonoch Tailteann, games of strength and skill dating from prehistoric times. Close by, on the hill-top, lie the ruins of Rath Dubh, or Black Fort, built by King Tuathal. In these once great halls cups were raised high as toasts were drunk, perhaps with heather wine, to the champions of the games. Here in the valley of the Boyne, you are surrounded by jewels in the crown of Irish history: Kells, where the famous Book of Kells was written; Tara, home of ancient Irish kings; and the Hill of Slane, where St. Patrick lit the paschal fire in A.D. 433.

One can only guess what part heather wine and *uisce beatha* played in those ancient times, but one thing we do know, these spirits are very much a part of the lore and the legends of this wondrous land.

The Scotch Mystique

Scotch whisky is made of grain, yeast, and water; fermented, then distilled, aged, and bottled. The process seems simple enough yet no spirit has as many subtle complexities in its making or is surrounded in as much lore and tradition. As many a traveler has found to his astonishment and delight after even a brief journey down the "Whisky Trail" in Scotland, once exposed to the Scotch whisky mystique, one may never again drink this remarkable beverage with indifference or lack of appreciation.

How, you ask, in this age of computers, lasers, and electronically controlled industry, can anything as simple as the distilling of Scotch whisky be characterized as complex? The answer is that making scotch is not complex—but it is surrounded by mystery (such as why the letter "e" is omitted from the word "whisky"). It is not what is known about the process of Scotch whisky production that is intriguing, but what is seemingly unknowable.

A case in point: Two identical casks of scotch aging in the

same warehouse, one on the earthen floor, the other on a rack nearby, twelve feet above the floor, will have different characteristics when sampled at the end of the aging period. The reason is known. It has to do with air circulation, since casks of whisky "breathe" as they age. But just *how* this can have such an effect on the finished whisky is a mystery.

Then there is the Laphroaig mystery. It seems that when some of the single-malt whisky produced by this highly respected distillery on the Isle of Islay (pronounced **eye-lah**) is put up in casks for aging, it takes on a seaweed tang in the ninth month. This completely disappears at the twelfth year, however. Some say that this is due to the sea washing against the distillery walls, but exactly *how* this affects the whisky is not so easy to explain.

Despite dedicated efforts to make surrogate scotch in other places as diverse as Asia and North America, the results have been a perfectly drinkable whisky, but lacking in those subtle qualities that would be considered attributes of a fine scotch.

There are two types of Scotch whisky: malt whisky, which is made in an old-fashioned pot still (similar to cognac) and grain whisky, which is made in a patent or continuous still, sometimes called a Coffey still after its inventor, Aeneas Coffey. Malt whisky is made entirely from malted barley, and grain whisky is made from malted barley combined with unmalted barley and corn. The malting process involves the soaking of barley for two to three days in water and then spreading it out over a wide area so it can germinate or sprout. During this period, which lasts from eight to twelve days, the enzyme diastase is released. The enzyme makes the starch in the barley soluble so it can be converted to sugar. During the malting process the rate of germination and temperature must be carefully controlled. In some places the barley is still spread out on a malting floor and turned by hand to regulate the germination activity. In modern facilities the malting is done in boxes or drums turned by machine while temperature-controlled air is blown through the germinating grain.

At precisely the right time, the germination is stopped by drying the green malt (malted barley) in a kiln. The peat that is used to fire the kiln is responsible for the smoky taste that is a characteristic of malt whisky. The dried malt then is ground in a grist mill and poured into a huge tank or tun, where the mash is mixed with hot water. The liquid soluble starch (wort) created by the malting process is, after eight hours, drawn off from the mash tun and transferred to the fermentation vats. Here, the wort is fermented by yeast for forty-eight hours. This converts the sugar in the wort to low-strength alcohol (wash) and various by-products that are not involved in the scotch-making process. These are then filtered out.

The malt whisky is distilled twice in large copper-pot stills. The distillation process involves heating the wash mixture until it is vaporized. The vapors are collected in a condenser that is cooled by water, causing them to return to a liquid state. The pot still (similar in principle to the old alembic used by alchemists) must be emptied and recharged after each distilling cycle. In the case of grain whisky, the patent still is continuous in its operation as it is in the form of a huge column, not a pot, and thus can be charged and emptied without interfering with the distillation process.

The raw whisky is now ready for maturation in oak casks. They may be new American white oak containers, used sherry butts, or even casks that have held other spirits such as American bourbon. The whisky must age for at least three years, although most are aged longer. Malt whiskies require longer maturation than grain whiskies—as long as fourteen or fifteen years. Some blenders say that everything that can be achieved in aging is realized before the fifteenth year. For grain whiskies, six to eight years is considered optimum. When aging is complete, the whisky is ready for the most important step of all: blending.

In Scotland a master blender holds a position of high esteem considering the fact that ninety-eight percent of all whiskies produced at Scotland's 116 malt-whisky distilleries and fourteen grain-whisky distilleries are used to make *blended* Scotch whisky. There is growing interest in the U.S. in single malt whiskies, and some of Scotland's finest, once reserved exclusively for blending, are becoming available for the first time (see "A Selection of 21 Outstanding Single Malt Whiskies").

The blender's task is to replicate the blend in use, week in and week out, year after year. Quality control and ensuring a consistent product is of prime importance. Creating new blends is challenging and exciting, but is only a small part of the blender's job. The average blend will involve from fifteen to fifty different whiskies, since each distillery produces a whisky that has unique flavor and aroma. This individuality is one of the great aspects of the scotch mystique: how malt whiskies can vary in taste, using the very same ingredients and distilled in the same way only a short distance from one another. Since the blender and his team must sample, in some instances, four hundred casks in a single day, he must rely on his nose and his ability to remember his individual olfactory experiences, much as an accomplished composer will remember tones, chords, and melodies. As a rule, blenders do not taste the whiskies they sample, but rely entirely upon their highly educated noses.

Blending is designed to achieve a synergistic effect in the end product, meaning that the whole will be far superior to any of the individual elements it contains. To aid the blender in the task of selecting components that will "marry well" when blended, a library of spirits is carefully assembled. (Certain whiskies "fight one another," causing the temperature in the vats to rise, while some components of one whisky will cancel out the qualities of another whisky and thus cannot be used in a particular blending formula.) The library will contain samples from perhaps a hundred distilleries. In addition, it will have samples of many different blends devised by the blender and his assistants as well as samples of blends, purchased on the open market, of many competing brands of scotch. Most important is the collection of "key" malt whiskies from the most important distilleries in the various areas of Scotland, classified by the types of scotch produced in each.

A Selection of 21 Outstanding Single Malt Whiskies

Aberlour, ten years old (Speyside): This highly regarded Speyside malt has a slightly nutty aroma, full robust fruity flavor with good mouth feel, and a light peaty finish with a pronounced presence of sherry from the casks.

Balvenie, fifteen years old (Speyside): The aroma swirls with orange, honey, molasses, nuts, and sherry. The flavor is bold and assertive, imbued with a full body and good balance. The fine, full finish has overtones of sherry, oak, and honey.

Benriach (Speyside): A mélange of fruit greets your nose and you must spend time sniffing since there are lots to choose from. Flavors are extensions of the aromas, with good body and character topped by a muted, mellow finish.

Bowmore, twenty-five years old (Islay): This remarkable malt goes far beyond the seaweed and peat reek one might expect on the Island of Islay, a storm-lashed bastion of the western Hebrides. The citrusy, sherry, honey, spicy, peppery-peat bouquet prepares you for what's to come: chocolate, vanilla, black walnuts, old wine, bourbon, and items from the spice rack all capped by a lingering aftertaste that you do not want to forget.

Cardhu, twelve years old (Speyside): As Speyside whiskies go, this is a very light single malt, which makes it a good let's-get-acquainted dram for the beginner. It has a pleasant, diaphanous bouquet; the flavor is mild, well-balanced with velvety mouth feel and a sweet, gentle finish. An important component of the Johnnie Walker blend.

The Century of Malts, Chivas Brothers: By any standard this is a unique product consisting of a hundred single malts from all parts of Scotland, skillfully selected and matched by Chivas Brothers Master Blender, Colin Scott. It must be tasted to be appreciated. The nose is an array of fruity, sweet aromas. The flavor is complex: mellow with great character and balance followed by a lingering finish with hints of toffee and smoke. An impressive work of art that has been described as "Scotland in a bottle."

Cragganmore, twelve years old (Speyside): The fact that many distillers point to this malt as an outstanding example of a Speyside Highland Whisky is borne out by its complex aroma of heather honey, fruit, spices, coffee, vanilla, and a touch of peat. The flavor carries over much of the aroma's promise with oak and herbal undertones. A long, velvety finish brings it all together—the hallmark of an exemplary single malt.

Glendronach, twelve years old (Speyside): This Highland distillery prides itself on making whisky using old-fashioned methods: barley is spread on the malting floor, watered, and then turned and raked by hand to achieve maximum germination. Only four distilleries in Scotland still employ malting floors. The malt is aged in sherry casks and bourbon barrels, yielding a full-bodied whisky with an assertive flavor,

Glenfiddich, (Speyside): The delicate, mild aroma of Glenfiddich is intertwined with delicate florals and herbals, with undertones of sherry that are repeated in the flavor, which is smooth and pleasing. The finish is soft and floral. This is a good entry-level malt for the novice; it is also a favorite of aficionados, which has made it the largest selling single malt in the world.

Glenkinchie, ten years old (Lowland): This light-bodied malt whisky has an aroma of new-mown hay with a nutty nose, a slightly herbal flavor, a delicate character, and a soft, smoky finish. Because of their natural lightness, Lowland malts are used extensively for blending.

The Glenlivet, twelve years old (Speyside): This is the top-selling single malt in the U.S. When you taste it, you'll know why. It is a very easy malt to make friends with. Its light body is deceptive, as it has a broad spectrum of fruit and candy-store flavors, with some of the floral accents experienced in the aroma. An undertone of mixed nuts, caramel, and sherry adds to the complexity and character. It is topped off by a lovely and lively finish. It is very popular with both beginners and old Highland hands.

Glenmorangie, ten years old (Northern Highlands): Here's your chance to put your nose to the test. This malt has a brilliant, complex, multifaceted bouquet. It wasn't until a Parisian perfume chemist identified twenty-three separate aromas in that bouquet that blenders realized what has long been known, but never proven in the laboratory: "The nose *knows.*" Some of the scents are almond, chocolate, cinnamon, hay, juniper, lemon, sage, tobacco, and vanilla. Many of these fragrances have been associated by blenders with Scotch whisky for years and Glenmorangie seems to be especially well-endowed; perhaps this is why it's the best-selling malt in Scotland.

Glenrothes, fifteen years old (Speyside): This single malt, which is new to the American market, is so highly regarded by other Scotch whisky distillers that almost all of the Glenrothes production until recently has been snapped up for blending purposes. The soft, full, rounded taste and aging in sherry casks and bourbon barrels results in a wonderful smoothness, making it ideal for blending in a light scotch like Cutty Sark. It is also ideal for initiating a would-be serious Scotch whisky lover into the inner circle.

Highland Park, twelve years old (Orkney Islands): Here is another easy-to-know single malt because of its depth of character and excellent balance combined with an agreeable medium body. Highland Park is one of the very few distilleries that still use a malting floor, which, they say, gives maximum quality control over the malt at a most crucial time before mashing. It has a heathery bouquet, slightly sweet, not too smoky with a touch of sherry. The care that is given to the malting comes through in the flavor that is smooth and well-rounded. The lingering finish is polished and memorable.

Laphroaig, ten years old (Island of Islay): This is a classic, traditional Islay (pronounced "eye-lah") single malt, laden with the tastes and scents of peat, seaweed, burnt heather, blackened barley, and other earthy constituents that characterize this whisky type. My father gave me my first taste of scotch with this advice: "Remember, son, scotch takes getting used to. It's an acquired taste, but worth the effort." Laphroaig is even more so, but it has built a loyal following.

Longmorn, fifteen years old (Speyside): The bouquet foretells of wonderful tastes that lie in wait: butterscotch, lavender, honey, caramel, vanilla, cinnamon, and orange blossoms all seem to come through one way or another in the flavors that result in depth of character which continues to the long finish, providing a silky, gratifying aftertaste.

Macallan, twelve years old (Speyside): Oloroso sherry, spices, oak, and bitter orange form the core of a delightful bouquet. Unlike some blenders who seem to more or less tolerate the flavor of aging the whisky in sherry casks, Macallan has given it center stage. The results are truly an impressive amalgamation between a fortified wine from sunny Spain and a pure malt whisky from the windswept moors of the Highlands. The flavor is a mirror image of the bouquet, with the addition of a honey-like texture and smoothness; a touch of creamy, toasted coconut; and a light undercurrent of citrus and oloroso. The finish, like the taste, lives up to great expectations.

Oban, fourteen years old (Western Highlands): When you pull the cork you are greeted by an agreeable combination of malt, peat, oak, and oatmeal cookies warm from the oven. At the first taste of this hearty malt one encounters an undercurrent of smokiness with touches of orange, honey, and vanilla, plus a good peaty balance which never becomes overly assertive. The mouth-feel is smooth and refined, which eventually becomes part of a pleasantly lingering finish.

Royal Lochnagar Selected Reserve (Highlands–Royal Deeside): This distillery is close to Balmoral Castle, residence of the Royal Family when they visit Scotland, which may explain the very royal manner in the way Royal Lochnagar is presented in an elegant, fitted oaken box. Sherry aroma, from the casks used for aging, is pronounced in the bouquet, with overtones of malt and smokiness and other subtle aromatics. The flavor is slightly fruity, oaky, and quite mellow, providing good mouth-feel and character, all well-balanced. The finish is soft with an undercurrent of sherry.

Strathisla, twelve years old (Speyside): Chocolate, caramel, heather honey, buttered scones, and other subtle aromatics makes inhaling this aroma a delight. The flavor has a pleasant woody character with a nice touch of smokiness that is perfectly balanced with other qualities resulting in a mellow, medium body, all of which contributes to a luxurious finish. If you are an admirer of Chivas Regal, you may recognize some of the elegant qualities that Strathisla contributes to that distinguished blended whisky.

Talisker, ten years old, (Isle of Skye): The nose will detect at first contact that this is a robust, authoritative malt whisky with overtones of peat, smoke, sea spray, burnt driftwood, and seaweed. The flavor is pronounced, but all of the stronger elements, such as peatyness and maltiness and smokiness, are held in balance, resulting in a round, medium whisky with touches of brine, iodine, and other oceanic influences that come to the surface during the finish. Talisker is a major contributor to the blends of both Johnnie Walker Red and Black.

When the blender goes to work he has a vast arsenal of flavors and aromas to choose from, many of which are well-known to him. In devising a blend, he strives to utilize each component in exactly the right proportion to achieve the optimum flavor, character, and balance in the finished product. A hypothetical blend might consist of the following: sixty-five percent grain whiskies made up of the products of two or three grain distilleries, and thirty-five percent malt whiskies comprised of products from ten to fifteen malt distilleries. The malts, by far the most important components in the blend, might be chosen as follows: four to six Highland malts for body, three to four Speyside malts for balance, three or four Lowland malts for lightness, and one or two Islay malts for accent.

When all of the matured whiskies are "called" from the warehouse by the blender and his staff, they will be "vatted" or mixed to exacting specifications and then returned to wood to marry for six to nine months. When the blend is checked before bottling, it will have achieved precisely the flavor, bouquet or aroma, body, and color that the blender expected. Into every bottle will go a symphonic melding of Scotland's finest—the grain, the sun, the rain, the soil, the water that coursed through Highland heather and bracken, and, finally, the yeast and wood and the coming together with all the science and art and care that man can muster.

And there will be something else that goes into every bottle of whisky—a generous portion of scotch mystique.

ABERDEEN SOUR

2 oz. scotch
1 oz. orange juice
1 oz. lemon juice
½ oz. triple sec

Mix all ingredients with cracked ice in a shaker or blender. Pour into a chilled Old Fashioned glass.

AFFINITY COCKTAIL No. 2

1 oz. scotch
1 oz. dry sherry
1 oz. port
Several dashes Angostura
    bitters
Lemon peel
Maraschino cherry

Stir all ingredients, except lemon and cherry, in a mixing glass with cracked ice and strain into a chilled cocktail glass. Twist lemon peel over drink and drop into glass and garnish with a cherry.

ARDMORE COCKTAIL

1 oz. scotch
½ oz. Cherry Marnier
½ oz. sweet vermouth
2 oz. orange juice

Mix all ingredients with cracked ice in a shaker or blender. Strain into a chilled cocktail glass.

ARGYLL COCKTAIL

1 oz. scotch
1 oz. calvados
½ oz. dry gin
1 tsp. heather honey or
    sugar syrup

Mix all ingredients, except lemon peel, with cracked ice in a shaker or blender. Pour into a chilled Old Fashioned glass. Twist lemon peel over drink and drop in.

AULD MAN'S MILK Cold

1 tsp. sugar syrup
1 whole egg
5 oz. heavy cream, or 3 oz.
    cream and 3 oz. milk
2 oz. scotch
Grated nutmeg

Beat egg separately with sugar syrup and add to a shaker or blender with cream, scotch, and cracked ice. Mix well and pour into a chilled Old Fashioned glass. Sprinkle with grated nutmeg.

BARTENDER'S SECRET NO. 21—Equal Servings

When filling a number of glasses from the same cocktail shaker or blender, don't fill the first glass to the top and then the remaining glasses. You will usually come out short on the last glass unless you are experienced. Experts fill each glass about half full and then return to glass number one and repeat the procedure. This will insure an equal portion for everyone.

BAIRN

1½ oz. scotch
¾ oz. Cointreau
Several dashes orange
    bitters

Mix all ingredients with cracked ice in a shaker or blender. Strain into a chilled cocktail glass.

BALLSBRIDGE BRACER

1½ oz. Irish whiskey
¾ oz. Irish Mist
3 oz. orange juice
1 egg white (for two drinks)

Mix all ingredients with cracked ice in a shaker or blender. Strain into a chilled Whiskey Sour glass.

BALLYLICKEY BELT

½ tsp. heather honey or to taste
1½ oz. Irish whiskey
Club soda
Lemon peel

Muddle heather honey with a little water or club soda until dissolved and pour in whiskey. Add several ice cubes and fill with club soda. Twist lemon peel over drink and drop into glass.

BALMORAL STIRRUP CUP

1½ oz. scotch
1 oz. Cointreau
Several dashes Angostura bitters

Mix all ingredients with cracked ice in a shaker or blender. Strain into a chilled cocktail glass.

BANCHORY COCKTAIL

1 oz. scotch
1 oz. medium sherry
1 tsp. lemon juice
1 tsp. orange juice
½ tsp. sugar syrup

Mix all ingredients with cracked ice in a shaker or blender. Strain into a chilled cocktail glass.

BANFF BANG

1½ oz. gin
½ oz. amontillado sherry
1 oz. scotch
Lemon peel

Mix gin and amontillado with cracked ice in a shaker or blender. Pour into a chilled Old Fashioned glass. Twist lemon peel over drink and drop in, and float scotch on top.

BARBARY COAST

¾ oz. scotch
¾ oz. light rum
¾ oz. gin
¾ oz. white crème de cacao
1 oz. cream

Mix all ingredients with cracked ice in a shaker or blender. Pour into a chilled Old Fashioned glass.

◗ BLACKTHORN No. 1

1½ oz. Irish whiskey
1½ oz. dry vermouth
Several dashes Pernod
Several dashes Angostura
  bitters

Mix all ingredients with cracked ice in a shaker or blender. Pour into a chilled Old Fashioned glass.

Sloe gin can be used in place of Irish whiskey.

BLACKWATCH

1½ oz. scotch
½ oz. curaçao
½ oz. brandy
Lemon slice
Mint sprig

Pour scotch, curaçao, and brandy into a chilled highball glass along with several ice cubes. Gently stir. Garnish with lemon slice and mint sprig.

BLOOD & SAND

¾ oz. scotch
¾ oz. cherry brandy
¾ oz. sweet vermouth
¾ oz. orange juice

Mix all ingredients with cracked ice in a shaker or blender. Pour into a chilled Old Fashioned glass.

BLUE FIRTH

1½ oz. scotch
½ oz. blue curaçao
Dash dry vermouth
Dash orange bitters

Mix all ingredients with cracked ice in a shaker or blender. Strain into a chilled cocktail glass.

BOBBY BURNS

1½ oz. scotch
½ oz. dry vermouth
½ oz. sweet vermouth
Dash Benedictine

Mix all ingredients with cracked ice in a shaker or blender. Strain into a chilled cocktail glass.

BONNIE PRINCE CHARLIE

1½ oz. scotch
½ oz. dry vermouth
Several dashes Pernod
Lemon peel

Mix all ingredients, except lemon peel, with cracked ice in a shaker or blender. Strain into a chilled Martini glass. Twist lemon peel over drink and drop in.

BOW STREET SPECIAL

1½ oz. Irish whiskey
¾ oz. triple sec
1 oz. lemon juice

Mix with cracked ice in a shaker or blender and strain into a chilled cocktail glass.

BRAEMAR COCKTAIL

1½ oz. scotch
½ oz. sweet vermouth
½ oz. Benedictine

Mix all ingredients with cracked ice in a shaker or blender. Strain into a chilled cocktail glass.

BRIGADOON

1 oz. scotch
1 oz. grapefruit juice
1 oz. dry vermouth

Mix all ingredients with cracked ice in a shaker or blender. Pour into a chilled Old Fashioned glass.

 BUNRATTY PEG

1½ oz. Irish whiskey
¾ oz. Irish Mist, amaretto, or Drambuie

Stir with ice and strain into a chilled cocktail glass or with ice cubes in an Old Fashioned glass.

CABER TOSS

1¼ oz. scotch
1¼ oz. gin
½ oz. Pernod

Mix all ingredients with cracked ice in a blender or shaker. Strain into a chilled cocktail glass.

CAITHNESS COMFORT

2–3 oz. scotch
½ oz. honey
½ oz. triple sec
6 oz. milk
1 oz. cream
Pinch grated nutmeg

Mix all ingredients except nutmeg in a shaker or blender with cracked ice and pour into a chilled Collins glass. Add pinch of grated nutmeg.

CAMPBELTOWN JOY

1½ oz. scotch
1 tsp. dry vermouth
½ oz. Drambuie
Dash orange bitters

Mix all ingredients with cracked ice in a shaker or blender. Strain into a chilled cocktail glass.

CELTIC BULL

1½ oz. Irish whiskey
2 oz. beef consommé or
    bouillon
2 oz. tomato juice
Several dashes
    Worcestershire sauce
Dash Tabasco sauce
Freshly ground pepper

Mix all ingredients with cracked ice in a shaker or blender. Pour into a chilled Old Fashioned glass.

◤ COCKTAIL NA MARA Cocktail of the Sea

2 oz. Irish whiskey
2 oz. clam juice
4 oz. tomato juice
½ oz. lemon juice
Several dashes
    Worcestershire sauce
Dash Tabasco sauce
Pinch white pepper

Stir all ingredients well in a mixing glass with cracked ice and pour into a chilled highball glass.

COLLODEN CHEER

1 oz. scotch
1 oz. dry sherry
½ oz. lemon juice
½ oz. *La Grande Passion*

Mix all ingredients with cracked ice in a shaker or blender. Strain into a chilled cocktail glass.

CONNEMARA CLAMMER

2 oz. *Irish whiskey*
2 oz. clam juice
3 oz. *V-8 juice*
1 tsp. lime juice
Several dashes
    Worcestershire sauce
½ tsp. horseradish
Several pinches freshly
    ground black or white
    pepper

Mix all ingredients with cracked ice in a shaker or blender. Strain into a chilled double Old Fashioned glass.

CORK COMFORT

1½ oz. *Irish whiskey*
¾ oz. sweet vermouth
Several dashes Angostura
    bitters
Several dashes Southern
    Comfort

Mix all ingredients with cracked ice in a shaker or blender. Pour into a chilled Old Fashioned glass.

DINGLE DRAM

1½ oz. *Irish whiskey*
½ oz. *Irish Mist*
Coffee soda
Dash crème de cacao
Whipped cream

Pour Irish whiskey and Irish Mist into a chilled highball glass along with several ice cubes. Fill with coffee soda. Stir gently. Add a float of crème de cacao. Top with dollop of whipped cream.

DUNDEE DRAM

1 oz. scotch
1 oz. gin
½ oz. Drambuie
1 tsp. lemon juice
Lemon peel
Maraschino cherry

Mix all ingredients, except lemon peel and cherry, with cracked ice in a shaker or blender. Pour into a chilled Old Fashioned glass. Twist lemon peel over drink and drop in. Garnish with cherry.

DUNDEE DUNKER

2 oz. scotch
6 oz. milk
1 tsp. golden syrup or honey
Grated nutmeg
Shortbread

Mix all ingredients, except nutmeg and shortbread, with cracked ice in a shaker or blender. Pour into a chilled Old Fashioned glass. Sprinkle with grated nutmeg. Dunk shortbread in mixture as you drink it.

ERIC THE RED

1½ oz. scotch
½ oz. Cherry Heering
1 tsp. dry vermouth

Mix all ingredients with cracked ice in a shaker or blender. Pour into a chilled Old Fashioned glass.

FLYING SCOT

1½ oz. scotch
1 oz. sweet vermouth
Several dashes sugar syrup
Several dashes Angostura
  bitters

Mix all ingredients with cracked ice in a shaker or blender. Pour into a chilled Old Fashioned glass.

GLASGOW

1½ oz. scotch
½ oz. crème de noyaux or
  amaretto
¼ oz. dry vermouth
½ oz. lemon juice

Mix all ingredients with cracked ice in a shaker or blender. Strain into a chilled cocktail glass.

GLENBEIGH FIZZ

1½ oz. Irish whiskey
1 oz. medium sherry
½ oz. crème de noyaux
½ oz. lemon juice
Club soda

Pour all ingredients, except club soda, with several ice cubes in a chilled highball glass and stir. Fill with club soda.

GLENEAGLES AERIE

1½ oz. scotch
½ oz. dry vermouth
½ oz. port
Dash orange bitters

Mix all ingredients with cracked ice in a shaker or blender. Strain into a chilled cocktail glass.

 THE GODFATHER

1½ oz. scotch, bourbon, or blended whiskey
¾ oz. Amaretto di Saronno

Mix with ice cubes in a chilled Old Fashioned glass.

GRAFTON STREET SOUR

1½ oz. Irish whiskey
½ oz. triple sec
1 oz. lime juice
¼ oz. raspberry liqueur

Mix all ingredients, except raspberry liqueur, with cracked ice in a shaker or blender and strain into a chilled cocktail glass. Top with raspberry liqueur.

GRETNA GREEN

½ oz. Falernum or heather honey
1½ oz. scotch
½ oz. green Chartreuse
1 oz. lemon juice

Mix Falernum or honey with a little water until dissolved and pour into a shaker or blender with scotch, green Chartreuse, and lemon juice, and mix thoroughly with cracked ice. Strain into a chilled cocktail glass.

HARRY LAUDER

1½ oz. scotch
1½ oz. sweet vermouth
½ tsp. sugar syrup

Mix all ingredients with cracked ice in a shaker or blender. Strain into a chilled cocktail glass.

HIGHLAND FLING No. 1

1½ oz. scotch
3 oz. milk
1 tsp. sugar syrup
Nutmeg

Mix all ingredients, except nutmeg, with cracked ice in a shaker or blender. Pour into a chilled Old Fashioned glass. Sprinkle with nutmeg.

HIGHLAND FLING No. 2

1½ oz. scotch
½ oz. sweet vermouth
Several dashes orange
  bitters
Olive

Mix all ingredients, except olive, with cracked ice in a shaker or blender. Pour into a chilled cocktail glass. Drop in olive.

HIGHLAND MORNING

1 oz. scotch
¾ oz. Cointreau
3 oz. grapefruit juice

Mix all ingredients with cracked ice in a shaker or blender. Pour into a chilled Old Fashioned glass.

INNISFREE FIZZ

2 oz. Irish whiskey
1 oz. lemon juice
1 oz. curaçao
½ tsp. sugar syrup or to taste
Club soda

Mix all ingredients, except club soda, with cracked ice in a shaker or blender. Strain into a chilled wine goblet and fill with club soda.

 INVERCAULD CASTLE COOLER

1½ oz. scotch
1 oz. Benedictine
Ginger ale

Pour scotch and Benedictine into a chilled highball glass, add several ice cubes, and fill with ginger ale. Stir gently.

INVERNESS COCKTAIL

2 oz. scotch
½ oz. lemon juice
1 tsp. orgeat syrup
1 tsp. triple sec or curaçao

Mix all ingredients, except triple sec, with cracked ice in a shaker or blender and strain into a chilled cocktail glass. Top with a float of triple sec or curaçao.

IRISH BUCK

1½ oz. Irish whiskey
Lemon peel
Ginger ale

Pour Irish whiskey into chilled highball glass with cracked ice. Twist lemon peel over drink and drop in. Add ginger ale.

IRISH FIX

2 oz. Irish whiskey
½ oz. Irish Mist
½ oz. lemon juice
½ oz. pineapple syrup or
    pineapple juice
Orange slice
Lemon slice

Mix all ingredients, except fruit slices, with cracked ice in a shaker or blender and pour into an Old Fashioned glass. Garnish with fruit slices.

If pineapple juice is used in place of pineapple syrup, add a little sugar syrup to taste.

IRISH KILT

1 oz. Irish whiskey
1 oz. scotch
1 oz. lemon juice
1½ oz. sugar syrup or to
    taste
Several dashes orange
    bitters

Mix all ingredients with cracked ice in a shaker or blender and strain into a chilled cocktail glass.

IRISH RAINBOW

1½ oz. Irish whiskey
Several dashes Pernod
Several dashes curaçao
Several dashes maraschino
    liqueur
Several dashes Angostura
    bitters
Orange peel

Mix all ingredients, except orange peel, with cracked ice in a shaker or blender. Pour into a chilled Old Fashioned glass. Twist orange peel over drink and drop in.

IRISH SHILLELAGH

1½ oz. Irish whiskey
½ oz. sloe gin
½ oz. light rum
1 oz. lemon juice
1 tsp. sugar syrup
2 peach slices, diced
5–6 fresh raspberries
Maraschino cherry

Mix all ingredients, except berries and cherry, with cracked ice in a shaker or blender. Pour into a chilled Old Fashioned glass. Garnish with raspberries and cherry.

J.J.'S SHAMROCK

1 oz. Irish whiskey
½ oz. crème de cacao (white)
½ oz. crème de menthe
  (green)
1 oz. milk

Mix in a shaker or blender with cracked ice and serve in a chilled cocktail glass.

JAPANESE FIZZ No. 2

2 oz. scotch
2 oz. dry red wine
½ oz. lemon juice
1 tsp. sugar syrup
Club soda
Pineapple spear

Mix all ingredients, except club soda and pineapple, with cracked ice in a shaker or blender. Pour into a chilled highball glass and fill with club soda. Decorate with pineapple.

 ## KERRY COOLER

2 oz. Irish whiskey
1½ oz. medium sherry
1 oz. orgeat syrup
½ oz. lemon juice
Club soda
Lemon slice

Mix all ingredients, except club soda and lemon slice, with cracked ice in a shaker or blender. Pour into a chilled highball glass and fill with club soda. Garnish with lemon slice.

KILDRUMMY

1½ oz. scotch
½ oz. sweet vermouth
Several dashes orange
  bitters
Several dashes Pernod

Mix all ingredients with cracked ice in a shaker or blender. Pour into a chilled Old Fashioned glass.

KINSALE COOLER

1½ oz. Irish whiskey
1 oz. Irish Mist
1 oz. lemon juice
Club soda
Ginger ale
Lemon peel

Mix Irish Mist, whiskey, and lemon juice with cracked ice in a shaker or blender. Pour into a chilled Collins glass. Fill with equal parts of club soda and ginger ale. Stir gently. Twist lemon peel over drink and drop in.

KISS ME AGAIN

1½ oz. scotch
Several dashes Pernod
1 egg white (for two drinks)
Orange slice

Mix all ingredients, except orange slice, with cracked ice in a shaker or blender and pour into a chilled cocktail glass.

LOCH LOMOND

1½ oz. scotch
½ oz. sugar syrup
Several dashes Angostura
   bitters

Mix all ingredients with cracked ice in a shaker or blender and pour into a chilled cocktail glass.

LOCH NESS

1½ oz. scotch
1 oz. Pernod
¼ oz. sweet vermouth

Mix all ingredients with cracked ice in a shaker or blender. Pour into a chilled Old Fashioned glass.

MAMIE TAYLOR

3 oz. scotch
½ oz. lime juice
Ginger ale
Lemon slice

Pour scotch and lime juice in a chilled Collins glass with several ice cubes. Fill with ginger ale and gently stir. Garnish with lemon slice.

MIAMI BEACH COCKTAIL

1 oz. scotch
1 oz. dry vermouth
1 oz. grapefruit juice

Mix all ingredients with cracked ice in a shaker or blender. Strain into a chilled cocktail glass.

 THE MINCH

1½ oz. scotch
1 tsp. peppermint schnapps
Club soda
Peppermint stick or candy
   cane (optional)

Mix all ingredients, except club soda and stick, with cracked ice in a shaker or blender. Pour into a chilled Old Fashioned glass. Fill with club soda. Decorate with peppermint stick or candy cane.

MODERN No. 2

3 oz. scotch
Several dashes Jamaica rum
Several dashes Pernod
Several dashes lemon juice
Several dashes orange
  bitters
Maraschino cherry

Mix all ingredients, except maraschino cherry, with cracked ice in a shaker or blender. Pour into a chilled Old Fashioned glass. Decorate with cherry.

MONTROSE MILK

2 oz. scotch
6 oz. chocolate milk
1 tsp. curaçao
Grated chocolate

Mix all ingredients, except chocolate, with cracked ice in a shaker or blender. Pour into a chilled double Old Fashioned glass. Sprinkle with grated chocolate.

MORNING GLORY

1 oz. scotch
1 oz. brandy
½ tsp. sugar syrup
Several dashes curaçao
Dash Pernod
Several dashes Angostura
  bitters
Club soda
Powdered sugar

Mix all ingredients, except club soda and powdered sugar, with cracked ice in a shaker or blender. Pour into a chilled Collins glass. Fill with club soda. Wet a barspoon with water and roll in a little powdered sugar. Use this spoon to stir the drink before serving.

MORNING GLORY FIZZ

2 oz. scotch
¼ oz. Pernod
½ oz. lemon juice
1 tsp. sugar
1 egg white (for two drinks)
Dash Peychaud's bitters
Club soda
Lemon slice

Mix all ingredients, except club soda and lemon slice, with cracked ice in a shaker or blender. Pour into a chilled Collins glass. Fill with club soda. Decorate with fruit slice.

PADDY COCKTAIL

1½ oz. Irish whiskey
¾ oz. sweet vermouth
Several dashes Angostura
   bitters

Mix all ingredients with cracked ice in a shaker or blender. Serve in a chilled cocktail glass.

PARKNASILLA PEG LEG

1½ oz. Irish whiskey
1 oz. coconut syrup
3 oz. pineapple juice
1 tsp. lemon juice
Club soda

Mix whiskey, coconut syrup, and fruit juices in a shaker or blender with cracked ice and pour into a chilled highball glass along with several ice cubes. Fill with club soda. Stir gently.

PERTH COCKTAIL

2 oz. scotch
½ oz. lemon juice
1 tsp. sugar syrup
Several dashes curaçao
Dash amaretto

Mix all ingredients with cracked ice in a shaker or blender. Pour into a chilled cocktail glass.

PRESTWICK

1½ oz. scotch
½ oz. sweet vermouth
Several dashes orange
   curaçao
Several dashes Drambuie
Orange peel

Mix all ingredients, except Drambuie and orange peel, with cracked ice in a shaker or blender. Pour into a chilled Old Fashioned glass. Twist orange peel over drink and drop in. Top with float of Drambuie.

PRINCE EDWARD

1½ oz. scotch
½ oz. Lillet blanc
¼ oz. Drambuie
Preserved orange slice

Mix all ingredients, except orange slice, with cracked ice in a shaker or blender. Pour into a chilled Old Fashioned glass. Garnish with orange slice.

PRINCES STREET

1½ oz. scotch
1 egg white (for two drinks)
1 tsp. sugar syrup
1 tsp. curaçao

Mix all ingredients with cracked ice in a shaker or blender. Strain into a chilled cocktail glass.

THE PURPLE HEATHER

1½ oz. scotch
½ oz. crème de cassis
Club soda

Mix scotch and crème de cassis in a highball glass with ice and fill with club soda.

P.V. DOYLE

1½ oz. Irish whiskey
¾ oz. green crème de menthe
1 oz. heavy cream
Maraschino cherry

Mix all ingredients, except maraschino cherry, with cracked ice in a shaker or blender and pour into a chilled cocktail glass.

 PYEWACKET'S REVENGE

1½ oz. scotch
6 oz. cola
Lemon peel

Pour scotch into a chilled double Old Fashioned glass along with several ice cubes. Fill with cola and stir gently. Twist lemon peel over drink and drop in.

REMSEN COOLER

2–3 oz. scotch
1 tsp. sugar syrup
Club soda
Lemon peel

Pour scotch and sugar syrup into a chilled Collins glass along with several ice cubes. Fill with club soda. Thoroughly stir. Twist lemon peel over drink and drop in.

For a gin Remsen Cooler, substitute gin for scotch and ginger ale for club soda.

◤ RING OF KERRY

1½ oz. Irish whiskey
1 oz. Bailey's Irish Cream
½ oz. Kahlua or crème de
   cacao
1 tsp. shaved chocolate

Mix all ingredients, except shaved chocolate, with cracked ice in a shaker or blender. Strain into a chilled cocktail glass. Sprinkle with shaved chocolate.

◤ ROB ROY

1½–2 oz. scotch
½ oz. sweet vermouth
Dash orange bitters
   (optional)
Maraschino cherry

Pour all ingredients, except cherry, into a mixing glass along with several ice cubes. Stir well. Strain into a chilled cocktail glass. Garnish with cherry.

◤ ROB ROY Dry

1½–2 oz. scotch
½ oz. dry vermouth
Dash Angostura bitters
   (optional)
Lemon peel

Stir all ingredients, except lemon peel, with ice in a mixing glass and strain into a chilled cocktail glass. Twist lemon peel over drink and drop into glass.

ROYAL DEESIDE

1 oz. scotch
1 oz. brandy
1 oz. Parfait Amour
Several dashes Pernod
Several dashes orange
   bitters

Mix all ingredients with cracked ice in a shaker or blender. Pour into a chilled Old Fashioned glass.

ROYAL ROB ROY

1½ oz. scotch
1½ oz. Drambuie
¼ oz. dry vermouth
¼ oz. sweet vermouth
Maraschino cherry

Mix all ingredients, except cherry, with cracked ice in a shaker or blender. Strain into a chilled cocktail glass and decorate with cherry.

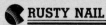 **RUSTY NAIL**

1½ oz. scotch
1 oz. Drambuie

Pour ingredients into a chilled
Old Fashioned glass along with
several ice cubes. Stir.

SCOTCH BUCK

2–3 oz. scotch
¼ oz. lime or lemon juice
Ginger ale
Lime or lemon wedge

Mix scotch and lime juice with
cracked ice in a mixing glass
and pour into a chilled highball
glass. Fill with ginger ale and
garnish with fruit wedge.

SCOTCH COOLER

3 oz. scotch
Several dashes white crème
   de menthe
Club soda

Pour scotch and crème de menthe
into a chilled highball glass.
Stir. Add several ice cubes. Top
with club soda.

SCOTCH FLIP

2 oz. scotch
1 egg white
½ oz. sugar syrup
Club soda

Mix all ingredients, except club
soda, with cracked ice in a
shaker or blender. Pour into a
chilled Old Fashioned glass.
Add club soda and stir gently.

SCOTCH HOLIDAY SOUR

2 oz. scotch
1 oz. Cherry Marnier
1 oz. lemon juice
½ oz. sweet vermouth
1 egg white (for two drinks)
Lemon slice

Mix all ingredients, except
lemon slice, with cracked ice in
a shaker or blender. Strain into
a chilled Whiskey Sour glass.
Garnish with lemon slice.

SCOTCH JULEP

6–8 mint leaves
1 oz. Drambuie
2 oz. scotch
Mint sprig

Muddle mint leaves, Drambuie,
and a little water together in a
chilled double Old Fashioned
glass. Fill with finely crushed ice
and add scotch. Muddle again and
add more scotch and more ice if
you wish. Garnish with mint sprig.

 ## SCOTCH MIST

1½–2 oz. scotch
Lemon peel

Pour scotch into a chilled Old Fashioned glass filled with crushed ice. Twist lemon peel over drink and drop into glass.

 ## SCOTCH ORANGE FIX

2 oz. scotch
½ oz. lemon juice
1 tsp. sugar syrup
1 tsp. curaçao
Orange peel cut in a long spiral

Mix all ingredients, except curaçao and peel, with cracked ice in a shaker or blender and pour into a double Old Fashioned glass. Add orange peel and additional ice. Top with curaçao.

 ## SCOTCH SANGAREE

1 tsp. heather honey or to taste
1½ oz. scotch
Lemon peel
Club soda
Grated nutmeg

Mix heather honey and a little water or club soda in a double Old Fashioned glass until honey is dissolved. Add scotch and a lemon twist, ice cubes, and fill with club soda. Sprinkle grated nutmeg over top.

 ## SCOTCH SMASH

6 mint leaves
Heather honey or sugar syrup
2–3 oz. scotch
Orange bitters
Mint sprig

Muddle honey or sugar with mint in a double Old Fashioned glass and fill with crushed ice. Add scotch and mix well with a barspoon. Add additional ice and scotch if desired. Top with orange bitters and a mint sprig.

 ## SCOTCH SOUR

1½ oz. scotch
½ oz. lemon juice
1 tsp. sugar syrup
Orange slice
Maraschino cherry

Mix all ingredients, except orange slice and maraschino cherry, with cracked ice in a shaker or blender. Strain into a chilled Whiskey Sour glass. Garnish with orange slice and cherry.

SCOTTISH COBBLER

1½ oz. scotch
½ oz. pineapple syrup, sugar syrup, or honey
½ oz. curaçao
Mint sprigs

Mix all ingredients, except mint, with cracked ice in a shaker or blender. Strain into a chilled Old Fashioned glass and garnish with mint sprigs.

SCOTTISH HORSE'S NECK

1 lemon peel, in long spiral
2–3 oz. scotch
½ oz. sweet vermouth
½ oz. dry vermouth

Place lemon peel in a chilled Collins glass with one end of peel hanging over rim. Pour in scotch, sweet and dry vermouths. Fill glass with cracked ice. Stir well and let stand for a few minutes before drinking.

SECRET

1½ oz. scotch
Several dashes peppermint schnapps
Club soda

Mix all ingredients, except club soda, with cracked ice in a shaker or blender. Pour into a chilled Old Fashioned glass. Fill with club soda.

 SERPENT'S TOOTH

¾ oz. Irish whiskey
1½ oz. sweet vermouth
½ oz. kümmel
¾ oz. lemon juice
Several dashes Angostura bitters
Lemon peel

Mix all ingredients, except lemon peel, with cracked ice in a shaker or blender. Pour into a chilled Old Fashioned glass. Twist lemon peel over drink and drop in.

 SHAMROCK No. 1

1½ oz. Irish whiskey
¾ oz. dry vermouth
1 tsp. green Chartreuse
1 tsp. green crème de menthe

Stir all ingredients with plenty of ice in a pitcher and strain into a chilled cocktail glass.

SHAMROCK No. 2

1½ oz. Irish whiskey
1½ oz. green crème de
  menthe
2 oz. heavy cream
Maraschino cherry

Mix all ingredients, except
cherry, with cracked ice in a
shaker or blender. Pour into a
chilled Old Fashioned glass. Garnish with maraschino cherry.

 ### SHAMROCK No. 3

1½ oz. Irish whiskey
¾ oz. green crème de
  menthe
4 oz. vanilla ice cream

Mix all ingredients in a blender
at high speed until smooth. Pour
into a chilled wine goblet.

 ### SHETLAND PONY

1½ oz. scotch
¾ oz. Irish Mist
Dash orange bitters
  (optional)

Mix all ingredients with cracked
ice in a mixing glass and strain
into a chilled cocktail glass.

SKIBBEREEN TONIC

2 oz. Irish whiskey
Tonic water
Lemon peel

Pour Irish whiskey into a chilled
Old Fashioned glass with several ice cubes. Fill with tonic
water. Twist lemon peel over
drink and drop in.

SKYE SWIZZLE

¾ oz. scotch
¾ oz. Jamaica rum
¾ oz. dry gin
1 tsp. lime juice
Several dashes sweet
  vermouth
Several dashes cherry
  brandy
Maraschino cherry

Mix all ingredients, except maraschino cherry, with cracked ice
in a shaker or blender. Pour into
a chilled Collins glass. Garnish
with cherry.

SPIRIT OF SCOTLAND

2 oz. scotch
¾ oz. Drambuie
¼ oz. lemon juice

Mix all ingredients with cracked ice in a shaker or blender and strain into a chilled cocktail glass.

STIRLING SOUR

1½ oz. scotch
½ oz. lime juice
1 tsp. sugar syrup or to taste
Several dashes Cointreau

Mix all ingredients with cracked ice in a shaker or blender. Pour into a chilled cocktail or Whiskey Sour glass.

STONEHAVEN

1½ oz. scotch
½ oz. Cointreau
½ oz. sweet vermouth
2 tsp. lime juice

Mix all ingredients with cracked ice in a shaker or blender. Pour into a chilled Old Fashioned glass.

THISTLE

2 oz. scotch
1 oz. sweet vermouth
Several dashes Angostura
  bitters

Mix all ingredients with cracked ice in a shaker or blender. Strain into a chilled cocktail glass.

 TIPPERARY

1 oz. Irish whiskey
1 oz. sweet vermouth
½ oz. green Chartreuse

Combine all ingredients with several ice cubes in mixing glass. Stir well and strain into a chilled cocktail glass.

TRILBY No. 2

¾ oz. scotch
¾ oz. sweet vermouth
¾ oz. Parfait Amour
Several dashes Pernod
Several dashes Angostura
  bitters

Mix all ingredients with cracked ice in a shaker or blender. Pour into a chilled Old Fashioned glass.

URQUHART CASTLE

1½ oz. scotch
Several dashes dry vermouth
Several dashes Cointreau
Several dashes orange
   bitters

Mix all ingredients with cracked ice in a shaker or blender. Pour into a chilled Old Fashioned glass.

WHISKEY MAC

2 oz. scotch
2 oz. ginger wine

Mix all ingredients with cracked ice in a shaker or blender. Pour into a chilled Old Fashioned glass.

 WICKLOW COOLER

1½ oz. Irish whiskey
1 oz. Jamaica dark rum
½ oz. lime juice
1 oz. orange juice
1 tsp. Falernum or orgeat
   syrup
Ginger ale

Mix all ingredients, except ginger ale, with cracked ice in a shaker or blender. Pour into a chilled Collins glass. Fill with ginger ale.

MONTEZUMA'S LEGACY: TEQUILA

Ay, Chihuahua!
—Uttered by an American friend in a
Mexican *cantina* upon taking his first drink
of straight tequila with lime and salt.

Legend has it that in ancient times a Toltec of royal blood discovered a miraculous potion in the heart of the great spiked maguey plant. He called it "honey water" (*aguamiel* in Spanish), for when it was fermented and imbibed, it produced a wondrous effect. (The sap or juice of the maguey is still referred to as *aguamiel* when making pulque, a fermented, mildly alcoholic beverage consumed fresh, like draft beer, in Mexico, where it is extremely popular.) To win favor with the king, he prepared a flask of this magic brew and dispatched his young and beautiful daughter, Princess Xochitl, to present this gift at the royal court. History does not tell us what the king thought of the gift, but he apparently was quite taken with Xochitl, who soon became Queen Xochitl and bore him a son.

From these auspicious beginnings have come pulque, which is probably the first alcoholic beverage to originate in the New World, and later, after the Spanish conquistadors imported the art of distillation, mescal, and its more refined cousin, tequila.

The reputation that tequila once had among the uninitiated as a raw, harsh beverage is undeserved. It probably resulted from tourists being subjected to cheap, unaged mescals or other forms of *aguardientes* distilled from coconuts, cane, corn, or pineapple. The alcoholic content of most tequila runs from 80 to 86 proof, which puts it in a class with most whiskeys, rum, gin, and vodka.

The subtle and elusive flavor of tequila perhaps accounts for its growing popularity in the U.S. Pungent and faintly yeasty, it defies more precise description, but marries well with other spirits and liqueurs and almost any kind of fruit juice. It is especially good with citrus fruits and does wonders for tomato juice, thus providing a proper foundation for a smashing Bloody Mary and similar concoctions employing the tomato.

As you might have guessed, most tequila is produced in and around the town of Tequila, about thirty-five miles from Guadalajara in the state of Jalisco. It is distilled from the juice that is extracted from the heart of the *agave tequilana weber* or so-called "blue agave," which is just one of the more than four hundred varieties of the agave or maguey plant. Of this extensive plant category only a few types of maguey may be used to produce mescal and only one, the *agave tequilana*, is used to make tequila.

In the area surrounding the town of Tequila—a strictly delimited zone, the boundaries of which are specified by the Mexican government—some forty to fifty distillers or *tequileros* cultivate the blue agave and make tequila. After a ten-year growing process, the heart of the agave is harvested and roasted in huge steam ovens. The hearts are then shredded, the juice pressed out, and sugar added for a four-day period of fermentation. After a double distillation (needed to bring the alcoholic content up to the proper level), the white spirit is ready for drinking, without further processing, like gin or vodka. A part of the production will be set aside and aged in wooden casks from a period of a few months to as long as seven years. During this period the tequila takes on a yellow or golden color and is marketed as *tequila añejo*. The older *añejos* command premium prices and are worth it to the tequila connoisseur since the aging process gives them a smooth, mellow finish comparable to fine old bourbon or cognac.

Whether you take tequila neat with salt and lime in the classic Mexican style or use it to build a zippy cocktail or a tall, refreshing summer cooler, tequila deserves knowing. The creative mixologist will find a challenge in devising tequila drinks because of its elusive and unique flavor characteristics, but the rewards and satisfaction are great, especially when you hit upon the right flavor combination resulting in a delicious recipe that is unlike any other.

The "Mexican Itch"—The Original Tequila Tot

No one who has reached his majority should be deprived of the opportunity to quaff a hearty peg of tequila *cantina*-style with coarse salt and fresh lime at least once. It is a moving experience, especially if one has a tender gullet. Here follows a memorable experience on the part of a Mexicophile companion on a journey of discovery south of the border:

"Tequila estilo Pancho Villa, por favor," croaks my hot and thirsty friend through parched throat as he swaggers up to the bar in the local *cantina*. The fact that a gringo from New York City would have the audacity to order Mexico's national spiritous drink "Pancho Villa style" naturally evokes a smile from the *cantinero* as he serves up a shot of white, unaged tequila, a wedge of lime, and coarse kitchen salt. Sometimes a glass of *sangrita*, a peppery mixture of tomato and orange juice, hot chilies, onion, and divers seasonings, is proffered as a chaser.

Now begins the venerable ritual of the "Mexican Itch." As an empathetic and rapt audience of local hombres watches appreciatively, my friend grasps the wedge of lime between the thumb and forefinger of his left hand, places a pinch of salt in the fleshy depression near the thumb on the back of the same hand, and with his right hand carefully lifts the shimmering glass of tequila until it is at eye level. Then, with the graceful, fluid motion of a matador executing a flawless *veronica* in the *corrida de toros*, the salt is deftly licked, the tequila is quaffed, and the lime is sucked, all of which is followed by a zesty draught of sangrita.

"Ay Chihuahua!" exclaims my friend as he gasps for air. The effect of this assault on the gullet is pronounced and instantaneous. The shock quickly passes, however, and is gradually replaced by a warm, pervasive sensation of well-being, a glow that suffuses the whole man as earthly cares begin to fade.

A more genteel version of the basic lime-tequila-salt combination (sans *sangrita*) is to be had in the Margarita, the major differences being that a pony of triple sec is added and the ingredients are mixed, with ice, in a cocktail shaker or blender instead of in the stomach. The effect is not as dramatic as when taking tequila neat, but it is pleasant and satisfying nevertheless.

Tequila's full potential as a key ingredient in the creation of a host of tempting drink recipes has yet to be fully exploited. One thing is evident: The Mexican Itch, a good-natured reference to the classic method of imbibing tequila, could spread rapidly beyond the borders of Mexico. If it follows the route of vodka, it promises to become epidemic. As to the cure for this contagious malady, there alas is none—only temporary remission.

Once you have the "Itch," as everyone in Mexico knows, you have it for life.

ACAPULCO BAY

1½ oz. Gran Centenario
   Plata Tequila
1 oz. Rhum Barbancourt
3 oz. pineapple juice
3 oz. grapefruit juice
1 oz. orgeat syrup or simple
   syrup
Pineapple stick

Mix all ingredients, except pineapple stick, with cracked ice in a shaker or blender and pour into a chilled Hurricane glass, with additional ice cubes if necessary. Garnish with pineapple stick.

Created by the author for Carillon Importers, Ltd.

ACAPULCO CLAM DIGGER

1½ oz. tequila
3 oz. tomato juice
3 oz. clam juice
½ tsp. horseradish
Several dashes Tabasco
   sauce
Several dashes
   Worcestershire sauce
Dash of lemon juice

Mix all ingredients thoroughly in a double Old Fashioned glass with cracked ice. Garnish with lemon slice. Clamato juice may be used in place of clam and tomato juice.

ACAPULCO ORANGE BLOSSOM

1½ oz. tequila
¾ oz. Benedictine
2 oz. orange juice

Mix all ingredients with cracked ice in a shaker or blender and strain into a chilled cocktail glass.

Created by the author for Benedictine Whitbread Enterprises, Inc.

BERTA'S SPECIAL

In the lovely old silver city of Taxco you may have the good fortune to come upon a famous watering place known as Bertita's Bar, renowned for a drink named after Bertha, the proprietor—who, some say, was the progenitor of the ubiquitous Margarita. In any event, the Bertha or Berta's Special (also known as the Taxco Fizz) is a mighty fine way to relax after a silver-shopping tour of the city.

2 oz. tequila
Juice of 1 lime
1 tsp. sugar syrup or honey
Several dashes orange bitters
1 egg white
Club soda
Lime slice

Mix all ingredients, except soda, in a shaker or blender with cracked ice and pour into a 14-oz. Collins glass. Fill with club soda, stir gently, and garnish with a lime slice if you wish.

BIG BLUE SHARK

1 oz. white tequila
1 oz. vodka
¾ oz. blue curaçao

Mix all ingredients with cracked ice in a shaker or blender, strain, and serve in a chilled cocktail glass.

BRAVE BULL

1½ oz. white tequila
¾ oz. *Kahlua*
Lemon peel

Mix all ingredients, except lemon peel, with cracked ice in a shaker or blender and pour into an Old Fashioned glass. Twist lemon peel over drink and drop into glass.

BUNNY BONANZA

1½ oz. tequila
1 oz. applejack
½ oz. lemon juice
1 tsp. simple syrup or maple syrup
Generous dash triple sec or curaçao
Lemon slice

Mix all ingredients with cracked ice in a shaker or blender and serve in a chilled Old Fashioned glass. Garnish with lemon slice.

BARTENDER'S SECRET NO. 22—Salt Tamer

A little salt goes a long way with some people, who find it interferes with their ability to taste certain essential flavors. A mixture of equal parts of salt and sugar instead of salt alone is a very palatable solution for any drink recipe that specifies a coating of salt on the rim of the glass.

CAFÉ AZTECA

1 oz. *Hornitos Sauza Tequila*
1 oz. *Kahlua*
1 cup *vanilla ice cream*
1 tsp. *instant coffee*
Whipped cream

Mill all ingredients, except whipped cream, with cracked ice in a blender and serve in a wine goblet. Top with whipped cream.

This is a house special drink of the **Hotel Marquis Reforma, Mexico City.**

CAFÉ DEL PRADO

1 tsp. *instant coffee*
2 tsp. *instant cocoa*
1½ oz. *tequila*
Whipped cream
Powdered cinnamon or nutmeg

Put coffee and cocoa in a mug and fill with boiling water. Add tequila, mix well, and top with whipped cream. Grate a little cinnamon or nutmeg on top.

CAN CAN

1½ oz. *white tequila*
½ oz. *dry vermouth*
4 oz. *grapefruit juice*
½ tsp. *sugar syrup or to taste*
Orange slice

Mix all ingredients, except orange slice, in a shaker or blender with cracked ice and pour into a double Old Fashioned glass. Garnish with orange slice.

¡CARAMBA!

1½ oz. *white tequila*
3 oz. *grapefruit juice*
1 tsp. *sugar or to taste*
Club soda

Mix all ingredients, except soda, in a shaker or blender with cracked ice, pour into tall highball glass, and top with club soda.

CAROLINA

3 oz. gold tequila
1 oz. cream
Generous tsp. grenadine
Generous dashes vanilla
    extract
1 egg white (for two drinks)
Powdered cinnamon
Maraschino cherry

Mix all ingredients, except cinnamon and cherry, in a shaker or blender with cracked ice, and pour into a chilled cocktail glass.

CATALINA MARGARITA

1¼ oz. tequila
1 oz. peach schnapps
1 oz. blue curaçao
4 oz. sweet-and-sour mix

Mix all ingredients with cracked ice in a shaker or blender and serve in a chilled Margarita glass.

This is a house speciality of **The Arizona Biltmore, Phoenix, Arizona.**

 CHANGUIRONGO

1½ oz. tequila
Orange, lemon-lime, ginger
    ale, or other flavored soda
Lemon or lime wedge

Put ice cubes in a tall highball or Collins glass, pour in tequila and soda, stir gently, and garnish with fruit wedge.

CHAPALA

1½ oz. tequila
¾ oz. orange juice
¾ oz. lemon juice
½ oz. grenadine or to taste
Generous dashes triple sec
Orange slice

Mix all ingredients, except orange, with cracked ice in a shaker or blender, pour into an Old Fashioned glass, and garnish with orange slice.

 CHAPULTEPEC CASTLE

1½ oz. tequila
1 oz. Grand Marnier
4 oz. fresh orange juice
Orange slice

Mix all ingredients in a shaker or blender with cracked ice and pour into a double Old Fashioned glass. Garnish with an orange slice if you wish.

CHERRY COCO

1½ oz. tequila
¾ oz. coconut cream
1 oz. lime or lemon juice
1 tsp. maraschino liqueur

Mix all ingredients in a shaker or blender with cracked ice and pour into a chilled Whiskey Sour glass or champagne tulip glass.

CINCO DE MAYO SALUTE

1½ oz. Gran Centenario
  Añejo Tequila
¾ oz. Amaretto di Saronno
¾ oz. coconut rum
¾ oz. lemon juice; or lime
  juice; or lemon juice and
  lime juice half-and-half
Lime slice

Mix all ingredients, except lime slice, with cracked ice in a shaker or blender and serve in a chilled cocktail glass. Garnish with lime slice.

Adjust measurements to suit individual tastes.

Created by the author for Carillon Importers, Ltd.

COCO LOCO

1 coconut, topped
1 oz. tequila
1 oz. gin
1 oz. light rum
1 oz. pineapple juice
½ fresh lime
Falernum or simple syrup to
  taste

Open fresh coconut by sawing off the top, taking care not to spill out the coconut water. Add some cracked ice to the coconut and pour in all the liquid ingredients. Squeeze lime over drink and drop in husk. Stir well, adding a little additional cracked ice if necessary.

DANIEL DE ORO

1½ oz. tequila
Orange juice
Damiana

Put some ice cubes in a tall Collins glass, pour in tequila, and fill with orange juice. Top with a float of Damiana.

This is a specialty of the **Su Casa Restaurant in Chicago.**

DON PEPE COCKTAIL

1½ oz. Gran Centenario
   Añejo Tequila
¾ oz. coconut rum
4 oz. pineapple juice
Pineapple slice

Mix all ingredients, except pine-apple slice, with cracked ice in a shaker or blender and pour into a chilled double Old Fashioned glass. Garnish with pineapple slice.

Created by the author for Caril-lon Importers, Ltd.

 ## EL CID

1½ oz. tequila
1 oz. lemon juice or lime
   juice
½ oz. orgeat syrup
Tonic water
Grenadine
Lime slice

Pour tequila, juice, and syrup into a tall Collins glass and mix well. Add cracked ice and fill with tonic. Top with a dash or two of grenadine and decorate with lime slice.

 ## EL TORO SANGRIENTO The Bloody Bull

1½ oz. tequila
3 oz. tomato juice
3 oz. beef consommé or
   bouillon
Dash lemon juice
Several dashes
   Worcestershire sauce
Pinch celery salt (optional)
Pinch white pepper

Mix all ingredients with cracked ice and serve in a double Old Fashioned glass.

ESMERALDA

1½ oz. tequila
Juice of 1 lime
1 tsp. honey
Dash Angostura bitters
   (optional)

Mix all ingredients in a shaker or blender with cracked ice, strain, and pour into a chilled cocktail glass.

FROSTBITE

1½ oz. white tequila
½ oz. white crème de cacao
¾ oz. blue curaçao
2 oz. cream

Mix all ingredients with cracked ice in a shaker or blender and pour into a chilled cocktail glass or Whiskey Sour glass.

 FROZEN MARGARITA

1½ oz. tequila
½ oz. triple sec
1 oz. lemon or lime juice
Salt or sugar/salt mixture
    (see Bartender's Secret
    No. 22)
Lime slice

Use 1½ to 2 cups of cracked ice for each drink. Add ice, tequila, triple sec, and juice to blender and mix for 5 to 10 seconds until slushy and firm (not watery) and pour into large chilled cocktail glass or wine goblet, the rim of which has been rubbed with lime juice and coated with salt. Garnish with lime slice.

Because of the large amount of ice used to make a frappé-style drink, larger glasses than would be used for a regular recipe are needed.

GENTLE BEN

1 oz. white tequila
1 oz. vodka
1 oz. gin
3 oz. orange juice
1 tsp. sloe gin (optional)
Orange slice

Mix all ingredients, except sloe gin, in a shaker or blender and pour into a double Old Fashioned glass. Float sloe gin on top of drink and garnish with an orange slice if you wish.

GENTLE BULL

1½ oz. tequila
¾ oz. coffee liqueur
¾ oz. cream

Mix all ingredients with cracked ice in a shaker or blender and pour into a chilled cocktail glass.

 ## GRAPESHOT

1½ oz. tequila
¾ oz. curaçao
1 oz. grape juice

Mix all ingredients with cracked ice in a shaker or blender, strain, and pour into a chilled cocktail glass.

GREEN IGUANA MARGARITA

1 oz. Midori melon liqueur
½ oz. tequila
2 oz. sweet-and-sour mix

Mix all ingredients with cracked ice in a shaker or blender and serve in a chilled Margarita glass, the rim of which has been dipped in salt.

 ## GRINGO SWIZZLE

2 oz. tequila
½ oz. crème de cassis or to taste
1 oz. lime juice
1 oz. pineapple juice
1 oz. orange juice
Ginger ale

Mix all ingredients, except ginger ale, in a shaker or blender with cracked ice and pour into a 14-oz. Collins glass. Add more ice if needed and fill with ginger ale.

GUADALAJARA

1½ oz. tequila
2–3 oz. grapefruit juice
1 tsp. almond extract
Dash lime juice
Dash triple sec or curaçao
Mint sprigs (optional)

Mix all ingredients, except mint, in a shaker or blender and pour into a chilled wine goblet. Garnish with mint.

HOT PANTS

1½ oz. tequila
¾ oz. peppermint schnapps
¾ oz. grapefruit juice
½ tsp. grenadine or to taste

Mix all ingredients in a shaker or blender with cracked ice, strain, and pour into a chilled cocktail glass. You may frost the rim of the glass with salt or salt/sugar mixture if you wish (see *Bartender's Secret No. 22*).

JUANITO'S TEMPTATION

1½ oz. Gran Centenario
   Reposado Tequila
1 oz. white crème de cacao
½ oz. Stolichnaya Vanilla
   Vodka
2 oz. cream
Toasted coconut
Maraschino cherry

Mix all ingredients, except coconut and cherry, with cracked ice in a shaker or blender and serve in a chilled cocktail glass. Sprinkle toasted coconut on top and garnish with a cherry.

Created by the author for Carillon Importers, Ltd.

 ## MARGARITA

1½ oz. tequila, white or gold
½ oz. triple sec
Juice of ½ large or one small
   lime
Coarse salt

Mix tequila, triple sec, and lime juice with cracked ice in a shaker or blender with plenty of cracked ice. Rub rim of a chilled cocktail glass with a piece of cut lime and dip the rim of the glass in a saucer of salt until it is evenly coated. Strain and pour Margarita mixture into glass and garnish with a thin slice of lime.

 ## MATADOR

1½ oz. tequila
3 oz. pineapple juice
1 oz. lime juice
½ tsp. sugar syrup or to taste

Mix all ingredients with cracked ice in a shaker or blender, strain, and pour into a chilled cocktail glass.

There are many variations of this drink. Some use honey, grenadine, coconut syrup, or triple sec as a sweetener, but they are all based on the pineapple/lime juice combination.

MEXICAN BULL SHOT

1½ oz. tequila
¾ oz. lime or lemon juice
4–6 oz. beef consommé
Generous dashes
   Worcestershire sauce
Pinch celery salt or celery
   seed

Mix all ingredients with ice in a double Old Fashioned glass and garnish with a lime wedge.

MEXICAN COFFEE

1½ oz. tequila
Kahlua or sugar syrup to
    taste
Strong hot black coffee
Whipped cream

Mix tequila and sweetener in a large mug, pour in hot coffee, and top with a generous dollop of whipped cream.

 MEXICAN MARTINI

1½ oz. Gran Centenario
    Añejo Tequila
½ oz. lemon juice
Several dashes Tabasco
    sauce, or to taste
Several dashes Agavero
    Tequila Liqueur or to taste
Salt
Lime wedge

Blend all ingredients, except salt and lime, with ice cubes in a mixing glass. To get a good balance, check for spiciness and sweetness and adjust by adding Tabasco or Agavero. Moisten rim of cocktail glass with lime, roll in salt, and strain in Martini.

Created by the author for Carillon Importers, Ltd.

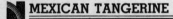 MEXICAN PEPPER POT

1½ oz. tequila
Dr Pepper
Lime wedge

Put ice cubes in a highball or Collins glass, pour in tequila, and fill with soda. Squeeze lime over drink and drop into glass.

MEXICAN TANGERINE

1½ oz. gold tequila
1 oz. Mandarine Napoleon
½ oz. grenadine
Juice of 1 small lime

Mix all ingredients in a shaker or blender with cracked ice, strain, and pour into a chilled cocktail glass.

MEXICOLA

1½ oz. tequila
Cola
Lemon twist

Put ice cubes in a tall highball glass, add tequila and cola, stir gently, and garnish with lemon twist.

MOCKINGBIRD

1½ oz. tequila
¾ oz. white crème de
   menthe
Juice of ½ lime

Mix all ingredients with cracked ice in a shaker or blender, strain, and serve in a chilled cocktail glass.

MONJA LOCA Crazy Nun

1½ oz. tequila
1½ oz. anisette

Fill an Old Fashioned glass with finely crushed ice, pour in tequila and anisette, and swizzle with a spoon, muddler, or swizzle stick. Use less anisette for a drier drink.

MONTEZUMA

1½ oz. tequila
1 oz. Madeira
1 egg yolk

Mix all ingredients in a shaker or blender with cracked ice, strain, and pour into a chilled cocktail glass.

MUCHACHA APASIONADO

1 oz. tequila
1 oz. La Grande Passion
Juice of ½ lime
½ tsp. amaretto
Dash grenadine

Mix all ingredients in a shaker or blender with cracked ice, strain, and serve in a chilled cocktail glass. Garnish with a lime slice if you wish.

PEACHTREE MARGARITA

1½ oz. tequila
1 oz. DeKuyper Peachtree
   Schnapps
Juice of 1 lime
Salt

Mix all ingredients with cracked ice in a shaker or blender, strain, and pour into a chilled cocktail glass that has been rimmed with salt, or use a salt and sugar mixture (see Bartender's Secret No. 22).

PIERRE MARQUES COOLER

1½ oz. Olé Tequila
½ oz. Strega
2 oz. cranberry juice
1 oz. pineapple juice

Fill a tall Collins glass with
cracked ice, add ingredients, and
stir well. You may mix in a
shaker or blender if you wish.

PIÑA

1½ oz. tequila
3 oz. fresh pineapple juice
1 oz. lime juice
1 tsp. honey or sugar syrup
Lime slice

Mix all ingredients with cracked
ice in a shaker or blender and
serve in an Old Fashioned glass.
Garnish with lime slice.

PIÑATA

1½ oz. gold tequila
1 oz. banana liqueur
1 oz. lime juice

Mix all ingredients with cracked
ice in a blender or shaker,
strain, and pour into a chilled
cocktail glass.

PRADO

1½ oz. tequila
½ oz. maraschino liqueur
¾ oz. lemon or lime juice
1 egg white (for two drinks)
1 tsp. grenadine
Maraschino cherry

Mix all ingredients in a shaker
or blender with cracked ice and
serve in a Whiskey Sour glass.
Garnish with a maraschino
cherry.

PRICKLY PEAR MARGARITA

1½ oz. Tequila Patron Agave
2½ oz. fresh lemonade
½ oz. triple sec
¾ oz. lime juice
1½ oz. prickly pear juice
Lime slice

Mix all ingredients, except lime
slice, with cracked ice in a
shaker or blender and serve in a
chilled double Old Fashioned
glass. Garnish with lime slice.

A popular house speciality of
**The Phoenician, Scottsdale,
Arizona.**

PRINCESS COCKTAIL

1 oz. tequila
1½ oz. La Grande Passion
Juice of ½ lime
Lime slice

Mix all ingredients with cracked ice in a shaker or blender, strain, and pour into a chilled cocktail glass. Garnish with a slice of lime.

ROSA MEXICANO'S POMEGRANATE MARGARITA

2 oz. tequila
½ oz. triple sec
1 oz. fresh lime juice
1 tbsp. fresh pomegranate
   juice
Coarse salt (optional)

Mix all ingredients, except salt, with cracked ice in a shaker or blender and pour into a chilled Margarita glass, the rim of which has been dipped in salt.

This is a special house drink of the **Rosa Mexicano, New York.**

ROSITA

1½ oz. tequila
1 oz. Campari
½ oz. dry vermouth
½ oz. sweet vermouth
Lemon or orange twist

Put some cracked ice into a double Old Fashioned glass, add all ingredients except fruit peel, and stir until well mixed. Squeeze fruit peel over drink and drop into glass.

ROUX-RAH!

6 oz. can of V-8 or tomato
   juice
½ tsp. soft blue cheese
½ tsp. fresh grated
   horseradish
1½ oz. Gran Centenario
   Plata or Reposado Tequila
Several dashes Tabasco
   sauce or to taste
Dash Worcestershire sauce
Lemon wedge

Using a barspoon, add several spoonfuls of V-8 or tomato juice to a chilled highball glass and mix with blue cheese until mixture is creamy. Stir in horseradish and remainder of juice, a little at a time, and mix well. Then stir in tequila, Tabasco, Worcestershire, squeeze of lemon, and ice cubes.

Created by the author for Michel Roux, President of Carillon Importers, Ltd.

ROYAL MATADOR

Whole pineapple
3 oz. gold tequila
1½ oz. framboise
Juice of 1 lime
1 tsp. orgeat syrup or
*   amaretto*

Remove top from pineapple and reserve with leaves intact. Carefully scoop out pineapple, being careful not to puncture the shell, which will be used to serve this drink. Place pineapple chunks in a blender and extract as much juice as possible or use a juice extractor. Strain pineapple juice and return to blender, adding tequila, framboise, lime juice, syrup, and cracked ice. Mix well and pour into pineapple shell, adding additional ice if needed. Replace top and serve with straws. Makes two drinks.

SANGRITA

Another favorite way of drinking tequila in Mexico is con *sangrita*, which means the tequila is tossed off neat and the sangrita is drunk as a chaser. Sangrita is traditionally a peppery mixture of tart oranges, tomato juice, onion, hot chilies, and other seasonings, which you can make to your own taste or buy bottled in stores that specialize in Mexican foods. Sangrita can also be used to make the spiciest Bloody Mary you've ever put a lip to.

2 cups tomato juice
1 cup orange juice
2 oz. lime juice
1–2 tsp. Tabasco sauce or to
*   taste*
2 tsp. finely minced onion
1–2 tsp. Worcestershire sauce
Several pinches white pepper
Celery salt or seasoned salt to
*   taste*

Blend well, strain, and chill in refrigerator. Yields about 3½ cups.

SAUZALIKY

1½ oz. tequila
3 oz. orange juice
Dash lime or lemon juice
½ ripe banana

Mix all ingredients with cracked ice in a shaker or blender and pour into a wine goblet.

SENORA LA ZONGA

1½ oz. tequila
1 oz. white crème de cacao
2 oz. evaporated milk
Dash vanilla extract
Dash orgeat syrup (optional)
Dash maraschino cherry
  juice

Mix all ingredients with cracked ice in a shaker or blender and pour into a chilled Whiskey Sour glass or a wine goblet. Almond extract may be used in place of orgeat syrup.

SLOE CABALLERO

1 oz. tequila
1 oz. sloe gin
1 oz. lime juice

Mix all ingredients in a shaker or blender with cracked ice, strain, and pour into a chilled cocktail glass.

 SNEAKY PETE

Some poorly made mescals—poor relations to tequila—were called "Sneaky Pete" because in addition to possessing the flavor characteristics of a good belt of battery acid, some of the delayed effects were memorable in the intensity of their manifestations and their reluctance to depart. Here is a civilized recipe using tequila and the popular tequila-pineapple-lime combination that is the basis of many recipes.

4 oz. tequila
1 oz. white crème de menthe
1 oz. pineapple juice
1 oz. lime or lemon juice
Lime slices

Mix all ingredients, except lime slices, in a shaker or blender with cracked ice, strain, and pour into chilled cocktail glasses. Garnish with lime slices. Makes two drinks.

BARTENDER'S SECRET NO. 23—Egg White

No one has ever devised a simple way to divide the raw white of an egg into two equal parts. When egg white is called for in a drink, one egg white can be overwhelming for a single recipe. Smart bartenders use one egg white for two drinks. "But my customer only ordered one drink," you say. Make two anyway. Somebody will drink the second one—maybe you at the end of your shift.

STEAMING BULL

1½ oz. tequila
3 oz. beef consommé or
    bouillon
3 oz. tomato juice
Generous pinches celery salt
    or celery seed
Generous dashes
    Worcestershire sauce
½ tsp. lemon juice (optional)

Heat all ingredients in a saucepan except tequila. Stir well and
heat to boiling point. Heat a
mug by rinsing with boiling
water, pour in tequila, and fill to
the brim with contents of
saucepan.

STRAWBERRY MARGARITA

1½ oz. tequila
½ oz. triple sec
½ oz. strawberry schnapps or
    strawberry liqueur
1 oz. lime juice
5–6 fresh or frozen
    strawberries (optional)

Mix all ingredients, except strawberries, in a shaker or blender
with cracked ice and pour into a
wine goblet. Garnish with strawberries. Rim of glass may be
frosted with salt or salt/sugar
mixture (see *Bartender's Secret
No. 22*).

SUBMARINO

1 oz. tequila in glass jigger
1 large mug or stein of beer

Fill mug with cold beer within
several inches of the rim and
drop jigger with tequila into the
mug. Some prefer to simply pour
the tequila into the beer while
others drink the tequila straight
and follow it with a beer chaser.

TEQUILA COCKTAIL

1½ oz. Gran Centenario
    Plata or Reposado Tequila
¾ oz. Agavero Tequila
    Liqueur
1 oz. lime juice
Salt (optional)
Lime slice

Mix tequila, Agavero, and lime
juice with cracked ice in a
shaker or blender and strain into
a chilled cocktail glass, the rim
of which has been moistened
with lime juice and dipped in
salt. Garnish with a lime slice.

Created by the author for Carillon Importers, Ltd.

TEQUILA COLLINS

1½ oz. white tequila
1 oz. lemon juice
Sugar syrup to taste
Club soda
Maraschino cherry

Put several ice cubes in a 14-oz. Collins glass, add tequila, lemon juice, and sweetener. Stir well, fill with club soda, and garnish with cherry.

TEQUILA COMFORT

1½ oz. tequila
1½ oz. Southern Comfort
3 oz. orange juice

Mix all ingredients with cracked ice in a shaker or blender and pour into a Whiskey Sour glass.

TEQUILA GIMLET

1½ oz. tequila
1 oz. Rose's lime juice
Lime wedge

Pour tequila and lime juice into an Old Fashioned glass with ice cubes, stir well, and garnish with lime wedge.

TEQUILA GHOST

1½ oz. white tequila
¾ oz. Pernod
½ oz. lemon juice

Mix all ingredients in a shaker or blender with cracked ice, strain, and pour into a chilled cocktail glass.

TEQUILA ICE-COFFEE

1½ oz. tequila
1 tsp. sugar or to taste
Dash lime or lemon juice
Strong black coffee

Add tequila, sugar, and fruit juice to a highball glass and fill with cracked ice and black coffee. Stir and serve.

TEQUILA MANHATTAN

1½ oz. gold tequila
Several dashes sweet
   vermouth
Lime slice

Mix tequila and vermouth with cracked ice in a shaker or blender, strain, and pour into a chilled cocktail glass and garnish with lime slice.

Some prefer a sweeter drink, and vermouth should be adjusted to individual taste. Dry vermouth may be used in place of sweet vermouth or vermouths may be used in combination to make a "perfect" Tequila Manhattan.

TEQUILA MARIA

1½ oz. tequila
4 oz. tomato juice
Juice of ¼ lime
½ tsp. fresh grated
   horseradish
Generous dashes
   Worcestershire sauce
Generous dashes Tabasco
   sauce
Generous pinch white
   pepper
Generous pinch celery salt
   or celery seed
Generous pinch tarragon,
   oregano, or dill

Stir all ingredients with cracked ice and pour into a chilled double Old Fashioned glass.

TEQUILA OLD FASHIONED

1 lump sugar
Several dashes Angostura
   bitters
1½ oz. gold tequila
Lemon twist

Place sugar cube in Old Fashioned glass and saturate with bitters. Muddle until sugar is dissolved, add ice, tequila, and a jigger or two of water. Stir well and garnish with lemon twist.

An interesting variation is to add an ounce of lime or lemon juice and enough additional sugar to sweeten to your taste.

TEQUILA ROSA

1½ oz. white tequila
¾ oz. dry vermouth
Dash grenadine
Lemon peel

Mix all ingredients, except lemon twist, with cracked ice in a shaker or blender, strain, and pour into a chilled cocktail glass. Twist lemon peel over drink and drop into glass.

TEQUILA RUSSIAN STYLE

1 bottle of tequila
Orange peel

Pour a bottle of tequila into a large, wide-mouthed container or decanter. Carefully remove the zest (the colored, outside part of an orange peel) of a selected orange with an unblemished skin. With patience, the entire outside of the peel can be cut off in a single, unbroken spiral, leaving the white, inner part of the peel on the orange. Gently force the zest into the container of tequila, seal, and let stand for several days. The flavored tequila can then be used to make any drink calling for tequila, or tossed off straight, as the Russians drink vodka.

TEQUILA SOUR

1½ oz. tequila
1 oz. lime juice or lemon juice
1 tsp. confectioner's sugar or to taste

Mix all ingredients in a shaker or blender with cracked ice, strain, and pour into a chilled cocktail glass.

This is also called a Tequila Daiquiri.

TEQUILA STINGER

1½ oz. gold tequila
¾ oz. white crème de
    menthe

Mix ingredients in a shaker or blender with cracked ice, strain, and pour into a chilled cocktail glass.

Next to the Margarita, the most popular tequila mixed drink is the Sunrise, which is essentially tequila, orange juice, and grenadine, which provides the "sunrise." Another version is made without orange juice and with crème de cassis substituted in place of grenadine.

 **TEQUILA SUNRISE No. 2**

1½ oz. tequila
Generous dash Cointreau or
    triple sec
Juice of ½ lime
Club soda
½ oz. crème de cassis
Lime slice

Mix tequila, cassis, and lime juice in a tall Collins glass with cracked ice. Fill with soda and top off with orange liqueur. Garnish with lime slice and stir gently.

 TEQUILA SUNRISE The Original

1½ oz. tequila
Juice of ½ lime
3 oz. orange juice
¾ oz. grenadine
Lime slice

Mix all ingredients, except grenadine and lime slice, in a shaker or blender with cracked ice and pour into a tall Collins glass with additional ice if needed. Slowly pour in grenadine. Do not stir. Garnish with lime slice.

TEQUILA TEA

1½ oz. tequila
Hot tea
Lemon slice
Sugar to taste (optional)

Pour tequila into a large mug, fill with tea, and garnish with lemon slice.

TEQUINI

2 oz. white tequila
Dash dry vermouth or to
    taste
Pepperoncini, olive, or lemon
    twist

Stir tequila and desired amount
of dry vermouth in a pitcher with
plenty of ice, strain, and pour
into a chilled cocktail glass. Garnish with pepperoncini, olive, or
lemon twist.

TIJUANA CHERRY

1 oz. tequila
1 oz. Cherry Heering
Juice of ½ lime or lemon

Mix all ingredients with cracked
ice in a shaker or blender,
strain, and serve in a chilled
cocktail glass.

T.N.T. (Tequila 'N' Tonic)

1½ oz. tequila
Tonic water
Lime wedge

Put ice cubes in a highball or
Collins glass, pour in tequila,
and fill with tonic. Garnish with
lime wedge.

TOREADOR

1½ oz. tequila
½ oz. crème de cacao
2 tbsp. whipped cream
Cocoa powder

Mix tequila and crème de cacao
in shaker or blender with
cracked ice, strain, and pour into
a chilled cocktail glass or goblet.
Top with whipped cream and
sprinkle a little cocoa over the
top.

TORRIDORA MEXICANO

1½ oz. tequila
¾ oz. coffee-flavored brandy
Juice of ½ lime

Mix all ingredients with cracked
ice in a shaker or blender,
strain, and pour into a chilled
cocktail glass.

TRIPLE ORANGE MARGARITA

1 oz. Gran Centenario Plata
    or Reposado Tequila
1 oz. Stolichnaya Orange
    Vodka
1 oz. triple sec
2 oz. orange juice
Mixture equal parts salt and
    sugar (optional)
Lime slice

Mix all ingredients, except salt and sugar mixture and lime slice, with cracked ice in a shaker or blender and strain into a chilled cocktail glass. Rim glass with salt and sugar mixture and garnish with lime slice. Adjust portions to suit your taste.

Created by the author for Carillon Importers, Ltd.

TURQUOISE MARGARITA

1½ oz. Jose Cuervo Gold
    Tequila
1 oz. blue curaçao
3 oz. Margarita mix
Dash Rose's lime juice
Lime wedge

Mix all ingredients, except lime wedge, with cracked ice in a shaker or blender and pour into a chilled Margarita glass, the rim of which has been dipped in coarse kosher salt. Garnish with lime wedge.

This is the house speciality of **The Inn on the Alameda, Santa Fe, New Mexico.**

 ## ZORRO

1½ oz. tequila
1 oz. slivovitz
1 oz. lime juice or lemon
    juice
1 tsp. sugar syrup or to taste

Mix all ingredients in a shaker or blender with cracked ice and pour into a chilled cocktail glass.

THE FLAVORFUL
WORLD OF
LIQUEURS

Double, double, toil and trouble;
Fire burn and cauldron bubble.
—*Macbeth*

The flavorful world of liqueurs and cordials has its origins in
the ancient lore of drugs and medicines. The use of roots,
barks, seeds, herbs, spices, fruits, flowers, and other flora has
been the basis of assuaging human ills since the beginning
of civilization, long before the art of distilling was known. The
discovery of the technique of distilling probably had the same
impact on the pharmacology of the Middle Ages as the discovery of antibiotics in the twentieth century had on modern
medicine.

We tend to look upon distilling in terms of beverage alcohol,
but the production of such spirits as brandy, vodka, and whiskey was actually only one of the many benefits of this new
technique. The still provided the basis of modern chemistry by
making it possible to extract many new compounds derived
from natural sources. Even in medieval times distilling made
possible a thriving perfume industry as well as greatly improved paints and varnishes. It also provided a practical
method of preserving the extracts of fruits, herbs, and other
biological substances long before the invention of refrigeration or reliable canning and bottling methods.

It was only natural that in medieval times people looked
upon alcohol as a highly valuable medicine. The restorative
effects of brandy were well-known. Of greater importance,
medicines that were perishable could be kept for extended
periods when alcohol was used in their preparation. Distilled
compounds were also in vogue for other reasons: as tonics,

disease preventives, love potions, and aphrodisiacs. More than a few experimenters hoped to produce a distillate that would eclipse every other medicine made heretofore: an elixir of life.

Many of our present-day liqueurs and cordials (the names are used interchangeably) were created in the continuing search for new medicines. Gin (though not a liqueur) is a good example. It was first made by Franciscus de la Boe, also known as Dr. Sylvius, a professor at the University of Leyden (Leiden). Looking for new medicines to combat tropical diseases contracted by sailors on Dutch East India Company ships, he steeped some juniper berries in alcohol, thus stumbling on a rudimentary gin. Called *jenever* in the Netherlands, the name was shortened to "gin" when it was distilled in England. Curaçao is a well-known liqueur that was created as a preventive against scurvy. In the seventeenth century it was not known that this malady was caused by a nutritional deficiency, but ship doctors noticed that when fresh fruit supplies ran out, sailors began getting sick. It was believed that the dried peel of curaçao oranges processed with alcohol and given to the seamen when fresh oranges were not available might turn the trick. It didn't (they were on the right track, since oranges are a natural source of vitamin C, the lack of which was causing all the trouble), but, according to all accounts, curaçao liqueur was a big hit on board.

Today, liqueurs have limited medicinal value, although many people swear that certain liqueurs can settle an upset stomach or, as a digestive aid, relieve an overly full one. Instead they are valued for their contributions to the flavor combinations in a vast range of mixed drinks. Liqueurs also are excellent flavor enhancers in cooking, and every chef has a repertoire of spirits that are used for flambé dishes, ice cream toppings, pastries, sorbets, puddings, sauces, ragouts, pâtés, soufflés, dessert crepes, game dishes, and fruits.

Liqueurs traditionally have been made by *infusion* (steeping flavoring agents in water, like making tea), *maceration* (steeping flavoring agents in alcohol for an extended period until most of the flavor has been extracted), and *distillation* (mixing flavoring agents with alcohol and distilling them together in a pot still). *Percolation*—similar to percolating coffee—is another, more modern method. Spirits are percolated or dripped through flavoring agents for long periods until optimum flavor and fragrance extraction is completed. All liqueurs are sweetened by various means and must, by law, contain at least 2.5 percent sugar by weight. Most liqueurs contain considerably more than that, the amount varying according to the formulas used by individual distillers.

Improvements are constantly being made in the state of the

art. For instance, we have seen the recent ascendence of a whole new category of cream liqueurs, which are produced in a variety of flavors. A technical breakthrough made it possible for the distiller to homogenize dairy cream with alcohol, yielding a stable end product requiring no refrigeration (at least not in temperate climes) with fairly long shelf life. Another improvement in the process of extracting flavors from various botanicals has brought forth a new wave of schnapps liqueurs, which are characterized by a very natural, intense fruit flavor and fragrance. These innovations are self-evident and significant, and consumers were quick to respond. As this is being written, there is little doubt that new taste experiences are being researched and developed for a vast audience of thirsty and appreciative consumers.

The many different types and brands of liqueurs and cordials are divided into two important categories. The first encompasses the full range of *generic* products. This category, which probably accounts for less than half of all liqueurs on the market, includes all of the basic flavors from whatever source that can be made by any distiller. Some of the most popular generic liqueurs are crème de cassis (black currants), crème de cacao (cocoa and vanilla), crème de menthe (peppermint), triple sec (oranges), crème de café (coffee), sloe gin (sloe berries), and many more. This group also includes the fruit-flavored brandies such as peach-flavored brandy, apricot-flavored brandy, cherry-flavored brandy, etc. These brandies are made in the U.S. and by law are sweetened (2.5 percent or more sugar). They should not be confused with the clear brandies distilled in Europe, such as kirschwasser, which contain no sweeteners. Both the so-called "true" brandies (framboise, mirabelle, fraise, kirsch, and others) and the flavored brandies are used extensively in mixed drinks. There is often confusion between liqueurs and brandies. A cherry liqueur, a cherry brandy, and a cherry-flavored brandy are all really quite different. The liqueur is quite sweet with a low alcoholic content (approximately 48 to 60 proof); a cherry brandy such as kirsch is not sweet at all and has a high alcoholic content (approximately 86 to 100 proof), and a cherry-flavored brandy may have a trace of sweetness with a medium-high alcoholic content (approximately 70 proof or more). In Europe, however, there are cherry brandies that are sweetened and look and taste exactly like a cherry liqueur and bottled at a relatively low (48 proof) alcoholic level. Therefore it pays to read labels and make tasting notes when liqueurs are concerned.

The second major category of liqueurs are *proprietary* brands such as Benedictine, Chartreuse, Drambuie, Grand Marnier, Cointreau, and Irish Mist, to mention but a few of the most famous names. All proprietary specialty liqueurs are made from formulas that are trade secrets, many of them closely guarded family recipes that have been handed down through many generations. Some of these liqueurs have become legendary, surrounded by colorful histories and lore. Benedictine is made from a closely guarded recipe created by Benedictine monks in 1510. Chartreuse, still made by the Carthusian brothers in France, originated in 1605. Drambuie, "Prince Charles Edward's Liqueur" is reputed to be made from a recipe that Bonnie Prince Charlie gave to a retainer in gratitude for loyal services rendered in 1745 after the battle of Culloden Moor. Irish Mist may be very close to a re-creation of the lost recipe for Irish heather wine, which disappeared from Ireland after the Rebellion of 1691, when much of the Irish nobility fled the country. Liquore Galliano was created in the late 1800s and named after Major Giuseppe Galliano, a hero of the Italo-Abyssinian War. And then there is Southern Comfort, a bourbon-based invention of a St. Louis bartender who discovered that peach liqueur seemed to have a real affinity for whiskey.

Almost every proprietary brand has an interesting story regarding its origins and development, and new stories are being written as new creations are brought into the marketplace.

Liqueurs are fascinating because they come to us from an ancient heritage, a bridge to the past. They are a part of the unending search for medicines to make life bearable, or love potions and aphrodisiacs to make life enjoyable, or the elusive elixirs of life to make it ageless. But even in ancient times, liqueurs were revered for another vital and practical function: to provide the means to enhance and improve all manner of food and drink. And so, liqueurs and cordials, even in this modern age, whatever the time or the season, give us a world of flavors at our fingertips.

ABBOT'S DELIGHT

1½ oz. Frangelico
3 oz. pineapple juice
½ small ripe banana, peeled and sliced
Several dashes Angostura bitters

Mix all ingredients with cracked ice in a blender until smooth and pour into a chilled parfait glass.

ABSINTHE DRIP FRAPPÉ

2 oz. Pernod (or other
absinthe substitute)
1 sugar cube
Club soda

Half fill a mixing glass with crushed ice and pour in Pernod. Place sugar cube on top of the ice and very slowly drip club soda on sugar cube until it is completely dissolved. Mix well with barspoon and strain into a chilled cocktail glass. Traditionally this drink is served with two straws that have been cut in half.

ACAPULCO JOY

1½ oz. Kahlua
1 oz. peach brandy
Large scoop vanilla ice
cream
½ ripe banana, peeled and
sliced
Pinch ground nutmeg
Maraschino cherry

Mix all ingredients, except nutmeg and maraschino cherry, in a blender until smooth and pour into a chilled wine goblet. Sprinkle with ground nutmeg and garnish with cherry.

ADIRONDACK SUNDAE

1½ oz. peppermint schnapps
½ oz. crème de cacao
Several dashes maraschino
liqueur
Scoop chocolate ice cream

Mix all ingredients in a blender until smooth and serve in a chilled parfait glass.

AKRON, OH!

1 oz. Droste Bittersweet
Chocolate
1 oz. peppermint schnapps
1 oz. white crème de cacao
Dash curaçao

Mix all ingredients, except curaçao, with cracked ice in a shaker or blender, pour into a chilled cocktail glass, and top with a curaçao float.

ALABAMA SLAMMER

1 oz. amaretto
1 oz. Southern Comfort
½ oz. sloe gin
Dash lemon juice

Mix amaretto, Southern Comfort, and sloe gin in a chilled highball glass with ice and add a dash of lemon juice. Stir well.

 ALFONSO SPECIAL

1½ oz. Grand Marnier
¾ oz. gin
1 tsp. dry vermouth
1 tsp. sweet vermouth
Several dashes Angostura
    bitters

Mix all ingredients with cracked ice in a shaker or blender and strain into a chilled cocktail glass.

ALICE MARSHALL

1½ oz. apricot brandy
1 oz. sloe gin
1 oz. cream
Dash cream or half-and-half
Large maraschino cherry

Mix all ingredients with cracked ice in a shaker or blender and strain into a chilled cocktail glass. Garnish with a large cherry.

AMSTERDAMER

1½ oz. advocaat egg liqueur
1½ oz. cherry brandy

Mix all ingredients with cracked ice in a shaker or blender and pour into a chilled cocktail glass.

ANTOINE'S TRIUMPH

1½ oz. praline liqueur
¾ oz. CocoRibe
½ oz. dark Jamaica rum
1 oz. whipped cream
1 tsp. chocolate shavings
1 tsp. grated coconut

Mix spirits with cracked ice in a shaker or blender and pour into a chilled Delmonico glass or parfait glass. Top with generous helping of whipped cream and sprinkle with chocolate shavings and grated coconut.

APASSIONATA

1½ oz. *La Grande Passion*
¾ oz. *amaretto*
4 oz. grapefruit juice
Red maraschino cherry
Green maraschino cherry

Mix all ingredients, except maraschino cherries, with cracked ice in a shaker or blender and pour into a large chilled goblet. Garnish with red and green cherries.

Created by the author for Carillon Importers Ltd.

 APPLE PIE

1½ oz. *DeKuyper Apple Barrel Schnapps*
1½ oz. *DeKuyper Cinnamon Schnapps*
Orange slice

Pour apple and cinnamon schnapps into a chilled cocktail glass with cracked ice and garnish with orange slice.

 **ARCTIC JOY**

1 oz. peppermint schnapps
1 oz. white crème de cacao
1 oz. light cream

Mix all ingredients with cracked ice in a shaker or blender and strain into a chilled cocktail glass.

 ARNAUD'S DELIGHT

1½ oz. *praline liqueur*
1 oz. light rum or vodka
2 oz. cream
½ oz. coconut cream

Mix all ingredients with cracked ice in a blender until smooth and pour into a chilled parfait glass.

 **AVERY ISLAND**

1½ oz. sloe gin
¾ oz. *Southern Comfort*
5 oz. orange juice
Orange slice

Mix all ingredients, except orange slice, with cracked ice in a shaker or blender and pour into a chilled Collins glass. Garnish with orange slice.

White rings and other blemishes on wooden tabletops caused by alcoholic beverage spills can usually be removed by the rapid application of a little first aid. Try rubbing the area with a cloth moistened with camphorated oil or turpentine. Some have found that sprinkling salt over the stain and rubbing with a cloth saturated with lemon oil is effective. Or you can flood the area with lemon oil, let stand for a few hours, and wipe off. Prompt action is important. Wood surfaces defaced by old stains must usually be refinished.

◤ BALLYLICKEY DICKIE

1½ oz. amaretto
1 oz. Irish cream
1 scoop vanilla ice cream
1 oz. slivered almonds
Pinch ground nutmeg
Pinch powdered cinnamon
Maraschino cherry

Mix all ingredients, except spices and maraschino cherry, in a blender until smooth and pour into a chilled wine goblet. Sprinkle with ground nutmeg and powdered cinnamon, and garnish with cherry.

BANANA ITALIANO

1 oz. Galliano
½ oz. crème de banane
1 oz. cream

Mix all ingredients with cracked ice in a shaker or blender and strain into a chilled champagne glass.

BARBELLA

2 oz. Cointreau
1 oz. sambuca

Mix all ingredients with cracked ice in a shaker or blender and pour into a chilled cocktail glass.

BARRACUDA No. 1

½ oz. Galliano
1 oz. gold rum
1 oz. pineapple juice
¼ oz. lime juice
¼ oz. sugar syrup
Champagne
Lime slice
Maraschino cherry
Pineapple shell, carved out
  (optional)

Mix all ingredients, except champagne, lime slice, and maraschino cherry, with cracked ice in a shaker or blender, pour into a fresh pineapple shell or a Hurricane glass, and fill with champagne. Stir gently and garnish with fruit.

BARRACUDA No. 2

1 oz. Benedictine
1 oz. gin
2 oz. grapefruit juice

Mix with cracked ice in a shaker or blender and serve in a chilled cocktail glass.

Created by the author for Benedictine Whitbread Enterprises, Inc.

BEE STING

1 oz. Benedictine
1 oz. bourbon
½ oz. lemon juice
2 oz. orange juice

Mix with cracked ice in a shaker or blender and pour into a chilled Delmonico glass.

Created by the author for Benedictine Whitbread Enterprises, Inc.

B-52

1oz. Grand Marnier
¾ oz. Kahlua
½ oz. Bailey's Irish Cream

Mix all ingredients with cracked ice in a shaker or blender and strain into a chilled cocktail glass.

BELGRADE BELT

1 oz. Grand Marnier
1 tsp. quetsch plum brandy
1 tsp. orange slice
Lemon slice

Combine all ingredients, except lemon slice, in a mixing glass, stir, and pour into a chilled deep-saucer champagne glass packed with cracked ice. Garnish with lemon slice.

BEVERLY'S HILLS

1½ oz. Cointreau
½ oz. cognac
¼ oz. Kahlua

Mix all ingredients with cracked ice in a shaker or blender and strain into a chilled cocktail glass.

 BIJOU MEDICI

½ oz. Grand Marnier
½ oz. Galliano
½ oz. gin
1½ oz. cream

Mix all ingredients with cracked ice in a shaker or blender and strain into a chilled cocktail glass.

BLACKJACK

1 oz. kirsch
½ oz. brandy
1 cup cold black coffee

Mix all ingredients with cracked ice in a shaker or blender and pour into a chilled wine glass.

BLANCHE

1 oz. Cointreau
1 oz. curaçao
1 oz. anisette

Mix all ingredients with cracked ice in a shaker or blender and strain into a chilled cocktail glass.

BLUE ANGEL

½ oz. blue curaçao
½ oz. crème de violette
½ oz. brandy
½ oz. lemon juice
½ oz. cream

Mix all ingredients with cracked ice in a shaker or blender and strain into a chilled cocktail glass.

BLUE BAR COOLER

½ oz. yellow Chartreuse
½ oz. cognac
Lemon-lime soda
Orange slice

Mix all ingredients, except soda and orange slice, with cracked ice in a shaker or blender, strain into a chilled Squall glass or wine goblet, fill with lemon-lime soda, and stir gently. Garnish with orange slice.

 BLUE COOL

1½ oz. peppermint schnapps
¾ oz. blue curaçao
Lemon-lime soda
Lemon wheel

Combine peppermint schnapps and curaçao in a chilled highball glass with several ice cubes and stir well. Fill with cold lemon-lime soda and stir gently. Slice lemon wheel halfway through and slip over rim of glass.

BLUE LADY

1½ oz. blue curaçao
½ oz. white crème de cacao
½ oz. light cream

Mix all ingredients with cracked ice in a shaker or blender and pour into a chilled cocktail glass.

BOURBON DELUXE

2 oz. bourbon
1 oz. praline liqueur

Pour ingredients into a chilled Old Fashioned glass with several ice cubes and stir gently.

BRYN MAWR COLLEGE COOLER

1½ oz. Malibu or CocoRibe
½ oz. dark Jamaica rum
Dash lime or lemon juice
Dash orgeat syrup
Scoop butter-pecan or rum-raisin ice cream
Maraschino cherry

Mix all ingredients, except maraschino cherry, in a blender until smooth. Serve in a chilled parfait glass or wine goblet. Garnish with cherry.

BUBBLING PASSION

1½ oz. La Grande Passion
Brut champagne or sparkling wine
Lemon peel

Pour La Grande Passion into a chilled champagne flute or goblet and fill with ice-cold champagne. Twist lemon peel over drink and drop into glass.

Created by the author for Carillon Importers Ltd.

CADIZ

¾ oz. *blackberry liqueur*
¾ oz. *amontillado sherry*
½ oz. *triple sec*
½ oz. *cream*

Mix all ingredients with cracked ice in a shaker or blender and pour into a chilled Old Fashioned glass.

CAFÉ KAHLUA

2–3 oz. *Kahlua*
1–½ oz. *gold Jamaica rum*
2 oz. *cream*
Cinnamon stick

Mix all ingredients, except cinnamon stick, with cracked ice in a shaker or blender, pour into a chilled Old Fashioned glass, and garnish with cinnamon stick.

CAFÉ LIGONIER

¾ oz. *crème de cacao*
¾ oz. *cognac*
1 cup *cold black coffee*
Cinnamon stick

Mix all ingredients, except cinnamon stick, with cracked ice in a shaker or blender and pour into a chilled highball glass. Garnish with cinnamon stick.

 CAFÉ ROMANO

1 oz. *sambuca*
1 oz. *Kahlua*
1 oz. *cream*

Mix all ingredients with cracked ice in a shaker or blender and strain into a chilled cocktail glass.

CALM VOYAGE

½ oz. *Galliano or Strega*
1 oz. *light rum*
½ oz. *passion fruit syrup*
½ oz. *lemon juice*
1 *egg white (for two drinks)*

Mix all ingredients with cracked ice in a blender until smooth and pour into a chilled champagne tulip glass.

CAPE COD COOLER

2 oz. *sloe gin*
1 oz. *gin*
5 oz. *cranberry juice*
½ oz. *lemon juice*
½ oz. *orgeat syrup*
Lime slice

Mix all ingredients, except lime slice, with cracked ice in a shaker or blender and pour into a chilled Collins glass. Garnish with lime slice and add extra ice if necessary.

CAP MARTIN

1 oz. crème de cassis
½ oz. cognac
1 oz. pineapple juice
Orange slice

Mix all ingredients, except orange slice, with cracked ice in a shaker or blender and strain into a chilled cocktail glass. Garnish with orange slice.

CAPRI

1½ oz. white crème de cacao
1½ oz. crème de banane
1 oz. cream

Mix all ingredients with cracked ice in a shaker or blender and strain into a chilled cocktail glass.

CARA SPOSA

1 oz. coffee-flavored brandy
   or *Tia Maria*
1 oz. triple sec
½ oz. cream

Mix all ingredients with cracked ice in a shaker or blender and strain into a chilled cocktail glass.

CARLOS PERFECTO

1½ oz. *Kahlua*
1½ oz. Spanish brandy
Cream

Mix all ingredients, except cream, with cracked ice in a shaker or blender, pour into a chilled Old Fashioned glass, and top with float of cream.

 CHARLOTTESVILLE, VA.

1½ oz. Southern Comfort
½ oz. Pernod
2 oz. orange juice
1 oz. lemon juice

Mix all ingredients with cracked ice in a shaker or blender and strain into a chilled cocktail glass.

CHARTREUSE COOLER

1½ oz. yellow Chartreuse
4 oz. orange juice
½ oz. lemon or lime juice
Bitter lemon soda or lemon-
   lime soda
Orange slice

Mix all ingredients, except soda and orange slice, with cracked ice in a shaker or blender and pour into a chilled Collins glass. Fill with bitter lemon or lemon-lime soda, stir gently, and garnish with orange slice.

 **CHERRY-M COLADA**

1½ oz. Cherry Marnier
1 oz. light rum (optional)
1 oz. coconut cream
4 oz. pineapple juice

Mix all ingredients with cracked ice in a shaker or blender and pour into a chilled double Old Fashioned glass.

Created by the author for Carillon Importers Ltd.

 CHERRY-M DAIQUIRI

1 oz. Cherry Marnier
1 oz. light rum
Juice of ½ (large) lime

Mix all ingredients with cracked ice in a shaker or blender and strain into a chilled cocktail glass.

Created by the author for Carillon Importers Ltd.

 CHERRY-M SOUR

1½ oz. Cherry Marnier
¾ oz. Bombay gin
Juice of ½ lemon

Mix all ingredients with cracked ice in a shaker or blender and strain into a chilled cocktail glass.

Created by the author for Carillon Importers Ltd.

 CHERRY TART

1½ oz. Cherry Marnier
¾ oz. white crème de cacao
1 oz. light cream

Mix all ingredients with cracked ice in a shaker or blender and strain into a chilled cocktail glass.

Created by the author for Carillon Importers Ltd.

 CHINCHILLA

1 oz. Benedictine
1 oz. triple sec
1 oz. light cream

Mix all ingredients with cracked ice in a shaker or blender and strain into a chilled cocktail glass.

Created by the author for Benedictine Whitbread Enterprises, Inc.

CHOLULA

1 oz. Benedictine
½ oz. Kahlua
¾ oz. cream

Mix with cracked ice in a shaker or blender and strain into a chilled cocktail glass.

Created by the author for Benedictine Whitbread Enterprises, Inc.

CHRYSANTHEMUM

1½ oz. Benedictine
1 oz. dry vermouth
Several dashes Pernod
Orange peel

Stir everything, except orange peel, with ice cubes in a mixing glass and strain into a chilled cocktail glass. Twist orange peel over drink and drop into glass.

Created by the author for Benedictine Whitbread Enterprises, Inc.

COCONUT COVE

1½ oz. CocoRibe
½ oz. lime juice
1 tsp. orgeat syrup or Falernum
½ ripe banana, peeled and sliced
Scoop vanilla ice cream

Mix all ingredients with cracked ice in a blender until smooth and pour into a chilled parfait or Squall glass.

CORAL GOLD

1 oz. Cointreau
1 oz. gold Barbados rum
½ oz. peppermint schnapps

Mix all ingredients with cracked ice in a shaker or blender and strain into a chilled cocktail glass.

CORDIAL MÉDOC CUP

1 oz. Cordial Médoc
½ oz. cognac
1 oz. lemon juice
1 tsp. sugar syrup or to taste
Brut champagne
Orange slice

Mix all ingredients, except champagne and orange slice, with cracked ice in a shaker or blender and pour into a chilled wine goblet. Fill with champagne, stir gently, and garnish with orange slice.

CORTINA CUP

2 oz. Strega
½ oz. peppermint schnapps
   or white crème de menthe
1 oz. orange juice
1 oz. lemon juice
½ tsp. Pernod
Orange slice

Mix all ingredients, except Pernod and orange slice, with cracked ice in a shaker or blender and strain into a chilled wine goblet. Float Pernod on top and garnish with orange slice.

COZUMEL CUP

1½ oz. crème de banane
1½ oz. white crème de
   menthe

Pour ingredients into a chilled Old Fashioned glass with several ice cubes and stir well.

CULROSS

1 oz. apricot-flavored brandy
1 oz. light rum
1 oz. Lillet blanc
½ oz. lemon juice

Mix with cracked ice in a shaker or blender and strain into a chilled cocktail glass.

CURAÇAO COOLER

1½ oz. blue curaçao
1 oz. light rum
5 oz. orange juice
1 oz. lime juice
Orange peel

Mix all ingredients, except orange peel, with cracked ice in a shaker or blender and pour into a chilled Collins glass. Twist orange peel over drink and drop into glass.

◣ DALE'S HERSHEY

1 oz. Vander Mint
1 oz. peppermint schnapps
½ oz. curaçao
Large scoop chocolate ice
   cream
1 tbsp. whipped cream
1 tsp. finely chopped Hershey
   chocolate kisses

Mix all ingredients, except whipped cream and chocolate kisses, in a blender for a few seconds until smooth. Top with whipped cream and garnish with chopped Hershey chocolate kisses.

DANISH SNOWBALL

2 oz. Cherry Heering
6 bing cherries, pitted and
    chopped
Large scoop New York cherry
    ice cream

Combine Cherry Heering and
chopped cherries in a mixing
glass and pour over ice cream,
which has been placed in a
chilled sherbet or wine glass.

DORCHESTER NIGHT CAP

1 oz. Galliano
1 oz. brandy
1 tsp. white crème de
    menthe

Stir all ingredients in a mixing
glass with cracked ice and
strain into a chilled brandy snifter filled with several ice cubes.
Serve with a straw.

Created for **The Dorchester,
London.**

DUCHESS

1 oz. Pernod
1 oz. dry vermouth
1 oz. sweet vermouth

Mix all ingredients with cracked
ice in a shaker or blender and
pour into a chilled cocktail
glass.

EAST SIDE

1 oz. amaretto
1 oz. light rum
½ oz. Malibu or CocoRibe
1 oz. cream
1 tsp. toasted, shredded
    coconut (optional)

Mix all ingredients, except coconut, with cracked ice in a
blender until smooth, pour into a
chilled wine goblet, and sprinkle
with shredded coconut.

ERMINE TAIL

1 oz. sambuca
½ oz. cream
Pinch instant espresso coffee
    powder

Pour sambuca into a pony glass
and, using the back of a spoon,
carefully pour cream into glass
so it floats. Dust top with powdered coffee.

FERRARI

2 oz. vermouth
1 oz. amaretto
Lemon twist

Pour vermouth and amaretto into a chilled double Old Fashioned glass with ice cubes, stir well, and add lemon twist.

FESTIVAL

¾ oz. crème de cacao
1 oz. apricot brandy
¾ tsp. cream
1 tsp. grenadine

Mix all ingredients with cracked ice in a shaker or blender and pour into a chilled cocktail glass.

FOREIGN AFFAIR

1 oz. sambuca
1 oz. brandy
Lemon peel

Mix all ingredients, except lemon peel, with cracked ice in a shaker or blender and strain into a chilled cocktail glass. Twist lemon peel over drink and drop into glass.

FRED FERRETTI'S DELIGHT

1 oz. grappa
1 oz. Strega
1 oz. orange juice
1 oz. lemon juice
Lemon peel

Mix all ingredients, except lemon peel, with cracked ice in a shaker or blender and strain into a chilled cocktail glass. Twist lemon peel over drink and drop into glass.

FRIAR TUCK

2 oz. Frangelico
2 oz. lemon juice
1 tsp. grenadine
Orange slice

Mix all ingredients, except orange slice and maraschino cherry, with cracked ice in a shaker or blender, pour into a chilled Old Fashioned glass, and garnish with orange slice.

FRISCO

1½ oz. Benedictine
1½ oz. bourbon
Lemon peel

Stir Benedictine and bourbon with ice cubes and strain into a chilled cocktail glass. Twist lemon peel over drink and drop into glass.

FUZZY FRUIT

1½ oz. DeKuyper Peachtree Schnapps
Grapefruit juice, chilled

Pour schnapps into a chilled highball glass with several ice cubes and fill with grapefruit juice.

FUZZY NAVEL

1½ oz. DeKuyper Peachtree Schnapps
Orange juice, chilled

Pour schnapps into a chilled highball glass with several ice cubes and fill with orange juice.

 GALATOIRÉS GLORY

2 oz. Southern Comfort
1 oz. cognac
½ oz. lemon juice
Several dashes grenadine

Mix all ingredients with cracked ice in a shaker or blender and pour into a chilled cocktail glass.

GALWAY GLADNESS

¾ oz. peppermint schnapps
¾ oz. Tia Maria
¾ oz. Bailey's Irish Cream
¾ oz. cream

Mix all ingredients in a blender for a few seconds until smooth and pour into a chilled wine goblet with several ice cubes.

 GEORGIA PEACH

1½ oz. DeKuyper Peachtree Schnapps
¾ oz. white crème de cacao
1 oz. cream
Peach slice

Mix all ingredients, except peach slice, with cracked ice in a shaker or blender, strain into a chilled cocktail glass, and garnish with fruit slice.

GLAD EYES

1½ oz. Pernod
½ oz. peppermint schnapps

Mix all ingredients with cracked ice in a shaker or blender and pour into a chilled cocktail glass.

GLOOM CHASER

1 oz. Grand Marnier
1 oz. curaçao
½ oz. lemon juice
¼ oz. grenadine

Mix all ingredients with cracked ice in a shaker or blender and pour into a chilled cocktail glass.

GOLD CADILLAC

2 oz. Galliano
1 oz. white crème de cacao
1 oz. cream

Mix all ingredients with cracked ice in a blender for 10 seconds and strain into a chilled cocktail glass.

GOLDEN DRAGON

1½ oz. yellow Chartreuse
1½ oz. brandy
Lemon peel

Stir Chartreuse and brandy with ice cubes in a mixing glass and strain into a chilled cocktail glass. Twist lemon peel over drink and drop into glass.

GOLDEN DREAM No. 1

1½ oz. Galliano
1 oz. Cointreau
1 oz. orange juice
1 tsp. cream

Mix with cracked ice in a shaker or blender and strain into a chilled cocktail glass.

 GOLDEN DREAM No. 2

1 oz. Irish cream
1 oz. Cointreau
1 oz. crème de banane
1 oz. cream
Orange slice

Mix all ingredients, except orange slice, with cracked ice in a blender, strain into a chilled Whiskey Sour glass, and garnish with orange slice.

● THE GRAND, GRAND COCKTAIL

1 oz. Cherry Marnier
1 oz. Grand Marnier
1 oz. cream or scoop vanilla
ice cream
Dash Bombay gin (optional)

Mix all ingredients with finely cracked ice in a blender and strain into a chilled cocktail glass. If ice cream is used, use generous scoop and mix in a blender for only a few seconds so mixture is slightly slushy.

Created by the author for Carillon Importers Ltd.

GRAND HOTEL

1½ oz. Grand Marnier
1½ oz. gin
½ oz. dry vermouth
Dash lemon juice
Lemon peel

Mix all ingredients, except lemon peel, with cracked ice in a shaker or blender and pour into a chilled cocktail glass. Twist lemon peel over drink and drop into glass.

GRASSE SUNSET

1½ oz. Pernod
¾ oz. Cointreau
½ oz. lime juice

Mix all ingredients with cracked ice in a shaker or blender and pour into a chilled cocktail glass.

● GRASSHOPPER

1 oz. green crème de menthe
1 oz. white crème de cacao
1 oz. light cream

Mix all ingredients with cracked ice in a shaker or blender and strain into a chilled cocktail glass.

◤ GREEN CHARTREUSE NECTAR

½ oz. green Chartreuse
1 oz. apricot schnapps

Combine all ingredients in a chilled Old Fashioned glass with several ice cubes and stir well.

GUILLOTINE

1 oz. Benedictine
¾ oz. gin
½ oz. lemon juice
½ tsp. sugar or to taste

Mix all ingredients with cracked ice in a shaker or blender and strain into a chilled cocktail glass.

Created by the aughor for Benedictine Whitbread Enterprises, Inc.

HALLEY'S COMFORT

1½ oz. Southern Comfort
1½ oz. peach schnapps
Club soda

Pour Southern Comfort and peach schnapps into a chilled Old Fashioned glass with several ice cubes and top with club soda.

HANG GLIDER

1½ oz. sloe gin
¾ oz. cherry liqueur or cherry brandy
6 oz. cola
Lemon slice

Add sloe gin and cherry liqueur into a tall, chilled cooler glass with several ice cubes. Fill with cold cola and garnish with a lemon slice. If you prefer a drier drink, substitute cherry brandy in place of cherry liqueur and add a dash or two of lemon juice.

HARVARD YARD

1 oz. gin
¾ oz. peppermint schnapps
½ oz. cranberry liqueur
Dash triple sec
Orange slice

Mix all ingredients, except orange slice, with cracked ice in a shaker or blender, strain into a chilled cocktail glass, and garnish with orange slice.

HOMECOMING

1½ oz. amaretto
1½ oz. Irish cream

Mix all ingredients for a few seconds with cracked ice in a shaker or blender and strain into a chilled cocktail glass.

HONG KONG SUNDAE

1 oz. Galliano
½ oz. Cointreau
Scoop orange or lemon
    sherbet

Mix all ingredients in a blender
until smooth and pour into a
chilled parfait glass.

HOOPLA

¾ oz. Cointreau
¾ oz. Lillet blanc
¾ oz. brandy
¾ oz. lemon juice

Mix all ingredients with cracked
ice in a shaker or blender and
pour into a chilled cocktail
glass.

ICE BOAT

1 oz. peppermint schnapps
1 oz. vodka

Combine all ingredients in a
mixing glass with several ice
cubes, stir well, and strain into a
chilled brandy snifter filled with
crushed ice.

IMPERIAL KIR

2 oz. crème de cassis
1 oz. kirsch
Champagne, sparkling wine,
    or white wine

Mix all ingredients, except champagne or wine, with cracked ice
in a shaker or blender and pour
into a large wine goblet. Fill
with cold champagne or wine
and stir gently.

IL PARADISO

1 oz. Tuaca
1 oz. curaçao
1 oz. cream

Mix all ingredients with cracked
ice in a blender for a few seconds and strain into a chilled
cocktail glass.

ITALIAN PACIFIER

1½ oz. white crème de
    menthe
Several dashes Fernet
    Branca

Pour crème de menthe into a
chilled sherry glass packed with
cracked ice and float Fernet
Branca on top.

IXTAPA

1½ oz. Kahlua
½ oz. tequila

Stir ingredients in a mixing glass with cracked ice and serve in a chilled cocktail glass.

JACARANDA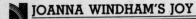

1 oz. Haitian rum
½ oz. peppermint schnapps
1½ oz. mango nectar
½ oz. cream
1 tsp. peach schnapps

Mix all ingredients, except peach schnapps, with cracked ice in a shaker or blender and pour into a chilled cocktail glass. Top with peach schnapps.

JOANNA WINDHAM'S JOY

1 oz. Southern Comfort
½ oz. gold tequila
6 oz. orange juice
Maraschino cherry
1 tsp. raspberry syrup

Mix all ingredients, except maraschino cherry and raspberry syrup, with cracked ice in a shaker or blender and pour into a chilled Collins glass. Garnish with cherry and float raspberry syrup on top.

JOHNNIE'S COCKTAIL

1½ oz. sloe gin
¾ oz. curaçao or triple sec
1 tsp. anisette

Mix all ingredients with cracked ice in a shaker or blender and pour into a chilled cocktail glass.

KAHLUA HUMMER

1 oz. Kahlua
1 oz. light rum
½ cup vanilla ice cream

Mix all ingredients in a blender until smooth and pour into a chilled parfait glass.

KAISER KOLA

1½ oz. kirschwasser
Cola
Lime wedge

Pour kirschwasser into a chilled highball glass with several ice cubes. Fill with cold cola and stir gently. Squeeze lime wedge over drink and drop into glass.

KAMIKAZE

1 oz. triple sec
1 oz. vodka
1 oz. lime juice

Mix with cracked ice and strain into a chilled cocktail glass.

KIRSCHWASSER RICKEY

1½ oz. kirschwasser
½ oz. lime juice
Lemon-lime soda
Several pitted black cherries, speared on cocktail toothpick

Pour kirschwasser and lime juice into a chilled highball glass with several ice cubes and fill with lemon-lime soda. Stir gently and garnish with speared black cherries.

KISS ME QUICK

2 oz. Pernod
½ oz. curaçao
Several dashes Angostura bitters
Club soda

Mix all ingredients, except club soda, with cracked ice in a shaker or blender and pour into a chilled brandy snifter. Fill with club soda and stir gently. Add additional ice if necessary.

KOWLOON

1 oz. Grand Marnier
1 oz. Kahlua
2–3 oz. orange juice
Orange slice

Combine all ingredients, except orange slice, in a mixing glass, stir well, and pour into a chilled wine glass with plenty of cracked ice. Garnish with orange slice.

KREMLIN COCKTAIL

1 oz. Tia Maria or crème de cacao
1 oz. vodka
1 oz. cream

Mix all ingredients with cracked ice in a blender for a few seconds until smooth and pour into a chilled cocktail glass.

LA BOMBA

1 oz. light rum
½ oz. curaçao
½ oz. anisette
½ oz. apricot brandy
½ oz. lemon juice
Pineapple stick or slice

Mix all ingredients, except pineapple stick or slice, with cracked ice in a shaker or blender, pour into a chilled cocktail glass, and garnish with pineapple.

 LA CONDAMINE

2 oz. Pernod
1 oz. gin
1 tsp. anisette
1 egg white (for two drinks)
Club soda

Mix all ingredients, except club soda, with cracked ice in a shaker or blender and pour into a chilled highball glass. Fill with cold club soda and stir gently.

LA GRANDE AFFAIRE

1½ oz. La Grande Passion
1 oz. Crème de Grand
   Marnier

Mix all ingredients briefly but briskly with cracked ice in a shaker or blender and strain into a chilled cocktail glass.

Created by the author for Carillon Importers Ltd.

LA GRANDE PASSION COCKTAIL

1½ oz. La Grande Passion
1 oz. Grand Marnier
Juice of ½ lemon
Sugar to taste (optional)

Mix all ingredients with cracked ice in a shaker or blender and strain into a chilled cocktail glass.

Created by the author for Carillon Importers Ltd.

LADY LOVERLY'S CHATTER

1½ oz. mirabelle or quetsch
½ oz. maraschino liqueur
2 oz. orange juice
1 oz. lemon juice

Mix all ingredients with cracked ice in a shaker or blender and strain into a chilled cocktail glass.

LAS HADAS

1 oz. sambuca
1 oz. Kahlua
Several coffee beans

Stir sambuca and Kahlua in a mixing glass with cracked ice and pour into a chilled wine goblet. Add additional ice if necessary and float coffee beans on top of drink.

LA VIE EN ROSE

1 oz. Pernod
1 oz. white crème de cacao
½ oz. vodka
2 scoops vanilla ice cream
¼ oz. grenadine
Long-stemmed red rose
    (optional)

Mix all ingredients, except rose, in a blender at high speed until smooth and pour into a large chilled champagne flute. Garnish with a red rose.

This grand prize winner in a Pernod recipe contest was created by Wendy Wells Clifford, Newburgh, New York.

THE LEAF

1 oz. melon liqueur
½ oz. white rum
2 oz. half-and-half

Mix all ingredients in a blender and pour into an Old Fashioned glass with several ice cubes.

 ## LEE KRUSKA'S BANANA COOLER

1½ oz. gold rum
1 oz. crème de banane
½ oz. 151-proof rum
4 oz. pineapple juice
1 oz. orange juice
½ oz. orgeat syrup
½ ripe banana, peeled and
    sliced
Lime slice

Mix all ingredients, except lime slice, with cracked ice in a blender until smooth and pour into a chilled Collins glass. Garnish with lime slice.

LEMONADE MODERNE

1½ oz. sloe gin
1½ oz. sherry
2 oz. lemon juice
1 oz. sugar syrup or to taste
Club soda
Lemon peel

Mix all ingredients, except club soda and lemon peel, with cracked ice in a shaker or blender and pour into a chilled highball glass. Fill with club soda and stir gently. Twist lemon peel over drink and drop into glass. Add additional ice cubes if necessary.

LIEBFRAUMILCH

1½ oz. white crème de cacao
1½ oz. heavy cream
Juice of 1 lime

Mix all ingredients with cracked ice in a shaker or blender and strain into a chilled cocktail glass.

LOLLIPOP

¾ oz. Cointreau
¾ oz. kirsch
¾ oz. green Chartreuse
Several dashes maraschino liqueur

Mix all ingredients with cracked ice in a shaker or blender and pour into a chilled cocktail glass.

LONDON FOG

½ oz. white crème de menthe
½ oz. anisette
Scoop vanilla ice cream

Mix all ingredients with cracked ice in a blender for a few seconds and pour into a chilled parfait glass. Do not overmix.

LOWER DARBY

1 oz. melon liqueur
1 oz. cream
Several dashes triple sec
Pinch of ground nutmeg

Mix all ingredients, except nutmeg, with cracked ice in a shaker or blender and strain into a chilled cocktail glass. Sprinkle with ground nutmeg.

LOVE

2 oz. sloe gin
1 egg white (for two drinks)
½ oz. lemon juice
Several dashes raspberry
  syrup or grenadine

Mix all ingredients with cracked ice in a shaker or blender and pour into a chilled cocktail glass.

MACARONI

1½ oz. Pernod
½ oz. sweet vermouth

Mix all ingredients with cracked ice in a shaker or blender and pour into a chilled cocktail glass.

 MAHARANI OF PUNXSUTAWNEY

1 oz. brandy
½ oz. crème de noyaux or
  amaretto
½ oz. kirsch
¼ oz. orgeat syrup
1 oz. lemon juice
Lemon slice

Mix all ingredients, except lemon slice, with cracked ice in a shaker or blender, pour into a chilled cocktail glass, and garnish with lemon slice.

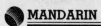 **MALIBU BUBY**

2 oz. Malibu
1 oz. gold Barbados rum
2 oz. orange juice
1 oz. lime juice
Several dashes curaçao
Maraschino cherry

Mix all ingredients, except maraschino cherry, with cracked ice in a shaker or blender, strain into a chilled wine glass, and garnish with cherry.

 MANDARIN

1 oz. Grand Marnier
½ oz. Cherry Marnier
2 oz. orange juice
1 oz. lemon juice
Several dashes orange
  flower water

Mix all ingredients with cracked ice in a shaker or blender and pour into a chilled cocktail glass. Sprinkle a little additional orange flower water on top, if you wish.

Created for the **Mandarin Oriental, Hong Kong.**

MARBELLA CLUB

1 oz. Grand Marnier
3 oz. orange juice
1 egg white (for two drinks)
Several dashes peach or
    orange bitters
Champagne
Maraschino cherry

Mix all ingredients, except champagne and maraschino cherry, with cracked ice in a shaker or blender and strain into a chilled wine goblet. Fill with cold champagne, stir gently, and garnish with cherry.

MARIE ANTOINETTE

1 oz. Kahlua
1 oz. crème de banane
Club soda

Mix all ingredients, except club soda, with cracked ice in a shaker or blender, pour into a chilled cocktail glass, and top with float of cold club soda.

MARMALADE

1 oz. Benedictine
¾ oz. curaçao
2 oz. orange juice

Mix with cracked ice in a shaker or blender and strain into a chilled cocktail glass.

Created by the author for Benedictine Whitbread Enterprises, Inc.

MARTINIQUE

1 oz. Benedictine
1 oz. light rum or Martinique
    rum
4 oz. pineapple juice

Mix with cracked ice in a shaker or blender and pour into a chilled highball glass with ice cubes.

Created by the author for Benedictine Whitbread Enterprises, Inc.

 MARY LYONS FIZZ

Brut champagne
Several dashes green
    Chartreuse
Several dashes cognac

Pour all ingredients into a chilled champagne tulip glass and stir gently.

MAURA'S COFFEE

1 oz. Irish cream
½ oz. Irish whiskey
5 oz. iced black coffee
1 oz. heavy cream

Mix all ingredients in a blender with a tablespoon of cracked ice until smooth and pour into a chilled wine goblet.

MAZATLÁN

1 oz. white crème de cacao
1 oz. light rum
½ oz. coconut cream
1 oz. cream

Mix all ingredients with cracked ice in a shaker or blender and pour into a chilled cocktail glass.

McCLELLAND

2 oz. sloe gin
1 oz. curaçao
Several dashes orange
    bitters

Mix all ingredients with cracked ice in a shaker or blender and strain into a chilled cocktail glass.

MELON PATCH

1 oz. melon liqueur
½ oz. triple sec
½ oz. vodka
Club soda
Orange slice

Combine melon liqueur, triple sec, and vodka in a chilled highball glass with several ice cubes and stir. Fill with club soda, stir gently, and garnish with orange slice.

 MIAMI MELONI

1 oz. melon liqueur
1 oz. light rum
1 oz. cream

Mix all ingredients with cracked ice in a shaker or blender and strain into a chilled cocktail glass.

MIDORI SOUR

2 oz. Midori melon liqueur
1 oz. lemon juice
1 tsp. sugar syrup

Mix all ingredients with cracked ice in shaker or blender and strain into a chilled Whiskey Sour glass.

MINTY MARTINI

2 oz. gin or vodka
1 oz. peppermint schnapps
Orange or lemon peel

Combine all ingredients, except peel, in a mixing glass with ice cubes, stir well, and strain into a chilled cocktail glass. Twist peel over drink and drop into glass.

MISTLETOE APERITIF

½ oz. Chambord
½ oz. Midori
½ oz. Grand Marnier

in a tall shot glass add Chambord, then gently pour Midori, the second layer, over the back of an inverted spoon so that it flows on top of the Chambord without mixing. Repeat the process using Grand Marnier. This makes a good holiday shooter, or you can flambé it by igniting the top with a match. Blow flame out after a few seconds and make certain the rim of the glass has cooled before drinking.

This is a signature drink of the **Contrapunto, New York.**

MOBILE BAY

1½ oz. Southern Comfort
1 oz. gin
1 oz. grapefruit juice
1 tsp. lemon juice

Mix all ingredients with cracked ice in a shaker or blender and pour into a chilled Old Fashioned glass.

MOCHA MINT

¾ oz. Kahlua or coffee-
  flavored brandy
¾ oz. crème de menthe
¾ oz. crème de cacao

Mix all ingredients with cracked ice in a shaker or blender and strain into a chilled cocktail glass.

MODERN No. 1

¾ oz. Scotch
1½ oz. sloe gin
Several dashes Pernod
Several dashes grenadine
Several dashes orange bitters

Mix all ingredients with cracked ice in a shaker or blender. Pour into a chilled Old Fashioned glass.

MOONGLOW

1 oz. Benedictine
1 oz. white crème de cacao
1 oz. cream

Mix with cracked ice in a blender until smooth and serve in a chilled cocktail glass.

Created by the author for Benedictine Whitbread Enterprises, Inc.

MOONSHINE COCKTAIL

1 oz. Galliano
¾ oz. white crème de cacao
¼ oz. orange juice
1 oz. vanilla ice cream

Mix all ingredients with cracked ice in a shaker or blender and pour into a large, chilled cocktail glass.

 MORGAN'S FAIR CHILD

1 oz. melon liqueur
½ oz. amaretto
Scoop vanilla ice cream
1 tbsp. whipped cream
Maraschino cherry

Mix all ingredients, except whipped cream and maraschino cherry, in a blender until smooth and pour into a chilled parfait glass. Top with whipped cream and garnish with cherry.

MORNING CALL

1 oz. peach schnapps
½ oz. white crème de cacao
2 oz. orange juice
1 egg white (for two drinks)
Maraschino cherry

Mix all ingredients except maraschino cherry, with cracked ice in a shaker or blender, strain into a chilled cocktail glass, and garnish with cherry.

MOULIN ROUGE

1½ oz. sloe gin
½ oz. sweet vermouth
Several dashes Angostura
  bitters

Mix all ingredients with cracked ice in a shaker or blender and pour into a chilled cocktail glass.

MOUNTAIN STRAWBERRY BREEZE

1½ oz. *DeKuyper Mountain
    Strawberry Schnapps*
1 oz. grapefruit juice
1 oz. orange juice
Orange slice

Combine strawberry schnapps,
grapefruit and orange juices in a
chilled highball glass with several ice cubes, stir, and garnish
with orange slice.

THE MYSTERY COCKTAIL

1 oz. Ricard
1–2 oz. *La Grande Passion*
Lemon peel

Mix all ingredients, except
lemon peel, with cracked ice in
a shaker or blender and strain
into a chilled cocktail glass.
Twist lemon peel over drink and
drop into glass.

Created by the author for Carillon Importers Ltd.

 ## NIGHTINGALE

1 oz. crème de banane
½ oz. curaçao
1 oz. cream
1 egg white (for two drinks)
Maraschino cherry

Mix all ingredients, except maraschino cherry, with cracked ice
in a shaker or blender, strain
into a chilled cocktail glass, and
garnish with cherry.

NINETEEN PICK-ME-UP

1½ oz. Pernod
¾ oz. gin
Several dashes sugar syrup
Several dashes Angostura
    bitters
Several dashes orange
    bitters
Club soda

Mix all ingredients, except club
soda, with cracked ice in a
shaker or blender, pour into a
chilled highball glass, and fill
with club soda. May be made as
a cocktail by omitting soda.

NORTHERN LIGHTS

1½ oz. Yukon Jack Canadian
    liqueur
4 oz. cranberry juice
4 oz. orange juice

Mix all ingredients with cracked
ice in a shaker or blender and
pour into a chilled highball
glass. Add several ice cubes if
necessary.

NUTCRACKER

1½ oz. DeKuyper Hazelnut
   Liqueur
½ oz. DeKuyper Coconut
   Amaretto
1½ oz. heavy cream

Mix all ingredients with cracked
ice in a shaker or blender and
strain into a chilled cocktail
glass.

 **NUTTY COLADA**

2–3 oz. amaretto
1 oz. gold rum (optional)
1½ oz. coconut syrup or to
   taste
2 oz. pineapple juice
Pineapple slice

Mix all ingredients, except pineapple slice, with cracked ice in a
blender until smooth, pour into a
chilled Squall glass or a Collins
glass, and garnish with pineapple slice.

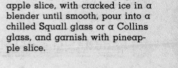 **OSTEND FIZZ**

1 oz. kirsch
1 oz. crème de cassis
Club soda
Lemon peel

Stir kirsch and crème de cassis
with ice cubes in a highball or
Collins glass until thoroughly
mixed and fill with cold club
soda. Twist lemon peel over
drink and drop into glass.

 **PACIFIC PACIFIER**

1 oz. Cointreau
½ oz. crème de banane
½ oz. light cream

Mix all ingredients with cracked
ice in a shaker or blender and
pour into a chilled Old Fashioned glass.

 PADDY'S DERIVATION

1½ oz. Irish cream
½ oz. apricot brandy
½ oz. Irish whiskey
Maraschino cherry

Mix all ingredients, except maraschino cherry, with cracked ice
in a shaker or blender, strain
into a chilled cocktail glass, and
garnish with cherry.

PALM BEACH POLO SPECIAL

1 oz. peppermint schnapps
1 oz. crème de banane
1 oz. light cream

Mix all ingredients with cracked ice in a shaker or blender and pour into a chilled Whiskey Sour glass.

PAPPY McCOY

1 oz. Jeremiah Weed Bourbon
   Liqueur
½ oz. tequila
½ cup orange juice

Mix all ingredients with cracked ice in a shaker or blender and serve in a chilled Delmonico glass.

PARKNASILLA PALMS

2 oz. Irish cream
½ oz. Cointreau
Orange peel

Mix all ingredients, except orange peel, with cracked ice in a shaker or blender for a few seconds and strain into a chilled cocktail glass. Twist orange peel over drink and drop into glass.

THE PASHA'S PASSION

1½ oz. Pistàchà
1 oz. crème de menthe

Mix all ingredients with cracked ice in a shaker or blender and strain into a chilled cocktail glass.

PASSION COLADA

1½–2 oz. La Grande Passion
4 oz. pineapple juice
1–2 oz. coconut cream,
   depending on sweetness
   desired
1 oz. light rum (optional)
Pineapple stick
Maraschino cherry

Mix all ingredients, except pineapple stick and maraschino cherry, with cracked ice in a shaker or blender and pour into a chilled double Old Fashioned glass. Garnish with pineapple stick and cherry.

This may be made very easily by using any of the popular prepared Piña Colada mixes in place of coconut cream and pineapple juice.

Created by the author for Carillon Importers Ltd.

PASSION SHAKE

3 oz. *La Grande Passion*
1 cup *whole milk*
1 *ripe banana, sliced*
½ pint *vanilla ice cream*
Grated nutmeg

Mix La Grande Passion, milk, and banana in a blender with a little cracked ice until banana is liquified. Add ice cream and blend for just a few seconds so ice cream is mushy. Serve in chilled parfait or sherbet glasses. Makes 2 drinks.

Created by the author for Carillon Importers Ltd.

PEACH BANG!

1 oz. *Southern Comfort or peach brandy*
1 oz. *peach schnapps*
2 oz. *peach nectar or juice from ½ cup ripe peaches, crushed*
Dash lemon juice
1 oz. *cream*
Brandied peach slice (optional)

Mix all ingredients, except peach slice, with cracked ice in a shaker or blender, pour into a chilled cocktail glass, and garnish with brandied peach slice.

PEACHES AND CREAM

1½ oz. *DeKuyper Peachtree Schnapps*
2 oz. *half-and-half or milk*

Mix all ingredients in a shaker or blender and pour into a chilled Old Fashioned glass with several ice cubes.

PEACHTREE TONIC

2 oz. *DeKuyper Peachtree Schnapps*
Tonic water
Orange slice

Pour schnapps into a chilled Collins glass with several ice cubes, fill with cold tonic water, and stir gently. Garnish with orange slice.

PERNOD COCKTAIL

½ oz. water
Several dashes sugar syrup
Several dashes Angostura
  bitters
2 oz. Pernod

Fill an Old Fashioned glass half full with crushed ice, add water, syrup, and bitters and stir well. Add Pernod and stir again.

PERNOD FLIP

1½ oz. Pernod
1 oz. heavy cream
½ oz. orgeat syrup or sugar
  syrup to taste
1 egg
Pinch ground nutmeg

Mix all ingredients, except nutmeg, with cracked ice in a blender until smooth and pour into a chilled wine goblet. Sprinkle with ground nutmeg.

PERNOD FRAPPÉ

1½ oz. Pernod
½ oz. anisette
Several dashes Angostura
  bitters

Mix all ingredients with cracked ice in a shaker or blender and strain into a chilled cocktail glass.

PERNOD PARADISE COOLER

1 oz. Pernod
1 oz. Kahlua
4 oz. half-and-half
1 oz. club soda
1 tsp. shredded coconut
Mint leaves
Red licorice stick (optional)

Mix all ingredients, except mint and licorice, with cracked ice for 20 to 25 seconds and pour into a chilled 8 oz. tumbler. Garnish with mint leaves and a red licorice stick.

This recipe won a grand prize in a Pernod contest and was created by Barbara Murphy, Yonkers, New York.

PERSIAN MELON

1½ oz. melon liqueur
⅔ oz. Pistàchà
1 tsp. lime juice
Ginger ale
2 blanched pistachio nuts
  (optional)

Combine all ingredients, except ginger ale and pistachio nuts, in a chilled highball glass with several ice cubes and stir well. Fill with cold ginger ale, stir gently, and garnish with pistachio nuts.

PEUGEOT

1½ oz. Cointreau
¾ oz. calvados
2 oz. orange juice

Mix all ingredients with cracked ice in a shaker or blender and strain into a chilled cocktail glass.

PICON

1 oz. Amer Picon
1 oz. sweet vermouth

Mix all ingredients with cracked ice in a shaker or blender and pour into a chilled cocktail glass.

PICON FIZZ

1½ oz. Amer Picon
¼ oz. grenadine
Club soda
½ oz. cognac

Pour Amer Picon and grenadine into a chilled highball glass, add several ice cubes and stir well. Fill with cold club soda, stir gently, and float cognac on top.

PICON ORANGE

2 oz. Amer Picon
2 oz. orange juice
Club soda

Mix Amer Picon and orange juice with cracked ice in a shaker or blender and pour into a double Old Fashioned glass. Fill with club soda and stir gently. Add additional ice cubes if necessary.

PICON SOUR

1½ oz. Amer Picon
½ oz. lemon juice
1 tsp. sugar syrup or to taste

Mix with cracked ice in a shaker or blender and strain into a Whiskey Sour glass.

 PIMLICO SPECIAL

1½ oz. brandy
½ oz. amaretto
½ oz. white crème de cacao

Mix all ingredients with cracked ice in a shaker or blender and pour into a chilled cocktail glass.

 **PIÑA KOALAPEAR**

2 oz. *DeKuyper Harvest Pear*
  Schnapps
1 oz. *CocoRibe*
1 oz. *cream*
Pear slice

Mix all ingredients, except pear
slice, with cracked ice in a
shaker or blender, pour into a
chilled cocktail glass, and garnish with pear slice.

 **PINK SQUIRREL**

1 oz. *crème de noyaux*
1 oz. *white crème de cacao*
1 oz. *cream*

Mix all ingredients with cracked
ice in a shaker or blender and
strain into a chilled cocktail
glass.

A Passel of Pousse-Cafés

The Pousse-Café is the multilayered wedding cake of the
mixed-drink world. A skillfully made Pousse-Café, consisting
of as many as seven different-colored layers of liqueurs, each
floating on the one beneath it and served in a tall, slim,
stemmed glass, is a spectacular drink creation. It requires patience, a precise knowledge of the specific gravity or relative
weight of each ingredient to be used, and a steady hand. A
simple miscalculation (all liqueurs of the same type may not
weigh exactly the same from brand to brand because proof
or alcoholic content, the amount of sugar used, and flavoring
agents will vary from one distiller to another), an ingredient
poured too hurriedly, or a jarred glass, and all is lost. The
rainbow magic of a Pousse-Café in the making can, in a trice,
turn into an expensive disaster. For this reason it is considered
poor form to order this drink in a busy bar and if you do, don't
be surprised if the bartender demurs.

A variety of Pousse-Café recipes follow, and none should be
regarded as completely fail-safe for the reasons given above.
It is suggested that you test any Pousse-Café concoction that
you intend to serve to guests; it will be time well spent because you will need to practice the delicate business of pouring each liquid ingredient down the side of a tilted glass or
over the back of an inverted barspoon or down the length of
a stirring rod. A pony or Pousse-Café glass is traditionally
used. The old-fashioned ones only had a capacity of two
ounces or less. If you can find a larger size, so much the better.
They make a better looking presentation of liqueurs, and if

you plan to build a Pousse-Café of the seven-layer type, you will need a big glass. Pousse-Café recipes always list ingredients in descending order, meaning that the heaviest liquids appear at the top of the list and should be poured into the glass first. Amount of each ingredient used depends upon the size of the glass and the number of different spirits called for in your recipe. As a rule, a teaspoon or ¼ ounce is standard.

ANGEL'S KISS

Crème de cacao
Crème yvette
Prunelle
Rich cream

Layer ingredients, one on top of the other in the order given in a Pousse-Café glass. For pouring instructions, see *Bartender's Secret No. 25.*

ANGEL'S TIT

Crème de cacao
Maraschino liqueur
Rich cream
Maraschino cherry

Layer ingredients, one on top of the other in the order given in a pony glass. Chill for a half hour before serving and garnish with a cherry. See *Bartender's Secret No. 25* for pouring instructions.

A CLASSIC POUSSE-CAFÉ

Raspberry syrup (or grenadine)
Crème de cacao
Maraschino liqueur
Curaçao
Crème de menthe (green)
Parfait Amour
Cognac

Layer ingredients one on the other in the order given, using a large liqueur glass or a Pousse-Café glass. For pouring instructions, see *Bartender's Secret No. 25.*

COPENHAGEN POUSSE-CAFÉ

Crème de banane
Cherry Heering
Cognac

Layer ingredients, one on top of the other in the order given in a pony glass. For pouring instructions, see *Bartender's Secret No. 25.*

OLD GLORY

½ oz. grenadine
½ oz. heavy cream
½ oz. crème yvette

Carefully pour each ingredient in the order listed into a large pony glass so that each liqueur floats on the one preceding it. See *Bartender's Secret No. 25* for pouring methods.

POUSSE L'AMOUR

½ oz. maraschino liqueur
1 egg yolk (unbroken)
½ oz. Benedictine
½ oz. cognac

Layer ingredients, one on top of the other in the order given in a Pousse-Café glass. For pouring instructions, see *Bartender's Secret No. 25*.

RUE DE LA PAIX POUSSE-CAFÉ

Benedictine
Curaçao
Kirschwasser

Layer ingredients, one on top of the other in the order given in a pony glass. For pouring instructions, see *Bartender's Secret No. 25*.

ST. MORITZ POUSSE-CAFÉ

Raspberry syrup
Anisette
Parfait Amour
Yellow Chartreuse
Green Chartreuse
Curaçao
Cognac

Layer ingredients in the order given, one on top of the other in a Pousse-Café glass. For pouring instructions, see *Bartender's Secret No. 25*.

SAVOY POUSSE-CAFÉ

Crème de cacao
Benedictine
Cognac

Layer ingredients, one on the other in a pony or Pousse-Café glass. For pouring instructions, see *Bartender's Secret No. 25*.

STARS AND STRIPES No. 1

Grenadine
Maraschino liqueur
Parfait Amour

Layer ingredients, in the order given, one on top of the other in a pony glass. See *Bartender's Secret No. 25* for pouring instructions.

STARS AND STRIPES No. 2

Crème de cassis
Green Chartreuse
Maraschino liqueur

Layer ingredients in the order given in a pony glass, one on top of the other. See *Bartender's Secret No. 25* for pouring instructions.

BARTENDER'S SECRET NO. 25—Precise Pouring

When making Pousse-Cafés, master bartenders usually pour liquid *slowly* over the back or round bottom of a barspoon that is held inside the glass very near the previous ingredient that has been poured. A stirring rod may be used in place of a spoon. Other bartenders prefer to pour liquid very slowly down the inside of the glass or down a glass stirring rod. Any agitation or rush of liquid will cause the layers to mix, at which point one must begin again. However, patience and adroit spoon-handling can produce a multi-hued libation fit for an empress.

QUEEN ELIZABETH WINE

1½ oz. Benedictine
¾ oz. dry vermouth
¾ oz. lemon or lime juice

Mix all ingredients with cracked ice in a shaker or blender and strain into a chilled cocktail glass.

 RAINBOW ROOM

1½ oz. Cointreau
1 oz. brandy
½ oz. peach schnapps

Mix all ingredients with cracked ice in a shaker or blender and strain into a chilled cocktail glass.

◪ RANCHO MIRAGE

1 oz. blackberry brandy
1 oz. gin
1 oz. crème de banane
1 oz. cream

Mix all ingredients with cracked ice in a shaker or blender and strain into a chilled cocktail glass.

RED DANE

2 oz. vodka
1 oz. Peter Heering

Combine all ingredients in a mixing glass with several ice cubes, stir, and strain into a chilled cocktail glass.

◖ REPULSE BAY SPECIAL

1½ oz. crème de banane
½ oz. peach schnapps
½ oz. grenadine
1½ oz. orange juice
1½ oz. cream

Mix all ingredients in a shaker or blender with cracked ice and strain into a chilled wineglass.

◖ RHETT BUTLER

1½ oz. Southern Comfort
½ oz. lime juice
1 tsp. curaçao
1 tsp. lemon juice
1 tsp. sugar syrup

Mix all ingredients with cracked ice in a shaker or blender and strain into a chilled cocktail glass.

◖ RICARD FLORIDIAN

1½ oz. Ricard
1 tsp. amaretto, crème de noyaux, or orgeat syrup
4 oz. grapefruit juice

Mix all ingredients with cracked ice in a shaker or blender and pour into a chilled Old Fashioned glass.

Created by the author for Carillon Importers Ltd.

RICARD ROSE

¾ oz. Ricard
1½ oz. dark rum
4 oz. cranberry juice

Mix all ingredients with cracked ice in a shaker or blender and pour into a chilled Old Fashioned glass or wine goblet.

Created by the author for Carillon Importers Ltd.

RICARD SATIN

3 oz. Ricard
2 oz. Bombay Gin
1 egg white
1 oz. cream (optional)
Sugar syrup to taste

Mix all ingredients with cracked ice in a shaker or blender and strain into a chilled cocktail glass. Makes 2 servings.

Created by the author for Carillon Importers Ltd.

 ## RIC-O-CHET

1½ oz. Ricard
1 oz. cognac
Champagne or sparkling wine

Pour Ricard and cognac into a large chilled wine goblet, add several ice cubes, and stir until cold. Remove ice cubes and fill with ice-cold sparkling wine.

Created by the author for Carillon Importers Ltd.

RIVER CLUB

¾ oz. peppermint schnapps
¾ oz. Kahlua
¾ oz. white crème de cacao

Mix all ingredients with cracked ice in a shaker or blender and pour into a chilled cocktail glass.

ROLLS ROYCE No. 2

1 oz. Cointreau
1 oz. cognac
1 oz. orange juice

Mix all ingredients with cracked ice in a shaker or blender and pour into a chilled cocktail glass.

 **ROMAN HOLIDAY**

½ oz. amaretto
½ oz. sambuca
½ oz. blackberry brandy
1½ oz. light cream

Mix with cracked ice in a blender and strain into a chilled cocktail glass.

ROMAN SNOWBALL

2–3 oz. sambuca
5 coffee beans

Fill a large tulip glass half full of finely crushed ice and pour in sambuca. Add coffee beans and serve with a straw. Chew beans after they have been steeped in sambuca for a few minutes.

 ROOTY TOOTY

2 oz. DeKuyper Old Tavern
   Rootbeer Schnapps
4 oz. orange juice

Mix all ingredients with cracked ice in a blender until smooth and pour into a chilled Old Fashioned glass.

RUBY FIZZ

3 oz. sloe gin
1 oz. lemon juice
1 tsp. sugar syrup
1 tsp. grenadine
1 egg white (for two drinks)
Club soda

Mix all ingredients, except club soda, with cracked ice in a shaker or blender and pour into a chilled highball glass. Fill with club soda and stir gently.

RUM DUM

1 oz. Barbados rum
½ oz. crème de cacao
½ oz. peppermint schnapps
½ oz. cream
1 tsp. maraschino liqueur

Mix all ingredients, except maraschino liqueur, with cracked ice in a shaker or blender, strain into a chilled cocktail glass, and top with maraschino liqueur.

ST. THOMAS SPECIAL

1½ oz. light rum
¾ oz. Cherry Heering
½ oz. cream

Mix all ingredients with cracked ice in a blender and pour into a chilled cocktail glass.

SAN FRANCISCO

1 oz. sloe gin
1 oz. dry vermouth
1 oz. sweet vermouth
Several dashes Angostura
    bitters
Several dashes orange
    bitters
Maraschino cherry

Mix all ingredients, except maraschino cherry, with cracked ice in a shaker or blender and pour into a chilled cocktail glass. Garnish with cherry.

 ## SATIN GLIDER

1 oz. peppermint schnapps
1 oz. white crème de cacao
½ oz. sambuca
1 oz. cream

Combine all ingredients with cracked ice in a shaker or blender and pour into a chilled cocktail glass.

 ## SCARLETT O'HARA

1½ oz. Southern Comfort
1½ oz. cranberry juice
½ oz. lime juice

Stir with cracked ice in a mixing glass and strain into a chilled cocktail glass.

SCHIEDAM SALUTE

1 oz. advocaat egg liqueur
2 oz. Jenever gin
1 oz. orange juice
½ oz. lemon juice
1 tsp. Galliano

Mix all ingredients with cracked ice in a shaker or blender and strain into a chilled Delmonico glass.

SENOR MÉDOC

1½ oz. Cordial Médoc
¾ oz. amontillado sherry

Stir ingredients in a mixing glass with ice cubes and pour into a chilled Old Fashioned glass. Add additional ice cubes if necessary.

SLOE GIN COCKTAIL

1½ oz. sloe gin
½ oz. dry vermouth

Mix all ingredients with cracked ice in a shaker or blender and strain into a chilled cocktail glass.

 SLOE GIN FIZZ

2–3 oz. sloe gin
½ oz. lemon juice
1 tsp. sugar syrup or to taste
Club soda
Lemon slice

Mix sloe gin, lemon juice, and syrup with cracked ice in a shaker or blender and pour into a chilled Collins glass. Fill with cold club soda and garnish with lemon slice. Stir gently.

SLOE SCREW

1½ oz. sloe gin
Orange juice

Pour sloe gin into a chilled Old Fashioned glass with several ice cubes, fill with orange juice, and stir.

 SNOW JOB

2 oz. pear schnapps
1 oz. heavy cream or half-and-half
Pinch ground cinnamon

Mix all ingredients, except cinnamon, with cracked ice in a shaker or blender, and sprinkle ground cinnamon on top.

SOMBRERO

1½ oz. Kahlua
1 oz. cream

Pour Kahlua into a chilled Old Fashioned glass with several ice cubes, then using the back of a spoon, carefully pour in cream so that it floats.

SPINNAKER

1 oz. Benedictine
1 oz. gin
4 oz. orange juice

Mix with cracked ice in a shaker or blender and pour into a chilled double Old Fashioned glass with ice cubes.

Created by the author for Benedictine Whitbread Enterprises, Inc.

SOUTH BEND

1½ oz. Irish cream
1½ oz. Frangelico
1 oz. orange juice
1 oz. cream

Mix all ingredients with cracked ice in a shaker or blender and pour into a chilled parfait glass.

 SOUTHERN STIRRUP CUP

1½ oz. Southern Comfort
¾ oz. light rum or gin
2 oz. cranberry juice
2 oz. grapefruit juice
½ oz. lemon or lime juice
Club soda
Mint sprigs

Mix all ingredients, except soda and mint, with cracked ice in a shaker or blender and pour into a chilled silver mug. Fill with cold club soda and stir gently. Garnish with mint sprig.

 STRAWBERRY COMFORT

1½ oz. Southern Comfort
½ oz. strawberry liqueur or
    strawberry schnapps
Lemon slice

Stir Southern Comfort and strawberry liqueur or schnapps in a mixing glass with several ice cubes and pour into a chilled Old Fashioned glass. Add additional ice cubes if necessary. Garnish with lemon slice.

STREGA DAIQUIRI

1 oz. Strega
1 oz. light rum
½ oz. lemon juice
½ oz. orange juice
½ tsp. orgeat syrup or to
    taste
Maraschino cherry

Mix all ingredients, except maraschino cherry, with cracked ice in a shaker or blender, strain into a chilled cocktail glass, and garnish with cherry.

STREGA FLIP

1½ oz. Strega
¾ oz. brandy
1 oz. orange juice
½ oz. sugar syrup
½ oz. lemon juice
1 egg
Pinch ground nutmeg

Mix all ingredients, except nutmeg, with cracked ice in a shaker or blender and pour into a chilled highball glass. Sprinkle with ground nutmeg.

STREGA SATIN

1½ oz. Strega
1 oz. vodka
2 oz. orange juice
Large scoop vanilla ice
cream

Mix all ingredients in a blender
until smooth and pour into a
chilled parfait or sherbet glass.
Serve with a straw.

SUISSESSE

1½ oz. Pernod
½ oz. anisette
1 egg white (for two drinks)
Several dashes cream
(optional)

Mix with cracked ice in a shaker
or blender and strain into a
chilled cocktail glass.

SUMATRA PLANTER'S PUNCH

1 oz. Swedish Punsch
1 oz. gold rum
2 oz. pineapple juice
1 oz. lime juice
1 tsp. 151-proof Demerara
rum

Mix all ingredients, except Demerara rum, with cracked ice in
a shaker or blender and pour
into a chilled Old Fashioned
glass. Top with 151-proof Demerara rum.

SUMMERTIME

1 tsp. white crème de
menthe or peppermint
schnapps
1 tsp. green crème de
menthe
Scoop vanilla ice cream

Mix all ingredients in a blender
for a few seconds until smooth
and pour into a chilled parfait
glass. Do not overmix.

 SUNDOWNER

1 oz. Benedictine
1 oz. light or gold rum
4 oz. orange juice

Mix with cracked ice in a shaker
or blender and serve in a chilled
highball glass with ice cubes.

Created by the author for Benedictine Whitbread Enterprises,
Inc.

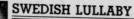 SWEDISH LULLABY

1½ oz. Swedish Punsch
1 oz. Cherry Marnier
½ oz. lemon juice

Mix all ingredients with cracked ice in a shaker or blender and strain into a chilled cocktail glass.

TAPPAN ZEE TOT

2 oz. blackberry brandy
1 oz. blackberry liqueur
½ oz. lime juice

Mix all ingredients with cracked ice in a shaker or blender and strain into a chilled cocktail glass.

 TAWNY RUSSIAN

1 oz. DeKuyper Coconut
  Amaretto
1 oz. vodka

Pour all ingredients into a chilled double Old Fashioned glass with several ice cubes and stir well.

TIGER TAIL

1½ oz. Pernod or Ricard
4 oz. orange juice
Dash triple sec
Lime wedge

Mix all ingredients, except lime wedge, with cracked ice in a shaker or blender, pour into a chilled Delmonico glass or wine glass, and decorate with lime wedge.

TIVOLI TONIC

2 oz. Cherry Heering
½ oz. lemon or lime juice
Tonic water
Lime slice

Pour liqueur and lemon or lime juice into a chilled highball glass and stir well. Add several ice cubes, fill with cold tonic water, and stir gently. Garnish with lime slice.

TRICYCLE

2 oz. triple sec
3 oz. orange juice
2 oz. cream

Mix all ingredients with cracked ice in a shaker or blender and strain into a chilled wine goblet.

TRI-NUT SUNDAE

Large scoop vanilla ice
　　cream
1 oz. Pistàchà
1 oz. Frangelico
1 oz. amaretto

Put ice cream in a large chilled
goblet or sherbet glass. Pour liqueurs individually on different
parts of the ice cream.

TUACA COCKTAIL

1 oz. vodka
1 oz. Tuaca
½ oz. lime juice

Mix all ingredients with cracked
ice in a blender or shaker and
strain into a chilled cocktail
glass.

 TUACA FLIP

3 oz. Tuaca
1 oz. cream (optional)
½ tsp. sugar syrup
1 egg
Pinch of ground nutmeg

Mix all ingredients, except
ground nutmeg, with cracked ice
in a shaker or blender, strain
into a chilled cocktail glass, and
sprinkle with nutmeg.

TURKEY TROT

2 oz. Wild Turkey bourbon
　　liqueur
1½ oz. Wild Turkey
Lemon peel

Pour bourbon liqueur and bourbon into a chilled Old Fashioned
glass with several ice cubes and
stir well. Twist lemon peel over
drink and drop into glass.

TYPHOON BETTY

1 oz. Cherry Marnier
½ oz. kirschwasser
½ oz. ginger-flavored brandy
1 piece preserved ginger
　　(optional)
Maraschino cherry

Mix all ingredients, except preserved ginger and maraschino
cherry, in a shaker or blender
and pour into a chilled cocktail
glass with plenty of cracked ice.
Garnish with ginger and cherry
speared together on a cocktail
toothpick.

VELVET HAMMER

1 oz. Cointreau
1 oz. white crème de cacao
1 oz. heavy cream

Mix all ingredients with cracked ice in a shaker or blender and strain into a chilled cocktail glass.

VICTORY

1½ oz. Pernod
¾ oz. grenadine or raspberry syrup
Club soda

Mix all ingredients, except club soda, with cracked ice in a shaker or blender, pour into a chilled highball glass, and fill with club soda. Stir gently.

VIKING

1½ oz. Swedish Punsch
1 oz. aquavit
1 oz. lime juice

Mix all ingredients with cracked ice in a shaker or blender and pour into a chilled cocktail glass.

VILLANOVA VICTORY CUP

1 oz. light rum
1 oz. strawberry liqueur
½ oz. kirschwasser
1 oz. orange juice
1 tsp. lemon juice
Large strawberry (optional)

Mix all ingredients, except strawberry, with cracked ice in a shaker or blender, strain into a chilled cocktail glass, and garnish with strawberry.

WALDORF

2 oz. Swedish Punsch
1 oz. gin
1 oz. lemon juice

Mix all ingredients with cracked ice in a shaker or blender and pour into a chilled cocktail glass.

WALLY HARVBANGER No. 1

1½ oz. Galliano
1½ oz. dark Jamaica rum
1 oz. orange juice
1 oz. pineapple juice
½ oz. lime juice
Pineapple stick

Mix all ingredients, except pineapple stick, with cracked ice in a blender until smooth, pour into a chilled Squall glass or brandy snifter, and garnish with pineapple stick.

WESTCHESTER EYE-OPENER

1½ oz. Benedictine
½ oz. cognac
1 egg
1 oz. cream

Mix all ingredients, except cream, with cracked ice in a shaker or blender and strain into a chilled cocktail glass. Top with float of cream and stir gently several times.

WETZLAR COFFEE

1 oz. kirsch
½ oz. crème de cacao
1 oz. cream
1 cup cold black coffee
1 egg white (for two drinks)

Mix all ingredients with cracked ice in a shaker or blender and pour into a chilled highball glass.

WHITE LADY No. 1

1½ oz. gin
¾ oz. Cointreau
¾ oz. lemon juice

Mix with cracked ice in a shaker or blender and strain into a chilled cocktail glass.

WHITE LADY No. 2

1½ oz. Cointreau
½ oz. brandy
¼ oz. white crème de
   menthe

Mix all ingredients with cracked ice in a shaker or blender and strain into a chilled cocktail glass.

WHITE LADY No. 3

1½ oz. gin
¼ oz. cream
1 tsp. sugar syrup or to taste
1 egg white (for two drinks)

Mix with cracked ice in a blender and strain into a chilled cocktail glass.

WHITE ORCHID

1½ oz. Benedictine
1½ oz. light cream

Shake well with cracked ice and strain into a chilled cocktail glass.

Created by the author for Benedictine Whitbread Enterprises, Inc.

WHITE VELVET

1½ oz. sambuca
1 tsp. lemon juice
1 egg white

Mix all ingredients with cracked ice in a blender at medium speed for 20 seconds and strain into a chilled cocktail glass.

YELLOW CHARTREUSE NECTAR

¾ oz. yellow Chartreuse
¾ oz. apricot schnapps

Combine all ingredients in a chilled Old Fashioned glass with several ice cubes and stir well.

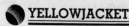 YELLOWJACKET

1 oz. Benedictine
1 oz. vodka
4 oz. orange juice

Mix with cracked ice in a shaker or blender and pour into a chilled Collins glass with ice cubes.

Created by the author for Benedictine Whitbread Enterprises, Inc.

YODEL

2 oz. Fernet Branca
3 oz. orange juice
Club soda

Pour Fernet Branca and orange juice into a chilled double Old Fashioned glass with several ice cubes, fill with club soda, and stir gently.

ZIHUATENEJO

1 oz. Galliano
1 oz. light rum
4 oz. orange juice
Scoop vanilla ice cream

Mix all ingredients in a blender until smooth and pour into a chilled Squall glass or wine goblet.

WONDROUS WAYS WITH WINE

Sine cerere et libero friget venus.
(Without bread and wine love grows cold.)
—Old Roman saying

Americans are discovering what our ancestors in wine-producing countries learned hundreds of years ago: that wine is a marvelous mixer, a delightful and satisfying ingredient for all manner of libations for social drinking and special occasions. A great burgeoning interest in wine has taken place in the U.S. in recent years. We have learned much about wine, and most important, we have learned to be comfortable with it and to enjoy it for what it is: a wholesome, natural, satisfying beverage that, when taken in moderation, of course, can be most beneficial in the pursuit of happiness and the enjoyment of life.

Here we are concerned with the everyday use of wine as an important ingredient in the "The New Mixology"—the creative approach to drink-making—rather than the lore and traditions of rare vintages. Wines of various kinds are adding a new dimension to cocktails, coolers, punches, and party drinks—an area of the beverage world ordinarily considered, with some notable exceptions, to be the domain of distilled spirits. This is a relatively recent point of view, however, for wine has been used in Europe since ancient times as a base ingredient in numerous drink recipes. Indeed, a number of recipes in this chapter are inventions from the eighteenth and nineteenth centuries, and some of the punch recipes in Chapter 13 had their origins in ancient Greece and Rome.

From the earliest times, wine has been flavored and sweetened in many ways. Sometimes this was done to improve the taste of a poor wine, but more often it was done to preserve the vintage from premature spoilage. Feasts and special religious and state occasions required something special in the way of food and drink. Then as now, new culinary creations were in order to commemorate a coronation, the wining of a battle, or a great wedding feast. One of the oldest accounts of a punch was given by Daniel, who described a dinner given by Belshazzar, the king of Babylon, for four hundred guests. The liquid refreshment included red wines, "a heady brew of barley and a wine of date palms stiffened with honey." (Daniel 5:1). In ancient Greece, Hippocrates, the father of medicine, originated a concoction consisting of wine sweetened with honey and flavored with spices such as cinnamon, which became known in various forms as Hippocras, a popular drink during the Middle Ages. In the Iliad, Homer describes a feast given by Nestor to celebrate his return from the Trojan wars. He writes that Hekemede, a lady of the house, prepared a punch made of Pramian wine (believed to be rather heavy and sweet, not unlike a ruby port) by mixing it with grated goat cheese, a sprinkling of barley, and accompanied with a raw onion to be eaten with the drink.

Many of today's fortified wines, such as sherry, port, and Madeira, as well as the so-called apéritif or aromatized wines, such as Dubonnet, Byrrh, and St. Raphael, have their roots in the flavored wines of old. Glühwein, a staple of après-ski hot drinks, is simply a modern-day Hippocras. And that German favorite, May Wine (maiwein), flavored with woodruff, an aromatic herb, follows the venerable tradition of flavoring wines with spices, herbs, fruits, and flowers. Most modern punches, flavored with fruits, and fruit-based liqueurs such as curaçao, spices, and sweetened with flavored syrups like orgeat or honey, are based upon ancient recipes. Sangria is a good example.

The modern mixologist looks upon wines ranging from table wines, dessert wines, and sparkling wines to highly flavored apéritif and specialty wines as important ingredients in the full spectrum of mixed drinks. Many of the wine cocktails and coolers in this chapter are simply recycled concoctions from recent times: the "Art Deco" drinks of the Roaring Twenties and the Thirties; the Belle Epoque libations of the last part of the 1800s; and the hearty grogs of the American colonial period. Other recipes are new innovations using wine as a basic and significant ingredient. Champagne (or comparable, good-quality sparkling wine) appears in many recipes. What could possibly be a better foundation for a refreshing tall drink or an elegant cocktail? The French showed us the way, and we are indebted to them.

They not only invented champagne, but taught us not to be afraid to mix it with other things that make good drinks.

 **ACHAMPAÑADO**

3–4 oz. dry vermouth
½ tsp. sugar syrup
Juice of ¼ lime
Club soda

Pour vermouth into a chilled collins glass with several ice cubes, add sugar syrup, lime juice, and stir until sugar syrup is dissolved. Fill glass with cold club soda and stir gently.

Vermouth and vermouth drinks such as the Achampañado are quite popular in many South American countries.

 ADDINGTON

2 oz. dry vermouth
2 oz. sweet vermouth
Club soda
Orange peel

Pour vermouths into a chilled Collins glass with several ice cubes, stir, and fill with club soda. Twist orange peel over drink and drop into glass.

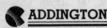 **ADONIS COCKTAIL**

3 oz. fino sherry
1 oz. sweet vermouth
Dash orange bitters
Orange peel

Mix sherry, vermouth, and bitters in a small pitcher with ice and strain into a chilled cocktail glass. Twist orange peel over drink and drop into glass.

AFFINITY COCKTAIL

1 oz. sweet vermouth
1 oz. dry vermouth
1 oz. scotch
Several dashes Angostura
  bitters
Maraschino cherry

Stir vermouths, scotch, and bitters in a mixing glass with ice cubes and strain into a chilled cocktail glass. Garnish with a cherry.

ALFONSO COCKTAIL

2 oz. Dubonnet rouge
1 tsp. curaçao or sugar syrup
  to taste
Several dashes Angostura
  bitters
Brut champagne
Lemon peel

Prechill all ingredients and pour Dubonnet, curaçao or syrup, and bitters into a chilled wine goblet and fill with champagne. Stir gently and garnish with lemon peel.

 AMERICANO

2 oz. sweet vermouth
2 oz. Campari
Club soda
Orange peel

Mix vermouth and Campari in a mixing glass with ice and strain into an Old Fashioned glass. Add several ice cubes and club soda. Twist orange peel over drink and drop into glass.

ANY PORT IN A STORM

3 oz. ruby port
1 oz. cognac
1 oz. lemon juice
1 tsp. maraschino liqueur
Club soda

Mix port, cognac, maraschino, and lemon juice with cracked ice in a blender or shaker and pour into a chilled Collins or highball glass. Add additional ice if necessary and fill glass with cold club soda.

APPETIZER

2–3 oz. Dubonnet rouge
Juice of 1 orange

Mix with cracked ice in a blender or shaker and strain into a chilled cocktail glass.

ARUBA COOLER

3 oz. dry vermouth
1½ oz. curaçao
Club soda

Pour dry vermouth and curaçao into a chilled highball glass with several ice cubes, fill with club soda, and stir gently.

AZZURRA

3 oz. Cinzano Bianco
½ oz. triple sec
Tonic water
Lemon peel

Pour Cinzano and triple sec into a chilled highball glass with several ice cubes and stir well. Fill with cold tonic water and stir gently. Garnish with a lemon peel.

Created by the author for Cinzano and the Azzurra, Italy's entry in the America's Cup trials at Newport, Rhode Island.

BAHIA

1½ oz. amontillado sherry
1½ oz. dry vermouth or
    sweet vermouth
½ tsp. Pernod or Herbsaint
Several dashes Peychaud's
    bitters, orange bitters, or
    Angostura bitters

Stir briskly with cracked ice in a pitcher or mixing glass and strain into a chilled cocktail glass.

 BAMBOO COCKTAIL

2 oz. fino sherry
2 oz. dry vermouth
Several dashes Angostura
    bitters

Stir with ice in a mixing glass and strain into a chilled cocktail glass.

BLACK PRINCE

1 oz. blackberry-flavored
    brandy
Dash lemon or lime juice
Brut champagne

Pour brandy into a chilled tulip glass, add lemon or lime juice, and fill with cold champagne.

 BLACK VELVET

½ pt. Guinness stout
½ pt. champagne

Prechill stout and champagne and pour carefully into a chilled highball or Collins glass. Stir gently so as not to lose the fizz.

BOB DANBY

2–3 oz. Dubonnet rouge
1 oz. brandy
Orange slice

Stir Dubonnet and brandy with several ice cubes in a mixing glass and strain into a chilled cocktail glass. Garnish with orange slice.

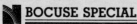 BOCUSE SPECIAL

½ oz. crème de cassis
½ oz. framboise
Brut champagne

Mix cassis and framboise briskly with several ice cubes in a mixing glass and strain into a chilled tulip glass. Fill with cold champagne and stir gently.

This is a favorite of the renowned French chef Paul Bocuse.

BONSONI

3 oz. sweet vermouth
1 oz. Fernet Branca
Lemon or orange peel

Stir vermouth and Fernet Branca briskly with ice cubes in a mixing glass and strain into a chilled cocktail glass. Twist lemon peel over drink and drop into glass.

THE BROKEN SPUR

3 oz. white port
½ oz. gin
½ oz. sweet vermouth
1 egg yolk
½ tsp. anisette
Grated nutmeg

Mix all ingredients, except nutmeg, with cracked ice in a blender and strain into a chilled cocktail glass. Sprinkle with a little grated nutmeg.

B.V.D.

1 oz. Dubonnet, St. Raphael, or Byrrh
1 oz. dry vermouth
1 oz. light rum
Orange peel

Mix all ingredients, except orange peel, with cracked ice in a small pitcher and strain into a chilled cocktail glass. Twist orange peel over drink and drop into glass.

BYCULLA

1 oz. sherry
1 oz. port
1 oz. Stone's ginger wine
1 oz. curaçao

Mix with ice cubes in a small pitcher and strain into a chilled cocktail glass.

BYRRH CASSIS

2–3 oz. Byrrh
1 oz. crème de cassis
Club soda

Mix Byrrh and cassis in a chilled wine goblet with several ice cubes and fill with club soda.

CANARIE D'OR

1 oz. cognac or armagnac
Brut champagne
½ oz. yellow Chartreuse

Prechill all ingredients and pour cognac into a chilled tulip glass. Fill with cold champagne and float yellow Chartreuse on top.

CHAMPAGNE BLUES

Brut champagne
Blue curaçao
Lemon peel

Prechill champagne and curaçao. Pour champagne into a chilled tulip glass and add curaçao to taste. Twist lemon peel over drink and drop into glass.

Created by the author for Nan and Ivan Lyons, writers of *Champagne Blues* and *Someone Is Killing the Great Chefs of Europe.*

CHAMPAGNE COCKTAIL

1 sugar cube
Several dashes Angostura
   bitters, orange bitters, or
   Peychaud's bitters
Champagne
Lemon or orange peel
   (optional)

Put a sugar cube in a chilled champagne tulip glass and saturate it with bitters. Fill with cold champagne and stir gently. Garnish with lemon peel if you wish.

CHAMPAGNE CUP

½ oz. cognac
½ oz. curaçao
Brut champagne
Orange slice
Mint sprig

Pour cognac and curaçao into a chilled large wine goblet, add a cube of ice, and fill with cold champagne. Stir gently and garnish with orange slice and mint sprig.

CHAMPAGNE CRUSTA

1 large orange
1 oz. cognac or armagnac
½ oz. kümmel
½ oz. lemon juice
½ tsp. sugar syrup or to taste
Orange bitters
Brut champagne

Select a large orange with an unblemished peel. Carefully remove peel by cutting it so that you have a long, continuous spiral of the zest (outer peel) of the orange. Place this in a large, chilled balloon glass or wine goblet. Mix brandy, kümmel, lemon juice, and syrup in a shaker or blender with cracked ice and strain into glass. Sprinkle generously with bitters and fill with cold champagne.

CHAMPAGNE NAPOLEON

½ oz. Grand Marnier
½ oz. curaçao
½ oz. maraschino liqueur
Several dashes rosewater
Brut champagne

Pour Grand Marnier, curaçao, and maraschino into a mixing glass with several ice cubes and stir briskly. Strain into a chilled tulip glass, sprinkle with rosewater, and fill with cold champagne.

 CHOCOLATE COCKTAIL

3 oz. ruby port
1 oz. yellow Chartreuse
1 egg yolk
1 tsp. grated chocolate

Mix all ingredients, except chocolate, with cracked ice in a blender or shaker and strain into a chilled cocktail glass. Sprinkle with grated chocolate.

COFFEE COCKTAIL No. 3

3 oz. ruby port
1 oz. cognac
1 egg yolk
½ tsp. sugar syrup
Dash curaçao
Grated nutmeg

Mix all ingredients, except nutmeg, with cracked ice in a blender or a shaker and strain into a chilled Delmonico glass.

CORONATION COCKTAIL No. 3

1 oz. sweet vermouth
1 oz. dry vermouth
1 oz. calvados or applejack
Several dashes apricot
   liqueur or apricot brandy

Stir briskly with cracked ice in a
mixing glass and strain into a
chilled cocktail glass.

COUNTRY CLUB COOLER

4 oz. Lillet blanc or dry
   vermouth
1 tsp. grenadine
Club soda or ginger ale
Orange peel

Pour Lillet and grenadine into a
chilled Collins glass, stir well,
and add several ice cubes. Fill
glass with cold soda and garnish with an orange peel cut
into a long spiral.

 DEATH IN THE AFTERNOON

1½ oz. Pernod
Brut champagne

Pour Pernod into a mixing glass
with several ice cubes and stir
briskly. Add Pernod to a chilled
tulip glass and fill with cold
champagne. Stir gently

This was purported to be a favorite of Ernest Hemingway's when
he lived in Paris in the 1920s. It
is said that he rotated Pernod as
an additive with cognac or green
Chartreuse; all calculated to put
a little extra bite into the
champagne.

DIABLO

1½ oz. white port
1 oz. dry vermouth
Dash lemon juice
Lemon peel

Mix port, vermouth, and lemon
juice with cracked ice in a
shaker and strain into a chilled
cocktail glass. Twist lemon peel
over drink and drop into glass.

 DUBONNET FIZZ

3–4 oz. Dubonnet rouge
½ oz. cherry brandy
2 oz. freshly squeezed
    orange juice
1 oz. freshly squeezed lemon
    juice
Club soda or champagne

Mix Dubonnet, brandy, and juices with cracked ice in a shaker or blender and strain into a chilled Collins glass. Add several ice cubes and fill with club soda or champagne.

DUCHESS COCKTAIL

1 oz. dry vermouth
1 oz. sweet vermouth
1 oz. Pernod
Orange slice

Stir vermouths and Pernod briskly with ice cubes in a mixing glass and strain into a chilled cocktail glass. Garnish with an orange slice.

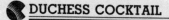 DUPLEX COCKTAIL

2 oz. dry vermouth
2 oz. sweet vermouth
Several dashes orange
    bitters

Stir briskly in a mixing glass with cracked ice and strain into a chilled cocktail glass.

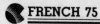 FRENCH 75

1 oz. lemon juice
½ oz. sugar syrup or to taste
1½ oz. cognac
Brut champagne

Mix lemon juice and syrup with several ice cubes in a chilled Collins glass until syrup is dissolved, add cognac, and fill with cold champagne. Stir gently.

Some recipe books specify gin in place of cognac for this drink. It may be palatable, but it is not a French 75. The French 75 was so named by American doughboys during World War I (after the renowned French Army field piece with a bore diameter measuring 75 millimeters), who found cognac and champagne very enjoyable and readily available.

◉ GENERAL HARRISON'S EGGNOG

1 whole egg
1 cup hard cider
1 tsp. sugar syrup or to taste

Mix all ingredients with cracked ice in a blender and pour into a chilled highball glass.

◉ THE GRAND SCREWDRIVER

Juice of 1 orange
1 oz. Grand Marnier
Brut champagne

Mix orange juice and Grand Marnier with cracked ice in a blender or shaker for a few seconds to chill, strain into a chilled large wine goblet, and fill with cold champagne. Do not add ice.

This drink is at its grandest when all ingredients are crackling cold.

GRAND SLAM

1½ oz. Swedish Punsch
1 oz. sweet vermouth
1 oz. dry vermouth

Stir all ingredients briskly with ice in a mixing glass and strain into a chilled cocktail glass.

GREEN ROOM

2 oz. dry vermouth
¾ oz. brandy
Several dashes curaçao
Orange peel

Stir vermouth, brandy, and curaçao briskly in a mixing glass with ice and strain into a chilled cocktail glass. Twist orange peel over drink and drop into glass.

IMPERIAL HOUSE BRACER cold

2 oz. port
1 oz. cognac
1 egg yolk
¾ oz. cream
Grated nutmeg

Mix all ingredients, except nutmeg, with cracked ice in a blender or shaker and strain into a chilled cocktail glass. Top with a sprinkle of nutmeg.

INCA COCKTAIL

1 oz. amontillado sherry
1 oz. dry vermouth
1 oz. sweet vermouth
1 oz. gin
1 tsp. orgeat syrup or sugar
  syrup to taste
Several dashes orange
  bitters

Mix with cracked ice in a
blender or shaker and pour into
a chilled Delmonico glass.

 ## J.P. FIZZ

3 oz. Dubonnet rouge
1 oz. gin or brandy
½ oz. curaçao
Club soda
Orange or lemon slice

Stir Dubonnet, gin, and curaçao
in a mixing glass with cracked
ice and strain into a chilled Collins glass. Add several ice cubes
and fill with cold club soda. Stir
gently and garnish with orange
slice or lemon slice.

 ## KIR

½ oz. crème de cassis
5 oz. dry white wine

Prechill cassis and wine and
mix together in a chilled wine
glass.

 ## KIR ROYALE

½ oz. crème de cassis
5–6 oz. Brut champagne

Mix cassis and cold champagne
gently in a chilled champagne
tulip glass.

LE COQ HARDY CHAMPAGNE COCKTAIL

1 sugar cube
Dash Angostura bitters or
  orange bitters
1 drop Fernet Branca
1 drop Grand Marnier
1 drop cognac
Brut champagne
Orange peel

Place sugar cube in a chilled
champagne tulip glass and saturate it with bitters, Fernet
Branca, Grand Marnier, and cognac. Fill with cold champagne.
Garnish with a small strip of orange zest (the outer, colored part
of the peel, not the white).

LITTLE BISHOP

2 oz. fresh orange juice
1 oz. lemon juice
1 tsp. sugar syrup or to taste
Dry red wine
½ oz. dark Jamaica rum
Orange slice

Mix orange juice, lemon juice, and syrup with cracked ice in a shaker or blender and strain into a chilled highball glass. Add an ice cube or two, fill with wine, and top with a float of rum. Garnish with an orange slice.

THE MAHARAJAH'S BURRA-PEG

1 sugar cube
Several dashes Angostura
  bitters
1–2 oz. cognac
Brut champagne

Saturate a sugar cube with bitters and put into a chilled balloon glass. Add chilled cognac and fill with cold champagne. Stir gently.

This is also known as the King's Peg and the Russian Cocktail. Some prefer this drink sans sugar and bitters.

MARAGATO SPECIAL

1 oz. dry vermouth
1 oz. sweet vermouth
1 oz. light rum
1 oz. lemon juice
½ oz. lime juice
½ oz. sugar syrup or to taste
Dash kirsch

Mix with cracked ice in a blender or shaker and strain into a chilled wine glass.

BARTENDER'S SECRET NO. 26—Room Temperature

Most wine books tell you to chill white wines and sparkling wines but to serve red wines at room temperature. The "room temperature" generally referred to is that which is found in Europe and especially England. Americans consider 72 degrees to be an acceptable room temperature. In England, 50 degrees or thereabouts is probably somewhere near the norm. A red wine served at 50 degrees will generally taste more sprightly than the same wine served at 72 degrees. A good sommelier knows that putting a *little* chill on even a distinguished red wine definitely makes it more palatable.

MIMOSA

6 oz. brut champagne
3 oz. fresh orange juice

Prechill orange juice and champagne and mix together in a chilled wine goblet. Proportions of wine and juice may be adjusted for individual tastes. If drink needs more chilling, add an ice cube or 2 tbsp. cracked ice.

NIGHTMARE ABBEY COCKTAIL

1½ oz. Dubonnet rouge
1 oz. gin
1 oz. orange juice
¾ oz. cherry brandy

Mix all ingredients with cracked ice in a shaker or blender and strain into a chilled cocktail glass.

NINETEEN

3 oz. dry vermouth
½ oz. gin
½ oz. kirsch
Several dashes Pernod
Several dashes sugar syrup
  or to taste

Mix all ingredients with cracked ice in a shaker or blender and strain into a chilled cocktail glass.

 **PACIFIC PALISADES**

1½ oz. Campari
1 oz. orange juice
Brut champagne

Mix Campari and orange juice in a chilled wine goblet with an ice cube and fill with cold champagne.

PANTOMIME

2 oz. dry vermouth
1 egg white (for two drinks)
Several dashes orgeat syrup
Dash grenadine

Mix all ingredients with cracked ice in a blender and strain into a chilled cocktail glass.

PHILOMEL COCKTAIL

2½ oz. amontillado sherry
1½ oz. St. Raphael
1 oz. light rum
1½ oz. orange juice
Pinch ground cayenne or
    white pepper

Mix all ingredients, except cayenne, with cracked ice in a blender or shaker and strain into a chilled wine goblet. Sprinkle with ground cayenne.

PICON COCKTAIL

2 oz. Amer Picon
2 oz. dry vermouth

Stir briskly with ice in a mixing glass and strain into a chilled cocktail glass.

PIZZETTI

1 oz. cognac
2 oz. orange juice
2 oz. grapefruit juice
Brut champagne

Mix cognac and fruit juices in a blender or shaker with cracked ice and strain into a chilled wine goblet. Fill with cold champagne and stir gently.

From the **Hotel de la Poste**, Cortina, Italy.

BARTENDER'S SECRET NO. 27—Sparkle Saver

Spare the fizz. And if the fizz comes from champagne or other good sparkling wine made by the time-honored *méthode champenois* (a natural way of making sparkling wine with a second fermentation in the bottle), all the more reason to preserve it. All mixologists should use care when using a sparkling wine in the making of mixed drinks, and especially punches, to stir the mixture gently so as not to dissipate the sparkle. And for the same reason, all swizzle sticks, those destructive devices no doubt invented by die-hard Prohibitionists to take the joy out of drinking champagne, should be seized and burned or otherwise obliterated. For this reason, a warning notice should be printed on every sparkling wine label:

> PLEASE SPARE THE SPARKLE
> Don't stir out in minutes
> what it took months of
> work by master winemakers
> to put into this bottle.

PORT MILK PUNCH

3–4 oz. ruby port
1 cup milk
1 tsp. superfine sugar or
   honey to taste
Grated nutmeg

Mix port, milk, and sugar with
cracked ice in a blender and
strain into a chilled Collins
glass. Sprinkle with nutmeg.

PORT SANGAREE

5 oz. port
1 tsp. sugar syrup or to taste
Grated nutmeg

Mix port and syrup with several
ice cubes in a large chilled wine
goblet until syrup dissolves.
Sprinkle with a little nutmeg.

A Sangaree, a gentle concoction
popular in a bygone era, is basically any wine, sweetened to
taste, served with or without ice
and topped with grated nutmeg.

PORT SNORT

2 oz. tawny port
2 oz. sloe gin
Lemon slice

Stir port and sloe gin briskly
with cracked ice in a mixing
glass and strain into a chilled
cocktail glass. Garnish with a
lemon slice.

PUENTE ROMANO SPECIAL

2–3 oz. cream sherry
¾ oz. brandy
1½ oz. orange juice
1 oz. heavy cream
Dash curaçao

Mix all ingredients with cracked
ice in a blender or shaker and
strain into a chilled Delmonico
glass.

Created by the author for the
Puente Romano, Marbella, Spain.

 RACE CUP COCKTAIL

1 oz. sweet vermouth
1 oz. tequila
3 oz. grapefruit juice

Mix all ingredients with cracked
ice in a shaker or blender and
strain into a chilled cocktail
glass.

RAYMOND HITCHCOCKTAIL

3 oz. sweet vermouth
2–3 oz. fresh orange juice
Several dashes orange
   bitters
Slice of pineapple

Mix vermouth, juice, and bitters with cracked ice in a shaker or blender and strain into a chilled Old Fashioned glass. Garnish with pineapple slice.

REFORM COCKTAIL

2 oz. fino sherry
1 oz. sweet vermouth
Several dashes orange
   bitters

Stir with ice in a mixing glass and strain into a chilled cocktail glass.

RHINE WINE SPRITZER

4 oz. Rhine, Mosel, or
   Johannisberg Riesling
   wine
Club soda or mineral water
Lemon or lime peel
   (optional)

Pour cold Rhine wine into a chilled wine goblet or highball glass with several ice cubes, and fill with cold club soda or sparkling mineral water. Twist lemon peel over drink and drop into glass.

This is the original Spritzer, but it can be made with any wine of your choice, a little ice, and sparkling water. The name comes from the German word *spritzig*, meaning fizzy, bubbly, and lively, which is what a well-made Spritzer should be.

RITZ FIZZ

4 oz. sauterne, barsac, or
   other sweet white wine
2 oz. dry vermouth
½ oz. kirsch
½ oz. peach-flavored brandy
½ tsp. orgeat syrup or sugar
   syrup to taste
Club soda
Orange peel

Combine sauterne, vermouth, kirsch, brandy, and syrup with ice cubes in a mixing glass. Stir well and pour into a large chilled wine goblet or large brandy snifter. Fill with club soda and garnish with an orange peel cut in a long spiral.

ROY HOWARD

2–3 oz. Lillet blanc
1 oz. brandy
1 oz. orange juice
Several dashes grenadine

Mix all ingredients with cracked ice in a shaker or blender and strain into a chilled cocktail glass.

 SANCTUARY

2 oz. Dubonnet rouge
1 oz. Amer Picon
1 oz. Cointreau
Lemon peel

Stir Dubonnet, Amer Picon, and Cointreau in a mixing glass with ice and strain into a chilled cocktail glass.

BARTENDER'S SECRET NO. 28—Opening Champagne

How do you open a bottle of champagne? By removing the wire fastener and foil that covers the crown of every champagne bottle and twisting the cork until it can be pulled out of the bottle. Right? Wrong. Experienced sommeliers and bartenders know that the easy way to open a bottle of champagne is to hold the cork in one hand and *turn the bottle* with the other. Try it, it works. Place the bottle upright on the bar or table and use a bar towel to get a firm grip on the cork, hold tightly and slowly turn the bottle with your other hand.

SATIN'S WHISKERS COCKTAIL

1½ oz. sweet vermouth
1½ oz. dry vermouth
1 oz. gin
½ oz. Grand Marnier
3–4 oz. fresh orange juice
Dash orange bitters

Mix with cracked ice in a blender or shaker and strain into a chilled wine glass.

SHERRY AND EGG

1 whole egg
Amontillado sherry

Carefully break an egg into a chilled wine glass, leaving the yolk intact. Fill with slightly chilled sherry.

Other wines such as such as port and Madeira may also be used. And some prefer spirits such as brandy and whiskey, which were popular combinations in the nineteenth century.

 **SHERRY COBBLER**

Several dashes curaçao
Several dashes pineapple
    syrup or sugar syrup
4 oz. amontillado sherry
Lemon peel
Pineapple stick
Mint sprig (optional)

Fill a large chilled wine goblet with crushed ice, add curaçao and syrup, and churn the glass with a barspoon. Then add sherry and churn until a frost appears on the outside of the glass. Add more ice, if necessary. Twist lemon peel over drink and drop into glass. Garnish with pineapple stick and mint sprig.

Cobblers may utilize fortified wines such as port, sherry, and Madeira; table wines, both red and white; dessert wines such as sauterne; and all spirits.

 **SHERRY EGGNOG**

3–4 oz. amontillado sherry
1 whole egg
1 cup milk
1 tsp. superfine sugar or
    brown sugar to taste
Grated nutmeg

Mix sherry, egg, milk, and sugar in a blender with cracked ice and strain into a tall Collins glass or wine goblet chilled in the refrigerator. Top with a sprinkling of nutmeg.

SHERRY SHANDY

2–3 oz. amontillado sherry
Several dashes Angostura or
    orange bitters (optional)
Ginger beer or ginger ale
Lemon slice

Mix sherry and bitters in a highball glass with several ice cubes, fill with cold ginger beer, and garnish with a lemon slice.

SHERRY SOUR

3 oz. fino sherry
1 oz. lemon juice
1 oz. orange or grapefruit
    juice
½ oz. sugar syrup or to taste
Maraschino cherry

Mix all ingredients, except cherry, with cracked ice in a shaker or blender and pour into a chilled Whiskey Sour glass. Garnish with a cherry.

SHERRY TWIST No. 1

3 oz. amontillado sherry
1 oz. Spanish brandy,
    cognac, or armagnac
1 oz. dry vermouth
½ oz. curaçao
Several dashes lemon juice
Pinch ground cinnamon

Mix all ingredients, except cinnamon, with cracked ice in a shaker or blender and strain into a chilled Delmonico glass. Top with ground cinnamon.

 SHERRY TWIST No. 2

3 oz. amontillado sherry
1½ oz. bourbon or blended
    whiskey
½ oz. curaçao
3 oz. fresh orange juice
½ oz. lemon juice
3 whole cloves
Pinch cayenne or ground
    white pepper

Mix all ingredients with cracked ice in a blender or shaker and strain into a chilled Old Fashioned glass or a wine goblet.

SHIP COCKTAIL

3 oz. amontillado or fino
    sherry
¾ oz. blended whiskey
¾ oz. light rum
1 tsp. sugar syrup or to taste
Several dashes orange
    bitters
Several dashes prune juice
    or prune syrup

Mix all ingredients with cracked ice in a shaker or blender and strain into a chilled cocktail glass.

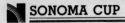

SONOMA CUP

3 oz. dry white wine
½ oz. Cointreau
3 oz. orange juice
Club soda

Mix all ingredients, except club soda, with cracked ice in a shaker or blender and pour into a chilled Collins glass. Fill glass with cold club soda and stir gently.

SOUL KISS

1 oz. Dubonnet or St. Raphael
1 oz. dry vermouth
1 oz. sweet vermouth
1 oz. orange juice

Mix with cracked ice in a blender or shaker and strain into a Delmonico glass.

SOUTHERN CHAMPAGNE COCKTAIL

1 oz. Southern Comfort
Dash Angostura or orange bitters
Brut champagne
Orange peel

Prechill all ingredients and pour Southern Comfort into a chilled tulip glass, add bitters, and fill with champagne. Twist orange peel over drink and drop into glass.

SOYER AU CHAMPAGNE

2 tbsp. vanilla ice cream
Several dashes curaçao
Several dashes maraschino liqueur
Several dashes cognac
Champagne
Orange slice
Maraschino cherry

Put vanilla ice cream into a chilled wine goblet or large champagne flute and mix with curaçao, maraschino, and cognac. Fill goblet with cold champagne and stir gently. Garnish with orange slice and maraschino cherry.

SPION KOP

2 oz. Dubonnet rouge
2 oz. dry vermouth
Orange peel

Stir Dubonnet and vermouth in a chilled Old Fashioned glass with ice cubes. Twist orange peel over drink and drop into glass.

STRAIGHT LAW COCKTAIL

2 oz. fino sherry
1 oz. gin
Lemon peel

Mix gin and sherry with ice in a small pitcher and strain into a chilled cocktail glass. Twist lemon peel over drink and drop into glass.

 TEMPTER COCKTAIL

2 oz. port
2 oz. apricot-flavored brandy

Stir with ice in a mixing glass and strain into a chilled cocktail glass.

THIRD RAIL

2–3 oz. dry vermouth
Several dashes curaçao
Several dashes peppermint
 schnapps
Lemon or orange peel

Stir vermouth, curaçao, and schnapps briskly with ice cubes in a mixing glass and strain into a chilled cocktail glass. Twist fruit peel over drink and drop into glass.

 **TINTON COCKTAIL**

2 oz. port
2 oz. applejack or calvados

Stir with ice in a mixing glass and strain into a chilled cocktail glass.

TINTORETTO

¼ cup pureed pears
1 oz. pear brandy
Brut champagne
Mint sprig (optional)

Puree a ripe pear using a sieve and spoon puree into a chilled balloon glass. Add brandy and cold champagne and a little cracked ice, if you wish (otherwise, prechill all ingredients). Garnish with a small mint sprig.

 TROLLHAGEN SPECIAL

1 oz. B&B liqueur
Brut champagne
Orange peel

Prechill B&B and pour into a chilled balloon glass. Fill with cold champagne and stir gently. Twist orange peel over drink and drop into glass.

TUXEDO

2–3 oz. fino sherry
½ oz. anisette
Several dashes maraschino
   liqueur
Several dashes Angostura
   bitters, orange bitters, or
   Peychaud's bitters

Mix with ice in a small pitcher
and strain into a chilled cocktail
glass.

VERMOUTH CASSIS

3 oz. dry vermouth
1 oz. crème de cassis
Club soda

Mix vermouth and cassis with
ice cubes in a chilled highball
glass and fill with cold club
soda.

VICTOR COCKTAIL

1½ oz. sweet vermouth
¾ oz. brandy
¾ oz. gin
Orange peel

Mix vermouth, brandy, and gin
with cracked ice in a shaker or
blender and strain into a chilled
cocktail glass. Twist orange peel
over drink and drop into glass.

WALTZING MATILDA

3–4 oz. dry white wine
1 oz. gin
1½ oz. passion fruit juice
¼ tsp. curaçao
Club soda, ginger ale, or
   lemon-lime soda
Orange peel

Mix wine, gin, passion fruit, and
curaçao with cracked ice in a
shaker or blender and pour into
a chilled Collins glass. Add several ice cubes and fill with cold
soda. Stir gently and twist orange peel over drink and drop
into glass.

 WEEP NO MORE

1½ oz. Dubonnet rouge
1½ oz. cognac
1½ oz. lime juice
Dash maraschino liqueur

Mix all ingredients with cracked
ice in a shaker or blender and
strain into a chilled cocktail
glass.

⚫ WHISPERS OF THE FROST

1 oz. ruby port
1 oz. fino sherry
1 oz. straight bourbon or
    straight rye whiskey
½ tsp. sugar syrup or to taste
Lemon peel

Stir port, sherry, bourbon, and syrup with cracked ice in a mixing glass until syrup is dissolved and strain into a chilled cocktail glass. Twist lemon peel over drink and drop into glass.

WINE COLLINS

4 oz. Madeira, port, or
    Marsala
½ oz. lime juice
Lemon-lime soda
Maraschino cherry

Pour wine and lime juice into a chilled Collins glass and stir with several ice cubes. Fill glass with cold lemon-lime soda, stir again, and garnish with a cherry.

WINE LEMONADE

Juice of large lemon
½ oz. sugar syrup or to taste
4 oz. dry or sweet, red, rosé,
    or white wine
Club soda
Lemon slice
Maraschino cherry

Pour lemon juice and syrup into a chilled Collins glass and stir until syrup is dissolved. Add wine and fill glass with cold soda. Stir gently and garnish with lemon slice and a cherry.

BARTENDER'S SECRET NO. 29—Vermouth Preserver

Vermouth is a popular, complex, aromatized wine with a relatively high alcoholic content (16 to 18 percent) that is indispensable to the making of many mixed drinks. If you buy a bottle of either sweet or dry vermouth and let it stand in your liquor cabinet for weeks after it has been opened, you will find the subtle flavor overtones that vermouth can impart to drinks will have disappeared. Store opened bottles of vermouth in your refrigerator. Unless you use a great deal of vermouth, buy the 375 ml bottle instead of the 750 ml size. It takes up less space in the refrigerator and, no doubt, will be used up before it becomes stale.

WYOMING SWING COCKTAIL

2 oz. sweet vermouth
2 oz. dry vermouth
3–4 oz. fresh orange juice
1 tsp. orgeat syrup or sugar
    syrup to taste
Orange slice

Mix with cracked ice in a
blender or shaker and serve in a
chilled highball glass. Add additional ice cubes if needed and
garnish with an orange slice.

YELLOW RATTLER

1 oz. dry vermouth
1 oz. sweet vermouth
1 oz. gin
2–3 oz. fresh orange juice

Mix with cracked ice in a
blender or shaker and serve in a
chilled wine glass.

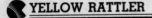 ZANZIBAR

2–3 oz. dry vermouth
1 oz. gin
¾ oz. lemon juice
1 tsp. sugar syrup or to taste
Several dashes orange
    bitters
Lemon peel

Mix all ingredients, except
lemon peel, with cracked ice in
a blender or shaker and strain
into a chilled Delmonico glass.
Twist lemon peel over drink and
drop into glass.

HOUSE SPECIALTIES FROM THE WORLD'S GREAT BARS

> There is nothing by which so much
> happiness has been produced as by
> a good tavern or inn.
> —Samuel Johnson

Good bartenders make good bars. And accomplished chefs fulfill the same role for restaurants. In both instances, the patrons may be glamorous, the decor may be stunning, and the service cheerful and competent, but if what is served is dreary, skimpy, and poorly made, many customers may come and go but few will ever become regulars. The professionalism required to operate a successful bar is detailed in the first chapters of this book. Here we are concerned with bartenders who are not only professional but also creative. Like their counterparts in the kitchen, they frequently devise a recipe that is unique (whether it be original or simply an innovative way of preparing a standard recipe) and which in time becomes a popular, widely acclaimed speciality of the house.

The cocktail is an American invention, and the mixologists who devised mixed drinks that have become classics are all a part of an American tradition. It is a creative tradition that has spread to every continent. Even in the most unlikely places, a traveler can stumble upon a small bar where an enterprising bartender has created a very special (and often a very good) house libation that is served with justifiable pride.

It was not always so, of course. A century ago, with the exception of a few of the more elegant restaurants in large cities, the American drinking scene was pretty much relegated to what was drawn from a keg or poured from a bottle. Early mixologists like Jerry Thomas, the legendary "professor" who created the spectacular Blue Blazer and is credited by many historians as the originator of the Manhattan and the Martinez, the forerunner of the Martini, helped lay the foundation for a gradual change in American tastes toward more genteel, more flavorful drinks. Others followed and made their contributions: Harry C. Ramos, who was renowned in New Orleans at the turn of the century for his creation, the Ramos Gin Fizz. The drink became so popular that on a busy night Harry would have as many as thirty shaker boys, who would pass ice-cold shakers down the line, each giving it a good buffeting as it passed by. And in New York, tales are still told about Johnnie Solon, head barman at the old Waldorf-Astoria, who created many concoctions such as the Bronx cocktail for the likes of J.P. Morgan, Jimmie Walker, and Buffalo Bill Cody. (When offered a drink by an admirer, Cody invariably would reply, "Sir, you speak the language of my tribe.")

In the Roaring Twenties an enterprising Scot from Dundee, Harry MacElhone, opened Harry's New York Bar in Paris. It quickly became known as a hangout for American expatriates such as F. Scott Fitzgerald, Ernest Hemingway, and George Gershwin, who wrote parts of his *An American in Paris* on the downstairs piano. Harry's also served American-style hot dogs and American cocktails such as some of Harry MacElhone's own inventions, including the Sidecar, the White Lady, and Death in the Afternoon, reputed to be a great favorite of Ernest Hemingway's. It was at this very bar that Fernand Petiot is credited with inventing the Bloody Mary.

Around the corner from Harry's New York Bar and just a short walk down the Rue de la Paix is Place Vendôme and the venerable Ritz Hotel. The bars in the Ritz also were creating American-style cocktails in the 1920s, and "style" is the right word for them. Beginning with inventions such as the Mimosa (champagne and orange juice) and Hemingway's Special (lime, bourbon, and a dash of Pernod), the Ritz bars have offered elegant and unusual refreshment to the rich and famous through the years, and the bartenders who created these inspired potations have become legends. Barmen like Frank Meyer, Georges (Sheuer) and Bertin (Jean Bernard Azimont) had an international following, and their handiworks still fill the drink menu at *Les Bars du Ritz*.

About the same time, an American bartender, Harry Craddock, took up residence at London's Savoy Hotel and made its American Bar a source of brilliantly conceived and executed original cocktails. He later compiled *The Savoy Cocktail Book*, a bibber's bible that has become a classic. His successor, Joe Gilmore, another inventive mixologist, carried on the Craddock tradition, devising many interesting new concoctions that helped make the Savoy famous.

The late Trader Vic (Victor Bergeron) was an indefatigable inventor of new and exciting drinks. He changed the drinking habits of the country (with his contemporary, Don the Beachcomber of Hollywood) and made exotic "Polynesian-style" rum drinks the rage in the 1940s and '50s. Trader Vic was proud of his prowess as a mixologist and enjoyed being called a "saloon keeper." Some of his famous drink inventions are the Mai Tai, the Fog Cutter, the Scorpion, and the Tortuga. Creativity in food and drink propelled Trader Vic's from a small Oakland, California, bar (originally known as "Hinky-Dinks") to a large food-products company and a chain of twenty restaurants worldwide, grossing in excess of $50 million a year.

The basis of selecting the establishments and recipes that appear here was not predicated upon size, success, or reputation, although all of these factors, of course, played a part. The primary consideration is creative, imaginative, innovative mixology; and a house policy of serving expertly made drinks. Apologies are in order for the very fine watering places, bartenders, and original recipes that could not be included due to space limitations. One fact, however, became quite obvious as the research for this chapter progressed: the number of good bars creating and promoting special house drinks à la New Mixology is growing and would in itself form the basis for a valuable drink-recipe book.

When you thumb through the wonderfully innovative mixed-drink recipes in this chapter—especially the many new entries—you will realize that this is The New Mixology in action. This dedicated search for flavor and good taste has become a part of an enlightened and informed lifestyle that will ultimately benefit those on both sides of the bar.

AL CAPONE

1½ oz. brandy
¾ oz. Marsala
Dash Drambuie

Mix with cracked ice in a shaker or blender and strain into a balloon glass.

Created by Raffaele de Martinis of the **Cavalieri Hilton International, Rome.**

ALOHA

1 oz. dark Jamaica rum
1½ oz. Myers's rum cream
   liqueur
½ oz. Rose's lime juice
2 oz. pineapple juice
2 oz. orange juice
1 oz. coconut syrup or to
   taste
Small scoop vanilla ice
   cream
Pineapple stick

Mix all ingredients, except pineapple stick, with cracked ice in a blender and pour into a chilled Hurricane or Collins glass. Do not overmix. Garnish with pineapple stick.

From the **Kahala Hilton Hotel, Honolulu.**

ANATOLE COFFEE

½ oz. Courvoisier
½ oz. Tia Maria
½ oz. Frangelico
Cold black coffee
Whipped cream
Chocolate shavings

Mix all ingredients, except whipped cream and chocolate, with a little cracked ice in a blender and pour into a chilled wine goblet. Top with whipped cream and sprinkle with shavings scraped from a bar of chocolate with a knife.

From **Loews Anatole Hotel, Dallas.**

AÑEJO HIGHBALL

1½ oz. añejo rum
½ oz. orange curaçao
¼ oz. lime juice
2 dashes Angostura bitters
Ginger beer
Lime wheel
Orange slice

Add rum, curaçao, lime juice, and bitters to a chilled highball glass and mix well. Add several ice cubes and fill with ginger beer. Garnish with lime wheel and orange slice.

Created by Dale DeGroff, Beverage Director of **The Rainbow Room, New York.**

THE ANNABELE SPECIAL

1½ oz. Benedictine
⅓ oz. dry vermouth
⅓ oz. lime juice

Mix with cracked ice in a shaker or blender and strain into a chilled cocktail glass. Proportions may be varied for individual tastes.

From **Annabele's, London.**

AZTEC

1 oz. gin
½ oz. cherry brandy
1 oz. Piña Colada mix
1 oz. orange juice
Pineapple slice
Maraschino cherry

Mix all ingredients, except pine-apple and cherry, with cracked ice in a shaker or blender and serve in a double Old Fashioned glass. Garnish with fruit.

From the **Arizona Biltmore, Phoenix.**

BATH CURE

1½ oz. dark Jamaica rum
1½ oz. brandy
1½ oz. vodka
2 oz. light Puerto Rican rum
1 oz. Puerto Rican gold rum
1 oz. 151-proof rum
½ oz. lime juice
1 oz. orange juice
1 oz. pineapple juice
1 oz. lemon juice
½ oz. grenadine
1 tsp. sugar syrup or to taste
Red, blue, and green
    vegetable coloring
Lime slice
Maraschino cherry

Mix all ingredients, except lime slice and cherry, with cracked ice in a blender and strain into a 14- or 16-oz..double Old Fashioned-style glass that has been frozen in a mold of shaved ice. Decorate sides of ice mold with red, blue, and green vegetable coloring. Garnish with lime slice and maraschino cherry and serve with two straws.

From the Pump Room, **Ambassador East Hotel, Chicago.**

BALTSCHUG COCKTAIL

1½ oz. vodka
1 oz. lemon juice
½ oz. raspberry syrup or
    grenadine
1½ oz. peach juice
1⅓ oz. orange juice
Assorted garnishes: orange
    slice, lemon slice, and
    maraschino cherry
    (optional)

Mix all ingredients, except garnishes, with cracked ice in a shaker or blender and strain into a chilled cooler glass with ice.

This is a special signature drink of the **Hotel Baltschug Kempinski Moskau, Russian Federation.**

BANANA CREAMSICLE

1½ oz. gin
¾ oz. crème de banane
1 slice ripe banana
Sprite
Assorted garnishes: end of a
banana, piece of banana
leaf, red cherry, lemon
slice (optional)

Mix gin, crème de banane, and banana with cracked ice in a blender at high speed so that banana is liquified. Pour into a chilled champagne glass and top with cold Sprite. In the original recipe the garnishes were fashioned into a woman perched on the rim of the champagne glass. The body was made from a banana, the banana leaf became a cape, the cherry was the head, and the lemon slice the hat.

This signature drink was the creation of the **Kempinski Hotel Beijing Lufthansa Center, Beijing.**

BARCELONA

¾ oz. Spanish brandy
¾ oz. Dry Sack Sherry
1 oz. orange juice
1 oz. heavy cream
1 oz. simple syrup
Cointreau
Powdered cinnamon

Mix all ingredients, except Cointreau and cinnamon, with cracked ice in a blender for a few seconds until mushy. Serve as a frozen drink in a chilled stemmed glass. Float a little Cointreau on top and dust with powdered cinnamon.

Created by Dale DeGroff, Beverage Director at **The Rainbow Room, New York.**

BELLINI

3 oz. pureed peaches
Dash lemon juice
Maraschino liqueur to taste
Brut champagne

Puree ripe peaches in a blender and spoon into a large, chilled wine goblet. Sprinkle with lemon juice and sweeten with maraschino liqueur. Fill with ice cold champagne.

From **Harry's Bar, Venice.**

BOLSHOI PUNCH

1 oz. vodka
¼ oz. light rum
¼ oz. crème de cassis
Juice of 1 lemon
1–2 tsp. sugar syrup or to taste

Mix all ingredients with cracked ice in a shaker or blender and strain into a chilled cocktail glass.

From the **Russian Tea Room, New York.**

BOSSA NOVA

1 oz. light Puerto Rican rum
1 oz. Galliano
¼ oz. apricot brandy
3 oz. pineapple juice
1½ oz. lemon mix
Pineapple slice
Maraschino cherry

Mix all ingredients, except pineapple slice and cherry, with cracked ice in a shaker or blender and pour into a chilled Squall glass or a ten-pin Pilsener glass. Garnish with pineapple slice and cherry.

From the **Sonesta Beach Hotel, Key Biscayne, Florida.**

THE "BOSS McCLURE" COCKTAIL

1 oz. cognac
1 oz. gin
½ oz. orange curaçao
½ oz. apricot liqueur
Lemon twist

Mix all ingredients, except lemon twist, with cracked ice in a shaker or blender and strain into a chilled cocktail glass. Garnish with lemon twist.

From the **Vista International Hotel, Washington, D.C.**

THE BOSTON RITZ FIZZ

Brut champagne
Dash amaretto
Dash blue curaçao
Dash lemon juice

In a chilled champagne glass fill two-thirds full with cold champagne and add amaretto, blue curaçao, and lemon juice.

This is a special signature drink of **The Ritz-Carlton, Boston.**

CAMEL PUNCH

1 oz. dark rum
¾ oz. vodka
½ oz. cherry brandy
½ oz. apricot brandy
3 oz. pineapple juice
1 tbsp. diced assorted fruits

Mix all ingredients, except fruits, with cracked ice in a shaker or blender and strain into a chilled Pilsener glass. Add additional ice cubes if necessary and garnish with diced fruits.

From the **Petra Forum Hotel, Petra, Jordan.**

CANGREJO COCKTAIL

2 oz. light rum
1 oz. Dubonnet rouge
½ oz. Campari
½ oz. lime juice
Sugar syrup to taste
Pineapple slice

Mix all ingredients, except pineapple, with plenty of cracked ice in a blender and pour into a double Old Fashioned glass.

From the **Cartagena Hilton, Cartagena, Colombia.**

THE CARIBE PIÑA COLADA

2 oz. dark rum
8 oz. light rum
2 oz. heavy cream
5 oz. coconut cream
10 oz. pineapple juice
Pineapple spears

Mix all ingredients with crushed ice in a blender for 10 seconds and serve in chilled Hurricane glasses or Poco Grande glasses. Garnish with pineapple spears. Makes 4 drinks.

From the **Caribe Hilton International, San Juan, Puerto Rico.**

The Piña Colada was invented by Ramón "Monchito" Marrero in 1958 at the Caribe Hilton.

CARNEGIE COCKTAIL

1¼ oz. scotch
1 oz. Bailey's Irish Cream
3½ oz. cranberry juice
Orange slice
Mint sprig

Mix scotch, Irish cream, and cranberry juice with cracked ice in a shaker or blender and pour over ice cubes in a chilled highball glass. Garnish with orange and mint.

Created by Joseph Reilly, **Hotel Inter-Continental, New York.**

CHAMPEARMINT

1 oz. Poire William Brandy
Dash vodka
4 oz. chilled champagne
Slice fresh pear
Several fresh mint leaves
Dash white crème de menthe

Pour brandy and vodka into a chilled champagne flute and fill with champagne. Garnish with pear slice and mint leaves. Pour dash of crème de menthe over pear slice.

This is a house specialty of the **Mark Hotel, New York.**

CIRAGAN COCKTAIL

½ oz. cognac
½ oz. Cointreau
½ oz. orange juice
Champagne

Mix all ingredients, except champagne, with cracked ice in a shaker or blender and strain into a chilled champagne glass. Fill glass with cold champagne.

This special house cocktail is a signature drink of the **Ciragan Palace Kempinski Hotel Istanbul, Turkey.**

CLARIDGE'S RENAISSANCE

1 oz. whiskey
1 oz. sweet vermouth
1 oz. orange juice
Dash Campari
Orange wedge

Mix whiskey and sweet vermouth with cracked ice in a shaker and strain into a chilled cocktail glass. Add a dash of Campari for color and garnish with an orange peel on the rim of the glass.

This is a special signature drink of **Claridge's and the Savoy Group, London.**

COLE PORTER

1½ oz. gin
3 or 4 small plum tomatoes, cooked and chilled
Dash Angostura bitters
Dash Worcestershire sauce
Dash lemon juice

Mix all ingredients with cracked ice in a blender until smooth and pour into a chilled Old Fashioned glass.

From the **Waldorf-Astoria Hotel, New York.**

COMET COCKTAIL

1 oz. rum
¾ oz. Chambord
¾ oz. strawberry liqueur
2–3 oz. sweet-and-sour mix
1 small scoop vanilla ice
  cream

Mix all ingredients in a chilled blender bowl until smooth and creamy. Do not overmix. Pour into a chilled wine goblet.

From the Sandpiper and Trade-winds Resort Hotels, St. Petersburg Beach, Florida.

◥ CONNAUGHT CELEBRATION

¼ oz. Benedictine
¼ oz. armagnac
1 oz. apricot nectar
Orange bitters
Champagne

Add Benedictine, armagnac, apricot nectar, and several dashes of orange bitters to a chilled champagne flute and fill with cold champagne.

This is a special signature drink of The Connaught and the Savoy Group, London.

CORPSE REVIVER

¾ oz. white crème de
  menthe
¾ oz. brandy
¾ oz. Fernet Branca

Mix with cracked ice in a shaker or blender and strain into a chilled cocktail glass.

This is a hangover straightener created by Joe Gilmore, the Savoy, London.

CROCODILE

1 oz. rum
1 oz. blue curaçao
2 oz. orange juice
3 oz. sweet-and-sour mix
Dash orgeat syrup

Mix all ingredients with cracked ice in a shaker or blender. Pour into a chilled Old Fashioned glass.

From Loews Anatole Hotel, Dallas.

CROWN JEWEL

1½ oz. light rum
½ oz. crème de noyaux
1¼ oz. lemon juice
1 oz. coconut cream
1 egg white (for two drinks)
Fresh whole strawberry

Mix all ingredients, except strawberry, with cracked ice in a blender until smooth, pour into a chilled wine goblet, and garnish with strawberry.

From the Fairmont Hotel, San Francisco.

CUPID'S BOW

½ oz. Cherry Heering
5 oz. brut champagne

Pour Peter Heering into a chilled tulip glass and fill with cold champagne.

From the **Drake Hotel, Chicago.**

DERBY DAIQUIRI

3 oz. light rum
2 oz. orange juice
1 oz. lime juice
1 oz. sugar syrup

Mix all ingredients with cracked ice in a shaker or blender and strain into a chilled wine glass.

From the **Mai-Kai Polynesian Restaurant, Fort Lauderdale, Florida.**

DESERT BREEZE

1 oz. gin
1 oz. blue curaçao
1 oz. coconut cream
½ oz. lemon juice
Lemon-lime soda
Pineapple stick

Mix all ingredients, except soda and pineapple, with cracked ice in a shaker or blender and serve in a tall, chilled chimney glass. Fill with soda and garnish with pineapple.

From the **Camelback Inn, Scottsdale, Arizona.**

DIAMOND CHAMPAGNE COCKTAIL

1 sugar cube
Angostura bitters
Splash of Sublime Orange
    Liqueur
Brut champagne
Stir stick with a cluster of
    crystallized sugar

Put sugar cube in a chilled champagne glass and soak with bitters. Add orange liqueur, fill with cold champagne, and garnish with crystallized sugar stick.

Created by Dale DeGroff, Beverage Director, **The Rainbow Room, New York.**

THE DOVE CHAMPAGNE COCKTAIL

1 sugar cube
3 dashes Angostura bitters
½ oz. brandy
½ oz. Grand Marnier
Brut champagne

Place sugar cube in a chilled champagne glass and saturate it with bitters. Add brandy and Grand Marnier and fill with cold champagne.

This is a special signature drink of **The Sign of the Dove, New York.**

EAST WINDS DELITE

2 oz. gold rum
½ oz. Galliano
1 oz. orange juice
½ oz. lime juice
Sugar syrup to taste
Dash grenadine

Mix with cracked ice in a shaker or blender and pour into a chilled Collins glass.

From **East Winds Inn, Castries, St. Lucia.**

FIVE-LEGGED MULE

1½ oz. gin
1 oz. Dubonnet rouge
1 oz. dry vermouth
Dash lemon juice
Dash grenadine

Mix all ingredients with cracked ice in a shaker or blender and strain into a chilled cocktail glass.

From the **Hotel Muehlebach, Kansas City, Missouri.**

FOUQUET'S PICK-ME-UP

1 oz. Grand Marnier
½ oz. kirsch
2 oz. orange juice
Brut champagne
Orange slice

Mix Grand Marnier, kirsch, and cold orange juice with cracked ice in a large, chilled wine goblet. Fill with ice-cold champagne, stir gently, and garnish with an orange slice.

From **Fouquet's Restaurant, Paris.**

FRANGIPANI

1¼ oz. dark rum
1¼ oz. Frangelico
½ oz. anisette
2½ oz. pineapple juice
Dash lime juice

Mix all ingredients with cracked ice in a shaker or blender. Pour into a chilled Squall glass or Poco Grande glass.

From **Marriott's Sam Lord's Castle, Barbados.**

FROSTED ROMANCE

1 oz. Chambord
¾ oz. white crème de cacao
2 scoops vanilla ice cream
Whipped cream

Mix all ingredients, except whipped cream, in blender until smooth and creamy. Do not overmix. Serve in a chilled balloon glass and top with whipped cream.

From the **Drake Hotel, Chicago.**

FROZEN PEACHTREE ROAD RACE

1¼ oz. peach schnapps
1¼ oz. vodka
2 oz. peach puree
2 oz. orange juice
Cranberry juice

Mix all ingredients, except cranberry juice, with two cups of crushed ice in a blender at high speed for a few seconds and serve in a chilled Collins glass. Top with a cranberry juice float. Serve with straws.

From the **Ritz-Carlton, Atlanta.**

GOLDEN TULIP

1 oz. vodka
½ oz. apricot brandy
½ oz. curaçao
½ oz. orange juice
½ oz. lemon juice
Orange slice
Maraschino cherry

Mix all ingredients, except orange and cherry, with cracked ice in a shaker or blender and strain into a chilled cocktail glass. Garnish with orange slice and cherry.

Created by Gerry Kooyman, **Hotel Pulitzer, KLM Royal Dutch Airlines, Amsterdam.**

GOOD AND PLENTY

1 oz. vodka
1 oz. *Kahlua*
Dash anisette
½ scoop vanilla ice cream

Mix all ingredients in a blender for a few seconds until smooth. Do not overmix or drink will become watery. Pour into a chilled wine goblet.

From the **Bonaventure Inter-Continental Hotel and Spa, Ft. Lauderdale, Florida.**

GREEN FANTASY

1 oz. vodka
1 oz. dry vermouth
1 oz. melon liqueur
Kiwi slices

Mix all ingredients, except kiwi, with plenty of crushed ice until drink is frappéed. Serve in a chilled balloon glass and garnish with kiwi slices.

From the **Vista International Hotel, New York.**

GRITTI SPECIAL

3 oz. Cinzano dry vermouth
2 oz. Campari
1 oz. China-Martini or Punt e
Mes

Mix well with ice cubes in a pitcher and strain into a chilled wine goblet.

From the **Gritti Palace, Venice.**

HANDLEBAR

1½ oz. scotch
¾ oz. Drambuie
½ oz. Rose's lime juice

Mix with cracked ice in a shaker or blender and strain into a chilled cocktail glass.

From the **Oak Room Bar, Hotel Plaza, New York.**

HALEKULANI SUNSET

1 oz. light rum
½ oz. triple sec
½ oz. grenadine
3 oz. guava nectar
1 oz. sweet-and-sour mix
Pineapple wedge
Orchid (optional)

Mix all ingredients, except pineapple wedge and orchid, with cracked ice in a shaker or blender and pour into a double Old Fashioned glass. Garnish with pineapple and orchid.

This is a signature house specialty of the **Halekulani, Honolulu.**

THE HARPOONER

1½ oz. light Puerto Rican
rum
1½ oz. Trinidad rum
1½ oz. light Jamaica rum
1½ oz. Haitian rum
1 oz. crème de cacao
½ oz. brandy
4 oz. pineapple juice
2 oz. lime juice
Dash Angostura bitters
Dash 151-proof Demerara
rum

Mix all ingredients, except Demerara rum, with cracked ice in a blender and pour into a chilled double Old Fashioned glass. Top off with Demerara rum.

From the **Crown Point Hotel, Tobago.**

HEAVENLY SPIRITS

1 oz. vodka
½ oz. amaretto
¼ oz. triple sec
¼ oz. Galliano
2 oz. orange juice

Mix all ingredients with cracked ice in a shaker or blender and strain into a chilled cocktail glass.

From the **Heaven Restaurant, Pittsburgh.**

HOT PINT

4 oz. blended whiskey
4 eggs
4 tbsp. sugar or to taste
1 qt. ale, heated

In each of 4 heat-proof mugs add 1 oz. whiskey, 1 egg, and sugar to taste. Stir well and pour in ale, heated almost to boiling point. Continue stirring to prevent egg from curdling. Hot ale is traditionally poured into mug from a height to make the drinks frothy. Makes 4 servings.

From the **Al Ain Inter-Continental Hotel, Abu Dhabi, United Arab Emirates.**

ICE CREAM COLADA

1½ oz. light rum
½ oz. banana, melon, or
    strawberry liqueur
2 scoops vanilla ice cream
3 oz. coconut cream
1 oz. heavy cream
4 oz. crushed pineapple
1 tsp. shredded coconut

Mix all ingredients, except shredded coconut, in a blender until smooth, pour into a chilled wine goblet, and sprinkle with coconut.

From the **Boca Raton Hotel and Club, Boca Raton, Florida.**

JERRY'S CHRISTMAS COCKTAIL

1½ oz. Irish whiskey
1 oz. Irish Mist
1 oz. lemon juice
1 egg white (for two drinks)
Ground nutmeg
Orange slice

Mix all ingredients, except nutmeg and orange, with cracked ice in a shaker or blender and pour into a chilled Delmonico glass or a wine glass. Sprinkle with nutmeg and garnish with orange slice.

Created by Jerry Fitzpatrick, **Gresham Hotel, Dublin.**

◤ JOHN'S TEQUILA CITRUS COOLER

1 oz. Herradura Tequila
1 oz. Cointreau
1 oz. fresh squeezed lime
2 oz. fresh squeezed orange
    juice
Splash blue curaçao
1 oz. club soda
Orange slice

Mix all ingredients, except club soda and orange slice, with cracked ice in a shaker or blender and serve in a tall, chilled cooler glass with ice cubes. Top with club soda and garnish with orange slice.

Created for the author by Miles Angelo, chef of **Arizona 206, New York.**

JUNGLE BIRD

1½ oz. dark rum
¾ oz. Campari
4 oz. pineapple juice
½ oz. lime juice
½ oz. sugar syrup or to taste
Maraschino cherry
1 lime slice
1 orange slice
Orchid (optional)

Mix all ingredients, except cherry, orange and lime slices, and orchid, with cracked ice in a shaker or blender and serve in special ceramic-bird container or use a chilled Hurricane glass. Garnish with cherry, orange and lemon slice, and an orchid.

From the **Kuala Lumpur Hilton, Kuala Lumpur, Malaysia.**

KENYA SIKU KUU

1 oz. Kenya white rum
1 oz. Cointreau
2 oz. passion fruit juice
Orange slice
Maraschino cherry
Mint sprig

Mix rum, Cointreau, and passion fruit juice with cracked ice in a shaker or blender and serve in a chilled cocktail glass. Garnish with orange, cherry, and mint.

From the **Mount Kenya Safari Club, Nanyuki, Kenya. Siku Kuu** means "Christmas."

KEVIN'S COFFEE

¾ oz. *Jamaica rum*
¾ oz. *Grand Marnier*
¾ oz. *Tia Maria*
Hot black coffee
Whipped cream
Pinch of powdered cinnamon

Mix spirits and coffee together in a large mug or Irish coffee glass, top with whipped cream and a pinch of cinnamon.

This can also be served as a cold drink. Mix spirits and cold black coffee in a blender with a little cracked ice and pour into a Squall glass or a large wine goblet. Add more ice cubes if needed, top with generous serving of whipped cream, and sprinkle with powdered cinnamon.

From the **Allendale Bar & Grill, Allendale, New Jersey.**

KILAUEA LAVA FLOW

1½ oz. *light rum*
3 oz. *Coco Lopez Syrup*
2 oz. *pineapple juice*
1 oz. *half-and-half*
2 oz. *pureed strawberries*

Pour pureed strawberries in the bottom of a chilled Hurricane glass. Mix other ingredients with cracked ice in a blender and pour into glass.

This is the signature drink of the **Hilton Waikoloa Village, Kamuela, Hawaii.**

THE KISS

1½ oz. *vodka*
¾ oz. *chocolate-cherry liqueur*
¾ oz. *heavy cream*
½ fresh strawberry

Mix all ingredients, except strawberry, with cracked ice in a shaker or blender and strain into a chilled cocktail glass. Garnish with strawberry.

From the **Grand Hyatt Hotel, New York.**

KOKONOKO

1½ oz. tequila
¾ oz. *La Grande Passion*
1 oz. pineapple juice
½ oz. coconut syrup or to
taste

Mix all ingredients with cracked
ice in a shaker or blender and
pour into a chilled Squall glass
or a Poco Grande glass. Garnish
with pineapple and orange
slices, if you wish.

From the **Kahala Hilton, Honolulu.**

LADY DI

1 oz. Benedictine
½ oz. tequila
1 oz. cream
½ tsp. orgeat syrup or to
taste

Mix with cracked ice in a
blender and pour into a chilled
cocktail glass.

Created by L. Baril, **Hotel Inter-
Continental, Paris.**

LADY KILLER

1 oz. gin
½ oz. apricot brandy
2 oz. passion fruit juice
2 oz. pineapple juice
Orange peel

Mix all ingredients, except orange peel, with cracked ice in a
shaker or blender and strain into
a chilled cocktail glass. Garnish
with orange peel.

From the **Kronenhalle, Zurich.**

LA PEROUSE DISCOVERY

1 oz. Tuaca
¾ oz. Kahlua
4 oz. black coffee
Whipped cream
Chocolate shavings

Blend all ingredients, except
whipped cream and chocolate,
with a little cracked ice in a
shaker or blender and pour into
a chilled parfait glass. Top with
a generous portion of whipped
cream and sprinkle with chocolate shavings scraped from a
chocolate bar with a kitchen
knife. This drink may also be
served hot in a mug or Irish coffee glass.

From the **Maui Inter-Continental
Wailea, Kihei, Maui, Hawaii.**

BARTENDER'S SECRET NO. 30—Dripless Coasters

Glass, metal, wood, or plastic, it makes no difference. When moisture forms on the outside of a glass and flows down onto the coaster, the coaster sticks to the glass and usually ends up on the floor or in your lap. You can easily make the best stick-proof coaster in the world by cutting circles out of carpet swatches or scraps. (a carpet store is the place to go) and gluing them to conventional coasters. Try it. It really works.

LODGE FIZZ

1½ oz. gin
½ oz. lemon juice
1 tsp. crème de noyaux
1½ oz. half-and-half
1 tsp. sugar syrup
Club soda

Mix all ingredients, except soda, with cracked ice in a shaker or blender and serve in a chilled Collins glass. Fill with cold club soda and stir gently.

From the **Lodge at Pebble Beach, Pebble Beach, California.**

LONG ISLAND ICED TEA

½ oz. gin
½ oz. vodka
½ oz. white tequila
½ oz. white rum
¼ oz. white crème de menthe
3 oz. sour mix
Cola
Lemon wedge
Mint sprigs (optional)

Mix all ingredients, except cola, lemon, and mint, with cracked ice in a blender and pour into a tall, chilled Collins glass. Fill glass with cold cola, stir gently, and garnish with lemon wedge and mint sprigs.

From the **United Nations Plaza Hotel, New York.**

MANDARIN PUNCH

1½ oz. dark Jamaica rum
½ oz. mandarine liqueur
2 oz. orange juice
2 oz. pineapple juice
Orange slice
Maraschino cherry

Mix all ingredients, except orange slice and cherry, with cracked ice in a shaker or blender and pour into a chilled highball glass. Add additional ice cubes and garnish with orange slice and cherry.

From the **Captain's Bar, Mandarin Oriental Hotel, Hong Kong.**

MANSION SMOOTHIE

1 oz. Bacardi Light
½ oz. amaretto
¼ oz. Kahlua
¼ oz. Cherry Heering
Pinch ground nutmeg

Mix all ingredients, except nutmeg, with cracked ice in a shaker or blender and pour into a chilled cocktail glass. Sprinkle top with ground nutmeg.

From the **Mansion on Turtle Creek, Dallas.**

MARQUIS ROYAL

4½ oz. champagne
¾ oz. Chambord
¼ oz. Cointreau
Fresh raspberry

Combine all ingredients, except raspberry, in a chilled flute champagne glass. Decorate with raspberry.

From the **New York Marriott Marquis Hotel, New York.**

THE MAYFAIR SPRITZER

4 oz. white wine (your
    favorite)
2 oz. club soda
Several dashes Campari

Pour chilled white wine into a chilled Collins glass, add several ice cubes and cold soda. Add several dashes of Campari and stir gently.

From the **Mayfair Regent Hotel, New York.**

MELANCHOLY BABY

1½ oz. gold rum
1 oz. crème de banane
¾ oz. wild strawberry
    liqueur
3 oz. pineapple juice
Lime slice

Mix all ingredients, except lime slice, with cracked ice in a shaker or blender and strain into a chilled tulip or parfait glass. Garnish with lime slice.

From **Pinehurst, Pinehurst, North Carolina.**

MEXICAN BOY

1½ oz. tequila
½ oz. melon liqueur
½ oz. lemon juice
½ oz. simple syrup or to taste
1 whole egg white (for two drinks)
Assorted garnishes: lime slice, melon ball, cloves, maraschino cherry (optional)

Mix all ingredients, except garnishes, with cracked ice in a blender and serve in a chilled tall champagne glass. The original recipe specifies a "Mexican Boy" garnish, using the melon ball for the head, cloves as eyes, a small slice of cherry for the mouth, and a lime slice for a hat.

This signature drink was created by Pauly Poon, bar captain at the **Kowloon Shangri-La, Hong Kong.** She won the grand prize for the Mexican Boy in a competition against contestants from 24 other hotels.

MEXICAN HOP

1½ oz. coffee-flavored brandy
2 oz. Irish cream
Pinch ground nutmeg or cinnamon

Mix with cracked ice in a shaker or blender and pour into a chilled Old Fashioned glass. Sprinkle with spice.

From **Innisbrook, Tarpon Springs, Florida.**

MIAMI VICE

1½ oz. white tequila
½ oz. blue curaçao
¼ oz. maraschino liqueur
½ oz. fresh lime juice
Top with Schweppes Bitter Lemon (to taste)
Maraschino cherry
Mint leaves (optional)

Mix all ingredients, except cherry and mint, with cracked ice in a shaker or blender and pour into a chilled cooler glass with several ice cubes. Garnish with cherry and mint leaves.

This drink is the house specialty of the **Kempinski Hotel Atlantic Hamburg, Germany.**

MIAMI WHAMMY

1½ oz. light rum
1½ oz. Nassau Royale
Orange slice

Add rum, liqueur, and ice cubes to a mixing glass, stir briskly, and strain into a chilled cocktail glass. Garnish with orange slice.

From the **Omni Hotel, Miami.**

MIDORI MARGARITA

1 oz. tequila
1 oz. Midori
1 oz. sweet-and-sour mix
Watermelon ball
Cantaloupe ball

Mix all ingredients, except melon balls, with cracked ice in a shaker or blender. Pour into a chilled cocktail glass, the rim of which has been moistened with lemon juice and rolled in salt. Garnish with melon balls skewered on toothpicks.

From the **Mansion on Turtle Creek, Dallas.**

MIMI COCKTAIL

1 oz. gin
½ oz. apricot brandy
½ oz. cognac
1 egg white (for two drinks)
Dash grenadine
Lemon juice
Powdered sugar

Mix gin, apricot brandy, cognac, egg white, and grenadine in a shaker or blender and pour into a chilled cocktail glass, the rim of which has been dipped in lemon juice and rolled in powdered sugar.

From the **Hotel George V, Paris.**

MIRAGE

1 oz. lime juice
¾ oz. Midori
1 bottle ginger beer
1 oz. vodka
¾ oz. strawberry liqueur
1 tsp. strawberry syrup (or to taste)
Mint sprig (optional)

Pour the first three ingredients into an ice-filled highball glass in the following order: lime juice, Midori, ginger beer. Do not stir—keep the ingredients separated. In a mixing glass with ice add the remaining ingredients: vodka, strawberry liqueur, and strawberry syrup, and mix well. Carefully strain over the back of a barspoon over the highball glass so that the mixture floats on top of the ingredients in the highball glass. Do not stir. Garnish with mint sprig.

This is a house speciality of **The Dorchester, London.**

MOUNT FUJI

1½ oz. gin
½ oz. lemon juice
½ oz. heavy cream
1 tsp. pineapple juice
1 egg white
Several dashes maraschino
    liqueur or cherry brandy
Maraschino cherry

Mix all ingredients, except maraschino cherry, with cracked ice
in a shaker or blender and pour
into a chilled Old Fashioned
glass. Garnish with cherry.

From the **Imperial Hotel, Tokyo.**

MUDSLIDE

1 oz. vodka
1 oz. Kahlua
1 oz. Bailey's Irish Cream

Mix with cracked ice in a shaker
or blender and serve in a chilled
cocktail glass.

From the **Allendale Bar & Grill,
Allendale, New Jersey.**

MURRAY'S BLUE PARADISE

1¼ oz. Malibu
¾ oz. blue curaçao
2 oz. pineapple juice
1¼ oz. Coco Lopez Cream of
    Coconut
Orange slice
Maraschino cherry

Mix all ingredients, except orange slice and cherry, in a
blender with plenty of crushed
ice. Blend only for a few seconds. Serve in a chilled balloon
glass.

This is a speciality of the **Elbow
Beach Bermuda Hotel, Bermuda.**

BARTENDER'S SECRET NO. 31—Bar Mixes

From time to time you will come across recipes that specify
so-called bar mixes such as sweet-and-sour and similar
lemon-lime combinations containing a sweetener and sometimes egg white to make a drink with a foamy head. Bar mixes
come in powdered as well as liquid versions. They have one
great advantage in that they offer an instantly ready drink
mix that yields consistent results when making drinks for a
large number of people. And, obviously, they fulfill a need
when on a camping trip or an extended cruise on a small boat
and fresh fruit is not available. For home drink-making, even
for fairly large groups, fresh or frozen fruit juices are undeni-
ably the best choice.

MYSTIC COOLER

1½ oz. vodka
½ oz. orange juice
½ oz. pineapple juice
½ oz. grapefruit juice
½ oz. crème de banane
1 tsp. grenadine
Lime slice

Mix vodka and fruit juices in a shaker or blender with cracked ice and pour into a chilled Collins glass. Float crème de banane on top and gently add float of grenadine. Top with lime slice.

From the **Royal Sonesta Hotel, New Orleans.**

THE NEW COSMO

1½ oz. Absolut Vodka infused
    with cranberries, oranges,
    and lemons (see below)
½ oz. Cointreau
½ oz. cranberry juice
½ oz. orange juice (for color)
Dash lime juice
Lime wedge

Mix all ingredients, except lime wedge, with cracked ice in a shaker or blender and strain into a chilled cocktail glass. Garnish with lime wedge.

To infuse vodka used in this drink, pour 4 oz. of vodka into a glass container with a tight-fitting top. Peel an orange and a lemon and add 3 orange and 3 lemon segments, along with 8 to 12 cranberries, to vodka. Cover and let stand for at least two days; strain and discard fruit. For a stronger flavor you may age the infusion longer, but replace old fruit with fresh fruit after a week.

This house speciality is a signature drink of **The Hilton at Short Hills, New Jersey.**

NUMERO UNO

1 oz. vodka
Juice of ½ lime
Sugar syrup to taste
Brut champagne
Mint sprig, slightly bruised

Mix vodka, lime, and sugar with cracked ice in a blender and strain into a chilled tulip champagne glass. Fill with cold champagne and garnish with mint sprig.

From **La Caravelle, New York.**

PALM COURT SPECIAL

2½ oz. Stolichnaya vodka
1 tbsp. Rose's lime juice
1 tbsp. fresh lime juice
Several dashes Cointreau

Mix all ingredients well in a mixing glass with cracked ice and strain into a chilled cocktail glass.

From the **Palm Court, Plaza Hotel, New York**.

PAPERBACK The Publisher's Special

1 oz. Lillet blanc
1 oz. gin
1 oz. framboise

Blend with ice in a mixing glass and strain into a chilled cocktail glass.

Created by Joe Gilmore, **Savoy, London**.

PEAR SOUR

2 oz. pear brandy or pear
    schnapps
1 oz. lemon juice
½ oz. sugar syrup or to taste
Brandied pear slice or
    canned pear slice

Mix all ingredients, except pear slice, in a shaker or blender with cracked ice and strain into a chilled cocktail glass. Garnish with pear slice.

From the **Four Seasons restaurant, New York**.

THE PETRIFIER

2 oz. cognac
2 oz. gin
2 oz. vodka
2 oz. triple sec
½ oz. Grand Marnier
Several dashes Angostura
    bitters
Grenadine to taste
Ginger ale
Orange slice
Maraschino cherry

Mix all ingredients, except ginger ale, orange slice, and cherry, with cracked ice in a shaker or blender and pour into a large goblet, beer schooner, or tankard, that has been well chilled. Add additional ice if necessary and fill with cold ginger ale. Garnish with orange slice and cherry.

Created by Andy MacElhone, **Harry's New York Bar, Paris**.

PINK APRICOT SOUR

1½ oz. apricot-flavored
 brandy
Juice of ½ lemon
½ oz. grenadine
Orange slice
Maraschino cherry

Mix all ingredients, except orange slice and cherry, in a blender with cracked ice and pour into a chilled balloon glass. Garnish with orange slice and maraschino cherry.

From **Ye Cottage Inn**, Keyport, New Jersey.

PINK PANTHER No. 1

2 oz. gin
2 oz. apple juice
4 oz. grapefruit juice
Dash grenadine (or enough
 to make a pink drink)
Mint sprigs

Mix all ingredients, except mint, with cracked ice in a shaker or blender and strain into a wine goblet that has been well chilled. Garnish with mint sprig.

From the **Sign of the Dove**, New York.

PINK SUNSET

1¼ oz. vodka
5 oz. cranberry juice
Lemon wedge
¼ oz. Mandarine Napoleon
Kiwi slice

Pour vodka and cranberry juice into a chilled 8-oz. glass with several ice cubes. Squeeze lemon into drink, float Mandarine on top, and garnish with kiwi.

This is the 50th anniversary signature drink of the **Beverly Hills Hotel**, Beverly Hills.

PINK SWAN

1½ oz. Bacardi Añejo Rum
½ oz. Cointreau
1 oz. sweet-and-sour mix
2 maraschino cherries
Sugar

Mix all ingredients, except sugar, with cracked ice in a blender and serve in a chilled Martini glass, the rim of which has been dipped in sugar.

This is a special signature house drink of the **Hotel Bel-Air**, Bel-Air, California.

PIRATE'S PASSION

1 oz. dark rum
½ oz. gin
1¼ oz. La Grande Passion
2 oz. orange juice
2 oz. pineapple juice
Dash grenadine

Mix all ingredients with cracked ice in a shaker or blender. Pour into a chilled Squall glass or a Poco Grande glass.

From **Marriott's Sam Lord's Castle, Barbados.**

PLAISIR D'AMOUR

1½ oz. Bacardi Rum
1 oz. Malibu
5 oz. pineapple juice
Dash lime juice
Dash grenadine
Brandied cherry
Mint sprig

Mix all ingredients, except cherry and mint, with cracked ice in a shaker or blender and strain into a chilled champagne glass. Garnish with brandied cherry and mint sprig.

This is the house signature cocktail of the **Hotel Meurice, Paris.**

POINSETTIA

½ oz. Cointreau or triple sec
3 oz. cranberry juice
3 oz. brut champagne

Prechill all ingredients, including glass. Mix Cointreau and cranberry juice in champagne glass and pour in champagne.

From **Windows on the World, New York.**

THE PRINCESS MARTINI

1½ oz. Stolichnaya Cristal
  Vodka
Splash crème de fraises
Twist of orange peel

Mix vodka and crème de fraises in a shaker with cracked ice and strain into a chilled Martini glass. Squeeze orange peel over glass and drop into drink.

This is a special house drink of the **Colony Pub Steakhouse, The Princess, Bermuda.**

▌ PURPLE RAIN

1 oz. blue curaçao
1 oz. vodka
2 cubes of pineapple
Juice of ½ lime
1 strawberry
Maraschino cherry

Mix all ingredients, except cherry, with cracked ice in a blender and serve in a chilled Squall or footed glass; garnish with cherry.

This is a house speciality of the **Grand Lido Negril, Jamaica.**

PUTTING GREEN

¾ oz. gin
1 oz. melon liqueur
1½ oz. orange juice
1½ oz. lemon juice
Green cherry
Orange slice

Mix all ingredients, except green cherry and orange slice, with cracked ice in a shaker or blender. Pour into a frosted Collins glass. Garnish with cherry and orange slice. This drink may also be served frozen or as a mist.

From the **Colonnade Hotel, Boston.**

RACQUEL WELCH

¾ oz. Tuaca
¾ oz. amaretto
¾ oz. white crème de cacao
Several dashes sweet cream

Mix all ingredients with cracked ice in a shaker or blender. Pour into a chilled wine glass.

Created by Bru Danger of the "21" Club, New York.

RAYON VERT

2 oz. dry vermouth
1 oz. Izzara
1 oz. blue curaçao
Dash orange curaçao
Dash framboise

Mix with cracked ice in a blender and strain into a chilled cocktail glass.

From **Hotel du Palais, Biarritz, France.**

RAZ-MA-TAZZ

1½ oz. brandy
2½ oz. raspberry liqueur
2½ cups French vanilla ice cream, softened
Fresh raspberries

Mix all ingredients, except fresh raspberries, in a blender until smooth. Pour into chilled parfait or sherbet glasses. Garnish with fresh raspberries. Makes 2 servings.

From the **Hyatt Regency, Atlanta.**

RED ROCK CANYON

1½ oz. vodka
¼ oz. crème de cassis
¼ oz. peach brandy
¼ oz. Cointreau
Several dashes Campari
Maraschino cherry
Orange slice

Mix all ingredients, except Campari, maraschino cherry, and orange slice, with cracked ice in a blender and pour into a chilled Collins glass. Top with Campari float. Garnish with cherry and orange.

From **Caesar's Palace, Las Vegas.**

THE REEF RUNNER

1 oz. Jumby Bay Rum
¼ oz. Midori
1 oz. orange juice
1 oz. cranberry juice
1 oz. pineapple juice
Splash Coco Lopez

Mix all ingredients with cracked ice in a shaker or blender and serve in a tall, chilled cooler glass.

This is a signature house specialty of **The Breakers, Palm Beach, Florida.**

REGISTRY SUNSET

½ oz. amaretto
½ oz. Grand Marnier
½ oz. crème de banane
Dash sweet-and-sour mix
Dash pineapple juice
Pineapple wedge
Fresh orchid

Mix all ingredients, except pineapple wedge and orchid, with cracked ice in a shaker or blender and strain into a chilled cocktail glass. Garnish with pineapple wedge and a fresh orchid.

From the **Registry Resort, Scottsdale, Arizona.**

REMINGTON FREEZE

1½ oz. Chambord
2 scoops vanilla ice cream
8 raspberries

Mix all ingredients, except 2 raspberries, with cracked ice in a blender until smooth. Pour into a chilled wine glass and garnish with raspberries. *Do not overmix or drink will become watery.*

From the **Remington on Post Oak Park, Houston.**

THE RHODODENDRON

1 oz. light rum
½ oz. crème de almond
¼ oz. lemon juice
¼ oz. lime juice
½ oz. sugar syrup
Mint sprig
Strawberry

Mix all ingredients, except mint and strawberry, with cracked ice in a shaker or blender and strain into a chilled cocktail glass. Garnish with mint sprig and strawberry.

This is a special house drink of **The Greenbrier, White Sulphur Springs, West Virginia.**

RITZ SPECIAL

2 oz. cognac
2 tsp. kirsch
2 tsp. sweet vermouth
2 tsp. crème de cacao

Mix with cracked ice in a shaker or blender and strain into a chilled cocktail glass.

From the **Hotel Ritz, Paris.**

RITZ SPECIAL PICK-ME-UP

¾ oz. cognac
¾ oz. Cointreau
4 oz. orange juice
Brut champagne

Mix all ingredients, except champagne, with cracked ice in a blender and pour into a chilled balloon glass. Fill with cold champagne and stir gently.

From the **Hotel Ritz, Paris.**

◤ ROBIN AND MIKE MARTINI

3 oz. Stolichnaya Vanilla
    Vodka
Several dashes Malibu
Several dashes pineapple
    juice
Maraschino cherry

Mix all ingredients, except cherry, with cracked ice in a shaker and strain into a chilled Martini glass. Garnish with cherry.

This is a house speciality of the **Fifty-Seven, Fifth-Seven Bar in the Four Seasons Hotel, New York.**

RODEO DRIVER

1½ oz. Cuervo 1800 Tequila
⅓ oz. Mandarine Napoleon
1 oz. sweet-and-sour mix
1 oz. pineapple juice
2 oz. club soda
Orange slice with cherry

Mix all ingredients—except orange slice with cherry and club soda—with cracked ice in a shaker or blender; pour into a chilled rocks glass and fill with soda. Garnish with orange slice with cherry.

This is a house speciality at **The Regent Beverly Wilshire, Beverly Hills.**

ROSALIE

½ oz. gin
½ oz. Grand Marnier
½ oz. Cointreau
½ oz. Campari
Dash grenadine

Mix with cracked ice in a shaker or blender and strain into a chilled cocktail glass.

Created by Fridrich Lechner, **Hotel Inter-Continental, Zagreb, Croatia.**

 SAVOY RESTORATION

1½ oz. vodka
1 oz. Campari
1 oz. crushed strawberries
Champagne
Whole strawberry

Mix vodka, Campari, and crushed strawberries with cracked ice in a shaker and serve in a chilled champagne glass, the rim of which has been dipped in sugar. Fill with cold champagne and garnish with a large strawberry.

This is a special signature drink of **The Savoy** and the **Savoy Group, London,** and was created to celebrate the restoration of The Savoy's famous lobby.

ST. GREGORY COCKTAIL

1 oz. apple brandy
½ oz. B&B liqueur
1 tsp. triple sec
½ oz. sweet-and-sour mix
Lime slice
Lemon slice

Mix all ingredients, except lime and lemon slices, with cracked ice in a blender for two seconds. Strain into a chilled cocktail glass. Garnish with fruit wheels.

Created by Sam Aronis, **Fairmont Hotel, San Francisco.**

SCOTTISH SUNSET

1 oz. scotch
1 oz. coconut rum
½ oz. Grand Marnier
4 oz. orange juice
1 oz. grenadine
Lime slice
Orange slice

Mix all ingredients, except lime and orange slices, with cracked ice in a shaker or blender and pour over ice cubes in a chilled highball glass. Garnish with lime and orange wheels.

Created by Gene Ciesielski, **Hotel Inter-Continental, Hilton Head, South Carolina.**

SCRATCH

Dash Salignac
Dash cranberry juice
Dash vodka
Champagne, chilled
Raspberry eau-de-vie
Lemon peel

Combine Salignac, cranberry juice, and vodka in chilled champagne glass. Fill with champagne and add float of raspberry brandy. Twist lemon peel over drink and drop into glass.

From the **Scratch Restaurant, Santa Monica, California.**

SEA PINE'S STRAWBERRY FREEZE

1½ oz. light rum
2 oz. orange juice
1 oz. coconut cream or to taste
4 large strawberries

Mix in a blender with cracked ice until smooth and pour into a chilled brandy snifter. Garnish with a strawberry.

From **Sea Pines Plantation, Hilton Head, South Carolina.**

747

1 oz. bourbon
½ oz. vodka
½ oz. Galliano
½ oz. white crème de cacao
1 oz. half-and-half

Mix with cracked ice in a blender and strain into a chilled wine goblet.

From **La Costa Hotel and Spa, Carlsbad, California.**

SNOWFLAKE

2 oz. Galliano
1 oz. white crème de cacao
3 oz. cream
3 dashes Pernod
Orange slice
Maraschino cherry

Mix all ingredients, except orange slice and cherry, with cracked ice in a blender and pour into a large, chilled brandy snifter. Garnish with orange slice and maraschino cherry.

From the **Warwick Hotel, Philadelphia.**

SPUMONI COFFEE

½ oz. Galliano
½ oz. Tuaca
½ oz. crème de cacao
1 cup hot black coffee
1 tbsp. whipped cream
Shaved chocolate

Mix liqueurs with steaming hot coffee in a large, heatproof mug, top with whipped cream, and sprinkle with chocolate shaved from your favorite chocolate bar.

From the **Panorama Room, Portland Hilton, Portland, Oregon.**

 STARS AND STRIPES No. 3

1 oz. bourbon
1 oz. Grand Marnier
½ oz. peach schnapps
2 oz. fresh orange juice
Maraschino cherry

Mix all ingredients, except cherry, with cracked ice in a shaker or blender and strain into a chilled cocktail glass. Garnish with cherry.

This special signature drink was created by David Greenwood, head barman of the Four Seasons Hotel, London.

STRAWBERRY MIMOSA

3½ oz. orange juice
3–4 large fresh strawberries
3½ oz. brut champagne

Mix orange juice and strawberries with a little shaved ice in a blender until smooth. Pour into a chilled wine goblet and add cold champagne. Stir gently so as not to lose the bubbles.

From the **New York Hilton, New York.**

TAHOE JULIUS

1½ oz. vodka
3 oz. orange juice
1 oz. half-and-half
1 egg
1 tsp. sugar syrup or to taste

Mix with cracked ice in a blender until smooth and strain into a chilled Squall glass or wine glass.

From **Harrah's Hotel and Casino, Lake Tahoe, Nevada.**

TOASTED ALMOND

1½ oz. Kahlua
1 oz. amaretto
1½ oz. cream or half-and-half
Pinch ground nutmeg or cinnamon

Mix all ingredients, except spice, with cracked ice in a shaker or blender and strain into a chilled cocktail glass. Sprinkle nutmeg or cinnamon on top.

From **Windows on the World, New York.**

TORTUGA

½ lime
1½ oz. 151-proof Demerara rum
1 oz. sweet vermouth
1½ oz. orange juice
1 oz. lemon juice
Dash curaçao
Dash crème de cacao
Dash grenadine
Mint sprig

Squeeze lime into a blender with cracked ice and add all other ingredients, except mint sprig, and serve with ice in the biggest glass you can find. Garnish with spent lime shell and mint sprig.

From **Trader Vic's, San Francisco.**

THE TOULOUSE STREET TWIST

1½ oz. Tanqueray Sterling Citrus Vodka
Domaine Chandon Brut Champagne
Lemon twist

Pour vodka into a chilled champagne glass and fill with cold champagne. Garnish with lemon twist.

This is the signature house speciality of **The Bistro at Maison de Ville, New Orleans.**

TROPICAL DECEMBER

1 oz. Mandarine Napoleon
1 oz. gin
½ oz. blue curaçao
4 oz. orange juice
2 oz. guava juice
2 oz. mango juice
Splash tonic water
Orange slice
Maraschino cherry
Mint sprig

Mix all ingredients, except tonic water, orange slice, cherry, and mint in a shaker or blender with cracked ice and pour into a tall, chilled Collins or iced-tea glass. Top with a splash of tonic and garnish with orange slice, cherry, and mint sprig.

From the **Hotel Inter-Continental Kinshasa, Zaire.**

TURNBERRY ISLE

1 oz. Malibu
¾ oz. Chambord
2 oz. sweet-and-sour mix
Whole strawberry
Pineapple slice

Mix all ingredients, except strawberry and pineapple, with plenty of cracked ice in a blender for 15 seconds until mushy; pour into a large red wine glass. Garnish with strawberry and pineapple slice.

This is a signature drink of the **Turnberry Isle Resort & Club, Aventura, Florida.**

VICTOR'S SPECIAL

1 oz. bourbon
1 oz. Grand Marnier
1 oz. lime juice
½ oz. sugar syrup or to taste
Dash grenadine
Lemon wedge
Pineapple slice or stick
Maraschino cherry

Mix all ingredients, except lemon wedge, pineapple, and cherry, with cracked ice in a shaker or blender and serve in a chilled wine goblet. Garnish with lemon wedge, pineapple, and cherry.

From the **Taj Mahal Inter-Continental Hotel, Bombay.**

VIKING COCKTAIL

1 oz. vodka
1 oz. Grand Marnier
1 oz. Campari or Cinzano
   Bitter
Dash lemon juice

Mix all ingredients with cracked ice in a shaker or blender and strain into a chilled cocktail glass.

Created by Bjarne Eriksen of the **Hotel Viking, Oslo.**

VOUVRAY SUMMER APERITIF

3 oz. vouvray wine
6 large strawberries
Dash grenadine

Place 5 strawberries (reserve 1 strawberry for garnish) and vouvray in a blender with 3 oz. of cracked ice, add a dash of grenadine, and blend until smooth. Pour into a chilled champagne glass or wine glass and garnish with whole strawberry.

From the **Jefferson Hotel, Washington, D.C.**

WAILEA TROPICAL ITCH

1 oz. blended whiskey
1 oz. dark Jamaica rum
½ oz. curaçao or triple sec
1 oz. orange juice
Dash Angostura or orange bitters
Pineapple stick
Maraschino cherry

Mix all ingredients, except pineapple and cherry, with cracked ice in a blender and pour into a chilled Hurricane glass. Garnish with pineapple stick and maraschino cherry.

From the **Wailea Beach Hotel, Maui, Hawaii.**

WHITE GHOST

1¼ oz. Frangelico
¾ oz. white crème de cacao
¼ oz. Chambord
2 oz. heavy cream
Fresh raspberry

Mix all ingredients, except raspberry, with cracked ice in a blender until smooth. Pour into a chilled cocktail glass. Garnish with fresh raspberry.

From the **New York Marriott Marquis Hotel, New York.**

WINDJAMMER

1½ oz. Jamaica rum
1½ oz. light rum
1½ oz. white crème de cacao
6 oz. pineapple juice
1 oz. heavy cream
Grated nutmeg

Mix all ingredients, except nutmeg, with cracked ice in a shaker or blender and pour into a double Old Fashioned glass. Sprinkle with grated nutmeg.

From the **Coral Harbor Restaurant, Nassau.**

WINDSOR ROMANCE

¾ oz. mint-chocolate liqueur
¾ oz. amaretto
¾ oz. gin
¾ oz. passion fruit juice

Mix all ingredients with cracked ice in a shaker or blender and strain into a chilled cocktail glass.

Created by Peter Dorelli, **The Savoy, London.** Concocted in honor of the wedding of the Prince and Princess of Wales.

YELLOWFINGERS

1 oz. blackberry brandy
1 oz. crème de banane
½ oz. gin
½ oz. heavy cream

Mix with cracked ice in a shaker or blender and strain into a chilled Old Fashioned glass.

Created by Louis Pappalardo, **Bull and Bear Bar, The Waldorf-Astoria Hotel, New York.**

ZAPATA

1 oz. tequila
½ oz. Campari
Juice of 1 orange

Mix all ingredients with cracked ice in a shaker or blender. Pour into a chilled champagne goblet.

Created by Bru Mysak of the **"21" Club, New York.**

PUNCHES:
THE TIMELESS
ALLURE OF THE
FLOWING BOWL

> There, gentlemen, is my champagne and my
> claret. I am no great judge of wine and I give
> you these on the authority of my wine
> merchant; but I can answer for my punch,
> for I made it myself.
>
> —Lord Pembroke

The punch bowl is the original community cocktail. And punches traditionally have been festive, culinary showpieces, concocted with great care and pride. The flowing bowl of a long past, more gracious era was the center of the party; the hub of a golden circle of family and friends; and perhaps the expression, "proud as punch," reflected the importance of the custom and circumstances of punch making and serving. Punches were never intended to be labor-saving devices or a means of do-it-yourself dispensing of refreshments for the multitude. Nor were they devised as a stratagem whereby a small amount of wines and spirits sufficient for the few could be stretched to serve the many. Unfortunately, punches have become equated with drab, uninspired drinks served on such auspicious occasions as the crowning of the new basketball queen or the dedication of the new department of sanitation incinerator and solid-waste compactor. We have all suffered from episodes of dreary liquid boredom or stomach-wrenching, acidic assaults from concoctions that were unfit for human consumption. It is our purpose here to provide some simple rules, which, if followed, will produce exemplary punches, together with a collection of good punch recipes, both modern and traditional, that have achieved gratifying results. (And see Chapter fifteen for nonalcoholic punches.)

The word "punch" is reputed to be a derivative of the Hindustani word *pānch*, meaning "five" (as in *panchāmrit*, a mixture of five ingredients), which is believed to be the basis for the "Rule of Five," the traditional means of making a punch. However, it is doubtful if the word "punch" originated in the Far East. As Congreve put it so memorably, "To drink is a Christian diversion, unknown to the Turk or the Persian." Some historians believe the name is of English origin and is a contraction of the word "puncheon," a small cask holding about eighty gallons of liquid. Mariners stored their wines and spirits in puncheons, and seamen in the British Navy in particular were often served their rum rations from these or similar small casks.

Liberally applied, the Rule of Five is summed up in the axiom: "One sour, two sweet, three strong, four weak," with the fifth element being spices and other flavorings. In olden times, this may have been a good working formula, but tastes change and so perhaps this has gone the way of the equal-parts-of-gin-and-vermouth Martini. The Rule of Five, whether or not applied literally, embodies a valid idea: balance. Good drink recipes must have balance as every professional mixologist knows. Anyone can have a go at making a new drink whether by the glass or by the bowl, but if the ingredients are not properly balanced, the results will be undistinguished, flat, and moribund. And it follows, the more ingredients, the more essential—and critical—the task of achieving balance. The Rule of Five is simply an effort, albeit arbitrary and inflexible, to produce a formula for balance in a punch.

Here follow the rules of punch making gleaned from many sources and put to test on many occasions. It is mostly just common sense based upon an old-fashioned idea that your guests deserve the best and a good host's primary responsibility is to see that this comes to pass.

THE RULES OF THE BOWL

1. A punch may be made in an engraved bowl of gold or cut crystal or English bone china. For entertaining, the more elegant, the better. For outdoor entertaining, a stockpot, kettle or other large cooking container; wooden bucket, a cut-down keg or steel drum, or even a hollowed-out ice cake will fill the bill, depending upon the theme of the party. Be sure the bowl is large so it can be properly chilled with a

large cake of ice. For hot punches, a heat-proof bowl is essential since an acceptable hot punch must be served piping hot, just as a cold punch should be served crackling cold. Since proper presentation is important in culinary matters, if you do not have the right kind of punch bowl, borrow one from a friend or rent one from a caterer.

2. Use only the finest ingredients, the freshest fruits and the best spices and mixers. Do not for a moment think that a substandard whiskey or wine will go unnoticed in the punch bowl because of the presence of many other ingredients. Each part, however small, contributes to or detracts from the whole. By the same token, stock enough supplies so that you will have adequate refills for the punch bowl. If the weather is hot, be guided by the old adage: generously estimate the amount of ice you think you need and get three times as much.

3. Planning the right type of punch is as important as planning the party. A light, not too authoritative punch is in order for a graduation party that many people of all age groups will be attending. Powerhouse mixtures such as Fish House Punch should be reserved for a small group of experienced drinkers who understand the perils of strong, seductively tasty potations. A summertime punch should be designed to be refreshing and thirst-quenching, whereas a cold weather concoction should be bracing and stimulating. If the group is made up of adults and teenagers, a second, nonalcoholic punch should be made. A well-made nonalcoholic punch can be just as appetizing and refreshing as the other kind.

4. For cold punches, all ingredients should be chilled in advance, including the punch bowl itself. If large ice cakes are not available, slabs of ice made by freezing water in milk cartons will do, or you can remove the dividers in your ice trays and make small slabs this way. *Ice cubes are out for punches.* They melt too quickly and create unwanted dilution. Fruit juices should be squeezed in advance and strained before using. It is important that your punch be clear, not murky. Do not fill the bowl with whole fruit. It does nothing for the punch but get in the way of serving and drinking. A few orange or lemon slices are sufficient. Remember that sugar and alcohol don't mix readily, so it is advisable to add fruit juices and other nonalcoholic ingredients with your sweetener first to make certain the sweetener is dissolved. Alcoholic beverages go in about an hour before the guests arrive to prevent excessive evaporation. Spar-

kling wines and mixers such as club soda and ginger ale are added just before serving and stirred into the punch gently to preserve carbonation.

5. The crucial point in the party will come when much of the punch has been drunk, much of the ice has melted, and it is recycling time. This does *not* mean getting more punch from the pantry and dumping it into the bowl; it means *renewing the bowl* by removing it from the table for a thorough rinsing, a filling of fresh ice, and preparing the punch as you did the first time around. If you have two punch bowls you can rotate, fine; otherwise your guests will have to wait a few minutes until the new punch (with clean cups) is brought in. It will be worth the wait, for everything will be fresh and clean and sparkling. The second serving will taste exactly like the first, if not better, and your guests will be the first to notice they are getting top-shelf treatment. This will do wonders for your reputation as a party-giver.

6. Punch cups are important for a crucial reason: you must know exactly how much you can put in them for serving purposes so you can estimate how much punch you will need for your guests. Generally, a punch cup serving is reckoned to be four ounces, since the traditional punch cup is smaller than a tea cup. For purposes of standardization, unless otherwise specified, all servings in this chapter will be four ounces.

7. Estimating the number of servings, and therefore the amount of punch makings you will need, is important since running out of food or beverages at a party is an affront to your guests and brands you as a poor planner or a niggardly host. Caterers who are pretty good at counting the house estimate that the average guest will consume between two and three cups. Some, of course, will have only one drink and others will have four or more. The important thing to remember is *no party-giver should expect to come out even.* You should plan, as insurance, to have food and beverages left over. For every quart of punch you will get about eight 4-ounce servings and about 8½ servings from a liter. A gallon of punch will yield thirty-two servings. There will actually be slightly more due to ice meltage, but this is not exactly a plus, since ice meltage and dilution should be held to a minimum. A watery punch is unforgivable. If you have punch left over, fear not, if it contains a nominal amount of alcohol; it will keep for several weeks in a tightly sealed container in your refrigerator.

If you will but follow the rules of the bowl, your punches will be legendary, you will be lionized, and your guests will love coming to your parties.

APPLEJACK PUNCH

2 750-ml. bottles applejack or calvados
1 pt. light rum
1 pt. peach-flavored brandy
1 pt. lemon juice
1 cup brandy
½ cup maple syrup or sugar syrup to taste
2 l. lemon-lime soda or 1 l. lemon-lime soda and 1 l. club soda
½ red apple thinly sliced

Prechill all ingredients and pour applejack, rum, peach brandy, brandy, lemon juice, and maple syrup into a chilled punch bowl with a large cake of ice. Stir well, adjust sweetness, and pour in soda. Stir gently and garnish with apple slices. Makes about 45 servings.

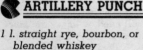

ARIZONA SUNSHINE

1 l. light rum
1 qt. vanilla ice cream
1 qt. cold black coffee

Mix all ingredients in a chilled punch bowl and ladle into punch cups. Makes about 24 cups.

ARTILLERY PUNCH

1 l. straight rye, bourbon, or blended whiskey
1 l. dry red wine
1 l. strong black tea
1 pt. dark Jamaica rum
1 pt. orange juice
1 cup brandy
1 cup gin
1 cup lemon juice
4 oz. Benedictine
Sugar syrup to taste
Lemon peels

Prechill all ingredients and put into a chilled punch bowl with a large cake of ice. Stir well, adjust sweetness, and garnish with a few lemon peels. Makes about 40 servings.

ASCOT CUP

2 750-ml. bottles red
   Bordeaux or California
   cabernet sauvignon
1 pt. fino sherry
½ cup cognac
½ cup curaçao
½ cup raspberry syrup
½ cup lemon juice
1 oz. framboise or raspberry
   liqueur
2 qt. club soda or 1 bottle
   each club soda and
   champagne
Orange and lemon slices,
   thinly sliced

Prechill ingredients and, except for club soda or champagne and fruit slices, put everything in a chilled punch bowl and stir well. Add a cake of ice and just before serving, gently stir in club soda or champagne. Garnish with a few orange and lemon slices. Makes about 37 servings.

AZTEC PUNCH

4 l. tequila
4 qt. grapefruit juice
2 qt. tea
1 cup lemon juice
1–2 cups orgeat or simple
   syrup
1 cup curaçao
1 oz. Angostura bitters
   (optional)
1 tsp. ground cinnamon

Chill all ingredients and mix in a large punch bowl with a cake of ice. Yields about 90 5-oz. servings.

BALLSBRIDGE BRACER PUNCH

2 750-ml. bottles Irish
   whiskey
½ pt. peach-flavored brandy
1 pt. fresh lemon juice
½ cup maple syrup or honey
   to taste
2 l. club soda or ginger ale
   or 2 750-ml. bottles
   champagne
Sliced brandied peaches
   (optional)

Prechill all ingredients and pour whiskey, brandy, lemon juice, and syrup (which has been dissolved in a little water) into a chilled punch bowl and mix well. Add a large cake of ice and just before serving, pour in club soda or ginger ale or champagne or any combination thereof (i.e., half soda, half ginger ale; half soda, half champagne, etc.), depending on the strength desired. Slice some brandied peaches thinly and put one slice in every cup of punch. Makes about 37 servings.

BALTIMORE EGGNOG

12 eggs
2 cups superfine or
   confectioner's sugar
1 pt. cognac
1 cup dark Jamaica rum
1 cup peach brandy or
   Madeira
3 pt. milk
1 pt. cream
Grated nutmeg

Separate eggs and beat yolks with sugar until thick and gradually stir in cognac, rum, and peach brandy (some recipes specify Madeira in place of peach brandy), milk, and cream. Keep in refrigerator until well chilled. In another bowl, beat egg whites until stiff. When ready to serve, transfer egg-yolk mixture to a chilled punch bowl and carefully fold in whites without beating or stirring. Makes about 28 servings.

Do not put any ice into the punch bowl.

BENGAL LANCER'S PUNCH

1 l. dry red wine
3 oz. gold Barbados rum
3 oz. curaçao
½ cup lime juice
½ cup pineapple juice
½ cup orange juice
2 oz. orgeat syrup or sugar syrup to taste
1 750-ml. bottle champagne
1 pt. club soda
Lime slices

Prechill all ingredients and put everything, except champagne and soda, in a chilled punch bowl with a cake of ice and stir well. Immediately before serving, add champagne and soda and stir gently. Garnish with a few lime slices. Approximately 24 servings.

 BOMBAY PUNCH

12 lemons
Sugar to taste
1 750-ml. bottle cognac
1 750-ml. bottle medium-dry sherry
½ cup maraschino liqueur
½ cup curaçao
4 750-ml. bottles brut champagne
2 l. club soda

Squeeze juice from lemons and sweeten to taste with sugar in a chilled punch bowl with a large cake of ice. Add cognac, sherry, maraschino, and curaçao and stir well. Immediately before serving, add cold champagne and club soda. Stir gently to preserve carbonation. Makes about 58 servings.

BOURBON PUNCH

2 l. straight Kentucky bourbon
1 pt. fresh orange juice
1 cup peach-flavored brandy
1 cup fresh lemon juice
⅔ cup orgeat syrup or sugar syrup to taste
2 qt. club soda or 2 750-ml. bottles champagne
12 maraschino cherries

Prechill all ingredients and, excepting club soda or champagne, put everything into a chilled punch bowl, stir well, and check sweetness. When ready to serve, add club soda or champagne, stir gently, and garnish with maraschino cherries. Makes about 42 servings.

BARTENDER'S SECRET NO. 32—Ice Cakes

Ice cakes for large punch bowls may not be easy to come by, but you can make your own by removing the separater inserts in your ice trays and freezing solid slabs of ice. This works well and three or four slabs will cool your punch very nicely.

BRANDY PUNCH

12 lemons
4 oranges
Superfine sugar
½ cup grenadine or
    raspberry syrup
1 cup curaçao
2 750-ml. bottles cognac
1 750-ml. bottle champagne
    or club soda

Squeeze juice from fruit and pour into a chilled punch bowl with ice cake. Add sugar and stir until sugar is dissolved. Add grenadine, curaçao, and cognac. Stir well and just before serving, add cold champagne and stir gently. Spiral peels from your oranges make a good garnish. Makes about 30 servings.

BUDDHA PUNCH

1 pt. Rhine wine or Riesling
1 cup light rum
1 cup orange juice
½ cup lemon juice
½ cup Cointreau
½ oz. kirschwasser
1 oz. sugar syrup or to taste
Several dashes Angostura
    bitters (optional)
1 750-ml. bottle sparkling
    Mosel or champagne
1 lime thinly sliced

Prechill all ingredients and put into a chilled punch bowl, excepting sparkling wine and lime slices, which will be added just before serving. Mix well and add a large cake of ice. Makes about 17 servings.

BURGUNDY PUNCH

2 750-ml. bottles red
    Burgundy
1 pt. orange juice
1 cup port
1 cup cherry brandy
½ cup lemon juice
1 oz. sugar syrup or to taste
1 l. club soda (optional)
Orange slices

Prechill all ingredients and pour into a chilled punch bowl with a cake of ice. Stir well and garnish with a few orange slices. If soda is used, add just before serving and stir gently. Makes about 22 servings.

CARDINAL PUNCH

2 750-ml. bottles dry red
 wine
1 pt. cognac
1 pt. Jamaica gold rum
3 oz. sweet vermouth
½ cup sugar syrup or to
 taste
1 750-ml. bottle brut
 champagne
2 l. club soda
Sliced oranges

Prechill all ingredients and put
red wine, cognac, rum, vermouth,
and sugar syrup in a chilled
punch bowl with a cake of ice.
Mix well and check sweetness.
Pour in cold champagne and club
soda and stir gently. Garnish with
a few thinly sliced orange peels.
Makes about 46 servings.

Some prefer more champagne
than club soda, so feel free to adjust quantities to suit your taste.

CELEBRITY PUNCH

1 750-ml. bottle gold rum
1 750-ml. bottle gin
1 l. grape juice
1 pt. orange juice
2 l. ginger ale
Small jar maraschino cherries
6 orange slices
6 lemon slices

Pour chilled spirits and fruit
juices into punch bowl with
large cake of ice and stir well.
Gently stir in ginger ale and jar
of cherries, including juice. Garnish with fruit slices. Makes
about 43 4-oz. servings.

CHAMPAGNE PUNCH

1 cup cognac
1 cup maraschino liqueur
1 cup curaçao
½ cup sugar syrup or to
 taste
2 750-ml. bottles brut
 champagne
1 l. club soda (optional)

Prechill all ingredients and pour
cognac, maraschino liqueur, curaçao, and syrup into a chilled
punch bowl with a cake of ice
and stir well. Just before serving,
add champagne and stir gently.
Add cold club soda to reduce potency and increase the fizziness,
if you wish. Makes about 19
servings.

DAVID EISENDRATH'S "FAMILY DRINK"

½ gal. blended pineapple-
 grapefruit juice
1 l. gold rum
1½ cups lemon juice
1½ cups Falernum

Mix well with ice in a blender and
serve in chilled Old Fashioned
glasses or mix without ice and
store in a gallon jug in the refrigerator. Mixture will keep well for
an extended period of time if
tightly sealed. Makes 30 servings.

● MICHAEL O'RIORDAN'S IRISH PUNCH

2 750-ml. bottles Irish
    whiskey
½ pt. Cointreau
1 pt. fresh lemon juice
½ pt. fresh orange juice
¼ cup raspberry syrup or
    grenadine
¼ cup sugar syrup or honey
    to taste
1 750-ml. bottle champagne
1 l. club soda
Fresh mint sprigs

Prechill all ingredients and pour
whiskey, Cointreau, lemon juice,
orange juice, raspberry syrup,
and sugar syrup into a chilled
punch bowl with a cake of ice
and mix well. Just before serving, pour in champagne and
club soda and stir gently. Garnish with mint sprigs. Makes
about 37 servings.

For a weaker punch, use 2 bottles of soda. For a special occasion, you may want to use 2
bottles of champagne and no
soda at all.

THE DEVIL'S CUP

1 cup cognac
½ cup lemon juice
2 oz. green Chartreuse
2 oz. yellow Chartreuse
2 oz. Benedictine
2 oz. sugar syrup or to taste
2 750-ml. bottles brut
    champagne
1 l. club soda

Prechill all ingredients and pour
cognac, lemon juice, liqueurs,
and syrup into a chilled punch
bowl with a cake of ice. Mix
well and check sweetness. Add
cold champagne and club soda
just before serving and stir gently. Makes about 27 servings.

DRAGOON PUNCH

2 small lemons, thinly sliced
¼ cup superfine sugar
1 l. ale
1 l. porter or a mixture of ½
    beer and ½ stout
1 cup amontillado sherry
1 cup brandy
2 750-ml. bottles champagne

Prechill all ingredients. Put a
cake of ice in a chilled punch
bowl, cover ice with lemon
slices, and cover lemons with a
thin coating of sugar. Bruise lemons with a muddler or a heavy
serving spoon. Add ale and porter or beer and stout mixture,
sherry, and brandy and stir well.
Just before serving, stir in champagne gently. Makes about 34
servings.

DUBONNET PUNCH

1 750-ml. bottle Dubonnet
  rouge
1 pt. gin or vodka
½ cup curaçao
Juice of 6 limes
1 pt. club soda
Lime peel cut in a spiral
Orange slices cut thin

Prechill all ingredients and add Dubonnet, gin or vodka, curaçao, and lime juice to a chilled punch bowl and mix well. Adjust sweetness by adding more curaçao. Just before serving, add club soda and stir gently. Garnish with lime peels and a few orange slices. Makes about 17 servings.

BARTENDER'S SECRET NO. 33—Punch Extender

Some punches, while flavorful, well-balanced, and hearty, like Fish House Punch, are simply too strong for protracted drinking. The solution is obviously to extend or dilute the mixture so the high alcoholic content is spread out over more servings. Instead of disturbing the flavor or balance by adding, say, more fruit juice, experienced bartenders opt for club soda. The sparkle adds to the punch and does not interfere with the basic recipe. If done with care (so as not to make the punch watery), this is a practical way to keep your guests from having an abbreviated evening.

EAST OF SUEZ

1 qt. hot tea
1 lemon, sliced thin
2 oz. lime juice
1 cup superfine sugar
½ pt. Batavia arak or
  Swedish Punsch
½ pt. triple sec or curaçao
1 pt. dark Jamaica rum
1 pt. cognac

Put tea, lemon slices, lime juice, and sugar into the flaming pan of a chafing dish and simmer over direct heat until all sugar is dissolved. Add arak, triple sec, and rum. Heat but do not boil. Warm some cognac in a ladle by keeping it partially submersed in the hot punch, ignite, and pour blazing into chafing dish. After a few moments, extinguish flames, then pour in remainder of cognac. Makes about 20 servings.

EGG NOG Basic

12 eggs
2 cups superfine sugar
1 pt. cognac
1 pt. dark Jamaica rum
3 pt. milk
1 pt. cream
Grated nutmeg

Separate eggs and beat yolks and sugar together until thick. Stir in cognac, rum, milk, and cream, and chill in refrigerator until needed. Just before serving, transfer egg mixture from refrigerator to a chilled punch bowl. Beat egg whites until stiff and carefully fold whites into the egg nog without beating or stirring. Sprinkle the top with nutmeg. Makes about 28 servings.

Do not put any ice in the punch bowl.

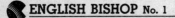 **EGG POSSET**

6 egg yolks
½ cup sugar or to taste
½ tsp. ground cinnamon
½ tsp. ground nutmeg
½ tsp. ground cloves
1 750-ml. bottle dry red wine

Beat egg yolks well with sugar and spices. Heat wine in a saucepan, bring to a simmer, and pour into egg mixture, stirring constantly. Serve in warmed cups. Makes 6 servings.

ENGLISH BISHOP No. 1

6 large oranges
Brown sugar
Whole cloves
3–4 cinnamon sticks
1 750-ml. bottle gold
   Barbados rum or dark
   Jamaica rum
½ gallon apple cider
Grated nutmeg

Dampen outside of oranges and coat with brown sugar, then stud each orange with about a dozen cloves. Place in a roasting pan and put in the broiler of a medium oven (350°) and brown well until juice begins to seep out of oranges. Quarter oranges and place in a heatproof punch bowl. Add cinnamon sticks and sprinkle a little more brown sugar on oranges. Pour in rum that has been warmed in a pan, ignite, and set ablaze for a few seconds. Extinguish by pouring in hot cider. Stir well and sprinkle with nutmeg. Makes 24 servings.

Some prefer a piece of orange with their punch, in which case a larger cup may be needed with teaspoons.

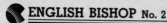

ENGLISH BISHOP No. 2

6 large oranges
Brown sugar
Whole cloves
3–4 cinnamon sticks
2 750-ml. bottles ruby port
1 cup cognac

Prepare oranges in oven as in the recipe above and place in the flaming pan of a chafing dish over direct heat. Add cinnamon sticks and port, cover, and simmer gently for 15 minutes, but do not boil. Pour in cognac (except for an ounce or two) gently so that it stays on top of wine mixture. Remove one orange, put into a ladle, and douse with several ounces of cognac, ignite, and lower blazing into pan, which in turn will ignite the contents of the chafing dish. After a few moments extinguish with the lid of the pan. Makes about 16 servings.

Some will want portions of orange with their punch, in which case a large cup may be needed and teaspoons provided.

ENGLISH CHRISTMAS PUNCH

2 750-ml. bottles dry red wine
3 cups strong tea
Juice of 1 large orange
Juice of 1 lemon
1 lb. superfine sugar
1 750-ml. bottle dark Jamaica rum

Heat wine, tea and fruit juices in a chafing dish or saucepan, but do not boil. This punch may be served from the chafing dish or transferred to a heatproof punch bowl. Put sugar into a large ladle and saturate with rum. If ladle is not large enough for all the sugar, put remainder in punch bowl. Ignite rum in ladle and pour blazing into punch. Stir well, extinguish flames, and then pour remainder of rum into punch. Stir again and serve. Makes about 27 servings.

FIRESIDE PUNCH

1 pt. strong hot black tea
1 cup fresh orange juice
½ cup fresh lemon juice
Brown sugar, maple syrup,
  or honey to taste
4 oz. curaçao
1 750-ml. bottle dark Jamaica
  rum

In a chafing dish or saucepan put in hot tea, fruit juices, and sugar, syrup, or honey, and mix well until sweeteners are dissolved. Add curaçao and rum and heat, but do not boil. Stir well and serve in warmed mugs. Makes slightly more than 14 cups.

FISH HOUSE PUNCH The Original

¾ lb. sugar or to taste
2 l. spring water
1 l. freshly squeezed lemon
  juice
½ cup peach brandy
1 l. cognac
2 l. dark Jamaica rum

Dissolve sugar in spring water, stir in lemon juice, and add peach brandy, cognac, and rum. Check sweetness and pour into a chilled punch bowl with a cake of ice. Makes about 52 servings.

This is America's most venerable punch from the State in Schuylkill club of Philadelphia, established in 1732. There are many variations of the original recipe, but it remains unsurpassed. Yes, George Washington drank here.

GUARDSMEN'S PUNCH

1 qt. green tea
1 cup brown sugar
Peel of 1 lemon
2 oz. port
1 750-ml. bottle scotch
1 cup cognac

Simmer tea, sugar, and lemon peel in the flaming pan of a chafing dish over direct heat until all sugar is dissolved. Add port and scotch and heat, but do not boil. Add all cognac to the pan, except several ounces for flaming. Pour reserved cognac into a ladle and warm by partially immersing in hot punch. Ignite cognac and pour blazing into pan. After a few moments, extinguish flame with pan lid. Makes about 17 servings.

HARVARD PUNCH

1 l. blended whiskey
1 pt. brandy
1 cup Grand Marnier or
   triple sec
1 cup orange juice
½ cup lemon juice
½ cup orgeat or sugar syrup
   to taste
2 750-ml. bottles champagne
   or 2 l. club soda or ginger
   ale
Orange and lemon slices

Mix all ingredients, except champagne or soda and fruit slices, in a large, chilled container or punch bowl, cover, and chill in refrigerator for one hour. When ready to serve, add a large cake of ice to bowl and pour in champagne or club soda or ginger ale, stir gently, and garnish with a few orange and lemon slices. Makes about 32 servings.

HOLIDAY PUNCH

1 l. gin
½ cup curaçao
5 cups orange juice
1½ cups lemon juice
2 oz. grenadine
1 l. lemon-lime soda
4 lemon slices
4 orange slices

Pour chilled gin, curaçao, fruit juices, and grenadine into a punch bowl with a cake of ice. Stir well, add soda, and stir again gently. Garnish with fruit slices. Makes about 32 servings.

JACK-THE-GRIPPER

1 750-ml. bottle applejack or
   calvados
Juice of 3 lemons
¼ cup maple syrup, honey,
   or sugar syrup
1 oz. ginger-flavored brandy
½ oz. Angostura bitters
   (optional)
Cinnamon sticks
Lemon peel
Boiling water

Heat applejack, lemon juice, and syrup in the flaming pan of a chafing dish over direct heat. Stir until syrup is dissolved. Add brandy, bitters, cinnamon, and a few pieces of lemon peel. Stir well and ignite. After a few moments, extinguish flames by adding a little boiling water or use pan lid. Makes about 8 servings.

JEFFERSON DAVIS PUNCH

12 750-ml. bottles Bordeaux
   or dry red wine
2 750-ml. bottles oloroso
   sherry
½ l. brandy
1 pt. freshly squeezed lemon
   juice
1 cup dark Jamaica rum
1 cup maraschino liqueur
5 l. club soda
5 l. ginger ale

Prechill all ingredients and pour red wine, sherry, brandy, lemon juice, rum, and maraschino into a punch bowl, cover, and refrigerate for 8 hours. When ready to serve, put in a large ice cake and pour in cold soda and ginger ale. Stir gently and garnish with a little fruit, if you wish. Makes about 186 servings.

J.P.'S PUNCH

2 qt. orange juice
1 qt. pineapple juice
1 cup lime juice
2 ripe bananas, peeled and
   sliced thin
2 oz. grenadine or raspberry
   syrup
1 750-ml. bottle dark Jamaica
   rum
1 l. gold Puerto Rican rum
12 maraschino cherries

Pour orange and pineapple juice into a chilled punch bowl with a large cake of ice. Put lime juice, bananas, and grenadine into a blender and mix until bananas are creamy. Pour into punch bowl with Jamaica rum and Puerto Rican rum and stir well. Garnish with maraschino cherries. Makes about 42 servings.

KENNETH BOLES' SHOOTING MIXTURE

3 750-ml. bottles cherry wine
1½ 750-ml. bottles cherry
   brandy
1 750-ml. bottle brandy

Mix all ingredients and refrigerate for several hours, covered, before serving. Shooting mixture may be stored in bottles in a cool place for future use. Makes 40 servings.

This wonderful restorative, designed to aid and comfort those who climb about on the cold and desolate moors of the Scottish Highlands in foul weather, is the invention of Kenneth Boles, a stalwart outdoorsman, guide, and good companion.

KRAMBAMBULI PUNCH

2 750-ml. bottles dry red
    wine
2 oranges
2 lemons
1 cup superfine sugar or to
    taste
1 pt. dark Jamaica rum
1 pt. Batavia arak or
    Swedish Punsch

Pour wine and the juice of oranges and lemons into the flaming pan of a chafing dish and heat over direct flame until mixture is hot. Add sugar and stir until dissolved. Put a little rum and arak into a long-handled ladle, warm by partially submerging in wine mixture, ignite, and pour flaming into chafing dish. Extinguish flames after a few moments and add remainder of rum and arak. Makes about 24 servings.

LA PALOMA PUNCH

1 l. tequila
½ cup maraschino liqueur
½ cup peach brandy
1 16-oz. can pineapple
    chunks with juice
2 l. lemon-lime soda
1 750-ml. bottle sparkling
    wine or champagne

Chill all ingredients in refrigerator and mix in a large punch bowl with a cake of ice. Add sparkling wine last and stir in gently. Yields about 35 servings.

MICHEL ROUX PUNCH

1½ cups La Grande Passion
1 cup Grand Marnier
1 cup Stolichnaya Vodka or
    Bombay Gin
1 cup Marnier-La Postolle
    Cognac
2 750-ml. bottles Champagne
    de Venoge Brut
1 l. club soda (optional)
1 orange, sliced thin

Prechill all ingredients and pour La Grande Passion, Grand Marnier, Stolichnaya Vodka or Bombay Gin, and Marnier-La Postolle Cognac into a chilled punch bowl with a cake of ice. Stir well and add cold champagne and some club soda, if you wish. Stir gently. Makes about 30 servings.

MULLED CLARET

2 oz. honey or sugar syrup to
    taste
1 750-ml. bottle red Bordeaux
1 pt. ruby port
1 cup brandy
6 whole cloves
Several cinnamon sticks,
    broken
½ tsp. grated nutmeg
Lemon peel

Dissolve honey with a cup of
water in the flaming pan of a
chafing dish over direct heat.
Pour in Bordeaux, port, brandy,
and add spices and lemon peel.
Heat over low flame, but do not
boil. Stir from time to time and
serve when hot. Makes 13
servings.

 MYRTLE BANK PUNCH

½ pt. fresh lime juice
½ cup maraschino liqueur
¼ cup orgeat syrup or
    Falernum to taste
1 oz. raspberry syrup or
    grenadine
1 750-ml. bottle 151-proof
    Demerara rum

Mix lime juice, maraschino, orgeat syrup, and raspberry syrup
with cracked ice in a blender
and pour into a chilled punch
bowl with a cake of ice. Pour in
Demerara rum and mix well.
Makes about 10 servings.

BARTENDER'S SECRET NO. 34—Flaming Punches

When flaming punches in a large container such as a chafing
dish or a heat-proof punch bowl, it is necessary to have a lid
handy to extinguish the flames in the container. In the case
of a large punch bowl for which no securely fitting lid is available, make a cover using two layers of very heavy institutional
aluminum broiling foil that is shaped so it will cover the bowl
tightly. In no instance should any punch mixture be flamed for
more than a few seconds because it allows too much alcohol to
burn away. Make certain a lid is close by before the flaming
process begins, since this is the only method for quickly extin-
guishing the flames in a container without damaging the
contents.

NEGUS

1 large lemon
6–8 sugar cubes
Boiling water
1 cinnamon stick
1 nutmeg, crushed
6 whole cloves
Several dashes lemon juice
   (optional)
1 750-ml. bottle port,
   Madeira, sherry, or dry
   red or white wine

Rub all of the zest (outside peel) off a lemon until only the white, inner peel shows, using as many sugar cubes as necessary. Put sugar cubes in a warmed pitcher and add enough boiling water to completely dissolve sugar. Add spices, some lemon juice, if you wish, and wine. Mix well and when ready to serve, pour in 2 cups of boiling water. Makes about 10 servings.

This "mull" (heated with hot water instead of a red-hot flip iron) was named for Colonel Francis Negus, who presumably enjoyed this daily "after his morning walk." He lived during the reign of Queen Anne.

OLD COLONIAL HOT TEA PUNCH

1 l. dark Jamaica rum
1 pt. brandy
3 pt. hot tea
1 pt. fresh lemon juice
½ cup honey, orgeat syrup,
   or sugar syrup to taste
3 oz. curaçao
½ lemon, thinly sliced

Mix rum, brandy, hot tea, lemon juice, honey or syrup, and curaçao in a saucepan and stir until honey or syrup is completely dissolved. Check for sweetness, and when cool, pour into a chilled punch bowl with a large cake of ice. Garnish with lemon slices. Makes about 30 servings.

OLD-FASHIONED WHISKEY PUNCH

1 l. blended whiskey
1 pt. dark Jamaica, gold
   Jamaica, or Barbados gold
   rum
1 pt. fresh lemon juice
1 pt. black tea, chilled
1 cup orgeat syrup or sugar
   syrup to taste
4 oz. curaçao
1 750-ml. bottle champagne
   brut
6 each, thin orange and
   lemon slices

Mix all ingredients, except champagne and fruit slices, in a punch bowl, cover, and chill for several hours in the refrigerator. When ready to serve, put a large ice cake in punch, add champagne, stir gently, and garnish with fruit slices. Makes about 30 servings.

OLD NAVY PUNCH

Juice of 4 lemons
Meat of 1 fresh pineapple or
    canned pineapple
1 750-ml. bottle dark Jamaica
    rum or Demerara rum (90
    proof)
1 pt. cognac
1 pt. peach-flavored brandy
    or Southern Comfort
Sugar syrup, orgeat syrup, or
    Falernum to taste
4 750-ml. bottles brut
    champagne

Put lemon juice, pineapple, rum, cognac, brandy, and syrup in a prechilled punch bowl and mix well. Add large ice cake and immediately before serving, pour in champagne and stir gently. Makes about 45 servings.

OLD OXFORD UNIVERSITY PUNCH

1 cup brown sugar
2 qt. boiling water
1 pt. lemon juice
1 750-ml. bottle cognac
1 750-ml. bottle 151-proof
    Demerara rum
Cinnamon sticks and whole
    cloves (optional)

Dissolve brown sugar with boiling water in the flaming pan of a chafing dish and then add lemon juice and cognac. Heat, but do not boil. Pour in Demerara rum, reserving several ounces for flaming. Warm remainder of rum in a ladle, ignite, and pour into chafing dish. After a few moments, extinguish flames with pan lid. Garnish with cinnamon sticks and whole cloves, if you wish. Makes 33 servings.

PARK AVENUE ORANGE BLOSSOM

2 qt. fresh orange juice
6-oz. jar maraschino cherries
3 750-ml. bottles brut
    champagne

Pour cold orange juice and cherries (with juice) into a prechilled punch bowl with a large cake of ice. Stir well and add cold champagne and stir gently. Serve in chilled 8-oz. champagne tulip glasses. Makes about 24 6-ounce servings.

BARTENDER'S SECRET NO. 35—Proper Tea

The making of tea for punches is important. You may get by with a teabag sloshed about in a cup of tepid water when making a cup of "Old Herbal Dreadful" tea for your aunt, but a liter or so of that very same tea can ruin a beautiful punch. Tea in punch is a balancer and a binder. It smooths out the punch and holds the disparate elements together. A strong tea is often called for in punches (green or black are usually specified, black being the odds-on favorite since it is "seasoned" or fermented after picking, while green tea is dried immediately after harvesting), but that does not mean bitter and overbrewed. On the other hand, a weak, bland tea does nothing for a punch except dilute it. To make a proper cup of tea, scald out a teapot, add a rounded teaspoon of tea leaves for each cup and fill pot with spring water just brought to a brisk boil. After three minutes of steeping—and *not* more than 5 minutes at the outside—stir tea and strain into cups. Remember, when a recipe calls for strong tea, it means fully brewed, but not harsh and bitter from oversteeping.

● PENNSYLVANIA HUNT CUP PUNCH

1 cup gold Puerto Rican, Barbados, Haitian, or Martinique rum
½ cup dark Jamaica rum or Rhum Negrita
½ cup Malibu or CocoRibe
½ cup peach brandy
Juice of 6 lemons
Juice of 1 large orange
Juice of 1 tangerine (or substitute another orange)
6 oz. can of pineapple juice or ¾ cup fresh pineapple juice
6–8 oz. Falernum or sugar syrup to taste

Mix all ingredients in a large container and allow to stand in the refrigerator, *tightly* covered, overnight. Serve in a chilled punch bowl with a large cake of ice. Makes about 12 servings.

This was created by the author for tailgate luncheons that precede this outstanding annual steeplechase and turf-racing event for charity.

PICCADILLY PUNCH

2 large lemons
12 whole cloves
2 cinnamon sticks
¼ tsp. grated nutmeg
1 cup superfine sugar
2 cups hot water or
   (optional) ruby port
1 750-ml. bottle cognac

Slice peel from lemons, stud with cloves, and place into the flaming pan of a chafing dish along with juice. Add cinnamon sticks, nutmeg, sugar, and hot water and simmer until all sugar is dissolved. Warm some cognac in a ladle, ignite, and pour blazing into chafing dish. Extinguish and then pour remainder of cognac into pan. Stir and serve. Makes about 11 servings.

Some recipes call for port in place of hot water, in which case the lemon juice and sugar would have to be adjusted for individual tastes.

PRINCE'S (PRINCESS'S) PUNCH

1 750-ml. bottle Benedictine
1 750-ml. bottle cognac
½–1 pt. fresh lemon juice,
   depending upon tartness
   desired
2 oz. sugar syrup or to taste
4 750-ml. bottles champagne
½ lemon thinly sliced
10 maraschino cherries

Prechill all ingredients and put Benedictine, cognac, lemon juice, and sugar syrup into a chilled punch bowl. Mix well and adjust sweetness. Just before serving, gently stir in champagne and garnish with lemon slices and cherries. Makes about 42 servings.

The secret of this punch is to use just the right amount of lemon juice, adding more lemon juice and sugar syrup as needed until the balance is just right.

QUEEN ANNE'S SHRUB

1 pt. lemon juice
Grated zest (outer peel) of 2
  lemons
2 lbs. sugar or to taste
2 750-ml. bottles brandy
2 750-ml. bottles dry white
  wine
Several strips of lemon peel
Mint sprigs (optional)

Clean out a large container with a tight-fitting lid with boiling water. In a small mixing bowl combine lemon juice, zest, and sugar and stir until sugar is dissolved. Pour into large container with brandy and 1 bottle of wine, reserving the other. Seal the container and store in a cool place for 5 or 6 weeks. To serve, strain shrub into a chilled punch bowl with a cake of ice, add second bottle of white wine, and garnish with long strips of lemon peels and several mint sprigs. Makes about 30 servings.

REGENT'S PUNCH

1 750-ml. bottle Rhine wine
2 750-ml. bottles Madeira
1 750-ml. bottle curaçao
1 750-ml. bottle cognac
1 pt. dark Jamaica rum
1 pt. tea
3 cups orange juice
5 oz. lemon juice
½ cup sugar syrup or to taste
3 750-ml. bottles champagne
2 l. club soda

Prechill all ingredients and mix in a chilled punch bowl with ice cake, reserving champagne and club soda until just before serving. When ready to serve, add champagne and soda and stir very gently. Makes approximately 83 servings.

ROMAN PUNCH

1 750-ml. bottle Haitian,
  Martinique, or Barbados
  rum
1 750-ml. bottle brut
  champagne
½ cup curaçao
1 cup lemon juice
¾ cup orange juice
1 tbsp. raspberry syrup or
  grenadine or to taste
Whites of 10 eggs
Orange peels

Mix all ingredients, prechilled, except egg whites and orange peels, in a chilled punch bowl with an ice cake. Check sweetness. Beat egg whites until fairly stiff and gently stir into punch. Garnish with a few orange peels. Makes about 20 servings.

ST. CECELIA SOCIETY PUNCH

6 limes, sliced thin
4 lemons, sliced thin
1 small ripe pineapple,
    skinned, cored, and sliced
    thin
1 cup superfine sugar
1 750-ml. bottle cognac
1 750-ml. bottle peach
    brandy
1 qt. iced tea
1 pt. dark Jamaica rum
1 cup curaçao
4 750-ml. bottles brut
    champagne
2 l. club soda

Place sliced limes, lemons, and pineapple in a large pot with a lid that fits securely. Spread sugar evenly over the fruit and muddle until sugar is pounded or pressed into the slices. Pour in cognac, cover, and let stand for 24 hours. Pour the entire contents of the pot into a chilled punch bowl containing a large cake of ice. Add chilled peach brandy, tea, rum, and curaçao, and stir well. Just before guests arrive, gently stir in cold champagne and club soda. Check sweetness and serve. Makes about 70 servings.

SANGRIA Basic

2 750-ml. bottles dry red
    wine
3 oz. curaçao
2 oz. brandy (optional)
Juice of 1 orange
Juice of 1 lemon or lime
4 oz. sugar syrup or to taste
1 l. club soda (optional)
6 each thin orange and
    lemon slices
1 fresh or brandied peach,
    sliced thin (optional)

Prechill all ingredients and mix wine, curaçao, brandy, fruit juices, and sugar syrup until well blended and strain into a chilled punch bowl with a cake of ice or serve from chilled pitchers. Add club soda, if you wish, and garnish with orange and lemon slices. A fresh or brandied peach may be added to the punch. Makes 24 servings.

Sangria is basically wine flavored with fresh fruits and sweetened to taste. Spirits are often added for flavor and soda may be used to provide fizziness. There are many recipes and variations.

SANGRIA Blonde

2 750-ml. bottles chablis,
  Mosel, Rhine wine, or
  California Johannisberg
  Riesling
2–3 oz. curaçao
1 oz. kirschwasser
½ cup orange juice, freshly
  squeezed
2 oz. lemon or lime juice
2 oz. sugar syrup or to taste
1 l. club soda
½ orange, sliced thin

Prechill all ingredients and pour
in wine, curaçao, kirsch, and
fruit juices and let steep for 30
minutes with a cake of ice. Just
before serving, pour in soda, stir
gently, and garnish with orange
slices. Makes about 25 servings.

SANGRIA Champagne

1 750-ml. bottle Riesling
  wine
1 generous cup grapefruit
  sections
2 oz. gin
1 oz. triple sec
1 oz. maraschino liqueur or
  sugar syrup to taste
3 oz. grapefruit juice
Several dashes lime juice
1 750-ml. bottle champagne
1 lime, sliced thin
Mint sprigs (optional)

Prechill all ingredients and mix
riesling, grapefruit, gin, triple
sec, maraschino liqueur, grapefruit and lime juices, in a chilled
punch bowl with a cake of ice.
Check sweetness and add more
lime juice if too sweet or more
maraschino or triple sec if too
tart. Pour in champagne and stir
gently. Garnish with lime sections and mint sprigs. Makes
about 16 servings.

SANGRIA Mexican

4 oz. gold tequila
1 bottle dry red wine
1 orange sliced
1 lemon sliced
1 lime sliced
2 oz. curaçao
1 fresh peach, peeled,
  quartered, and studded
  with cloves
2–3 cinnamon sticks
Club soda or sparkling wine
  (optional)

Mix all ingredients, except
peach, cinnamon, and soda or
sparkling wine, in a punch bowl
in which has been placed a cake
of ice. Add peach and cinnamon
and soda or sparkling wine if
more dilution is required. Makes
8 servings.

SEWICKLEY HEIGHTS GUN CLUB PUNCH

1 qt. pineapple juice
1 qt. grapefruit juice
1 qt. orange juice
1 l. dark Jamaica rum
1 pt. gold rum
1 6-oz. jar maraschino
    cherries
1 qt. lemon-lime soda
½ tsp. powdered cinnamon

Pour pineapple, grapefruit, and orange juice into a prechilled punch bowl with a large cake of ice. Add Jamaica rum and mix well. Take cup of gold rum and the entire contents of a jar of cherries and mix in a blender until cherries are chopped fine and pour into punch bowl with remainder of gold rum. Stir well and just before serving, add lemon-lime soda and stir gently. Sprinkle with powdered cinnamon. Makes about 40 servings.

SHAMROCK PUNCH

2 750-ml. bottles Irish
    whiskey
½ pt. Irish Mist
1 pt. fresh lemon juice
½ cup honey or sugar syrup
    to taste
2 750-ml. bottles champagne,
    or 1 bottle champagne
    and 1 bottle club soda
Fresh shamrocks or clover

Prechill all ingredients and pour whiskey, Irish Mist, and lemon juice into a chilled punch bowl with a cake of ice. Add honey after dissolving it in a cup with a little warm water and mix well. Immediately before serving, pour in champagne and stir gently. Garnish with a few fresh shamrocks. Makes about 33 servings.

For a less potent punch, use club soda in place of champagne.

SHANGHAI PUNCH

2 qt. hot black tea
1 750-ml. bottle cognac
1 pt. curaçao
1 pt. dark Jamaica or
    Demerara rum
2 cups lemon juice
1½ oz. orgeat syrup
1 oz. orange flower water
Orange peel
Lemon peel
Cinnamon sticks

Mix all ingredients, except orange and lemon peels and cinnamon sticks, in the flaming pan of a chafing dish over direct heat and bring to simmering. Serve steaming in mugs with a garnish of orange and lemon peel and a stick of cinnamon. Makes about 35 servings.

This recipe is from Shanghai and was popular with the White Russian colony before World War II.

SHERRY TWIST PUNCH

1 750-ml. bottle amontillado
   sherry
1 pt. Spanish brandy or
   armagnac
½ pt. dry vermouth
½ pt. curaçao
Juice of 1 lemon
Ground cinnamon

Prechill all ingredients and mix
(except for cinnamon) in a
chilled punch bowl with a cake
of ice. Sprinkle powdered cinnamon over punch. Makes about 15
servings.

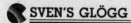 ## SVEN'S GLÖGG

½ gal. dry red wine
1 pt. port
½ cup dry vermouth
1 cup blanched almonds
1 cup seedless raisins
¼ cup dried bitter orange
   peel
4 cinnamon sticks
1½ tbsp. cardamom seeds
1 tbsp. whole cloves
1 tsp. aniseed
1 tsp. fennel seed
⅔ cup granulated sugar
1 pt. vodka
1 pt. cognac
1 pt. rye whiskey or blended
   whiskey

Pour red wine, port, and vermouth
into a large bowl. Add almonds
and raisins. Put orange peel, cinnamon sticks (broken), cardamom,
cloves, aniseed, and fennel seed
into a cloth bag and add it to the
wine mixture. Cover and let stand
overnight. Transfer all ingredients
from bowl to a saucepan and heat
over a low flame. Add sugar to
taste and allow to simmer for a
few minutes, but do not boil. Remove from heat, add vodka, cognac and rye, cover pan, and heat
until punch reaches boiling point.
Remove cloth bag and pour punch
into the flaming pan of a chafing
dish (or a warmed heat-proof
punch bowl); cover and heat over
a low fire. Just before serving, put
an ounce or two of warmed cognac
in a long- handled ladle, ignite, remove lid (be sure to stand away
from chafing dish), and pour flaming liquid into punch. Allow to
blaze for a few moments and extinguish by covering with lid. Serve
in cups with spoons. Be sure to put
a helping of almonds and raisins
into each cup along with the
glögg. Makes about 33 servings.

Glögg is traditionally served with
ginger snaps and is a great favorite in Sweden during the Christmas season. Every family has a
treasured recipe for this festive
punch. This is one of them.

BARTENDER'S SECRET NO. 36—Taste Testing

No professional chef or experienced cook would dream of serving a soup, sauce, or other made-from-scratch recipe without tasting it during the course of preparation. All recipes are subject to change and modification depending on the nature of the available ingredients and the taste preferences of the one who is doing the cooking. Complicated punches and other mixed drinks are no different. They must always be checked for flavor before serving (unless you have made the recipe many times) and especially for sweetness. If a punch turns out to be too sour or too sweet despite the fact that you have followed the recipe assiduously, adjustments should be made until you are satisfied with the results.

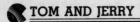 TOM AND JERRY

12 eggs
2½ lbs. superfine sugar
1½ tsp. ground cinnamon
½ tsp. ground cloves
½ tsp. ground allspice
¼ tsp. cream of tartar
4 oz. dark Jamaica rum
1 l. bottle brandy, bourbon, or rum
Boiling water, milk, or coffee

Separate eggs. Beat yolks with 2 lbs. sugar (reserving remainder for the whites), ground cinnamon, cloves, and allspice until they are smooth and creamy, then add rum gradually, stirring constantly. In another bowl, beat egg whites with a pinch of cream of tartar until soft peaks form, then beat in remainder of sugar until peaks stiffen. Carefully fold whites into yolks. This batter is the basis of individual servings. When ready to serve, scald out a Tom and Jerry mug or other heatproof container and put a ladleful of the batter into a cup. Add 2 oz. of brandy or bourbon or rum or any combination that suits your taste (i.e., half brandy and half rum), fill with boiling water or milk and sprinkle with nutmeg.

This recipe is based on the original created by the famous mixologist Jerry Thomas, and adjusted to modern tastes. Sugar and other ingredients may be varied.

TRADER VIC'S TIKI PUNCH

1 pt. Cointreau or triple sec
1 pt. gin
¾ cup fresh lime juice
4 750-ml. bottles champagne

Prechill all ingredients and pour Cointreau, gin, and lime juice into a chilled punch bowl with a cake of ice. Mix well, let stand an hour, and check sweetness, adding more lime juice or Cointreau to suit your taste. Just before serving, add champagne and stir gently. Makes about 35 servings.

VICTORIA PARADE PUNCH

1 750-ml. bottle blended
  whiskey, scotch, or
  bourbon
1 750-ml. bottle dark Jamaica
  rum
1 750-ml. bottle Benedictine
1 750-ml. bottle cherry
  brandy
1 pt. Darjeeling tea
1 cup orange juice
4 oz. lemon juice
4 oz. sugar syrup, pineapple
  syrup, or Falernum
Orange and lemon slices

Chill all ingredients and mix together in a large punch bowl with a cake of ice. Stir well, adjust sweetness, and serve. Makes about 33 servings.

WASSAIL BOWL

1 cup brown sugar
2 tsp. grated nutmeg
2 tsp. powdered ginger
3 cinnamon sticks, broken
½ tsp. mace
6 whole cloves
6 allspice berries
3 750-ml. bottles Madeira,
    sherry, port, or Marsala
6–8 eggs
1 cup cognac or gold rum
4 baked apples, cored but
    not skinned

Put sugar and spices in a saucepan or the flaming pan of a chafing dish over direct heat and add a cup or two of water. Bring to a boil and stir well until all sugar is dissolved. Add wine and heat, but do not boil. Separately, beat egg yolks and egg whites and fold together, then pour eggs into a warmed, heat-proof punch bowl. Add the hot wine mixture to the punch bowl a little at a time, stirring constantly until all wine has been blended with the eggs. Stir briskly and add cognac. Stir again and add baked apples. Makes about 28 servings. Put a bit of baked apple into each cup.

This traditional English Christmas punch can be made with wine, beer, cider, ale, or any combination thereof.

WOODCHOPPER'S PUNCH

1 l. fresh lemon juice
1 pt. maple syrup
6 cinnamon sticks or 1 tsp.
    powdered cinnamon
2 750-ml. bottles straight rye,
    bourbon, or Canadian
    whisky

Simmer lemon juice, maple syrup, and cinnamon in a saucepan until maple syrup is dissolved. Stir well and check sweetness. Pour in whisky, mix well, and serve in warmed mugs. This punch may also be served cold in a pitcher or a punch bowl with ice. Makes about 25 servings.

◗ XALAPA PUNCH

2 l. hot, strong black tea
Zests (outside peel) of 2 large
    oranges, grated
1½ cups sugar syrup or
    honey to taste
1 750-ml. bottle gold rum
1 750-ml. bottle applejack or
    calvados
1 750-ml. bottle dry red wine
12 thinly sliced orange and
    lemon sections

Pour hot tea into a saucepan with
orange zest (only the colored peel of
the orange, not the white) and let
steep until tea cools. Add sugar or
honey and mix thoroughly until dissolved. Stir in spirits and wine and
chill in refrigerator, covered, for an
hour or two before serving in a
chilled punch bowl with a cake of
ice. Garnish with orange and lemon
sections. Makes about 40 servings.

◗ YARD OF FLANNEL

1 l. ale
4 eggs
3 tbsp. superfine sugar or to
    taste
½ tsp. ground nutmeg
½ tsp. ground ginger,
    cinnamon, or allspice
½ cup Martinique, Haitian,
    gold Jamaica, or other
    aromatic rum
Boiling water

Heat ale in a saucepan over low
heat. In a small bowl, beat eggs
with rum, sugar, and spices and
pour into a pitcher that has been
rinsed with boiling water. In a second pitcher, also rinsed with boiling water, pour hot ale from the
saucepan and very gradually add
to egg mixture, stirring constantly
until well blended. Before serving
in heated mugs, pour mixture from
one pitcher to another until frothy.
Makes 4 servings.

 ZOMBIE PUNCH

2 750-ml. bottles gold Puerto
    Rican rum
1 750-ml. bottle dark Jamaica
    rum
1 pt. 151-proof Demerara rum
1 pt. curaçao or triple sec
1 pt. lime juice
1 pt. orange juice
1 cup lemon juice
1 cup papaya juice or
    pineapple juice
1 cup passion fruit juice or
    La Grande Passion
½ cup grenadine
2 oz. Pernod
Pineapple slices

Mix all ingredients well in a
chilled punch bowl, add a large
cake of ice, and let stand for several hours in a cool place or in
your refrigerator. Garnish with a
few thin pineapple slices. Makes
about 42 servings.

Fruit-juice proportions depend
upon the freshness and availability of tropical fruits. Feel free to
adjust quantities to suit your
taste.

HOT DRINKS:
THE FIRE SPIRITS

When you and I went down the lane
  with ale mugs in our hands,
The night we went to Glastonbury
  by way of Goodwin Sands.
         —G. K. Chesterton

You have made your last run down the mountain. It is dusk and you have begun to feel the pervasive, penetrating cold despite your vigorous activity on the ski slopes. In the main hall of the lodge a great fire roars in the hearth, and as you and your companions begin to thaw out in front of the fire a waiter appears holding a tray of steaming mugs. "What is it?" you ask as you deftly lift one from the tray and to your lips in a quick, sweeping motion. Suddenly the heady aroma of spirits and spices assails your nose and you take a sip of the burning liquid. The waiter answers your question, but you do not hear. The burning sensation has cascaded down your throat, and your whole being is suffused with what seems to be a burgeoning wave of warmth and, at the same time, a soothing sensation of glorious relaxation and well-being.

You have fallen under the spell of the fire spirits, an unfailing antidote for cold that has restored life to body and spirit for all manner of men and women from ancient times. Hot drinks are well-known for their restorative properties and it is no secret in cold countries that hot alcoholic beverages are consumed with gusto and great regularity. In olden days, hot drinks were indeed the original "central heating." The Colonial tavern in America was a good example. The taproom was the social center, dominated by a great fireplace and a cheerful, blazing fire that had an important function aside from providing heat and light on cold, wintry nights. In the fireplace were kept the flip irons or loggerheads (also called "hottles" and "flip dogs," but not "pokers," as pokers were designed for fire tending, not drink-making), which were used to mull the drinks that were served in large mugs, tankards, bowls, cups, or whatever would survive a sudden dose of heat. Wines, spirits, beers, ales, and divers mixtures known by such names as "Kill-Divil," "Rattle Skull," and "Whistle-Belly Vengeance" were regularly "frothed" using a red-hot flip iron. The resulting burnt flavor was highly prized by our Colonial forebears.

Few of these hot potations have survived the passing of the years except for the name "flip" (derived from "flip iron") and the recipe itself: a mix of wine or spirits, beer or ale, eggs, sugar, cream, and spices which lives on, though without the use of beer or ale, and which may be served hot or cold. Another hand-me-down is the phrase "being at loggerheads," which alludes to disputes and spirited debates during which opponents would use loggerheads to make their point. Many early American inns and taverns were centers of discourse, for they fulfilled the functions of meeting place, public forum, social club, restaurant, and town saloon.

Modern hot libations are no longer mulled with a flip dog but flamed instead. (No doubt, as this is being written, some enterprising pub owner is preparing to feature hot drinks heated with a red-hot iron and they'll become the rage!) To the unitiated, blazing drinks may seem to be the pursuit of fools who are (1) showing off; (2) burning up good spirits to no worthy end; and (3) taking a chance on starting a fire or injuring someone. There is, of course, an element of truth in all of these assertions, depending on who is doing the drink-making and under what circumstances.

There is a certain amount of show in any pyrotechnical display, especially at the bar or your dining table, but if that were the only purpose—a spectacle—then it probably wouldn't be worth the effort. Proper flaming of drinks adds flavor that cannot be achieved by conventional methods: sugar and syrups are carmelized; essential oils from citrus peels are ignited; butter, spices, and flavorings are enhanced; and spirits undergo chemical changes that can produce new and intriguing flavors. Not all recipes for flamed drinks yield optimum results. This is a matter of experimentation and experience. In any event, the flaming process should last no more than ten or fifteen seconds, so the amount of alcohol that is burned away is negligible. A far more important consideration is safety. Fire is not a toy to be played with by the inexperienced, the foolhardy, or the inebriated. See Bartender's Secret No. 38 for detailed safety rules on how to flame drinks for festive, flavorful, and harmless enjoyment.

 AZTEC CUP

Scant cup milk
1 tsp. cocoa
1 tsp. sugar or to taste
1 oz. Gran Centenario
  Reposado Tequila
½ oz. triple sec
Whipped cream

Heat milk in a saucepan, but do not boil. Rinse a large, heat-proof mug with hot water; discard and add cocoa, sugar, and a little hot milk from the saucepan. Mix briskly until mixture is creamy and smooth. Pour remainder of hot milk from saucepan and stir in tequila and triple sec. Top with whipped cream.

Created by the author for Carillon Importers, Ltd.

 BEACHCOMBER'S BRACER

1 tsp. honey or sugar syrup
Dash lemon juice
Boiling water
1 oz. bourbon or rye
1 oz. light Jamaica rum
1 oz. curaçao
Dash Angostura bitters

Dissolve honey with lemon juice and a little boiling water in a heat-proof mug and add bourbon, rum, curaçao, and a dash of bitters. Fill mug with boiling water and stir well.

 THE BLACK STRIPE

2 tsp. molasses or honey
Boiling water
Lemon peel
Cinnamon stick
2–3 oz. dark Jamaica rum
Ground nutmeg

Dissolve molasses in a heat-proof mug with a little boiling water. Add lemon peel and cinnamon stick and more boiling water. Float rum on top and blaze for a few seconds, if you wish. Stir to extinguish flames and top with a sprinkling of nutmeg.

BLUE BLAZER

4 oz. scotch
4 oz. boiling water
2 tsp. sugar
2 small lemon peels

Pour scotch into one warmed mug and boiling water into the other. Ignite scotch, and while blazing, pour back and forth between the two mugs. Extinguish and serve drink in two mugs. Add 1 tsp. sugar to each mug, stir well, and garnish with lemon peels. Makes two drinks.

Warning: Professional bartenders attempting to make this drink are cautioned to practice with cold water first to avoid scalding themselves and innocent bystanders at the bar.

BUKHARA COFFEE

1 oz. Stolichnaya Vanilla
  Vodka
¾ oz. Bailey's Irish Cream
½ oz. crème de cacao
1 cup freshly made coffee,
  hot or cold
Whipped cream

Mix vodka, Bailey's Irish Cream, and crème de cacao in a large heated mug, pour in boiling hot coffee, and top with whipped cream. For a cold drink, chill all ingredients until ice cold, mix in a chilled stemmed glass, and top with whipped cream. A scoop of vanilla or chocolate ice cream may be added to cold versions.

Created by the author for Carillon Importers, Ltd.

CAFÉ AGAVERO

1 oz. Agavero Tequila
  Liqueur
1 oz. Stolichnaya Coffee
  Vodka
6 oz. black coffee
1 oz. cream or to taste
1 tsp. crème de cacao

Stir all ingredients, except crème de cacao, in a large heat-proof mug that has been warmed by a rinsing of boiling water. Float crème de cacao on top of drink and serve immediately. Adjust proportions to suit your taste.

Created by the author for Carillon Importers, Ltd.

CAFÉ AMARETTO

1 cup hot, strong black
  coffee
1 oz. amaretto
½ oz. cognac
1 tbsp. whipped cream

Pour amaretto into coffee and stir well. Float cognac on top, using the back of a spoon, and top with a generous portion of whipped cream.

 CAFÉ BRÛLOT Basic

Several cinnamon sticks
8 whole cloves
4–5 sugar cubes, depending
  on sweetness desired
Outer peel (zest) of ½ orange
Outer peel (zest) of ½ lemon
4 oz. cognac
1 pt. strong hot black coffee

Place all ingredients, except cognac and coffee, in a brûlot bowl or chafing dish. Soften sugar cubes with a little water and mash them into orange and lemon peels with a muddler. Add warmed cognac and mix well with other ingredients in bowl. Ignite and blaze for a few seconds and pour in hot coffee. Ladle into demitasse cups. Makes four servings.

CAFÉ BRÛLOT GRAND MARNIER

2 sugar cubes
2 cinnamon sticks
8 whole cloves
Outer peel (zest) of ½ orange
Outer peel (zest) of ½ lemon
Small piece of vanilla bean
3 oz. Grand Marnier
2 oz. cognac or dark rum
1 pt. hot, strong black coffee

Put all ingredients, except spirits and coffee, in a brûlot bowl or a chafing dish. Moisten sugar cubes with a little water and mash into orange and lemon peels with a muddler or heavy spoon. Add warmed Grand Marnier and cognac and mix well. Place a small sugar cube in a ladle and add a tbsp. of cognac that has been warmed. Ignite and pour blazing into bowl. After a few seconds pour in coffee and stir. Makes four demitasse servings.

CAFÉ CHAPULTEPEC

1 cup hot black coffee
1 oz. Gran Centenario
   Reposado Tequila
1 oz. Agavero Tequila
   Liqueur
½ oz. Stolichnaya Coffee
   Vodka
Several dashes of
   Stolichnaya Cinnamon
   Vodka
Whipped cream

Rinse out a large mug with boiling water, discard water, and add very hot coffee, Reposado Tequila, Agavero liqueur, coffee vodka and stir well. Sprinkle and top with whipped cream. Serve with a spoon. Adjust sweetness by using more or less Agavero liqueur.

Created by the author for Carillon Importers, Ltd.

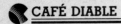 CAFÉ DIABLE

2 cinnamon sticks
8 whole cloves
6 whole coffee beans
2 oz. cognac
1 oz. Cointreau
1 oz. curaçao
1 pt. hot, strong black coffee

Place all ingredients, except coffee, in a chafing dish or *brûlot* bowl and warm over low, direct heat. Ignite and blaze for a few seconds and pour in coffee. Mix well. Makes four demitasse servings.

CAFÉ DIANA

6 oz. Southern Comfort
½ tsp. lemon juice
4 minced maraschino
   cherries
2 tsp. maraschino cherry
   juice
½ tsp. ground ginger
1 large segment cocktail
   orange preserved in syrup
2 tsp. cocktail orange syrup
8 whole cloves
Several pinches powdered
   cinnamon
Several pinches powdered
   nutmeg
4 cups hot, strong black
   coffee
4 small cinnamon sticks

Put all ingredients, except hot coffee, in the flaming pan of a chafing dish and stir well. When heated (do not boil), ignite and blaze for a few seconds. Pour in hot coffee, stir well, and serve in warmed cups with cinnamon sticks. Makes four servings.

CAFÉ DORN

1 pt. hot, strong black coffee
4 pieces lemon peel
4 pieces orange peel
4 cinnamon sticks
12 whole cloves
Honey or sugar syrup to
  taste
1½ oz. Benedictine
1½ oz. kümmel
1½ oz. dark Jamaica rum
7 oz. cognac
4 tbsp. whipped cream

Mix coffee, fruit peels, spices, honey, Benedictine, kümmel, rum, and 3 oz. of cognac in a saucepan or chafing dish and bring to a simmer. Do not boil. Ladle into warmed mugs or cups and add 1 oz. of cognac to each cup. Top with a generous tablespoon of whipped cream. Serves four.

● CAFÉ JEAVONS

1 tsp. coconut syrup
Hot black coffee
1 oz. dark Jamaica rum
1 oz. cognac
Orange peel
1 generous tbsp. vanilla ice
  cream
Pinch ground cinnamon

Pour coconut syrup and hot coffee into a large, heat-proof mug that has been rinsed with hot water. Stir until syrup is dissolved. Add rum, cognac, orange peel, and ice cream float. Sprinkle with cinnamon.

CAFÉ NAPOLEON

2 tbsp. honey
Outer peel (zest) of ½ orange
1 tsp. lemon juice
2–3 cinnamon sticks
8 whole cloves
4 cups hot, strong black
  coffee
2 oz. B&B liqueur
1 oz. kümmel
1 oz. gold rum
1 oz. cognac
Whipped cream
Grated nutmeg

Put all ingredients, except spirits, whipped cream, and nutmeg, into the flaming pan of a chafing dish over direct heat and bring to a simmer, but do not boil. Add B&B, kümmel, and rum and stir well. Warm cognac in a ladle over hot water, ignite, and pour blazing into chafing dish. Stir and serve in large cups or mugs, top with whipped cream, and sprinkle with nutmeg. Makes four servings.

BARTENDER'S SECRET NO. 37—Hot Cups

Serving a hot drink in a cold glass is as bad as serving hot food on a cold plate. Glasses used for hot beverages should be rinsed in hot water so they are thoroughly warmed before serving. Actually, the best container for a hot drink is a china cup, and better still is an earthenware mug because it holds the heat longer. When pouring very hot drinks into cups and glasses, be sure to place a spoon in the container to prevent cracking. Silver, pewter, and copper mugs should be used with care in the service of very hot drinks. The excellent heat conductivity of these metallic containers can cause minor burns to the lips and mouth.

CAFÉ ROYALE No. 1

4 sugar cubes
1 pt. hot, strong black coffee
4 oz. 100-proof bourbon

Place sugar cube in each of 4 warmed demitasse cups and fill almost full of hot coffee. Carefully float 1 oz. of bourbon in each cup, ignite, and flame for a few seconds. Stir with spoon to extinguish the flames. Serves four.

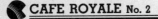

CAFÉ ROYALE No. 2

4 sugar cubes
1 pt. hot, strong black coffee
4 oz. cognac

Place sugar cube in each of 4 demitasse cups that have been rinsed with boiling water. Fill each cup nearly full with hot coffee and carefully float an ounce of cognac in each cup. Ignite, flame for a few seconds, and stir with a spoon to extinguish the flames. Serves four.

CAFÉ WELLINGTON

½ cup whipping cream
¼ tsp. instant coffee
2 tsp. coconut syrup
1 oz. light rum
Hot black coffee

Blend whipping cream with instant coffee until it stands up in stiff peaks. In a heat-proof cup add coconut syrup and a little coffee and stir until syrup is dissolved. Add rum and stir well while filling cup with more coffee. Top with whipped cream. Whipped-cream mixture is sufficient for from four to six cups of coffee.

CAPETOWN COFFEE

1 cup hot black coffee
1 tbsp. coconut cream or to taste
1½ oz. bourbon, rye, or blended whiskey
1 tbsp. whipped cream

In a warmed mug put hot coffee and coconut cream and stir until cream is dissolved. Add whiskey, stir, and top with whipped cream.

CHARTREUSE CHOCOLATE KISS

½ oz. green Chartreuse
1 cup hot chocolate
1 heaping tbsp. whipped cream
Chocolate shavings

Pour Chartreuse into a warmed, heat-proof mug, fill with hot chocolate, and garnish with dollop of whipped cream and chocolate shavings.

CHOKLAD PRINS BERTIL

1 cup hot chocolate
1½ oz. Grand Marnier or triple sec
½ oz. cognac (optional if triple sec is used in place of Grand Marnier)
1 heaping tbsp. whipped cream

Scald a heat-proof mug with boiling water and fill with steaming hot chocolate. Add Grand Marnier or triple sec and cognac and stir well. Top with whipped cream.

Created by the author for H.R.H. Prince Bertil of Sweden.

COFFEE GROG

1 tsp. butter
1 tbsp. brown sugar or 1 tsp. coconut syrup
Grated nutmeg
12 whole cloves
4 cinnamon sticks
4 small slices lemon peel
4 small slices orange peel
1 cup dark Jamaica rum
Hot, strong black coffee
Whipped cream (optional)

Cream butter with brown sugar and several pinches of nutmeg and into each of 4 flame-proof mugs add some of the butter-sugar mixture, 3 cloves, and 1 each cinnamon stick, lemon peel, orange peel, and 2 oz. of rum. Stir well and ignite and blaze for a few seconds. Pour in coffee and stir well. Top with whipped cream, if you wish. Makes four servings.

Be sure to warm rum in advance so it will flame.

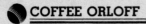 COFFEE ORLOFF

¾ oz. vodka
¾ oz. Tia Maria
1 cup hot black coffee
¾ oz. Crème de Grand
    Marnier

Scald a large cup or mug with boiling water and add vodka, Tia Maria, and steaming black coffee. Stir well and carefully float Crème de Grand Marnier on top.

COMFORTABLE COFFEE COCKTAIL

1½ oz. Southern Comfort
1 oz. Kahlua
Several dashes orange
    bitters
Lemon peel
Orange peel
Pinch powdered cinnamon

In a saucepan, heat 2 oz. of water and all other ingredients, except cinnamon, to the simmering point. Pour into a warmed, heat-proof mug and sprinkle with powdered cinnamon.

COSSACK COFFEE

1 oz. Stolichnaya Coffee
    Vodka
1 oz. Stolichnaya Cinnamon
    Vodka
1 cup strong, hot black
    coffee
Whipped cream

Mix coffee vodka and cinnamon vodka in a large, heated mug. Fill with hot coffee and top with a generous dollop of whipped cream.

Created by the author for Carillon Importers, Ltd.

DOWN EAST HOT BUTTERED RUM

2 tsp. brown sugar
1 cup apple cider
Cinnamon stick
4 whole cloves
1 piece lemon peel
2 oz. gold label rum
Small pat butter
Grated nutmeg

In a warmed, heat-proof mug, add sugar and a little cider that had been heated to the boiling point. Stir until sugar is dissolved and add cinnamon, cloves, lemon peel, and rum. Fill with hot cider, stir, and top with butter and grated nutmeg.

FLAMING HOT BUTTERED RUM

1 tbsp. brown sugar
Cinnamon stick
Lemon peel or orange peel
Whole cloves
Boiling water
2–3 oz. dark Jamaica rum
Pinch of sugar
½ oz. 151-proof Demerara
  rum
Pat of butter
Grated nutmeg

Rinse a large, heat-proof mug with boiling water, add sugar, cinnamon stick, and a lemon or orange peel studded with cloves. Pour in enough boiling water to dissolve sugar and stir in rum. Fill mug with boiling water and place pat of butter on top of drink. Warm Demerara rum in a ladle, into which you have put a pinch of sugar, by partially immersing the bowl in hot water. Ignite rum and pour blazing into mug. Add a little additional butter, if you wish, and sprinkle with nutmeg.

 FLAMES OVER JERSEY

2 oz. applejack or apple
  schnapps
4 oz. apple cider or apple
  juice
Pinch ground cinnamon
Pinch ground nutmeg
¼ baked apple
½ oz. 151-proof Demerara
  rum

Into the flaming pan of a chafing dish or saucepan, put all ingredients except Demerara rum, and heat over a low flame until apple is warmed through (do not boil). Just before serving, warm Demerara rum in a ladle over hot water, ignite, and pour blazing into pan. After a few seconds extinguish flame with pan lid and serve in a warmed mug or wine goblet with a spoon.

FUZZY NUT

1½ oz. DeKuyper Peachtree
  Schnapps
½ oz. amaretto
5 oz. hot chocolate
Marshmallow or whipped
  cream
Pinch ground cinnamon

Combine Peachtree Schnapps, amaretto, and hot chocolate in a warm mug and stir. Garnish with marshmallow or dollop of whipped cream and sprinkle ground cinnamon on top.

GINGER PEACHY TOM AND JERRY

1 egg
½ oz. orgeat syrup or to taste
Pinch ground ginger
Pinch ground cinnamon
1 oz. peach-flavored brandy
1 oz. light rum or cognac
1 oz. milk
1 oz. cream
Pinch ground nutmeg

Beat egg yolk in a small bowl, add orgeat syrup, ground ginger, and cinnamon, and blend well. Beat egg white separately in a small bowl until stiff, carefully fold yolk mixture into white, and spoon egg mixture into a large, warmed mug. Combine peach brandy, rum or cognac, milk, and cream in a small saucepan, heat, and pour into mug while stirring constantly. Sprinkle with topping of ground nutmeg.

GLÜHWEIN

5 oz. Madeira or dry red wine
Lemon peel
Orange peel
Small cinnamon stick, broken
Several whole cloves
Pinch of ground nutmeg
1 tsp. honey or to taste

Heat all ingredients in a saucepan and stir until honey is dissolved. Do not boil. Serve in a warmed, heat-proof mug.

GOLDEN GROG

¾ oz. straight rye or bourbon
¾ oz. gold Jamaica or Barbados rum
¾ oz. Cointreau
1 tsp. orgeat syrup or Falernum to taste
Boiling water
Cinnamon stick
Lemon or orange slice

Put rye, rum, Cointreau, and syrup into a warmed, heat-proof mug, fill with boiling water, and stir well. Garnish with cinnamon stick and lemon or orange slice.

◗ GOODNIGHT SWEETHEART HOT MILK PUNCH

1 tsp. superfine sugar
1 cup milk
1 oz. dark Jamaica rum
1 oz. cognac
1 oz. gin or vodka
Dash Angostura bitters
Grated nutmeg

Dissolve sugar in milk and heat in saucepan. When milk is hot, add rum, cognac, gin, and bitters. Heat again and stir well. Pour mixture into a blender and mix at high speed. Pour into a mug that has been rinsed with boiling water and top with a sprinkling of nutmeg.

GRINGO GROG

1 tsp. brown sugar or to taste
3 whole cloves
Cinnamon stick
Boiling water
2 oz. tequila
Pat of butter
Grated nutmeg

Rinse out a heat-proof mug with boiling water, add brown sugar, cloves, cinnamon, and pour in enough boiling water to dissolve sugar. Add tequila and fill mug with boiling water. Top with butter and sprinkling of nutmeg.

◗ HIGHLAND HOT MILK PUNCH

2 oz. scotch
1 oz. Drambuie
½ oz. sugar syrup or to taste
1 whole egg, beaten
1 cup milk
Pinch powdered cinnamon

Heat all ingredients, except cinnamon, in a saucepan over low heat, stirring from time to time to prevent milk from scorching. Rinse a heat-proof mug with boiling water and fill with hot punch. Sprinkle cinnamon on top.

HOT APPLE BANG!

1 oz. applejack
1 oz. apple schnapps
4 oz. apple cider or apple
     juice
½ oz. maple syrup or sugar
     syrup to taste
Several whole cloves
Slice of baked apple
     (optional)
Cinnamon stick
Pat butter
Grated nutmeg
Lemon slice

Rinse a heat-proof mug with boiling water, add applejack, schnapps, cider, and maple syrup that has been heated (but not boiled) in a saucepan, and stir well. Stud baked apple with cloves and add to mug with cinnamon stick. Add additional hot apple cider, top with butter and nutmeg, and garnish with lemon slice.

 # HOT BENEFACTOR

1 tsp. sugar syrup or to taste
2 oz. Jamaica rum
2 oz. dry red wine
Lemon slice
Grated nutmeg

Add syrup to saucepan with a little hot water and stir until sugar is dissolved. Add rum and wine, and heat until it begins to simmer. Serve in warmed, heat-proof mug with lemon slice and a sprinkling of grated nutmeg.

 # HOT BRANDY FLIP

2 oz. brandy (rum, whiskey,
     or gin may be used)
1 whole egg
1 tsp. sugar syrup or to taste
Grated nutmeg

Mix all ingredients, except nutmeg, in a blender and pour into a saucepan. Heat gently and pour into a warm Delmonico glass and sprinkle with nutmeg.

Some recipes call for 2 to 4 oz. of milk, which may be used for those liking a longer drink.

 # HOT BRICK TODDY

¼ tsp. powdered cinnamon
1 tsp. sugar syrup
1 pat butter
Boiling water
2 oz. bourbon, rye, Canadian,
     or blended whiskey

In an Old Fashioned glass that has been rinsed in hot water, add cinnamon, syrup, and butter and enough boiling water to combine ingredients. Add whiskey and fill with boiling water.

HOT BULL

2 oz. vodka or tequila
3 oz. tomato juice or V-8 juice
3 oz. beef consommé or bouillon
Several dashes Worcestershire sauce
Several dashes Tabasco sauce
Dash lemon juice
Pinch celery seed or celery salt
Dash white pepper

Heat all ingredients in a saucepan until steaming, but do not boil. Serve in a warmed, heatproof mug.

HOT BUTTERED BOURBON

1½ oz. bourbon
1 oz. Wild Turkey Bourbon Liqueur
6 oz. apple cider or apple juice
Cinnamon stick
Pat of butter
Pinch ground nutmeg
Pinch ground ginger

Heat bourbon, bourbon liqueur, and apple cider or juice in a saucepan and pour into a warmed mug. Add cinnamon stick and butter and stir. Sprinkle with ground nutmeg and ginger.

HOT BUTTERED RUM Basic

1 generous tbsp. brown sugar
1 cinnamon stick
Lemon peel
6 whole cloves
Boiling water
2–3 oz. dark Jamaica rum
Pat of butter
Grated nutmeg

Rinse a large mug with boiling water and add brown sugar, cinnamon stick, and a lemon peel studded with cloves. Pour in a little boiling water and stir until sugar is dissolved. Add rum and fill with boiling water. Stir, then place pat of butter on top of drink, and sprinkle with grated nutmeg.

◥ HOT BUTTERED SOUTHERN COMFORT

2 oz. Southern Comfort
½ oz. curaçao
Whole cloves
Cinnamon stick
Orange or lemon slice
Pat of butter
Grated nutmeg

Heat all ingredients, except butter and nutmeg, in a saucepan with a cup of water, stir well, and pour, steaming, into a mug that has been rinsed with boiling water. Top with butter and a sprinkling of nutmeg.

HOT DAMN!

1 egg yolk
1 tbsp. superfine sugar
6 oz. milk
1 oz. brandy
1 oz. dark Jamaica rum
½ oz. crème de cacao
Grated nutmeg

Beat egg with sugar and stir in milk. Put brandy, rum, and crème de cacao into a saucepan over low heat and add egg mixture, stirring constantly until hot. Pour into a warmed mug and top with grated nutmeg.

HOT EGGNOG

1 egg
Pinch of salt
1 tbsp. superfine sugar
1 cup hot milk
2–3 oz. warm brandy
Pinch ground nutmeg

Place egg and salt in a mixing bowl and beat until egg is thick; add sugar and beat until blended. Add hot milk and brandy, mix well by hand or in a blender, and pour into a warmed mug that has been rinsed in hot water. Sprinkle with ground nutmeg.

HOT KENTUCKY TODDY

Honey or sugar syrup to
  taste
Dash orange bitters
4 whole cloves
2–3 oz. bourbon
Lemon slice
Boiling water
Grated nutmeg

Put all ingredients, except nutmeg, in a warmed, heat-proof mug and fill with boiling water. Stir well and sprinkle with nutmeg.

HOT MILK PUNCH Basic

2–3 oz. whiskey, gin, rum,
brandy, or vodka
1 cup milk
1 whole egg (optional)
1 tsp. sugar syrup or to taste
Pinch powdered nutmeg,
cinnamon, or allspice

Heat all ingredients, except
spice, in a saucepan over low
heat, stirring regularly to make
certain milk does not scorch.
When piping hot, pour into a
heat-proof mug that has been
rinsed in boiling water and top
with nutmeg or spice of your
choice.

If glasses are used, be certain to
warm them in advance and keep
a long spoon in the glass when
pouring in hot liquid to prevent
cracking.

HOT NAIL

2 oz. scotch
1 oz. Drambuie
Dash lemon juice
Lemon slice
Orange slice
Boiling water
Cinnamon stick

Pour Drambuie, scotch, and
lemon juice into a warmed mug,
add lemon and orange slices
and boiling water. Garnish with
cinnamon stick.

HOT PASSION

1½ oz. La Grande Passion
1 cup hot black coffee
1 oz. Crème de Grand
Marnier

Pour La Grande Passion into a
steaming cup of black coffee and
gently spoon on Crème de
Grand Marnier so it floats on
top.

HOT PORT FLIP

3 oz. port, Madeira, or
Marsala
1 egg
1 tsp. superfine sugar
2 oz. heavy cream
Pinch grated nutmeg

Heat wine in saucepan, but do
not boil. Beat egg with sugar in
a bowl using a whisk, blend in
cream, and pour into saucepan
with wine, stirring constantly.
Serve in a warmed mug and
sprinkle with nutmeg.

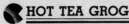

HOT TEA GROG

1 oz. dark Jamaica rum
1 oz. cognac
½ tsp. honey or to taste
Several cloves
Cinnamon stick
Pinch grated nutmeg
1 cup hot tea

Mix all ingredients together in a saucepan, heat, and pour into a warmed mug.

HOT TEA TODDY

1½ oz. gold rum
½ tsp. honey or to taste
Pinch powdered cinnamon
Lemon slice or orange slice
1 cup hot tea
Candied ginger

Heat all ingredients, except ginger, in a saucepan until steaming hot and pour into a warmed cup or mug. Garnish with a large piece of candied ginger.

HOT TODDY Basic

2–3 oz. whiskey, brandy, rum, gin, or vodka
1 oz. sugar syrup or to taste
4 whole cloves
Generous pinch powdered cinnamon
Lemon slice
Boiling water
Grated nutmeg
Cinnamon stick

Warm a mug or Old Fashioned glass and add all ingredients, except nutmeg, and fill with boiling water. Stir and top with grated nutmeg. Garnish with cinnamon stick, if you wish.

Any type of whiskey, rum, or brandy will make a good toddy. It is a matter of personal preference. Measurements are approximate, depending on how strong, sweet, or spicy you want your toddy to be.

IMPERIAL HOUSE BRACER Hot

2 egg yolks
3 oz. cream or half-and-half
3 oz. ruby port
2 oz. cognac
Grated nutmeg

Beat egg yolks and beat in cream. Gradually mix in port, using a whisk, and then add cognac. Heat in a saucepan over low heat, stir well, and serve in warmed wine goblets or mugs. Sprinkle with grated nutmeg. Makes two servings.

INDIAN SUMMER

Pinch confectioner's sugar
Pinch powdered cinnamon
2 oz. apple schnapps
5 oz. hot apple cider
Cinnamon stick

Wet the rim of a heat-proof mug
and roll in a mixture of half cinnamon and half sugar. Add
warmed apple schnapps and
mix in mug with hot apple cider.
Garnish with cinnamon stick.

 IRISH COFFEE Basic

Hot black coffee
1 tsp. sugar syrup or
    superfine sugar
1½ oz. Irish whiskey
1–2 tbsp. whipped cream

Rinse a wine glass or goblet
with hot water, add a little hot
coffee and sugar, and stir until
sugar is dissolved. Add whiskey,
fill with hot coffee, allowing
room for topping. Cover with a
generous amount of whipped
cream. Do not stir. Sip coffee
through whipped cream.

Some recipes call for heavy
cream—unwhipped—as a top-
ping. This is a matter of individual taste.

JACK'S APPLE

2 oz. applejack
4 oz. hot apple cider
1 tsp. honey
Pinch ground nutmeg
Pinch ground cinnamon
Slice baked apple

Heat applejack and cider in a
saucepan and stir in honey until
dissolved. Pour into a warmed,
heat-proof mug and sprinkle
with ground nutmeg and cinnamon. Garnish with baked apple
slice.

JAMAICA COFFEE

½ oz. cognac
½ oz. Tia Maria
½ oz. dark Jamaica rum
Hot black coffee
1 heaping tbsp. whipped
    cream
Pinch ground cinnamon
Pinch ground ginger

Warm cognac, Tia Maria, and
rum in a saucepan, ignite, and
pour quickly into a warmed,
heat-proof mug. Fill with hot coffee, top with whipped cream,
and sprinkle top with cinnamon
and ginger.

JERSEY FLASH

1 tsp. honey or sugar syrup
4 whole cloves
Pinch cinnamon
Lemon peel
2 oz. gin
Hot apple cider or apple
  juice
Grated nutmeg

Rinse out a heat-proof mug with boiling water and add honey, cloves, cinnamon, lemon peel, and a little boiling water to dissolve honey. Pour in warmed gin, ignite, blaze for a few seconds, and fill mug with hot cider. Sprinkle with grated nutmeg.

JERSEY TODDY

1 tsp. honey
Boiling water
Several dashes Angostura
  bitters
2–3 oz. applejack or calvados
Lemon peel
Cinnamon stick

Put honey in a warmed, heat-proof mug and add enough boiling water to dissolve honey. Add bitters, apple jack, and fill with boiling water. Garnish with lemon peel and cinnamon stick.

KENT'S CORNERS HOT CUP

5 oz. cider
2 oz. dark Jamaica rum
1 oz. maple syrup or to taste
½ tsp. lemon juice
Cinnamon stick

Heat all ingredients in a saucepan and bring to boiling point, but do not boil. Serve in a warmed mug.

THE LOCOMOTIVE

6 oz. dry red wine
½ oz. curaçao
½ oz. maraschino liqueur
  (optional)
½ oz. honey or sugar syrup
  to taste
1 egg
Lemon slice
Ground cinnamon

In the flaming pan of a chafing dish (or a saucepan) mix red wine, curaçao, maraschino, and honey until honey is dissolved. Gradually warm wine over direct heat (but do not boil), stir in a lightly beaten egg, and bring to a simmer. Pour into a warmed, heat-proof mug, add lemon slice and pinch of cinnamon.

LONDON DOCK

½ oz. honey or sugar syrup
1½ oz. dark Jamaica rum
1½ oz. dry red wine
Lemon peel
Cinnamon stick
Grated nutmeg

Dissolve honey with a little boiling water in a heat-proof mug. Add remainder of ingredients, except nutmeg, and fill mug with boiling water. Top with grated nutmeg.

MEXICAN COFFEE

1 oz. Kahlua
½ oz. tequila
Hot black coffee
1 generous tbsp. whipped cream
Pinch ground cinnamon

Pour Kahlua, tequila, and hot coffee into a warmed mug or Irish coffee glass, stir well, and top with whipped cream and a sprinkling of cinnamon.

BARTENDER'S SECRET NO. 38—Flaming Safely

What is the best way to flame drinks? Answer: safely. As everyone knows, alcohol is a flammable substance. What many people do not know is that when alcohol is warmed it begins to vaporize, and this vapor is very flammable indeed. For this reason, alcohol used for all flambé food dishes and flaming hot drinks must be warmed or it will not ignite unless the proof is very high (100 to 151). Professionals always treat alcohol with respect. Here are some safety rules: Do not use large amounts of alcohol to flame drinks. A scant ounce is sufficient. When heating spirits in a saucepan or chafing dish, stand well back and do not bend over to look into the pan. When igniting spirits in a brightly lit room, it is best to dim the lights because the flames from alcohol are almost invisible in daylight. Do not place uncorked bottles of spirits near any open flame. Never pour spirits from a bottle into a flaming dish (fire may blow back). Never flame anything in a large pan or chafing dish with people sitting at the table (it could spill over). Instead, do your flaming on a cart or serving table. And never flame anything near draperies, curtains, or in the vicinity of party decorations such as paper bunting, streamers, and other flammable festoons, trimmings, and table coverings.

 MIKE GILL'S GROG

1 750-ml. bottle Haitian or
    Martinique rum
1 pt. orange juice
1 cup brandy
½ cup kümmel
½ cup Benedictine
½ cup lemon juice
½ cup Falernum or honey to
    taste
1 cup canned pineapple,
    cubed with juice
1 liter spring water

Mix all ingredients in a sauce-pan and heat until simmering. Serve in warmed mugs with a pineapple cube. Makes about 26 servings.

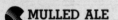 MRS. CAHILL'S IRISH COFFEE

Hot, strong black coffee
2 oz. Irish whiskey
½ oz. Kahlua or Irish Mist,
    depending on sweetness
    desired
Orange peel
1–2 tbsp. whipped cream

Rinse a wine goblet, mug, or a beer schooner with hot water and fill, leaving room at the top, with hot coffee. Stir in whiskey and Kahlua or Irish Mist. Add a slice of the outer zest of an or-ange peel and top with a gener-ous serving of whipped cream.

MULLED ALE

1 cup ale
Small piece whole ginger
1 pat butter (optional)
1 tsp. sugar
1 or 2 eggs (depending on
    richness desired)

Put ale, ginger, butter, and sugar into a saucepan and heat to the boiling point, but do not boil. In a bowl, beat the eggs with a ta-blespoon of cold ale and pour into saucepan. Pour ale mixture back and forth between two saucepans to froth, return to heat, and serve hot in a warmed mug.

The alternative method of prepa-ration is to plunge a red-hot poker or flip iron into a large tan-kard containing this mixture.

MULLED CIDER

2 oz. gold Jamaica, Barbados,
  or Haitian rum
Dash Angostura bitters
4 whole cloves
Cinnamon stick
Pinch ground allspice
1 tsp. honey or sugar syrup
  to taste
1 cup apple cider or apple
  juice
Lemon twist

Heat all ingredients in a saucepan and strain into a warmed
mug.

An alternative method of making
this drink is to put all ingredients into a tankard and froth by
plunging a red-hot poker into the
mixture.

MULLED CLARET

5 oz. red Bordeaux
1 oz. port
¾ oz. brandy
Pinch ground cinnamon
Pinch grated nutmeg
Several whole cloves
Lemon peel

Heat all ingredients in a saucepan (do not boil) and pour into a
warmed mug.

PEDRO MacDONALD'S CUP

1½ oz. scotch
2 oz. cream or oloroso sherry
½ tsp. lemon juice
1 tsp. sugar syrup or honey
  to taste
Several dashes Angostura
  bitters
Several dashes orange
  bitters
Cinnamon stick
Orange peel

Heat all ingredients with 2 oz. of
water in a saucepan and pour
into a heat-proof mug.

⬤ PUERTO BANUS BRUNCH SPECIAL

1½ oz. light rum
1 oz. cream sherry
4 oz. orange juice
1 tsp. honey or to taste
Several dashes Angostura or
    orange bitters
Cinnamon stick
Orange slice

Heat all ingredients, except orange slice, and pour into a warmed mug or Old Fashioned glass. Garnish with orange slice.

⬤ ROCK AND RYE TODDY

3 oz. rock and rye
Dash Angostura bitters
Lemon slice
Cinnamon stick
Boiling water
Grated nutmeg

Rinse a heat-proof mug with hot water and add rock and rye, bitters, lemon slice, and cinnamon stick. Fill with boiling water and stir well. Sprinkle with grated nutmeg.

⬤ RUMFUSTIAN

2 egg yolks
1 tsp. sugar or to taste
1 cup ale
2 oz. gin
2 oz. sherry
Cinnamon stick
Several whole cloves
Lemon peel
Grated nutmeg

Beat egg yolks in a bowl with sugar. In a saucepan, bring ale, gin, sherry, cinnamon, cloves, and lemon peel to the boiling point (but do not boil), then pour in egg mixture, stirring briskly with a whisk. Serve in a warmed mug and top with grated nutmeg.

◼ SHEILA GOODMAN'S GINKEN SOUP

1½ cups canned or
    homemade chicken soup
1 oz. gin
Pinch white pepper
½ tsp. chopped parsley

If canned or packaged, prepare soup according to directions, heat in a saucepan, and add gin when simmering, but do not boil. Add pepper and parsley, and serve piping hot in a large mug.

BARTENDER'S SECRET NO. 39—Hot Spirits

Piping hot drinks are much to be desired, especially when there is a chill in the air. Drinks can be made with boiling hot ingredients as long as they are *nonalcoholic*. Wines and spirits should never be boiled. Why let all the zip in your drink go up in steam? Also, many liqueurs and almost all wines do not stand up well to high heat and develop an off flavor. Care should be taken when heating alcoholic ingredients over an open flame. Use small quantities and a low flame. Spirits are volatile materials that can ignite and flare up, causing singed hair and eyelashes, and in some cases minor burns.

ST. VINCENT HOT BUTTERED RUM

1 tbsp. brown sugar
Small lemon peel or orange
  peel
Whole cloves
Cinnamon stick
2 oz. dark or gold Jamaica rum
1 oz. crème de cacao
Pat butter
Grated nutmeg

Put brown sugar into a warmed, heat-proof mug with peel studded with cloves and cinnamon stick. Pour in a little boiling water and stir until sugar is dissolved. Add rum, crème de cacao, and fill with boiling water. Stir and top with butter and grated nutmeg.

SKI LIFT

1 oz. DeKuyper Peachtree
  Schnapps
½ oz. CocoRibe
5 oz. hot chocolate
Marshmallow or whipped
  cream
Pinch ground cinnamon

Combine schnapps, coconut rum, and hot chocolate in a warm mug and stir. Garnish with marshmallow or dollop of whipped cream and sprinkle cinnamon on top.

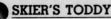 SKIER'S TODDY

1 cup hot chocolate
¾ oz. *Kahlua, Tia Maria,* or
   crème de cacao
¾ oz. triple sec
Several marshmallows or
   whipped marshmallow
   topping

Rinse out a large mug with boiling water, add steaming hot chocolate, and stir in liqueurs. Top with marshmallow.

SLALOM STEAMER

½ oz. package hot cocoa mix
½ tsp. instant coffee
Boiling water
1½ oz. gold Puerto Rican,
   Barbados, or Jamaica rum
Ground cinnamon or nutmeg

Add cocoa mix and coffee to a warmed mug and fill almost to the top with boiling water. Stir in rum and mix well. For a richer drink use milk instead of water. Sprinkle with ground cinnamon or nutmeg.

STEAMING MARY

2 oz. vodka
5 oz. tomato juice or V-8
   juice
1 tbsp. hot barbecue sauce
   or to taste
½ tsp. lemon juice
Several dashes Tabasco
   sauce
Pinch white pepper
Small pat butter
Pinch ground or chopped dill

Heat vodka, tomato juice, barbecue sauce, lemon juice, Tabasco, and white pepper in a saucepan to a simmer, but do not boil. Pour into a warmed mug and top with butter and a sprinkling of dill.

TOM AND JERRY Individual

1 egg
½ oz. sugar syrup or to taste
1 oz. dark Jamaica rum
1 oz. cognac
Grated nutmeg

Separate egg and beat the yolk and white individually. Fold white and yolk together, add syrup, and put into a warmed, heat-proof mug. Add rum and cognac and fill with boiling water. Sprinkle with grated nutmeg.

Some recipes call for additional spices such as ground cinnamon, cloves, and allspice. This is a matter of individual taste.

VESUVIO

1 cup hot strong black coffee 1 oz. sambuca 1 sugar cube	Fill warmed cup with hot coffee and, using an inverted teaspoon, carefully float half of the sambuca on top of the coffee. Place a sugar cube in a spoon and pour remainder of sambuca into spoon. Ignite and dip blazing spoon into cup. Let cup flame for a few seconds and stir coffee to extinguish flames.

WINDJAMMER Hot

Peel of half a large orange Brown sugar 2 oz. gold Jamaica or Barbados rum 1 oz. rock and rye 1 oz. curaçao Lemon peel Boiling water	Cut orange peel in a thin spiral, moisten, and coat with brown sugar. Place spiral in a heat-proof mug, add about ½ oz. of warmed rum, and flame until sugar is carmelized. Add remainder of rum, rock and rye, curaçao, and lemon peel, fill with boiling water, and stir well.

WINTER PASSION

1 oz. La Grande Passion 1 cup hot tea Milk or cream (optional)	Add La Grande Passion to hot tea and add milk or cream, if you wish. Stir and serve.

GOOD DRINKS
SANS SPIRITS

With a little creative planning and care,
the nonalcoholic drink can be just
as appetizing and satisfying as any other
kind of liquid refreshment
that you serve to your guests.
> —John Poister

A good drink has nothing to do with how big it is, how strong
it is, or how much alcohol it contains—whether a big slug, just
a little, or none at all. The recipes in this chapter have been
carefully researched and tested. Many are outstanding, meaning that the recipes produce predictable results, and are flavorful, refreshing, and satisfying. They can be served at any
social occasion with pride and will taste just as good sans
spirits as the alcoholic kind. The New Mixology in drink-
making should not be relegated only to alcoholic drinks. There
are times when, for whatever reason, anyone may choose to
have light, nonalcoholic refreshment in place of conventional
cocktails, wine, or beer. Rather than restricting the nondrink-
ing guest to soda pop, tea, or coffee, the considerate host will
provide a selection of imaginative, well-made, flavorful beverages without alcohol that will be appropriate to the occasion
and do honor to the nonimbibing guest.

Time was when the selection of fruit juices was limited to
lemon, lime, grapefruit, pineapple, and orange; and not always fresh, but canned or frozen. Today with greatly improved
transportation from tropical growers and streamlined distribution to the market, the resourceful host will find a large selection of tropical fruits that were rarely seen in the U.S. just a
few years ago. Freezing and canning methods have also improved greatly, so that exotic fruits, which are quite acceptable for drink-making purposes, may be had out of season.
Party planners will find that many alcoholic coolers, party

drinks, and punches are excellent even when the alcohol is omitted.

With a little creative planning and care, the nonalcoholic drink can be just as appetizing and satisfying as any other kind of liquid refreshment that you serve to your guests. This includes attention to proper glassware and attractive garnishes as well as the other essentials of good mixology.

Gone are the days when the well-meaning host would say, "Oh, just have one," to the nonimbibing guest. However well intended, this is misdirected hospitality and unnecessary. Instead the nondrinker should be presented with a good drink sans spirits that will make other, drinking guests exclaim, "That looks great. I'll have one!"

AILEEN PETERSON'S CIDER CUP

1 cup fresh apple cider
1 cup hot tea
1 tsp. brown sugar or to taste
Dash orange juice
Dash lemon juice
Pinch powdered cinnamon
Pinch grated nutmeg
2 cinnamon sticks

Mix all ingredients, except cinnamon sticks, in a saucepan over low heat and bring to a simmer. Serve in warmed mugs and garnish with cinnamon sticks. Makes two servings.

APRÈS TENNIS BRACER

1 oz. canned frozen orange juice concentrate
Ginger ale
Orange slice

Spoon orange juice concentrate into a 10-oz. glass and fill with cold ginger ale. Add an ice cube or two, if you wish, and garnish with orange slice. Stir gently.

ARYAN

½ cup plain yogurt
½ cup cold spring water
2 tsp. dried mint leaves or fresh mint, finely chopped
Pinch salt

Mix all ingredients in a blender until smooth and serve in a chilled goblet. Add several ice cubes, if you wish.

BANANA MILK SHAKE

1 cup whole milk
1 small ripe banana or a half
   of a medium-size banana
2 scoops vanilla, butter
   pecan, or coconut ice
   cream
Powdered cinnamon or
   grated nutmeg

Mix all ingredients, except cinnamon or nutmeg, in a blender and pour into a 10-oz. glass. Sprinkle top with cinnamon or nutmeg.

BERRY COLA

1 12-oz. can cola
2–3 oz. cranberry-raspberry
   drink
Juice of ½ lemon or lime
Lemon wheel

Pour cold cola, cranberry-raspberry drink, and lemon juice into a chilled 14-oz. cooler glass. Stir gently and garnish with lemon wheel.

 BLACK COW

Root beer
2 scoops vanilla ice cream

Put scoops of ice cream into a chilled 12- or 14-oz. glass and fill with cold root beer. Stir gently and serve with a spoon.

BREAKFAST EGGNOG

1–2 oz. frozen orange juice
   concentrate or 2–3 oz.
   fresh orange juice
¾ cup whole milk or skim
   milk, very cold
1 egg
Powdered cinnamon or
   grated nutmeg

Mix all ingredients, except spice, in a blender until smooth and foamy. Pour into a chilled goblet and sprinkle with cinnamon or nutmeg or both.

BUTTERMILK BOUNTY

1 tsp. honey
1 cup buttermilk
¼ cup ripe banana, thinly
   sliced
¼ cup ripe pear, peeled and
   chopped
Pinch powdered cinnamon

Dissolve honey with a little buttermilk in a cup and pour into a blender. Add remaining milk, banana, and pear. Blend until smooth and pour into a chilled wine glass. Sprinkle with cinnamon.

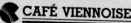

CAFÉ VIENNOISE

1 cup cold strong black
   coffee
1 oz. heavy cream
1 tsp. chocolate syrup
½ tsp. powdered cinnamon
Pinch grated nutmeg

Mix coffee, cream, chocolate, and cinnamon in a blender until smooth and pour into a Squall glass or a wine goblet. Sprinkle with nutmeg.

This elegant coffee is often served with a generous topping of whipped cream.

A CALF SHOT

6 oz. beef consommé or
   bouillon
½ oz. lemon juice
Several dashes
   Worcestershire sauce or to
   taste
Several pinches celery salt
   or celery seed
Several pinches white
   pepper

Stir well with ice cubes in a mixing glass and pour into a chilled Old Fashioned glass. Add additional ice cubes if necessary.

CARIBBEAN CELEBRATION PUNCH

1 cup pineapple, chopped
1 cup orange sections
1 cup grapefruit sections
1 package frozen
   strawberries, thawed
1 pt. orange juice
1 cup grapefruit juice
1 cup papaya juice
1 cup guava juice
1 cup passion fruit juice
1 6-oz. jar maraschino
   cherries
2 l. ginger ale
1 l. lemon-lime soda
1 l. club soda
1 banana, thinly sliced
1 lime, thinly sliced

Prechill all ingredients and mix pineapple, orange, and grapefruit sections in a blender; add strawberries and orange juice until fruit is pulverized but still chunky. Remove and set aside. Then mix grapefruit, papaya, guava, passion fruit juices, and maraschino cherries in a blender until cherries are pulverized. Pour into a chilled punch bowl and mix in fruit from the first blending and stir well. Chill with a large cake of ice. Just before serving, gently stir in ginger ale and soda. Garnish with thinly sliced banana and lime. Makes about 55 servings.

CHERRY VELVET

Several scoops New York
  cherry or vanilla ice cream
¼ cup cream or half-and-half
6 maraschino cherries
1 tbsp. maraschino cherry
  juice

Mix all ingredients in a blender
for a few seconds until cherries
are pulverized and serve in a
chilled goblet.

 CHOCOLATE MALTED

1 cup whole milk
2 scoops chocolate ice cream
¼ cup chocolate syrup
2 generous tbsp. malt
  powder

Mix in a blender until smooth
and pour into a chilled 10-oz.
glass with straws.

CREAMSICLE

Several scoops vanilla ice
  cream
1 cup fresh orange juice
1 tsp. orgeat syrup or
  almond extract

Mix all ingredients in a blender
for a few seconds until smooth
and serve in a chilled goblet.

DOWN EAST DELIGHT

½ cup fresh orange juice
2 oz. grapefruit juice
2 oz. cranberry juice
1 oz. orgeat syrup or honey
  to taste
Maraschino cherry

Mix all ingredients, except
cherry, with cracked ice in a
blender or shaker and pour into
a chilled Old Fashioned glass.
Garnish with a cherry.

 EGGNOG FOR ONE

1 whole egg
2 tsp. superfine sugar
Pinch salt
Several dashes vanilla
  extract
1 cup milk
Grated nutmeg or powdered
  cinnamon

Beat egg with sugar and salt until
well blended and smooth, and
spoon into a chilled highball glass.
Add vanilla and a little cold milk
and stir briskly. Add remainder of
milk, stir again, and top with nutmeg or cinnamon.

Ice is not used in the making of
this drink, so make certain all ingredients are prechilled.

FISHERMAN'S CUP

2–3 oz. tomato juice
2 oz. clam juice
2 oz. sauerkraut juice
½ tsp. horseradish
Several dashes Tabasco
    sauce
Several dashes
    Worcestershire sauce
Dash lemon juice

Stir all ingredients with several ice cubes or mix with cracked ice in a shaker or blender and pour into a chilled highball glass.

This is an excellent party punch. Increase quantities, mix well in a chilled punch bowl, taste for seasoning, and chill with a large cake of ice.

FLORIDA PUNCH

2 qt. fresh orange juice
1 qt. fresh grapefruit juice
2 l. ginger ale
1 cup fresh lime juice
1 cup orgeat syrup or sugar
    syrup to taste
½ cup grenadine

Chill all ingredients in advance and mix in a chilled punch bowl with a large cake of ice. Makes about 46 servings.

GARDEN CUP

1½ cups buttermilk
¼ cup ripe avocado, mashed
¼ cup cucumber, peeled,
    seeded, and finely
    chopped
1 tsp. onion, finely chopped
1 tsp. parsley, finely chopped
Pinch celery salt or to taste
Pinch white pepper

Mix all ingredients in a blender until smooth and serve in chilled wine goblets or parfait glasses. Makes two drinks.

GENTLE SEA BREEZE

½ cup cranberry juice
½ cup grapefruit juice

Mix in a blender until foamy and pour into a 12-oz. glass with several ice cubes.

GINGER PEACHY SHAKE

1 cup milk
¼ cup fresh or frozen
    peaches, sliced thinly or
    chopped
2 scoops peach or vanilla ice
    cream
¼ tsp. powdered ginger
¼ tsp. powdered cinnamon
Whipped cream (optional)

Mix peaches with a little milk in a blender until peaches are pulverized, add remainder of milk, ice cream, and spices. Blend for a few seconds until mixture is smooth and pour into a tall, chilled glass. Top with a mound of whipped cream, if you wish.

ICE-BREAKER PUNCH

1 6-oz. can frozen orange
    juice
1 6-oz. can frozen grapefruit
    juice
1 6-oz. can frozen pineapple
    juice
1 qt. ginger ale
1 qt. lemon-lime soda
½ cup liquid Piña Colada
    mix or to taste
½ tsp. powdered cinnamon
½ tsp. grated nutmeg
1 small ripe banana, thinly
    sliced

Prepare frozen fruit juices according to instructions on cans and pour into a chilled punch bowl with a large cake of ice. Gently stir in ginger ale and lemon-lime soda and sweeten to taste with Piña Colada mix. To make blending easier, dilute Piña Colada mix with a little fruit juice or water before mixing in punch. Sprinkle punch with cinnamon and nutmeg to taste and garnish with banana slices. Makes about 35 servings.

GINGER SNAPPER

2 oz. orange juice
2 oz. grapefruit juice
2 oz. cranberry juice
1 tbsp. ginger marmalade
½ tsp. freshly grated ginger
Orange slice

Mix all ingredients, except orange slice, with cracked ice in a shaker or blender until marmalade is dissolved and pour into a chilled Old Fashioned glass or tumbler. Add additional ice, if you wish, and garnish with orange slice.

JOHN'S JUICE

3 cups fresh orange juice
1 tbsp. liquid Piña Colada
    mix

Mix in an electric blender until Piña Colada mix is dissolved and chill in the refrigerator until cold.

JONES BEACH COCKTAIL

5 oz. beef consommé or
    bouillon
3 oz. clam juice
Juice of ½ lemon or lime
½ tsp. horseradish
Several dashes
    Worcestershire sauce
Pinch celery salt or celery
    seed

Mix all ingredients with cracked
ice in a shaker or blender and
serve in a chilled highball glass
with ice cubes.

JUNGLE COOLER

4 oz. pineapple juice
2 oz. orange juice
1 oz. liquid Piña Colada mix
½ oz. passion fruit juice
Pineapple slice

Mix all ingredients, except pineapple slice, with cracked ice in a
blender or shaker and pour into
a tall, chilled Collins glass. Garnish with a pineapple slice.

KEYPORT COCKTAIL

5–6 oz. clam juice
1 oz. seafood cocktail sauce
    or to taste
½ oz. lemon juice
Several dashes Tabasco
    sauce
Several dashes
    Worcestershire sauce
Several pinches celery salt
Lemon slice

Mix all ingredients, except
lemon slice, with cracked ice in
a shaker or blender and strain
into a chilled Old Fashioned
glass. Garnish with a lemon
slice.

THE LONE PRAIRIE OYSTER

1 tsp. Worcestershire sauce
½ tsp. cider vinegar
1 tsp. cocktail sauce (red)
Several dashes Tabasco
    sauce
Pinch celery salt
Pinch cayenne
Dash Angostura bitters
    (optional)
1 egg yolk

In a chilled wine goblet, mix all
ingredients, except egg yolk,
with a spoon until well blended.
Carefully add egg yolk to glass
so that it is unbroken.

The contents of entire glass are
to be swallowed in one gulp
without breaking the egg yolk.

MILKMAID'S COOLER

¾ cup buttermilk
¾ cup tomato juice
Dash lemon juice
Pinch white pepper
Pinch dried basil
Dash Worcestershire sauce
  (optional)

Prechill all ingredients and mix in a blender until smooth. Serve in a tall, chilled Collins glass.

 MOCHA COFFEE

½ cup strong black coffee
½ cup hot chocolate
1 tbsp. whipped cream
Pinch powdered cinnamon,
  grated nutmeg, or grated
  orange peel

Combine coffee and chocolate in a warmed mug, stir, top with a generous spoonful of whipped cream, and sprinkle with pinch of cinnamon, nutmeg, or orange peel.

MOCK MARGARITA

1 oz. fresh lime juice
1 oz. Rose's lime juice
½ oz. orgeat syrup or Piña
  Colada mix
1 egg white (for two drinks)
Maraschino cherry with a
  dash of juice
Lime slice

Mix all ingredients, except cherry and lime slice, with cracked ice in a blender until frothy. Check for sweetness and add more syrup if necessary. Pour into a chilled Margarita glass and garnish with cherry and lime slice.

 MULLED CIDER

2 cinnamon sticks, broken
12 whole cloves
1 tsp. allspice berries
½ gallon apple cider
½ cup brown sugar or to
  taste
Dried apple rings
Whole cinnamon sticks

Put broken cinnamon sticks, cloves, and allspice into a cheesecloth bag and place in a saucepan with cider and brown sugar. Stir and heat over a low flame and simmer for a few minutes until spice flavors have an opportunity to dissipate. Remove spice bag and ladle into warmed cups in which you have put an apple ring and a cinnamon stick. Makes 16 servings.

NEW YORK EGG CREAM

½ cup cold milk
2 or 3 tbsp. chocolate-
   flavored syrup
Ice-cold seltzer water

Add milk and chocolate syrup in a chilled highball glass and mix well. Fill glass with seltzer, stir gently, and serve with an iced-tea spoon and a straw.

Egg cream is a New York City tradition which dates from the early 1900s or even earlier. It contains no egg and no cream, and probably never did. Purists maintain it should be made the old-fashioned way with U-Bet Chocolate Syrup and seltzer squirted out of a siphon bottle.

ON TO OMSK!

5 oz. beet borscht
½ tsp. lemon or lime juice
½ tsp. horseradish
Several dashes Tabasco
   sauce or to taste
Several dashes
   Worcestershire sauce
2 tbsp. plain yogurt or sour
   cream

Stir all ingredients, except yogurt, with cracked ice in a mixing glass and strain into a chilled Old Fashioned glass. Top with yogurt or sour cream.

ORANGE FLOWER COOLER

3 oz. orange juice
3 oz. grapefruit juice
1 tsp. maraschino cherry juice
6 maraschino cherries
½ tsp. orange flower water

Mix all ingredients with cracked ice in a blender until cherries are pulverized and pour into a chilled goblet or Collins glass. Add additional ice, if necessary.

ORANGE JUICE SUPREME

6 oz. fresh orange juice
2–3 preserved cocktail
   orange sections with syrup
1 tsp. orange marmalade
Several dashes lime or
   lemon juice
Several dashes raspberry
   syrup or grenadine

Mix with cracked ice in a blender or shaker until orange sections are pulverized and marmalade is dissolved. Pour into a tall, chilled highball or Collins glass. Add additional ice, if you wish.

ORGEAT COCKTAIL

1 oz. lemon juice
¾ oz. orgeat syrup or to taste
1 egg white
Maraschino cherry

Mix with cracked ice in a blender or shaker and strain into a chilled cocktail glass.

BARTENDER'S SECRET NO. 40—Rim Dips

To give a cocktail added flavor and appetite appeal, you can frost the top of the glass in many interesting ways similar to the method used to decorate a Margarita, which consists of moistening the rim with a little lime or lemon juice, shaking off the excess liquid, and then dipping the glass into a bed of salt. Try rimming your glass with zesty fruit juices such as cranberry, grape, pineapple, orange, and grapefruit or syrups such as apple-cinnamon, blueberry, raspberry, strawberry, orgeat, or Falernum (see Chapter 2, "A Collection of Fine Flavorings and Exotic Sweeteners"). Sweeteners such as orange blossom or buckwheat honey, a good grade of light molasses, chocolate, or corn syrup provide a flavorful base for your dips. Experiment with dips using raw sugar crystals or brown sugar, or crush assorted hard candies into a coarse powder using a mortar and pestle or by wrapping hard candies in a towel and cracking them into tiny pieces with a rolling pin. Whatever you use as a dip, the particles must be small enough to adhere to the moistened rim of the glass.

PALM GROVE COOLER

2 oz. orange juice
1 oz. guava juice
1 oz. grapefruit juice
1 oz. pineapple juice
½ oz. lime juice
½ oz. grenadine
1 small, ripe banana
Several dashes Angostura
  bitters
Club soda
Pineapple slice
Maraschino cherry

Mix all ingredients, except soda, pineapple slice, and cherry, with cracked ice in a blender and pour into a tall, chilled Collins glass and fill with cold club soda. Stir gently and garnish with pineapple slice and maraschino cherry.

PLANTER'S PAUNCH

2 oz. pineapple juice
2 oz. orange juice
1 oz. lime or lemon juice
1 oz. coconut syrup or to
   taste
1 oz. passion fruit juice
½ oz. grenadine
6 maraschino cherries
Club soda
Pineapple slice
Orange slice

Mix all ingredients, except soda, orange slice, and pineapple slice, with cracked ice in a blender until cherries are crushed. Pour into a chilled Collins glass. Add cold club soda and stir gently. Garnish with pineapple slice and orange slice.

PLUM JOY

Juice of 2 plums
½ cup cold water
1 oz. lemon juice
½ oz. sugar syrup or to taste
2 tbsp. plum jelly
Lemon-lime soda

Mix all ingredients with cracked ice in a blender and strain into a large Collins glass. Fill with lemon-lime soda, stir gently, and add additional ice if necessary.

PONY'S NECK

1 large lemon or orange
Ginger ale
½ tsp. lime juice
Dash Angostura bitters
   (optional)
Maraschino cherry

Carefully peel the outer layer (zest) of a lemon or orange in a thin, unbroken spiral that is then fitted into a highball or Collins glass with one end hooked over the rim of the glass. Add several ice cubes and fill with cold ginger ale. Stir in lime juice and bitters gently, and garnish with a maraschino cherry.

POOR SUFFERING BUSTARD

Dash Angostura bitters
6 oz. ginger beer
1 tsp. Rose's lime juice
Cucumber slice
Lemon slice
Mint sprig

Swirl bitters around a chilled Old Fashioned glass and empty. Add several ice cubes, fill with cold ginger beer, and garnish with cucumber, lemon, and mint. Stir gently.

RASPBERRY-MA-TAZZ

5 oz. pineapple juice
12 raspberries or 6
   strawberries
1 small, ripe banana
Grated nutmeg

Mix all ingredients, except nutmeg, with cracked ice in a blender and pour into a chilled highball glass. Sprinkle with grated nutmeg. Add additional ice, if necessary.

RASPBERRY SODA

¼ cup frozen or fresh
   raspberries
2 scoops raspberry sherbet,
   raspberry ice, or vanilla
   ice cream
Creme soda, lemon-lime
   soda, or club soda
Whipped cream
Whole raspberry

Blend raspberries with several tbsp. sherbet in a blender until pulverized. If frozen raspberries are used, be sure to add some of the syrup. Pour into a chilled 12-oz. glass, add remainder of sherbet, fill with cold soda, stir gently, and garnish with a topping of whipped cream dotted with a whole raspberry.

ROYAL CHOCOLATE-NUT SHAKE

½ cup chunky peanut butter
½ cup chocolate syrup
1 cup whole milk
2 scoops chocolate, vanilla,
   or butter pecan ice cream
Whipped cream (optional)

Mix peanut butter and chocolate syrup with a little milk in a blender until mixture is smooth. Add remainder of milk and ice cream and mix for a few seconds until smooth. Top with mound of whipped cream, if you wish.

BARTENDER'S SECRET NO. 41—Fire Spray

For those who enjoy a pyrotechnical display with their cocktails, a lemon, lime, orange, or grapefruit peel squeezed over their drink and instantaneously ignited with a match provides a festive touch. The volatile essential oils in the peel, when released, produce a very fine spray that creates a flash when set afire. When rubbed on the rim of a glass, the peel leaves an often intense residual flavor that many drinkers find appealing. The amount of flame generated is minuscule, so one need not be diffident about flambéeing their apéritif.

SHIRLEY TEMPLE

4 oz. ginger ale
1 tsp. grenadine
Orange slice
Lemon peel
Maraschino cherry

Pour ginger ale and grenadine into a chilled wine glass with an ice cube and stir gently. Garnish with orange slice, lemon peel, and maraschino cherry.

STEPPES SHAKE

½ cup diced, ripe cantaloupe
½ cup sliced, ripe banana
½ cup plain yogurt
1 tsp. sugar syrup or honey to taste
Several dashes lemon juice

Mix all ingredients in a blender until smooth and pour into a tall, chilled Collins glass or large wine goblet.

Other fruit combinations may be used. If honey is used as a sweetener, dissolve it with a little water before putting into blender.

SUNSET COOLER

½ cup cranberry juice
2–3 oz. fresh orange juice
Dash lemon juice
Ginger ale
Lemon slice

Mix cranberry juice, orange juice, and lemon juice with cracked ice in a shaker or blender and strain into a tall, chilled Collins glass. Add several ice cubes and fill glass with cold ginger ale. Garnish with lemon slice.

T. M. HUNT'S CUP

½ cup fresh orange juice
2 scoops vanilla ice cream
Several dashes vanilla extract
1 tsp. honey or sugar syrup to taste
1 egg (optional)
Pinch powdered cinnamon
Pinch grated nutmeg

Mix cold orange juice, ice cream, vanilla, honey, and egg in a blender until honey is dissolved and mixture is smooth but not watery. Pour into a chilled Collins glass or large goblet and sprinkle with cinnamon and nutmeg.

Honey will mix more easily if you dissolve it with a little milk or water in a cup before adding to blender.

TRANSFUSION

3 oz. grape juice
6 oz. ginger ale
Several dashes lime juice
Lime slice

Pour grape juice and ginger ale into a chilled highball glass with several ice cubes, add lime juice, stir gently, and garnish with lime slice.

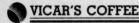 VICAR'S COFFEE

1 cup strong black coffee
½ tsp. orgeat syrup
Several pinches powdered
    cinnamon
1–2 scoops chocolate ice
    cream
Whipped cream
Grated nutmeg

Put cold coffee, syrup, cinnamon, and ice cream into a blender and mix for a few seconds until smooth but not watery. Serve in a chilled wine goblet and top with a generous mound of whipped cream and sprinkle with nutmeg.

VIRGIN MARY

6 oz. tomato juice or V-8
    juice
1 tsp. dill, chopped
1 tsp. fresh lemon juice
¼ tsp. Worcestershire sauce
Several pinches celery salt
    or celery seed
Pinch white pepper
Several dashes Tabasco
    sauce

Stir all ingredients well in a mixing glass and pour into a chilled highball glass with several ice cubes.

▧ YE COTTAGE COCKTAIL

3 oz. tomato or V-8 juice
3 oz. clam juice
Several dashes Tabasco
    sauce
Several dashes
    Worcestershire sauce
½ tsp. lemon juice
Fresh dill, finely chopped (or
    dried dill may be
    substituted)

Mix all ingredients, except dill, with cracked ice in a shaker or blender and pour into a chilled Old Fashioned glass or a highball glass. Top with chopped dill.

This is a refreshing drink at any time of the day or night. Some will want to add a jigger of vodka, but it is just as good without.

GLOSSARY

Abbott's Bitters See Chapter 2 under *A Battery of Bitters*.

Abricotine The proprietary name for an apricot liqueur made by the French house of Garnier.

Absinthe An anise-flavored, high-proof liqueur now banned due to the alleged toxic effects of wormwood, which reputedly turned the brains of heavy users to mush.

Advocaat A bottled eggnog mixture made with brandy and eggs that originated in the Netherlands. Also spelled Advockaat.

Afri-Koko A chocolate-coconut cordial made in the West African county of Sierra Leone.

Aguardiente "Burning water" and well named for this generally high-powered, low-quality, brandy-like spirit popular in parts of Spain and South America.

Airelle An eau-de-vie made from the red mountain cranberry (see *Myrtille*).

Amaretto A generic cordial invented in Italy and made from apricot pits and herbs, yielding a pleasant almond flavor.

Amer Picon See Chapter 2 under *A Battery of Bitters*.

Anesone The ouzo of Italy; an anise-based absinthe substitute.

Angostura Bitters See Chapter 2 under *A Battery of Bitters*.

Anisette A very sweet, anise-based generic liqueur. That produced by the firm of Marie Brizard is generally considered to be an outstanding example of this cordial.

Applejack Sometimes called apple brandy, this spirit, distilled from apples, is aged in wooden barrels like whiskey (see *Calvados*).

Apéritif See Chapter 1 under *The Language of Mixology*.

Apricot Brandy Rarely made as an eau-de-vie, this spirit is usually available in the U.S. as apricot-*flavored* brandy.

Apry An apricot cordial made by the firm of Marie Brizard.

Aquavit See Chapter 4 under *Flavored Vodkas*. Also spelled *Akvavit*.

Armagnac See Chapter 6.

Amontillado An amber, medium-dry sherry often possessing a nutty flavor and excellent as an apéritif or mixed-drink ingredient.

Asbach Uralt An excellent German brandy, similar to cognac, and matured in oak barrels.

Arak (Also *Arrack* and *Arrak*) A generic term that refers to various spirits made in parts of the Pacific, Southeast Asia, and the Middle East. See *Batavia Arak*.

Aurum A fine, golden orange liqueur from Italy.

B&B A mixture of cognac and Benedictine, yielding a drier product than Benedictine alone.

Bacardi See Chapter 5.

Barack Palinka An outstanding eau-de-vie distilled from apricot fruit and stones by the Austrian firm of Zwack.

Barbados rum See Chapter 5.

Batavia Arak A rich, pungent, aromatic rum made from malted rice and molasses and aged in barrels like cognac in Indonesia.

Batida (Brazil) Any drink made with fruit and rum, often referred to as "sugarcane brandy."

Benedictine A venerable, complex, aromatic herbal liqueur invented by a Benedictine monk in the early sixteenth century, but now purely a commercial enterprise and generally recognized to be one of the world's top five proprietary liqueurs.

Bergamot A brandy-based liqueur made in Germany from bergamot, a very flavorful citrus fruit.

Bitters See Chapter 2 under *A Battery of Bitters*.

Blackberry Popular as a cordial and as a flavored brandy in the U.S.

Blended whiskey See Chapter 7.

Boker's Bitters See Chapter 2 under *A Battery of Bitters*.

Boonekamp See Chapter 2 under *A Battery of Bitters*.

Borovicka A Czechoslovakian juniper brandy that bears a greater resemblance to gin than to brandy.

Bourbon See Chapter 7.

Bronte An English herbal liqueur made of fruits and spices, also known as Yorkshire liqueur.

Byrrh An aromatic apéritif wine from France with overtones of orange and quinine.

Cachaca Distilled directly from sugarcane sap, it has a sweet taste, a subtle rum flavor with overtones of vanilla and various herbal flavors.

Caipirinha A cocktail (from the Portuguese word *caipira* or peasant) made with cachaca, lime juice, and sugar—a Brazilian Daiquiri.

Calisay A liqueur specialty from Barcelona used for flavoring and as a digestif with strong quinine overtones.

Caloric Punsch See *Swedish Punsch*.

Calvados One of the most important eaux-de-vie distilled from the apples of Normandy and considered the quintessential apple brandy, especially that classified as *Calvados du Pays d'Auge*.

Campari A popular Italian bitter apéritif with a brilliant red hue and strong quinine underpinnings.

Canadian whisky See Chapter 7.

Cerise See *Kirsch*.

Certosa Liqueurs of various colors and flavors faintly reminiscent of Chartreuse distilled by an order of monks near Florence, Italy.

Chambord A liqueur made in France from black raspberries and various other fruits.

Chartreuse One of the royal family of great proprietary liqueurs, this complex formulation in green and yellow versions has been made by the Carthusian monks near Grenoble since 1605.

Cherry Heering See *Peter Heering*

Cherry liqueurs Like orange liqueurs, these are usually compounded with fruit, flavorings, and sweeteners. A few outstanding names include Cherry Marnier (France), Cherry Heering (Denmark), DeKuyper (the Netherlands), Cheristock (Italy), Rocher Cherry Brandy (France), Grant's Morella Cherry Brandy (England), Cerasella (Italy), and Wisniak (Poland). Maraschino liqueur, like cherry cordials, is made by many distillers, but the world's largest producer of maraschino is the Luxardo firm of Torreglia, Italy.

China-Martini See Chapter 2 under *A Battery of Bitters*.

Chocolate liqueurs Crème de cacao, a very popular, generic chocolate liqueur available in the traditional cocoa color or clear for mixed drinks, is manufactured by many producers worldwide including such famous names as Bols, DeKuyper, Garnier, Marie Brizard, and Hiram Walker. There are also speciality chocolate liqueurs such as Vandermint and Royal Mint-Chocolate Liqueur, mint-chocolate mixtures; Sabra, a chocolate-orange cordial from Israel; Marmot from Switzerland with little pieces of chocolate in the liqueur; Droste Bittersweet Chocolate Liqueur, and chocolate-coconut combinations such as Afri-Koko and Choclair. Some distillers, like Hiram Walker, market a line of flavored chocolate cordials using orange, raspberry, cherry, and other fruits.

Coffee liqueurs Crème de mocha or créme de café are generic coffee-based liqueurs made by a number of producers. Specialty proprietary brands like Kahlua from Mexico and Tia Maria from Jamaica have become famous. Other specialties included Pasha Turkish Coffee Liqueur, Gallwey's Irish Coffee Liqueur, and Coffee Espresso from Italy.

Chouao An area in Venezuela reputed to grow some of the world's finest cocoa beans, which explains why the name is sometimes used on crème de cacao labels.

Cognac See Chapter 6.

Cointreau A famous proprietary brand of triple sec that is popular straight and as a versatile ingredient for many mixed drinks.

Coing A rare eau-de-vie made from quince.

Cordial Médoc A complex, proprietary liqueur produced in Bordeaux, France, with a brandy base and overtones of raspberry, orange, cacao, and other flavorings.

Crème liqueurs The prefix *crème* indicates that sugar is basic to these formulations that encompass a full spectrum of flavorings. Here are a few:

Crème de almond (almond)
Crème de banane (banana)
Crème de cacao (cocoa-vanilla)
Crème de cassis (black currants)
Crème de celeri (celery)
Crème de d'anana (pineapple)
Crème de menthe (peppermint)
Crème de noisette (hazelnuts)

Crème de noyaux (bitter almond

Crème de mocha (coffee)

Crème de rose (vanilla and roses)

Crème de thé (tea)

Crème de vanilla (vanilla beans)

Crème de violette (violets)

Crème yvette (violets)

Curaçao An intense orange liqueur made from the peels of green oranges from the island of Curaçao. In clear, orange, and blue colors.

Cynar An aromatized wine from Italy flavored with the artichoke.

Cuarenta y Tres A brandy-based proprietary liqueur from Spain containing 43 ingredients and a hint of vanilla. Also known as *Licor 43*.

Damiana A French proprietary liqueur specialty.

Danziger Goldwasser Originally made in Danzig by the firm of Der Lachs (established 1598) and popularly known as *eau-de-vie de Danzig*, Goldwasser is characterized by little bits of gold leaf that float around in the bottle and a spicy, citrus flavor.

Demerara rum See Chapter 5.

Drambuie Drambuie, the great proprietary liqueur of Scotland made of scotch and heather honey, is considered to be one of the top five world-class formulations. Reputed to have been Bonnie Prince Charles's own family recipe.

Dubonnet A famous aromatized wine of French origin, available in red and white with a flavor base of quinine. Now made in the U.S.

Eaux-de-vie Literally "waters of life," which was once used to describe all distilled spirits, but now generally encompassing only clear distillates such as the fruit brandies made in Europe (i.e., framboise, kirsch, mirabelle, calvados, quetsch, etc.).

Estomacal-Bonet A Spanish liqueur similar to the specialty of the Basque country, Izzara.

Falernum See Chapter 2 under *A Collection of Fine Flavorings*.

Fernet Branca See Chapter 2 under *A Battery of Bitters*.

Fino A light, dry, fragrant sherry type usually drunk cold.

Fior d'Alpe An Italian proprietary liqueur instantly recognizable by a twig in the bottle festooned with rock-candy crystals. Made from a venerable herbal recipe.

Fleurs d'Acacia An Alsatian eau-de-vie made from acacia flowers.

Forbidden Fruit An American creation, one of the few grapefruit liqueurs.

Fraise The French word for strawberry generally refers to the clear eau-de-vie fruit brandy, but may also designate a liqueur (crème de fraise).

Framboise Usually denotes an eau-de-vie made from raspberries, but can also be used to identify a liqueur made from raspberries (crème de framboise).

Frangelico A proprietary liqueur with a pronounced hazelnut flavor.

Framberry A brand name for a raspberry liqueur produced by the Alsatian firm of Dolfi.

Galliano A sweet, spicy, herbal liqueur popular taken neat and as a mixed-drink ingredient. Named in honor of an Italian war hero, Major Giuseppe Galliano.

Genever See Jenever.

Gentiane An eau-de-vie made from gentian root.

Gilka A famous German name long associated with kümmel, a liqueur with a distinctive caraway-cumin flavor. The Dutch firm of Bols in the Netherlands also claims to have fathered this spirit in the sixteenth century.

Gin See Chapter 3.

Glayva A Scottish proprietary liqueur with a scotch-whiskey base similar to Drambuie.

Goldwasser See Danziger Goldwasser.

Grand Gruyere An herbal liqueur from Switzerland.

Grand Marnier One of the top five world-class proprietary liqueurs, with a distinctive curaçao-cognac flavor that is highly prized by connoisseur, chef, and mixologist.

Grappa A popular Italian pomace brandy made from grape, pulp, skin, and seeds that are the residue from the wine press after the juice has been extracted (see Marc).

Groseille Currants, both red and white, which are sometimes made into an eau-de-vie.

Herbsaint An absinthe substitute similar to Pernod made in New Orleans.

Hollands gin See *Jenever.*

Himbergeist A German eau-de-vie, literally "spirit of raspberry."

Houx A rare and expensive eau-de-vie made from holly berries in Alsace.

Irish cream liqueur A popular sweet, rich liqueur made with cream, Irish whiskey, and sweeteners homogenized into a well-balanced cordial. Bailey's began it all, quickly followed by other brands such as Carolan's, Dunphy's, Emmet's, O'Darby's, St. Brendan's, Waterford, and others.

Irish Mist This excellent proprietary liqueur, like Drambuie, utilizes heather honey and has a similarly legendary provenance, believed by some to be a re-creation of Ireland's lost heather wine dating back to the pre-Christian era. A spicy, sweet concoction with an Irish-whiskey base.

Irish whiskey See Chapter 8.

Izzara The liqueur of the Basques; an herbal mixture with an armagnac base and, like Chartreuse, available in both green and yellow versions.

Jaegermeister See Chapter 2 under *A Battery of Bitters.*

Jenever A distinctive spirit, not at all like London or dry gin, with a malty flavor that is very popular in the Netherlands, where it originated in the seventeenth century (also spelled *Genever* and known as *Schiedam* or *Hollands gin*).

Kahlua Mexico's famous *licor de café*, sweet, rich, flavorful, and well balanced.

Kirsch (Also *Kirschwasser*) A trenchant eau-de-vie made from cherries and distilled by producers in a large area around the Rhine where Germany, France, and Switzerland share common borders.

Kümmel An old, generic liqueur available in both dry and sweet versions, made with caraway, cumin, coriander, and various other herbs. Some distinguished brands include Allasch, Bolskümmel, and Gilka.

La Grande Passion A fine proprietary specialty liqueur made in France by Marnier-Lapostolle, the firm that makes Grand

Marnier. Pronounced passion-fruit flavor with an armagnac base.

Lakka A liqueur made from the Arctic cloudberry by the firm of Marli in Turku, Finland.

Lillet A popular French apéritif wine that is available in red and white versions.

Liqueur d'Anis An aniseed liqueur such as anisette.

Liqueur d'Or An herbal specialty liqueur produced by the firm of Garnier and similar to yellow Chartreuse in flavor and character.

Licor 43 See *Cuarenta y Tres.*

Lochan Ora A proprietary liqueur made of Scotch whisky, honey, and various herbs. Similar to Drambuie.

Madeira Fortified wines from the Portuguese island of Madeira, blended, like sherry, using the *solera* system so that young wines are blended with older ones in successive stages to achieve consistent quality. Madeiras range from very dry to very sweet and are as highly prized in the kitchen as they are drunk as an apéritif or as a dessert wine.

Malaga A sweet, fortified wine from southern Spain.

Malibu A Caribbean coconut-flavored rum originally from Barbados.

Mandarine Napoleon A medium-sweet, well-balanced tangerine liqueur with a cognac base. Made in Brussels.

Manzanilla The driest of all sherries, which is made in the area surrounding Sanlucar de Barrameda in the "Sherry Triangle" of southern Spain.

Maraschino A sweet liqueur made from Marasca cherries, which grow in Dalmatia bordering on the Adriatic Sea (see *Cherry liqueurs*).

Marc A pomace brandy from France, principally from Burgundy, similar to grappa, which comes from Italy. The grape skins, stems, and pulp that are used to make this eau-de-vie give it a characteristic woody taste.

Marsala A robust, Madeira-like, fortified wine from Sicily ranging from dry to very sweet, with a distinctive flavor that makes it excellent for cooking as well as drinking.

Mastikha An anise-based liqueur from Greece.

Mazarine A proprietary liqueur from the house of Cusenier from a seventeenth century recipe. Suggestive of yellow Chartreuse with a spicy, herbal flavor.

Mead A honey wine of ancient origins that is still made in England, parts of Europe, and the U.S.

Mesimara A liqueur made from the wild Arctic bramble by Marli of Turku, Finland.

Metaxa A popular Greek brandy that has been sweetened to give it a liqueur quality.

Midori A honeydew melon flavored liqueur from the Japanese house of Suntory.

Mirabelle A popular eau-de-vie distilled from the yellow plum.

Mistra Italian ouzo, an anise-based liqueur.

Moscato A fortified wine made from the Muscat grape in various countries such as Italy, Spain, and Portugal.

Mûre An eau-de-vie made from the blackberry or mulberry.

Myrtille An eau-de-vie made from the whortleberry or hurtleberry (also bilberry), a large species encompassing several varieties. Sometimes referred to as airelle.

Ojen A Spanish, anise-based, absinthe-type liqueur sans wormwood, which has been banned from spiritous beverages.

Okolehao A distillate of rice, taro root, and molasses from Hawaii that is guaranteed to loosen up the luau.

Oloroso A rich, sweet sherry type that is popular as an after-dinner drink.

Orgeat A syrup with a pronounced almond flavor, which makes it a good sweetener for desserts and mixed drinks.

Ouzo An anise-based, sweet liqueur that is the national spiritous drink of Greece.

Parfait Amour The elixir of "perfect love" is a sweet, perfumed liqueur with hints of flowers, spices, and fruit, and a mauve color that apparently had great appeal to women in the nineteenth century.

Pasha A Turkish coffee liqueur.

Pastis A French generic term for all anise-based, absinthe-type liqueurs.

Pastis de Marseilles A proprietary anise-based liqueur from the city of the same name.

Peppermint schnapps An intensely mint-flavored liqueur that is lighter and less sweet than older mint-based liqueurs such as crème de menthe.

Pernod A famous proprietary absinthe-type liqueur from France without the wormwood ingredient that was a part of the original absinthe formula.

Persico A peach liqueur with overtones of almond and other fruits and flavorings made by the Dutch firm of Bols.

Peter Heering A famous proprietary cherry liqueur from Denmark with a rich, full-bodied, intense cherry flavor. Formerly known as Peter Heering. The name was changed to Cherry Heering to afford better copyright protection for the brand.

Pimento Dram A Jamaican specialty liqueur, this spicy, zesty, tropical elixir is made from the flower buds of the pimento tree.

Pineau des Charentes A *mistelle* (grape juice to which sufficient alcohol has been added to stop fermentation) from the cognac area in France, prized as an apéritif.

Pisco An unusual brandy from Muscat wines made in and around Ica, Peru, on the coastal desert south of Lima. Made famous as the main ingredient in Pisco Punch.

Pistàchà A pistachio-flavored liqueur produced by Cointreau, Ltd. in the U.S.

Poire Williams An exceedingly fine eau-de-vie made from the Williams or Bartlett pear.

Port (Porto) Port or Porto (*Vinho do Porto*), its official designation, is the great fortified wine of a strictly controlled area of the Douro region of Portugal. Port has been used as a generic term to describe port-type wines wherever they may have been produced, but since 1968, only wines produced in Portugal may use the Porto appellation.

Praline A New Orleans liqueur that re-creates the butter-pecan–brown-sugar–vanilla flavor of the traditional praline candy.

Prunelle The French name for the sloeberry, source of sloe gin, which can also be made into a delightful eau-de-vie. The sloeberry is not a berry but a wild plum and, for the record, sloe gin is not a gin, but a very fruity liqueur that is the base of the Sloe Gin Fizz.

Punt e Mes A famous proprietary apéritif wine from Milan with intriguing orange-quinine flavors.

Quetsch An eau-de-vie made from the purple plum.

Quinquina An apéritif wine with a quinine flavor base.

Raki A Turkish liqueur with a sweet licorice flavor.

Raspberry See *Framboise*.

Ricard A popular French pastis with a pronounced anise-licorice flavor in the absinthe tradition.

Rock and Rye A generic liqueur made with whiskey, whole fruits, and sweetened with rock-candy crystals. Sometimes taken as a hot toddy to alleviate cold symptoms.

Roiano A proprietary Italian liqueur made from various herbs with an anise-vanilla-spice flavor reminiscent of Galliano.

Rum See Chapter 5.

Rye whiskey See Chapter 7.

Sabra A chocolate-orange liqueur from Israel.

Sake A unique Japanese brewed beverage that is not a rice wine as some mistakenly suppose, and not a spirit since it is not distilled. It is nevertheless a versatile product that may be drunk hot or cold or used to make mixed drinks such as a vodka or gin Martini.

Sambuca An anise-like Italian liqueur, but not made with aniseed, but the elder *Sambucus nigra*. Traditionally drunk after dinner with coffee beans.

Schiedam gin See *Jenever*.

Schnapps The word "schnapps" (from the German word *schnappen*, meaning "snap") refers to a tot of vodka, gin, brandy, or other spirit. In Scandinavia the word is *snaps* and almost always means akvavit. Today in the U.S., the term has taken on a new meaning to identify a whole new generation of intensely flavored, sweet, inexpensive liqueurs of moderate strength (22 to 30 percent alcohol by volume). The DeKuyper brands of Apple Barrel Schnapps and Peachtree Schnapps, while not the first in the U.S. market, are generally credited with launching the "schnapps sweep" due to technical breakthroughs that yielded a fresh rather than "cooked" fruit flavor. Other flavors such as cola, cinnamon, root beer, cranberry, butterscotch, strawberry, hazelnut, apricot, and other types proliferated from a number of distillers, making the schnapps category an overnight success.

Scotch See Chapter 8.

Sherry One of the classic fortified wines produced in a restricted area known as the "Sherry Triangle" that surrounds the city of Jerez de la Frontera in the south of Spain between Seville and Cadiz. Sherry ranges in color from straw to dark amber and in taste from very dry (Manzanilla) to very sweet, which is designated a cream sherry. All sherries exported from Spain are blends using the *solera* method (i.e., maturing young wines by blending them with other wines in successive stages to achieve predictable quality and consistency).

Slivovitz A plum brandy similar to quetsch, aged in wood, but classified as an eau-de-vie. Made in Croatia and some other parts of Eastern Europe.

Sloe gin A sweet, fruity liqueur made from the sloeberry or wild plum (also called prunelle and blackthorn) that is popular mainly in mixed drinks.

Sommer Garden A proprietary liqueur from Odense, Denmark, purported to be the world's first after-dinner liqueur without sugar (it is sweetened with saccharin).

Southern Comfort A popular proprietary liqueur from St. Louis used extensively in mixed drinks and often described as a peach whiskey.

Steinhager A unique German gin made exclusively from juniper berries that are crushed, fermented, distilled, and then redistilled with grain neutral spirits. Its name comes from the Westphalian town of Steinhagen. It is also known by its generic name, *wacholder*.

Stonsdorfer See Chapter 2 under *A Battery of Bitters*.

Strawberry See *Fraise*.

Strega A sweet, spicy, proprietary liqueur from Italy reputed to be made from over 70 ingredients.

Sureau An eau-de-vie from Alsace made from elderberries.

Swedish Punsch This sweet, spicy liqueur is popular in Sweden, especially during the winter months due to its legendary warming qualities, hence its other name, Caloric Punsch. The predominant flavor is Batavia arak, an aromatic rum from Indonesia.

Tequila See Chapter 9.

Tia Maria A venerable coffee liqueur from Jamaica with a pleasant aroma and overtones of tropical spices in its flavorings.

Triple sec A generic liqueur made by many producers, varying in its orange flavor, aroma, and sweetness. Made from sweet and bitter oranges, this clear liqueur is probably best characterized by the Cointreau brand.

Tuaca An Italian, brandy-based, proprietary liqueur with the suggestion of many flavors such as vanilla, citrus, almond, coconut, orange, and cocoa, among others.

Van Der Hum A brandy-based tangerine liqueur made in South Africa from Dutch origins.

Vandermint A "liquid after-dinner chocolate mint" perhaps best describes this proprietary liqueur from the Netherlands.

Verveine du Velay A French herbal liqueur made from plants of the genus *Verbena*. Popular as a digestif.

Vieille Cure A complex, aged liqueur of the herbal type from Bordeaux, reputedly made from over 50 ingredients and available in yellow and green, suggestive of Chartreuse.

Vodka See Chapter 4.

Whiskey liqueurs Drambuie, Irish Mist, Glayva, and Lochan Ora are examples of whiskey liqueurs made with Scotch and Irish whiskey bases. American whiskey liqueurs include Wild Turkey Liqueur made from bourbon; and George M. Tiddy's Canadian Liqueur and Yukon Jack, both made from Canadian whiskies.

Wishniak (Wisniak) A wild-cherry liqueur that originated in Poland and is now made in other parts of Eastern Europe.

INDEX